Commerce and Manners in Edmund Burke's Political Economy

Although many of Edmund Burke's speeches and writings contain prominent economic dimensions, his economic thought seldom receives the attention it warrants. *Commerce and Manners in Edmund Burke's Political Economy* stands as the most comprehensive study to date of this fascinating subject. In addition to providing rigorous textual analysis, Collins unearths previously unpublished manuscripts and employs empirical data to set out a rich historical and theoretical context for Burke's economic beliefs. Collins integrates Burke's reflections on trade, taxation, and revenue within his understanding of the limits of reason and his broader conception of empire. Such reflections demonstrate the ways that commerce, if properly managed, could be an instrument for both public prosperity and imperial prestige. More important, *Commerce and Manners in Edmund Burke's Political Economy* raises timely ethical questions about capitalism and its limits. In Burke's judgment, civilizations cannot endure on transactional exchange alone, and markets require ethical preconditions. There is a grace to life that cannot be bought.

Gregory M. Collins is Postdoctoral Associate and Lecturer in the Program on Ethics, Politics, and Economics at Yale University.

Commerce and Manners in Edmund Burke's Political Economy

GREGORY M. COLLINS
Yale University

 CAMBRIDGE
UNIVERSITY PRESS

CAMBRIDGE
UNIVERSITY PRESS

University Printing House, Cambridge CB2 8BS, United Kingdom

One Liberty Plaza, 20th Floor, New York, NY 10006, USA

477 Williamstown Road, Port Melbourne, VIC 3207, Australia

314–321, 3rd Floor, Plot 3, Splendor Forum, Jasola District Centre, New Delhi – 110025, India

79 Anson Road, #06–04/06, Singapore 079906

Cambridge University Press is part of the University of Cambridge.

It furthers the University's mission by disseminating knowledge in the pursuit of education, learning, and research at the highest international levels of excellence.

www.cambridge.org
Information on this title: www.cambridge.org/9781108489409
DOI: 10.1017/9781108776813

© Gregory M. Collins 2020

First published 2020

Printed in the United Kingdom by TJ International Ltd. Padstow Cornwall

A catalogue record for this publication is available from the British Library.

Library of Congress Cataloging-in-Publication Data
NAMES: Collins, Gregory M., 1986– author.
TITLE: Commerce and manners in Edmund Burke's political economy / Gregory M. Collins.
DESCRIPTION: Cambridge, United Kingdom ; New York, NY : Cambridge University Press, 2020. | Includes bibliographical references and index.
IDENTIFIERS: LCCN 2019049024 (print) | LCCN 2019049025 (ebook) | ISBN 9781108489409 (hardback) | ISBN 9781108776813 (epub)
SUBJECTS: LCSH: Burke, Edmund, 1729–1797 – Political and social views. | Economics – Great Britain – History – 18th century. | Political science – Great Britain – History – 18th century. | Rationalism – History – 18th century.
CLASSIFICATION: LCC HB103.B87 C65 2020 (print) | LCC HB103.B87 (ebook) | DDC 381.01–dc23
LC record available at https://lccn.loc.gov/2019049024
LC ebook record available at https://lccn.loc.gov/2019049025

ISBN 978-1-108-48940-9 Hardback

To Rochelle

Contents

List of Figures	*page* xi
List of Tables	xii
Acknowledgments	xiii

Introduction	1
The Problem: Markets and Social Order	1
Interpretations of Burke's Political Economy	8
Terminology of Political Economy and Burke's Use of Empirical Information	12
Conclusion	14

PART I BIOGRAPHY

1 Biography and Burke's Authority as a Political Economist	19
1.1 The Roots of Burke's Interest in the Science of Political Economy	19
1.2 Burke as a Political Economist	27
1.3 Conclusion	31

PART II MARKET ECONOMIES

2 *Thoughts and Details on Scarcity*, Supply and Demand, and Middlemen	37
2.1 Introduction	37
2.2 The Stresses of England's Agricultural Economy in the 1790s and the Drafting of *Thoughts and Details*	38
2.3 The Laws of Supply and Demand, Wages, and Price Theory	44
2.4 Middlemen	57
2.5 The 1772 Repeal of Statutes Banning Forestalling, Regrating, and Engrossing	70
2.6 Conclusion	76

3   Agricultural Policy, Labor, and Wealth Redistribution   78
    3.1 Introduction   78
    3.2 The Corn Laws and Export Bounties   78
    3.3 Enclosure   88
    3.4 Labor, the Laboring Poor, and the Rich as Trustees   92
    3.5 Wealth Redistribution and Equality in *Thoughts and Details* 109
    3.6 Conclusion   114

4   Markets, Rationalism, and the Hayek Connection   117
    4.1 Introduction   117
    4.2 England's Grain Trade and National Policy   118
    4.3 Voluntary Contracts and Market Exchange   119
    4.4 Incentive, Reciprocity, and Commercial Virtues   123
    4.5 Laissez-Faire and the Role of State Regulation   127
    4.6 Rationalism in *Thoughts and Details*   131
    4.7 Rationalism and the Hayek Connection   136
    4.8 Burke and Adam Smith   139
    4.9 Conclusion   143

PART III   THE BRITISH CONSTITUTION AND ECONOMICAL REFORM

5   The British Constitution: Burke's Program of Economical
    Reform and the Role of the State   151
    5.1 Introduction   151
    5.2 Wyvill's Movement and the Spirit of Constitutional Reform   153
    5.3 *Speech on Economical Reform* I: Private Land, Contracts,
         and the Board of Trade   159
    5.4 *Speech on Economical Reform* II: Pensions, Costly Offices,
         and the Civil List   169
    5.5 Aftermath and Influence   189
    5.6 Burke's Trustee Theory of Representation and His Conception
         of Reform   191
    5.7 Conclusion   199

PART IV   FOREIGN TRADE

6   *Account of the European Settlements in America*, the British
    West Indies, and the Free Port Act of 1766   209
    6.1 Introduction   209
    6.2 British Commercial Policy and the Navigation Acts   213
    6.3 An Account of the European Settlements in America   217
    6.4 The British West Indies and the Free Port Act of 1766   235
    6.5 Conclusion   245

7   *Observations on a Late State of the Nation* and the Political
    Economy of Anglo-American Imperial Relations   248
    7.1 British Imperial Policy and the American Colonies   248

7.2   Observations on a Late State of the Nation   251
7.3   The American War and the Navigation Acts: *Speech
       on American Taxation* and *Speech on Conciliation with America*   275
7.4   Conclusion   297

8   Anglo-Irish Commercial Relations, *Two Letters on the Trade
     of Ireland*, and the Politics of Free Trade   299
8.1   Introduction   299
8.2   The Commercial Tensions between England and Ireland   300
8.3   The Irish Trade Bills and *Two Letters on the Trade of Ireland*   306
8.4   Irish Trade, Nature, Principle, and Prudence   322
8.5   Pitt's Commercial Propositions   334
8.6   The Anglo-French Commercial Treaty of 1786   337
8.7   The Question of Mercantilism Revisited   339
8.8   Conclusion   342

PART V   INDIA

9   Britain's East India Company, Indian Markets, and Monopoly   347
9.1   Introduction   347
9.2   The Politics of the East India Company   350
9.3   Burke's General Principles of Trading Monopolies   356
9.4   *Ninth Report of Select Committee* I: Markets and the Corruption
       of Supply and Demand Laws   358
9.5   *Ninth Report of Select Committee* II: Monopoly   366
9.6   Conclusion   369

10   *Speech on Fox's India Bill*, Six Mercantile Principles,
      and the Danger of Political Commerce   371
10.1   The East India Company, *Eleventh Report of Select Committee*,
        and *Speech on Fox's India Bill*   371
10.2   *Speech on Fox's India Bill* and the Destruction of the Local
        Economy and Culture   384
10.3   Political Commerce, Avarice, and Arbitrary Rule   390
10.4   Conclusion   397

PART VI   THE FRENCH REVOLUTION

11   *Reflections on the Revolution in France*: Property, the Monied
      Interest, and the *Assignats*   405
11.1   Introduction   405
11.2   The Political Economy of the Ancien Régime   407
11.3   Property as a Constitutional Bulwark   411
11.4   The French Revolution's Attack on Church Property   419
11.5   The Monied Interest and the *Assignats*   427
11.6   The Relation between the Monied Interest and the Landed Interest   447

12 The Real Rights of Men, Manners, and the Limits of Transactional
    Exchange   460
    12.1 The Real Rights of Men and the Menace of French Revolutionary
          Equality   460
    12.2 The Impact of Abstract Theory on Political Economy
          and the General Bank and Capital of Nations   478
    12.3 Manners and Ethics as a Preconditions for Commerce
          and the Scottish Enlightenment   487
    12.4 The Limits of Voluntary Contracts and Transactional Exchange 503
    12.5 *Third Letter on a Regicide Peace* and the Political Economy
          of England   509
    12.6 Conclusion   516

Conclusion   526
    Burke's Economic Thought   526
    The Relationship between Burke's Economic Thought and Political
    Theory and the Question of Burke's Conservativism   529
    Applications for Today   533

Bibliography   537
Index   557

Figures

2.1 Wheat prices, 1780–1803   *page* 39
2.2 *Oracle* advertisement for Burke's letter to Arthur Young
    on rural economy (1795)   42
4.1 *Memoir Written on a Visit to Lord Lauderdale with Mr Burke
    and Adam Smith* (1784)   140
5.1 *An Account of All the Civil List Expences*, 1761–1768   157
6.1 External trade of England and Wales in the eighteenth century,
    by decade   216
7.1 British imports from Guadeloupe and Martinique
    in 1761 and 1762   254
7.2 British imports from Guadeloupe, Martinique, and Havana
    in 1763   254
7.3 British exports to Jamaica, 1764–1767   258
7.4 English exports to North America, the West Indies, and Africa
    in 1704   284
7.5 English exports to North America, the West Indies, and Africa
    in 1772   284
8.1 Percentage of total exports from Ireland traded to Great Britain,
    by decade   302
8.2 External trade of England and Wales with Ireland, 1750–1780   303
8.3 Ships entering Bristol from transatlantic destinations, 1754–1797   318
11.1 *Assignat* issued during the French Revolution   435

Tables

3.1 English enclosure bills, 1789–1796   *page* 91
5.1 Burke's program of economical reform   179

Acknowledgments

A book such as this one reflects a blend of private labor and the diffused wisdom of the many. Much of this wisdom derived from David Bromwich, Bryan Garsten, Harvey Mansfield, and David Walsh, to whom I owe a deep debt of gratitude for their support and guidance throughout this project.

All Burke scholars – and I am no exception – are beneficiaries of the painstaking research conducted by the editors of *The Writings and Speeches of Edmund Burke* (Oxford: Clarendon Press, 1970–), as well as by the biographers of Burke, including, most recently, Richard Bourke and F. P. Lock. The hardworking editorial team at Cambridge University Press, including Robert Dreesen, Jackie Grant, and Catherine Smith, made this project possible and exhibited professionalism and diligence. Ryan Patrick Hanley and Frederick G. Whelan read the manuscript anonymously and provided constructive feedback that sharpened its argument and structure. The manuscript was greatly improved by the copy-editing prowess of Matt Sparrow. Thank you.

I am grateful for the institutional support from the Acton Institute, Claremont Institute, Institute for Humane Studies, Intercollegiate Studies Institute, Jack Miller Center, Koch Foundation, and the Russell Kirk Center; and for the opportunity to present parts of my research on this book at the Abigail Adams Institute, American Political Science Association meetings, New England Political Science Association meetings, Northeastern Political Science Association meetings, the Political Economy Project at Dartmouth College, the Center for the History of Political Economy at Duke University, the Elm Institute, the Mont Pelerin Society, and the West Hartford (CT) Toastmasters Club.

I am also appreciative of the many people who have provided professional encouragement and intellectual insight into matters of political and economic thought during the composition of this manuscript. Among them include: Roberto Alejandro, Scott Alford, Hadley Arkes, Nigel Ashford, Morton Blackwell, David Bobb, Joshua Bowman, Bruce Caldwell, Gregory Clark,

Henry Clark, Ian Crowe, Dan Cullen, William Doyle, Paul Dudenhefer, Kelli
Farnham, Emily Finley, Kayla Garthus, Nicole Gordon, John Grove, Rudy
Hernandez, Patrick Hough, Lee Edwards, Warren M. Elofson, Kelli Farnham,
Justin Garrison, Sheldon Goldman, Matthew Green, Phillip Henderson, Doug
Irwin, Kerry Joyce, Boris Kasputin, Daniel Klein, Robert Lacey, Yuval Levin,
Alan Levine, Mordechai Levy-Eichel, David Lindauer, Mary Longnecker,
Joshua Lynn, Daniel Mahoney, Samuel Moyn, Jeff Nelson, Saskia Niehoff,
Eduardo Schmidt Passos, Mimi Perlman, Ronald Pestritto, Danilo
Petranovich, Richard Reinsch, Frances Rosenbluth, Nina Rosenwald, Greg
Smith, Jason Sorens, Luke Sheahan, Steven B. Smith, Brad Thompson, Sarah
Walton, Stephen Watts, Greg Weiner, Susan Krauss Whitbourne, Peter Wicks,
George F. Will, Robinson Woodward-Burns, David Woronov, and Michael
Zuckert. My former colleagues in the Department of Politics at Catholic
University and Department of Political Science at Yale University, as well as
my current colleagues in the Ethics, Politics, and Economics Program at Yale,
have been a pleasure to work with. Special thanks to Dr. Robert Carangelo,
Craig Alver, and Dr. Khayyam Durrani as well.

My study of Burke would not have been possible without the research
assistance from the dedicated staffs at the Bass Library (Yale), British Library,
British Museum, W. E. B. DuBois Library (UMass Amherst), Edinburgh
University Library, Lewis Walpole Library (Yale), Mullen Library (Catholic
University), Sheffield Archives, Sterling Memorial Library (Yale), and Trinity
College Library (located in Hartford, Connecticut). Graeme Siddall, Stephen
Willis, Jennifer Gloede, Kay Peterson, Tim Knebel, Chris Rawlings, Danielle
Spittle, Paul Barnaby, Cherrod Parker, Raghavi Govindane, and Walter
McElrath were particularly helpful in various capacities throughout this
project, such as locating documents and images for this book, authorizing
permissions requests, and providing technical support.

Portions of this book have expanded upon articles published in the *Review of
Politics*, *Journal of the History of Economic Thought*, and *Perspectives on
Political Science*. I am solely responsible for any errors herein.

I first gained an appreciation for the intersection between politics and
philosophy after writing a paper on Enlightenment thinkers for Brad Walker's
World History course at Needham High School, located in Needham,
Massachusetts. I am also grateful to have had the opportunity to take classes
taught by Bob Baker and Max Hekler, among many teachers at Needham High,
who helped cast the roots of my intellectual development throughout my high
school years. Roberto Alejandro's courses on ancient and modern political
thought at UMass Amherst, and Hadley Arkes's course on political and moral
philosophy, titled Political Obligations, at Amherst College, deepened my
interest in pursuing an academic career in political theory. My friends in
the informal intellectual club I have participated in for over a decade now,
titled the "Panera Club" (ambitiously modeled after Burke's "Club," absent the
powdered wigs), have refined my thinking throughout the years.

My passion for political philosophy and political economy derives from my father, Thomas Collins, who first introduced me to these subjects. Thank you for your continued support and philosophical engagement. My mother, Sandra Charton, has also been a strong source of intellectual encouragement and discussion, as have my two sisters, Samantha and Nicole. My father, mother, and Samantha read portions of the manuscript and offered thoughtful feedback; my mother's unsparing eye for strong prose was a particularly useful guide as I edited my chapters.

My grandparents, Thomas and Rose Collins and Seymour and Estelle Charton, and my great aunt, Mary Odian, were exemplars of the moral inheritance that binds generations together. Nancy and Richard Gauvin, my caring in-laws, generously tolerated my teeming bookshelves whenever they visited our apartment during the drafting of this manuscript. Most important, I am forever indebted to my wife, Rochelle, for her abiding love and support, and for Grace, our daughter, both of whom have taught me that there is indeed a grace to life that cannot be bought.

Introduction

THE PROBLEM: MARKETS AND SOCIAL ORDER

Was Edmund Burke moved by the abstract spirit of the French Revolution? Ever since he condemned the event in *Reflections on the Revolution in France* in 1790, Burke has acquired a lasting reputation as the foremost critic of the Revolution and a sworn defender of tradition. In the *Reflections*, he scolds French revolutionaries for seeking to remodel French society on a foundation of theoretical rights claims removed from the steady pulse of historical experience. Burke attacked this philosophy as "mazes of metaphysic sophistry."[1]

But was Burke's mind tempted by the same mazes? Consider: One key strand of French revolutionary ideology defended the authority of nature as a basis for opposing the government's infringement on property rights. The French Revolution's *Declaration of the Rights of Man*, passed by the Revolution's National Constituent Assembly in August 1789, established the "natural, unalienable, and sacred rights of man," one of which was "property."[2] Abbé

---

[1] Paul Langford, gen. ed., *The Writing and Speeches of Edmund Burke*, vol. VIII, *The French Revolution 1790–1794* (Oxford: Clarendon Press, 2007), 72. The following are the editors for the individual volumes of *The Writings and Speeches of Edmund Burke*: T. O. McLoughlin and James T. Boulton (Vol. I: *The Early Writings*); Paul Langford (Vol. II: *Party, Parliament, and the American Crisis 1766–1774*); Warren M. Elofson and John A. Woods (Vol. III: *Party, Parliament, and the American War 1774–1780*); P. J. Marshall and Donald C. Bryant (Vol. IV: *Party, Parliament, and the Dividing of the Whigs 1780–1794*); Marshall (Vol. V: *India: Madras and Bengal 1774–1785*); Marshall (Vol. VI: *India: The Launching of the Hastings Impeachment 1786–1788*); Marshall (Vol. VII: *India: The Hastings Trial 1789–1794*); L. G. Mitchell (Vol. VIII: *The French Revolution 1790–1794*); and R. B. McDowell (Vol. IX: *I: The Revolutionary War 1794–1797; II: Ireland*). These sources will be labeled as "Langford, *Writings and Speeches*," with the corresponding volume and page number.

[2] "Declaration of the Rights of Man – 1789," *The Avalon Project*, Yale Law School, accessed August 17, 2017, http://avalon.law.yale.edu/18th_century/rightsof.asp. Article 17 states that property "is an inviolable and sacred right."

Sieyès, a revolutionary and Roman Catholic clergyman who helped draft the declaration, protested Mirabeau's resolution calling to confiscate French church property by stating, "I don't see how a simple declaration can change the nature of rights."[3]

A related feature of French revolutionary thought was the endorsement of a free domestic trade seasoned with the principles of rationality. Condorcet, a leader of the Revolution and a chief enthusiast of Enlightenment notions of reason, argued for liberty of commerce in the grain industry as late as June 1793.[4] Pierre Samuel Dupont de Nemours,[5] an early supporter of the Revolution whose conception of natural law was central to his economic thought,[6] claimed that "freedom of exchange ... serves the general good, for it engenders competition."[7] In general, many members of the educated classes on the eve of the Revolution defended the notion spread by Adam Smith and the économistes, or Physiocrats, the school of eighteenth-century French economists who championed a free grain trade, that the liberal circulation of goods should not be disturbed by the regulatory designs of the state.[8]

In *Thoughts and Details on Scarcity*, his primary economic tract written five years after the *Reflections*, Burke displayed a similar commitment to the inviolability of property and to the belief that the natural order sanctioned the free diffusion of commerce. In the writing, he summons rationalist principles of political economy to resist government intervention in the domestic grain trade. The "laws of commerce," Burke insists, are the "laws of nature, and consequently the laws of God."[9] Here the intrigue in the relationship between his intellectual thought and the French Revolution arises: does Burke's invocation of general principles – "laws of nature" and "laws of God" – overlap with French revolutionaries' embrace of abstract theory as a justification for their economic doctrine?

To further complicate matters, the ancien régime, the French government before the Revolution, had carried out a program of *dirigisme* by issuing heavy

[3] Simon Schama, *Citizens: A Chronicle of the French Revolution* (New York: Alfred A. Knopf, 1989), 485.

[4] Emma Rothschild, "Adam Smith and Conservative Economics," *The Economic History Review* 45 (1992): 83.

[5] De Nemours was a Physiocrat.

[6] James L. McLain, *The Economic Writings of Du Pont de Nemours* (Newark: University of Delaware Press; London: Associated University Presses, 1977), 163. McLain writes that "natural law remained at the foundation of Du Pont's view of the economy."

[7] Florin Aftalion, *The French Revolution: An Economic Interpretation*, trans. Martin Thom (Cambridge: Cambridge University Press, 1990), 46.

[8] Aftalion, *Economic Interpretation*, 46. Note that Smith held fundamental differences from the Physiocrats on economic matters. See Richard Whatmore, "Adam Smith's Role in the French Revolution," *Past & Present* 175 (2002): 72.

[9] Langford, *Writings and Speeches*, IX, 137.

regulations of the country's trade of grain and other commodities.[10] French revolutionaries created a free internal grain trade,[11] at least temporarily. On principle, then, did Burke's political economy in *Thoughts and Details* militate against the *dirigiste* policies of prerevolutionary France? In addition, Turgot, a French statesman associated with the Physiocrats who supported market freedom, had gradually eliminated restrictions on the country's grain trade as a French minister in the ancien régime under Louis XVI in the mid-1770s. (He was dismissed soon thereafter, and his economic reforms were reversed.) Yet a footnote to the 1803 edition of the *Reflections* included an attack from Burke on French *philosophes* for allying themselves with the monied interest, which had connections with Turgot and other men of finance under the ancien régime; this alliance, in Burke's view, helped fuel the animosity toward the landed classes and higher social orders that precipitated the Revolution.[12]

Most famously, Burke in the *Reflections* issues a glittering endorsement of Britain's rich tradition of inherited privileges and rights. "We have an inheritable crown; an inheritable peerage; and an house of commons and a people inheriting privileges, franchises, and liberties, from a long line of ancestors," he writes.[13] For Burke, England's hereditary nobility and medieval inheritance laws, such as primogeniture entail, preserved the strength of landed aristocracies and sustained the delicate equilibrium of English constitutional government. How, then, could the thinker who wrote the *Reflections*, considered the authoritative Western defense of cultural traditionalism in modernity, also compose a tract called *Thoughts and Details*, in which the same writer provided steadfast support for Enlightenment, market-based principles that were perceived by contemporaries as a threatening force to settled social conventions?

This book attempts to answer that question. It will explore Burke's conception of political economy and his understanding of the relationship between commerce and manners. That Burke might hold significant insights into economics may come as a surprise to some readers. He has been characterized, among many labels, as a conservative, liberal, natural law theorist, traditionalist, historicist, reactionary, reformer, romantic, imperialist, anti-imperialist, empiricist, utilitarian, and Aristotelian, but rarely is he considered to be a profound thinker on matters relating to trade, public finance, taxation, and revenue. Such neglect most likely stems from the enduring influence of Burke as a foe of the French Revolution, a defender of party

---

[10] Aftalion, *Economic Interpretation*, 11–15, 31–47, 198–199. There were brief spurts of implementing free trade policies. Consult also Whatmore, "Adam Smith's Role in the French Revolution," 71.
[11] Aftalion, *Economic Interpretation*, 54. The exportation of grain was still prohibited.
[12] Langford, *Writings and Speeches*, VIII, 162, including 162n1.
[13] Langford, *Writings and Speeches*, VIII, 83.

government, and an antagonist of abstract theory, all of which have overshadowed his contributions to the history of economic thought.

The following chapters seek to change this impression. Burke's political economy warrants serious attention because it provided a distinctive approach to the study of economics that blended considerations of morality, religion, and empire into its examination of modern commercial phenomena. As demonstrated by *Thoughts and Details*, Burke certainly had a strong command of supply and demand laws for the time period in which he lived, particularly for someone who had served in the British Parliament, a body populated by landed gentlemen who were generally uninterested in penetrating the mystifying intricacies of commercial activity.[14]

Yet no greater mistake can be made than to assume that *Thoughts and Details* captures the range and depth of Burke's conception of political economy. In the many speeches and writings he drafted throughout his life that touched upon commerce and trade, Burke did not isolate these subjects from their wider ethical and social contexts, but rather integrated and synthesized them in a way that reflected an enlightened comprehension of the relationship between economics and morals unusual for his time. As will be shown throughout this book, and in particular its final chapters on the French Revolution, religion and virtue were indispensable parts of Burke's capacious understanding of economics. Without probing these intersecting parts of Burke's political economy, we will be deprived of the philosophic maturity needed to achieve a proper understanding of the ethical and cultural foundations of commercial prosperity.

Scholars have already made great strides in broadening our apprehension of Burke by refuting caricatures of him as a coldhearted reactionary and drawing attention to the many ways in which he was a dedicated reformer in the eighteenth century.[15] While such studies have focused on Burke's attempt to balance his instinct for political and social reform with his disposition to conserve institutions, this book examines the specific application of his political philosophy to his economic thought. What did Burke think about free markets and free trade? Did Burke detect sparks of friction between his embrace of commercial liberty and his defense of long-lasting custom? How did he negotiate the tensions between exchange economies and morality? If Burke was indeed a conservative, was he conserving a pattern of human behavior, capitalism, which was, and is, a socially disruptive phenomenon?

---

[14] Burke retired from Parliament the year before he drafted *Thoughts and Details*.

[15] See, among many, James Conniff, *The Useful Cobbler: Edmund Burke and the Politics of Progress* (Albany: State University of New York Press, 1994); Richard Bourke, *Empire & Revolution: The Political Life of Edmund Burke* (Princeton: Princeton University Press, 2015); David Bromwich, *The Intellectual Life of Edmund Burke: From the Sublime and Beautiful to American Independence* (Cambridge, MA: The Belknap Press, 2014); and Jesse Norman, *Edmund Burke: The First Conservative* (New York: Basic Books, 2013).

Another way to frame these questions is to compare Burke's economic thought with that of perhaps the most famous advocate of free trade in British history, Adam Smith.[16] This relationship has been called the "Burke-Smith Problem,"[17] and can be captured in a single historical idiosyncrasy suggested at the outset of this introduction: Smith served as an intellectual inspiration for French revolutionaries[18] – yet Burke, while endorsing many of the same policy prescriptions as Smith, has achieved a reputation as the most celebrated critic of revolution in modernity.

How, then, could a proponent of settled habit, Burke, support the commercial policies of a thinker, Smith, whose economic thought departed from previous paternalistic understandings of the proper way to establish and maintain social order? How could Burke's firm belief in the sociability of man be compatible with the notion – articulated by many disciples of Smith, if not by Smith himself – that the elementary unit of economic activity is the individual? Did Burke support Smith's idea of an "Invisible Hand"? Did he fully champion Smith's system of natural liberty? If so, is there not a contradiction in Burke's philosophy? Did Burke offer a convincing way of overcoming the Burke-Smith Problem, if there is one to begin with? In the latter half of the nineteenth century, German scholars famously introduced the idea of "Das Adam Smith Problem," which highlighted the possible discrepancy between Smith's defense of self-interest in *The Wealth of Nations* and his embrace of sympathy in *The Theory of Moral Sentiments*.[19] Is there also "Das Edmund Burke Problem," a seeming disjunction between Burke's support for market economies in *Thoughts and Details* and his traditionalist persuasions in the *Reflections*?

Liberty and Virtue

These questions merge with the second theme of this book. The rise in opposition to globalization and neoliberalism in the United States and Europe has highlighted a noticeable amount of friction between elitism and populism that has simmered for decades, symbolizing the enduring struggle in the West to balance the protection of economic liberty with a commitment to sustaining the deeper chords of local community.

---

[16] Admittedly, there is great debate over the extent to which Smith endorsed free trade.
[17] Donald Winch, "The Burke-Smith Problem and Late Eighteenth-Century Political and Economic Thought," *The Historical Journal* 28 (1985): 231–247. See also Winch, *Riches and Poverty: An Intellectual History of Political Economy in Great Britain, 1750–1834* (Cambridge: Cambridge University Press, 1996), 138–141, 166–220; and Irving Kristol, *The Neoconservatism Persuasion: Selected Essays, 1942–2009*, ed. Gertrude Himmelfarb (New York: Basic Books, 2011), 304–305.
[18] See Whatmore, "Adam Smith's Role in the French Revolution," 65–89; and Rothschild, "Adam Smith and Conservative Economics," 74–96.
[19] See Keith Tribe, "'Das Adam Smith Problem' and the Origins of Modern Smith Scholarship," *History of European Ideas* 34 (2008): 514–525.

Burke's economic thought catches the essence of this conflict: How should the West understand the relationship between commerce and virtue in general? How can a political community conserve the strength of culture and religion while securing the right to pursue profit? How can it relax the strains in the simultaneous attempt to preserve political stability and encourage economic change? Does market activity fuel unbounded individualism? If so, how can societies temper its self-destructive consequences?[20] Such questions posed difficult challenges for thinkers and statesmen in Burke's age, during which there existed irrepressible tensions, particularly in England, between retaining the authority of ancient morals and extolling the spirit of material acquisition.

Such tensions further reflect the two most powerful political identities in the United States today, conservatism and liberalism. Modern conservatism is associated with the blending of traditional morality with competitive capitalism. Modern liberalism is associated with mixing a need for social change with an unease over the impact of unfettered markets on the well-being of individuals. In the context of history, however, the release of markets from external controls, such as the church, the state, and the guild, heralded a pivotal shift away from traditional understandings about the moral need to discipline man's acquisitive instincts While freedom of commerce existed to a more limited degree before the eighteenth century, its transformation into the energizing lifeblood of European civilization, touching the deepest crevices of human activity, was an eminently new phenomenon that blossomed in Burke's day.

We must, however, remind ourselves that the struggle between commerce and virtue does not fall neatly along contemporary ideological lines in American politics. Just as liberals harbor grave apprehensions toward the excesses of commercial culture, so do conservatives. And just as liberals have attempted to revive the idea of local community, so too have conservatives.[21]

It is also worth noting that many distinguished European thinkers in the seventeenth, eighteenth, and nineteenth centuries who supported dynamic commercial activity espoused religious beliefs that shunned traditional Christian orthodoxy and objected to the state establishment of a church.

---

[20] To claim that incoherence may persist in Burke's support for both tradition and economic liberty is not to contend that his life and thought were stuck in an irrepressible psychoanalytic conflict, as Isaac Kramnick suggested in *The Rage of Edmund Burke: Portrait of An Ambivalent Conservative* (New York: Basic Books, 1977). It is, rather, to stress that Burke's engagement with the seeming uncertainties of commercial society reflected intellectual and practical reflection on matters relating to markets and virtue. Burke's conclusions on the merits and demerits of exchange economies derived from contemplation and application, not inner torment.

[21] For a liberal perspective, see Robert D. Putnam, *Bowling Alone: The Collapse and Revival of American Community* (New York: Simon & Schuster, 2000); and Michael J. Sandel, *What Money Can't Buy: The Moral Limits of Markets* (New York: Farrar, Straus and Giroux, 2012). For a conservative perspective, see Patrick J. Deneen, *Why Liberalism Failed* (New Haven: Yale University Press, 2018); and Alasdair MacIntyre, *After Virtue: A Study in Moral Theory* (Notre Dame: University of Notre Dame Press, 1984).

These thinkers included John Locke, Voltaire, Adam Smith, Joseph Priestley, Richard Price, and John Stuart Mill. And David Hume, who did support state establishment, nevertheless displayed an antagonism toward religion that revolted against Burke's firm theism. Leading public intellectuals in the twentieth century in favor of libertarian capitalism, including F. A. Hayek, Milton Friedman, and Ayn Rand, hesitated to embrace religious faith.[22]

Moreover, the thinkers spanning from the Enlightenment period to today that tend to be placed in the conservative[23] or counter-Enlightenment tradition did not embrace commercial societies with the same measure of intensity and conviction as the philosophers just mentioned, if they did reflect deeply on the role of market economies at all. In the English-speaking world, these figures included Romantic poets such as Samuel Coleridge, William Blake, and Robert Southey; prominent twentieth-century American thinkers such as Russell Kirk, Richard Weaver, and Robert Nisbet; and contemporary writers such as Patrick Buchanan, Patrick Deneen, and Claes Ryn. At its most doctrinaire level, traditional conservatism has emphasized strict class distinctions, granted priority to social order over economic liberty, and professed a contempt for political, social, and economic egalitarianism.

These historical divisions expose one of the most consequential developments in Western civilization: the shift from classical and medieval Judeo-Christian perspectives on the need to tame man's biological impulses for commodious self-preservation with liberal modernity's defense of material self-preservation as a dignified human pursuit. According to the former view, worship of the divine and the exercise of rationality defined the essence of human beings and distinguished them from irrational animals. Yet modernity's consecration of productivity, utility, profit, and industry in the pursuit of meeting our basic demands for food and shelter delivered a shock

---

[22] For Hayek, see Kenneth G. Elzinga and Matthew R. Givens, "Christianity and Hayek," *Faith & Economics* 53 (2009): 53–68. For Friedman, see "'Your World' Interview with Economist Milton Friedman," *Fox News*, November 16, 2006, accessed September 12, 2017, www.foxnews.com /story/2006/11/16/your-world-interview-with-economist-milton-friedman.html. For Rand, see Jennifer Anju Grossman, "Can You Love God and Ayn Rand?" *Wall Street Journal*, November 10, 2016, accessed September 13, 2017, www.wsj.com/articles/can-you-love-god-and-ayn-rand-1478823015. Richard A. Epstein, another prominent advocate of economic liberty, says he is a "rather weak, non-practicing Jew." See Epstein, "The Libertarian: Discrimination, Religious Liberty and How We Undervalue Free Association," *The Federalist*, April 2, 2015, accessed September 12, 2017, http://thefederalist.com/2015/04/02/the-libertarian-discrimination-religious-liberty-and-how-we-undervalue-free-association/. Tyler Cowen, a leading contemporary libertarian, has said he doesn't believe in God. See Cowen, "Why I Don't Believe in God," *Marginal Revolution*, May 25, 2017, accessed September 12, 2017, http://marginalrevolution .com/marginalrevolution/2017/05/dont-believe-god.html. Of course, there have been orthodox religious conservatives within the past century who have been drawn to the power of free markets, such as Michael Novak. See Novak, *The Spirit of Democratic Capitalism* (New York: Touchstone, 1983). And there have been many secularists who have endorsed socialism.

[23] Admittedly, "liberal" and "conservative" thought did not exist before the nineteenth century.

to traditional understandings of man. According to this reasoning, modern man has allowed his passions for earthly satisfaction to overwhelm his higher capacities to exercise reason and prepare for the afterlife. In doing so, he has striven to conquer nature rather than seek to understand it. The modern claim to personal autonomy, including the right to capitalist acquisition, subverted traditional reason, morality, and faith. The individual in modernity triumphed over the social group in classical and medieval communities.[24]

In taking into consideration this dramatic interaction between markets and morals, including in Burke's age, relations between commerce and tradition have exhibited a far greater volatility than political classifications suggest today. This book will attempt to draw out and elucidate such historical tensions through careful examination of Burke's economic thought. It is animated by two paramount questions: What were the principles of his conception of political economy? And what do his insights teach us about the relationship between commerce and virtue today? The answer to the first question will help us gauge the extent to which he supported or opposed the abstract ideology of the French Revolution. The answer to the second question will help us elevate economic discourse above conversations about tax rates and trade policy in a manner that promotes a deeper understanding of the preconditions of human flourishing.

INTERPRETATIONS OF BURKE'S POLITICAL ECONOMY

Alfred Cobban was one of the first twentieth-century scholars to highlight the possible incoherence between Burke's potent defense of tradition in the *Reflections* and his vigorous support for commercial activity in *Thoughts and Details*. In *Edmund Burke and the Revolt against the Eighteenth Century*, Cobban writes that Burke's economic ideas were "utterly alien"[25] from his political ideas, a conclusion Judith N. Shklar echoes.[26] Burke discussed property "as though it were one of those abstract rights he is elsewhere so

---

[24] For various arguments elaborating on these points, see, among many, Hannah Arendt, *The Human Condition* (Chicago: The University of Chicago Press, 1998); Leo Strauss, *Natural Right and History* (Chicago and London: The University of Chicago Press, 1965); Eric Voegelin, *The New Science of Politics: An Introduction* (Chicago and London: The University of Chicago Press, 1987); and David Walsh, *The Growth of the Liberal Soul* (Columbia and London: University of Missouri Press, 1997). Most recently, see D. C. Schindler, *Freedom from Reality: The Diabolical Character of Modern Liberty* (Notre Dame: University of Notre Dame Press, 2017); Deneen, *Why Liberalism Failed*; and Steven B. Smith, *Modernity and Its Discontents: Making and Unmaking the Bourgeois from Machiavelli to Bellow* (New Haven and London: Yale University Press, 2016).

[25] Alfred Cobban, *Edmund Burke and the Revolt against the Eighteenth Century: A Study of the Political and Social Thinking of Burke, Wordsworth, Coleridge and Southey* (London: George Allen & Unwin, 1962), 196.

[26] Judith N. Shklar, *After Utopia: The Decline of Political Faith* (Princeton: Princeton University Press, 1969), 225.

fond of abusing," even though, Cobban adds, Burke was not persuaded by Lockean justifications for property rights.[27]

An alternative interpretation has been put forth by Francis Canavan. In *The Political Economy of Edmund Burke: The Role of Property in His Thought*,[28] the only book to date that has focused exclusively on Burke's economic thought, Canavan strongly emphasizes Burke's advocacy of prescriptive property rights as a pillar of his conception of political economy. This approach represents a tendency to locate Burke's political economy comfortably within the conventional Whig tradition, a view shared by J. G. A. Pocock and James Conniff as well.[29]

An additional pattern in interpreting Burke's economic theory is to characterize it in the tradition of classical economic liberalism or bourgeois capitalism, as exemplified in the writings of C. B. Macpherson, Frank Petrella, Jr., and Isaac Kramnick.[30] Petrella argues that Burke was a "conservative classical economic thinker"[31] who supported the economic tenets of classical liberalism, such as competitive markets, supply and demand laws, and free trade. He also notes that one can reconcile Burke's conservatism with his fondness for market capitalism because he championed an ethic of incremental reform, which allowed for the conservation of the institutions and customs that perpetuated economic order.[32] Petrella does not, however, elaborate on the primacy of the role of landed property in Burke's thought, as Canavan does.

One more view portrays Burke's political economy as a manifestation of practical statesmanship, seeking to prevent commercial activity from tilting both too far in the direction of free markets and too close to the permanent grasp of government planners. Rod Preece, for instance, disputes the idea that Burke was a laissez-faire economic liberal and instead describes his economic theory as "discriminatory

---

[27] Cobban, *Edmund Burke and the Revolt against the Eighteenth Century*, 193. Gertrude Himmelfarb, Isaac Kramnick, Rod Preece, and Michael L. Frazer also endorse this view. See Himmelfarb, *The Idea of Poverty: England in the Early Industrial Age* (New York: Vintage Books, 1985), 71; Preece, "The Political Economy of Edmund Burke," *Modern Age* 24 (Summer 1980): 268; and Frazer, "Seduced by System: Edmund Burke's Aesthetic Embrace of Adam Smith's Philosophy," *Intellectual History Review* 25 (2015): 357–372.

[28] Francis Canavan, *The Political Economy of Edmund Burke: The Role of Property in His Thought* (New York: Fordham University Press, 1995).

[29] See J. G. A. Pocock, *Virtue, Commerce, and History: Essays on Political Thought and History, Chiefly in the Eighteenth Century* (Cambridge: Cambridge University Press, 1985), 194; and Conniff, *Useful Cobbler*, 3.

[30] See C. B. Macpherson, *Burke* (Oxford and New York: Oxford University Press, 1990), 53; Frank Petrella, Jr., "Edmund Burke and Classical Economics" (PhD thesis, Notre Dame, 1961); and Kramnick, *Rage of Edmund Burke*, 158.

[31] Petrella, "Edmund Burke and Classical Economics," 5. See also Petrella, "Edmund Burke: A Liberal Practitioner of Political Economy," *Modern Age* 8 (Winter 1963–64): 52–60.

[32] Petrella, "Edmund Burke and Classical Economics," 130–134.

interventionism."[33] James Conniff adopts this perspective, arguing that the laissez-faire passions in *Thoughts and Details* were calmed by Burke's focus on prudence and advocacy for government intervention in the British slave trade.[34] Nobuhiko Nakazawa suggests that at the heart of Burke's political economy was a nuanced conception of public finance, not the rigid dogma of free markets.[35]

Based on this brief survey, most secondary interpretations of Burke's economic thought, some of which overlap, can be placed in the categories of traditional Whiggism, free market classical liberalism and capitalism, or prudential statesmanship. There is much truth to these views, but they also carry limitations. First, locating Burke's economics in the Whig tradition minimizes the broader significance of his reflections on trade that transcended the time period in which he lived. The intellectual salience of Burke's defense of commercial activity in the eighteenth century, for example, is not that Burke was promoting a Whig economic agenda, but that his thought conveyed a possible defiance of traditional orthodoxy from theologians and defenders of a settled social order who had emphasized for centuries the malign effects of ungoverned commerce. This difference attains even greater significance in light of the conventional belief that Burke was a starry-eyed romantic for long-lost customs.

Second, positioning Burke in the tradition of classical liberalism and capitalism encounters difficulties. The term "classical liberalism" did not exist in Burke's day. More important, thinkers associated with "classical liberalism" embodied a wide spectrum of beliefs about the proper relation among politics, economics, and society. Thomas Hobbes called for a strong state – a Leviathan – in order to preserve social order. John Locke supported a limited state in order to secure the individual right to private property. Adam Smith did not accept the idea of an abstract state of nature espoused by Hobbes and Locke, yet in many ways he continued the Lockean tradition of endorsing the individual right to pursue profit. The Physiocrats, like Smith, praised the virtues of a free internal grain trade, but tended to submit to hardened abstract axioms Smith was keen on avoiding. Like Smith, Burke did not embrace a Lockean state of nature – but, like Locke (and Smith, and the Physiocrats), he supported the right to trade freely. Burke was also a resilient defender of the state establishment of a church, a position that creates significant tensions with many thinkers in the classical liberal tradition. Such differences show that the placement of Burke's economic thought in the framework of classical liberalism

---

[33] Preece, "Political Economy of Edmund Burke," 273.

[34] Conniff, *Useful Cobbler*, 113–136. See also Conniff, "Burke on Political Economy: The Nature and Extent of State Authority," *Review of Politics* 49 (1987): 490–514.

[35] Nobuhiko Nakazawa, "The Political Economy of Edmund Burke: A New Perspective," *Modern Age* 52 (Fall 2010): 285–292.

understates key philosophical differences between Burke and other liberal thinkers on questions concerning commerce and virtue.

Similar to "classical liberalism," the word "capitalism" was not used in Burke's time.[36] Yet we often characterize a belief in free markets before the nineteenth century as an expression of support for capitalism. This is done with reasonable justification, since contemporary terms can help clarify the underlying similarities between historical patterns of thought and modern ideas about politics, economics, and culture. But an exclusive reliance on such a method can also obscure the differences between the thinking of historical figures, like Burke, and modern classifications of political and economic viewpoints.

"Capitalism" is an apt example. The suffix "ism" denotes an ideology of thought. Burke was indeed a firm backer of market liberty, but he never transformed his support for free commerce into an ideology in itself. In fact, one of Burke's principal messages in the *Reflections* is that consecrating transactional exchange as an unassailable instrument of social organization threatens the moral fabric of civil order. Thus the portrayal of Burke's thought as a defense of capitalism wrongly suggests an undisciplined attraction to uncompromising ideology; and it further struggles to explain the nuances in his economic reflections that convey an uncommon self-awareness of the limits of exchange economies. We must also remember that when Burke died in 1797, he had not witnessed the full might of industrialization with which modern "capitalism" is associated, even if the roots of the Industrial Revolution had sprouted in his day. For these historical and conceptual reasons, this book will avoid when at all possible to depict Burke's political economy as a doctrine of "capitalism."

Yet, taking the opposite approach – defining Burke's economic thought merely as an exercise in piecemeal political prudence – neglects to recognize the primacy of conviction that motivated his statesmanship. The general interpretation of Burke that emerged in the nineteenth century, and one that has persisted to this day, regarded his public actions as gestures of cautious, utilitarian calculation and political opportunism untethered from general principles.[37]

---

[36] "Capitalism," according to Fernand Braudel, was first employed in the mid-nineteenth century by antagonists of market economies such as Louis Blanc and Pierre-Joseph Proudhon. See Braudel, *The Wheels of Commerce*, vol. II, *Civilization & Capitalism 15th–18th Century*, trans. Siân Reynolds (New York: Harper & Row, 1982), 237.

[37] For variations of this theme, see Henry Thomas Buckle, *History of Civilization in England*, vol. I (London: Longman, etc., 1864), 417–418, 422; John Morley, *Burke* (London: Macmillan and Co., 1879); Leslie Stephen, *History of English Thought in the Eighteenth Century*, vol. II (Cambridge: Cambridge University Press, 2012); Frank O'Gorman, *Edmund Burke: His Political Philosophy* (Bloomington: Indiana University Press, 1973); Lewis Namier, *The Structure of Politics at the Accession of George III* (London: Macmillan, 1982); Namier, *England in the Age of the American Revolution* (London: Macmillan, 1963); and Namier, "The Character of Burke," *Spectator*, 19 December 1958, 895–896.

Burke himself said in the *Reflections* that prudence was the "first of all virtues."[38] But this was certainly not the only virtue, or the last virtue, that he championed with force and clarity in the eighteenth century. Burke's engagement with matters of commerce and revenue certainly took into consideration existing political constraints and interests. Nevertheless, they also reflect a general coherence of thought on political economy that spanned his entire public and private life.

It is the premise of this book, therefore, that our comprehension of Burke's theory of political economy should not be limited by a particular political tradition, such as Whiggism, or seen through a modern lens, such as classical liberalism, or denoted by an ideological category, such as capitalism. Rather, this inquiry seeks to illuminate Burke's theoretical observations on the interaction between commerce and morals and locate them in wider intellectual contexts. In addition, this book will attempt to broaden the dimensions of Burke's economic thought beyond his comments on the importance of protecting landed property, which Canavan adequately discusses in his book. It will examine Burke's endorsement of landed property rights, but it will lay a sharper accent than Canavan does on his thought regarding mobile property – including the grain trade, public finance, and foreign commerce – that remains underappreciated and underexplored in the study of his economic theory.

TERMINOLOGY OF POLITICAL ECONOMY AND BURKE'S USE OF EMPIRICAL INFORMATION

The difficulties in describing Burke's economic thought as an affirmation of "capitalism" bring to light other terms this book will use that require brief elucidation. (Analysis of some terms will be expanded upon in various chapters.) "Liberalism" in the United States and Europe today is associated with government regulation of the economy, a strong welfare state, mass democratic participation, and a secular worldview. In Burke's time, however, the adjective "liberal" – without the "ism" suffix – in the context of economics connoted the dynamic of a free flow of goods emancipated from government restrictions. Therefore, this book will use "liberal" to embody a conception of economics that exudes firm support for market competition and free trade, not state regulation.

"Free trade" is another phrase that warrants scrutiny. Today "free trade" has acquired a life of its own as a self-sustaining economic doctrine. In the eighteenth century, however, a clear definition of "free trade" was still beginning to acquire visible form, and its meaning could suggest different things in different contexts to different audiences. For example, Adam Smith's

---

[38] Langford, *Writings and Speeches*, VIII, 113. Burke also stated in *Appeal from the New to the Old Whigs*, "Prudence is not only the first in rank of the virtues political and moral, but she is the director, the regulator, the standard of them all" (Langford, *Writings and Speeches*, IV, 383).

championing of "free trade," like Burke's, still accommodated support for some government regulations of foreign trade, most famously the Navigation Acts.[39] It follows from such provisos that advocacy for "free trade" did not necessarily convey the notion that all state entanglements in foreign commerce should be struck down, or struck down all at once. With these qualifications, however, "free trade" will be used when appropriate for lack of a more effectual term to capture the essence of the concept.

Because Burke's economic thought was neatly woven into his beliefs about ethics and society, this book will also employ the term "civil society." Civil society is characterized today as the zone of social interaction between the individual and the government in which voluntary associations, such as families, churches, and civic organizations, flourish.[40] Burke, however, tended to use "civil society" consistent with its traditional meaning as the general domain in which human beings engaged in social and political activity, including economic activity. This domain included social groups, but they also included the individual and the government. The significance of Burke's notion of civil society will emerge later in this book's discussion of the conceptual disharmonies between Burke and modern classical liberals and libertarians concerning the idea of a state. Therefore, this book will typically use "civil society" as Burke understood it.[41]

"Political economy" itself can be defined in a number of ways. Strictly speaking, it was recognized in the eighteenth century as the study of public finance, the science of establishing sufficient revenue streams for the people and the state.[42] In a larger sense, political economy was grasped as the examination of the relationship between commercial activity and foreign and domestic political affairs. In its broadest conception, the study of political economy spanned the comprehension of commercial, political, cultural, and moral influences on civil society. Because landed property played an influential role in informing Burke's beliefs on these matters, this book's notion of "political

---

[39] In particular, the Act of Navigation of 1660.

[40] For the intellectual roots of this concept, see Alexis de Tocqueville, *Democracy in America*, trans. and ed. Harvey C. Mansfield and Delba Winthrop (Chicago and London: The University of Chicago Press, 2000); and Georg Hegel, *Philosophy of Right*, trans. T. M. Knox (Oxford: Clarendon Press, 1958).

[41] For a deeper exploration into Burke's notion of civil society, see Richard Boyd, "'The Unsteady and Precarious Contribution of Individuals': Edmund Burke's Defense of Civil Society," *Review of Politics* 61 (1999): 465–491.

[42] Adam Smith described political economy "as a branch of the science of a statesman or legislator" that pursued "two distinct objects; first, to provide a plentiful revenue or subsistence for the people, or more properly to enable them to provide such a revenue or subsistence for themselves; and secondly, to supply the state or commonwealth with a revenue sufficient for the publick services. It proposes to enrich both the people and the sovereign" (Smith, *An Inquiry into the Nature and Cause of the Wealth of Nations*, vol. I, eds. R. H. Campbell and A. S. Skinner (Indianapolis: Liberty Fund, 1981), 428).

economy" will blend the aforementioned definitions of the word with his reflections on land.

In addition to terminology, this book's use of empirical information requires brief explanation that will be drawn out in later chapters. Books on Burke explore his political and intellectual activities almost exclusively through historical inquiry and textual interpretation of his speeches and writings. The following chapters will investigate Burke's thought using historical and textual methods as well, but they will also thread empirical evidence into such analysis, such as import and export trade data and grain prices. This will be done for two principal reasons. First, it will help evoke a sharper historical context for the debates and controversies of political economy Burke confronted in his political life.

More significant, Burke himself employed empirical data as an important supplement to his reflections on commercial activity. Awareness of Burke's use of data will thus place us in a better position to discern Burke's epistemic approaches to the study of political economy, for he understood this information to be a valuable analytic tool when testing the truth of man's theoretical assertions about commerce and revenue. Burke's application of empirical knowledge also reinforced his general maxim that the weight of experience elevates our understanding of human nature and human flourishing. Burke was not a strict empiricist, but this book will attempt to be faithful to the shrewd way in which he introduced statistical knowledge to enhance his method of argument.

CONCLUSION

Because this is a book tracing the principles of Burke's economic thought, it is not intended to be an exhaustive history of commercial society in the eighteenth century, nor of his private affairs regarding trade and personal finance. Our appreciation for Burke can be deepened, however, by acquainting ourselves with particular references and allusions that decorated his commentary. Therefore, most chapters include a section that outlines the contemporary milieu at the time of his writings and speeches on political economy. Every effort has been made to be as historically accurate as possible in these sections. Since this book is intended for both Burke scholars and the general public, those who are already familiar with eighteenth-century English politics are welcome to skip over such sections, while those less familiar with the subject are encouraged to read them.

The structure of this book begins with Burke's elementary principles of political economy and then ascends higher to examine his more philosophic meditations on commerce and manners. Chapter 1 provides a sketch of Burke's background, placing an emphasis on his engagement with matters relating to economics. It further demonstrates that he acquired a well-earned reputation in his political life as an authority on commerce and markets. Chapters 2, 3, and 4 explore Burke's commentary in *Thoughts and Details* and elsewhere on the domestic grain market, including his observations on supply and demand laws, wage labor, middlemen, and the corn bounty. Chapters 3 and 4 also discuss his more theoretical remarks on wealth redistribution, equality, and the role of rationality in regulating commercial exchange. Chapter 5 addresses Burke's plan for government reform, *Speech on Economical Reform*, and its relevance to his economic theory and conception of the role of the state.

The remaining chapters widen the geographical and intellectual scope of Burke's reflections on commerce. Chapter 6 investigates his early thoughts and legislative activity relating to the political economy of British colonization, including *An Account of the European Settlements in America* and the Free Port Act of 1766. Chapter 7 probes Burke's views on British foreign trade in the aftermath of the Seven Years War and on Anglo-American trade relations, as expressed in *Observations on a Late State of the Nation*, *Speech on American Taxation*, and *Speech on Conciliation with America*. Chapter 8 considers his remarks in *Two Letters on the Trade of Ireland* on Anglo-Irish trade and on the link between commerce and nature. This chapter also describes two important instances in which Burke suspended his support for free trade. Chapters 9 and 10 inspect Burke's critique in *Ninth Report of Select Committee* and elsewhere of Britain's East India Company, the chartered corporation that enjoyed a commercial monopoly in the East Indies. Chapters 11 and 12 analyze Burke's commentary in the *Reflections* and in his additional writings and speeches on the political economy of the French Revolution, including his profound statements on the interaction between ethics and economics.

The subject of political economy was not a tangential concern for Burke during his political life but an object of sustained inquiry in his thought and statesmanship. And, as we shall see, his engagement with matters of commerce and property would come into contact with celebrated thinkers such as Adam Smith and F. A. Hayek. Burke's considered ruminations on markets, foreign trade, and public finance would address some of the most formative political controversies in the history of modern Western civilization, including the Anglo-American and Anglo-Irish imperial relationships; British India and the East India Company; slavery; and the French Revolution. Yet Burke also confronted lesser-known affairs that carried a lasting influence on the political economy of Britain, such as commercial policy in the West Indies; the corn bounty; and prohibitions on middleman trading practices. The age of Burke was in many ways an inflection point for the historical development and public understanding of modern economics.

Burke's sophisticated fusion of philosophic and cultural insights with his study of commerce and property should not hide the imperfections in his economic thought. His thought is burdened by inherent limitations, first and foremost, because he did not write a comprehensive treatise on political economy such as Smith's *Wealth of Nations*. Much of his commentary on public affairs was written in different political settings, and addressed to different audiences, without seemingly being bound by any organizing principle. Therefore, Burke at times does not follow his arguments to their logical consequences, or does not seriously explore plausible alternatives to his own conclusions. In addition, while Burke did hold an advanced understanding of economics for his age, his command of particular subjects, such as finance, varied with his opportunity to immerse himself in such issues at the necessary level of detail. Finally, because Burke lived during a time before the advent of mass industrialized economies, we must be cautious before asserting that he would have supported particular policy prescriptions for modern nation-states.

Yet such constraints also furnish benefits in the study of Burke's economic thought. The pedagogical significance of his conception of political economy, then, arises from its tendency to escape modern classifications of economic viewpoints. It incorporated elements of classical liberalism but was not classical liberalism. And while Burke's economic thought retained insights from premodern philosophers and clerics, it was not an orthodox expression of classical or medieval perspectives on commerce. The conclusions Burke draws from his observation of economic phenomena are also not predictable; we shall learn that on certain points they overlapped with critics of capitalism in modernity.

In the end, by taking into serious account Burke's political economy, we can broaden our comprehension of the strengths and limitations of market liberty and become more aware of the possibilities of integrating the pursuit of profit with the ethical preconditions of freedom. For Burke's economic thought offers a mediating path forward for modern commercial society between excessive government intervention and individualism that retains the fruits of private market exchange while protecting against its baser effects, thereby providing timely lessons about the possible harmony between liberty and virtue.

PART I

BIOGRAPHY

I

Biography and Burke's Authority as a Political Economist

An Irishman, one Mr. Burke, is sprung up in the House of Commons, who has astonished every body with the power of his eloquence, his comprehensive knowledge in all our exterior and internal politics and commercial interests.[1]

Charles Lee, 1766

If I had not deemed it of some value, I should not have made political oeconomy an object of my humble studies, from my very early youth to near the end of my service in parliament, even before, (at least to any knowledge of mine) it had employed the thoughts of speculative men in other parts of Europe.[2]

Edmund Burke, 1796

1.1 THE ROOTS OF BURKE'S INTEREST IN THE SCIENCE OF POLITICAL ECONOMY

A brief background on Burke's biography, with particular emphasis on matters regarding commerce and agriculture, will help us discover the roots of his interest in political economy.[3] Burke was born on January 12, 1730[4] in Dublin, Ireland. He grew up in Dublin, but his childhood included temporary

---

[1] Edward Langworthy, ed., *Memoirs of the Life of the Late Charles Lee, Esq.* (London: J. S. Jordan, 1792), 297.

[2] Langford, *Writings and Speeches*, IX, 159.

[3] The biographical information on Burke was culled from the following sources: F. P. Lock, *Edmund Burke*, vol. I, *1730–1784* (Oxford: Clarendon Press, 2012); Lock, *Edmund Burke*, vol. II, *1784–1797* (Oxford: Clarendon Press, 2009); Bourke, *Empire & Revolution*; Carl B. Cone, *Burke and the Nature of Politics: The Age of the American Revolution* (Lexington: University of Kentucky Press, 1957); and Cone, *Burke and the Nature of Politics: The Age of the French Revolution* (Lexington: University of Kentucky Press, 1964).

[4] Some scholars contend that Burke was actually born in 1728 or 1729. See Bourke, *Empire & Revolution*, 29n8.

stays in the countryside, where his mother's extended family lived. Burke's childhood school at Ballitore was also in a rural area. Burke, who was baptized into the Established Church of England, was raised in moderate circumstances by an Anglican father, an attorney,[5] and Catholic mother. At the time, the penal codes, a series of anti-Catholic laws established in Ireland by the Irish Parliament, a body controlled by the Protestant elite, circumscribed the liberties of Catholics to practice their religion, inherit and acquire property, and pursue educational and employment opportunities. Burke would come to criticize the codes in his discussion of Irish property rights later in his life.

Burke attended Trinity College Dublin from 1744 to 1748. Outside of his formal education, he helped organize a range of social and intellectual activities during this time period. Burke was an active member of a student debating club[6] that discussed, among many topics, subjects relating to political economy, including: the influence of commerce in promoting wealth and discouraging idleness; the connection between trade and virtue; the merits of promoting the woolen or linen manufacture for Ireland; the role of luxury in the decline of Rome; the negative commercial impact of French global power on British trade; taxes on absentee Irish landlords; the advantages of power over riches; the confusion and instability wrought by a multiplicity of laws; printing rights and monopoly; the wisdom of laws banning the consumption of spirits; and appropriate punishment for the stealing of property.[7]

Burke wrote for and was the lead editor of *The Reformer*, a weekly literary paper founded when he was an undergraduate.[8] The *Reformer* contains some of Burke's earliest published reflections on political economy, including commentary on the impoverished condition of Irish peasants.[9] One of his essays in the periodical intriguingly noted that "[n]othing comes to its height at first, and the Spirit of encouraging Trade, may at length rise to Science."[10] While Burke was primarily attracted to literature and history in his youth, his activity for the *Reformer*, combined with his active participation in the student club while at Trinity College, illustrates a ripe and probing mind on subjects

---

[5] There is some debate about whether Burke's father conformed to the Church of Ireland to advance in the legal profession. See Lock, *Edmund Burke*, vol. I, 4–6 and Bourke, *Empire & Revolution*, 31.

[6] Arthur P. I. Samuels writes that the club was "the first of which there is any record in the United Kingdom." See Samuels, ed., *The Early Life Correspondence and Writings of The Rt. Hon. Edmund Burke* (Cambridge: Cambridge University Press, 1923), 203.

[7] Samuels, *Early Life Correspondence and Writings*, 233–293.

[8] The *Reformer* continued to be published after he left the school. Burke graduated from Trinity College Dublin in February 1748. The *Reformer* was published every week in Dublin from January 28 to April 21, 1748 (Langford, *Writings and Speeches*, I, 65). F. P. Lock, however, questions whether Burke should be considered the chief influence behind the *Reformer* (*Edmund Burke*, vol. I, 56–59).

[9] See "Labor, the Laboring Poor, and the Rich as Trustees," Chapter 3. The *Reformer*'s essays were signed by letters, not by the names of the individual authors.

[10] Langford, *Writings and Speeches*, I, 93–94.

relating to commerce, wealth, and property in the infancy of his intellectual development.

Multiple accounts testify to Burke's bookish curiosity and the determined vigor with which he engaged in private study, which quite possibly included examination of commercial matters. Richard Shackleton, a lifelong friend and fellow student of Burke, wrote that he was "a lad of most promising genius, of an inquisitive and speculative cast of mind" who "read much while he was a boy, and accumulated a stock of learning of great variety." His "memory was extensive."[11] Burke's brother, Richard, reportedly quipped that "while we were at play, he was always at work."[12] James Prior, an early biographer of Burke, wrote that "the cultivation of mind was with him not merely a duty, but an overpowering passion, which swallowed up every other."[13] Burke would retain this uncommon work ethic in Parliament on legislative matters relating to trade and agriculture, among many topics.

Burke returned his attention to the issue of Irish Catholic poverty in the early 1760s, when he was in Dublin serving as the private secretary to William Gerard Hamilton, a parliamentarian and then-Chief Secretary for Ireland, during sessions of the Irish Parliament in 1761 and 1762.[14] While he was in Ireland and after traveling back to England, Burke's conscience was struck by the conflict between the so-called Whiteboys, a poverty-stricken class of Catholic farmers, and anti-Catholic Protestant landlords, which flared up in the final months of 1761. Burke was sympathetic to the grievances aired by the Whiteboys; he believed that the punishment inflicted on the protestors was excessive, and became more attentive to the injustices occasioned by the popery laws. Burke most likely began to write *Tracts relating to Popery Laws*, his essay excoriating the penal code's oppression of Irish Catholics, in 1762.[15]

In 1750, two years after he graduated from Trinity College, Burke left Ireland and traveled to London to study for the bar, as he was considering becoming a lawyer like his father. Burke abandoned this aspiration during the decade and concentrated his efforts on literary writings. He published his first two major works, *A Vindication of Natural Society* and *A Philosophical Enquiry into the Origin of our Ideas of the Sublime and Beautiful*, in 1756 and 1757, respectively.

---

[11] *The Leadbeater Papers: A Selection from the MSS. and Correspondence of Mary Leadbeater*, vol. II, *Unpublished Letters of Edmund Burke: and the Correspondence of Mrs. Richard Trench and Rev. George Crabbe* (London: Bell and Daldy, 1862), 113.

[12] Arthur Lensen Woehl, "Burke's Reading" (PhD thesis, Cornell University, 1928), 39.

[13] James Prior, *Life of the Right Honourable Edmund Burke* (London: George Bell & Sons, 1878), 13.

[14] Burke returned to Ireland from 1763 to 1764 and in 1766 and 1786. See Lock, *Edmund Burke*, vol. I, 2n2.

[15] See Lock, *Edmund Burke*, vol. I, 194; Bourke, *Empire & Revolution*, 238–241; and Conor Cruise O'Brien, *The Great Melody: A Thematic Biography and Commented Anthology of Edmund Burke* (Chicago: The University of Chicago Press, 1993), 44–46.

The *Vindication* was a satire exposing and ridiculing the deistic rationalism of Lord Bolingbroke, a Tory politician and thinker influenced by John Locke and Francis Bacon. The *Philosophical Enquiry* was a work on taste, or what we would call aesthetics, that described how the sublime is a nonrational sensation distinct from the beautiful. These writings did not address economic subjects in particular, but they do supply theoretical insights into Burke's political thought that would come to inform his views on commerce and markets.

It was in 1757 that Burke married Jane Nugent, the daughter of an Irish Catholic physician. By all accounts Burke was a devoted husband and father. Most likely referring to the milieu of eighteenth-century British politics, Elizabeth R. Lambert writes that Burke "is probably singular among married public figures for not being charged with having either real or imagined affairs."[16] Jane gave birth to a son, Richard, in 1758, while a second son, Christopher, died before his sixth birthday.[17] Burke was a doting father who was fiercely protective of Richard.[18] Social relations in Burke's life were defined by love and obligation.

Burke helped found and edit the *Annual Register*, a literary and historical journal, in April 1758. He most likely was the primary (and anonymous) editor of the journal from 1758 to 1764. Upon becoming secretary to the Marquess of Rockingham in 1765, Burke maintained a more tenuous connection to the periodical thereafter.[19] The composition of the *Annual Register* included, among various sections, a review essay of the previous year's political affairs and a book review.[20] Although not every view in the publication can be attributed to Burke, the selection of the published material and the general argument of its essays do illuminate clues about his political and economic interests, and the general development of his intellectual thought, during his emergence as a mature thinker.

Burke's editorial duties for the *Annual Register* overlapped with his service to Hamilton. In 1763, while still working for him, Burke was awarded an annual pension of £300, billed to the Irish Establishment.[21] Two years later, in July 1765, Burke became the private secretary to the Marquess of Rockingham, a wealthy and influential aristocrat who was the leader of a Whig faction in Parliament. Later that year Burke won election to the

---

[16] Elizabeth R. Lambert, *Edmund Burke of Beaconsfield* (Newark: University of Delaware Press, 2003), 73.

[17] Jane may have experienced up to two miscarriages.

[18] Lambert, *Edmund Burke of Beaconsfield*, 89–90.

[19] See Bertram D. Sarason, "Edmund Burke and the Two *Annual Registers*," *PMLA* 68 (1953): 496–508.

[20] Consult T. O. McLoughlin, *Edmund Burke and the First Ten Years of the "Annual Register," 1758–1767* (Salisbury: University of Rhodesia, 1975).

[21] Burke to William Gerard Hamilton, [March 1763], in Thomas W. Copeland, ed., *The Correspondence of Edmund Burke*, vol. I (Cambridge: Cambridge University Press, 1958), 163–166.

House of Commons, representing Wendover, and entered Parliament for the first time in January 1766.

At this point, Burke did not possess a landed estate in England. (He had inherited an estate in Ireland from Garrett after the latter died in 1765.) Such was a political liability in eighteenth-century English politics. The weight of political authority for a Member of Parliament derived from the ownership of landed property, as illustrated by the Parliamentary Qualification Act of 1711, which had imposed property requirements for members. Englishmen believed that stable land, not transient commercial wealth, was tied to the general interests of the community, and that the pedigree of a statesman was built on his ancestral connections to inherited property.

Burke addressed this shortcoming in 1768 by purchasing an estate named Gregories, later called Butler's Court. Furnishing a necessary element of permanency in his life, this acquisition reflected Burke's attempt to "cast a little root" in England.[22] It covered around 600 acres.[23] With generous financial assistance from his friends, Burke paid just in excess of £20,000 for the land,[24] worth roughly half a million dollars in mid-twentieth century America.[25] Gregories was a section of a manor formerly owned by the seventeenth-century poet Edmund Waller and located at the market town of Beaconsfield, in the county of Buckinghamshire. (Beaconsfield was fewer than twenty-four miles from London.) The estate consisted of a central residence with two stories and two smaller two-story houses on either side, connected to the main residence by colonnades that gave the property a shine of royal grandeur. Carl B. Cone writes that the purchase "elevated his social status and brought to him the deep personal satisfaction of owning property and living magnificently."[26]

Burke was committed to the improvement of Gregories. He himself farmed more than 400 acres of productive land,[27] which covered arable and grass land. George Lipscomb, a physician and writer who had completed a sweeping survey of Buckingham estates called *The History and Antiquities of the County of Buckingham* in 1847, described Burke's stewardship of his property this way:

> Mr. Burke's purchase was also rendered of more than triple value, by the activity of his genius; for his comprehensive mind, which embraced every thing both useful and profound, induced him to apply himself to the pursuits of agriculture with so much assiduity, that he very soon astonished the literary circle amongst whom he had

---

[22] Burke to Richard Shackleton, 1 May 1768, in *Correspondence of Edmund Burke*, vol. I, 351.
[23] Burke to Richard Shackleton, 1 May 1768, in *Correspondence of Edmund Burke*, vol. I, 351. This section relied on the following sources concerning Burke's purchase and stewardship of his estate: Lambert, *Edmund Burke of Beaconsfield*; Lock, *Edmund Burke*, vol. I, 249–258 and 315–319; Cone, *Age of the American Revolution*, 123–143; George Lipscomb, *The History and Antiquities of the County of Buckingham*, vol. III (London: J. & W. Robins, 1847), 191–192; and Cone, "Edmund Burke, the Farmer," *Agricultural History* 19 (1945): 65–69.
[24] Lock, *Edmund Burke*, vol. I, 250–253.   [25] Cone, *Age of the American Revolution*, 129.
[26] Cone, *Age of the American Revolution*, 123.   [27] Lock, *Edmund Burke*, vol. I, 316.

accustomed to move, by his improvements at Gregories, which soon presented a very different character from that plain sombre habitation, when he first took possession of it.[28]

Lipscomb wrote that he "soon became one of the most successful practical farmers in Buckinghamshire."[29] The estate satisfied Burke's hunger to become a respected landed aristocrat, achieve mastery of husbandry, and earn a reputation for political and social integrity.

Arthur Young, a leading eighteenth-century English authority on agricultural economics and a friend of Burke, reported in 1771 that Burke's labor force consisted of one bailiff, two boys, and six other laborers. The farm's main crops were wheat, barley, clover, and turnips. The farm included forty swine, fourteen cows, six horses, and six young cattle.[30] Burke's superintendence over the property was known for its judicious openness to experimentation and innovation, and for its serious attention to the best agricultural techniques regarding the feeding of stock, the cultivation of soil, and the rotation of crops. For example, Young reported that Burke used advanced draining techniques to make a ten-acre field dry enough to cultivate crops: "[T]he drains answered extremely well, for the land has since been quite dry."[31]

Burke also displayed his ingenuity by "deep ploughing" farmland ten to twelve inches in the ground. Young noted that this was "double what the farmers ever attempt."[32] This decision "surprized [Burke's] bailiff," who thought Burke's crops would be "utterly ruined." Yet "a regular and unbroken success in every one has convinced him, that deep ploughing is not so pernicious a practice as he apprehended."[33] Overall, Cone concludes, the farm yielded a modest profit.[34] F. P. Lock, a more recent biographer, writes that the estate's value did not grow significantly under Burke's stewardship.[35]

Burke's zest for farming and creative agricultural techniques was not unusual for the time period in England. Still, multiple contemporary accounts testified to his achievements in productivity and efficiency.[36] The *Annual Register* published an excerpt from Bisset's biography of Burke in the journal's 1798 edition, one year after he died, which remarked that "as a farmer [Burke] was

[28] Lipscomb, *History and Antiquities*, 191.   [29] Lipscomb, *History and Antiquities*, 192n1.
[30] Arthur Young, *The Farmer's Tour Through the East of England*, vol. IV (London: W. Strahan, 1771), 77. See also Lock, vol. I, *Edmund Burke*, 316.
[31] Young, *Farmer's Tour*, 80. See also Cone, *Age of the American Revolution*, 139–140; and Cone, "Edmund Burke, the Farmer."
[32] Young, *Farmer's Tour*, 79.   [33] Young, *Farmer's Tour*, 79.
[34] Cone, *Age of the American Revolution*, 137.   [35] Lock, *Edmund Burke*, vol. I, 257.
[36] See the views of Young and James Boswell in Cone, "Edmund Burke, the Farmer," 65–69; and the comments of Mrs. Montagu in Cone, *Age of the American Revolution*, 138. Also, Prior reported in *Life of Edmund Burke* that "[Burke's] knowledge of farming, and of stock live and dead, was so highly estimated by his neighbours as to occasion frequent applications for advice upon such matters" (420–421).

the most successful of the neighbourhood, without any unusual expence."[37] His "taste displayed itself in various improvements of its natural beauties; and he bestowed much attention on farming."[38]

Burke's agricultural ingenuity even inspired Mary Leadbeater, the daughter of Richard Shackleton,[39] to draft a poem describing the Gregories estates in flowery language. Comparing Burke to Virgil, she wrote that he "Improves with skilful industry the soil, / Cheers the poor peasant, and rewards his toil."[40] Burke himself called agriculture his "favourite study" and "favourite pursuit."[41] In essence, it is hard to avoid the conclusion that Burke's experiences as a farmer helped inform his views in *Thoughts and Details*, a tract whose prime objects of discussion were the agricultural economy and employment relations between farmers and laborers.

Even with his flair for agriculture, the estate remained a heavy financial obligation that saddled Burke throughout his life. He experienced a piling clutter of interest payments, multiple mortgages, indebtedness, and litigious neighbors,[42] not to mention the heightened social anxiety that accompanied such problems. Lock characterizes Burke's purchase of the estate as "imprudent."[43] Cone calls attention to his "extreme carelessness in financial affairs."[44] Burke himself admitted that his personal matters, financial and otherwise, were "always in a State of embarrassment and confusion."[45] There is little evidence Burke made serious attempts to change his financially injudicious behavior. Yet the social and political advantages conferred by the estate must have exceeded these drawbacks for Burke, for he stayed active in its agricultural affairs up until his final years.

One reason Burke frequently found himself in a precarious financial position was because of his tender generosity to friends, employees, and tenants. According to historical accounts, he treated his laborers well and paid them

---

[37] "Characters," *The Annual Register, For the Year 1798* (London: T. Burton, 1800), 329.

[38] "Characters," *Annual Register, For the Year 1798*, 329. Of course, Burke's personal connections to the *Annual Register* may have prompted the publication to exaggerate his prowess as a husbandman.

[39] Richard was Burke's friend. Richard's father, Abraham, founded and managed the Quaker school at Ballitore that Burke attended as a youth.

[40] Mary Leadbeater, *Poems by Mary Leadbeater* (Dublin: Martin Keene, 1808), 99. See also Peter Burke, *The Public and Domestic Life of the Right Hon. Edmund Burke* (London: Nathaniel Cooke, 1854), 124–126.

[41] Prior, *Life of Edmund Burke*, 33.

[42] Burke was involved in property disputes at least twice with Edmund Waller, an irritable neighbor of Burke and the descendant of the poet whose manor Burke had purchased, regarding a wooded lane and a small pond. See Lambert, *Edmund Burke of Beaconsfield*, 65–67.

[43] Lock, *Edmund Burke*, vol. I, 256.   [44] Cone, *Age of the American Revolution*, 134.

[45] See "Edmund Burke's Character of His Son and Brother," in P. J. Marshall and John A. Woods, eds., *The Correspondence of Edmund Burke*, vol. VII, *January 1792–August 1794* (Cambridge: Cambridge University Press, 1968), 591.

handsomely relative to the standard pay at the time.[46] Burke was not
overzealous in demanding rent from his tenants, and he frequently entertained
guests at his estate, conveying a warmhearted hospitality.

Burke showed sweet compassion toward the poor. "He was remarkable
for hospitality," the *Annual Register* reported soon after he passed
away.[47] He was an active member of a community group that looked
after the infirm. Burke was also the source for other plans to help
ameliorate the misfortunes of the impoverished in his neighborhood,
such as creating local welfare institutions, which were not ubiquitous in
rural areas at the time. Burke sought to spread lessons of piety, industry,
and loyalty among the needy.[48] He would later establish a school for
children of destitute French émigré families who had fled the French
Revolution.[49] Burke's altruism prompted James Prior to write, "With
the poor in this neighborhood [in Wycombe] he was generally
a favourite, having the address to converse much with them, visit their
cottages, overlook or regulate their pastimes as well as their labours,
without losing any thing of his dignity."[50]

In 1772, during his tenure as MP for Wendover, Burke received an offer to
serve as a supervisor on a commission assigned to examine the misconduct of
Britain's East India Company in British India. The Company, a chartered
trading company that enjoyed an exclusive commercial monopoly on overseas
trade in South Asia, had been facing heightening public scrutiny at the time over
its maladministration on the subcontinent. Burke declined the offer, but he
would later play a significant role in investigating Company delinquencies as
a prominent member of the House of Commons' Select Committee on India in
the early 1780s.

Following his representation of Wendover, Burke would go on to serve as an
MP for Bristol, a bustling trading hub, from 1775 to 1780. Bristol's active
merchant class represented a thorn in the side of Burke's statesmanship,
however, since his sympathy for free trade was often in conflict with Bristol
traders' support for commercial protectionism. The city was also a powerful
purveyor of the Atlantic slave trade.

Burke's final service in Parliament was to represent Malton, a small borough
in Yorkshire, starting in 1780. He was appointed as Paymaster of the Forces, the
de facto banker for the British army, in Rockingham's second administration in
1782, and reappointed under the Fox-North coalition in 1783. Burke's most
famous writing, *Reflections on the Revolution in France*, which issued a fierce
attack on the French Revolution, was published in 1790. Burke retired from

[46] See Cone, *Age of the American Revolution*, 139.
[47] "Characters," *Annual Register, For the Year 1798*, 329.
[48] Prior, *Life of Edmund Burke*, 422.
[49] See "Labor, the Laboring Poor, and the Rich as Trustees," Chapter 3.
[50] Prior, *Life of Edmund Burke*, 423.

Parliament in June 1794, and was later awarded a government pension.[51] He passed away in July 1797.

1.2 BURKE AS A POLITICAL ECONOMIST

One final matter requires attention before examining the substance of Burke's political economy: did the British thinker-statesman reflect upon commercial matters with adequate seriousness to even warrant a study of his economic theory? We must first begin by noting that Burke's library included writings that discussed commerce and trade, such as William Combe edition of Adam Anderson's *An Historical and Chronological Deduction of the Origin of Commerce* and Malachy Postlethwayt's *Dictionary of Commerce*. The library also carried a copy of Adam Smith's *Wealth of Nations*, although this particular edition was published after Burke's death.[52] The presence of such writings in his private possessions suggests an attraction to questions of trade that would endure throughout his intellectual and political life.

Burke himself testified to this attraction in *Letter to a Noble Lord* (1796), when he defended his government pension by contrasting his industrious service in Parliament with the indolence of the Duke of Bedford, who had previously criticized Burke's "most extravagant pension" in a speech in the House of Lords – extravagant particularly for someone who, according to the duke, was a "preacher of economy."[53] In the letter, Burke first highlights the diligence with which he studied the science of political economy when discussing his efforts in crafting the Economical Reform Bill and its more condensed version, the Civil List Bill of 1782, both of which aimed to diminish the Crown's influence in Parliament and limit government expenditures.

Yet such bills, in Burke's telling, were part of his broader effort to examine the subject of political economy as it related to the British Empire: "The first session I sat in Parliament, I found it necessary to analyze the whole commercial, financial, constitutional and foreign interests of Great Britain and it's Empire."[54] Indeed, for someone piqued by questions of commerce and empire, Burke entered Parliament at an opportune moment: the Stamp Act of

---

[51] Consult H. V. F. Somerset, "Some Papers of Edmund Burke on His Pension," *The English Historical Review* 45 (1930): 110–114.

[52] Consult *Catalogue of the Library of the Late Right Hon. Edmund Burke* (1833).

[53] *St. James's Chronicle*, issue 5912, 12–14 November 1795.

[54] Langford, *Writings and Speeches*, IX, 159. He issued a similar statement more than twenty years prior in regard to the American colonies. Upon being elected to the House of Commons in 1765, Burke noted in *Speech on Conciliation with America*, "I was obliged to take more than common pains, to instruct myself in every thing which relates to our Colonies" (Langford, *Writings and Speeches*, III, 106). And in *Speech on Economical Reform* (1780), Burke remarked that the

1765, which the Rockingham ministry, of which Burke was emerging as a prominent member, repealed in 1766, was a hotly debated topic in the context of Anglo-American imperial relations. This Act was among the most important policies impacting the commercial activity Burke was referring to in his comments just noted.

In the next paragraph of *Letter to a Noble Lord*, Burke strengthens his assertion that he devoted copious energy to his evaluation of economic matters:

> Does his Grace think, that they who advised the Crown to make my retreat easy, considered me only as an oeconomist? That, well understood, however, is a good deal. If I had not deemed it of some value, I should not have made political oeconomy an object of my humble studies, from my very early youth to near the end of my service in parliament, even before, (at least to any knowledge of mine) it had employed the thoughts of speculative men in other parts of Europe. At that time, it was still in it's infancy in England, where, in the last century, it had it's origin.[55]

It is significant that Burke here is dignifying the study of political economy, for he had famously condemned "oeconomists," along with "sophisters" and "calculators," in the *Reflections* just six years prior for destroying the spirit of chivalry that had preserved social order in Christian Europe.[56] Based on this sharp attack in the *Reflections*, one suspects he would repudiate any notion suggesting that the study of economics was a worthy endeavor.

For the time being, however, we can make a provisional distinction that will acquire greater clarification later in this book: in Burke's judgment, his critique of "oeconomists" in the *Reflections* targeted the zealous schemes of French intellectuals, financiers, and legislators fond of employing abstract theory in the service of social engineering, while his favorable reference to his efforts as an "oeconomist" in *Letter to a Noble Lord* signaled a detached commitment to inquire into matters of public finance and commercial activity with impartiality, seeking not to innovate but to understand.

Burke expresses two other noteworthy points in his comments. First, he claims he studied political economy from his youth to his final days in Parliament, thereby reinforcing his own self-assessment that he examined markets and public administration with sustained reflection throughout his entire life. Second, by asserting that he was ahead of his time in his engagement with political economy, a discipline that was still in its "infancy" in England and elsewhere in Europe, Burke is attempting to convey that he was an authoritative *and* prescient thinker on subjects relating to commerce, revenue, and taxation.[57]

"pretended objects" of Britain's Board of Trade had been "much the objects of my study" (Langford, *Writings and Speeches*, III, 534).

[55] Langford, *Writings and Speeches*, IX, 159–160.

[56] Langford, *Writings and Speeches*, VIII, 127.

[57] Keep in mind that Burke's self-congratulatory declarations of his hard work in *Letter to a Noble Lord* were presented in the context of his attempt to justify his government pension.

Burke's next comments in *Letter to a Noble Lord* build upon this effort to assert his authority on political economy by suggesting that he participated in economic debates with other leading thinkers of this time. "Great and learned men thought my studies were not wholly thrown away, and deigned to communicate with me now and then on some particulars of their immortal works," he writes. "Something of these studies may appear incidentally in some of the earliest things I published."[58] Scholars have speculated that one of the "[g]reat and learned men" Burke is referring to here is Adam Smith.[59] Most likely he did have in mind Smith, but existing correspondence between the two thinkers does not include any penetrating philosophical exchange over commercial matters.

In addition to noting his personal efforts in exploring the anatomy of political economy, Burke insinuates that his economic ideas commanded influence in the House of Commons. "Gentlemen are very fond of quoting me" he insists regarding his Economical Reform Bill.[60] Supporters and critics of the bill, even if the latter disagreed on its substance, generally praised his speech defending the legislation.[61] And in referring to his general studies of political economy, Burke remarks that the "House has been witness to their effect, and has profited of them more or less for above eight and twenty years."[62] In sum, Burke's defense of his pension in *Letter to a Noble Lord* relies on his assertion that he admirably served the British government and the English nation at large, and that this service was demonstrated, at least in part, by comprehending the intricate dimensions of Britain's economic system as a legislator in Parliament.

Contemporary Accounts of Burke's Knowledge on Matters Relating to Political Economy

Was Burke justified in claiming that he was an astute thinker on commercial subjects? Indeed, Burke's contemporaries took notice of the uncommon breadth and depth of his economic wisdom even prior to his entry into Parliament. In

---

[58] Langford, *Writings and Speeches*, IX, 160.
[59] See Jacob Viner's "Guide to John Rae's *Life of Adam Smith*," in John Rae, *Life of Adam Smith* (New York: Augustus M. Kelley, 1965), 25; Canavan, *Political Economy of Edmund Burke*, 116–117; Petrella, "Edmund Burke and Classical Economics," 4; and Jerry Z. Muller, *The Mind and the Market: Capitalism in Western Thought* (New York: Anchor Books, 2003), 115. See also *The Monthly Review*, vol. XIX (London: R. Griffiths, 1796), 315n.
[60] Langford, *Writings and Speeches*, IX, 158.   [61] See Lock, *Edmund Burke*, vol. I, 454.
[62] Langford, *Writings and Speeches*, IX, 160. In the early years of his parliamentary service, Burke helped craft the Free Port Act of 1766. See "The British West Indies and the Free Port Act of 1766," Chapter 6. Burke also wrote *Short Account of a Late Short Administration* in 1766, which outlined Rockingham's legislative achievements throughout the previous year, including the Free Port Act. In addition, Burke engaged in a wide-ranging study of the financial and commercial impact of the Seven Years War on Britain and France in *Observations on a Late State of the Nation* (1769).

September 1759, seven years before Burke began his tenure as an MP, William Markham, a friend of his at the time, wrote a letter to the Duchess of Queensbury in which Markham said that "[Burke's] chief application has been to the knowledge of public business, and our commercial interests; that he seems to have a most extensive knowledge, with extraordinary talents for business."[63]

The Duke of Grafton remarked in October 1766 that Burke was the "readiest man upon all points perhaps in the whole House."[64] Two months later, Charles Lee[65] observed that "[a]n Irishman, one Mr. Burke, is sprung up in the House of Commons, who has astonished every body with the power of his eloquence, his comprehensive knowledge in all our exterior and internal politics and commercial interests."[66]

In 1772, in a House debate on regulating imports and exports of corn, Burke gave an "excellent speech" that was "full of that knowledge which he possesses of these matters; and explained, with that distinction of which he is master, both the effect of supply and trade."[67] The editors of the 1800 edition of *Thoughts and Details* explained that this oration was "admired at the time for its excellence, and described as abounding with that knowledge in œconomics, which he was then universally allowed to possess, and illustrated with that philosophical discrimination, of which he was so peculiarly a master."[68] Two years after his speech on corn bounties, in his first election speech to voters at Bristol, Burke admitted that commerce had "ever been a particular and a very favorite object of my study, in its principles, and in its details."[69]

Even more, *The London Magazine* reported in 1776 that there was "no subject that comes under discussion, whether politics, finances, commerce, manufactures, internal police, &c. with all their divisions and subdivisions, which he does not treat in so masterly and technical a manner as to induce such as hear him to imagine he had dedicated a considerable portion of his life to the investigation of that particular subject."[70] And James Boswell's *Life of Johnson* includes an anecdote conveyed by Dr. Samuel Johnson in 1777 in which Richard Jackson, a British statesman, told Dr. Johnson that "there was

---

[63] William Markham to the Duchess of Queensbury, 25 September 1759, in *Correspondence of William Pitt, Earl of Chatham*, vol. I (London: John Murray, 1838), 432.

[64] Duke of Grafton to the Earl of Chatham, 17 October 1766, in *Correspondence of William Pitt, Earl of Chatham*, vol. III, eds. William Stanhope Taylor and John Henry Pringle (London: John Murray, 1839), 110.

[65] Lee was an officer in the British Army and, later, major general of the American colonies' Continental Army.

[66] Langworthy, *Memoirs of the Life of the Late Charles Lee*, 297.

[67] *Cobbett's Parliamentary History of England*, vol. XVII, *1771–1774* (London: T. C. Hansard, 1813), 479.

[68] Edmund Burke, *Thoughts and Details on Scarcity, Originally Presented to the Right Hon. William Pitt, in the Month of November 1795* (London: F. and C. Rivington, 1800), vi.

[69] Langford, *Writings and Speeches*, III, 59–60.

[70] *The London Magazine, For the Year 1776*, vol. 45 (London: R. Baldwin, 1776), 526.

more good sense upon trade in [Johnson's account of his journey to the Western Islands of Scotland], than he should hear in the House of Commons in a year, except from Burke."[71] Dr. Johnson said of Burke, "Take up whatever topick you please, he is ready to meet you."[72]

We should also mention that Burke's acute interest in agricultural and welfare economics, in addition to imperial commerce, was noticed by contemporaries. According to James Prior, Burke

surprised a distinguished literary and political character who about this time paid him a visit, by entering into a history of rural affairs, of the rents, taxes, and the variations in the poor's rates of fifty parishes in the county during several consecutive years; as well as the improvements adopted by the neighbourhood in tillage and grazing – all with the fulness of a farmer who had little else to attend to, though it might be supposed that the contentions attendant on public life, had left little time for retaining such details.[73]

Burke's insatiable thirst for knowledge on agricultural economics applied to France as well. During his only known sojourn to the country in 1773, he "inquired about payments of labourers, & other farm business" according to Richard, Burke's son.[74]

On a personal note, Charles O'Hara, Burke's friend, utilized Burke's knowledge of tilling for his own cultivation. "You have given me the principle of the new husbandry, fertilizing and cleansing the ground, which was all I wanted," O'Hara told him in a letter.[75] O'Hara suggested that Burke's technique was more straightforward than one offered by Arthur Young, the renowned agriculturalist: "I neither mean to compliment you, nor to flatter you, when I say that you have recovered my mind from the confusion which Mr. Young had thrown me into."[76] The earth gave Burke bountiful possibilities for the practice of husbandry and the stirring of his imaginative and intellectual faculties on the mystery of economics.

I.3 CONCLUSION

Contemporary testimonials, and Burke's meticulous study of issues relating to political economy, still did not qualify him as an economist – a professional designation that in any case hardly yet existed. Burke did not write about political economy as exhaustively as contemporaries Adam Smith and Josiah

[71] James Boswell, *The Life of Samuel Johnson, LL.D.*, vol. II (London: Henry Baldwin, 1791), 133.
[72] Boswell, *Life of Samuel Johnson*, vol. II, 339. [73] Prior, *Life of Edmund Burke*, 421.
[74] Lock, *Edmund Burke*, vol. II, 249n17.
[75] O'Hara to Burke, 11 September 1772, in Ross J. S. Hoffman, *Edmund Burke, New York Agent with His Letters to the New York Assembly and Intimate Correspondence with Charles O'Hara 1761–1776* (Philadelphia: The American Philosophical Society, 1956), 531.
[76] O'Hara to Burke, 11 September 1772, in Hoffman, *New York Agent*, 531. O'Hara further notes in the letter, "[U]pon the whole, I was led to think, and your letter confirms me in the opinion, that the land of Ireland is in general richer than that of England."

Tucker, or Arthur Young and Sir James Steuart. Burke never published his own *Wealth of Nations*, or, for that matter, his own *Four Tracts on Political and Commercial Subjects*, as Tucker had.[77] Even more, his principal economic writing, *Thoughts and Details*, is short and addressed a particular historical circumstance.

In addition, while some of Burke's economic arguments were fresh and distinctive, others were not original nor elaborated upon in great detail. Burke's mastery of economic issues fell short of full elucidation. He displayed a strong understanding of supply and demand laws and the competitive price system for the time period, was attentive to the complicated nature of fluid market activities, and became a recognized expert on the commercial interests of the British Empire. Yet he did not sufficiently elaborate on some key implications of his economic thought, such as whether asymmetric information between the seller and the buyer made buyers more prone to price manipulation in the eighteenth century, or whether state regulations were appropriate to address the adverse effects of externalities.

Evidence also suggests that his knowledge of public finance early in his parliamentary career lacked sufficient rigor. Sir George Colebrook observed, for instance, that Burke "did not pretend to understand finances, and would not enter on the subject"[78] – a statement touched with a measure of irony, for Burke would later demonstrate an impressive understanding of public finance in *Speech on Economical Reform*, the *Reflections*, and other speeches and writings. In *Observations on a Late State of the Nation*, published in 1769, Burke most likely relied on arguments relating to finance and taxes presented by William Dowdeswell, who had served as Chancellor of the Exchequer in the first Rockingham administration.[79] Burke did not refrain from employing the economic knowledge of other peers as well: in the 1780s, his comprehensive *Ninth Report*, which detailed the abuses of Britain's East India Company in India,[80] called on the expertise of Philip Francis, who had been a member of the Bengal Council in India, to write sections on monopolies held by the Company in South Asia.

Nevertheless, Burke's consistent theoretical and practical engagement with political economy – as a writer on commercial affairs, as a legislator in Parliament, and as a farmer – testifies to a thoughtfulness on economic matters that transcended a mere passing fancy in ad hoc policy debates. He showcased an exceptional array of knowledge relating to commerce, markets, landed property, and public finance in a host of speeches and writings, including

---

[77] Josiah Tucker, *Four Tracts on Political and Commercial Subjects* (Glocester: R. Raikes, 1774), http://oll.libertyfund.org/titles/tucker-four-tracts-on-political-and-commercial-subjects. Consult George Shelton, *Dean Tucker and Eighteenth-Century Economic and Political Thought* (London and Basingstoke: The Macmillan Press, 1981).

[78] Langford, *Writings and Speeches*, II, 106.   [79] Langford, *Writings and Speeches*, II, 106.

[80] See Chapter 9.

Thoughts and Details (1795); the *Reflections* (1790); *Tracts Relating to Popery Laws* (1765); *Observations on a Late State of the Nation* (1769); *Speech on American Taxation* (1774); *Speech on Conciliation with America* (1775); *Two Letters on the Trade of Ireland* (1778); *Speech on Economical Reform* (1780); *Sketch of a Negro Code* (1780); *Ninth Report of Select Committee* (1783); *Speech on Fox's India Bill* (1783); and *Third Letter on a Regicide Peace* (1797).

Therefore, *Thoughts and Details*, while important, was not the only writing in which Burke examined economic matters with a diligent application of mind. As the following analysis will show, they tugged at Burke's intellectual disposition throughout his entire adult life, for he held a genuine fascination for and appreciation of the connections and dependencies between politics and economics in an age when the kinetic movements of mobile property still puzzled the minds of men. Even though he was not a professional economist, Burke's reflective attitude toward commerce and manufactures, reinforced by contemporary recognition of his economic literacy and the authority he commanded in Parliament, signals that his commentary on political economy should be studied with heightened seriousness.

PART II

MARKET ECONOMIES

2

Thoughts and Details on Scarcity, Supply and Demand, and Middlemen

> Of all things, an indiscreet tampering with the trade of provisions is the most dangerous, and it is always worst in the time when men are most disposed to it: that is, in the time of scarcity.[1]
>
> Edmund Burke, *Thoughts and Details on Scarcity*, 1795

2.1 INTRODUCTION

Burke discerned poetry in the elusive motions of England's internal grain trade. He provides his most considered thoughts on this trade in his primary agricultural tract, *Thoughts and Details*, which offers the sharpest insights into the theoretical foundations of his economic thought. In *Thoughts and Details*, Burke expresses vehement opposition to state interference in the domestic provisions market. He registers firm disapproval of parliamentary efforts to establish a new minimum wage, regulate contractual agreements between farmers and laborers, and create public granaries, among a variety of proposals suggested at the time to mitigate the pressures of material want felt by the laboring classes. The thrust of Burke's argument is that the exchange of grain within England flowed with full vigor and effect when the scope of government intervention in the economy was tightly confined.

The following three chapters will explain the general principles of Burke's support for market liberty, as articulated in *Thoughts and Details* and in his other speeches and writings that addressed England's agricultural economy. This chapter will discuss his thoughts on supply and demand laws, wage labor, and the competitive price system. It will also examine his support for middlemen trading activities, a key strand of Burke's economic thought that remains vastly underappreciated. In addition to probing the conceptual

---

[1] Langford, *Writings and Speeches*, IX, 120.

substance of *Thoughts and Details*, this chapter will highlight specific government policies Burke championed throughout his parliamentary career that furnished concrete examples of his sympathy for market economies.

Chapter 3 will explore one exception to Burke's fondness for government restraint in the agricultural economy, the corn bounty, as well his views on enclosure. It will also examine his deeper reflections on the relationship between the rich and the poor, and on conceptions of equality and wealth redistribution. Chapter 4 will broaden the philosophical frame of our discussion by investigating the social and epistemological foundations of Burke's economic thought. With the passage of time, Burke has acquired a reputation as a statesman of conservative persuasions. It is now time to discover how he held liberal sentiments as well.

2.2 THE STRESSES OF ENGLAND'S AGRICULTURAL ECONOMY IN THE 1790S AND THE DRAFTING OF THOUGHTS AND DETAILS

Thoughts and Details was not a systematic treatise. Its genesis was a private letter Burke wrote at the behest of War Secretary Henry Dundas and later distributed to William Pitt the Younger, England's First Lord of the Treasury, Britain's de facto prime minister, in early November 1795.[2] Dundas and Pitt had solicited Burke's thoughts – by then Burke had retired from Parliament – on the high cost of corn and other economic hardships. At the time Burke drafted the letter, England was groaning under the weight of severe social and economic stresses stemming from the feeble harvests of 1794 and 1795, as well as from war, famine, and the rising cost of food provisions.[3] Figure 2.1 shows the upsurge of wheat prices in 1795 and 1796. They increased by more than 50 percent from 1794 to 1796.[4]

Additional forces scraped up against each other in the late eighteenth century that further escalated the rising distempers in English society, including population growth, industrialization, international trade, and commercialization. The spike in population was a particularly noticeable trend of this time period; it rose 38 percent between 1781 and 1811, and almost doubled from 1771 to 1831.[5] It was only three years after Burke drafted his economic tract that Thomas Malthus anonymously published *An Essay on the*

---

[2] See Burke to William Pitt, [7] November 1795, in R. B. McDowell, ed., *The Correspondence of Edmund Burke*, vol. VIII, *September 1794–April 1796* (Cambridge: Cambridge University Press, 1969), 337–338; and Langford, *Writings and Speeches*, IX, 119.

[3] See Roger Wells, *Wretched Faces: Famine in Wartime England, 1793–1801* (New York: St. Martin's Press, 1988) for a comprehensive picture of this fraught time period.

[4] According to Gregory Clark, wheat cost 6.34 shillings per bushel in 1794 and 9.53 shillings per bushel in 1796. Note in Figure 2.1 that wheat prices increased even more in 1800, when *Thoughts and Details* was first published, and in 1801.

[5] Phyllis Deane and W. A. Cole, *British Economic Growth 1688–1959: Trends and Structure* (Cambridge: Cambridge University Press, 1967), 6.

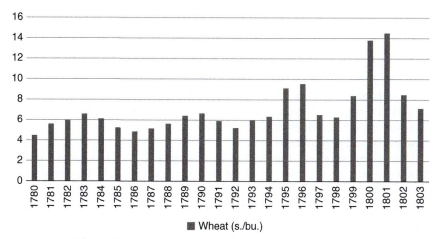

FIGURE 2.1 Wheat prices, 1780–1803
Source: Gregory Clark, University of California Davis, http://faculty.econ.ucdavis.edu
/faculty/gclark/data.html.

Principle of Population, in which he famously argued that the human population increased at a higher rate than that of the food supply and thus would face famine and misery if not checked by positive or preventive measures.[6]

Even more, England, long an exporter of grain, became a net importer in the 1750s and 1760s.[7] The percentage of imports that were grains rose from less than 1 percent in 1772 to 4.4 percent in 1790 and 8.7 percent by 1800.[8] In general, agricultural productivity in England lost vigor from 1740 to 1790 after flourishing between 1660 and 1740.[9] As John Bohstedt writes, "Proto-industrial England" from 1740 to 1820 was "becoming a market-dependent consumer society and economy just at a point when growth in domestic food production tapered off."[10]

These strains triggered food riots and social unrest. Public hostility to market fluctuations tended to derive from the aggravation of bread prices rather than

---

[6] See Thomas Malthus, *An Essay on the Principle of Population,* ed. Geoffrey Gilbert (Oxford: Oxford University Press, 1993).

[7] B. R. Mitchell, *British Historical Statistics* (Cambridge: Cambridge University Press, 1988), 221. Britain had more wheat imports than exports in the late 1750s, but reliable data is not available from 1759 to 1764. As Mitchell shows, Britain's wheat imports greatly exceeded wheat exports in 1765, and again in 1767 and 1768.

[8] R. P. Thomas and Donald McCloskey, "Overseas Trade and Empire 1700–1860," in *The Economic History of Britain since 1700,* vol. I, *1700–1860,* eds. Roderick Floud and Donald McCloskey (Cambridge: Cambridge University Press, 1981), 92.

[9] Wally Seccombe, *A Millennium of Family Change: Feudalism to Capitalism in Northwestern Europe* (London and New York: Verso, 1995), 203.

[10] John Bohstedt, *The Politics of Provisions: Food Riots, Moral Economy, and Market Transition in England, c. 1550–1850* (Farnham, England: Ashgate, 2010), 107.

from the level of wages.[11] The unpredictability of such price swings frequently induced popular outrage, particularly in eighteenth-century England, where disaffected laborers sometimes seized provisions and dictated the cost of goods during times of material deprivation. While protests drew serious attention to economic stresses in the market of provisions, they would, at times, explode into mob riots. 1766, the year Burke first entered Parliament, witnessed this phenomenon; more than 100 food riots took place that year.[12] Although rioters did not refrain from criticizing dealers, they tended to direct their ire toward exporters of corn.[13]

The "climactic year" for food riots was 1795, E. P. Thompson writes.[14] Almost 200 such protests occurred in 1795 and 1796.[15] Legislators and citizens offered a slew of policy proposals to remedy the pain experienced by the struggling classes. These measures included the government regulation of wages adjusted to the cost of living; the regulation of the corn, or wheat, trade; the establishment of public granaries; and self-imposed rationing on the part of wealthy families. Other proposed reforms included increasing potato consumption, farming unused land, and giving up the use of hair powder.[16] The British government also considered buying corn abroad, with the aim of distributing it to areas of want.[17] Donald Grove Barnes writes of this period, "[T]he suffering experienced by the lower classes was almost unprecedented."[18]

In addition, in May 1795, justices of the peace in Speenhamland, Berkshire, a location not too distant from where Burke's estate was located,[19] had created a means-tested government welfare program in which local parishes provided a subsidy to the working poor and nonworking poor to meet minimum levels of subsistence.[20] Following the Speenhamland laws, the program spread to other counties, particularly in southern rural areas where agricultural laborers were hit especially hard by the fury of economic pressures. As Gertrude Himmelfarb explains, the Speenhamland system signaled that "the problem of poverty had attained

---

[11] E. P. Thompson, *The Making of the English Working Class* (New York: Vintage Books, 1966), 63.

[12] Bohstedt, *Politics of Provisions*, 105.   [13] Bohstedt, *Politics of Provisions*, 105, 112–113.

[14] Thompson, *Making of the English Working Class*, 65.

[15] Bohstedt, *Politics of Provisions*, 167.

[16] Langford, *Writings and Speeches*, IX, 25–26. See also Walter M. Stern, "The Bread Crisis in Britain, 1795–96," *Economica* 31 (1964): 168–187.

[17] The British government did decide to buy corn from abroad.

[18] Donald Grove Barnes, *A History of English Corn Laws: From 1660–1846* (London and New York: Routledge, 2014), 72.

[19] Today it would take around an hour to drive from Beaconsfield, near where Burke's estate was located, to Berkshire.

[20] See Himmelfarb, *Idea of Poverty*, 65–66 and 84. This form of welfare relief first emerged in parishes in the 1750s. See Steven King, *Poverty and Welfare in England 1700–1850: A Regional Perspective* (Manchester: Manchester University Press, 2000), 34.

a new urgency and, more important, that the solutions themselves were becoming problematic, if only because the costs had become so burdensome."[21]

The additional historical contingency looming over *Thoughts and Details* was revolutionary France's efforts to alleviate its own harsh economic hardships, such as the rising cost of provisions, by experimenting with the policy of *dirigisme*. Derived from the Latin word *dirigere*, meaning "to direct," *dirigisme* was a meddling system of government intervention in which the state played an active role in managing the economic activity of the nation. Motivated by this idea, the French revolutionary government had attempted to supervise its internal trade in 1793 by regulating the cost of the grain supply and redistributing provisions.[22]

British newspapers reported these measures to English readers starting in September 1793.[23] Some in England became enamored by the regulatory measures, enough so that Burke was worried that the allure of *dirigisme* would tempt Englishmen to clamor for similar policies of wealth redistribution in the country in the 1790s. In this historical context, then, one can interpret *Thoughts and Details* not simply as an account of Burke's economic doctrine but also, much like the *Reflections*, as a cautionary attempt alerting the English to the radical egalitarianism lurking within Jacobin economic policy.

We must not underestimate the importance of the debate Burke confronted in England in the 1790s over whether to regulate the provisions market. It was at this moment that patterns of free market thinking that had spread throughout the eighteenth century collided powerfully with prevailing attitudes in favor of government intervention. "[I]deological debate over paternalist market regulation versus laissez faire reached a climax in this period because it was critical to the politics of provision in more ways than one," Bohstedt writes.[24] Foremost among these implications was the belief that corn dealers took advantage of markets to raise prices and secure exorbitant profit, all to the detriment of consumers. *Thoughts and Details*, therefore, is not only an essential text in the study of Burke's economic thought, but also exemplified a significant debate in the political economy of the early modern period that had been simmering in England for decades.

On December 9, 1795, a minimum wage bill was introduced in Britain's House of Commons by Samuel Whitbread.[25] The bill would have amended the Statute of Artificers of 1563, an Elizabethan Act that shifted the locus of regulatory authority over employment and wages in England's labor market

---

[21] Himmelfarb, *Idea of Poverty*, 66.   [22] Bourke, *Empire & Revolution*, 888–889.
[23] Bourke, *Empire & Revolution*, 888–889.   [24] Bohstedt, *Politics of Provisions*, 171.
[25] Whitbread, ironically enough, was sympathetic to Adam Smith's economic philosophy. See Rothschild, "Adam Smith and Conservative Economics," 84.

Speedily will be published,

A LETTER from the Right Honourable
EDMUND BURKE, to ARTHUR YOUNG,
Esq. Secretary to the Board of Agriculture, on the
projects talked of in Parliament, for an increase of
Wages to Day Labourers in Husbandry, and other
topics of rural œconomy.
  Printed for F. and C. Rivington, No. 62, St. Paul's
Church-yard.

FIGURE 2.2 *Oracle* advertisement for Burke's letter to Arthur Young on rural economy
(1795)
© British Library Board
Source: *The Oracle, Public Advertiser*, 17 December 1795, British Library

from traditional guilds to the state.[26] Whitbread's bill, which failed due to
parliamentary reluctance to control wages and Pitt's pledge to draft a new
poor law, would have vested justices of the peace with the authority to set
minimum wage rates of agricultural workers. (Whitbread reintroduced the bill
in 1800, but it failed to pass again.) Charles James Fox had previously opposed
regulating wages, but this time he threw his support behind the bill. Pitt resisted
the measure, insisting that free market principles should be allowed to operate
unimpeded.[27]

   This parliamentary debate about wage rates may have triggered Burke to
revise and build upon the original draft of *Thoughts and Details* with an eye
toward publication. Eight days after Whitbread's bill was introduced, the
Oracle reported that a letter from Burke to Arthur Young, Secretary to the
Board of Agriculture at the time, would be "speedily" published regarding the
"projects talked of in Parliament, for an increase of Wages to Day Labourers in
Husbandry, and other topics of rural œconomy"[28] (Figure 2.2).

   Then, on December 28, 1795, *The Times* published a brief notice that lent
a tantalizing glimpse into Burke's beliefs on the matter:

It is said to be the opinion of Mr. Burke, that it is an unwise measure to raise the price of
labour by any settled regulation. Wages, like every thing else, ought to find its own level.
If wages are to be regulated by the Justices, the consequence, he says, will be, that the
farmers will be delivered over, bound hand and foot, to the mercy of the landowners;
instead of this, he proposes that labour should be left to regulate itself.[29]

---

[26] See Donald Woodward, "The Background to the Statute of Artificers: The Genesis of Labour
      Policy, 1558–63," *The Economic History Review* 33 (1980): 32–44; and E. K. Hunt and
      Mark Lautzenheiser, *History of Economic Thought: A Critical Perspective*, 3rd ed. (Armonk,
      NY and London: M. E. Sharpe, 2011), 22.
[27] See Rothschild, "Adam Smith and Conservative Economics," 85.
[28] *The Oracle, Public Advertiser*, 17 December 1795, British Library. The *Morning Chronicle*
      announced the same message on 18 December.
[29] *The Times*, 28 December 1795, British Library.

One year later, when Burke started drafting *Third Letter on a Regicide Peace*, he wrote in the letter that a recent writing of his on the role of government intervention in the agricultural economy "may yet see the light."[30]

The final version of *Thoughts and Details* was collated by Burke's executors and published in 1800, three years after Burke passed away, at a time when rising provisions costs again provoked public debate over the merits of state interference in the agricultural economy.[31] It combined his original memorandum to Dundas and Pitt with three fragments of his letter to Young.[32] As F. P. Lock notes, Young generally embraced the cause of market liberty, but in late 1795 he had expressed support for the government regulation of wages, which perhaps explains why Burke chose to write his letter to Young.[33]

While *Thoughts and Details* has had a negligible long-term impact on the history of political and economic thought in comparison to many of Burke's other writings and speeches, the memorial most likely commanded some immediate influence in the British government, according to the editors of the tract in 1800. It was "believed at the time," they wrote, that it was "not wholly unproductive of good."[34] The memorial had been "communicated" to "several members of the King's Government."[35] Burke's preference for government restraint was satisfied. The parliamentary inquiry into the high price of corn was "silently dropped."[36] Ministers "repressed in others, or where they could not entirely controul, interposed to moderate and divert, that restless spirit of legislation."[37] The idea of public granaries was "abandoned."[38] The editors noted that a proposal to limit forestalling – a trading practice Burke defended throughout his political life, as we shall learn in this chapter – was defeated as well at the time.[39]

---

[30] Langford, *Writings and Speeches*, IX, 355. Burke had begun writing *Third Letter on a Regicide Peace* by the end of 1796, a little more than a year after he first started drafting his memorandum on the agricultural economy. *Third Letter* was published in November 1797. See Langford, *Writings and Speeches*, IX, 296–297.

[31] See Figure 2.1.

[32] Langford, *Writings and Speeches*, IX, 120. According to the editors of the 1800 edition, the fragments in Burke's letter to Young consisted of the following sections in *Thoughts and Details*: "There is an implied contract, much stronger than any instrument or article of agreement" to "as the exercise of a virtue most suitable to a being sensible of it's own infirmity" (Langford, *Writings and Speeches*, IX, 123–129); "It is a perilous thing to try experiments on the farmer" to "thus compelling us to diminish the quantity of labour which in the vulgar course we actually employ" (Langford, *Writings and Speeches*, IX, 130–132); and "It is one of the finest problems in legislation" to the end (Langford, *Writings and Speeches*, IX, 143–145).

[33] Lock, *Edmund Burke*, vol. II, 514. [34] Burke, *Thoughts and Details*, xi.

[35] Burke, *Thoughts and Details*, xi. [36] Burke, *Thoughts and Details*, xi.

[37] Burke, *Thoughts and Details*, xi.

[38] Burke, *Thoughts and Details*, xi. C. R. Fay backs this account. The British government considered creating new public granaries, he explains, but "dropped" the idea "in the face of a scathing onslaught from Edmund Burke." See Fay, *The Corn Laws and Social England* (Cambridge: Cambridge University Press, 1932), 36.

[39] Burke, *Thoughts and Details*, xi.

Although *Thoughts and Details* exhibits an impressive vigor of mind, it is not the greatest example of Burke's felicity of prose. The letter is scattered and pedantic, and Burke himself admitted it was "(hurriedly) scribbled."[40] The purpose of the following thematic structure, therefore, is to provide *Thoughts and Details* with a coherence and lucidity in order to apprehend patterns of Burke's economic commentary that warrant amplification in the study of his intellectual thought. For, while supply and demand laws certainly did not comprise the whole of Burke's conception of political economy, they did embody his grasp of its functional anatomy.

2.3 THE LAWS OF SUPPLY AND DEMAND, WAGES, AND PRICE THEORY

Burke's opposition to state intervention in the domestic agricultural economy bursts through in his very first statement in *Thoughts and Details*. "Of all things, an indiscreet tampering with the trade of provisions is the most dangerous," he writes, "and it is always worst in the time when men are most disposed to it: that is, in the time of scarcity."[41] In cautioning against state intrusion into the circulation of food and goods,[42] Burke here immediately displays his firm objection to the idea that government could channel provisions to needy areas in an effectual fashion, especially in times of economic dislocation, when men were most eager to seek relief from the state to remedy hardship.

Burke's advocacy for government restraint in *Thoughts and Details* is informed by a fluency in the laws of supply and demand. "The moment that Government appears at market, all the principles of market will be subverted," he writes in his discussion opposing the establishment of public granaries.[43] Upsetting supply and demand laws would create distortions and inefficiencies in the corn market, sowing economic disorder at the expense of the public.

Burke's embrace of supply and demand laws can be grasped through his conception of labor. He understands labor not as a static activity, frozen in time, but as a "commodity" – a good that can be traded – which, "like every other, and rises or falls according to the demand."[44] This statement formed part of Burke's response to the contemporary argument, raised in Parliament and other forums of public discourse, that laborers' wage rates had not grown concomitantly with the rise in the price of provisions. Burke insists in *Thoughts and Details* that wages had been increased twice in his lifetime, and had more than matched the cost of provisions within the previous twenty years.

---

[40] Burke to William Pitt, [7] November 1795, in *Correspondence of Edmund Burke*, vol. VIII, 337.
[41] Langford, *Writings and Speeches*, IX, 120.
[42] Note, however, that in modifying "tampering" with "indiscreet," Burke suggests that "discreet" government intervention in the economy might be tenable.
[43] Langford, *Writings and Speeches*, IX, 135.   [44] Langford, *Writings and Speeches*, IX, 122.

(The latter claim is still being contested by economic historians.[45]) Burke maintains that the wage hikes had borne "a full proportion to the result of their labour,"[46] thereby announcing his conviction that the salary of a laborer should be commensurate with his toil.

Burke then illuminates his stern opposition to the idea of increasing the minimum wage by evoking the presence of Sisyphus:

> If we were wildly to attempt to force [wages] beyond [the result of their labour], the stone which we had forced up the hill would only fall back upon them in a diminished demand, or, what indeed is the far lesser evil, an aggravated price of all the provisions, which are the result of their manual toil.[47]

Burke's beliefs about supply and demand laws are making a visible appearance here, seeking to correct the economic misconceptions held by champions of government regulation: raise the wage above a certain threshold, and the result would be a decrease in the demand for labor, a fundamental premise of supply and demand principles.[48] Since labor would become more expensive for the employer, he would be less likely to hire the laborer. The additional hazard of wage increases, Burke writes, is that the price of food would climb as well, leading to inflation.[49] To protect against these pernicious effects, labor, Burke insists later in *Thoughts and Details*, "must be subject to all the laws and principles of trade"[50] because it was an article of exchange rather than an activity immune from market forces. Consequently, the laws of supply and demand must not be distorted by "regulations foreign to them," which "may be totally inconsistent with those principles and those laws."[51] Such comments

---

[45] For a challenge to Burke's claim, see, for example, Seccombe, *A Millennium of Family Change*, 203: "[n]ominal wage hikes did not keep pace with food price increases over the last six decades of the eighteenth century." Generally, agricultural wages grew significantly in the last half of the eighteenth century. But their purchasing power was more limited because prices also increased. Real wages, then, grew moderately at best, and, in the period 1795–1796, may have decreased in some areas. See Langford, *Writings and Speeches*, IX, 122n1. But also consult M. W. Flinn, "Trends in Real Wages, 1750–1850," *The Economic History Review* 27 (1974): 395–413. See page 408 in particular: "Contrary to the very commonly made generalization that rapidly rising prices tended to erode real wages during the French Wars, it seems that for many groups of workers ... wage rates in general broadly kept pace with rising prices."

[46] Langford, *Writings and Speeches*, IX, 123. In arguing in favor of the minimum wage, Whitbread had used Richard Price's index detailing the cost of provisions. From this information Whitbread determined that prices had significantly exceeded wages. See Raymond G. Cowherd, "The Humanitarian Reform of the English Poor Laws from 1782 to 1815," *Proceedings of the American Philosophical Society* 104 (1960): 335.

[47] Langford, *Writings and Speeches*, IX, 123.

[48] See Thomas Sowell, *Basic Economics: A Citizen's Guide to the Economy* (New York: Basic Books, 2004), 163.

[49] Burke does not specify the connection between wage hikes and food prices, but he is suggesting that sellers, in order to preserve profit margins, would have to compensate for the added costs of labor by increasing the market prices of goods.

[50] Langford, *Writings and Speeches*, IX, 126.   [51] Langford, *Writings and Speeches*, IX, 126.

illustrate why Burke, according to the editors of the 1800 edition of *Thoughts and Details*, thought that the "unrestrained freedom of buying and selling is the great animating principle of production and supply."[52]

The economic tract was not the first time Burke connected the rate of pay with the amount of labor. More than twenty years prior, in a letter to Garret Nagle written in August 1771, Burke had remarked, "I have always found, that the Labour of men is nearly in proportion to their pay."[53] Burke does not elaborate on this idea in the letter, but the insight offers an earlier glimpse into his wage theory that would come to guide the economic reasoning in *Thoughts and Details*. Burke's principle of proportionality pushed against prevailing mercantilist wisdom in the eighteenth century about the relationship between wages and work ethic. While this latter perspective was not uniform and static, it generally held that high wages would encourage men to become less attentive to their responsibilities as laborers.[54] Burke, as did Adam Smith and other lesser-known writers, questioned this presumption by claiming that the prospect of high wage rates would motivate laborers to work with more diligence, not less.[55]

It is noteworthy, however, that Burke, in disapproving of Whitbread's minimum wage bill, does not expressly condemn the two previous wage hikes he cites briefly. This decision can possibly be attributed to his implicit support for particular wage increases depending on historical circumstance, or to his exercise of prudence in refusing to call for the suppression of all existing market regulations at that time. Burke never makes clear in *Thoughts and Details* which reason explains his noticeable hesitation to criticize these two salary increases.

In addition to his theoretical pronouncements about supply and demand laws, Burke summons the wisdom of experience when outlining their concrete effects in the marketplace. "I sold my wheat at 14l. a load ... when at the end of the season, if I had then had any to sell, I might have got thirty guineas for the

---

[52] Burke, *Thoughts and Details*, vi.

[53] Burke to Garrett Nagle, 23 August 1771, in Lucy S. Sutherland, ed., *The Correspondence of Edmund Burke*, vol. II, *July 1768–June 1774* (Cambridge: Cambridge University Press, 1960), 234.

[54] See Istvan Hont and Michael Ignatieff, "Needs and Justice in the *Wealth of Nations*: An Introductory Essay," in *Wealth & Virtue: The Shaping of Political Economy in the Scottish Enlightenment*, eds. Hont and Ignatieff (Cambridge: Cambridge University Press, 1985), 4–5; and Mokyr, *Enlightened Economy*, 267–268. Note, however, that there was a strain of mercantilist thought in the eighteenth century, even before 1750, that entertained the possible benefits of high wages. See Richard C. Wiles, "The Theory of Wages in Later English Mercantilism," *The Economic History Review* 21 (1968): 113–126. Mercantilism also held that high wages would inhibit competitive prices in international markets, in turn hurting the home country's balance of trade.

[55] For Smith, see *Wealth of Nations*, vol. I, 99. For additional writers on this subject, see A. W. Coats, "Changing Attitudes to Labour in the Mid-Eighteenth Century," *The Economic History Review* 11 (1958): 35–51.

same sort of grain," he writes in *Thoughts and Details*.[56] Burke acknowledges the unforgiving harvest of 1794–1795 – "never had I grain of so low a quality" – but mentions that he "sold one load for 21l."[57] "At the same time," he continues, "I bought my seed wheat (it was excellent) at 23l. Since then the price has risen, and I have sold about two load of the same sort at 23l."[58]

Such comments echo an observation Burke had made seventeen years prior during a parliamentary debate in May 1778, when Britain was deliberating over whether to enhance trade relations with Ireland, an idea he passionately championed at the time. He remarked in the debate, "The experience of every day tells us, that where the price of labour is highest, the manufacture[r] is able to sell his commodity at the lowest price."[59] Burke thus gave his supply and demand convictions a textured dimension throughout his life when he appealed to the experiences of market actors. His thorough analysis of the relationship between supply and demand principles and the crop in general validates the testimony from contemporaries, as outlined in Chapter 1, that his husbandry was informed by a penetrating mind keenly observant of the natural laws of commerce.

Burke embeds the importance of experience in his reflections in *Thoughts and Details* by landing a soft jab at Charles James Fox, who had suggested in the House of Commons that the "evil" of the price increase in meat and dairy products, in addition to bread, stemmed from an increase in consumption, among "a variety of causes, complicated in their nature, and extensive in their operations."[60] Burke notes in the memorial that Fox "insinuated a suspicion of some unfair practice"[61] on the part of traders. Today we would call this practice price gouging.

Carrying on his implicit dialogue with Fox, Burke acknowledges his preeminence by calling him a "leading member of great ability."[62] But then he insists that Fox was "*little conversant in these matters*" relating to the price fluctuations of the provisions market.[63] Fox had grown up as the pampered son of Henry Fox, a wealthy and influential British statesman, and acquired a reputation for indulgences in women, drinking, and gambling. The younger Fox was a distinguished Whig legislator and harbored a charismatic disposition, but he was not known as a farmer or a serious student of the agricultural economy.[64] Burke's point in *Thoughts and Details* was that such feeble experience and knowledge about supply and demand laws displayed a gross ignorance of their complex effects. For Burke, those who were immediately

---

[56] Langford, *Writings and Speeches*, IX, 137. [57] Langford, *Writings and Speeches*, IX, 138.
[58] Langford, *Writings and Speeches*, IX, 138. [59] Langford, *Writings and Speeches*, IX, 522.
[60] *Cobbett's Parliamentary History of England*, vol. XXXII, *Comprising the Period from the Twenty-Seventh Day of May 1795, to the Second Day of March 1797* (London: T. C. Hansard, 1818), 239.
[61] Langford, *Writings and Speeches*, IX, 139. [62] Langford, *Writings and Speeches*, IX, 139.
[63] Langford, *Writings and Speeches*, IX, 139.
[64] L. G. Mitchell, *Charles James Fox* (Oxford: Oxford University Press, 1992), 183–185.

involved in the practical activities of husbandry and dealing, such as farmers and traders, were more attuned to the unpredictable nature of oscillating prices.

Burke makes a further attempt to weave supply and demand principles within the fabric of experience by showing how the rising cost of provisions arose from a complicated chain of factors that could not be reduced to a single cause. In a serpentine but detailed breakdown[65] of this series of interrelated events, Burke traces how the deficiency of the wheat and barley harvests in 1794 helped explain the rise in malt prices; and how the scarcity of peas, barley meal, and beans, which were used in corn countries to feed swine, led to the spike in bacon and pork prices.[66] He then calls attention to the law of supply and demand: "This failure of so very large a supply of flesh in one species, naturally throws the whole demand of the consumer on the diminished supply of all kinds of flesh, and, indeed, on all matters of human sustenance."[67]

Burke applies this chain of reasoning to sheep and lambs as well, attributing their rise in food costs to scarcity and their low quality to harsh environmental conditions. The final cause of dear food prices Burke discusses is the prohibition of the distillery, which had produced spirits made from wheat, malt, and barley but was temporarily banned in June 1795.[68] The distilling and brewing industries in the eighteenth century maintained a distinctive relationship with members of the agricultural economy. The industries bought malt and barley from the farms, and they also created waste products for hogs and cattle to consume as feeding-stuffs, in turn playing an integral role in the provisions market. From the mid-1750s onward, however, the number of hogs used by distillers decreased as the industry became less competitive and duties rose.[69]

Burke was deeply conscious of the indirect impact of the distillery on the growth in food costs. When the distillery was open, he explains in *Thoughts and Details*, hogs were fed with the "waste wash"[70] of the distilling process and did not require the typical amount of corn used by farmers to fatten them. Burke is not explicitly clear on this point, but he seems to be suggesting that the

---

[65] Burke's attention to detail in this section is evidence of his passion as a farmer. It also suggests his implicit recognition that Young, one member of his audience in the letter, was well-versed in agricultural economics, as Young in fact was.

[66] Langford, *Writings and Speeches*, IX, 139–140.

[67] Langford, *Writings and Speeches*, IX, 140. Petrella uses this quotation to highlight Burke's failure to discuss the idea that the rise in prices of flesh would increase the demand for substitute goods. "What Burke did not conclude, yet could have concluded given his knowledge of demand, supply and price," Petrella writes, "was that the price increase, greater in the case of the former good than in the case of the latter goods, would cause a change in demand for particularly and generally related goods with consequent price reactions" (Petrella, "Edmund Burke and Classical Economics," 49–50).

[68] Langford, *Writings and Speeches*, IX, 141n1.

[69] See Peter Mathias, "Agriculture and the Brewing and Distilling Industries in the Eighteenth Century," *The Economic History Review* 5 (1952): 249–257, for a review of the relationship between the distillery and brewing industries and the agricultural economy.

[70] Langford, *Writings and Speeches*, IX, 141.

consumption of corn did increase unnecessarily because hogs were not able to eat distillers' waste. Hence they had to be fed corn, and subsequently prices rose to meet the increased demand (as the supply of corn had not caught up with this demand). Another implication considered by Burke was that the poor harvests of 1794 and 1795 enhanced the cost of country-fed hogs and the demand for other farm animals. "It is an odd way of making flesh cheap," he writes, "to stop or check the distillery."[71] Checking the distillery meant that fewer hogs and cattle would be nourished. Peter Mathias highlights Burke as one shrewd observer at the time who had drawn attention to this complex market interaction between the closure of distilleries and the price of hogs.[72]

Burke outlines additional uses of the distillery that had contributed to commercial vigor, waste management, and revenue production. The distillery encouraged international trade, and was "of great use ... to our fisheries and to our whole navigation."[73] The distilling process also used low-quality corn, malt, and barley that Burke hints would have been wasted otherwise. Finally, the consumption of alcohol generated a "great revenue" that could be used as an incentive to buy corn overseas or to produce more of it in England.[74]

By providing a concrete description of the many factors that contributed to high corn prices, Burke pours empirical substance into his initial theoretical claims in *Thoughts and Details* about market economies. In his judgment, competitive prices of agricultural economic activity could not be explained away by individual causes stripped of circumstance, such as unfair practices or increased consumption, for the impact of a poor harvest yielded wide-ranging consequences. "All the productions of the earth link in with each other," he writes.[75] A harmonizing interdependence emerged among crops, animals, and environmental conditions that shaped market phenomena. Similarly, the price of corn, Burke notes, was "the result of the expence of all the operations of husbandry."[76] Prices reflected a mysterious constellation of variables in the agricultural economy. Burke's comments on the complexity of markets denote his ability to peer at a single issue – in this case, high provisions costs – and then shift his eyes to the broader trends responsible for its manifestation, reflecting an uncommon ability to bring clarity to chaos in the study of political economy.

Nature and Price Theory

Even though Burke suggests that complex market phenomena could not be attributed to single human causes, he does connect the laws of supply and demand to the natural order of Providence. When describing that labor is

---

[71] Langford, *Writings and Speeches*, IX, 141.
[72] Mathias, "Agriculture and the Brewing and Distilling Industries," 253.
[73] Langford, *Writings and Speeches*, IX, 141.   [74] Langford, *Writings and Speeches*, IX, 141.
[75] Langford, *Writings and Speeches*, IX, 140.   [76] Langford, *Writings and Speeches*, IX, 127.

a commodity, Burke writes, "This is in the nature of things; however, the nature of things has provided for their necessities."[77] He refers again to nature later in *Thoughts and Details*, when he cautions against the idea that the government or the privileged classes were competent enough to supply the poor with sufficient provisions. In the most emphatic statement of his entire thought regarding the connection between market economies and the natural order, Burke writes that "the laws of commerce" were the "laws of nature, and consequently the laws of God."[78]

Burke sprinkles "natural" and its cognates in his other writings and speeches related to the free movement of commerce that precede *Thoughts and Details*.[79] In 1770, when opposing a bill in the House of Commons that would have renewed the ban on corn exportation, Burke referred to the "natural price which grain brings at an universal market."[80] In 1775, in *Speech on Conciliation with America*, Burke denounces the idea that the vibrant trade between England and its North American colonies was "unnatural."[81] In 1778 Burke contends, in the context of Anglo-Irish commercial relations, that men should be permitted to use their "natural advantages" to trade freely.[82] To "force nature" through unnecessary trade restrictions would only sow discord and confusion.[83]

The attempt to connect supply and demand laws with nature was not atypical in the eighteenth century. The Physiocrats invoked a more regimented conception of natural law to advance their vision of a free grain trade, and their idealist conceptions of society in general.[84] The Scottish Enlightenment spread the conception that the ordering of nature allowed economic freedom governed by the prerogatives of supply and demand to satisfy man's need for food and shelter. Adam Smith, the leading defender of commercial enterprise among Scottish Enlightenment thinkers, famously characterized free markets in the *Wealth of Nations* as "the system of natural liberty"[85] or "the natural system of perfect liberty."[86] Note, however, that some of Burke's remarks predate the *Wealth of Nations*, so it is safe to assume that his theory of nature in relation to market order did not originally derive from Smith's book, which was first published in 1776.[87]

---

[77] Langford, *Writings and Speeches*, IX, 122–123.

[78] Langford, *Writings and Speeches*, IX, 137.

[79] He also uses "natural" when describing the hierarchy of labor (see "Wealth Redistribution and Equality in *Thoughts and Details*," Chapter 3) and in contexts unrelated to economic matters.

[80] J. Wright, ed., *Sir Henry Cavendish's Debates of the House of Commons*, vol. II (London: Longman et al., 1841), 56.

[81] Langford, *Writings and Speeches*, III, 114.   [82] Langford, *Writings and Speeches*, IX, 510.

[83] Langford, *Writings and Speeches*, IX, 510.

[84] Consult Thomas P. Neill, "The Physiocrats' Concept of Economics," *The Quarterly Journal of Economics* 63 (1949): 532–553.

[85] Adam Smith, *An Inquiry into the Nature and Causes of the Wealth of Nations*, vol. II, eds. R. H. Campbell and A. S. Skinner (Indianapolis: Liberty Fund, 1981), 687.

[86] Smith, *Wealth of Nations*, vol. II, 606.

[87] For my challenge to the idea that Burke was a "disciple" of Smith, see "The Irish Trade Bills," Chapter 8.

Burke's belief that the laws of commerce reflected the laws of nature carries profound implications for how we characterize his political orientation. Orthodox medieval perspectives on commerce summoned nature as an authority to *temper* man's base impulses toward material self-preservation. "The law of nature had been invoked by medieval writers as a moral restraint upon economic self-interest," R. H. Tawney writes.[88] Yet, in the 1600s, this understanding of nature was transformed to justify, not curb, human appetites.

Similarly, in *Thoughts and Details*, Burke inverts the conception of nature from a standard of restraint into a basis for human freedom. He does not employ nature to argue for government supervision of man's market instincts, but rather to defend the economic liberties of individuals to pursue profit and material comfort.[89] To the extent that political and economic thought in the Middle Ages can be classified as "conservative" and "traditional," Burke's idea of nature in the tract, not unlike the economic theories of his contemporaries, telling reformulated conservative and traditional understandings of the word as it related to the exchange of goods.

The idea of nature in Burke's commentary on supply and demand laws also holds implications for secondary literature on Burke. Before the publication of Peter J. Stanlis's book *Edmund Burke and the Natural Law*,[90] scholarship did not attempt to trace a strong connection between natural law and Burke's political thought. In light of Stanlis's illumination of elements of natural law in Burke's philosophical doctrine, however, Burke's gestures to "nature" in relation to political economy do not seem so unusual. Admittedly, traditional natural law does not necessarily capture the idiosyncrasies of the "natural law" of the market, as conceptualized by Burke and the Scottish Enlightenment. But Burke's appeal to sources other than tradition or history, the two considerations most commonly associated with Burke's political philosophy, demonstrates that the summoning of nature in his thought is not as aberrant as conventional accounts would suggest.

Yet Burke goes beyond appealing to nature in his comments. Being that he was the foremost advocate of prudence in the late eighteenth century, not to mention a leading antagonist of French revolutionaries' tendency to wield rationalist arguments in the service of their muscular political agenda, it is striking that he would draw a direct line from the laws of commerce – supply and demand principles – to God's will. Is Burke not sacrificing his own philosophy of prudence on the altar of free market ideology? By invoking God in the name of commercial liberty, is he not succumbing to the very temptation of categorical abstractionism that he famously accused French

---

[88] R. H. Tawney, *Religion and the Rise of Capitalism: A Historical Study* (London and New York: Verso, 2015), 183.

[89] As we shall see, for Burke, the protection of commercial enterprise was grounded in morality.

[90] Peter J. Stanlis, *Edmund Burke and the Natural Law* (Shreveport and Lafayette, LA: Huntington House, 1986).

ideologues and their English sympathizers of disseminating? These questions will soon be addressed.

Price Theory

The second key implication of Burke's embrace of supply and demand principles is its smooth relation with his price theory, which can be divided into two areas of inquiry: the source of value in markets, and the consequences of the unnatural distortion of value. First, for Burke, the demand of the consumer determines the price, not the desires of the seller. "When any commodity is carried to market," Burke writes in *Thoughts and Details*, "it is not the necessity of the vender, but the necessity of the purchaser that raises the price."[91] Therefore, "The only question is, what is it worth to the buyer?"[92] Burke recognizes the power of supply and demand laws in this discussion when he affirms, "If the goods at market are beyond the demand, they fall in their value; if below it, they rise."[93] An oversaturation of products necessitates the decline in their price, while a scarcity of provisions occasions a spike in their cost. Forced commerce distorts markets.

By asserting that the market value of a good or service relied on consumer preference, Burke underscored what came to be one of the principal insights of classical economics: consumers, not producers, ultimately decided the value of commodities in free economies. "By the late nineteenth century," Thomas Sowell writes, "economists had given up the notion that it is primarily labor which determines the value of goods." He continues: "On the contrary, it was the value of the goods to the consumers which made it worthwhile to produce those goods – provided that the consumer was willing to pay enough to cover their production costs." This shift "marked a revolution in the development of economics."[94]

Burke accepts such realities of price fluctuations without criticism in *Thoughts and Details*. Although he never asserts a normative claim about the morality of supply and demand forces, his analysis of market prices bends toward exceeding approval, not condemnation. Such implicit assent achieves greater force in the memorial when he describes the price distortions caused by the tinkering hands of government. If an "authority comes in and forces the buyer to a price," Burke claims, the buyer in this case being the farmer, who was responsible for hiring laborers and providing equipment, the intervention amounts to "an arbitrary division of his property among [the farmer and his laborers]."[95] For Burke, third-party intervention in prices, epitomized by the state regulation of wages between the farmer and laborer, was an unjustified invasion into a consensual process through which value was best determined by

---

[91] Langford, *Writings and Speeches*, IX, 126.   [92] Langford, *Writings and Speeches*, IX, 126.
[93] Langford, *Writings and Speeches*, IX, 126.   [94] Sowell, *Basic Economics*, 177.
[95] Langford, *Writings and Speeches*, IX, 126.

autonomous parties. Such arbitrary power revolted against the laws of supply and demand that Burke ascribed to the laws of nature, and ultimately to the laws of God.

Burke never uses the phrase "unintended consequences" in *Thoughts and Details*, but the undertones of this idea clearly suffuse the writing. In Burke's judgment, government intrusion into the natural ordering of prices provoked unanticipated effects that extended beyond the immediate policy proposal, such as a decrease in consumer demand. "If a commodity is raised by authority above what it will yield with a profit to the buyer, that commodity will be the less dealt in,"[96] he writes, reinforcing his understanding of supply and demand laws. Burke continues:

If a second blundering interposition be used to correct the blunder of the first, and an attempt is made to force the purchase of the commodity (of labour for instance), the one of these two things must happen, either that the forced buyer is ruined, or the price of the product of the labour, in that proportion, is raised. Then the wheel turns round, and the evil complained of falls with aggravated weight on the complainant.[97]

Burke is arguing that raising the value of a commodity above its market price will lower its demand, signaling his awareness of the principle of inverse proportionality in price theory. The attempt to alleviate this negative repercussion by mandating the purchase of the commodity would be another "blunder" and yield two more noxious outcomes: the oppression of the consumer (if forced to buy the good, he might not be able to afford it, and therefore could suffer financial ruin) and the increase in the costs of goods. Thus begins a self-perpetuating cycle of unintended consequences, swallowing up the liberties of both consumers and producers.

In this environment of aggravated commodity costs, including the increased cost of agricultural labor, the best-case scenario for the laborer was continual employment. But, Burke goes on to say, "[I]f the price of the corn should not compensate the price of labour, what is far more to be feared, the most serious evil, the very destruction of agriculture itself, is to be apprehended."[98] Burke implies in this case that the laborer would lose his job, and that the agricultural industry would perish from the shortage of workers.

Taking into account Burke's analysis of the agricultural economy so far, we can start to discern in the background of *Thoughts and Details* a faint silhouette of F. A. Hayek.[99] In a series of books and articles in the twentieth century, the Austrian economist famously drew attention to the innumerable complexities of market exchange, in which the competitive price system represented

---

[96] Langford, *Writings and Speeches*, IX, 127.   [97] Langford, *Writings and Speeches*, IX, 127.
[98] Langford, *Writings and Speeches*, IX, 127.
[99] Linda C. Raeder has noticed their similarities as well. See Raeder, "The Liberalism/Conservatism of Edmund Burke and F. A. Hayek: A Critical Comparison," *Humanitas* 10 (1997): 70–88.

a spontaneous process of the satisfaction of individual desires in commercial society.[100] "The continuous flow of goods and services is maintained by constant deliberate adjustments, by new dispositions made every day in the light of circumstances not known the day before," he wrote of this dynamic process, which he characterized as one of "rapid adaptation to changes in the particular circumstances of time and place."[101] According to Burke, the "particular circumstances of time and place" of agricultural economic phenomena helped explain fluctuations in grain prices.

Such prices conveyed fluid knowledge that could not be fully comprehended by the solitary intellect, nor could be imputed to a single cause. Burke's detailed explanation of the spike in food costs mirrors this understanding: he was aware that a range of agricultural and environmental factors contributed to changes in food prices, and therefore could not be explained away by facile explanations such as "unfair practice[s]," as Burke had characterized Fox's superficial inferences. For Hayek and Burke, the free-flowing price system in market economies channeled disparate pieces of information in a way that steered commerce toward efficient ends, inducing economic freedom to public prosperity, and individual liberty to social cohesion.

In addition, Burke and Hayek (and the Austrian School of economics in general[102]) held that the true value of goods and services was determined by the subjective preferences of consumers, not by the wishes of the sellers. This idea aligns neatly with Burke's aforementioned claim that the buyer, not the vendor, raises the price. The implication for Burke, as it was for Hayek and the Austrian School, was that goods and services did not contain an intrinsic, objective value, but simply reflected the personal tastes and inclinations of consumers, as shown by Burke's previously mentioned observation, "The only question is, what is it worth to the buyer?" Consumers as well as producers and dealers derived individual agency from the wheel of exchange. Although their respective economic thought was not fully synonymous,[103] Burke's and Hayek's reflections on the virtues of the competitive price system bear an intriguing resemblance worthy of attention.

Burke's judgment that consumers, not sellers, set market value helps explain his conspicuous refusal to condemn the price system in *Thoughts*

---

[100] See, in particular, F. A. Hayek, "The Use of Knowledge in Society," *The American Economic Review* 35 (1945): 519–530; and Hayek, *The Constitution of Liberty*, ed. Ronald Hamowy (Chicago: The University of Chicago Press, 2011).

[101] Hayek, "Use of Knowledge," 524.

[102] To argue that Burke's particular beliefs about prices, and supply and demand, reflect the Austrian School's understanding of these particular issues is not to argue that Burke would have adopted all philosophical tenets of the school. He would have fundamentally disagreed with some of the movement's thinkers for being too sympathetic to the primacy of individualism, and for analyzing human action through the prism of rational utility maximization. In addition, as with most intellectual schools, the "Austrian School," admittedly, does not reflect a uniform perspective on all economic matters.

[103] Consult Chapter 12.

and Details for hurting the customer and taking advantage of the laborer. Consider an alternative point of view, famously espoused later by Karl Marx in his *Economico-Philosophical Manuscripts of 1844*, which, while written in different economic circumstances, addressed a similar question of employer-employee relations. "[T]he worker sinks to the level of a commodity and, indeed, of the most miserable commodity; that the worker's misery is inversely proportional to the power and scope of his production," Marx writes.[104] He continues: "[T]he necessary result of competition is the accumulation of capital in a few hands and thus the most frightful restoration of monopoly."[105] According to Marx, market capitalism, by reducing labor to an article of trade and human relations to conditional monetary contracts, authorized capitalists to exploit the worker and sink his dignity.

Burke's commentary in the *Reflections* about the limits of transactional exchange actually corresponds in part with Marx's critique of "callous 'cash payment'" in bourgeois society.[106] In *Thought and Details*, however, he reverses the belief that the market exploits the laborer: because the prices of goods and services in markets ultimately stemmed from the behavior of the buyers, consumers and workers held a firm amount of autonomy in exchange economies.[107] Under Burke's reasoning, a dealer was in many ways at the mercy of the buyer, for a trader would never be able to sell a product unless he fulfilled the need of a potential consumer. Since a laborer was also a consumer, he retained economic power by influencing the value of goods in the mart. Burke's grasp of the relationship between supply and demand laws and prices in *Thoughts and Details* challenged contemporary thinking that market activity vested producers, employers, and middlemen[108] with the authority to maltreat consumers, one of the central critiques of market economies that has persisted to this day.[109]

Burke and Slavery

We should briefly mention, however, that Burke held deep reservations over applying the competitive price system to the trafficking of human beings. As P. J. Marshall shrewdly observes, the Free Port Act of 1766, of which Burke played an important role in drafting, had the effect of promoting the expansion

---

[104] Eugene Kamenka, ed., *The Portable Karl Marx* (New York: Penguin Books, 1983), 131.
[105] Kamenka, *Portable Karl Marx*, 131.   [106] See Kamenka, *Portable Karl Marx*, 206.
[107] Of course, Burke and Marx were writing in different economic circumstances.
[108] See the next section, "Middlemen."
[109] For example, in the 2014 edition of his bestselling book *Capital in the Twenty-First Century*, Thomas Piketty writes, "The entrepreneur inevitably tends to become a rentier, more and more dominant over those who own nothing but their labor." See Piketty, *Capital in the Twenty-First Century*, trans. Arthur Goldhammer (Cambridge, MA and London: The Belknap Press, 2014), 571.

of the African slave trade.[110] Yet Burke had also criticized slavery throughout his public and private life for violating the principles of justice and liberty.[111] For our purposes, there are at least three points in his reflections on the subject that are relevant for studying his political economy: he raised urgent moral questions about conceiving the sale of Africans like any other trade; he was aware that the slave trade was driven by economic forces, chiefly the demand for slave labor; and, in his criticism of and attempt to gradually eliminate the trade, he aimed to provide slaves with greater opportunities to acquire and retain property, among various reforms of the institution he proposed throughout his life.

Burke had drawn attention to the poor treatment of slaves as early as 1757, when *Account of the European Settlements in America* was published.[112] One of the earliest writings to criticize slavery in the eighteenth century,[113] the book suggested a number of ideas to alleviate the harsh condition of enslaved Africans, such as allotting them parcels of land and offering additional employment opportunities.[114] The *Account*'s discussion of slavery will be examined in closer detail in Chapter 6, but the important observation here is that the writing's recommendations to slowly expand the liberties of slaves reflected Burke's belief in the power of autonomy to stimulate man's capacity for industry and invest him in the well-being of his community. The recommendations also anticipated Burke's more comprehensive effort to reform the slave trade twenty-three years later.

This effort was *Sketch of a Negro Code*. Drafted in or around 1780, the code was Burke's formal plan for the incremental abolition of the slave trade. He sent it to Henry Dundas in April 1792, when the House of Commons was debating the merits of immediate and gradual abolition.[115] The *Sketch* was one of the

---

[110] P. J. Marshall, *Edmund Burke & the British Empire in the West Indies: Wealth, Power, & Slavery* (Oxford: Oxford University Press, 2019), 122.

[111] For a broader examination into Burke's views on slavery, see Gregory M. Collins, "Edmund Burke on Slavery and the Slave Trade," *Slavery & Abolition* 40 (2019): 494–521; Marshall, *Edmund Burke & the British Empire in the West Indies*; Robert W. Smith, "Edmund Burke's Negro Code," *History Today* 26 (1976): 715–723; Nina Rodgers, "Edmund Burke and the Abolition of the Slave Trade," in Allan Blackstock and Eoin Magennis, eds., *Politics and Political Culture in Britain and Ireland 1750–1850: Essays in Tribute to Peter Jupp* (Belfast: Ulster Historical Foundation, 2007), 91–106; and Christopher Leslie Brown, *Moral Capital: Foundations of British Abolitionism* (Chapel Hill: The University of North Carolina Press, 2006).

[112] See "*An Account of the European Settlements in America*," Chapter 6.

[113] See Thomas Clarkson, *The History of the Rise, Progress, and Accomplishment of the Abolition of the African Slave-Trade by the British Parliament*, vol. I (London: Longman, etc., 1808), 55–56.

[114] *Account*, vol. II, 131.

[115] Consult Burke to Henry Dundas, 9 April 1972, in *Correspondence of Edmund Burke*, vol. VII, 122–125.

earliest pamphlets supporting such a policy in the eighteenth century,[116] and made a favorable impression upon William Wilberforce, the great anti-slavery campaigner.[117]

Burke first clarifies in the beginning of the *Sketch* that termination of the slave trade would align with "the principles of true religion and morality."[118] Yet he realized that moral suasion alone would not be sufficient to end the practice, for the continuing demand for slaves would perpetuate it beyond any ethical limits. The "true origin of the trade was not in the place it was begun at, but at the place of its final destination," Burke wrote in 1792.[119] Recognizing this cold reality of human trafficking, the *Sketch* proposes a dizzying array of rules regulating the treatment of slaves and the condition of slave ships, with the ultimate intention of escalating the trade's costs high enough that it would smother the incentive to deal Africans. Similar to the ideas in the *Account*, it further granted slaves the liberties to acquire and inherit property, pursue educational and employment opportunities, and take time off from labor for religious worship.[120]

The *Sketch*, and Burke's general approach to the slavery question, thus signified the harmonizing convergence of his moral philosophy, conception of reform, and understanding of supply and demand laws: the proposal identified a social wrong, proposed a method to steadily eliminate it, and employed the sheer weight of regulatory power to discourage demand and make it too burdensome to preserve. In a speech in May 1778 on the African Company, the *General Advertiser* reported Burke had "confessed" that he was "no advocate for a trade which consisted, in the greatest measure, of mens bodies, and not of manufactures."[121] The natural laws of commerce should govern the circulation of material goods, but not the trafficking of human beings, for slavery shocked the principles of humanity. Supply and demand stopped at the soul.

2.4   MIDDLEMEN

Some of Burke's most underappreciated comments in *Thoughts and Details* concern the hidden function of the middleman in exchange economies.[122] These

---

[116] Christopher L. Brown, "Empire without Slaves: British Concepts of Emancipation in the Age of the American Revolution," *The William and Mary Quarterly* 56 (1999): 273–306. See also Brown, *Moral Capital: Foundations of British Abolitionism* (Chapel Hill: The University of North Carolina Press, 2006), 228–229.

[117] Stanhope MSS 731 (12) Wilberforce to Tomline (Pretyman), 15 May 1806.

[118] Langford, *Writings and Speeches*, III, 563.

[119] Burke to Henry Dundas, 9 April 1972, in *Correspondence of Edmund Burke*, vol. VII, 123.

[120] See *Sketch of a Negro Code*, in Langford, *Writings and Speeches*, III, 562–581.

[121] *General Advertiser*, 14 May 1778.

[122] See Thomas Sowell, "Are Jews Generic?", in Sowell, *Black Rednecks and White Liberals* (San Francisco: Encounter Books, 2005), 65–110.

men were typically noncitizens of countries or empires who traded and invested in commodities and financial resources, standing between the producer and the consumer as vessels of intermediary exchange. The modus operandi of middlemen would be to buy low and sell dear. They would also often serve as moneylenders, providing credit to borrowers in exchange for eventual repayment on the principal plus interest. The role of the middleman has spanned across races, ethnicities, religions, and geographical regions, including in England, Ireland, and India in Burke's age.[123]

Three main ways English middlemen typically intervened in market activity were through the trading practices of forestalling, regrating, and engrossing, various methods in which dealers would buy up and resell provisions to consumers.[124] Traditionally these were all banned under English statutory law, and forestalling was also illegal under common law.[125] The dark undertones of William Blackstone's descriptions of these practices in his *Commentaries on the Laws of England*, reinforced by their placement under the section "Public Wrongs" in the *Commentaries*, provided legal fuel to the classic portrayal of middlemen as greedy dealers who inflated prices and harmed the consumer for the intent of striking a quick profit.[126]

With this thick stigma percolating throughout the economic atmosphere of early modern England, it comes as no surprise that the laws passed under Edward VI and Queen Elizabeth were designed to limit the influence of middlemen – specifically those who practiced forestalling, regrating, and

---

[123] For Ireland, see Maureen Wall, "The Rise of a Catholic Middle Class in Eighteenth-Century Ireland," *Irish Historical Studies* 11 (1958): 91–115. For India, see Chapters 9 and 10. For information on the experience of middleman minorities, see Sowell, "Are Jews Generic?"

[124] William Blackstone, basing his descriptions of the trading activities on statutes passed under Tudor King Edward VI in the sixteenth century, defined forestalling as "the buying or contracting for any merchandise or victual coming in the way to market; or dissuading persons from bringing their goods or provisions there; or persuading them to enhance the price, when there; any of which practices make the market dearer to the fair trader" (Blackstone, *Commentaries on the Laws of England*, vol. II, ed. Thomas M. Cooley (Chicago: Callaghan and Company, 1876), 158). Regrating was "the buying of corn, or other dead victual, in any market, and selling it again in the same market, or within four miles of the place" (158). Blackstone, referring to regrating, continues: "For this also enhances the price of the provisions, as every successive seller must have a successive profit" (158). Engrossing was the "getting into one's possession, or buying up, large quantities of corn, or other dead victual, with intent to sell them again" (158).

[125] See Wendell Herbruck, "Forestalling, Regrating and Engrossing," *Michigan Law Review* 27 (1929): 366; William L. Letwin, "The English Common Law Concerning Monopolies," *The University of Chicago Law Review* 21 (1954): 355–385; and R. H. Britnell, "Forstall, Forestalling and the Statute of Forestallers," *The English Historical Review* 102 (1987): 89–102. As Britnell observes, recorded measures against forestalling dated back to the thirteenth century.

[126] Blackstone wrote that engrossing "must of course be injurious to the public" because it permitted "one or two rich men to raise the price of provisions at their own discretion" (*Commentaries*, vol. II, 118).

engrossing – by trying to ensure that the goods of producers were bought directly by purchasers for immediate use.[127] Yet the trade restrictions and public shame did not halt the trading practices. Through the sixteenth century and up until the Restoration period starting in 1660, a "corn-importing middleman organization was developed," Ray B. Westerfield writes,[128] and continued to spread.

Nevertheless, the public's bitter attitude toward middlemen lingered into the late eighteenth century. Although England was transitioning to a commercial society in Burke's age, dealers still faced sharp antipathy from lawmakers and the public for pursuing an entrepreneurial ethic that pressed against Aristotelian and Christian notions of moral economic exchange. They served as an especially glaring target in times of want and despair. Attacks on middlemen reached a high-pitched crescendo during the bread crisis in the mid-1790s, as exemplified by Thomas Pownall's *Considerations on the Scarcity and High Prices of Bread-Corn and Bread at the Market*. Published around the same time Burke sent *Thoughts and Details* to Henry Dundas and William Pitt, the writing targeted forestallers and regraters for contributing to bread shortages and aggravating the cost of provisions.[129]

In his younger days, Burke actually conveyed a similarly distrustful attitude toward the acquisitive impulse. The *"Desire of Lucre,"* he wrote in the *Reformer*, had "become almost the general Spring of Action," and had "never produced any but mean ones." It was a passion "unworthy of a Gentleman." Burke further regretted that men were not encouraged to pursue higher objects in life. The "young Gentlemen of this Age, partly from Nature, partly from Education, have got a low kind of Prudence," he observed, "and are taught to think every Thing that does not Gratify the Senses, unsubstantial and trifling, and fit only for romantick Heads."[130] We may take such comments to reflect general youthful apprehensions of the impact of luxury and vanity on taste and high culture in Burke's age.

As an adult, however, Burke grew to embrace a more salutary conception of the desire for gain in the wider social order. In one of the most neglected areas of his economic thought, he defends middlemen in *Thoughts and Details* against

[127] The laws were enforced with varying degrees of effort. See Ray B. Westerfield, *Middlemen in English Business: Particularly between 1660 and 1760* (New Haven: Yale University Press, 1915), 139.

[128] Westerfield, *Middlemen in English Business*, 133.

[129] See Thomas Pownall, *Considerations on the Scarcity and High Prices of Bread-Corn and Bread at the Market; Suggesting the Remedies in a Series of Letters* (Cambridge: Francis Hodson, 1795). In the same year as Pownall's tract, a handbill from Retford implored the public to "stand Flast and True and see your Selves Righted (or be starved and pined to Death)." It then attacked middlemen: "[f]or those Cruall Villions the Millers Bakers etc Flower Sellers rases Flowe under a Comebination to what price they please on purpose to make an Artificall Famine in a Land of plenty" (Fay, *Corn Laws and Social England*, 44).

[130] Langford, *Writings and Speeches*, I, 93.

this charge with sturdy conviction, seeking to explode the delusions of the public keen on attacking their profit-seeking activities. He acknowledges in the writing that they were "hated and maligned"[131] by both farmers and consumers. But then Burke proceeds to endorse their practices against charges that they tormented other market participants by monopolizing capital. Two guiding threads connected together his reflections on the matter: middlemen served a beneficial purpose in market economies; and regulatory attempts to extinguish them would create far more destructive problems than the laws intended to solve.

Burke first insists that middlemen should "be left to their free course,"[132] governed by the natural laws of the market. He does not reprobate their trading activities, nor lambastes their commercial success. "[T]he more they make, and the richer they are, and the more largely they deal, the better both for the farmer and consumer, between whom they form a natural and most useful link of connection," he states.[133] Burke's approval of middlemen here rests on two observations simmering beneath the surface of the text. First, the accumulation of wealth on the part of middlemen ends up spreading material advantages to others engaged in private economic activities. Second, the role of the middleman as a common link between the farmer and the consumer illuminates the symbiotic connections among all participants in exchange economies.

Burke does not immediately elaborate on these points. His discussion of market prices two paragraphs later, however, provides a clearer window into the theoretical basis of his appraisal of middlemen. He states that the "balance between consumption and production makes price,"[134] ratifying his confidence in supply and demand laws as a means to equity in the process of barter. Moreover, "The market settles, and alone can settle, that price,"[135] which thereby produces a fusion of interests between market actors. Yet those who wish to disrupt this balance and issue an "arbitrary regulation" would "directly lay their *axe* to the root of production itself."[136]

Burke is somewhat ambiguous here, but it appears that he is referring to farmers as well as middlemen – indeed the groups could overlap – in defending their trading activities against accusations of price gouging. Burke acknowledges they both performed a crucial, and similar, function in competitive price systems. "What is true of the farmer is equally true of the middle man," he remarks.[137] Raising suspicions about the farmer's economic behavior conveys a fallacious assumption that he "takes unfair advantages by delay."[138] Burke ostensibly means that the farmer would intentionally withhold the selling of his commodities in the mart temporarily in order to swell their

[131] Langford, *Writings and Speeches*, IX, 132.　　[132] Langford, *Writings and Speeches*, IX, 132.
[133] Langford, *Writings and Speeches*, IX, 132.　　[134] Langford, *Writings and Speeches*, IX, 133.
[135] Langford, *Writings and Speeches*, IX, 133.　　[136] Langford, *Writings and Speeches*, IX, 133.
[137] Langford, *Writings and Speeches*, IX, 132.
[138] Langford, *Writings and Speeches*, IX, 134. This quotation is in parentheses in the text.

demand and raise their price. He then insinuates that circulating such suspicions was unfair to the middleman as well: "[O]n the part of the dealer, it gives rise obviously to a thousand nefarious speculations."[139]

Burke had in mind not only Charles James Fox's comments in the House of Commons, as discussed, that attributed the "evil" of aggravated prices to "a variety of causes, complicated in their nature, and extensive in their operations."[140] In late October 1795, the Duke of Portland sent a circular letter to officials in England, Wales, and Scotland that addressed the price of grain. The letter asked them to organize meetings for magistrates for "the Purpose of procuring an Account of the State of the late Crop."[141] And a member of Parliament's Select Committee on the high price of corn at the time said that "the Produce of Wheat has proved so far deficient, as to require the Adoption of the speediest and most effectual Measures for the Remedy or Alleviation of so great an Evil."[142]

Burke displays a noticeable unease over these sentiments. "I confess I do not clearly discern its object," he writes of the circular letter.[143] His deeper apprehension was that the inquiry would "raise some alarm"[144] over the trading practices that he justifies in *Thoughts and Details*, which, he thinks, would excite public anger. Burke was also concerned that the inquiry would lead to "the French system of putting corn into requisition,"[145] thereby prompting the British government, like the indulgent French state, to threaten private property and tighten its grasp over the grain trade.[146]

Based on his comments about middlemen and market prices so far, one can surmise the logic behind Burke's assertion that the former promoted the well-being of the farmer and the consumer. Because middlemen buy and sell products according to supply and demand laws in market economies, they played a pivotal role in facilitating, rather than obstructing, the movement of goods to communities in need. Therefore, the middleman's steady accumulation of riches did not prevent other market participants from amassing wealth; instead, it contributed to the greater good by reflecting the balance of wants among market actors – a balance that was met when a product was sold by a middleman and bought by a consumer at an agreed-upon price. Burke, in other words, is subtly invoking his own concept of the Invisible Hand – the "benign and wise disposer of all things," as he calls it in *Thoughts and*

[139] Langford, *Writings and Speeches*, IX, 134.
[140] *Cobbett's Parliamentary History of England*, vol. XXXII, 239.
[141] *Journals of the House of Commons*, vol. 51 (London: H.M. Stationery Office, 1803), 85.
[142] *Journals of the House of Commons*, vol. 51, 85.
[143] Langford, *Writings and Speeches*, IX, 133. [144] Langford, *Writings and Speeches*, IX, 133.
[145] Langford, *Writings and Speeches*, IX, 133.
[146] Burke does admit that the French principles that dictated the regulation of grain were "full of that violence *which here* is not much to be feared" (Langford, *Writings and Speeches*, IX, 133).

Details[147] – to demonstrate how the handiwork of a mysterious force allowed the self-interest of middlemen to spawn broader public opulence.

Burke's remarks in *Appeal from the New to the Old Whigs* (1791) complement these insights. When discussing his belief in a "true natural aristocracy,"[148] he applauded "rich traders," who "from their success are presumed to have sharp and vigorous understandings, and to possess the virtues of diligence, order, constancy, and regularity, and to have cultivated an habitual regard to commutative justice."[149] Prominent traders possessed an acute mind and induced the spread of commercial virtues fundamental to the flourishing of exchange economies. More important, by referencing commutative justice, Burke was suggesting that the activities of traders promoted a measure of equity in market transactions. Consumers as well as merchants profited from the commercial nourishment of the community.

Elsewhere Burke recognized the salutary impact of middlemen on the distribution of foreign commerce. In *Speech on St Eustatius* (1781), an oration in which he assailed British conquerors' treatment of the community of St. Eustatius,[150] a Dutch island, Burke defended the Jewish people, who had lived on the island, for their vital role in establishing an international network of communication channels and credit markets. "From the east to the west, from one end of the world to the other, they are scattered and connected," Burke noted.[151] They were "the links of communication in the mercantile chain; or to borrow a phrase from electricity, the conductors by which credit was transmitted through the world."[152] Jews provided the connections and capital integral for the vigorous diffusion of trade across the globe.

In fact, Burke was so distraught over the conquerors' brutal treatment of Samuel Hoheb, a Jewish factor for an Amsterdam company whose property was usurped in St. Eustatius (and who was then forcibly sent to St. Kitts), that he petitioned the House of Commons in 1782 to provide compensation to Hoheb.[153] Hoheb's trauma exemplified the gross injustices perpetrated on the island against the Jewish people: "The poor Jews at St. Eustatius were treated in a worse manner, if possible, than all the other inhabitants; they were stripped of all their money."[154] Hoheb was "treated in the most harsh manner" because

---

[147] Langford, *Writings and Speeches*, IX, 125.   [148] Langford, *Writings and Speeches*, IV, 448.

[149] Langford, *Writings and Speeches*, IV, 449.

[150] Burke was also quite aware that the plunder of the island undermined British traders' interests in the West Indies. See Langford, *Writings and Speeches*, IV, 66–67.

[151] Langford, *Writings and Speeches*, IV, 74.   [152] Langford, *Writings and Speeches*, IV, 74.

[153] Langford, *Writings and Speeches*, IV, 109n4. During a speech on the plundering of St. Eustatius in December 1781, Burke went so far as to hold up a piece of linen from Hoheb's coat that Hoheb used to conceal his money during the British pillage of the island (Langford, *Writings and Speeches*, IV, 109). For the petition, see *Journal of the House of Commons*, vol. 38 (London: H.M. Stationery Office, 1803), 672–673. For Burke's discussion of the persecution of other Jews, see Langford, *Writings and Speeches*, IV, 75–76.

[154] Langford, *Writings and Speeches*, IV, 109.

"he had endeavoured to carry away some of his own money."[155] For Burke, the Jews were fully within their right to employ personal means to secure their assets in the face of pillage.

Burke's comments on the role of Jews in threading intricate webs of connections and credit throughout many nations hint at a further insight into the contribution of middlemen in markets: they added *value* to goods. They did this by transporting commodities from the producer to local or foreign markets for consumer purchase; by improving their quality and then reselling them; by finding more efficient ways to organize their distribution; and by serving as harmonizing conduits between two trading parties who otherwise remained segregated because of social status or cultural barriers, among various reasons.[156] There are inklings and shades of these arguments in Burke's discussion of middlemen.

Yet Burke does not clarify how this kind of economic value aligned with his understanding of the implied contract in market economies, a concept that will be discussed in Chapter 3. Allow us to extend his reasoning here. Just as reciprocal exchange generates a mutual set of contractual obligations between the employer and the employee that cannot be communicated in statutes, the middleman adds a hidden value to goods that cannot necessarily be observed by the public, articulated by the philosopher, or written into laws by the legislator. Physical labor can literally be seen and understood as contributing value to society, such as a farmer growing crops for consumption. In contrast, a tradesman, by transferring a product from one geographical location to another, does not appear to add any tangible worth to the good, at least compared to the toil of the manual laborer.

The mystery of such added value has helped fuel an instinctual hostility toward middlemen in history. "Activities that appear to add to available wealth, 'out of nothing', without physical creation and by merely rearranging what already exists, stink of sorcery," F. A. Hayek writes.[157] "[A]s soon as knowledge – which was not 'open' or visible – was introduced as an element in competition, knowledge not possessed by other participants, and which must have seemed to many of them also to be beyond the possibility of possession," he continues, "the familiarity and sense of fairness vanished."[158] The idea of unarticulated knowledge transmitted by middlemen – prerational, intuitive, and difficult to capture in words – is eminently reconcilable with Burke's commentary on the utility of implied contracts and the limitations of abstract reason. While he moves toward this understanding in *Thoughts and Details*, however, he does not discuss it with sufficient clarity.

---

[155] Langford, *Writings and Speeches*, IV, 109–110.
[156] See Westerfield, *Middlemen in English Business*, 349–369; Sowell, "Are Jews Generic?"; and F. A. Hayek, *The Fatal Conceit: The Errors of Socialism*, ed. W. W. Bartley III (Chicago and London: The University of Chicago Press, 1991), 89–94.
[157] Hayek, *Fatal Conceit*, 91.   [158] Hayek, *Fatal Conceit*, 91.

Burke broadens his defense of middlemen trading practices by attempting to puncture the common prejudice that middlemen helped the rich and hurt the impoverished. He does so by painting a distinction between the monopoly of capital and the monopoly of authority. The monopoly of capital for Burke was "a great benefit, and a benefit particularly to the poor."[159]

Burke then explains that a middleman with capital of a hundred pounds could not live on an annual profit of 10 percent, which would amount to living on ten pounds per year. But a middleman with ten thousand pounds could flourish with a profit margin of 5 percent, since he would be able to live on five hundred pounds per year.[160] Greater capital accumulation thus required less of a profit margin for the trader to live comfortably. Burke states that "these principles [of the monopoly of capital] are plain and simple," although he does not elucidate this point in the memorandum.[161]

Still, Burke here introduces an additional dimension into his belief that the healthy pursuit of enlightened self-interest engendered public prosperity. In this case, he specifically integrates the acquisition of capital with the interests of the lower social and economic classes. The preservation of market freedom would allow middlemen, some of whom might hail from modest circumstances, to trade goods and services for a profit, thereby setting the conditions for them to live with sufficient nutriment. Limiting the economic freedom to make money, Burke suggests, would obstruct the ability of the ordinary middleman, and any other market actor who did not come from family wealth, to earn an honest living.

Accordingly, the menace to market economies in Burke's view was not a monopoly of capital but a monopoly of authority. He describes this latter form of monopoly during his discussion of the proposal to establish public granaries[162] in *Thoughts and Details*. Burke assails the proposal for a number of reasons. Politically speaking, public granaries would unleash distempers targeting the granaries, their administrators, and the towns in which they would operate.[163] Burke then lists practical objections to the plan: it would incur high expenses; it would require a legion of bureaucrats to run; the capital necessary to purchase the grain would be prohibitive; it would breed corruption

---

[159] Langford, *Writings and Speeches*, IX, 133.   [160] Langford, *Writings and Speeches*, IX, 133.
[161] Langford, *Writings and Speeches*, IX, 133.
[162] Burke writes that one purpose of the idea is "to subject the farmer to the consumer, by securing corn to the latter at a certain and steady price" (Langford, *Writings and Speeches*, IX, 134).
[163] If public granaries are created, writes Burke, "I should not like to answer for the safety of the granary, of the agents, or of the town itself, in which the granary was erected – the first storm of popular phrenzy would fall upon that granary" (Langford, *Writings and Speeches*, IX, 134). Burke does not identify the source of this fury. Would it be the surrounding economic climate of uncertainty? Would it be the attempt to regulate the economy? Would it be the inefficient administration of the granaries?

and waste; and the public would become angry over the low quality of the corn.[164]

But the ultimate motive behind the push to set up public granaries in every market town, Burke suspects, was to "extinguish"[165] and "destroy"[166] what was "commonly called the middle man."[167] He believed that state-financed granaries would injure the corn dealer to the point at which his role would be eliminated in the grain trade. The transformation of a monopoly of capital into a monopoly of authority would then be set in motion, generating odious effects: "[B]y incurring a voluntary loss to carry the baker to deal with Government," Burke explains, the government would need to create the new trades of a "miller or a mealman, attended with a new train of expences and risks."[168] If the miller and mealman succeeded in the grain trade, "so as to exclude those who trade on natural and private capitals,"[169] the consequence would be one that critics of middlemen aimed to prevent in the first place. The miller and mealman, Burke writes, "will have a monopoly in their hands, which, under the appearance of a monopoly of capital, will, in reality, be a monopoly of authority, and will ruin whatever it touches. The agriculture of the kingdom cannot stand before it."[170]

Instead of the middleman holding a monopoly on capital, in other words, the two new government-backed positions would possess a monopoly of raw political power. This intrusion of the miller and mealman into the natural grain trade, a trade normally facilitated by middlemen in a free market, would give rise to unrestrained political and economic domination over others in civil society. It would cause "ruin," including the ruin of the agricultural economy.

Burke is drawing attention to a principle of his political economy spanning beyond the maxims of supply and demand laws: an improper and arbitrary invasion of brute political force into markets produces destructive repercussions. It crushes the middleman – the individual, in Burke's judgment, who served as a fulcrum for the steady circulation of goods in exchange economies. And once "all the principles of market"[171] were disrupted by government intervention in the grain trade, that government would "speedily become a bankrupt, and the consumer in the end will suffer."[172] Burke suggests that the farmer might not suffer from the regulation if market competition for grain persisted. Yet if the government purchased corn all at once, it would "instantly raise the market upon itself,"[173] occasioning an artificial spike in

[164] Langford, *Writings and Speeches*, IX, 134.   [165] Langford, *Writings and Speeches*, IX, 134.
[166] Langford, *Writings and Speeches*, IX, 135.   [167] Langford, *Writings and Speeches*, IX, 135.
[168] Langford, *Writings and Speeches*, IX, 135. The traditional role of the miller was to convert corn into meal and flour at his mill, but he also engaged in controversial trading practices similar to those of a merchant, such as engrossing. The mealman was in the wholesale and retail trades of meal (coarse powder ground from the edible part of a grain) and flour. See Westerfield, *Middlemen in English Business*, 167–168 and 171–172.
[169] Langford, *Writings and Speeches*, IX, 135.   [170] Langford, *Writings and Speeches*, IX, 135.
[171] Langford, *Writings and Speeches*, IX, 135.   [172] Langford, *Writings and Speeches*, IX, 135.
[173] Langford, *Writings and Speeches*, IX, 135.

supply. If the government purchased the commodity consistent with market forces, it would "produce no effect, and the consumer may as well buy as he wants."[174]

Once again, even though Burke does not invoke the phrase "unintended consequences" in *Thoughts and Details*, this is the concept that permeates his discussion of granaries. In addition to his remarks on the malign effects of government intervention in the grain trade, keep in mind Burke's previous observations that granaries would inflame the public; incur enormous financial costs; require the administration of a labyrinth of state employees; disseminate a low quality of corn; and fail to meet the needs of consumers. Ultimately, state supervision would compel the inefficient distribution of provisions, which would discourage middlemen from channeling them to communities in need. Burke's critique of public granaries confirms his suspicion that they would generate far more harm than good to the people. They would, in other words, foster unintended consequences.

Three more points bring clarity to Burke's discussion of middlemen and public granaries. First, that Burke defends the monopoly of capital for middlemen does not mean he endorses the monopoly of local markets. In the first case, the middleman, Burke indicates, should be guaranteed the use of the *individual* capital he earns. But regarding the second instance, Burke throughout his political life opposed the idea that traders deserved the protection of a monopoly over the *collective* trade of goods in the domestic marketplace. For example, while he defended the East India Company as a legitimate chartered institution that enjoyed a legal monopoly over foreign trade, he denounced the firm's monopolistic control over the local economy in India.[175]

Second, Burke does not wholly condemn the idea of public granaries. In *Thoughts and Details*, he recognizes their limited utility in small jurisdictions like Geneva. "A little place like Geneva ... might find some resource in state granaries, and some revenue from the monopoly of what was sold to the keepers of public-houses," Burke writes.[176] In his view, however, special conditions rendered Geneva a more profitable location for granaries than other geographical areas, such as its small population, limited territory, and reliance on neighboring powers for its existence.[177] Burke's consideration of public granaries illustrates that his apparent embrace of laissez-faire economics exhibits a greater flexibility than commentators have suggested.

For Burke, not only did different market actors encounter a variety of commercial opportunities, and thus should be secured the blessing of economic liberty to pursue them, but different political jurisdictions also presided over dissimilar economic and geographical environments. What works for one territory may not work for another, Burke conveys in *Thoughts*

---

[174] Langford, *Writings and Speeches*, IX, 135.   [175] See Chapters 9 and 10.
[176] Langford, *Writings and Speeches*, IX, 135.   [177] Langford, *Writings and Speeches*, IX, 135.

and Details, because of the incongruities of time and place. Economies were comprised of many intricate ingredients, such as geography, culture, and climate, and of many *degrees* of ingredients, such as varying levels of soil fertility. Mandating a uniform principle on diverse territories overlooked such wide-ranging social and economic considerations that otherwise steered the flow of commerce to disparate markets.

Burke expands upon these reflections in his discussion of the futility of state granaries in papal territories, which were responsible for supplying grain to Rome. He asserts in *Thoughts and Details* that the areas of such territories in which those granaries operated were "utterly ruined."[178] Burke contrasts these territories with ecclesiastical jurisdictions without similar forms of government intervention, and insists these freer areas were "highly flourishing."[179]

Burke appears to have learned about the grain trade of Geneva and Rome from a book written by Ferdinando Galiani, an Italian economist, called *Dialogues sur le commerce des bleds*, or *Dialogues Concerning the Trade in Wheat*. It is worth briefly reviewing Galiani's argument because it mirrors Burke's economic thought in important respects. As Gilbert Faccarello explains, Galiani argued that tenets of free markets should take into account a range of variables, such as the unique geopolitical state of affairs of the sovereign state in question the quantity of its resources, and the fertility of its land. Geneva, for instance, was encircled by strong states and could be starved to death by a blockade. Consequently, the debate over the sovereignty's grain trade was a political question as much as an economic one, and hence the government had a role to play in regulating it.[180] As a result, Galiani cautioned that a general economic proposition might need to be amended based on the specific circumstances of each territory.[181]

Burke himself acknowledges that it would be impractical to reform the grain system in Rome, and that it did "keep bread and all other provisions equally subject to the chamber of supply, at a pretty reasonable and regular price."[182] The other positive effect was that it maintained the tranquility of the poor. Yet he returns to his theme of the unintended consequences of regulating the grain supply: "[T]he quiet of the town is purchased by the ruin of the country, and the ultimate wretchedness of both."[183] While free commercial trade afforded reciprocal benefits to market participants, Rome's type of grain regulation produced public hardship.

The third and final point about Burke's commentary on middlemen in *Thoughts and Details* concerns his notion of the vitality of local knowledge

---

[178] Langford, *Writings and Speeches*, IX, 136.   [179] Langford, *Writings and Speeches*, IX, 136.
[180] Gilbert Faccarello, "*'Nil Repente!'*: Galiani and Necker on Economic Reforms," *The European Journal of the History of Economic Thought* 1 (1994): 527–528.
[181] In light of the overlap between Burke and Galiani, it is not a coincidence that Galiani has been identified as a precursor to the Austrian School of economics. See Robert W. McGee, "The 'Austrian Economics' of the Early Italian Economists," *Austrian Economics Newsletter* 6 (Spring 1987): 9–10.
[182] Langford, *Writings and Speeches*, IX, 136.   [183] Langford, *Writings and Speeches*, IX, 136.

and circumstance. When discussing his opposition to public granaries, Burke claims that the current climate was not the ideal environment to keep wheat in granaries. Instead, he insists that the "best, and indeed the only good," granary was the "rick-yard of the farmer, where the corn is preserved in it's own straw, sweet, clean, wholesome, free from vermin and from insects, and comparatively at a trifle of expence."[184] Burke here signals that crops were best cultivated under the private stewardship of the farmer and his laborers, rather than under the public administration of many officials, and at a fraction of the cost. This understanding is consistent with the chief message of *Thoughts and Details* that the internal grain trade should be left in the hands of private market actors.

For Burke, then, the farmer was solely responsible for financing and caring for his crop. "All this is done at the expence of the undertaker, and at his sole risk," he writes, in reference to storing wheat in rickyards and barns. "He contributes to Government; he receives nothing from it but protection; and to this he has a *claim*."[185] The undertaker in the eighteenth century came to be seen as an entrepreneur, such as a middleman, one who both committed himself to some commercial endeavor and faced heightened risk if he failed to complete his project.[186] Burke is thus uncovering an additional layer to his economic thought: he is suggesting that the person who was in the best place to realize his self-interest would also face immediate consequences if he made improvident decisions ruinous to his well-being.

Accordingly, financial indiscretion, or mere indolence, would injure the undertaker. By blending this insight into his discussion on the limitations of public granaries, moreover, Burke intimates that government officials would not face the sudden impact of their unwise choices in the grain market. The implication is that such officials would not display the same level of caution or wisdom as middlemen, since the ramifications of the former's choices would be felt by others – distressed laborers – and not themselves.

Is Burke's treatment of middlemen in *Thoughts and Details* too willing to grant sympathy to their profit-driven activities? In the tract he does not give serious consideration to the possibility that tradesmen might combine together to artificially raise prices or deceive the public into buying a product. Such practices would distort the natural formation of market prices, thwart the efficient dispersal of goods, and necessitate government intervention to alleviate economic hardship, thereby subverting the very principles of market exchange that Burke himself advocated. Adam Smith famously assailed merchants in the *Wealth of Nations* for their propensity to combine together for nefarious purposes and swindle the public,[187] but Burke does not broach

---

[184] Langford, *Writings and Speeches*, IX, 135.   [185] Langford, *Writings and Speeches*, IX, 135.
[186] See Alfred Marshall, *Principles of Economics*, vol. I (London: Macmillan and Co., 1895), 40; and Bert F. Hoselitz, "The Early History of Entrepreneurial Theory," *Explorations in Entrepreneurial History* 3 (1951): 193–220.
[187] See Smith, *Wealth of Nations*, vol. I, 267, 462.

this prospect in *Thoughts and Details*. (He would, however, do so on matters relating to foreign commerce in *Observations on a Late State of the Nation*.[188]) As discussed, Burke does consider the possible threat of monopoly of capital, which he dismisses, but his inattention to the prospect of any conceivable machinations on the part of traders appears blithe, even in an ad hoc tract.

Burke's praise of middleman, and of the pivotal function of nonphysical labor in civil society, marked key shifts away from the traditional perspective on morals and markets in classical antiquity and Christian Europe. According to this view, only manual labor was a noble human endeavor in the agricultural economy, as symbolized by the independent farmer who toiled by the sweat of his brow, embodying republican virtue, integrity, and self-sufficiency. He did not produce goods for pure commercial motives but for the fulfillment of man's basic needs for food and shelter. And he was the cornerstone of political and social stability. "For having no great abundance of possessions, they are kept busy and rarely attend the assembly; and since they lack the necessities of life they are constantly at work in the fields, and do not covet the possessions of others," Aristotle writes in the *Politics*, representing the classic Greek expression of the yeoman farmer.[189]

Burke himself referenced this specific quotation from Aristotle when attacking the French Revolution's war on landed property,[190] for he did hold, like Aristotle, that landed property provided the necessary weight to lend stability to political communities.[191] Nevertheless, Burke's praise of middlemen in *Thoughts and Details* differs from the Aristotelian critique of commercial enterprise. "The first essential responsibility" of the state official, Aristotle writes in *Politics*, "is control of the market-place: there must be some official charged with the duty of seeing that honest dealing and good order prevail."[192] The acquisition of goods that concerns "trade and depends on exchange" is "justly regarded with disapproval, since it arises not from nature but from men's gaining from each other."[193] Although the source of Aristotle's antagonism toward moneymaking was drawn more from philosophical considerations than from the principle of utility, it is evident that Burke offers a degree of dignity to the activity of the middleman that Aristotle, and pagan philosophers in general, did not.

It is further striking how Burke's vigorous defense of middlemen departed from conventional Christian notions of a moral economy. There have certainly been strands of Christian thought that have conveyed sympathy toward commerce and trade – and in fact some concepts of modern economics have roots in Scholasticism[194] – but the middleman had often been seen with an eye

---

[188] See "*Observations on a Late State of the Nation*," Chapter 7.
[189] Aristotle, *The Politics*, trans. T. A. Sinclair (London: Penguin Books, 1981), 368.
[190] See Langford, *Writings and Speeches*, IX, 374.   [191] See Chapter 11.
[192] Aristotle, *Politics*, 380–381.   [193] Aristotle, *Politics*, 87.
[194] Raymond De Roover, "Scholastic Economics: Survival and Lasting Influence from the Sixteenth Century to Adam Smith," *The Quarterly Journal of Economics* 69 (1955): 161–190.

of distrust from authorities in the Christian tradition. The early Church Fathers represented this tendency. Saint John Chrysostom, for example, wrote that "no Christian should be a merchant; if he wishes to be one, let him be chased out of the church of God." There was also a lingering presumption that an individual's accumulation of wealth necessarily deprived others of the same. "No one can gain without another man losing," Saint Jerome argued.[195] Burke's recognition that middlemen promoted the diffusion of resources to the many clearly diverges from this zero-sum reasoning.

That Burke's positive assessment of middlemen drifts away from such negative impressions of traders has lasting implications for how we grasp his philosophical beliefs. In a sense, he did harbor traditionalist persuasions, as illustrated by his condemnation of the French Revolution and his efforts to renew Europe's code of chivalry in an age of radical innovation. But Burke's alliance with a group whose commercial activity has been morally denounced throughout human history invites us to modify the view that Burke can be comfortably located in conventional Aristotelian and Christian intellectual frameworks. He certainly aspired to recover the ancient wisdom of the past in his political thought; and he – like Aristotle and Christian theologians – certainly granted priority to ethical virtue over economics in civil society, as Chapters 11 and 12 will detail. But Burke's elevation of dealing in *Thoughts and Details* communicates a revision to these traditions that provided greater accommodation for the pursuit of profit as a tenable, even praiseworthy, human endeavor.

2.5   THE 1772 REPEAL OF STATUTES BANNING FORESTALLING, REGRATING, AND ENGROSSING

Burke's defense of middlemen and supply and demand laws in *Thoughts and Details* captured the economic principles behind his attempt in 1772 to repeal English statutes that prohibited the trading practices of forestalling, regrating, and engrossing.[196] This episode is one the most overlooked aspects of Burke's parliamentary career, yet it is central to understanding his staunch defense of free commerce in the internal grain market in an era of popular contempt toward dealers.

Burke was the chief legislator who orchestrated the termination of the statutes. Or, at least he took credit in playing a leading role: in a letter to Arthur Young in late May 1797, two months before Burke passed away and at a time when Parliament was considering resurrecting the laws,[197] he contended that he had pushed for the repeal "of the absurd code of Statutes,

---

[195] Jacob Viner, "Early Attitudes toward Trade and the Merchant," in Viner, *Essays on the Intellectual History of Economics*, ed. Douglas A. Irwin (Princeton: Princeton University Press, 1991), 40.

[196] 12 Geo. III c. 71.

[197] See *Journals of the House of Commons*, vol. 52 (London: H.M. Stationery Office, 1803), 625.

against the most useful of all trades, under the invidious Names of forstalling and regrating,"[198] a belief he shared with Adam Smith.[199] In the letter, Burke conveyed an antipathy to the state regulation of provisions that he exhibited in *Thoughts and Details*, and that he previously demonstrated throughout his legislative activities campaigning for the nullification of the bans in 1772. "I am extreamly sorry," he wrote to Young, "that any one in the House of Commons should be found so ignorant and unadvised, as to wish to revive the senseless, barbarous and, in fact, wicked regulations made against the free trade in matter of provision, which the good sense of late Parliaments had removed."[200]

Young granted weight to Burke's claim. The statutes, he remarked, "were repealed by motion of the Right Hon. Mr. Burke, so convinced was he from much evidence, that those laws had no other tendency but by restriction to *raise* instead of lowering prices; as I know from conversations which I had the honour of formerly holding with him."[201] And Sir Gilbert Blane, a Scottish naval surgeon and an authority on the agricultural economy who would give testimony to a committee in the House of Commons on the bread market, reported in 1800 that the "preamble to the statute of 1772, and the speeches in the debate, particularly that of Mr. Burke, set the impolitic tendency of the ancient law in the strongest point of view."[202]

Scant historical evidence exists of Burke's speeches in support of the legislation. But the law's purpose and preamble summoned a robust statement of pro-market principles which reflected Burke's judgment that the bans generated great disadvantages to the internal market of provisions. The bill was proposed "for remedying the evils occasioned by the laws"[203] against forestallers, engrossers, and regrators. The preamble to the repeal explained:

Whereas it hath been found by experience that restraints laid by several statutes upon the dealing in corn, meal, flour, cattle, and sundry other sorts of victuals, *preventing a free trade in the said commodities,* have a tendency to discourage the growth and to enhance the price of the same, which statutes, if put in execution, would bring great distress upon

---

[198] Burke to Arthur Young, 23 May 1797, in R. B. McDowell, ed., *The Correspondence of Edmund Burke*, vol. IX, *Part One: May 1796–July 1797*; John A. Woods, ed., *Part Two: Additional and Undated Letters* (Cambridge: Cambridge University Press, 1970), 362.

[199] Smith, *Wealth of Nations*, vol. I, 534.

[200] Burke to Arthur Young, 23 May 1797, in *Correspondence of Edmund Burke*, vol. IX, 361–362.

[201] Arthur Young, ed., *Annals of Agriculture, and Other Useful Arts*, vol. VII (Bury St. Edmund's: J. Rackham, 1786), 47.

[202] Sir Gilbert Blane, *Inquiry into the Causes and Remedies of the Late and Present Scarcity and High Price of Provisions* (London, 1817), 286. For Blane's testimony, see *Reports from Committees of the House of Commons*, vol. IX, *Provisions; Poor: 1774 to 1802* (House of Commons, 1803), 68–69. For background on Blane, see Mary Wharton, "Sir Gilbert Blane Bt (1749–1834)," *Annals of the Royal College of Surgeons of England* 66 (1984): 375–376.

[203] Egerton MS. 236, f. 180, British Library.

the inhabitants of many parts of this kingdom, and in particular upon those of the cities of London and Westminster.[204]

The editors of the latest and most comprehensive volumes of Burke's writings and speeches write that this preamble "strongly suggests" Burke's involvement in its drafting.[205]

The *Journals of the House of Commons'* description of the legislative activity surrounding the repeal further suggests Burke's heavy hand in its creation. It was ordered that "Mr. Burke do make the Report from the Committee of the whole House" to whom the bill was committed. Then, "Mr. Burke accordingly reported" the amendments the committee had added to the bill; he "read the Report in his Place; and afterwards delivered the Bill, with the Amendments, in at the Clerk's Table," after which the House agreed to the amendments.[206]

Burke's distaste for bans against forestalling, engrossing, and regrating was revived over a decade later, when aggravated prices again raised public concerns about the efficacy of unfettered markets. The City of London gave voice to these apprehensions in 1787 by petitioning the House of Commons to restore the prohibitions against regrating and forestalling.[207] In his *Speech on Motion for a Bill against Forestalling*, however, Burke was quick to ridicule the idea. His speech – embroidered with substance, sarcasm, and wit – fortified his endorsement of ungoverned commerce in the domestic provisions market, and supplied deeper clues about the reasons motivating his efforts in 1772 to nullify the statutes.

Burke first intimates a telling irony in the City of London's petition: one of its sources, the group of aldermen, was straining to alert legislators to the supposed economic stresses at the time – yet they themselves appeared not to be suffering terribly from the price increases. The petition against forestalling and regrating, Burke remarks, "came from the Aldermen concerned in it after dinner, for their Petition had all the marks of plenitude and fullness about it."[208] He then urges his opponents to be attentive to the frequent fluctuations of market prices; on some days costs will increase, but on other days they will decrease. Burke "begged them at all events not to be uneasy, for if meat had been a little dear, when the price of feeding cattle was also dear, it would be considerably cheaper day after day."[209] Prices will diminish in the long run. This subtle insight reveals the enlargement of Burke's analytic mind in his assessment of economic phenomena: the merit of voluntary exchange should not be judged

[204] "The Policy of a Repeal of the Corn Laws," *The British and Foreign Review; or, European Quarterly Journal*, vol. 12 (London: Richard and John Edward Taylor, 1841), 474.
[205] Langford, *Writings and Speeches*, IV, 241n3.
[206] *Journals of the House of Commons*, vol. 33 (H.M. Stationery Office, 1804), 759.
[207] See *Cobbett's Parliamentary History of England*, vol. XXVI, *Comprising the Period from the Fifteenth of May 1786, to the Eighth of February 1788* (London: T. C. Hansard, 1816), 1167–1168.
[208] Langford, *Writings and Speeches*, IV, 241–242.
[209] Langford, *Writings and Speeches*, IV, 242.

based on single moments frozen in time, but rather on a long view of the benefits of a competitive price system adjusting to the temporal vagaries of market activity.

Burke also marks the broad scope of his economic diagnosis in the speech by calling attention to the variety of factors that mitigated temporary price increases in particular industries. Even if meat was dear, he observes, "[T]here was already plenty of nice lamb at market, and in consequence of the kindness of Providence lately showered down upon the earth, the green peas were coming in, and every other luxury, both of meat and vegetables."[210] A free market, suffused with all its deep complexities and rapid movements, enabled a wide range of products to reach London, including "muslins, silks, and spices and teas from the East; of lumber, and staves and rice from the West; of furs, and timber, and hemp, and pitch and tar, from the North; of slaves, and gold dust, and drugs, and colours from the South."[211] The temporary depression of one market did not necessarily curb the prosperity of other markets.

Burke's deeper aim in his speech was to discourage champions of commercial regulation from attacking the underlying sources of commercial prosperity, producers and traders. "While they had plenty of provisions," the *Morning Chronicle* reported him saying, "[Burke] advised them not to want to go to loggerheads with the providers, but to let them fatten as well as themselves."[212] Such providers included "Forestallers and Regrators" in the domestic provisions market and the "factor, the warehouseman, and the merchant" in the foreign trade market.[213] Burke is insinuating a clear implication of the proposed statutory bans, taken in the context of his entire speech: state supervision of producers and middlemen disrupted the movement of goods and checked the growth of public riches. It was in this part of his speech that Burke admitted he was the "humble instrument" of the 1772 repeal against forestalling, regrating, and engrossing.[214]

Burke thus argues that the easy flow of domestic trade, not the stiff hand of government regulation, promoted commercial prosperity. In the speech he asks Paul Le Mesurier, one of the London aldermen who supported banning forestalling and regrating, "whether he was not aware that a free commerce was the species of commerce most likely to flourish and prosper?"[215] Burke presses further: "Let him therefore ask himself whether a free commerce in provisions was not likely to make a plentiful and a cheap market."[216] The release of commerce from the watchful eye of government brought about at least two salutary advantages to the public: it occasioned the diffusion of goods to the many – a "plentiful" market; and kept costs low – a "cheap" market.

[210] Langford, *Writings and Speeches*, IV, 242.   [211] Langford, *Writings and Speeches*, IV, 243.
[212] Langford, *Writings and Speeches*, IV, 242.
[213] Langford, *Writings and Speeches*, IV, 242–243.
[214] Langford, *Writings and Speeches*, IV, 242.   [215] Langford, *Writings and Speeches*, IV, 242.
[216] Langford, *Writings and Speeches*, IV, 242.

Burke's statement to the aldermen was not among his most impressive speeches, but its persuasive force most likely projected some degree of influence in Parliament. Le Mesurier agreed not to further pursue the motion since it "did not meet with the concurrence of the House."[217] When the motion to refer the petition to a House committee was put up to a vote, it was defeated.[218] (Burke did offer to reconsider the motion in August.[219]) As Gilbert Blane later noted, "So great was the impression made on the members of the legislature" by the "enlightened view" of free markets espoused by Burke in his speech that the House of Commons "refused even to take [the City of London's petition] into consideration."[220] Blane explained that a similar petition introduced in 1796, one year after Burke wrote *Thoughts and Details* and two years after he left Parliament, was rejected again by the House.[221]

The noteworthy aspect of the City of London's petition in 1787 was its appeal to the authority of ancestral wisdom – a kind of reasoning Burke employs famously in the *Reflections* – as a vindication for the revival of the bans against forestalling, regrating, and engrossing. According to the petition, the rise in the price of provisions in 1787 was generated, at least in part, by the 1772 repeal of the trading laws that "the wisdom and experience of our ancestors had found necessary to prevent."[222] The city was partially correct in its invocation of history: because the prohibitions had been indelible features of statutory law for centuries, the 1772 ban symbolized a rather abrupt departure from England's traditions of regulating the grain trade (with, albeit, varying degrees of enforcement).

One, then, must not underestimate the boldness of Burke's mission to overturn the statutes against forestalling, regrating, and engrossing in 1772. Public disapproval of forestalling remained so intense in the 1760s, due to aggravated corn prices, that King George III felt compelled to issue a proclamation in 1766 urging his subjects to help enforce anti-forestalling statutes.[223] Many petitions were presented to Parliament in that decade from concerned citizens who claimed that the trading practices had inflated the price of provisions.[224] Forestallers in general were so denigrated in the eighteenth century that citizens offered rewards to individuals who exposed them.[225]

---

[217] *Cobbett's Parliamentary History of England*, vol. XXVI, 1170.
[218] *Cobbett's Parliamentary History of England*, vol. XXVI, 1172.
[219] Langford, *Writings and Speeches*, IV, 243.
[220] Blane, *Inquiry into the Causes and Remedies*, 286.
[221] Blane, *Inquiry into the Causes and Remedies*, 286.
[222] *Cobbett's Parliamentary History of England*, vol. XXVI, 1167–1168.
[223] Herbruck, "Forestalling, Regrating and Engrossing," 382. See also Letwin, "English Common Law Concerning Monopolies," 371.
[224] Herbruck, "Forestalling, Regrating and Engrossing," 379–380.
[225] Herbruck, "Forestalling, Regrating and Engrossing," 365.

It is most likely no coincidence that such opposition to the statutory bans on middlemen trading practices gained momentum[226] around the time when Burke entered Parliament in 1766. In April 1767, a House committee of which Burke was a member concluded that "the several Laws relating to Badgers, Engrossers, Forestallers, and Regraters, by preventing the Circulation of, and free Trade in, Corn and other Provisions, have been the Means of raising the Price thereof in many Parts of this Kingdom."[227] This message is a seamless precursor to Arthur Young's remark that Burke insisted the bans "had no other tendency but by restriction to *raise* instead of lowering prices."[228]

In addition, although Burke formally relinquished editorial duties of the *Annual Register* prior to the start of his parliamentary service in 1766, his view in support of free commerce may have carried weight at the journal after he left it. In response to King George's attempt to enforce the statutes proscribing the trading practices, the 1767 edition of the *Annual Register* stated that the existing bans were "dark in the construction, and extremely difficult in the execution."[229] Enforcing them would "have an effect contrary to the intentions of the council, and by frightening dealers from the markets, would increase that scarcity it was designed to remedy."[230] These comments fit neatly with Burke's remarks in *Thoughts and Details* that outlined the counterproductive effects of domestic grain regulations. Such noticeable movement in favor of annulling the trading bans in late eighteenth-century England disclosed Burke's commitment to, and influence in, reducing the Britain government's supervision over middlemen activities.

The Whig political tradition certainly encouraged the growth of the commercial economy. But scholars have underestimated Burke's specific efforts in this regard. Donald Winch writes that Burke's appraisal of middlemen was "merely defending the status quo."[231] Carl Cone states that Burke's views in 1772 and 1787, and in *Thoughts and Details*, "expressed views that were in harmony with the spirit of the age."[232] If Burke was defending the status quo, and if he was expressing views in harmony with his time period, it was because he helped create this status quo in the latter half of the eighteenth century that displayed, through legislative initiative, greater sympathy to the activities of middlemen.

---

[226] See Letwin, "English Common Law Concerning Monopolies," 371.

[227] *Journals of the House of Commons*, vol. 31 (London: H.M. Stationery Office, 1803), 291.

[228] Young, *Annals of Agriculture*, 47.

[229] "The History of Europe," *The Annual Register, For the Year 1767* (London: J. Dodsley, 1768), 40.

[230] "History of Europe," *Annual Register, For the Year 1767*, 40. Note that the *Annual Register* wrote in a different section that the cure to distress in the provisions market should not begin by "extirpating engrossers and regraters, nor by destroying rats and sparrows, those great forestallers of the public markets." In this section of the periodical, however, the writer considers the possibility of having government regulate the riches of prosperous men to pay off the national debt, indicating a sympathy to wealth redistribution Burke did not convey in his life. See "Essays," in *Annual Register, For the Year 1767*, 171.

[231] Winch, *Riches and Poverty*, 210.   [232] Cone, *Age of the French Revolution*, 490.

Although Burke's efforts helped abrogate the statutory bans against forestalling, regrating, and engrossing, the repeal did not end the debate over their legality under common law. The common law case *Rex v. Rusby* (1800) was evidence of this ongoing controversy, and demonstrated Burke's lingering influence in public discourse on the question of a free internal trade even after he passed away.[233] John Rusby was a trader at the time who had been accused of regrating thirty quarters of oats in November 1799. Lord Kenyon supported the jury's conclusion that Rusby was guilty of violating the common law prohibition of regrating. The argument from the prosecution and Kenyon dripped with emotion. Kenyon stated, "[T]hough in an evil hour all the statutes which had been existing above a century were at one blow repealed" – ostensibly referring to the Burke-led repeal of the practices in 1772 – "yet, thank God, the provisions of the common law were not destroyed."[234] The public was so enraged by Rusby's conduct, as conveyed by the impassioned statements from Kenyon and the jury, that a London mob destroyed his house and tried to lynch him.[235]

Burke's endeavors to repeal laws banning middlemen trading practices had a lasting impact, however. Following the era of Kenyon, forestalling was no longer prosecuted under common law. In 1844 Parliament repealed the remaining statutes that circumscribed the trading activity, and formally eliminated the common law restrictions against forestalling, regrating, and engrossing.[236] In the end, Burke's defense of middlemen from the 1760s to his final days illustrated a firm commitment to market liberty, thereby conveying strong degree of sympathy for one of the most maligned human groups in European civilization, one that offended the traditionalist sensibilities with which Burke is often associated.

2.6 CONCLUSION

As we shall see, Burke believed that a broad harmonious connection linked religion and manners with modern commercial activity. Similar to his reformulation of "nature" to defend commercial enterprise, however, Burke's endorsement of supply and demand principles and the competitive prices system in the provisions market indicates key tensions with traditional conventional classical and Christian critiques of market activity. His political philosophy stressed the importance of seeking guidance from the distilled wisdom of the past, but his economic thinking in *Thoughts and Details* does not *directly* tap into the vast repository of classical and Christian thought to inform his views on supply and demand laws, wages, and

---

[233] See discussion of this case in Barnes, *History of English Corn Laws*, 81–82; and Letwin, "English Common Law Concerning Monopolies," 372.

[234] Letwin, "English Common Law Concerning Monopolies," 372.

[235] Rusby ended up appealing the case. This time the court was split on whether forestalling, regrating, and engrossing were illegal under common law. See Barnes, *History of English Corn Laws*, 82.

[236] See Letwin, "English Common Law Concerning Monopolies," 372–373.

prices, as evidenced by his approval of middlemen trading practices.[237] Scholastic thinkers of political economy offered fragmentary insights into the merits of competitive exchange, but generally they were far more apprehensive than Burke about the benefits of widespread commerce, and approached economics through a sharper lens of formalism.[238] Furthermore, Burke's treatment of labor as a commodity – something tradable, ephemeral, movable – indicated a noticeable shift away from social and economic structures under feudalism, in which peasants were provided modest opportunities to cultivate land that were not contingent on the vagaries of commercial society and the forces of supply and demand in competitive labor markets. Yet the question remains: were there any exceptions to Burke's opposition to government intervention in private economic activity?

---

[237] As will be discussed, Burke does invoke Christianity in *Thoughts and Details* in his discussion of charity to the poor. See "Labor, the Laboring Poor, and the Rich as Trustees," Chapter 3. Of course, strands of classical and Judeo-Christian political thought have been employed to defend competitive price systems. See Novak, *Spirit of Democratic Capitalism.*

[238] See De Roover, "Scholastic Economics: Survival and Lasting Influence from the Sixteenth Century to Adam Smith."

3

Agricultural Policy, Labor, and Wealth Redistribution

> Such is the event of all compulsory equalizations. They pull down what is above. They never raise what is below.[1]
>
> Edmund Burke, *Thoughts and Details on Scarcity*, 1795

3.1 INTRODUCTION

Did Burke always support government restraint in the internal grain trade? As this chapter will seek to demonstrate, there was at least one powerful exception to his preference for a free market: the export bounty. In addition, *Thoughts and Details* raises further questions about Burke's views on particular policies pertaining to the agricultural economy of England that he clarifies in his parliamentary speeches and private notes, such as the enclosure movement and the Poor Removals Bill. This chapter will explore these subjects and other related items.

It will also discuss the broader implications of Burke's approach to the study of rural economics, such as his belief in the responsibility of the affluent to help the needy in trying times, as articulated in *Thoughts and Details* and exemplified in his public and private life. The chapter will conclude by probing Burke's conception of economic equality and his distrust of government-mandated wealth redistribution in seeking to mitigate the distresses of the laboring classes. For Burke, forced equality in the agricultural economy would condemn all men and women to poverty, rather than elevate them to prosperity.

3.2 THE CORN LAWS AND EXPORT BOUNTIES

While the primary focus of *Thoughts and Details* was England's domestic provisions market, this market carried important influence in the nation's

[1] Langford, *Writings and Speeches*, IX, 127.

foreign grain trade as well. Allow us to take a temporary detour away from the economic tract, then, and explore Burke's insights into the Corn Laws and export bounties that he expressed decades before its publication. Not unlike his commentary on middlemen, Burke's remarks on these policies tend to be neglected in the examination of his thought. Yet they remain an integral part of his conception of political economy, and illuminate his beliefs on a critical matter of English agriculture in the eighteenth century: whether the government should encourage the importation or exportation of wheat, a crop Burke called the "noblest grain" in *Thoughts and Details*.[2]

The general aim of the Corn Laws was, as Charles Smith explained, "to prevent Grain from being at any Time, either so dear that the poor cannot subsist, or so cheap that the Farmer cannot live by growing of it."[3] Their guiding principles were to encourage importation by setting low duties when prices were dear and discourage importation by setting high duties when prices were cheap. The export bounty was also intended to foster agricultural cultivation. As a result, the Corn Laws tended to maintain a price for grain that advantaged landowners and English producers seeking to reap profit from the provisions trade.[4]

Accordingly, export bounties were dangled to domestic producers as an incentive for tillage. Yet exports were proscribed when the prospect of scarcity emerged. Grain imports were allowed only when provisions reached a particular price determined by law, a decision prompted by the thinking that domestic producers at that point would not need protection from foreign competition. Otherwise, imports were inhibited by tariffs. The Corn Laws had some effect, at the very least, in expanding the grain market. Referring to the controversial Act of 1689, which revived the export bounty, Donald Grove Barnes writes that "there is no doubt that the policy did increase the production of wheat and other grain by widening the market."[5] The impact of the Corn Laws was weakened by defects in their administration and irregularities in their enforcement, however.

The Corn Laws did not attract sustained political scrutiny from agricultural and commercial interests prior to 1750. But they began to command greater national attention in the latter half of the eighteenth century, at a time when Burke was progressively attaining prominence as an eloquent legislator and careful thinker on the subject of political economy. The political implications of the laws were wide-

---

[2] Langford, *Writings and Speeches*, IX, 137.

[3] Charles Smith, *Three Tracts on the Corn-Trade and Corn-Laws* (London: J. Brotherton, 1766), 72. For Smith's contribution to the Corn Law debate in eighteenth-century England, see Richard Sheldon, "Practical Economics in Eighteenth-Century England: Charles Smith on the Grain Trade and the Corn Laws, 1756–72," *Historical Research* 81 (2008): 636–662.

[4] This survey of the Corn Laws relies primarily on Smith, *Short Essay on the Corn Trade*, 71–92; Barnes, *History of English Corn Laws*, 8–48; and Fay, *Corn Laws and Social England*, 1–34. See also Westerfield, *Middlemen in English Business*, 161–165.

[5] Barnes, *History of English Corn Laws*, 15.

ranging. The bounty on exports was funded by receipts from taxation, placing financial encumbrances on the Exchequer. The landed gentry harbored a vested interest in supporting the bounty, insisting that the general public benefited from the encouragement of grain, and would complain bitterly when grain prices fell. Yet rioters attacked corn dealers and granaries during times of perceived scarcity, signaling their discontent over the odious effects of exportation. Manufacturers grew disenchanted from the realization that the export bounties were, in effect, subsidizing inexpensive provisions to England's foreign rivals.

Although the Corn Laws generally favored producers, the price of grain actually declined from 1689, when the export bounty was implemented, to the mid-1700s because of moderate advances in agricultural technology and productivity.[6] The intersecting interests of the landed aristocracy, manufacturers, and consumers, combined with a string of weak harvests from the 1750s to the early 1770s, elevated the Corn Laws to an object of heightened public concern soon before Burke's entry into Parliament. In 1765, around the same time that England had become a net importer of grain, corn exports were suspended and corn imports were permitted duty-free. These measures were intended to support imports and hinder exports – the opposite priorities of the previous Corn Laws – and remained in place until 1773.

The early 1770s in particular witnessed a flurry of legislative activities, in which Burke played a prominent role, that attempted to address the uncertainties of the grain market. In addition to his orchestration of the 1772 repeal of statutes banning forestalling, regrating, and engrossing, he was an active participant in parliamentary debates over the Corn Laws. On November 16, 1770, for example, he spoke often during a discussion in the House of Commons over whether to continue the suspension of corn exports, and to suspend the distilling process that converted wheat into wine and spirits.[7]

Burke argued against the regulations. "There are no such things as a high and a low price," he insisted during the debate. "It resolves itself into an encouraging and a discouraging price." Burke contended further that prices should accord with the demands of the market, and that the swings in prices were induced by the export regulations. "We have nothing to look to, but the natural price which grain brings at an universal market," he stated. "There may be a fluctuation of price; but the want of exportation is the cause of that fluctuation."[8] The artificial suppression of grain disrupted the operation of supply and demand laws and the functioning of the competitive price system, a verdict in close agreement with *Thoughts and Details*.

---

[6] Note, however, that Donald Grove Barnes writes that the "effect of improvements in agriculture during the first half of the eighteenth century on the increased production and exportation of grain may be overestimated." The "effect was not, as a rule, felt until after 1760" (*History of English Corn Laws*, 14).

[7] Wright, *Sir Henry Cavendish's Debates of the House of Commons*, vol. II, 55–56.

[8] Wright, *Sir Henry Cavendish's Debates of the House of Commons*, vol. II, 56.

Burke also resisted the idea to check the distillery. The reasoning behind this proposal was to ensure that wheat, in a time of scarcity, would be used for provisions rather than spirits. Burke's principal message, however, was that England's grain economy was marked by a dramatic interdependency of parts. It thus made no sense to confine the use of a crop to one specific purpose – the consumption of food – when the use of corn for an object seemingly unrelated to this purpose might also impact the provisions market.[9] "Every grain is a manufacture, to ten times its value," Burke said. "Then, the refuse is not lost. It enters in the food of your hogs."[10]

Burke was delivering the same reasoning he conveyed twenty-five years later in *Thoughts and Details*: the distilling process created refuse for hogs to eat; this process thus encouraged the fattening up of pigs for the English to slaughter and consume for themselves. Inhibiting the distillery, therefore, limited the quantity of food that people could enjoy. "I shall live and die in this principle – that your corn is a branch of your manufactures, in all its parts," Burke avowed.[11] Because the influence of corn reached the outer edges of England's agricultural economy, the regulation of its trade would spawn unintended consequences far beyond the discouragement of exports. Burke's parliamentary efforts in support of corn exports disclosed his strength of conviction in support of free trade measures, even when – or especially when – he was in the minority; the original motion preserving the ban on corn exportation that Burke had criticized passed 155 to 16.[12]

Burke's endorsement of the free provisions trade, and of the competitive price system, was even more pronounced in a parliamentary debate earlier in the year. In February 1770, the House debated whether to allow the exportation of malt. An MP proposed an amendment calling for the exportation of wheat flour and barley as well. Thomas Townshend opposed the additional measure. "[W]e are not ripe for the amendment," he said.[13] Burke responded to Townshend in characteristic fashion, blending well-timed levity with sharp insight into the intricate connections of market phenomena:

In my opinion, we are ripe for the question till we are rotten. There is no such thing as the landed interest separate from the trading interest. What God has joined together, let no man separate. He who separates the interest of the consumer from the interest of the grower starves this country. Turn your land into trade. Export, that you may keep your

[9] Burke puts forth the same argument in regard to wool exports. "Why do you suffer your wool to be exported? Do not the people want clothes? Why export linen and cloth?" See Wright, *Sir Henry Cavendish's Debates of the House of Commons*, vol. II, 56.

[10] Wright, *Sir Henry Cavendish's Debates of the House of Commons*, vol. II, 56.

[11] Wright, *Sir Henry Cavendish's Debates of the House of Commons*, vol. II, 56.

[12] Wright, *Sir Henry Cavendish's Debates of the House of Commons*, vol. II, 57.

[13] J. Wright, ed., *Sir Henry Cavendish's Debates of the House of Commons*, vol. I, *May 10, 1768– May 3, 1770* (London: Longman et al., 1841), 476.

corn at home. Make things dear, that they may be cheap. These are all paradoxes; but nevertheless true. You are going upon particular, local, narrow, sentiments.[14]

These are some of the most telling comments from Burke about England's agricultural economy prior to *Thoughts and Details*. They capture his embrace of the fundamental principles of supply and demand: the undisturbed flow of provisions supplies a sufficient quantity of corn for home consumption. Price increases in one realm will lower costs in other areas of the economy. Cutting off the means of production and trade will deprive consumers of goods. Land should serve not merely as a ballast of stability but also as a lively incubator for industry.

The remarks also outline the broader implications of Burke's theory of political economy. Opposing the exportation of wheat flour and barley reflected a form of prejudice – "particular, local, narrow, sentiments" – ignorant of the advantages that accompanied the widespread diffusion of grain, an insight he would elaborate on in his commentary on the Irish trade bills. And Burke's stress on the reconciliation between the landed interest and the trading interest foreshadows his later discussion of the matter in the *Reflections*, in which he drew attention to the historical division between the two interests in France. Burke's sympathies for the natural laws of commerce in the internal grain industry coalesced decades before his drafting of *Thoughts and Details*.

Pownall's Act of 1773

A powerful test of Burke's ability to balance economic conviction with political prudence, however, emerged during an important debate on corn bounties in 1772. In April of that year, Thomas Pownall had introduced a number of resolutions in the House of Commons to regulate the corn trade that included the export bounty.[15] Donald Grove Barnes writes that Burke and Pownall were "principally responsible" for the restrictions concerning the bounty proposal.[16] Although the bill garnered wide appeal in the Commons, the House of Lords eliminated the bounty provision. The parliamentary divide over the bounty, which reflected sharper political frictions between the chambers at the time, was in many ways rooted in political posturing: the House of Commons claimed the exclusive privilege to draft money bills, yet the decision by the House of Lords to remove the export bounty offended this principle, according to MPs in the Commons. Burke himself waxed indignant at the Lords' decision to strike out the bounty. "Can liberty exist a moment," he asked, if the House of Commons

---

[14] Wright, *Sir Henry Cavendish's Debates of the House of Commons*, vol. I, 476. The House withdrew the amendment but agreed to the original motion permitting malt exports.

[15] See Barnes, *History of English Corn Laws*, 42–43; Fay, *Corn Laws and Social England*, 29–31; and Lock, *Edmund Burke*, vol. I, 320–323 for historical background on Pownall's act.

[16] Barnes, *History of English Corn Laws*, 42.

allowed the upper chamber to "lay their sacrilegious hands upon this holy of holies, this palladium of the constitution?"[17] The Commons rejected the bill.

After Parliament issued a series of temporary acts to strengthen England's grain trade in late 1772, the body renewed its effort to enact a more permanent law in the spirit of Pownall's previous bill. It succeeded: a law was passed in 1773[18] that permitted wheat imports when prices matched or exceeded 48s., if dealers paid a nominal duty of 6d. per quarter.[19] Exports were forbidden if wheat prices attained or exceeded a price of 44s.; previously the threshold was set above 48s. (In general, annual statutes had prohibited exports up until 1773.[20]) The law did provide a wheat bounty of 5s. if prices sunk below 44s.[21] Rye, beans, barley and malt, oats, and peas were also regulated under the law.[22]

Pownall's act ostensibly benefited consumers. By lowering the price at which the bounty would be discontinued, the legislation in effect narrowed its influence, thereby reducing, if slightly, the vested interest of exporters; and by easing restrictions on imports, it encouraged the purchase of goods from abroad, which would evidently decrease prices. This legislation was "the most important" such Corn Law since the Act of 1689, C. R. Fay writes.[23] As Fay explains, however, it did not mark a clear reversal of traditional corn policy, but an attempt at restoring the just proportions between supply and demand that had been rattled by shocks to the market and by demographic shifts, such as the increase in industrial population, in the 1760s and early 1770s.

Burke communicated lukewarm support for the final version of Pownall's bill, even though he had a hand in crafting it. During parliamentary debate, he registered his "protest against the general principles of policy" of the legislation because he thought they were "extremely dangerous." But Burke accepted the measure because it was "prudent to yield to the spirit of the times"[24] – a curious comment seemingly at odds with his trustee theory of representation.[25] One strand of Burke's criticism of the bill actually lent support to a particular policy of government interventionism: the export bounty on corn.

This is one of the rare instances when Burke explicitly defended a regulation of the internal grain economy. His argument was that grain prices had declined since the inauguration of the export bounty. Why should the English halt a policy "of which the utility has thus been ascertained by the most unerring

---

[17] *Parliamentary History of England*, vol. XVII, 513.   [18] The act took effect starting in 1774.
[19] "s." denoted shilling and "d." denoted pence. Consult Fay, *Corn Laws and Social England*, 29.
[20] Bohstedt, *Politics of Provisions*, 112n31.   [21] See Barnes, *History of English Corn Laws*, 43.
[22] *Customs Tariffs of the United Kingdom, from 1800 to 1897. With Some Notes Upon the History of the More Important Branches of Receipt from the Year 1660* (London: Her Majesty's Stationery Office, 1897), 231–232.
[23] Fay, *Corn Laws and Social England*, 29.
[24] *Cobbett's Parliamentary History of England*, vol. XVII, 480.
[25] See "Burke's Trustee Theory of Representation and His Conception of Reform," Chapter 5.

of guides, experience?"[26] If history revealed that a policy conferred an advantage to the public, such as, in Burke's view, the bounty, there was no compelling reason to end it. Burke reinforced this point in draft notes for a speech on the Corn Laws (most likely for the one quoted in this subsection), in which he criticized supporters of the bill for moving "from experience to experiment, from a good which we enjoy to an advantage which we may never arrive at."[27] This is the prudent Burke with which we are familiar, granting priority to the tried and true over the slippery speculations of untested theory.

Burke further maintained in Parliament that the corn bounty provided necessary support for British traders to compete in the foreign market:

The intention of the bounty is only to enable our merchants to bring the British corn to foreign markets upon a par with what is furnished by the countries where it is sold. The bounty, therefore, is only meant to defray the expence of exportation, and without it you will never be able to export, except when there is a famine abroad.[28]

Therefore, as Burke wrote in draft notes for a speech on the Corn Laws (again, most likely for the one cited in this subsection), the bounty established "two principles": it was to "encourage" British agriculture "in preference to foreign agriculture"; and to encourage British navigation "in preference to foreign Navigation."[29]

Hence Pownall's bill would erode the foundations of public opulence. It would discourage tillage, fuel greater scarcity, increase prices – and condemn landed cultivators and the underclass in the process. The corn trade, which was "the source of much wealth and prosperity" of the nation, would be lost, as Burke argued in his parliamentary speech. Additionally, "Will not the landed interest be deeply affected by that event? Will not less corn be grown? Will not less then come to market? Will not the price be enhanced, and the very poor, whom you mean to serve, most essentially injured?"[30] Burke believed that landed proprietors concurred with this assessment: in his draft notes, he claimed that "[e]very Gentleman" agreed "that the farmer ought to be *encouraged* by a *bounty on the foreign market*."[31]

We should note that Burke did not necessarily apply his reasoning in support of the corn bounty to other trades in the early 1770s. In 1770, a Linen Bill was proposed in Parliament that would have provided bounties for striped and checked linen in order to aid English traders competing with Dutch merchants in the West Indies. Regulations of the linen market spanned back to the seventeenth century, when England enacted a progressive series of import

---

[26] *Cobbett's Parliamentary History of England*, vol. XVII, 480–481.
[27] MSS. at Sheffield, Bk. 18–2.   [28] *Cobbett's Parliamentary History of England*, vol. XVII, 481.
[29] WWM/BkP/18/1.   [30] *Cobbett's Parliamentary History of England*, vol. XVII, 481.
[31] WWM/BkP/18/2.

duties, starting in 1690, in order to fund its military expeditions.[32] And in 1743, England established export bounties on linen, which was the "first positive official encouragement" to the linen industry among the British Isles that was implemented in the nation, writes N. B. Harte.[33] As a result, a wall of protection was formed around the nation's linen interest that shielded it from the full might of foreign competition. The price of custom duties on linen imports increased 100 percent from 1690 to 1704 and again from 1748 to 1779.[34]

Burke objected to the extension of the bounties for striped and checked linen. In his view, producers should make goods in accord with the demands of consumers, not the preferences of government. "To make a manufacture rise from the Treasury, & not from the market, is a bad principle,"[35] Burke observed, expressing a criticism of the law that Adam Smith would later articulate in the *Wealth of Nations*.[36] For to "give a man a monopoly, & a bounty too, is an absurdity."[37] The subsidizing of particular industries could have a negative influence on other manufactures: "[W]hen you give an artificial encouragement one way, you hurt another."[38] Even though Burke opposed linen bounties in principle, he was willing to accept their reduction, rather than outright abolition, on grounds of prudence. During debate over the Linen Bill, Burke voiced his support for the linen bounty to be 1/2*d*. instead of 1*d*.; the former passed committee.[39]

Because the corn bounty was an exception to Burke's broad endorsement of a free grain market, was he not inconsistent in opposing the "artificial encouragement" of the linen bounty but championing this government stimulant of grain? It is hard to avoid this conclusion. Perhaps Burke's experience as a farmer led him to think that the bounty supplied special advantages to the agricultural economy as a whole. Or maybe Burke's unshakable belief that the landed aristocracy should command disproportionate representation in the national legislature inspired him to grant support for the policy. And it is certainly plausible, if not likely, that Burke's high regard for the landed interest in general prompted him to approve of the corn bounty.

---

[32] Moderate import duties already existed. See N. B. Harte, "The British Linen Trade with the United States in the Eighteenth and Nineteenth Centuries," *Textile Society of America Symposium Proceedings* (1990): 16.

[33] N. B. Harte, "The Rise of Protection and the English Linen Trade, 1690–1790," in *Textile History and Economic History: Essays in Honour of Miss Julia de Lacy Mann*, eds. N. B. Harte and K. G. Ponting (Manchester: Manchester University Press, 1973), 99.

[34] See Harte, "British Linen Trade with the United States in the Eighteenth and Nineteenth Centuries," 16. See also Harte, "Rise of Protection and the English Linen Trade."

[35] "Debates of the House of Commons," 1770, Egerton MS 222, fo. 60, British Library.

[36] Smith, *Wealth of Nations*, vol. II, 644.

[37] "Debates of the House of Commons," 1770, Egerton MS 222, fo. 60, British Library.

[38] "Debates of the House of Commons," 1770, Egerton MS 222, fo. 63, British Library.

[39] Lock, *Edmund Burke*, vol. I, 293.

Burke's reasoning in favor of the export bounty reflected arguments that were commonly voiced from the 1750s through the 1770s, when a flood of pamphlets were issued in defense of the bounty in the midst of a burgeoning number of attacks from opponents on its merit. Arthur Young, one of the most vocal champions of the export bounty, also rationalized the policy by contending that it lowered grain prices, invigorated agricultural productivity, and served as the key to general commercial prosperity, among various salutary effects it fostered.[40]

In the *Wealth of Nations*, however, Adam Smith denounced the export bounty for thwarting, rather than encouraging, opulence. He argued further that grain prices in France also fell during the same period in which English corn prices declined, yet French exports had faced a general prohibition. (Smith attributed the fall in prices to the rise in the real value of silver, a claim that has proven to be historically inaccurate,[41] and to the stable political and legal foundations of Britain as a result of the Glorious Revolution.) Smith held that the bounty imposed two different taxes on the public, one that arose from the costs needed to finance it, and the second that reflected "the advanced price of the commodity in the home-market," which the people, as consumers of corn, would need to pay.[42]

Burke does not seriously confront these objections in his remarks on the bounty. Interestingly enough, historical evidence suggests that he may have discussed Pownall's law with Smith, and may have attempted to convince him that it was a better option than any alternative at the time seeking to promote the grain trade, as will be discussed in Chapter 4. Smith did remark in the *Wealth of Nations* that the law was perhaps the best that could be expected in accordance with the "temper of the times."[43]

Donald Grove Barnes concludes that the export bounty did not occasion wholly positive or wholly negative effects. Moreover, he explains, "The Corn Law of 1773 has been held up as a landmark by both friends and opponents of protection for agriculture."[44] Barnes further points out that both Young and Smith (and, by implication, Burke) were guilty of inconsistencies and post hoc rationalizations in their arguments.[45] In Burke's favor, even if he showed a lapse of consistency in championing the corn bounty and opposing the linen bounty, we can say, at the very least, that his assessment of the merit of the former was informed by the test of experience – history, he argued, showed the agriculture improved when the policy was implemented – rather than by the dictates of

[40] See Barnes, *History of English Corn Laws*, 27–29.
[41] See Barnes, *History of English Corn Laws*, 28.   [42] Smith, *Wealth of Nations*, vol. I, 508.
[43] Smith, *Wealth of Nations*, vol. I, 543. See "Burke and Adam Smith," Chapter 4.
[44] Barnes, *History of English Corn Laws*, 43.
[45] To make the intellectual idiosyncrasies of this debate even more intriguing, Thomas Pownall attributed Smith's reasoning in opposition to the export bounty to Jacques Necker – the French finance minister whom Burke extolled for his efforts in strengthening the foundation of French public finance. See Smith, *Wealth of Nations*, vol. I, 507n8.

theory, a manner of reasoning harmonious with his political thought. Nevertheless, Burke's positions on bounties leave unresolved questions that he did not fully answer in his reflections on the grain trade.

Burke, however, supplied additional reasons in his draft notes for his reticence toward Pownall's 1773 act that yield more clues into his economic thought. First, he conveyed that agricultural bounties should be settled on a stable regulatory basis in order to reduce sudden unpredictability in the market, so that the farmer "may correctly know" what the "encouragement of his Market is." He thus would face "as little as an uncertainty as possible on the prospects when which he is to till his Lands." This was one of the "[p]rinciples in which we all agree." The other was that "the farmer should be encouraged by a Bounty." Therefore, the "End of our Deliberation ought to be, as much as possible to establish these two principles" on "the steadiest of least variable foundations."[46] Merge these comments with Burke's remarks in *Thoughts and Details*: because farming was fraught with risk, it was an imperative for government to form orderly and consistent laws in support of agricultural activity. Regulations should be stable, as well as beneficial. Indeed, sometimes the benefit of a regulation stemmed from its very stability.

In addition, in his parliamentary speech, Burke questioned why Pownall's law enacted permanent measures to address what was a temporary evil of dearth, and subsequently linked this reasoning with his resistance to discontinuing the bounty.[47] After defending the export bounty, Burke actually transitioned into submitting an argument in opposition to government intervention: the cure for temporary distress was hard work, not state regulation. "[I]f they would be relieved, they must relieve themselves by an increase of industry," he declared. "There is no other possible remedy."[48]

The other alternatives, charity and government assistance, would "prove ineffectual." Burke then uttered some of his most intriguing comments about the poor in his entire life:

If the people of England should take it in their head to idle away one day extraordinary, no human contrivance could indemnify them. For what, I beseech you, are charity and alms and parish rates, the only succedaneum, but part of their own property, of the public stock? Let me tell you, it is not we that are charitable to them, but they to us. We hoard up a portion of what is produced by their labour, and, when we give it back, we give back but their own. Let us not, however, open our hands precipitately or indiscreetly, and endeavour to persuade them that we can give a relief, which is actually out of our power. Let us rather inculcate this maxim, that they must work out their salvation with their own hand. When the crops fail in this kingdom, what foreign country can give it aid?[49]

In times of temporary want, the people must combat their distress through increased diligence and industry. Other proposed remedies could not replace

<hr />

[46] WWM/BkP/18/3. [47] *Cobbett's Parliamentary History of England*, vol. XVII, 480.
[48] *Cobbett's Parliamentary History of England*, vol. XVII, 481.
[49] *Cobbett's Parliamentary History of England*, vol. XVII, 481.

this ethic of fortitude as an antidote to misfortune and a spring for prosperity. Burke is calling attention to the importance of commercial virtue in conquering the wicked effects of scarcity.

The second argument in Burke's comments is even more fascinating. He is contending that the distribution of charity and parliamentary aid would simply return the fruits wrought by the people to themselves. The source of public stock was the labor carried out by the commoners in private.[50] Burke's intimation is that the propertied ruling classes held the duty to ensure that the lower orders profited in some way from their individual exertions – which, in this instance, meant that lawmakers should encourage habits of private industry, rather than give the false hope that state welfare could alleviate private deprivation.

3.3 ENCLOSURE

The Corn Laws were not the only significant feature of England's internal economy at the time of Burke's swift emergence as a philosopher-statesman in the 1760s and 1770s. The enclosure movement, starting from 1765 – one year before Burke entered Parliament – to 1815, also marked a defining characteristic of the nation's agricultural milieu. Enclosure, a practice spanning back to the dissolution of the manor in the fourteenth century, was the method by which a farmer would surround a small parcel of land with fences and other physical barriers in order to discourage the movement of men or animals onto the property. The farmer would then obtain a title to the property. "[I]t was a sign of exclusive ownership of the part enclosed as opposed to community ownership," Donald Grove Barnes writes.[51] The traditional system of common arable land allowed farmers to till on open fields accessible to anyone, but it tended to be a wasteful and disjointed process.

Burke offered scattered thoughts on enclosure throughout his life, but he generally viewed it favorably as a movement that promoted the efficient production of crops. Some of Burke's most extended comments on the process were presented in one of his letters to the *Public Advertiser* that he drafted during the *Nullum Tempus* affair,[52] in which he addressed ministers' complaints that the claim of prescription would inhibit their ability to improve forest lands. In the letter, Burke affirms that enclosure had already occasioned the amelioration of land. "Many Tracts of Land have been enclosed and improved Many Houses erected by the rich, many Cottages built by the poor, many rights of Common of various kinds exercised from very remote times," he states.[53] Notice Burke's

---

[50] See also Burke's manuscript notes WWM/BkP/18/13: "from what fund must this Charity come. Why from the Labour and only from the Labour of the poor themselves."

[51] Barnes, *History of English Corn Laws*, 100.

[52] The letter went unpublished. For background on the affair and Burke's commentary on it, see Langford, *Writings and Speeches*, II, 75-86.

[53] Langford, *Writings and Speeches*, II, 84.

observation that the process advantaged *different* social orders: enclosure was a vehicle for the construction and improvement of housing that benefited both the rich and the poor.

Burke acknowledges that the general enclosure of waste lands would produce a "great and solid Benefit" to England,[54] regardless of whether the lands were possessed by the Crown or the people. He insists, however, that the process be transparent, systematic, and impartial. Enclosure must be "carried on openly in the face of day, with a quiet and deliberate procedure, not in a manner that is clandestine surreptitious and precipitate."[55] It "must be pursued with due Notice to and full consent of all the Parties; carried into execution by impartial reputable and intelligent commissioners, and not the lowest Slaves and Tools of single Interest only."[56]

Therefore, Burke states, "Under such qualifications I do not know a more diffusive Benefit that could be conferred on the publick than the reclaiming of the great Wastes and Forests of this Kingdom."[57] Yet he retained apprehensions that the Crown would abuse the process to disturb the settled possessions of the poor.[58] On the subject of enclosure in the letter, then, Burke integrates a sense of approval with a whisper of hesitation: he identified the consolidation of land with the improvement of residences for the affluent and the indigent, but he also thought that royal prerogative could be exercised under the guise of enclosure to threaten the prescriptive property holdings of the latter.

Burke conveyed an even greater fondness for enclosure in privately written remarks that were interspersed with his draft notes for his speech on the Corn Laws. "I am on principle strongly a friend to enclosure – and particularly to the enclosure of Wastes and Commons of Pastures," he asserts in the notes.[59] Let us not overlook his summoning of the phrase "on principle"; the suggestion in this comment is that, similar to his reflections on enclosure during the *Nullum Tempus* affair, Burke is emitting an awareness that the process could be prone to misapplication and abuse.

Burke continues:

When so great, (though gradual) a Change was making in the whole oeconomy of this Country, I could have wished the opportunity had been taken even to introduce not only correctives but *improvements* which might be of infinite advantage and might have tended further to recommend the excellency of this principle.[60]

Enclosure was a potentially bountiful source for the advancement of England's agricultural economy. A greater emphasis on improvement would have drawn out its fullest potentialities for public advantage.

---

[54] Langford, *Writings and Speeches*, II, 84.   [55] Langford, *Writings and Speeches*, II, 84.
[56] Langford, *Writings and Speeches*, II, 84.   [57] Langford, *Writings and Speeches*, II, 85.
[58] See Burke's thoughts on this matter during the *Nullum Tempus* affair in Langford, *Writings and Speeches*, II, 84–85.
[59] WWM/BkP/18/4.   [60] WWM/BkP/18/4.

Burke then appears to have itemized, and edited, a number of criteria to govern this principle of enclosure:

~~Melioration~~
Consent of the Proprietor
Indemnification
Melioration of the Common Interests
Consent will be heard in all those things.[61]

We should not disregard the importance of the first word. By writing "Melioration" before crossing it out, and then listing "Consent of the Proprietor" below that, Burke's notes suggest that the most important criterion to guide the process, in his judgment, was not the likelihood of bettering the property, but the assent of the party whose land would be consolidated into a larger farm. Once again, Burke is hinting at the possibility that enclosure could be abused while still preserving his support for it on principle.

Even more, Burke's reference to the "Consent of the Proprietor" illuminates the more fundamental moral dilemma: was enclosure responsible for depriving peasants of their previous rights to use common lands? Put another way, because Parliament, which was populated by the landed aristocracy, passed enclosure bills, was Burke's social class at fault for limiting the freedoms of the lower orders? Burke does not offer answers to these questions in his scattered commentary on the movement.

In *Third Letter on a Regicide Peace*, which he began drafting less than a year before he would pass away, Burke maintained that the rise of enclosure was a sign of agricultural progress and public opulence. He framed this point in the context of his argument that Britain's involvement in the French Revolutionary Wars did not diminish the nation's economic strength. "To what ultimate extent, it may be wise or practicable, to push inclosures of common and waste lands, may be a question of doubt, in some points of view," Burke writes. "[B]ut no person thinks them already carried to excess." Furthermore, "[T]he relative magnitude of the sums, laid out upon them, gives us a standard of estimating the comparative situation of the landed interest."[62] Enclosure may have limits, Burke intimates, but it still remained within those confines in the mid-1790s. And measuring its diffusion throughout England was a worthwhile endeavor because the process was a gauge of the prosperity of landed proprietors.

Burke proceeds to argue that the growth of enclosure did not appear to be stymied by Britain's military conflict with France. "The greatest number of inclosing bills, passed in any one year of the last peace, does not equal the smallest annual number in the war; and those of the last year exceed, by more than one half, the highest year of peace," he contends.[63] Burke observes further

---

[61] WWM/BkP/18/4.   [62] Langford, *Writings and Speeches*, IX, 372.
[63] Langford, *Writings and Speeches*, IX, 372.

TABLE 3.1 *English enclosure bills, 1789–1796*

Inclosure bills			
4 Yrs. of Peace.		**4 Yrs. of War.**	
1789	＿＿ ＿＿ 33	1793	＿＿ ＿＿ 60
1790	＿＿ ＿＿ 25	1794	＿＿ ＿＿ 73
1791	＿＿ ＿＿ 40	1795	＿＿ ＿＿ 77
1792	＿＿ ＿＿ 40	1796	＿＿ ＿＿ 72
	138		282

Source: Report of the Lords Committee of Secrecy (1797), Appendix 44

that the number of enclosure bills during the four years of war up to that point (1793–1796) "more than doubled" the four years of peace (1789–1792) preceding the period.[64] Using information from a report from a Committee on Waste Lands, Burke includes a table to brace his argument with empirical support (Table 3.1).[65]

Activating his instinct for data, Burke underlines his argument: enclosure was a token of growing industry and affluence. The number of enclosure bills continued to ascend during military hostilities. Therefore, war did not necessarily thwart the expansion of enclosure.[66]

Other references to enclosure in Burke's writings and speeches are sparse. In an essay for the *Reformer*, Burke offered a vignette about a "Gentleman of Fortune" who oversaw the amelioration of his estate and treated his tenants warmly.[67] The gentleman had gained possession of an estate that was uncultivated. "[N]othing could be in a worse Condition than his Estate," Burke writes.[68] There was "not a Bush, not a tolerable Enclosure, much less Habitation, to be seen."[69] As we can see by these comments, he associated the absence of enclosure with underdeveloped land early in his adult life. Burke illustrated a similar connection in *Tracts relating to Popery Laws* (1765), when he remarked that a short land tenure was a hindrance to "raise enclosures" in order to ameliorate the estates of Irish Catholic families.[70] In *Address and Petition* (1764), Burke also observed that the penal codes discouraged the

---

[64] Langford, *Writings and Speeches*, IX, 372–373.

[65] See Langford, *Writings and Speeches*, IX, 372.

[66] Of course, Burke does not entertain the counterfactual: would not enclosure have achieved even greater progress if Britain had not become involved in the French Revolutionary Wars? And he does not mention that the greatest proportional increase in enclosure bills – 60 percent – in the periods he listed occurred between 1790 and 1791, not between 1793 and 1796.

[67] See "Labor, the Laboring Poor, and the Rich as Trustees."

[68] Langford, *Writings and Speeches*, I, 99.   [69] Langford, *Writings and Speeches*, I, 99.

[70] Langford, *Writings and Speeches*, IX, 476.

"melioration of land" by "inclosure," one of a variety of practices he thought was "very necessary" for the cultivation of property in Ireland.[71]

In *Speech on Economical Reform*, in which Burke outlined his plan to reform the British constitution, he recommended that forest land under the general dominion of the Crown, but utilized as common land in practice, be "valued on an inclosure" for public advantage.[72] In a private letter late in his life, he referenced an "enclosure of a wretched farmyard" in a tongue-in-cheek passage.[73] Even more intriguingly, in his history of Buckingham, George Lipscomb made reference to the "beautiful enclosures" of Burke's estate, suggesting Burke made use of the practice.[74] In the end, we may take Burke's position on enclosure to be one of cautious yet steady support, aware of the possibility of abuse but alert to its benefits, as long as the process was governed by the hands of order and transparency. This view reflected an attraction to the spirit of agricultural improvement that characterized his economic thought – and, it is safe to say, that motivated his own innovative farming activities.

3.4   LABOR, THE LABORING POOR, AND THE RICH AS TRUSTEES

Allow us to return to *Thoughts and Details*. All of Burke's aforementioned beliefs about the fluidity of supply and demand laws and the cultivation of land in agricultural economies hold profound implications for his nuanced discussion of "labor" in the economic tract. In addition to treating labor as a commodity, and thus an article of trade, Burke attempts to show in the memorial that "labor" was a devious word that represented vastly different types of employment on the farm. "[T]his very broad generic term, *labour*, admits, at least, of two or three specific descriptions," he writes.[75] The term required "nicer distinctions and sub-divisions."[76] In his subsequent description of these categories, Burke submits that proposals to increase the wages of laborers did not take into account the intricate complexities of labor. "Encrease the rate of wages to the labourer, say the regulators – as if labour was but one thing and of one value," he remarks, revealing his irritation with the tendency to reduce the concept of labor to deadening simplicities.[77]

Burke attempts to bring out the many dimensions of the concept in *Thoughts and Details* by dividing it into three classifications. The first was husbandry that could be completed by able-bodied men, aged from twenty-one to fifty years old.[78] What one man sacrificed in energy, Burke explains, he could make up for it

---

[71] Langford, *Writings and Speeches*, IX, 430.   [72] Langford, *Writings and Speeches*, III, 506.
[73] Burke to Lord Auckland, 30 October 1795, in *Correspondence of Edmund Burke*, vol. VIII, 334.
[74] Lipscomb, *History and Antiquities*, 191. On a different note, remember that Burke thought that the reaction against the protestors who started the Whiteboy Disturbances – protestors whose discontent was stirred by the enclosure of common land – was overwrought.
[75] Langford, *Writings and Speeches*, IX, 127.   [76] Langford, *Writings and Speeches*, IX, 127.
[77] Langford, *Writings and Speeches*, IX, 127.
[78] See Langford, *Writings and Speeches*, IX, 127–128 for Burke's description of this first category.

with his experience. Burke acknowledges that, even within this category, there existed among men great diversity of work ethic, strength, and skill. Yet he concludes that the exertions of groups of five workmen would generally correspond with those of other such groups, since one laborer would be competent, one would be incompetent, and three would be middling on average. Therefore, Burke remarks, "[A]n error with regard to the equalization of their wages by those who employ five, as farmers do at the very least, cannot be considerable."[79] This comment signals an implicit concession that wage regulations for this platoon of physically capable men might not produce negative effects, but only if every type of laborer fell into one of these three categories of competency (or incompetency).

Burke's second category includes the husbandry of those who were unable to complete the same amount of labor as the able-bodied men working full-time. Like the first classification, Burke admits that the second group consisted of a medley of people. His two subdivisions under this head included men in physical decline (over the age of fifty), and women, who did not necessarily work full-time and who carried other responsibilities such as "gestation, nursing, and domestic management."[80] Burke's third category is the labor of children. Children do grow "from less to greater utility," he explains, "but with a still greater disproportion of nutriment to labour than is found in the second of these sub-divisions."[81]

We must pause and note that Burke's observations about child labor were not new in *Thoughts and Details*. In 1752, more than forty years prior to his drafting of the tract, he praised the contributions of young girls in spinning wool. When staying at a summer house at Turlaine near a location with a strong cloth industry, Burke noticed that the area was "a place of very great trade in making fine cloths, in which they employ a vast number of hands."[82] These hands included those of female children: "[L]ittle girls of six or seven years old at the wheel" could earn "three shillings and sixpence a week each, which is more than their keeping can amount to."[83] Indeed, the populous countryside was "the only one I ever saw where children are really an advantage to their parents."[84] This experience attests to Burke's awareness that the patchwork of distinctions among groups of laborers included varying abilities of dexterity, experience, work ethic, age, sex, and physical strength.

[79] Langford, *Writings and Speeches*, IX, 128.   [80] Langford, *Writings and Speeches*, IX, 128.

[81] Langford, *Writings and Speeches*, IX, 128.

[82] Edmund Burke to Richard Shackleton, 28 September 1752, in Charles William, Earl Fitzwilliam and Sir Richard Bourke, eds., *Correspondence of the Right Honourable Edmund Burke: Between the Year 1744, and the Period of His Decease, in 1797*, vol. I (London: Francis & John Rivington, 1844), 28–29.

[83] Edmund Burke to Richard Shackleton, 28 September 1752, in William and Bourke, *Correspondence of the Right Honourable Edmund Burke*, vol. I, 30.

[84] Burke to Richard Shackleton, 28 September 1752, in William and Bourke, *Correspondence of the Right Honourable Edmund Burke*, vol. I, 30.

The implications of Burke's classificatory system in *Thoughts and Details*, therefore, surpass questions about the merits of state-mandated wage hikes or the definition of "labor." For Burke, a uniform wage hike was cold and inflexible, failing to account for the multiplicity of human differences responsible for suffusing the term "labor" with a layered richness. His shrewd attention to the deeper dimensions of this seemingly simple economic concept parallels his discussion of the variety of factors that influenced the rise in food costs in the 1790s. In both cases, Burke's underlying purpose was to expose the limits of theoretic rationalism in describing the complicated operation of market economies, as will be discussed in greater detail in Chapter 4.

Burke's additional aim in highlighting different subdivisions of laborers was to challenge the public tendency in the late eighteenth century to indiscriminately expand the definition of the "labouring poor" beyond the conceptual integrity of its traditional understanding. This phrase, its origins dating back to Tudor England,[85] had crept into political discourse in England concerning the merit of providing government relief for distressed workers (and, in fact, had been employed frequently by Adam Smith in the *Wealth of Nations*[86]). *St. James's Chronicle*, for instance, published an article in early October 1795 calling for the regulation of the flour and wheat industries in order to alleviate the condition of the "labouring poor."[87]

Parliamentary debates in 1796 also employed the phrase. When discussing an earlier form of his minimum wage law in February of that year, Samuel Whitbread had "appealed to the sense of the House, whether the situation of the *labouring poor* in this country was such as any feeling or liberal mind would wish?" (italics added).[88] William Pitt, who opposed the bill, was described as saying, "The present situation of the *labouring poor* in this country, was certainly not such as could be wished, upon any principle, either of humanity, or policy"[89] (italics added). That Pitt used the phrase further explains why Burke was so intent in *Thoughts and Details* on clarifying its meaning, since Pitt had requested a copy of Burke's original memorandum to Dundas.

Burke had detected conceptual imprecision in this language, noticing that poor laborers were being lumped together with the nonworking poor by both supporters and opponents of the state regulation of wages in husbandry. In *Third Letter on a Regicide Peace*, he observed that the "poor" had previously been characterized as the "sick and infirm; for orphan infancy; for languishing

---

[85] See E. Royston Pike, ed., *Human Documents of Adam Smith's Time*, vol. 5 (London and New York: Routledge, 2010), 154.

[86] See, for example, Smith, *Wealth of Nations*, vol. I, "Of the Wages of Labour," 82–104. Smith does not use the word as a crutch to support wealth redistribution, however, as Burke believed rabble-rousers were doing in the 1790s.

[87] Bourke, *Empire & Revolution*, 891.

[88] *Cobbett's Parliamentary History of England*, vol. XXXII, 703.

[89] *Cobbett's Parliamentary History of England*, vol. XXXII, 705.

and decrepid age."[90] The problem from Burke's perspective was that the press and legislators were collapsing the distinction between commoners who possessed the capacity to work with the sick, the young, and the old, whose physical constitution limited their ability to perform manual labor.

Yet the precision of the phrase bore more than conceptual implications. In light of the French revolutionaries' impulse to regulate France's economy in the 1790s, Burke was concerned while drafting *Thoughts and Details* that rhetorical flourishes in Britain to assist the "laboring poor" would be brandished to justify a national policy of wealth distribution, thereby infecting England's commercial system with radical egalitarian influences. The consequence was that politicians were pitting the rich against the poor, inflaming the dark passions of Jacobin class warfare that Burke had so readily denounced in the *Reflections*.

With this historical backdrop in mind, one of Burke's tasks in *Thoughts and Details* was to define "laboring poor" with exactness and clarity. He writes in the tract, "The labouring people are only poor, because they are numerous."[91] Burke continues: "Numbers in their nature imply poverty. In a fair distribution among a vast multitude, none can have much."[92] The "poor" for Burke did not denote a specific amount of wealth, or a specific level of living standards. The phrase, rather, suggested a *relative* condition, not a fixed numerical figure, in a social environment constituting a mixed mass of people. For "when we speak of Poverty we must speak of something comparative," Burke observed earlier in the context of Anglo-Irish relations.[93] Burke's insinuation is that the "poor" could still enjoy a reasonable standard of living; they might just not reach the same altitude of prosperity as more affluent families.

Burke marks his aversion to sentimentalizing the laboring poor by scorning such corruption of political vocabulary. "Nothing can be so base and so wicked as the political canting language, 'The Labouring *Poor*,'" he writes in *Thoughts and Details*. "Let compassion be shewn in action, the more the better, according to every man's ability, but let there be no lamentation of their condition."[94] Pity will provide "no relief to their miserable circumstances," and in fact will insult their "miserable understandings"[95] (ostensibly understandings of their impoverished condition). Burke is arguing that public effusions of sentiment for the needy would not tangibly improve their low circumstances. In these comments, however, he does distinguish between excessive sentimentality and genuine compassion; the latter, Burke suggests, was manifested in acts of charity.

The intellectual roots of Burke's antipathy to the phrase "labouring poor" lie in his early work on taste, the *Philosophical Enquiry*. One of Burke's chief arguments in the writing is that words – specifically, compound abstract words

[90] Langford, *Writings and Speeches*, IX, 355. [91] Langford, *Writings and Speeches*, IX, 121.
[92] Langford, *Writings and Speeches*, IX, 121. [93] MSS. at Sheffield, Bk. 8–173.
[94] Langford, *Writings and Speeches*, IX, 121. [95] Langford, *Writings and Speeches*, IX, 121.

like virtue and honor – do not necessarily reflect real essences, for they could connote an emotion detached from the circumstances that provoked their usage in the first place.[96] "The sounds [of words] being often used without reference to any particular occasion, and carrying still their first impressions, they at last utterly lose their connection with the particular occasions that gave rise to them; yet the sound without any annexed notion continues to operate as before," Burke writes.[97] In addition, "[T]here are words, and certain dispositions of words, which being peculiarly devoted to passionate subjects, and always used by those who are under the influence of any passion; they touch and move us more than those which far more clearly and distinctly express the subject matter."[98] Words charged with passion could affect the imagination of men – but they could also offend the authenticity of truth.

Eloquence could thus distort, rather than sharpen, man's comprehension of reality. "A very great part of the mischiefs that vex the world, arises from words," Burke wrote to Richard Burke in 1792 in reference to the word Protestant in the phrase "Protestant Ascendancy." "People soon forget the meaning, but the impression and the passion remain."[99] These insights capture Burke's suspicion of the term "labouring poor": it evoked the image of an impoverished laborer stretched to the edge of starvation, condemned to hard toil without receiving fair recompense for his work. As Burke argues in *Thoughts and Details*, however, this class was experiencing a rise in living standards at the same time public agitators were calling for government to relieve it of hardship.

In other words, the innocence of an original word, harmonious to the ears and soothing to the heart, could transform into a fixed distortion of reality. Burke's analysis of the phrase "Protestant Ascendancy" reflected this danger. "[T]he poor word ascendancy, so soft and melodious in its sound, so lenitive and emollient in its first usage," Burke observed in his letter to Richard Burke, "is now employed to cover to the world, the most rigid and perhaps not the most wise of all plans of policy."[100] Notice this observation's implications for Burke's grasp of rationality in relation to his political economy: the initial meaning of a word – in this case, "ascendancy" – was enlarged to explain and vindicate the Protestant Ascendancy's misrule over Irish Catholics. Similarly, for Burke, public agitators widened the definition of "labouring poor," conflating poor people capable of labor with poor people incapable of labor, as a rhetorical device to justify schemes of wealth redistribution.

Accordingly, Burke's nuanced portrayal of "labor" and "laboring poor" illustrates his attempt to expose the limits of economic rationalism in

---

[96] See Dixon Wecter, "Burke's Theory concerning Words, Images, and Emotion," *PMLA* 55 (1940): 167–181.
[97] Langford, *Writings and Speeches*, I, 310.   [98] Langford, *Writings and Speeches*, I, 319.
[99] Burke to Richard Burke, *post* 19 February 1792, in Langford, *Writings and Speeches*, IX, 647.
[100] Langford, *Writings and Speeches*, IX, 644.

understanding the mysterious inner workings of private market activity. Not only did uniform wage regulations overlook the complicated nature of various forms of employment, but the temptations of Jacobinism in England compounded such ignorance by fueling a levelling spirit: men progressively exploited the phrases to evoke pity in order to serve broader political aspirations of forced egalitarianism. The simplification of the complex, combined with the politicization of the private, defined Jacobin ideology and threatened the very character of English social and economic order.

The Rich as Trustees for the Poor

That Burke attacked the phrase "labouring poor" did not mean he repudiated the principle of charity. On the contrary, throughout his political and private life he maintained that the rich retained the sacred duty to help the needy. This moral obligation was finely woven into Burke's economic thought, for he did not separate commercial matters from ethical considerations in his conception of political economy. The relationship between the well-off and the poor, he believed, was steered by a transactional spirit on a surface level, but secured by the seal of trust connecting the souls of men. The rich were "trustees" for "those who labour," Burke writes in *Thoughts and Details*.[101] Yet attempts to confiscate wealth from the rich to ease the destitute condition of the poor would only hurt the latter, since the rich were the ones who provided wages and nutriment to the common laborers in the first place. Burke's reasoning in this context is bathed in the presence of an Invisible Hand-type force; he claims that the rich, "[w]hether they mean it or not ... do, in effect, execute their trust – some with more, some with less fidelity and judgment."[102] Regardless of whether the affluent intend to help the poor in particular instances, the result of their actions as employers bestowed positive benefits upon wage laborers.

According to Isaac Kramnick, however, Burke's ardent defense of supply and demand laws appeared to neglect the concerns of the indigent. Burke thought that it was "unjust" to "aid the poor," Kramnick argues.[103] But Burke contradicts this portrayal in *Thoughts and Details* when he declares that Christians held the moral responsibility to provide sufficient nutriment to the impoverished when market principles failed. "Without all doubt, charity to the poor is a direct and obligatory duty upon all Christians," he avows.[104] Charity should be left in private hands, at the giver's discretion, which would not only encourage the rich to assist the needy but also create a heightened sense of fulfillment on the part of the benefactor.[105] Burke's trustee conception of the rich further undermines Kramnick's claim.

---

[101] Langford, *Writings and Speeches*, IX, 121.   [102] Langford, *Writings and Speeches*, IX, 121.
[103] Kramnick, *Rage of Edmund Burke*, 160.   [104] Langford, *Writings and Speeches*, IX, 129.
[105] Langford, *Writings and Speeches*, IX, 129. "[T]he manner, mode, time, choice of objects, and proportion, are left to private discretion; and perhaps, for that very reason it is performed with

Nevertheless, Burke does unintentionally release a coldness of sentiment in his discussion of the poor in *Thoughts and Details*. He goes so far as to insist it would be folly to think that the rich could supply them with "those necessaries which it has pleased the Divine Providence for a while to with-hold from them."[106] Burke is suggesting that a scarcity of goods stemmed from a supernatural force that intentionally deprived the lower classes of provisions, at least temporarily.

How can we sort out such ambiguities in Burke's thought on the relationship between the rich and the poor? His reflections can be clarified by examining his earliest writings as a young thinker, when he wrote for and edited the *Reformer*, the weekly periodical he helped found before he graduated from Trinity College. In *Reformer No. 7*,[107] an essay on Irish poverty marked by Swiftian undertones, Burke argues that affluent landowners possessed the moral duty to be charitable toward the less fortunate. He does so by introducing the parable of a "Gentleman of Fortune,"[108] whose actions, in Burke's telling, helped relieve the condition of his tenants and promote public prosperity.

Originally the gentleman inherited an estate that included a large number of tenants who paid a high rent. The estate itself was not cultivated. According to Burke, the Gentleman of Fortune responded to this feeble state of affairs by aiding and rewarding the hardworking poor:

> He found his Leases out, but he did not study, with the Greediness of a young Heir, how to raise the Price nor Value of his Lands, nor turn out all his poor Tenants to make room for two or three rich. He retained all those to whose honest Industry he had been Witness, and lowered his Rents very considerably; he bound them to plant certain Quantities of Trees, and make other Improvements.[109]

Consequently, the condition of the estate improved, rent was paid, and tenants acquired wealth. Throughout this process the Gentleman of Fortune did not spend his energies organizing wasteful horse races and assemblies, which encouraged "Drinking and Idleness."[110] Rather, he promoted a new "*Manufacture*" that "employed the whole Town, and in Time made it opulent."[111]

---

the greater satisfaction, because the discharge of it has more the appearance of freedom; recommending us besides very specially to the divine favour, as the exercise of a virtue most suitable to a being sensible of it's own infirmity."

[106] Langford, *Writings and Speeches*, IX, 137.

[107] Burke was one of a few collaborators of the periodical. F. P. Lock makes the convincing case that *Reformer No. 7* is Burke's work. See Lock, *Edmund Burke*, vol. I, 56–59.

[108] The anonymous writing *A View of the Grievances of Ireland by a True Patriot* (Dublin: George Faulkner, 1745) recounts a story resembling Burke's narrative.

[109] Langford, *Writings and Speeches*, I, 99–100.   [110] Langford, *Writings and Speeches*, I, 100.

[111] Langford, *Writings and Speeches*, I, 100. Burke makes this point about the modesty of the rich elsewhere. In a poem on Ballitore School, which Burke attended as a youth, he remarked favorably upon the "just use of Wealth without the show" of Abraham Shackleton, an

Burke is highlighting the paternalistic touch of the Gentleman of Fortune. The gentleman held, and met, the ethical responsibility to treat his poorer tenants well. He was charitable, not avaricious. He reduced rents to a sum affordable to the estate's existing tenants, rather than discard them and bring in more affluent tenants who could pay higher rates. The property owner also displayed an itch of ingenuity and economy: he ameliorated the land, encouraged honest industry, and stimulated new productive capacities, all the while checking the temptation to finance extravagant projects. Observe in this portrayal that Burke does not erect a stark division between economic advancement and ethics. The gentleman was concerned with material improvement as well as ancient virtue.

In Burke's story, the Gentleman of Fortune did not regret shunning the pursuit of fancy objects or services. "I keep no *French* Cook" the gentleman says proudly.[112] Instead he served his fellow human beings and the nation at large: "I am satisfied I am making Numbers happy, without Expence to myself, doing my Country Service without Ostentation, and leaving my Son a better Estate without oppressing any one."[113] Guided by an ethic of modesty and a fidelity to helping others, the Gentleman of Fortune advanced the public welfare, and warmed his own soul in the process.

Burke is famous for his celebrated "trustee" theory of representation in his political thought, which declared that an elected representative should make informed and independent judgments on legislative matters even if they defied the public will of his constituents.[114] As shown by his reference to the rich as a "trustee" of the needy in *Thoughts and Details*, and by his portrait of the Gentleman of Fortune, Burke also carried a "trustee" notion of the relationship between the rich and the poor in his economic thought: the upper classes were the faithful guardians of the lower classes and were governed by the moral imperative to aid them – by offering reasonable rents, encouraging good habits and discouraging bad behavior, and setting the example of a responsible citizen. Although Burke does paint an idealized portrait of the landed aristocrat, the relevant insight for our purposes is his belief that a tender chord of trust aligned the ethical responsibilities of the rich with the practical interests of the poor. The failure of the privileged orders to meet this commitment was a violation of trust – a trust that lied beyond the dictates of supply and demand laws.

Reformer No. 7 is also noteworthy for Burke's expression of sympathy for the mean condition of the Irish poor under the penal codes, which Burke no doubt witnessed growing up in Ireland. "Their Cloaths so ragged, that they

---

influential figure in Burke's youth and the founder of the school (Samuels, *Early Life Correspondence and Writings*, 17).
[112] Langford, *Writings and Speeches*, I, 100. [113] Langford, *Writings and Speeches*, I, 100.
[114] See Burke's "Speech at the Conclusion of the Poll," given on November 3, 1774, in Langford, *Writings and Speeches*, III, 63–70.

rather publish than conceal the Wretchedness it was meant to hide; nay, it is no uncommon Sight to see half a dozen Children run quite naked out of a Cabin," he writes in the essay.[115] Burke further highlights the ignorance of those who claimed that Irish peasants' "Sloth" was the "cause of their Misery."[116] In modern parlance, he is rebuking the idea of "blaming the victim" – in this case, the Irish – for the inferior state of Ireland's living standards and economic development.

Burke thus declares that it "is the Care of every wise Government to secure the Lives and Properties of those who live under it."[117] Moreover, "Why should it be less worth Consideration, to make those Lives comfortable, and these Properties worth preserving?"[118] Britain's oppressive imperial policy failed to protect the Irish people's possession of property and wealth. Indeed, Irish agricultural workers could use a portion of what they earned to cultivate crops and construct cabins, but they were not paid in cash,[119] which explains Burke's comment that "[m]oney is a Stranger to them."[120] He is suggesting that wider institutional factors were at play that discouraged the rise in mobility among Irish laborers.

Burke has in mind Britain's suppression of the Irish people's freedom to reap what they had sown. "[S]ure it is hard, that those who cultivate the Soil, should have so small a Part of its Fruits," he comments, most likely thinking of the oppressive nature of the penal codes.[121] Burke acknowledges that some might live in greater comfort than others, but he highlights the wide discrepancy between the rich and the poor, which offended the natural equality of man and was a "Blasphemy on Providence."[122] Government held the responsibility to establish the conditions under which men and women would be rewarded for their toil.

This section in the *Reformer* also releases a scent of Burke's moderate egalitarian proclivities – but ones that were distinct from the later impulses of Jacobinism. Burke advocates not the government redistribution of wealth to remedy Irish impoverishment but instead the idea that the Irish, rather than just royalty, should benefit from the fruits afforded by the enjoyment of property: "Our modern Systems hold, that the Riches and Power of Kings are by no means their property, but a Depositum in their Hands, for the Use of the People."[123] And while Burke is known for his defense of landed aristocrats, he is quite critical of them in this case for failing to use their estates for the public good. Narrow-minded, self-interested propertied gentlemen were "liable to the same or a greater Reproach than a Prince who abuses his Power."[124]

[115] Langford, *Writings and Speeches*, I, 97.   [116] Langford, *Writings and Speeches*, I, 98.
[117] Langford, *Writings and Speeches*, I, 96.   [118] Langford, *Writings and Speeches*, I, 96.
[119] See Langford, *Writings and Speeches*, I, 97n1.   [120] Langford, *Writings and Speeches*, I, 97.
[121] Langford, *Writings and Speeches*, I, 98.   [122] Langford, *Writings and Speeches*, I, 98.
[123] Langford, *Writings and Speeches*, I, 98.   [124] Langford, *Writings and Speeches*, I, 98.

Such insights, while not original, fortify the message of his parable about the Gentleman of Fortune: the rich harbor the sacred responsibility to help the poor. An implicit trust binds the two groups together, derived from a common human ground and from the economic reality that the luxuries of the rich were produced by the efforts of the lower classes. Hence the poor should be granted similar opportunities for gain and be treated with dignity by higher social orders.

One final statement of Burke's in *Reformer No. 7* is worthy of our attention because it blends his criticism of the pretensions of the nobility with his egalitarian leanings:

The Riches of a Nation are not to be estimated by the splendid Appearance or luxurious Lives of its Gentry; it is the uniform Plenty diffused through a People, of which the meanest as well as greatest partake, that makes them happy, and the Nation powerful.[125]

Burke, whether he realizes it or not, is questioning a key strand of contemporary wisdom holding that a country's material affluence could be evaluated accurately based on the amount of wealth possessed by the rich and powerful. Instead, as he suggests in these comments, the circulation of goods among different classes, spanning the "meanest" to the "greatest" people, was the true measure of public prosperity and happiness. The illusion of select riches may deceive observers into miscalculating the wealth of nations.

Burke's School for French Émigrés

Burke's acts of benevolence testified to his deepest beliefs about the responsibilities of the fortunate to the needy. In addition to his efforts aiding disadvantaged members of his neighborhood, Burke, almost two years after retiring from Parliament, founded a school in April 1796 for poor children of French émigrés who had been persecuted during the French Revolution.[126] He wanted the institution to become a kind of military academy. In preparing to open the school, Burke proposed that the state provide selective subsidies to fund its operating costs, and envisioned that it could be housed in an unused building rented by the British government.[127] Such thinking implies a belief that government did have some role to play in education, but he did not elaborate on the idea in his writings and speeches.

The institution sat around three miles northwest from Burke's estate and taught a maximum of sixty boys. Burke aimed to preserve the spirit of French

---

[125] Langford, *Writings and Speeches*, I, 96.
[126] See the following sources that provided much of the biographical information on Burke's school for émigrés: Prior, *Life of Edmund Burke*, 431–436; Lock, *Edmund Burke*, vol. II, 548–554; John Timbs, *Anecdote Lives of William Pitt, Earl of Chatham, and Edmund Burke* (London: Richard Bentley & Son, 1880), 314–316.
[127] "Burke's Proposal for a School at Penn," in *Correspondence of Edmund Burke*, vol. VIII, 396–397.

heritage by granting patronage and administrative authority to French émigré nobles and bishops, demonstrating his inclination to respect differences of lifestyle and culture. He visited the school frequently and exerted a fatherly presence over the schoolchildren. "His smiles might be said to have gladdened the hearts of the exiles" reported a school treasurer who had worked at the school after Burke passed away.[128]

Burke bequeathed in his will that the institution would be led by his faithful group of friends who were trustees at the school. Many students educated there achieved successful careers back in France during the Bourbon Restoration, according to the treasurer.[129] The institution was taken over by the French government that year, and remained open until 1820. In the end, the emigrant school was Burke's signature act of philanthropic benevolence. It also fulfilled his yearning for an active lifestyle and shifted his mind away from the intermittent despondency that plagued his final years. In many ways, the institution embodied Burke's self-recognition as a Gentleman of Fortune (albeit one who came from a modest background) who possessed the moral duty to aid those stranded at the margins.

Poor Removals Bill

As a legislator, Burke acted on behalf of the poor in a less direct, yet still significant, way. In 1774, a proposed parliamentary measure called the Poor Removals Bill would have circumscribed the ability of magistrates to return indigent immigrants back to their parish of origin, a power vested in them under the 1662 Settlement Act.[130] In *Speech on Poor Removals Bill*, Burke approved of the new legislation by arguing that the Act's restrictions on the autonomy of movement marked the depths of human bondage. "[I]f you will not let me live where I please, which necessarily implies in it, where I can best maintain and support myself, I am a slave" he declared in describing the perspective of the poor immigrant under the old law.[131] For Burke, state officials should not carry the authority to dictate where people should live: "[T]he power of tying down a man to reside in any place, or expelling him from any other, ought not to reside in Justices [of the Peace], nor any men."[132]

Instead, individuals, including paupers, should have the liberty to choose the location of their residency, which would allow them to seek additional employment opportunities. In this light, Burke detected a perverse incentive in the Settlement Act: it dissuaded the poor from traveling to other parishes to pursue new lines of work. "[Y]ou have laws that operate in a retrograde manner from the place of consumption to the place of production," Burke observed in notes for the speech. Such movement represented the direct opposite of the

---

[128] Prior, *Life of Edmund Burke*, 432.   [129] Prior, *Life of Edmund Burke*, 433.
[130] Langford, *Writings and Speeches*, II, 401–402.
[131] Langford, *Writings and Speeches*, II, 402.   [132] Langford, *Writings and Speeches*, II, 402.

natural flow of goods[133] As he wryly remarked in *Speech on Poor Removals Bill*, "Manufacture calls them to one place, the laws hurry them back to the other."[134]

This consequence was part of the "amazingly mischievous tendency"[135] of England's Poor Laws, the laws first implemented in the sixteenth century that were designed to provide relief to the needy, such as the Settlement Act. This mischievous tendency was to punish the industrious as if the pursuit of employment were a misdeed. They "suffer their best virtue to produce all the consequences of vice," he wrote in his notes for the speech.[136] Burke was drawing attention to the unanticipated effects of benevolent intentions: "[S]uch cruelty has arisen out of best national Charity in the world."[137] Be alert to the unintended consequences of legislation designed to help the poor.

Therefore, the Poor Laws contravened the iron laws of morality and right. The "arbitrary power of removal and restraint is a subversion of natural justice, a violation of the inherent rights of mankind, and not justified by the true policy of a commercial nation, but totally repugnant thereto," he contended.[138] Burke made these comments in a draft resolution that aimed to examine and reform the structure of the Poor Laws. The resolution called for a committee to report on "the most effectual means of restoring the labouring part of this kingdom to that liberty which all free and industrious subjects ought to enjoy, of exercising their industry wherever they shall find it most to their advantage."[139]

Based on Burke's engagement with the Poor Removals Bill and the Poor Laws, we can begin to peel back an additional layer to his theory of political economy: he championed not only the free flow of commerce but also the free movement of people, which, in his view, encouraged the mobility of labor – a market activity that generated advantages for manufacturers as well.[140] Discouraging the mobility of labor, however, shocked the principles of economic equity and natural justice. Burke's efforts in seeking to reform the Poor Laws occasioned a modest end. In 1795, the Settlement Act was modified to afford more protections for the poor to move and reside in different parishes, but the defects of the law still persisted.[141]

---

[133] Eg. MS. 253, p. 63.   [134] Eg. MS. 253, p. 63.

[135] Langford, *Writings and Speeches*, II, 403.   [136] Eg. MS. 253, p. 63.

[137] Eg. MS. 253, p. 63.

[138] Charles William, Earl Fitzwilliam and Sir Richard Bourke, eds., *Correspondence of the Right Honourable Edmund Burke: Between the Year 1744, and the Period of His Decease, in 1797*, vol. IV (London: Francis & John Rivington, 1844), 463.

[139] William and Bourke, *Correspondence of the Right Honourable Edmund Burke*, vol. IV, 464.

[140] This helps explain why the manufacturing interest supported the Poor Removals Bill. See Lock, *Edmund Burke*, vol. I, 359.

[141] See John J. Clarke, *Social Administration Including the Poor Laws* (London: Sir Isaac Pitman & Sons, 1922), 35; and Stuart Peterfreund, "Burke and Hemans: Colonialism and the Claims of Family," in *Global Romanticism: Origins, Orientations, and Engagements, 1760–1820*, ed. Evan Gottlieb (Lewisburg, PA: Bucknell University Press, 2015), 32. Clarke notes that Burke led efforts to change the Act, although I cannot find other sources to verify this claim.

In his speech supporting the Poor Removals Bill, Burke attempted to discredit a different argument related to population that was used to support the legislation. Lord Clare had remarked that the bill would encourage population growth, which, he claimed, had witnessed a decline.[142] Burke avowed that the population was ascending, as indicated by the increased cultivation of soil and consumption of food.[143] Moreover, emigration from England was not a cause for anxiety. "I should not be concerned if 40,000 emigrants went every day to America," Burke said, "as long as the cultivation of our soil is the effect of industry, and that industry is protected by the free constitution of this country."[144] Freedom of movement did not hinder the capacity of Englishmen to produce, as long as their liberties were secured by the sturdy edifice of constitutional government.

Burke's comments in this context illustrate his pronounced distrust of zero-sum economic thinking. "Let [emigrants] be flourishing and happy. They will not enjoy their fortune at the expence of Britain," he argued.[145] Even if people were leaving England, the prosperity of industry would encourage more births: "[T]hey will be speedily replaced, and our numbers never decline."[146] Just as foreign commercial intercourse did not deprive one nation of the fruits of trade, emigration did not necessarily condemn one nation to indigence.

Burke also anticipated lines of reasoning that would appear during the tendentious debate in the 1790s about the relationship between food prices and population growth, among various factors, in the English agricultural sector, as discussed in Chapter 2. For Burke, population growth was a positive pattern, signaling economic growth and collective prosperity. "There is nothing so much mistook as the principles of population," he remarked in his speech on the Poor Removals Bill, twenty-four years before Thomas Malthus's *An Essay on the Principle of Population* would be published.[147]

In another comment on the Poor Removals Bill, Burke revealed a further dimension to his conception of the poor. He noted that transforming the voluntary duty of benevolence into compulsory welfare drains the element of compassion from society, and in its place fuels social animosity: "[W]hen from the moment you take the people of England out of the course of occasional charity, and put them under the tutelage of Police: when you change the voluntary, free duty of Charity, into [taxation] obliged to be enforced by law: from that moment the [result] will be your business to cure."[148] Consequently, "[T]he people began to consider the poor not as an

---

[142] Langford, *Writings and Speeches*, II, 403n5.
[143] Burke appeared correct in his assessment about the growing population.
[144] Langford, *Writings and Speeches*, II, 403.   [145] Langford, *Writings and Speeches*, II, 403.
[146] Langford, *Writings and Speeches*, II, 403.   [147] Langford, *Writings and Speeches*, II, 403.
[148] Eg. MS. 253, pp. 63–64; and Langford, *Writings and Speeches*, II, 403n4.

object of compassion" but as "tax Gatherers."[149] The indigent were "lookd [sic] upon with abhorrence, and dread,"[150] which provoked further civil strife among parishes.

Burke's message is that forced assistance dissolves the tender chords of affection and sympathy that naturally motivate the fortunate to help the impoverished. This belief explains why Burke insisted in *Thoughts and Details* that "charity to the poor" was "a direct and obligatory duty upon Christians."[151] It also clarifies his opposition to the expansion of government subsidies for the poor, a stand he took dating back to his earliest days in Parliament. In November 1766, soon after Burke entered the House of Commons in January of that year, George Grenville introduced an amendment to offer welfare benefits to the needy. Burke protested the measure on personal and principled grounds.[152] In his judgment, the Gentleman of Fortune and other privileged members of civil society – not coercive state policies – exhibited real compassion when donating aid voluntarily from the warmth of their own hearts.

Burke's Trustee Theory of Representation and Political Economy

An additional ingredient of Burke's trustee theory of political economy mirrors a tenet of his trustee theory of political representation, which we shall discuss in greater detail in Chapter 5. In the latter theory, which he outlined in *Speech at the Conclusion of the Poll*, Burke raised the implicit assumption that the people might not know what was in their best interests. Therefore, it was the duty of the legislator to refine or even rebuff the wishes of his constituents, who might be misinformed about the issue at hand, in order to arrive at an independent and sober judgment in Parliament that would aim to promote the common good.

Burke applies this notion of representation to his economic thought. In *Thoughts and Details*, he remarks that even if the people in cities and towns cry out for the regulation of provisions, their instructions should not necessarily be followed, since their feelings might cloud their judgment. Their opinion "ought, in *fact*, to be the *least* attended to upon this subject" because of their "utter ignorance of the means by which they are to be fed" – the complicated nature of the cultivation and distribution of crops.[153] Burke is quite critical of urban dwellers in this regard: he assails them in the tract for claiming to possess sufficient knowledge about the complex operations of farming. He even uses a line from Horace's *Epistles* – "*Fruges consumere nati*," meaning, "born only

---

[149] Eg. MS. 253, p. 64.   [150] Eg. MS. 253, p. 64.
[151] Langford, *Writings and Speeches*, IX, 129.
[152] Burke describes Grenville's plan this way: "Grenville tried another amendment, (by way of a little, and indeed a very little bait for popularity) containing a proposal for supplying the poor out of the sinking fund" (Burke to Charles O'Hara, [*post* 11 November 1766], in *Correspondence of Edmund Burke*, vol. I, 278).
[153] Langford, *Writings and Speeches*, IX, 129.

to consume the fruits of the earth"[154] – to emphasize in a pejorative fashion how little townspeople knew about the economics of husbandry. Burke's trustee model of political economy, then, suggests that the wise statesman should resist popular calls for regulation and instead heed his own deliberative judgment on matters of public policy, which may or may not reflect the tribunal of collective opinion. The people entrust representatives to make sound decisions; representatives violate this trust if their decisions became subservient to the whims of public desire.[155]

The Insolvent Debtors Bill

A test of Burke's trustee theory of representation regarding public policy was the Insolvent Debtors Bill. In February 1780, Lord Beauchamp introduced a bill in Parliament that would have provided additional relief to insolvent debtors languishing in prison. The legislation struck a nerve with Burke's mercantile constituents in Bristol, many of whom relied on credit to finance their commercial endeavors. Burke recognized the importance of credit in market economies. "[Credit] is given, because capital *must* be employed; that men calculate the chances of insolvency; and they either withhold the credit, or make the debtor pay the risque in the price," he remarked in *Speech at Bristol Previous to the Election* on September 6, 1780, three days before he would terminate his reelection campaign for a seat representing Bristol.[156] For Burke, capital investment was essential to the functioning of commercial economies but also carried heightened risk, which was reflected in the dispensation of credit.

Yet, in *Speech on Insolvent Debtors Bill*, Burke supported Beauchamp's bill on the grounds of benevolence. As the *Morning Chronicle* wrote describing the speech, "[N]o man whose breast was not steeled against the impulse of humanity, could have heard him unmoved."[157] Burke went so far as to support the "white-washing clause," which would have gone further than Beauchamp's bill by relieving honest debtors of all financial obligations while securing their property against future claims from creditors.[158] Bristol constituents were unconvinced by his reasoning and removed much of their support for Burke.[159] The bill was greeted with sharp resistance in the House of Commons and encountered repeated delay thereafter.[160]

Burke elaborated on his opposition to the bill in *Speech at Bristol Previous to the Election*. He remarked that existing law relating to civil debt was premised

---

[154] Langford, *Writings and Speeches*, IX, 129 and 129n3.
[155] See Chapter 8 for the application of Burke's trustee theory of representation to the Irish trade bill debates.
[156] Langford, *Writings and Speeches*, III, 637.   [157] Langford, *Writings and Speeches*, III, 553.
[158] Langford, *Writings and Speeches*, III, 553.   [159] Langford, *Writings and Speeches*, III, 552.
[160] Langford, *Writings and Speeches*, III, 553.

on the misguided assumption that all debtors were solvent. This was not the case, and thus the debtor was forced to "be coerced his liberty until he makes payment."[161] Their imprisonment for life represented a "miserable mistaken invention" that changed a "civil into a criminal judgment, and to scourge misfortune or indiscretion" with an unreasonable punishment.[162] Burke's argument rested on the principle of punitive proportionality: men in debt to creditors who were otherwise law-abiding individuals did not deserve to be treated like dangerous criminals.

Burke delivered a number of other arguments in defense of the bill in *Speech at Bristol Previous to the Election*. He revived his appeal to the principle of fairness: "I know that credit must be preserved; but equity must be preserved too."[163] Besides, Burke noted, the principle of credit was not even threatened by Beauchamp's bill. Additionally, the procedures for condemning debtors to prison were carried out in an arbitrary fashion; and the creditor did not gain utility from the existing arrangement. "[I]f the few pounds of flesh were not necessary to his security," Burke stated, "we had not a right to detain the unfortunate debtor, without any benefit at all to the person who confined him."[164] The public would also become increasingly restless over the growing expenses of prison administration. Ultimately, the legal implications of financial and commercial enterprise should not be judged the same way as criminal law. "The counting-house has no alliance with the jail," Burke quipped.[165]

Because many of his Bristol constituents did not support Beauchamp's bill, Burke's endorsement of it cannot be seen as a political ploy. Instead, it may be taken as an expression of his genuine sympathy for the plight of debtors – a plight to which he could relate. Burke suffered chronic indebtedness throughout his life, due to his own financial imprudence and charitable giving, among a variety of reasons.[166] The intensity of his struggles reached a crescendo in June 1795, after he had retired from Parliament and two years before he would pass away, when Burke feared that he would be sent to debtors' prison.[167] To be in a precarious financial state was not unusual for British legislators in the eighteenth century, inclined to living beyond their income, but it does expose a gap between Burke's declared faith in prudence and his own personal shortcomings. And while no available historical evidence confirms that Burke's discomfiting experiences with debt directly shaped his views on Beauchamp's bill, it is not hard to imagine that they influenced his beliefs about the merits and demerits of debtors' prison, at least in part.

---

[161] Langford, *Writings and Speeches*, III, 635.
[162] Langford, *Writings and Speeches*, III, 635–636.
[163] Langford, *Writings and Speeches*, III, 636. [164] Langford, *Writings and Speeches*, III, 637.
[165] Langford, *Writings and Speeches*, III, 637. [166] See Lock, *Edmund Burke*, vol. II, 502–506.
[167] Burke to Walker King, 30 June 1795, in *Correspondence of Edmund Burke*, vol. VIII, 280. Due to pressure from creditors, Burke actually contemplated the prospect of having to leave England.

In the same discussion on debtors' prisons in *Speech at Bristol Previous to the Election*, Burke praised the exertions of John Howard on behalf of the needy. Howard, a philanthropist and prison reformer, had traveled throughout Europe to undertake a rigorous study of the incarcerated poor starting in the 1770s. As Burke explained in the speech, he sought to "plunge into the infection of hospitals; to survey the mansions of sorrow and pain; to take the gage and dimensions of misery, depression, and contempt; to remember the forgotten, to attend to the neglected."[168] In the case of prisons, Howard discovered that there was not "more than one prisoner for debt in the great city of Rotterdam," in Holland.[169] Burke's appraisal of Howard illuminated his own concern for the less fortunate.

What can we glean from this extended discussion of Burke's direct and indirect engagement with matters relating to the poor and poverty in eighteenth-century England? Burke's attitude toward the lower social orders continues to be misunderstood. In the late 1700s, he acquired a reputation as a blind defender of the interests of the landed aristocracy at the expense of the impoverished. In *Rights of Man*, Thomas Paine famously captured this view by condemning Burke for lamenting the demise of the French monarchy and nobility while overlooking the torment of the poor in the *Reflections*. "He pities the plumage, but forgets the dying bird," Paine said of Burke.[170] Burke's scathing attack on the Revolution in the *Reflections* certainly feeds this interpretation, strands of which have endured to this day. Jennifer Pitts, for example, notes Burke's "often staggering indifference to the suffering of the poor."[171] And recall Kramnick's contention that Burke believed it was immoral to aid the indigent.

Taking into account his writings and speeches on the subject, as well as his private endeavors, this view demands rethinking. Burke, in fact, did exhibit a lasting concern for the poor, for he harbored a firm belief in the power of private charity and the morality of market liberty (not to mention the justness in granting leniency to struggling debtors) to advance the interests of the disadvantaged. Such imperatives, he maintained, would ease the mean condition of laborers in a far more effectual fashion than state meddling in the market or public expressions of pity. The privileged orders carried the moral duty to aid the poor, such as by establishing educational institutions, as exemplified by Burke's school for French émigrés; the Poor Removals Bill defended the freedom of movement for struggling laborers to pursue work in different parishes; the repeal of laws banning middlemen trading practices would reduce the cost of provisions for consumers in the long run, in his

---

[168] Langford, *Writings and Speeches*, III, 638.   [169] Langford, *Writings and Speeches*, III, 637.
[170] Thomas Paine, *Rights of Man: Being an Answer to Mr. Burke's Attack on the French Revolution* (London: J. S. Jordan, 1791), 26.
[171] Jennifer Pitts, *A Turn to Empire: The Rise of Imperial Liberalism in Britain and France* (Princeton and Oxford: Princeton University Press, 2006), 62.

judgment; restrictions on minimum wage hikes encouraged agricultural employment for the lower classes; and securing the liberties of impoverished laborers to establish free contracts with employers, as Burke contends in *Thoughts and Details*, enhanced the prospect that they would receive sufficient wages, nutriment, and shelter.

Furthermore, as will be discussed, Burke opposed a bill regulating the sale of butcher's meat because it narrowed the market preferences of consumers from modest backgrounds; he argued for the relaxation of the penal codes in order to afford oppressed Irish Catholics greater opportunities to cultivate their land and bequeath their property to future generations; and, in his attack on Warren Hastings and the East India Company in the 1780s and 1790s, he implored the British government to respect the property rights of natives in India.

This is not to say that the amelioration of the poor was the principal object of Burke's legislative activities in Parliament, or that he insisted that the state held no role to play in helping them. (Indeed, as discussed, he broached the idea of, and possibly received, a government subsidy for his school for French émigrés.) And Burke was not solely an advocate of the indigent in his political career, since he was a firm, if not uncritical, defender of the hereditary aristocracy. (Remember also that the corn bounty Burke championed tended to benefit the landowning class.) Yet he displayed a keen awareness that market liberty, gentlemanly responsibility, and voluntary charity bestowed many advantages on lower orders and on society as a whole, and strengthened the ties of compassion that bound all men and women together. Burke's diligent exertions throughout his public life in promoting the cause of economic freedom for the lower classes and in laying stress on the ethical obligation of the rich to aid the poor – not to mention his private charitable efforts – demonstrate a stronger concern for the needy than scholars have suggested.

3.5 WEALTH REDISTRIBUTION AND EQUALITY IN THOUGHTS AND DETAILS

Burke's trustee notion of the relationship between the rich and the poor is a thread of his larger argument in *Thoughts and Details* that attacks the idea of wealth redistribution in the name of abstract equality. For Burke, the rich were not only the trustees of the poor but also the "pensioners of the poor."[172] Just as the poor[173] depended on the rich to provide them with the means for nutriment and lodging, the rich depended on the poor for labor. Disrupting this delicate relationship through government force would sow social distrust and inflict grave injury on both. Equality in theory would collapse into disorder in reality.

---

[172] Langford, *Writings and Speeches*, IX, 121.
[173] This section will label struggling agricultural workers "the poor" with the awareness of Burke's criticism of those using the term to describe a variety of laborers with different skill sets and experiences.

In crafting this argument in *Thoughts and Details*, Burke first makes a pragmatic, empirical claim. The rich were "so extremely small, that if all their throats were cut, and a distribution made of all they consume in a year, it would not give a bit of bread and cheese for one night's supper to those who labour, and who in reality feed both the pensioners [the rich] and themselves."[174] The total amount of wealth owned by the most affluent members of society, if taken by the state and reallocated to individuals, would still not be able to furnish adequate nutriment to struggling laborers. Hence "the throats of the rich ought not to be cut, nor their magazines plundered."[175] Such reasoning captures an inductive tendency in Burke's mode of thought throughout his adult life: he begins at an empirical assertion – the reapportionment of riches would not meet the needs of the public – and then arrives at a principled claim – the state should not seize private property.

One must pause, however, and ask whether Burke is engaging in hyperbole in insinuating that English radicals were calling to kill the rich in order to feed the poor. Certainly there were no major movements in England in the 1790s that resembled the French Revolution's swift and violent seizure of the wealth of the French aristocracy and the Gallican Church. Yet Burke's reference to "cut[ting]" the "throats of the rich" should not be taken literally. Consistent with the flair for metaphor he exhibited in his other writings and speeches, Burke here is activating his imaginative capacities to make the hard analytic point that the rich should not be targeted – whether through violent or peaceful means – for their wealth. Even more moderate measures considered in Burke's time to reduce social and economic disparities, such as reforming the laws of primogeniture entail, were met with resistance by Burke.

Burke continues that the confiscation of wealth from affluent employers would deprive them of the resources necessary to distribute sufficient wages, food, and shelter to laborers. Attacking the rich, therefore, would be hurting the poor. "When the poor rise to destroy the rich, they act as wisely for their own purposes as when they burn mills, and throw corn into the river, to make bread cheap," Burke remarks.[176] This comment is representative of the deepest anxiety conveyed throughout *Thoughts and Details*: the levelling impulses of Jacobin extremism might inflame the English government and the public into supporting the usurpation of property, wealth, and resources.

In Burke's judgment, then, government efforts to regulate wages embodied a dangerous scheme to impose an equality of wealth on an unequal society:

A perfect equality will indeed be produced; that is to say, equal want, equal wretched-ness, equal beggary, and on the part of the partitioners, a woeful, helpless, and desperate disappointment. Such is the event of all compulsory equalizations. They pull down what

---

[174] Langford, *Writings and Speeches*, IX, 121.   [175] Langford, *Writings and Speeches*, IX, 121.
[176] Langford, *Writings and Speeches*, IX, 121.

is above. They never raise what is below: and they depress high and low together beneath the level of what was originally the lowest.[177]

These sentences mark a fundamental truth of Burke's beliefs about government wealth distribution: the state reallocation of wealth would reduce all men to indigence. A naturally developing equality of wealth through private market activity, he suggests, was palatable, if not desirable. "Compulsory" equalization, however, was dreadful, for it might bring about equality – but such equality would be equally wretched conditions, not equally prosperous people. Coerced equality as an idea translates into inescapable poverty as a fact.

Such horrors arose from a denial of a basic reality about market economies, namely that civil society has limited resources. A natural inequality thus emerges among many people, as we recall from Burke's discussion of poverty in *Thoughts and Details*. Allow us to repeat his comments on the matter here: the sheer numbers of the laboring poor "imply poverty," for in "a fair distribution among a vast multitude, none can have much."[178] Poverty is the natural condition of man because the unequal distribution of resources is natural. Yet, as the next subsection discusses, Burke also placed emphasis on the growth in living standards among the lower classes as a mark of social advance, even if the members of such classes were considered poor in late eighteenth-century England compared to the hereditary aristocracy.

Compulsory equalization, then, would hurt those with wealth, aggravate the social condition of those without it, and excite civil unrest. These views illustrate a crucial lesson connecting Burke's economic thought with his broader political philosophy: the belief that inherent injustices exist in a society because of inequalities in wealth ignores the infinite variety of experiences, circumstances, and backgrounds of individuals. By trying to press an abstract conception of uniform equality upon a mixed variety of men and women, the state neglects to cherish and protect the richness of man's diversity.

We can apply this principle to Burke's discussion of labor in the agricultural economy. Labor was complex not only because men and women worked different hours, under different conditions, and with different skill sets; even more, labor itself occasioned a hierarchy of function. Burke explains in *Thoughts and Details* how husbandry included three levels of operation – *instrumentum vocale*, or slaves; *semivocale*, cattle; and *instrumentum mutum*, carts and other production tools – that reflected a "natural and just order" and a "chain of subordination" in the agricultural economy[179]: the "beast is as an

---

[177] Langford, *Writings and Speeches*, IX, 127.   [178] Langford, *Writings and Speeches*, IX, 121.

[179] Langford, *Writings and Speeches*, IX, 125. In *Account of the European Settlements*, in the context of their proposal for Britain to people its West Indian colonies with Englishmen, the Burkes write, "Indubitably the security, as well as the solid wealth of every nation, consists principally in the number of low and middling men of a free condition, and that beautiful gradation from the highest to the lowest, where the transitions all the way are almost imperceptible. To produce this

informing principle to the plough and cart; the labourer is as reason to the beast; and the farmer is as a thinking and presiding principle to the labourer."[180]

Such variations were necessary to encourage the efficient cultivation of crops for the market. Any attempt to disrupt this chain was singularly "absurd" when it effected a "practical operation," in which the corruption of a natural order was especially prone "to an erroneous judgment."[181] Burke's idea of market inequality, then, included disparities in the possession of wealth and distinctions in the kinds of labor. Schemes on the part of the state to ignore or alter these differences would shock the imperatives of nature.

This is not to say Burke believed that particular people were suited to perform specific tasks according to their natural constitution, a belief volunteered by Aristotle in his qualified defense of slavery in the *Politics*.[182] Burke's argument is not that some men were natural slaves, condemned to toil in the fields under the watchful eye of their master. Instead, the division of labor required the separation of tasks in order to ensure the optimal production of crops. Confusion about these roles would frustrate agricultural efficiency – to the detriment of both the farmer, seeking to extract profit from his landed investments, and of the laborer, seeking to earn a wage, food, and shelter. Maintaining the natural hierarchy of labor function promoted the interests of market participants and advanced the cause of economic prosperity.

Poverty as a Relative Condition

Before proceeding, we should not overlook the implication of Burke's aforementioned remark that the existence of poverty was due to the multitudes of people. His larger point is that poverty– much like the "poor" – was a relative term rather than a static condition. Even if a person's social status was modest in relation to members of privileged orders this did not necessarily mean that they were suffering under the weight of extreme indigence. "[T]he condition of those who labour ... is on the whole extremely meliorated, if more and better food is any standard of melioration," Burke states in *Thoughts and Details*.[183] In other words, men and women who were thought of as poverty-stricken in mid-1790s England benefited from a higher standard of living than in previous years, even if the wealth gap between the rich and the poor persisted.

Burke pursues a similar line of argument in his discussion on scarcity in the memorial. Scarcity, like poverty, was not a fixed definition but a relative

---

ought to be the aim and mark of every well regulated commonwealth, and none has ever flourished upon other principles." See Burke and William Burke, *An Account of the European Settlements in America*, vol. II (London: R. and J. Dodsley, 1760), 118.

[180] Langford, *Writings and Speeches*, IX, 125.   [181] Langford, *Writings and Speeches*, IX, 125.
[182] Aristotle, *Politics*, 66–75.   [183] Langford, *Writings and Speeches*, IX, 122.

concept. "Never since I have known England, have I known more than a comparative scarcity," Burke contends. "The price of wheat, taking a number of years together, has had no very considerable fluctuation, nor has it risen exceedingly until within this twelvemonth."[184] The apparent scarcity and poverty of mid-1790s England did not impose anticipated pain on the population: "Even now, I do not know of one man, woman, or child, that has perished from famine."[185] The relative character of scarcity and poverty, Burke suggests, should encourage people to think carefully about the actual health of the provisions markets, and to question whether the distresses of England's population were as cruel as agitators claimed.

Burke insists, then, that discussion about poverty should take into account the steady rise in living standards. "[E]ven under all the hardships of the last year," he writes in *Thoughts and Details*, "the labouring people did, either out of their direct gains, or from charity ... fare better than they did, in seasons of common plenty, 50 or 60 years ago; or even at the period of my English observation, which is about 44 years."[186] Relative poverty is mitigated by the growth in public opulence, indicating that accumulated riches in market economies reach society's lower classes as well as its affluent orders. Material progress advantages the poor.[187]

Final Thoughts on Equality in *Thoughts and Details*

Even though Burke condemned the manifestation of Jacobin equality in the form of wealth redistribution, he praised a different notion of equality grounded in the common nature of man.[188] This conception carries significant implications for his economic thought: as we shall learn, Burke believed that men should be preserved the right to use the fruits of their labor, regardless of their ethnic or religious background. True equality in a market society was the equal right to own property and cultivate resources for one's private enjoyment – a type of equality that, in Burke's view, would be destroyed by the muscular levelers of Jacobin equality.

An additional implication of Burke's idea of economic equality in *Thoughts and Details* lies in his heavy stress on the reciprocity of trade. He argues that suppressing the producer's impulse to generate profit would reduce him to being a "slave of the consumer."[189] This status benefited neither him nor the consumer; in contrast, the equal condition of trading partners, standing on

---

[184] Langford, *Writings and Speeches*, IX, 143.   [185] Langford, *Writings and Speeches*, IX, 143.
[186] Langford, *Writings and Speeches*, IX, 122.
[187] This insight predated Burke's time. John Locke observed in the late seventeenth century that a king in the Americas, ruling a "large and fruitful" yet underdeveloped territory, "feeds, lodges, and is clad worse than a day Labourer in *England*." See Locke, *Two Treatises of Government*, ed. Peter Laslett (Cambridge: Cambridge University Press, 1993), 297.
[188] See Stanlis, *Edmund Burke and the Natural Law*.
[189] Langford, *Writings and Speeches*, IX, 130.

the same plane of economic liberty, gave rise to a synthesis of mutual advantage. "No slave was ever so beneficial to the master as a freeman that deals with him on an equal footing by convention," Burke writes, "formed on the rules and principles of contending interests and compromised advantages."[190] The opportunity to sell and purchase goods was an essential precondition for the real economic equality of man.

3.6   CONCLUSION

Burke's survey of market phenomena in *Thoughts and Details* – on supply and demand laws, wage labor, price theory, and the role of government welfare – is distilled to its core in one of the most dramatic statements in the memorial. "The great use of Government is as a restraint," Burke insists.[191] He continues in the next paragraph:

> To provide for us in our necessities is not in the power of Government. It would be a vain presumption in statesmen to think they can do it. The people maintain them, and not they the people. It is in the power of Government to prevent much evil; it can do very little positive good in this, or perhaps in any thing else.[192]

Government is not capable of furnishing provisions to the people necessary to sustain their well-being. To believe otherwise would be to hold a pretense of knowledge – Burke's "vain presumption" – about the seeming fitness of public officials to coordinate the exchange of economic resources in an effectual manner.

The "zealots of the sect of regulation"[193] – Englishmen sympathetic to schemes of government intervention and wealth redistribution – harbored this vain presumption. From Burke's perspective, however, the state should primarily act as a restraint against arbitrary power, not as an engine for commercial growth, because it was capable of fulfilling the responsibilities of the former but not the latter. The role of government in the internal grain trade was to establish the conditions for farmers and laborers to engage in voluntary and mutually beneficial exchange.

In light of his opposition to the state supervision of the market, it comes as no surprise that Burke completes his tract with how he starts it: by cautioning against excessive government intrusion into private economic activity. "My opinion is against an over doing of any sort of administration," Burke declares at the conclusion of *Thoughts and Details*, "and more especially against this most momentous of all meddling on the part of authority; the meddling with the subsistence of the people."[194] The provisions trade is a delicate creature; rash attempts to disturb the operation of supply and

---

[190] Langford, *Writings and Speeches*, IX, 130.   [191] Langford, *Writings and Speeches*, IX, 120.
[192] Langford, *Writings and Speeches*, IX, 120.   [193] Langford, *Writings and Speeches*, IX, 126.
[194] Langford, *Writings and Speeches*, IX, 145.

demand principles will aggravate, rather than alleviate, social and economic hardship. Burke's stark warnings at the outset and culmination of the memorial about granting government the power to agricultural provisions clinches his argument in favor of market liberty.

Does Burke's firm support for free markets in *Thoughts and Details* display a consistency with his other commentary about the internal grain market and state welfare for the poor? As this chapter has outlined, Burke's embrace of a free domestic grain trade and his objection to the expansion of state welfare to the poor in *Thoughts and Details* reflect a chain of statements in favor of internal market liberty spanning his entire legislative career (the corn bounty excepted).

In summarizing this claim, we should first note that *Thoughts and Details* captured Burke's broader antipathy for government intervention, and for the influence of French Jacobinism on English economic policy, in the 1790s. When Arthur Young visited Burke at Beaconsfield the spring following the drafting of *Thoughts and Details*, he embarked on a five-hour walk with him, during which Burke, according to Young, discussed "French madness, price of provisions, the death of his son, the absurdity of regulating labour, the mischief of our Poor-laws, and the difficulty of cottagers keeping cows."[195] Burke was "absolutely inimical to any regulation whatever by law; that all such interference was not only unnecessary but would be mischievous."[196]

Exhibiting his fondness for empirical information in testing the truth of man's claims, Burke also undertook a "very careful examination of many bakers, butchers, and excisemen" in his neighborhood and concluded from this inquiry that the consumption of the people "was not lessened in the material articles of bread, meat, and beer." In addition, the poor had not "been distressed further than what resulted immediately from that improvidence which was occasioned by the Poor-laws."[197]

One of Burke's letters to Young in late May 1797, written less than two months before Burke's death, mirrored both his insights in *Thoughts and Details* and the conversation he had with Young at Beaconsfield: "My constant opinion was, and is, that all matters relative to labour, ought to be left to the conventions of the parties. That the great danger is in Governments intermeddling too much."[198] He goes on to condemn the "senseless, barbarous," and "wicked" regulations controlling the internal grain trade.[199] Notice that the intensity of his anti-regulatory message here – "senseless" and "barbarous" and "wicked" – matches the high temperature of his passions in

---

[195] Arthur Young, *The Autobiography of Arthur Young*, ed. M. Betham-Edwards (London: Smith, Elder, & Co., 1898), 257.
[196] Young, *Autobiography of Arthur Young*, 258.
[197] Young, *Autobiography of Arthur Young*, 258.
[198] Burke to Arthur Young, 23 May 1797, in *Correspondence of Edmund Burke*, vol. IX, 361.
[199] Burke to Arthur Young, 23 May 1797, in *Correspondence of Edmund Burke*, vol. IX, 361.

Thoughts and Details. In essence, Burke harbored a constant belief in the virtue of government restraint up until his final years.

Burke's suspicion of government regulations and welfare programs in the domestic economy spanned back to his first year in Parliament. Allow us to briefly review the evidence: in November 1766, in his first session in the House of Commons, Burke resisted George Grenville's proposals to aid the poor.[200] In 1770, he argued that promoting a manufacture through the Treasury, rather than the market, was a "bad principle,"[201] and that there were "no such things as a high and a low price."[202] He expressed his belief that the toil of the laborer was proportional to market wages in 1771.[203] Burke led parliamentary efforts to repeal the laws banning forestalling, regrating, and engrossing in 1772, and reaffirmed his disapproval of them in 1787. Burke supported freedom of movement, and subsequently the mobility of labor, in 1774 in his speech on the Poor Removals Bill.

In the same year, he also argued that compulsory charity dissolved social relations between the affluent and the poor. Burke opposed regulating the butchers' meat market in 1776.[204] And he praised "laudable avarice" as the great engine of industry in 1765, thirty years before he again defended the concept in *Thoughts and Details.*[205] He expressed a fondness for the same principle in 1780.[206] We may conclude, then, that the tract did not mark a shift in the principles of Burke's economic thought, for it reinforced a steady – though not blind – confidence in the laws of supply and demand and market liberty that he exhibited throughout his life.[207]

---

[200] Burke to Charles O'Hara, [*post* 11 November 1766], in *Correspondence of Edmund Burke*, vol. I, 278.

[201] "Debates of the House of Commons," 1770, Egerton MS 222, fo. 60, British Library.

[202] Wright, *Sir Henry Cavendish's Debates of the House of Commons*, vol. II, 56.

[203] Burke to Garrett Nagle, 23 August 1771, in *Correspondence of Edmund Burke*, vol. II, 234.

[204] See "Rationalism and the Hayek Connection," Chapter 4.

[205] Langford, *Writings and Speeches*, IX, 477.

[206] In *Speech on Economical Reform*, Burke says, "Interest, the great guide of commerce, is not a blind one. It is very well able to find its own way; and its necessities are its best laws" (Langford, *Writings and Speeches*, III, 535). He states in the same speech, "An honourable and fair profit is the best security against avarice and rapacity; as in all things else, a lawful and regulated enjoyment is the best security against debauchery and excess" (531). See "*Speech on Economical Reform* I: Private Land, Contracts, and the Board of Trade," Chapter 5.

[207] See Gregory M. Collins, "Edmund Burke on the Question of Commercial Intercourse in the Eighteenth Century," *Review of Politics* 79 (2017): 565–595 for additional discussion on the possible reasons for Burke's passionate pro-market convictions in the tract.

4

Markets, Rationalism, and the Hayek Connection

[I]nterest, habit, and the tacit convention, that arise from a thousand nameless circumstances, produce a *tact* that regulates without difficulty, what laws and magistrates cannot regulate at all.[1]

Edmund Burke, *Thoughts and Details on Scarcity*, 1795

4.1 INTRODUCTION

While Burke's thoughts on supply and demand laws, prices, and labor offer much insight into his economic mind, they merely touch the surface of the deeper philosophic substance of *Thoughts and Details*. Accordingly, this chapter will address the more fundamental questions he raises in the tract about the broader social advantages and epistemological foundations of market liberty. One of the memorial's more profound lessons penetrates to the very nature of free exchange: voluntary market contracts occasion a harmony of interest for each party involved in the agreement. Burke also puts forth a conception of commercial virtue in *Thoughts and Details* invites us to compare it with time-honored understandings of morality in European civilization. More important, Burke's grasp of the role of rationality in political economy warrants elaboration because it carries serious implications for our attempt to locate his commentary in the intellectual traditions of economic thought. Before exploring his thoughts on these matters, however, let us expand our knowledge of the specific policy proposals that motivated Burke to condemn state intervention and praise consensual exchange in *Thoughts and Details*, which will help us strengthen our appreciation of his attempt to link circumstance to theory in the writing.

---

[1] Langford, *Writings and Speeches*, IX, 128.

4.2   ENGLAND'S GRAIN TRADE AND NATIONAL POLICY

At the time Burke was drafting *Thoughts and Details,* the idea of instituting a new minimum wage had acquired public traction as a way to relieve struggling laborers of economic deprivation. Before Samuel Whitbread introduced his minimum wage bill in December 1795, justices of the peace in the county of Suffolk, located in East Anglia, had recommended that the wages of workers be raised to keep pace with rising corn prices. One of the Members of Parliament who represented Suffolk referred to this proposal during parliamentary debate on November 25, 1795.[2] This reference may have served as the trigger for Burke's discussion in *Thoughts and Details* about the role of justices of the peace in regulating the salaries of laborers.

In addition to Suffolk, a court of mayoralty in Norwich, also located in East Anglia, requested on October 21, 1795 that the city's MPs "bring forward and support such Measures as may have the most probable tendency to reduce the present exorbitant prices of every Necessary of life." This proposal was submitted under the rationalization that the city's magistrates, by "a regard for the welfare and safety of the State," were "intrusted with the police of a populous commercial city – as Members of a Christian community."[3] The attitude that justices of the peace in Suffolk and Norwich could, and should, set wage rates was grounded in historical and legal precedent. They had been nationally authorized to determine the salaries of laborers ever since the Statute of Artificers was passed under Elizabeth I, although the statute was not enforced rigorously throughout time.[4]

Debating the merit of increasing the minimum wage, then, was not a speculative exercise at the time Burke wrote *Thoughts and Details.* Yet it was not the only regulatory policy Burke confronts in the memorial at length. In 1795 the British government bought corn in international markets and distributed it domestically to distressed areas. In light of this trade, there were growing calls to establish public granaries,[5] such as the proposal put forth by

---

[2] See William Woodfall, ed., *An Impartial Report of the Debates That Occur in the Two Houses of Parliament,* vol. I (London: T. Chapman, 1795), 487. See also Langford, *Writings and Speeches,* IX, 123n1.

[3] *Morning Post,* issue 7399, 26 October 1795.

[4] Local authorities were able to set wage rates before the Statute of Artificers; the 1563 statute, however, established a system that gave official state sanction to magistrates to regulate economic matters. See R. H. Tawney, "The Assessment of Wages in England by the Justices of the Peace," *Vierteljahrschrift für Sozial- und Wirtschaftsgeschichte* 11 (1913): 315. See also Samuel Mencher, *Poor Law to Poverty Program: Economic Security Policy in Britain and the United States* (Pittsburgh: University of Pittsburgh Press, 1967), 29.

[5] The idea of public granaries was not novel. London established its first one in 1440. See Bruce M. S. Campbell et al., *A Medieval Capital and Its Grain Supply: Agrarian Production and Distribution in the London Region c. 1300* (Belfast: The Queen's University of Belfast and the Centre for Metropolitan History, Institute of Historical Research, University of London, 1993), 104. See also Jordan Claridge and John Langdon, "Storage in Medieval England: The Evidence from Purveyance Accounts, 1259–1349," *The Economic History Review* 64 (2011): 1242–1265.

Thomas Pownall.[6] In *Considerations on the Scarcity and High Prices of Bread-Corn and Bread at the Market*,[7] he wrote that "Great cities" and "great towns" such as London and Bristol, the city Burke previously represented, as well as other manufacturing districts, should,

as a measure of political œconomy, establish magazines, so as to be enabled to meet an approaching scarcity and enhancing price, whether real or artificial, with corn, at all times *in sufficient quantity*, to prevent such scarcity; *and at prices*, proportioned to a due profit on one hand, and to the scale of the wages of labour on the other.[8]

Pownall was giving voice to the central economic concerns in the mid-1790s, the aggravated cost and perceived scarcity of provisions, in order to vindicate his proposal for public granaries.

Also keep in mind that the movement in the 1790s in support of state economic regulations occurred around the same time that French Jacobin policies of wealth redistribution were attracting the interest of English MPs, including radical Whigs, in the House of Commons. Burke's concerns about the minimum wage thus stretched beyond the regulation's immediate policy implications. His underlying worry was that hasty legislation would engender even more tensions and anxieties in the fragile agricultural economy; that it would impose an inflexible national policy prescription on local English communities; and that the general government impulse to regulate social and economic relationships between farmers and laborers would unsettle the delicate harmony that emerged between the two parties. This final consideration is the first object of inquiry in this chapter.

4.3 VOLUNTARY CONTRACTS AND MARKET EXCHANGE

The heart of Burke's argument in *Thoughts and Details* about voluntary contracts between farmers and laborers rests on the idea of a synthesis of individual initiative: the pull of enlightened self-interest encourages one party to enter into a conditional arrangement with another in order to satisfy their private aims in the mart. The silent wizardry of supply and demand laws enables both parties to gain advantages from such contracts; and it further promotes the common good by encouraging the smooth distribution of provisions and the regular payment of wage labor. Hence free exchange between consenting parties spawns the blessing of collective benefit. From Burke's perspective, tinkering by the state would disrupt this natural symmetry that blossomed from the incentive structure of voluntary agreements between free persons.

Henry VIII also instituted a public granary system before abandoning the project. See Westerfield, *Middlemen in English Business*, 140.
[6] See "Middlemen," Chapter 2 for Pownall's rebuke of middlemen in the same tract.
[7] Consult "Middlemen," Chapter 2.   [8] Pownall, *Considerations on the Scarcity*, 55–56.

Burke presents this reasoning in *Thoughts and Details* by summoning his concept of the "implied contract." He asserts that an independent agreement between a laborer and his employer should not be subject to arbitrary taxation by justices of the peace:

There is an implied contract, much stronger than any instrument or article of agreement, between the labourer in any occupation and his employer – that the labour, so far as that labour is concerned, shall be sufficient to pay to the employer a profit on his capital, and a compensation for his risk; in a word, that the labour shall produce an advantage equal to the payment. Whatever is above that, is a direct *tax*; and if the amount of that tax be left to the will and pleasure of another, it is an *arbitrary tax*.[9]

A set of incentives and expectations arises from an agricultural employment arrangement, the foremost being that wages will be commensurate with the profit the laborer helps generate for the farmer. Burke's insinuation, when taken in the context of his discussion of commercial virtues in *Thoughts and Details*, is that an implicit awareness surfaces between the employer and laborer of the obligations that stem from a consensual market agreement: the farmer should treat his employees well, and the laborer should work with diligence. We shall elaborate on these virtues in the next section.

It is paramount that Burke distinguishes the strength of this "implied" contract with "any instrument or article of agreement" – formal legal contracts, statutes, judicial orders, and executive edicts. By issuing this distinction, he suggests that the spark of reciprocal interest was not a literal command carved meticulously into stone by political authorities, but instead stemmed from the intuitive understanding of each party that one stood to gain in some way by serving the needs of the other. Although such contracts were legally protected and enforced, their origin lay in the human inclination to seek out others for a self-interested purpose, rather than in the stiff dictates of political coercion, and they were sustained by a sense of mutual trust.

In Burke's view, a tax upset this natural equipoise of voluntary contracts by distorting the equality between the payment of the wage and the advantage of labor. Burke explains in the quotation that this tax could be direct or arbitrary. He reserves his scorn especially for the latter kind because of its autocratic nature, one determined by "will and pleasure" and unchecked by any legal constraints. The chief similarity between direct and arbitrary taxes, however, was that both threatened the fragile balance that emerged from consensual participation in employment contracts.

Arbitrary taxation exposed two particular problems for Burke: confusion over the role of the judge in economic transactions, and the presumption of knowledge from such judges in assuming they could identify the best interests of the mutual parties involved. The first issue arose from the failure to distinguish between "convention" and "judicature,"[10] as Burke writes in *Thoughts and*

---

[9] Langford, *Writings and Speeches*, IX, 123.   [10] Langford, *Writings and Speeches*, IX, 124.

Details. "Convention" in this context signified organic employment contracts between parties who freely chose to enter into them. For Burke, the authority of a judge[11] did not grant him the power to infringe on this voluntary contract by regulating the terms of the agreement, such as setting wage rates. The magistrate "cannot dictate the contract," Burke writes.[12] Instead, "It is his business to see that it be *enforced*; provided that it is not contrary to pre-existing laws, or obtained by force or fraud."[13]

The role of the judge was to help carry out the existing contract or determine whether it violated existing law. Burke's next sentence distills the crux of his indictment of judges who assumed the role of the legislator: "If he is in any way a maker or regulator of the contract, in so much he is disqualified from being a judge."[14] The magistrate should not be an innovative lawmaker, issuing third-party commands that control social and economic relations between the employer and the employee. If the magistrate acts as a lawmaker, he corrupts the integrity of his office which, Burke suggests, was grounds for discharge. Judicial intrusion into voluntary market activities lied beyond the scope of magistrates' legal authority, in other words, and was the parent of public confusion and arbitrary government.

The second problem, one that carried deeper philosophical implications than controversies over the role of the judiciary, was the question of knowledge. Burke asks hypothetically in *Thoughts and Details* which party was best suited to gauge his own self-interest: the individuals who were "mutually concerned in the matter contracted for," or those who "can have none, or a very remote interest in it, and little or no knowledge of the subject"?[15] Burke's conclusion is the former. He writes:

[F]or what man, of any degree of reflection, can think, that a want of interest in any subject closely connected with a want of skill in it, qualifies a person to intermeddle in any the least affair; much less in affairs that vitally concern the agriculture of the kingdom, the first of all it's concerns, and the foundation of all it's prosperity in every other matter, by which that prosperity is produced?[16]

These comments, when united with his previous quotation about the implied contract, shine bright light on one of the most persistent messages in *Thoughts and Details*: the producers, consumers, and middlemen who engage in market exchange can better discern their self-interest than parties not immediately involved in the transaction. Magistrates are distant from the private activities of individuals, lacking the same wellspring of knowledge about the specific circumstances of time and place as the contracted parties. In contrast, market participants, due to their direct engagement in the voluntary agreement, possess

---

[11] Burke uses "judge" to refer to the magistrate, or justice of the peace, who held the power to regulate wages.
[12] Langford, *Writings and Speeches*, IX, 124.   [13] Langford, *Writings and Speeches*, IX, 124.
[14] Langford, *Writings and Speeches*, IX, 124.   [15] Langford, *Writings and Speeches*, IX, 123.
[16] Langford, *Writings and Speeches*, IX, 123.

such knowledge, skills, and experience necessary to arrive at an informed opinion about whether employment contracts will satisfy their particular preferences in the agricultural economy.

For Burke, then, a free contract produced a kind of homeostasis – a process of absorbing, mixing, and balancing a variety of market desires into a harmony of human association. A contract is a "matter of discretion and of interest between the two parties," and the parties are "the masters"; but if they do not hold command over their decisions to enter into and fulfill their contract, then "they are not free, and therefore their contracts are void."[17] Discretion steers the decision-making of the parties immediately involved, while interest is the germ that prompts them to enter into contracts in the first place. State officials should not attempt to control either.

Burke does not endorse the advantages of mutual commercial agreements with blind deference. He writes in *Thoughts and Details* that it is better to reserve a zone of autonomy for individuals to enter into contracts as long as "there is no force or fraud, collusion or combination."[18] As stated previously, Burke writes that judges should enforce the law, not create new regulations, insofar as the contract did not contravene existing legislation or was not established by "force or fraud."[19] Such qualifications do convey a subtle awareness that some contractual agreements could be tainted by compulsion and deception.

Burke glides over this implication in *Thoughts and Details*, however. One important critique of the idea that voluntary exchange induces mutual benefits is that contracts are plagued by asymmetric information – one party holds more information about the quality of the goods or service in the transaction than the other party and therefore is capable of exploiting the deal to their advantage. Burke gives little indication in the memorial that he considers this possibility, or similar instances of market failure such as moral hazard and adverse selection, to be defects of free markets that demanded state intervention. For example, he does not reflect on whether an employer might intentionally minimize to a prospective employee the rigor of the agricultural labor to be performed, or the harsh conditions under which he would work. For that matter, Burke also does not entertain the prospect that the future employee might exaggerate his skills in husbandry or his work ethic in order to convince the employer to agree to the contract.

Indeed, scholarship by Gwenda Morgan and Peter Rushton,[20] E. P. Thompson,[21] and John Bohstedt[22] suggests that relations between employers and employees in the latter half of eighteenth-century England

---

[17] Langford, *Writings and Speeches*, IX, 124.   [18] Langford, *Writings and Speeches*, IX, 123.
[19] Langford, *Writings and Speeches*, IX, 124.
[20] Gwenda Morgan and Peter Rushton, "The Magistrate, the Community and the Maintenance of an Orderly Society in Eighteenth-Century England," *Historical Research* 76 (2003): 54–77.
[21] Thompson, *Making of the English Working Class*.   [22] Bohstedt, *Politics of Provisions*.

were more tumultuous than Burke leads the reader to believe in *Thoughts and Details*, particularly in times of economic uncertainty. In one case study, Morgan and Rushton discovered that it was not unusual for employees to issue complaints to the local magistrate claiming that they were abused or not trained properly. Others charged that their employers withheld their wages or did not pay them all. Workers were not entirely innocent of misconduct, however: employers and masters themselves would file complaints protesting that employees would not complete their tasks; in fact, more than 70 percent of their cases involved this charge.[23] Surely any educated person at the time, and especially a careful thinker like Burke, would have been aware of such cases of abuse and fraud in employment contracts, even – or especially – at a time when England's economy was growing tremendously in the eighteenth century.

We must briefly clarify the distinct nature of Burke's argument in favor of voluntary contracts with reference to the Middle Ages. The idea of a mutually advantageous relationship itself was not a self-contained concept within classical economics. Under feudalism, the lord and the vassal each had their own self-interested reason to enter into a partnership, formalized through a ritual called the commendation ceremony. The lord received obedience and loyalty from the vassal, including military and administrative service, and the vassal would receive protection, aid, and land tenure rights from the lord. "In this feudal arrangement," George H. Sabine writes, "there was an aspect of mutuality, of voluntary performance, and of implied contract which has almost wholly vanished from modern political relationships."[24]

Burke's "implied contract" between the employer and laborer in *Thoughts and Details* is of a different nature. His idea of a mutually beneficial relationship in the agricultural economy was one driven largely by the hidden incentive structure of supply and demand laws. Feudal arrangements, though shifting and heterogeneous throughout the Middle Ages, were defined not by the profit incentive but by duties of allegiance and obedience. As we have learned, Burke did not divorce traditional conceptions of paternalism and the element of trust from market activity. One of the most dramatic features of his economic thought in *Thoughts and Details*, however, is that he reframes the feudal understanding of mutual interest grounded in explicit moral duty into a market understanding of reciprocal benefits based on commercial virtue and implicit moral duty. What, specifically, constituted these commercial virtues and implied duties?

4.4   INCENTIVE, RECIPROCITY, AND COMMERCIAL VIRTUES

While Burke does not make explicit use of the phrase "commercial virtues" in *Thoughts and Details*, his description of the incentive structure of market

---

[23] Morgan and Rushton, "The Magistrate, the Community and the Maintenance," 64.
[24] George H. Sabine and Thomas Landon Thorson, *A History of Political Theory*, 4th ed. (Fort Worth, TX: The Dryden Press, 1978), 207.

transactions strikes a resonant chord with the concept today, which we associate with industry, frugality, and hard work. In discussing this matter in the memorandum, Burke first reasserts his belief that contracts signified a unity of interest between parties. "[I]n the case of the farmer and the labourer, their interests are always the same," he writes, "and it is absolutely impossible that their free contracts can be onerous to either party."[25]

Burke then proceeds to draw out the specific benefits for each party that blossomed from the fulfillment of the terms of contract. These included material conveniences and the easing of the mind:

It is the interest of the farmer, that his work should be done with effect and celerity: and that cannot be, unless the labourer is well fed, and otherwise found with such necessaries of animal life, according to it's habitudes, as may keep the body in full force, and the mind gay and cheerful.[26]

The farmer harbors an acute interest in ensuring that husbandry is practiced with efficiency and purpose. This can be done only if the laborer is well-nourished and has access to other basic requirements necessary to sustain his livelihood. In meeting the laborer's need for nourishment, then, the farmer promotes the physical strength and emotional well-being of his employee. Furthermore, the laborer gains advantages from this arrangement, including the health of the body, the tranquility and optimism of the mind, and employment in comfortable work conditions.

But if the employer struggles to reap material reward from labor, the incentive system that would normally benefit the employee collapses:

[I]f the farmer ceases to profit of the labourer, and that his capital is not continually manured and fructified, it is impossible that he should continue that abundant nutriment, and cloathing, and lodging, proper for the protection of the instruments he employs.[27]

Therefore, it is in the collective interest of both the farmer and the laborer to help produce a profit on the farm. Otherwise, the former will not be able to earn additional wealth, and the latter will be deprived of food and shelter.

Which commercial virtues, then, blossom from this incentive structure? Agricultural workers must demonstrate a strong work ethic, discipline, and dexterity in order to assist their employer in generating profit. They must show industry, efficiency, and vigor, as well as personal responsibility for their own physical and mental well-being. "Patience, labour, sobriety, frugality, and religion, should be recommended to them," Burke writes in describing the habits that should be encouraged among poor laborers.[28] In his *Third Letter on a Regicide Peace*, he repeats these virtues, with the

---

[25] Langford, *Writings and Speeches*, IX, 124–125.
[26] Langford, *Writings and Speeches*, IX, 125.   [27] Langford, *Writings and Speeches*, IX, 125.
[28] Langford, *Writings and Speeches*, IX, 121.

exception of labor.[29] He further encouraged "sentiments of piety, loyalty, order, and industry" among the poor in his neighborhood at Beaconsfield.[30]

Indeed, spanning all the way back to the *Account*, Burke detected a connection between labor and industry – and mental repose. In their discussion of slavery in the British West Indies, the Burkes write, "The mind goes a great way in every thing; and when a man knows that his labour is for himself; and that the more he labours, the more he is to acquire, this consciousness carries him through, and supports him beneath fatigues, under which he otherwise would have sunk."[31] The prospect of accumulation motivated the worker to toil laboriously, even, or especially, in times of distress.

The absence of such commercial virtues bred dire psychological effects. In the *Philosophical Enquiry*, Burke contends that indolence was the cause of "[m]elancholy, dejection, despair, and often self-murder."[32] Hence the "best remedy for all these evils is exercise or *labour*," which "is not only requisite to preserve the coarser organs in a state fit for their functions, but it is equally necessary to these finer and more delicate organs, on which, and by which, the imagination, and perhaps the other mental powers act."[33] Because the incentive structure of agricultural markets also inspires the farmer to be a responsible steward of his land, workers, and tools, Burke observes in *Thoughts and Details*, a synchronization of effort emerges between consenting parties in a system of voluntary exchange, fostering collective virtue in the service of commercial advantage.

Burke's identification of commercial virtues, when integrated with his concept of the "implied contract," contains echoes of William Blackstone's understanding of a similar idea. In the *Commentaries*, Blackstone wrote that there was a type of contract "implied by reason and construction of law" in which everyone who enters into an employment arrangement, among various undertakings, "contracts with those who employ or entrust him, to perform it with integrity, diligence, and skill."[34] The parties may consent to enter into the contract, but they do not necessarily come to an agreement about, or write down in great detail, every single expectation and obligation that may arise from its terms. The performance of contracts, Burke and Blackstone infer, derives from the implicit understanding that they demand the fulfillment of duties that transcend the written word and express verbal consent. "The law evidently holds people to this standard because it recognizes pre-existing

---

[29] The "affected pity" for the laboring poor teaches them to "seek resources where no resources are to be found, in something else than their own industry, and frugality, and sobriety" (Langford, *Writings and Speeches*, IX, 355).

[30] Prior, *Life of Edmund Burke*, 422.   [31] *Account of the European Settlements*, vol. II, 128.

[32] Langford, *Writings and Speeches*, I, 288.   [33] Langford, *Writings and Speeches*, I, 288.

[34] Blackstone, *Commentaries*, vol. II, 132. For additional commentary on Burke's and Blackstone's idea of an implied contract, see Frederick G. Whelan, "The Place of Contract in Burke's Political Theory," in Whelan, *The Political Thought of Hume and His Contemporaries: Enlightenment Projects Volume I* (New York and London: Routledge, 2015), 106–110.

moral norms as binding and hence assumes that all transactions partake of a larger implicit contract to observe them," Frederick G. Whelan writes in describing the notion of the implied contract in Burke's and Blackstone's thought.[35]

This aspect of Burke's economic theory holds a number of implications for his political theory. As we shall see in Chapters 11 and 12, Burke broadened his conception of the implied contract to encompass an understanding of the ethical underpinnings of social and economic order. In addition, the implied contract in Burke's political economy reflected a key tenet of his moral philosophy: a particular state of affairs demands the discharge of particular responsibilities. "The situation of man is the preceptor of his duty," he said in *Speech on Fox's India Bill*.[36] Rather than interpreting this remark as a statement of moral relativism, it may rather be taken as the recognition that men and women were required to carry out specific obligations relevant to the distinctive ethical dilemmas they faced under varying circumstances.[37] In the case of agricultural employment contracts, laborers held the specific obligation to be diligent and efficient, while farmers held the specific obligation to serve as stewards of their workers and tools.

The important point to remember about Burke's notion of the implied contract, however, is that Burke believed such duties emerged from an incentive structure, not from unconditional acts of charity. This view captured one of the critical modifications of classical and Christian conceptions of virtue, according to which men and women consciously acted in ways to meet a defined social aim, such as helping the needy. By contrast, Burke's commentary in *Thoughts and Details* illustrated a notion of agricultural employment that was chiefly inspired by healthy self-interest.

Furthermore, the commercial virtues Burke spotlights in the economic tract were pursued not as ends in themselves but to the extent they helped the individual fulfill his terms of the contract. Thomas Aquinas described the habit of Christian charity, the greatest theological virtue, as "not only to the love of God, but also to the love of our neighbor."[38] Burke's political theory, and the example he set in his private life, certainly affirmed Thomistic conceptions of the virtue of almsgiving and philanthropy. Besides his statement that "charity to the poor is a direct and obligatory duty upon all Christians,"[39]however, Burke's attention to this consideration in *Thoughts and Details* is scant. In his primary economic writing, he indicates that incentives were more effectual than pure acts of benevolence in helping to alleviate material want.

---

[35] Whelan, "Place of Contract in Burke's Political Theory," 109.

[36] Langford, *Writings and Speeches*, V, 404.

[37] Consult Whelan, "Place of Contract in Burke's Political Theory," 103–106.

[38] Thomas Aquinas, *Summa Theologica*, vol. III, trans. Fathers of the English Dominican Province (Allen, TX: Christian Classics, 1981), II-II, Q. 25, Art. 1, 1280.

[39] Langford, *Writings and Speeches*, IX, 129.

Burke's comments on the balance of interests in a system of voluntary exchange invites us to consider whether that the stability of transactional partnerships may actually have been more tenuous than he suggests in *Thoughts and Details*. If the farmer is not able to produce a profit, the laborer, as noted earlier, will be deprived of the advantages of food, clothing, and shelter that were generated from the set of incentives inherent in the original contract. Would not this very loss of necessities endanger the life of the agricultural worker? Did, then, the seeming stability of mutual employment agreements stand on a more precarious foundation than Burke insinuates, particularly if charity was inadequate to meet the needs of struggling laborers?

Burke does say that the laborer is tasked with ensuring that the farmer receives financial reward from his investment in labor. "It is therefore the first and fundamental interest of the labourer, that the farmer should have a full incoming profit on the product of his labour," he avers.[40] The collective pursuit of profit benefits the employer and employee, a phenomenon Burke calls "self-evident."[41] What he is really hinting at in *Thoughts and Details* is that the material, physical, and emotional well-being of the contracted laborer was influenced in important ways by his capacity to help his employer produce this profit. For Burke, such an arrangement was typically sufficient to ease social and economic hardship. If this was not sufficient, he believed that private acts of benevolence could make up for the limits of supply and demand laws. As he writes, "Whenever it happens that a man can claim nothing according to the rules of commerce, and the principles of justice, he passes out of that department, and comes within the jurisdiction of mercy."[42]

4.5 LAISSEZ-FAIRE AND THE ROLE OF STATE REGULATION

Can Burke's defense of voluntary exchange, and of free markets generally, be portrayed accurately as a blessing for laissez-faire economics? A number of scholars have put forth this interpretation, including C. B. Macpherson, who wrote that Burke "had no doubts" about the "virtue of *laissez-faire* at home."[43] Recall also that Alfred Cobban, Judith Shklar, and Gertrude Himmelfarb argued that Burke's strident pro-market beliefs in *Thoughts and Details* were in conflict with his political theory emphasizing the importance of prudence and moderation.

We should be careful before applying this label to Burke's economic thought, however. If one defines laissez-faire as the idea that the state should play no or

---

[40] Langford, *Writings and Speeches*, IX, 125.   [41] Langford, *Writings and Speeches*, IX, 125.
[42] Langford, *Writings and Speeches*, IX, 129.
[43] Macpherson, *Burke*, 53. Similarly, Isaac Kramnick writes that "[b]y far the most important statement by Burke of the basic bourgeois principles of a laissez-faire state and economic order is found in his essay *Thoughts and Details on Scarcity* of 1795" (*Rage of Edmund Burke*, 158).

almost no role in the economy, then Burke was not an orthodox laissez-faire economic thinker. There is a difference between providing a firm, though not blind, endorsement of market liberty, on the one hand, and calling for a radical minimalist state, on the other. If we integrate *Thoughts and Details* within his broader conception of political economy as a whole, we find that Burke, while a proponent of a free internal grain trade, does accommodate government intervention in important respects.

First, remember that Burke makes a demonstrated effort in the tract to distinguish between direct taxes and arbitrary taxes. The implied contract between the farmer and laborer, he writes in the memorial, signals the mutual understanding "that the labour shall produce an advantage equal to the payment."[44] Burke claims that any regulation above this threshold is a "*direct tax*" – and if the tax is levied by the "will and pleasure" of a third party, it is an "*arbitrary tax.*"[45] Burke refers multiple times to the arbitrary exercise of legal power to regulate employment transactions – "arbitrary taxation,"[46] an "arbitrary division of his property,"[47] and "arbitrary regulation."[48] With this distinction in mind, an attentive reading of Burke's commentary suggests he opposed the exercise of unrestrained and inconsistent regulatory authority, not any type of regulation per se.

In addition, it is worth reviewing other examples in Burke's economic thought that permits a measure of government intervention in the economy. In *Thoughts and Details*, Burke opposes calls for another minimum wage hike, but he does not condemn the two previous wage increases.[49] He also concedes that public granaries might serve a useful purpose in small territories that faced unique geopolitical challenges, such as Geneva.

Moreover, Burke supported the export bounty on corn, as discussed, and communicates a measure of sympathy in *Thoughts and Details* for the use of public revenue to fund an import bounty on corn.[50] He argued that taxes did not necessarily decrease consumption nor imperil the overall health of Britain's economy during times of war.[51] Burke championed the broad expansion of metropolitan authority to regulate the slave trade out of existence, as illustrated

---

[44] See Langford, *Writings and Speeches*, IX, 123.

[45] See Langford, *Writings and Speeches*, IX, 123.

[46] See Langford, *Writings and Speeches*, IX, 123.

[47] See Langford, *Writings and Speeches*, IX, 126.

[48] See Langford, *Writings and Speeches*, IX, 133.

[49] See Langford, *Writings and Speeches*, IX, 123. "Wages have been twice raised in my time, and they bear a full proportion, or even a greater than formerly, to the medium of provision during the last bad cycle of twenty years."

[50] In *Thoughts and Details*, Burke writes, "The domestic consumption of spirits, produced, without complaints, a very great revenue, applicable, if we pleased, in bounties to the bringing corn from other places, far beyond the value of that consumed in making it, or to the encouragement of it's encreased production at home" (Langford, *Writings and Speeches*, IX, 141).

[51] See "*Observations on a Late State of the Nation*," Chapter 7; and "*Third Letter on a Regicide Peace* and the Political Economy of England," Chapter 12.

by *Sketch of a Negro Code.*[52] He sought to preserve the older system of the Navigation Acts, which aimed to confine the flow of British goods within the British Empire.[53] Even more, Burke defended Britain's hereditary aristocracy, particular corporate privileges, and the inheritance law of primogeniture entail, a practice that Adam Smith criticized for hindering agricultural development. Most important, Burke resisted the contractarian thinking popular in the eighteenth century that extolled free commercial relations as the stimuli of social order and the antidote to conflict in civil society.[54] He was not a starry-eyed apologist for laissez-faire economics.

In fact, Burke himself insists in *Thoughts and Details* that government should perform positive functions in a commonwealth:

That the State ought to confine itself to what regards the State, or the creatures of the State, namely, the exterior establishment of its religion; its magistracy; its revenue; its military force by sea and land; the corporations that owe their existence to its fiat; in a word, to every thing that is *truly and properly* public, to the public peace, to the public safety, to the public order, to the public prosperity.[55]

Government holds tightly constrained but vital responsibilities in a political community. It should promote a common religion,[56] create a stable legal system, generate public revenue, maintain a military, and charter specific trading companies. That Burke includes state-backed corporations, such as Britain's East India Company, within this framework further confirms his resistance to laissez-faire economics, at least in the realm of foreign trade, as Chapters 9 and 10 will explore in greater detail.

Burke's remarks in *Third Letter on a Regicide Peace*, which he first began drafting in late 1796, just over a year after he started writing *Thoughts and Details*, contain an echo of this commentary in the economic tract. In *Third Letter*, Burke writes

Let Government protect and encourage industry, secure property, repress violence, and discountenance fraud, it is all that they have to do. In other respects, the less they meddle in these affairs the better; the rest is in the hands of our Master and theirs.[57]

Similar to *Thoughts and Details*, Burke in *Third Letter* hints at a key distinction between the exterior responsibilities of the state – create the conditions for industry to prosper and promote law and order – and the interior activities of the people,

---

[52] See "The Laws of Supply and Demand, Wages, and Price Theory," Chapter 2.
[53] See "The American War and the Navigation Acts: *Speech on American Taxation* and *Speech on Conciliation with America*," Chapter 7.
[54] See Chapter 12.   [55] Langford, *Writings and Speeches*, IX, 143.
[56] Burke also displayed sympathy toward religious minorities. See Michael W. McConnell, "Establishment and Toleration in Edmund Burke's 'Constitution of Freedom,'" *The Supreme Court Review 1995* (1995): 393–462.
[57] Langford, *Writings and Speeches*, IX, 355.

which, in his view, should be generally left to flourish free from unnecessary government meddling.

In other words, the state was indispensable to preserving social order and market liberty by upholding the rule of law. This point is essential to grasping Burke's conception of the relationship between government and commercial activity: Burke believed that to the extent that the state should intervene to enforce the law, it should do so with a steadiness of hand and force of execution – but it should not overwhelm the people with a torrent of rules. "In it's preventive police [the state] ought to be sparing of its efforts," he writes in *Thoughts and Details*, "and to employ means, rather few, unfrequent, and strong, than many, and frequent, and, of course, as they multiply their puny politic race, and dwindle, small and feeble."[58] Burke suggests that the salutary effect of state intervention was inversely proportional to the scope of its activity: the more regulations government enacted, the less effectual and meaningful they became.

Burke culminates his defense of the rule of law in the memorial by clarifying his distinction between higher and lower duties of government. The higher duty, the first duty of state officials, was to form laws that fulfilled the national responsibilities of government, such as the common defense and the preservation of public order. The lower duty of governing local communities, Burke suggests, should be reserved for the autonomous groups within those jurisdictions. If government officials creep beyond the confines of such higher responsibilities, they will not succeed in accomplishing their goals:

[A]s [statesmen] descend from the state to a province, from a province to a parish, and from a parish to a private house, they go on accelerated in their fall. They *cannot* do the lower duty; and, in proportion as they try it, they will certainly fail in the higher. They ought to know the different departments of things; what belongs to laws, and what manners alone can regulate. To these, great politicians may give a leaning, but they cannot give a law.[59]

Such comments not only illuminate Burke's allegiance to the rule of law, however. They also underscore his stress on the importance of local knowledge in *Thoughts and Details*. State officials who attempt to regulate the habits and customs of different communities are destined to meet failure, Burke insinuates, because remote legislators and magistrates do not possess the necessary level of information about particular social and economic circumstances required to effectively govern those communities. Parishes and families can largely rule themselves.

Burke is also intimating a notion of what today in America is called an "unwritten constitution," the patchwork of a culture's norms, customs, and traditions that antedate legal regulations of human conduct.[60] This unwritten

---

[58] Langford, *Writings and Speeches*, IX, 143.

[59] Langford, *Writings and Speeches*, IX, 143–144.

[60] Tocqueville provided the classic expression of this concept in *Democracy in America*. See also O. A. Brownson, *The American Republic: Its Constitution, Tendencies, and Destiny* (New York: P. O'Shea, 1866).

constitution is a particular *ethos*, blending civic culture with ethical habituation that prepares a people for self-rule (albeit, in Burke's case, under a limited constitutional monarchy) without demanding excess reliance upon the guidance of the state.

For Burke, then, private market arrangements should be governed not by public officials but by the civilizing influence of "manners." Manners, while not sufficient in themselves, tend to smooth out whatever coarse disagreements may arise between individuals in the mart and in the broader society in general. We will discuss this insight at greater length in Chapters 11 and 12. Burke does admit in the block quotation that legislators may "give a leaning" to nudge people toward adopting particular manners, but he suggests that this leaning carries inherent limitations compared with the greater capacity of a people to regulate their own conduct voluntarily.

Furthermore, in mentioning the "different departments of things," Burke conveys that any attempt to govern human activities requires a careful consideration of place and context: a market interaction between two consenting parties is a private affair,[61] and constitutes a wholly different category of human activity than criminal behavior, for instance. Burke avows that the state should intervene in the latter but not the former, since one primary function of government he lists in *Thoughts and Details* is to preserve public peace – not tinker with the market arrangements between employers and employees.

4.6 RATIONALISM IN THOUGHTS AND DETAILS

The significance of Burke's reproach of wage regulations transcends specific questions over judicial power, regulatory authority, or arbitrary taxation. There is a deeper philosophical component to his advocacy of government restraint, one that discloses a clearer picture of his conception of rationalism in relation to his comments on the internal grain trade in *Thoughts and Details*. For Burke, differences in judgment about the virtues of government intervention were, at root, disagreements over the efficacy of abstract reason in regulating the private affairs of producers, consumers, and middlemen.

The Intellectual Roots of Burke's Distrust of Abstract Reason

In order to understand Burke's distaste for abstract reason in *Thoughts and Details*, we must briefly probe the intellectual origins of this attitude in his early writings. *A Vindication of Natural Society* offers such an opportunity. Written

---

[61] This is not to say that Burke believed the consequences of private economic activity remained in the private sphere. Burke understood voluntary market transactions to hold public benefits, as will be discussed in Chapter 4.

in 1756, the *Vindication*, the first published book in Burke's life, was his attempt to ridicule Lord Bolingbroke's belief that a revival of natural reason and natural religion could alleviate the miseries and divisions of civil society. Burke, posing in the *Vindication* as a "Noble Writer" reflecting Bolingbroke's position, argues that disparities and inequalities in society developed because of man's rejection of reason. "[I]n proportion as we have deviated from the plain Rule of our Nature, and turned our Reason against itself, in that Proportion have we increased the Follies and Miseries of Mankind," the Noble Writer professes.[62] This remark captures one of Burke's underlying motifs in the *Vindication*: Bolingbrokean conceptions of natural reason failed to recognize the many complexities of man's condition in civil society that escaped the pretensions of stiff logic.

Additionally, in the *Philosophical Enquiry*, Burke refuses to assent to the idea that strict definitions of terms can fully grasp the reality of things. "For when we define, we seem in danger of circumscribing nature within the bounds of our own notions, which we often take up by hazard, or embrace on trust, or form out of a limited and partial consideration of the object before us," he writes in describing the word "taste," "instead of extending our ideas to take in all that nature comprehends, according to her manner of combining."[63] Fixed meanings of terms often revealed the perimeters of human knowledge rather than the varieties of nature, which man can grasp only in part. A "clear idea is therefore another name for a little idea."[64]

This lesson applied to political knowledge as well. "No lines can be laid down for civil or political wisdom," Burke commented later in *Thoughts on the Present Discontents*, his writing in defense of party government. "They are a matter incapable of exact definition. But, though no man can draw a stroke between the confines of day and night, yet light and darkness are upon the whole tolerably distinguishable."[65] Such remarks in the *Vindication*, *Philosophical Enquiry*, and *Thoughts on the Present Discontents* – not to mention his similar insights in the *Reflections* – all illuminate Burke's attention to the limits of individual reason in understanding the composite mysteries of society that lied beyond the precepts of formal deduction.

Even Burke's specific discussion of beauty in the *Philosophical Enquiry* relates to this matter. In his famous distinction between beauty – defined by qualities such as smallness and smoothness – and the sublime, created by the feeling of terror, he argued that beauty was not characterized by proportion, unlike traditional Platonic conceptions of the idea. Burke's perspective was that beauty based on proportion imposed a rigidly abstract view on aesthetic images, which reflected human beings' haughty confidence in their ability to evaluate form based on man-made measurements. "For there is in mankind an unfortunate propensity to make themselves, their views, and their works, the

[62] Langford, *Writings and Speeches*, I, 172.   [63] Langford, *Writings and Speeches*, I, 197.
[64] Langford, *Writings and Speeches*, I, 235.   [65] Langford, *Writings and Speeches*, II, 282.

measure of excellence in every thing whatsoever," he laments.[66] The artificial creation of formal gardens exposed this pretense of taste embraced by proponents of the concept of proportional beauty. "But nature has at last escaped from their discipline and their fetters; and our gardens, if nothing else, declare, we begin to feel that mathematical ideas are not the true measures of beauty," Burke writes.[67] The natural bloom of gardens, emancipated from inflexible mandates seeking to thrust proportion and uniformity upon the spontaneity and complexity of nature, displayed the essence of real beauty.

Abstract Reason in *Thoughts and Details*

Burke's doubt about the credibility of abstract reason and the omniscient power of the human mind animates his criticism of government regulations in *Thoughts and Details*. In the memorial, he argues that justices of the peace, and lawmakers in general, do not possess the deep reservoir of local knowledge necessary to enact laws that will benefit the laboring classes. Regarding wages and contracts between farmers and laborers, Burke writes:

Legislative acts, attempting to regulate this part of oeconomy, do, at least, as much as any other, require the exactest detail of circumstances, guided by the surest general principles that are necessary to direct experiment and enquiry, in order again from those details to elicit principles, firm and luminous general principles, to direct a practical legislative proceeding.[68]

He reinforces this message when discussing the failure of uniform wage regulations to embody the varieties of labor in the agricultural economy. In reference to his aforementioned description of the different categories of labor in Chapter 3, which he admits is an "inferior" classificatory system,[69] Burke writes that it

is introduced to shew, that laws prescribing, or magistrates exercising, a very stiff, and often inapplicable rule, or a blind and rash discretion, never can provide the just proportions between earning and salary on the one hand, and nutriment on the other: whereas interest, habit, and the tacit convention, that arise from a thousand nameless circumstances, produce a *tact* that regulates without difficulty, what laws and magistrates cannot regulate at all.[70]

These two quotations establish some of the most important philosophical themes in *Thoughts and Details* because they integrate Burke's general support for a free grain trade with his deeper theoretical convictions about abstract reason. The themes will be addressed under the following headings: the dissonance between legislative rules and experiential complexities; the question

---

[66] Langford, *Writings and Speeches*, I, 263.   [67] Langford, *Writings and Speeches*, I, 263.
[68] Langford, *Writings and Speeches*, IX, 124.   [69] Langford, *Writings and Speeches*, IX, 128.
[70] Langford, *Writings and Speeches*, IX, 128.

of knowledge; the primacy of self-regulation; and the imperfections of economic rationalism.

First, for Burke, the steeled rigidity of legislative mandates cannot capture the heartbeats of experience in social and economic affairs: fluid and intuitive agreements, practices, and understandings between flesh-and-blood human beings. Cold bureaucratic rules do not reflect the many unstated expectations and obligations inherent in the implied contract between the farmer and laborer. And, unlike free-flowing prices, state edicts cannot be changed quickly, but only after being sanctioned through formal institutional procedures.

Second, Burke illustrates the difficulty of economic policy in advancing the well-being of producers and consumers because of the inherent limitations of human knowledge. In his judgment, effectual state regulations of market activity demand a vast amount of information about particular situations, labor contracts, and relationships. They require the "exactest detail of circumstances" in order to arrive at a sound regulation. And, as Burke outlines in the first block quotation, market regulations face a double barrier of epistemological certitude: first, they must discover general principles about the best way to dictate "experiment and enquiry" regarding economic activity. Then, informed by the intricate details of local circumstance, legislation must create new principles to apply to a "practical legislative proceeding." Such is· a looming standard for lawmakers, in Burke's judgment. By contrast, private market contracts signal many intuitions of agreement between the farmer and laborer on a local level that the individual mind cannot fully penetrate.

This pretense of knowledge inspired passionate cries for the state to intervene in economic affairs. The individual who champions wage regulations "supposes or pretends that the farmer and the labourer have opposite interests."[71] He presumes that "the farmer oppresses the labourer; and that a gentleman called a justice of peace, is the protector of the latter, and a controul and restraint on the former."[72] Yet the magistrates who set wage rates "confide more in their abilities than is fit, and suppose them capable of more than any natural abilities, fed with no other than the provender furnished by their own private speculations, can accomplish."[73]

From Burke's perspective, then, wage regulations were not simply a question of authority; they also represented a swollen sense of confidence and importance on the part of the regulators by suggesting that public officials possessed sufficient information to control the labor market in a way that would help the needy. If the magistrate could not apprehend the blur of details within fluid and private market relations, how could he be certain that the law would actually benefit either the farmer or the laborer? The idea that a distant statesman, removed from the rhythmic pulse of local economic activity, knew

---

[71] Langford, *Writings and Speeches*, IX, 124.   [72] Langford, *Writings and Speeches*, IX, 124.
[73] Langford, *Writings and Speeches*, IX, 124.

the best interests of contracting parties better than they did themselves revealed a case of exploded ignorance.

Third, in his comments, Burke suggests that the gift of self-regulation, rather than the magistrate, effectively mediates relationships between employers and employees. The "tact" that "regulates without difficulty" is the guiding hand of the market, weaving and threading seemingly disparate economic activities into a steady but lively social order. This self-organizing principle escapes conceptual definition, for it remains beyond the capacities of the human intellect to articulate verbally with precision. The implication is that the power of self-regulation drastically reduces the importance of the regulator. For Burke, if individuals can make informed decisions about their particular social and economic circumstances, they will not need regulators to establish wage rates and terms of contract for them.

These three principles are the pillars for the fourth conclusion we can derive from the preceding quotations: Burke's thought signals his broad disgust with the intrusion of abstract rationality into organic social arrangements. He uses the word "rational" or its cognates in *Thoughts and Details* once, and not in the context of abstract thinking.[74] Yet the philosophical basis for his critique of government intervention in the letter rests on a conception of the limits of theoretic reason. This understanding emerges in *Thoughts and Details* in his comment that the rationality of economic legislation, intended to correct the seeming injustices of the labor market, was embodied by the "surest general principles," "firm and luminous general principles," and "very stiff, and often inapplicable rule[s]," as Burke writes.

In his view, however, these mandates simplified the intuitive and elusive realities of free-flowing market activities. The gap between stiff legislative principles and concrete market experience mirrors the vast space separating abstract reason from circumstance. This kind of reason is thus incapable of coordinating the diffusion of goods to many consumers, thereby severing the link between private market activity and the common good. To the extent that the abstract rationality of state edicts was true, its applicability to specific economic conditions was false.

Consider Burke's description of the different types of labor, as discussed in Chapter 3. He submits this classificatory framework to show that the imposition of a single numerical wage neglects to take into account the diversity of agricultural labor. Do men who work part-time deserve the same salary as men who work full-time? Do children who work less than their mothers deserve the same wage? Should an older man with fewer agricultural skills be paid the same as a younger man with greater dexterity? Should a younger man with limited experience be paid the same as an older man with more experience? Government wage mandates did not accurately reflect the "just proportions" between a laborer's earnings and an employer's provision of

---

[74] Burke refers to the "happiness of the rational man" (Langford, *Writings and Speeches*, IX, 122).

food and shelter, as Burke contends. Economic legislation that cements general principles into law overlooks the "thousand nameless circumstances" of convention, contract, and custom.

What Burke is really arguing is that market regulations, at least those he elaborates on in *Thoughts and Details*, are fruitless attempts to quantify the unquantifiable. Although legislators and magistrates possessed greater political and legal power than the common man, they simply were not capable of measuring the experiences and struggles of the laboring classes through strict numerical calculation. Laws, as Burke observes, will struggle to compute "just" wages with precision because of the constraints of human knowledge in determining what exactly constitutes a "just" salary. Burke's argument is not that the internal grain trade should be free of all rules, but that many of those rules can be best formed through private interactions between individual parties, not by men in government. Abstract reason was an insufficient guide for the enrichment of a people and the establishment of justice in a commercial economy.

4.7 RATIONALISM AND THE HAYEK CONNECTION

Drawing from Burke's insights into the limits of economic rationalism, we can now firmly discern the philosophical compatibility between Burke and Hayek on the subject of political economy. In his many writings, Hayek, like Burke, praises the price system in free markets for channeling the flow of resources with greater efficiency than could the single human mind or multiple minds. Hayek's endorsement of market prices is part of his broader defense of market activity, in which he argues that theoretic rationalism cannot capture the complexities of private economic activity that, fastened by the rule of law, produces a largely self-regulating harmony.

In other words, Hayek professes a deep contempt for the idea that rational economic planning, as embodied in government-mandated laws regulating prices, wages, and contracts, can distribute resources in a more judicious manner than individuals can on the basis of organic association. For Hayek, individuals have a mixed assortment of goals and preferences in civil society, and seek to fulfill these wants in markets. How, then, would it be possible for state officials, detached from the lived experience of these individuals, to identify their many inclinations and wishes? "[I]t would be impossible for any mind to comprehend the infinite variety of different needs of different people which compete for the available resources and to attach a definite weight to each," he writes in *The Road to Serfdom*.[75] For Hayek and Burke, even the brightest individual mind is only aware of a minuscule portion of the sweeping index of knowledge necessary to ensure the smooth coordination of economic activity.

[75] F. A. Hayek, *The Road to Serfdom*, ed. Bruce Caldwell (Chicago: The University of Chicago Press, 2007), 102.

Therefore, rather than reflecting the French school of "constructivist rationalism," which elevated abstract reason above concrete experience as the touchstone of knowledge, Burke, according to Hayek in the *Constitution of Liberty*, exemplified the "British tradition."[76] This latter tradition recognized that social institutions and practices, such as market activity, blossomed from the slowly accumulated insights and discoveries of knowledge spanning generations. The British tradition, Hayek writes, comprehended "how institutions and morals, language and law, have evolved by a process of cumulative growth and that it is only with and within this framework that human reason has grown and can successfully operate."[77] The flowing channel of collective wisdom, instead of the expertise of the solitary mind, was the lifeblood of civilization.

Hayek's insights display a noticeable continuity with Burke's critical assessment of wage and labor regulations in *Thoughts and Details*. The two thinkers both condemned the rationalism lurking within laws and edicts that ignored the sheer multiplicity of situations and conditions in dynamic market economies. For Burke, "interest, habit, and the tacit convention" facilitated a liberal system of exchange, similar to how Hayek's notion of experiential knowledge guided the coordination of economic activities throughout the generations. In their judgments, abstract rationalism stiffened the diversity of circumstance into rules of steel.

In other words, government restraint allowed private men and women to use their specific knowledge of time and place to satisfy their market desires, thereby permitting an element of flexibility and adaptation in the exercise of individual judgment. As Hayek explains, the "particular circumstances of time and place" relies on the premise that "practically every individual has some advantage over all others in that he possesses unique information of which beneficial use might be made, but of which use can be made only if the decisions depending on it are left to him or are made with his active coöperation."[78]

This remark is strongly compatible with *Thoughts and Details*. For Burke and Hayek, an individual is in a far better position than a government official, or any other person for that matter, to assess which goods and services will satisfy his market preferences because he knows a great deal more about his life than third parties. As we shall see in our discussion of the French Revolution, Burke's and Hayek's respective thought was not synonymous, and there even remains friction between Hayek's notion of spontaneous order and Burke's conception of the growth of civilization. For now, however, we may take note of their shared conclusion that the locus of epistemological authority in exchange economies should reside in those immediately involved in producing, consuming, and trading, since the mysterious motions of commerce were too elusive to be fully understood by fallible men in power.

---

[76] Hayek, *Constitution of Liberty*, 110. [77] Hayek, *Constitution of Liberty*, 112.
[78] Hayek, "Use of Knowledge," 521–522.

The Butcher's Meat Bill

Consider an episode in Burke's life that is rarely discussed but nevertheless captured his critique of abstract reason and defense of the virtues of local knowledge. In March 1776, the House of Commons debated a piece of legislation called the Butcher's Meat Bill, which would have increased regulations of the meat trade of butchers. It mandated that livestock, upon reaching the market, be slaughtered only after a certain period of time in order to ensure high quality meat.[79] Advocates of the bill argued that the quick slaughter of animals, without giving them time for rest, would produce tainted meat for consumer purchase.

Burke opposed the legislation in *Speech on Butcher's Meat Bill*, which he presented to Parliament on March 26, 1776. He first claims in the speech that the bill would encourage a monopoly by hurting small butchers who, not being able to afford to keep the animals they might buy, would not purchase them in warm weather.[80] This point hints at Burke's aversion to economic monopoly. His next argument signals a keen awareness of the particular circumstances of time and place. According to *St. James's Chronicle*, Burke "insisted that poor People would buy Meat a little tainted, and that Means might be devised by Salt, Spices, etc. to preserve it from Putrefaction, so as in the End, to render it both wholesome and palatable Food."[81] While consumers of fortunate means may prefer to buy higher quality beef at a dear price, individuals from more modest backgrounds may choose to accept the trade-offs of purchasing lower quality food at a cheaper cost.

Burke is calling attention to the colorful diversity of preference in market economies: particular individuals desire particular goods of particular qualities at particular prices. Disturbing the natural circulation of trade, then, would prevent individuals from purchasing goods agreeable to their unique tastes and expectations. In this case, Burke conveyed that the Butcher's Meat Bill would generate the unintended consequence of harming the poor by limiting their access to meat. As he understood the issue, consumers of humble means harbored deeper knowledge about their personal circumstances than legislators, and were thus in a better position to judge whether market prices were commensurate with variations in the quality of goods offered in the mart. Regulating the meat market in this manner, to employ Hayekian lexicon, reflected a gross pretense of knowledge.

---

[79] Langford, *Writings and Speeches*, III, 224.

[80] Langford, *Writings and Speeches*, III, 224–225.

[81] Langford, *Writings and Speeches*, III, 225. Burke also notes that wine had once been considered poisonous before experience showed that it actually generated "Chearfulness and good Humour."

4.8 BURKE AND ADAM SMITH

Hayek located Adam Smith as well as Burke in the "British tradition" of anti-rationalist liberty because Smith, like Burke (and, we should add, David Hume), nursed a sharp distrust of planned systems of economic organization, in Hayek's judgment.[82] When examining Burke's approach to political economy, it is indeed difficult to ignore intriguing intellectual relationship between Burke and Smith, both of whom were active in similar literary and social circles in the latter half of the eighteenth century.[83] As Robert Bisset reported in an early biography of Burke, Smith, according to Burke, "told him, after they had conversed on subjects of political economy, that he was the only man, who, without communication, thought on these topics exactly as he did."[84] Both thinkers embraced the general principles of market liberty, contended that a providential force transformed enlightened self-interest into collective advantage, and believed that the spread of commerce promoted public opulence and the common good. More deeply, Burke's and Smith's economic thought anticipated Hayek's important insight that the limits of the individual intellect posed great difficulties for government officials to effectively coordinate the distribution of resources in a complex society.

Such similarities between Burke and Smith explain Burke's attraction to the commercial principles outlined in the *Wealth of Nations*. According to Dugald

---

[82] Hayek, *Constitution of Liberty*, 110.

[83] For instance, they were members of Samuel Johnson's famed London-based Literary Club, which also included, at various points, Edward Gibbon, Joshua Reynolds, and Oliver Goldsmith. Burke was one of the original members of the Club. Smith was elected in 1775, the calendar year before the *Wealth of Nations* was published. Yet they probably did not meet each other for the first time until two years later, in 1777 (Ernest Campbell Mossner and Ian Simpson Ross, eds., *The Correspondence of Adam Smith* (Indianapolis: Liberty Fund, 1987), 47n4). See, among many, the following sources for additional information on their personal and intellectual relationship: Rae, *Life of Adam Smith*, 46–47, 387–397, including Jacob Viner's "Guide to John Rae's *Life of Adam Smith*," 23–33; C. R. Fay, "Burke and Adam Smith: Being a Lecture delivered at The Queen's University of Belfast" (Belfast: Queen's University of Belfast, 1956); Kevin M. Wagner, "Understanding the Divisions Within Conservative Thought: Edmund Burke vs. Adam Smith," *Florida Political Chronicle* 21 (2012): 11–24; Himmelfarb, *Idea of Poverty*, 66–71; William Clyde Dunn, "Adam Smith and Edmund Burke: Complementary Contemporaries," *Southern Economic Journal* 7 (1941): 330–346; and Winch, *Riches and Poverty*, 125–220. See also my article on their respective views on Britain's East India Company: "The Limits of Mercantile Administration: Adam Smith and Edmund Burke on Britain's East India Company," *Journal of the History of Economic Thought* 41 (2019): 369–392.

[84] Robert Bisset, *The Life of Edmund Burke*, vol. II (London: George Cawthorn, British Library 1800), 429. Even though there remains no hard historical evidence to confirm this anecdote, that Bisset's biography was published in 1800, only three years after Burke passed away, suggests that Bisset's retelling of the story may not have strayed too far from the truth. Note that Bisset first published his biography of Burke in 1798, but it does not appear that he included this anecdote between Burke and Smith in it. See Bisset, *The Life of Edmund Burke* (London: George Cawthorn, British Library, 1798).

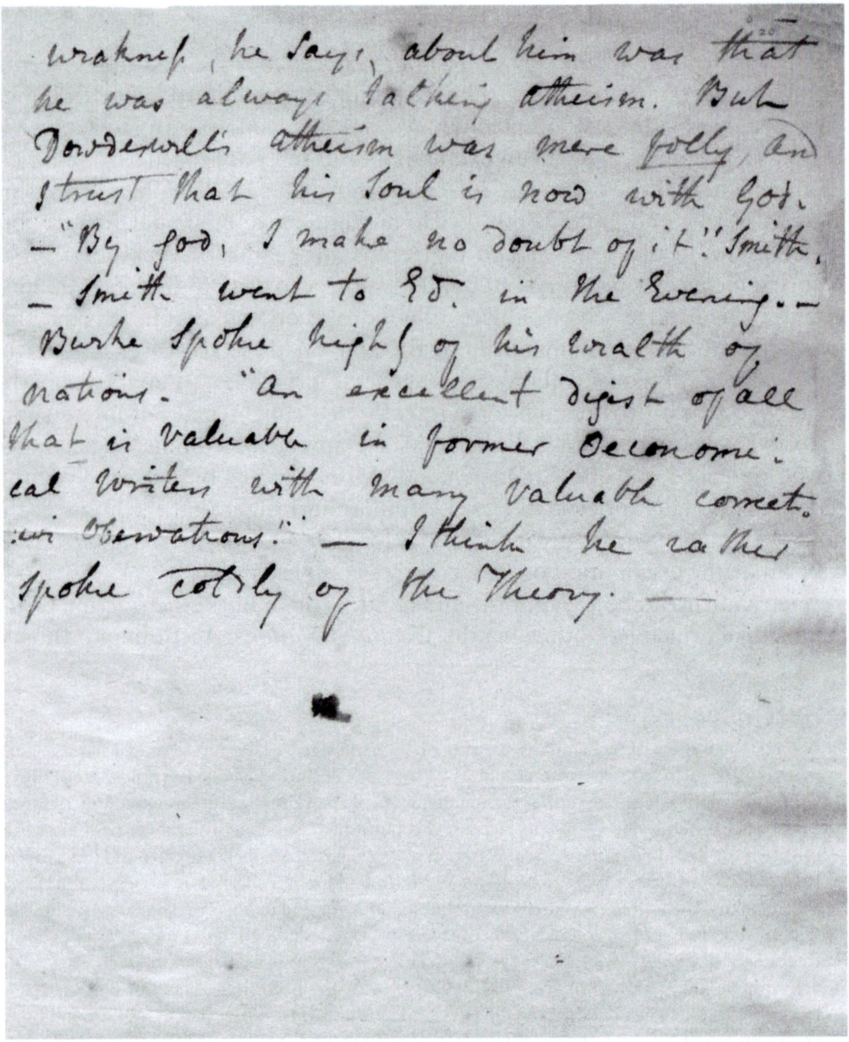

20
weakness, he says, about him was that
he was always talking atheism. But
Dowdeswell's atheism was mere folly, and
I trust that his Soul is now with God.
—"By god, I make no doubt of it!" Smith.
— Smith went to Ed. in the Evening.—
Burke spoke highly of his Wealth of
nations. "An excellent digest of all
that is valuable in former Oeconomical Writers with many valuable correct-
-ive Observations!" — I think he rather
spoke coldly of the Theory. —

FIGURE 4.1 *Memoir Written on a Visit to Lord Lauderdale with Mr Burke and Adam Smith* (1784)
Source: Edinburgh University Library, Dc.6.111, ff. 18–20

Stewart, Burke noted in a conversation in 1784 that the book was an "excellent digest of all that is valuable in former Oeconomical writers" and included "many valuable corrective" observations.[85] See Figure 4.1.

[85] Dugald Stewart, *Memoir Written on a Visit to Lord Lauderdale with Mr Burke and Adam Smith* (1784), Dc. 6.111, Edinburgh University Library, Centre for Research Collections. This excerpt

Even more, according to the editors of the 1800 edition of *Thoughts and Details*, Burke was "consulted, and the greatest deference was paid to his opinions by Dr. Adam Smith, in the progress of the celebrated work on the Wealth of Nations."[86] (Historical evidence suggests Burke exerted some, but not a strong, influence on the composition of the *Wealth of Nations*, as will be described shortly.) It is also worth noting that the *Annual Register*, the periodical Burke edited and wrote for up until the mid-1760s, published a favorable review, and excerpted the introduction, of the *Wealth of Nations* in 1776. The review praised the work's "sagacity and penetration of mind, extent of views, accurate distinction, just and natural connection, and dependence of parts."[87] Clearly Smith's economic thought enticed the mind of Burke.

Burke's Influence on the *Wealth of Nations*

The general symmetry of Burke's and Smith's support for market liberty did include digressions and strains in their respective beliefs on the pace of commercial reform. Recall that Burke, in *Letter to a Noble Lord*, may have been referring to Smith when he claimed that "[g]reat and learned men" had "deigned to communicate" with Burke on matters of political economy.[88] Then consider a compelling argument Jacob Viner has put forth about Burke's possible limited influence on the *Wealth of Nations*, and on Smith's science of political economy: in 1773, Burke begrudgingly supported Pownall's Act, the bill that reformed, but still retained, British bounties on grain exports.[89] In a subsequent edition of the *Wealth of Nations*, most likely the one published in 1778,[90] around a year after Burke probably met Smith for the first time, Smith inserted into the text the following remarks about the legislation, with reference to the distinguished Athenian lawgiver Solon:

So far, therefore, this law seems to be inferior to the antient system. With all its imperfections, however, we may perhaps say of it what was said of the laws of Solon, that, though not the best in itself, it is the best which the interests, prejudices, and temper of the times would admit of. It may perhaps in due time prepare the way for a better.[91]

---

from Stewart's memoir appears to be the strongest evidence to date demonstrating Burke's embrace of the economic principles in the *Wealth of Nations*.

[86] Burke, *Thoughts and Details*, vi.

[87] "The Account of Books for 1776," *The Annual Register, For the Year 1776* (London: J. Dodsley, 1788), 241. The review notes Smith's "diffuse" writing style. It is interesting that this remark is similar to Burke's comment in his September 1759 letter to Smith that the *Theory of Moral Sentiments* was "too diffuse" at times (Mossner and Ross, *Correspondence of Adam Smith*, 47).

[88] Langford, *Writings and Speeches*, IX, 160.

[89] See "The Corn Laws and Export Bounties," Chapter 3.

[90] See Viner, 26n23, in Rae, *Life of Adam Smith*.

[91] Smith, *Wealth of Nations*, vol. I, 542–543.

These comments possibly reflect a conversation Smith had with Burke, after the initial publication of the *Wealth of Nations* in 1776, about the prudence in modifying trade regulations in an incremental fashion rather than in a single stroke.

Such speculation is further fueled by an anecdote offered by Francis Horner, a Scottish statesman and political economist, in 1804. Horner wrote that Burke, in response to Smith's admonition that the 1773 bounty law had not been fully repealed, told Smith that "it was the privilege of philosophers to conceive their diagrams in geometric accuracy: but the engineer must often impair the symmetry, as well as simplicity of his machine, in order to overcome the irregularities of friction and resistance."[92]

What is more interesting is that Smith added in a Part VI to the sixth edition of the *Theory of Moral Sentiments*,[93] published soon before Smith passed away in 1790, that also referenced Solon in the context of prudence, though not necessarily in specific regard to political economy. "[L]ike Solon, when [the statesman] cannot establish the best system of laws, he will endeavour to establish the best that the people can bear," he wrote.[94] Smith also highlighted the primacy of moderation when he conceded in the *Wealth of Nations* that the incremental reduction of colonial trade regulations, rather than their immediate abolition, might be the wisest course to take in the reform of commercial policy.[95]

This is not to claim that Burke exerted a significant influence on Smith's thought or vice versa. Because both men were independent thinkers, it remains difficult to gauge whether one gained a wholly new insight into an economic subject from the other. In addition, they did not hold the same judgments on all matters relating to political economy, such as the East India Company[96] and the corn bounty.[97] Such differences in many ways reflected the political constraints Burke faced as an elected representative, a consideration we shall explore in greater detail in his discussion of free trade. Furthermore, as will be examined in Chapter 12, perhaps the most important intellectual disparity between Burke and Smith, and Burke and the Scottish Enlightenment in general, stemmed from deeper theoretical

---

[92] Frank Whitson Fetter, ed., *The Economic Writings of Francis Horner in the Edinburgh Review 1802–6* (London: The London School of Economics and Political Science, 1957), 98.

[93] "Introduction," in Adam Smith, *The Theory of Moral Sentiments*, eds. D. D. Raphael and A. L. Macfie (Indianapolis: Liberty Fund, 1984), 44.

[94] Smith, *Theory of Moral Sentiments*, 233. I thank Erik Matson for alerting me to Smith's reference to Solon in this text. Note also that Smith referenced Solon multiple times in the *Lectures on Jurisprudence* in different contexts. See Adam Smith, *Lectures on Jurisprudence*, eds. R. L. Meek, D. D. Raphael, and P. G. Stein (Indianapolis: Liberty Fund, 1982), 38, 62, 64, 130, 228, 231, 410, 462.

[95] See Smith, *Wealth of Nations*, vol. II, 606.

[96] See Collins, "Limits of Mercantile Administration."

[97] See "The Corn Laws and Export Bounties," Chapter 3.

divisions concerning the relation between commerce and virtue in understanding the growth of civilization.

We may conclude for now, however, that Burke and Smith carefully navigated the tension between the pursuit of economic liberty and the pressures of politics in the eighteenth century. While the two thinkers retained the view that many commercial restrictions were unnecessary, they also recognized that existing political and social prejudices posed a hindrance at times to the advancement of freedom. They formed a symbiotic power in this regard: while Smith was proposing a grander theoretical blueprint for an economic environment governed by the natural laws of commerce, Burke was active in the British Parliament in seeking to apply the principles of market liberty to concrete legislation.

4.9 CONCLUSION

Taking into account the last three chapters, allow us to submit some final thoughts on *Thoughts and Details*. Although the memorial serves as the fulcrum for understanding Burke's economic thought, it must be restated that the writing suffers from limitations intrinsic to ad hoc tracts. As mentioned, Burke originally wrote the memorandum in a conditional fashion; he addressed a particular historical situation, the severe social and economic stresses in mid-1790s England; and he delivered his critique of government intervention in response to particular legislative proposals, such as regulating wages and establishing public granaries. The letter was short and poorly organized, and Burke admitted he wrote it in a hasty fashion.

Even with such limitations, *Thoughts and Details* offers the sturdiest philosophical foundation among all of Burke's writings and speeches for his defense of market liberty. It furnishes his most considered statements on the limits of human knowledge in regulating the circulation of scarce resources, and illuminates his enlightened comprehension of the inner workings of the competitive price system and supply and demand laws. The tract further reveals Burke's keen awareness of the varieties of labor in agriculture and the complexities of market phenomena in general. Understanding his economic thought is not possible without grasping his insights into these crucial themes in *Thoughts and Details*.

The conclusion to Chapter 3 argued that Burke's embrace of market liberty was consistent throughout his public life. Yet this judgment still does not resolve perhaps the most pressing question in the study of *Thoughts and Details*: did Burke's support for the natural laws of commerce contradict his broader political thought that praised the virtues of prudence and tradition, as many scholars have argued?[98] Judith Shklar, representing this perspective, insists that there is "no trace" of the "complexities of social life" in Burke's economic

---

[98] See "Interpretations of Burke's Political Economy," Introduction.

reflections in *Thoughts and Details* and elsewhere.[99] She argues that Burke "was one of the first social theorists to base his economic and political ideas on entirely opposed principles."[100]

These comments illustrate perhaps the most fundamental misinterpretation of *Thoughts and Details* as a vindication of abstract economic principles over the complexity of economic circumstance. For Burke, a defense of the natural laws of commerce protected, rather than offended, the varieties of human experience. A free market in grain permitted Englishmen and women to make economic decisions based on their private desires unique to their particular circumstances. The competitive price system reflected the infinite fluctuations of production and consumption. And the preservation of supply and demand laws enabled farmers and laborers to make contingent employment arrangements based on their shifting preferences.

Such fluid activity in the market exemplified the many dimensions of social life that could not be measured by a ruler. We may apply this observation to his broader political theory. As Burke wrote in the *Reflections*, "The nature of man is intricate; the objects of society are of the greatest possible complexity; and therefore no simple disposition or direction of power can be suitable either to man's nature, or to the quality of his affairs."[101] Rigid government edicts and the simplistic contrivances of radical constitutions – such as the new constitution of revolutionary France – scorned the complexity of man, while state restraint preserved and nourished its diffuse parts. This powerful convergence of Burke's economic thought and political thought draws out his sensitivity to the complicated character of human activity and human association.

Hence Burke is at pains in *Thoughts and Details* to highlight the intrinsic constraints of human knowledge. Economic regulations "never can provide the just proportions between earning and salary on the one hand, and nutriment on the other."[102] Safeguarding the integrity of Burke's "implied contract" from the designs of state supervision, then, affirmed the multilayered realities of market exchange. "[I]nterest, habit, and the tacit convention" emerged from "a thousand nameless circumstances" to produce public prosperity.[103] National legislators and local magistrates were not capable of anticipating these nameless circumstances; therefore, their efforts to produce fair wages and prices would struggle to promote fair employment contracts between farmers and laborers and equitable dealing on the part of middlemen. For Burke, the strict boundaries of the human intellect imposed heavy constraints on legislators and administrators to coordinate the efficient flow of resources according to notions of abstract reason.

Yet even if Burke's defense of market principles illustrated his recognition of social complexity, does his appraisal of voluntary contracts in general signal a shift away from his impassioned support for tradition in the *Reflections* and

[99] Shklar, *After Utopia*, 225.   [100] Shklar, *After Utopia*, 225.
[101] Langford, *Writings and Speeches*, VIII, 112.
[102] Langford, *Writings and Speeches*, IX, 128.   [103] Langford, *Writings and Speeches*, IX, 128.

elsewhere? This possibility first demands clarification of Burke's conception of "tradition." In the *Reflections*, he defended the rich heritage of British constitutional liberty not for the sake of blind veneration but for allowing for the conservation of the kingdom's best traditions and reformation of its worst practices. The wheel of change was thus fundamental to Burke's embrace of "tradition" – and to his embrace of progress: social growth required perpetual adaptations and modifications to settled customs and institutions. A refusal to reform presaged the demise of civil society.

These tenets of Burke's political thought align with his support for market liberty. Man's needs for food and shelter were best met by the easy flow of goods in mediums of market exchange: as Burke explains in *Thoughts and Details*, the competitive price system permitted constant adjustments and readjustments to shifting human preferences and to the supply and demand of provisions. Yet forced supervision of market activity, such as the government regulation of wages and the control of resources, marked a departure away from the steady self-regulation of voluntary contracts in the internal grain trade, thereby sowing the seeds for even more instability in the agricultural economy that had already been rattled by poor harvests. Burke's endorsement of market liberty and front against the arbitrary power of the magistracy, then, was also an endorsement of socioeconomic order, relative to the unpredictable conditions of farm management, such as the weather.

On this note, C. B. Macpherson has argued that Burke's support for exchange economies was a defense of a traditional social and economic model that had been cemented by the Glorious Revolution in 1688–1689. "[B]y Burke's time the capitalist order *had in fact been* the traditional order in England for a whole century," Macpherson writes because the Glorious Revolution had affirmed the principles of property law and the political institutions necessary for sustained capitalist production and accumulation.[104] J. G. A. Pocock posits an overlapping argument. "The defence of a commercial order in politics, society and morality, wherever it occurs down to Burke's time and after, is invariably a defence of the Whig regime and generally of natural aristocracy," he writes.[105]

There were, of course, general liberalizing tendencies in British politics following the Glorious Revolution. Macpherson's and Pocock's interpretations, however, understate the novelty of the efforts Burke undertook to facilitate economic reform in his age. Burke's stances against laws banning forestalling, regrating, and engrossing, in 1772 and 1787, offer telling examples. His efforts during these episodes were not a mere renewal of British traditions of economic liberty; they constituted a swift rejection of laws that had been carved into national statutes since the reign of Edward VI in the sixteenth century (which, albeit, were enforced to varying degrees). Local attempts to prevent forestalling in English cities and towns, we should note, including those implemented by guilds, dated back further to the late thirteenth

---

[104] Macpherson, *Burke*, 63.   [105] Pocock, *Virtue, Commerce, and History*, 195.

century.[106] And, as we shall learn, Burke initiated his campaigns in support of West Indian and Anglo-Irish trade at times when trade restrictions had been increasing, not decreasing.

In addition, while the steady exchange of goods certainly existed in pre-eighteenth-century Britain, the widespread diffusion of commerce had a particularly distinctive impact on the time period in which Burke was active in public life. Assuming that the start of the Industrial Revolution can be dated roughly to 1760, Burke's defense of commercial activity, including but not limited to the grain trade, was a defense of a relatively new phenomenon in British society – and a bold one at that, considering that the concomitant forces of population growth and industrialization aggravated the social and economic difficulties facing struggling laborers in England's agricultural sector. For Burke, the principles of supply and demand preserved market order. But this type of market order, of which he was a prominent advocate, acquired a wholly new form in late eighteenth-century Britain.

We may take Burke's praise of market liberty to be consistent with his broader conception of tradition, then, not necessarily because it was a seamless empirical reflection of established practices and attitudes in English society at the time. Instead, Burke's support for freedom of exchange was harmonious with the conceptual substance of his notion of tradition: human activities require the space to adjust to shifting circumstances. The growth of civilization called for the refinement of past practice. Liberty in the mart – not restrictions on trading activities – permitted economic corrections and reforms to emerge over time. By breaking with lingering English traditions and opinions hostile to forestalling, regrating, and engrossing and reforming Britain's commercial system, among various economic policies he pressed for, Burke was not blindly venerating the past. Rather, he was upholding two key functions of his understanding of tradition as the root of change and the edifice of ordered liberty. Modifying convention to meet the new demands of markets served as an engine of preservation and improvement.

Returning to the arguments posed by Himmelfarb and others, the additional defect of their contention that Burke's rationalist principles of political economy in *Thoughts and Details* breach his defense of tradition and prudence is the assumption that reason is at fundamental odds with tradition. Burke famously declared that the prejudices of tradition, properly understood, reflected, rather than militated against, reason by representing the accumulated wisdom of many generations. He understood that the collected knowledge of market order derived

---

[106] Britnell, "Forstall, *Forestalling and the Statute of Forestallers*," 89–102. As Britnell explains, this conception of forestalling was distinct from the older idea of *forstall*, the act of ambushing a person, typically carrying merchandise, on a highway. This definition did not relate directly to the market activities of middlemen. Furthermore, note that the Crown and local courts sometimes defined forestalling in different ways, and that enforcement against offenders was applied inconsistently, if at all.

its nourishment from the principles and application of supply and demand laws. In Burke's judgment, the perverse form of rationality – Jacobin ideology – was the presumption that the state could, and should, contravene such laws for the ostensible benefit of the people. Government paternalism would shatter the delicate frame of market wisdom built up from the natural course of free commerce.

Yet how could Burke's endorsement of market liberty signal a defense of economic order if the fluctuations of the grain trade in mid-1790s England encouraged disorder in communities? Burke was conscious that the agricultural sector was prone to temporary instabilities stemming from the unpredictability of weather conditions and agricultural cultivation, as mentioned, such as the weak harvests of 1794 and 1795. But this reality of the agricultural economy in the eighteenth century confirmed Burke's broader conception of market order in *Thoughts and Details*: a steady adherence to supply and demand laws would be able to absorb these shocks in the long run and reestablish economic activity on a firmer basis. Burke believed that transactional exchange in itself was not sufficient to preserve European civilization. But he did maintain, as he outlined in *Thoughts and Details*, that market economies were more likely than arbitrary government intervention to satisfy the needs of producers and consumers in an effectual and orderly fashion. Tact, indeed, could regulate without difficulty.

PART III

THE BRITISH CONSTITUTION AND ECONOMICAL REFORM

5

The British Constitution: Burke's Program of Economical Reform and the Role of the State

Prudence, and a calm review of the financial powers of a country, were the first objects of a Statesman.[1]

Edmund Burke, *Speech on Army Estimates*, 1778

Here Lieth Ed Burke [reads one], Oeconomist Extraordinary to his Majesty,
To Save his breath He welcom'd death.[2]

All Alive or the Political Churchyard, 1783

5.1 INTRODUCTION

Even though Burke was a proponent of market liberty, he maintained that there was a role – an important role – for the state in civil society. Burke touched upon this matter briefly in *Thoughts and Details*, arguing that government should provide for the common defense, maintain order, charter corporations, and raise revenue. Because of the tract's ad hoc nature, however, he does not sufficiently elaborate on these roles, giving the false impression that his vision of the state was conceived through a tight libertarian framework.

Burke's *Speech on Economical Reform* helps fill this gap by giving harder definition to his conception of the state. Secondary accounts of the oration focus heavily on its constitutional and political implications, and for appropriate

---

[1] Langford, *Writings and Speeches*, III, 396. This speech on December 14, 1778 was different from Burke's *Speech on the Army Estimates* of 1790, when Burke first introduced his thoughts on the French Revolution in a public forum.
[2] Nicholas K. Robinson, *Edmund Burke: A Life in Caricature* (New Haven and London: Yale University Press, 1996), 52. The quotation was from a contemporary political cartoon. See the British Museum 6256, 9 August 1783, published by B. Pownall.

reasons. *Speech on Economical Reform* has earned a lasting reputation for displaying Burke's earnest efforts to reduce the corruption and patronage of the Crown in England during the latter part of the American war, and was part of his broader attempt to rescue the integrity of the British constitution from its baser administrative deformities.[3] Additionally, the speech reflected Burke's celebrated trustee theory of representation in action: he lent a sensitive ear to the popular movement at the time remonstrating in support of government reform, and employed his own independent judgment to channel the movement's energies into a systematic program of institutional change.

Yet *Speech on Economical Reform* does more than present a laundry list of government offices to cut, for the speech also supplies significant clues about his conception of political economy, broadly construed. It elucidates Burke's beliefs on markets, contracts, and commerce that have been neglected in secondary accounts of the speech, and provides commentary on profit and transactional exchange that anticipate some of his most profound remarks in the *Reflections* on the underlying character of civil order. The address casts further light on Burke's vision of reform as a program of principle. These insights do not constitute the heart of *Speech on Economical Reform*, but they do outline contours of Burke's economic theory that merit our heightened attention. When taken together, they reveal a body of thought both sympathetic to markets and aware of their limits in assessing the true value of public service.

More important, *Speech on Economical Reform* tackles an elemental question of statesmanship that would occupy Burke's mind throughout his entire political life, and in particular regard to the East India Company and the French Revolution: how can a state secure a steady revenue stream while preserving the liberties of the people? For a functioning state, government needs money; but for a free state, its subjects need liberty. This seeming contradiction was the underlying puzzle motivating Burke's engagement with matters of public finance in *Speech on Economical Reform* and his other writings and speeches.

In *Letter to a Noble Lord*, published more than two decades after he gave *Speech on Economical Reform*, Burke presented a key distinction between parsimony and economy that would shape his efforts in reforming the administrative structure of the British government:

[M]ere parsimony is not oeconomy ... Expence, and great expence, may be an essential part in true oeconomy. If parsimony were to be considered as one of the kinds of that virtue, there is however another and an higher oeconomy. Oeconomy is a distributive virtue, and consists not in saving, but in selection. Parsimony requires no providence, no sagacity, no powers of combination, no comparison, no judgment ... The other oeconomy has larger views. It demands a discriminating judgment, and a firm sagacious mind.

---

[3] For a study of Burke's influence on public administration theory, see Akhlaque Haque, "Edmund Burke: Limits of Reason in Public Administration Theory" (PhD thesis, Cleveland State University, 1994).

It shuts one door to impudent importunity, only to open another, and a wider, to unpresuming merit. If none but meritorious service or real talent were to be rewarded, this nation has not wanted, and this nation will not want, the means of rewarding all the service it ever will receive, and encouraging all the merit it ever will produce. No state, since the foundation of society, has been impoverished by the species of profusion.[4]

Cheapness was not a virtue in public administration, much less in human affairs. The wisdom of economy lied in the ability of statesmen to dispense reward when reward was warranted and restrict reward when it was not. Responsible statesmanship reflected prudence of selection and discretion of judgment, not cold miserliness.

Speech on Economical Reform, then, is as significant for what it defends as for what it seeks to change: by endeavoring to reform the British government, Burke is announcing his firm belief *in* the state as an essential constituent of civil society. For him, tightening the scope of government created the institutional conditions necessary for public officials to carry out their responsibilities in an effectual manner. A leaner bureaucracy bred a selective yet vigorous state. The principles of public administration animating *Speech on Economical Reform* are fundamental to Burke's conception of political economy.

5.2 WYVILL'S MOVEMENT AND THE SPIRIT OF CONSTITUTIONAL REFORM

As the British government imposed costly taxes to finance loans for its war against the Americans in the late 1770s, Englishmen grew increasingly dispirited over what they perceived to be corruptions of the government's administrative practices. Empirical observation suggests that nefarious patronage did not increase dramatically under King George III and Lord North in the 1770s and early 1780s, if at all.[5] Nevertheless, with popular confidence in the North ministry diminishing rapidly, the public believed that the government was in severe need of institutional correction in order to cleanse itself of the political and financial improprieties of the Crown and Parliament.[6]

In late 1779, Reverend Christopher Wyvill, a wealthy Anglican clergyman from Yorkshire, set in motion a reform movement, the Yorkshire Association,

---

[4] Langford, *Writings and Speeches*, IX, 162.
[5] See Ian R. Christie, *Myth and Reality in Late-Eighteenth-Century British Politics and Other Papers* (Berkeley and Los Angeles: University of California Press, 1970), 299–300.
[6] The following sources were used for background information on the political context of *Speech on Economical Reform*: Langford, *Writings and Speeches*, III, 30–35, 466–467, 476, 481–483; Langford, *Writings and Speeches*, IV, 46, 65; Lock, *Edmund Burke*, vol. I, 446–459; Bourke, *Empire & Revolution*, 425–428; E. A. Reitan, "The Civil List in Eighteenth-Century British Politics: Parliamentary Supremacy versus the Independence of the Crown," *The Historical Journal* 9 (1966): 318–337; and Ian R. Christie, "Economical Reform and 'The Influence of the Crown', 1780," *The Cambridge Historical Journal* 12 (1956): 144–154.

which proposed remedies for such ailments.[7] The movement desired institutional changes in Parliament, including shorter electoral terms and the expansion of country seats in the House of Commons, and economical reform, such as the curbing of corruption in government and the reduction of royal sinecures. Although Wyvill's vision prompted the interest of churchmen and the propertied classes, strands of the movement expressed sympathy for more extreme constitutional alterations to the elemental structure of the British government, including universal male suffrage.

These radical exhortations stirred anxieties among the Rockingham Whigs, an opposition party at the time whose members, including Burke, were committed to sustaining the aristocratic traditions of the British constitution. In late 1779 and early 1780, however, even the Rockinghams could not ignore the speed and force of the reform movement. More than half of the counties in England had issued petitions for economical reform by April 1780, and around one-fifth of the total electorate had signed these petitions, according to conservative estimates from Ian R. Christie.[8]

In the unfolding drama inspired by Wyvill's movement, Burke and the Rockingham Whigs confronted the opportunity to fight the undue influence of George III in the House of Commons and purify government of its most profligate financial malignancies and superfluities – two prime objects of "economical reform," as understood in eighteenth-century England's vocabulary. But the Rockingham faction aimed to distinguish itself from the radical strands in Wyvill's movement by undertaking a more moderate approach to political reform, one that would restrain or abolish the British government's worst deformities while shielding the constitution from the provocations of radical egalitarian sentiment.

Burke first introduced the Rockinghams' general plan to the House of Commons on December 15, 1779, little more than two weeks after Wyvill had invited county freeholders to a meeting at York to draft a petition for Parliament in favor of government reform.[9] "[T]he whole of our grievances are owing to the fatal and overgrown influence of the Crown; and that influence itself to our enormous prodigality," Burke asserted in his first speech on the plan, *Speech on Public Expenses*.[10] He explained that his reforms would save £200,000 per year and "cut off the quantity of influence" representing the offices of fifty MPs.[11] Most important, the foremost aim of Burke's scheme

---

[7] See Ian R. Christie, "The Yorkshire Association, 1780–4: A Study in Political Organization," *The Historical Journal* 3 (1960): 144–161.

[8] Ian R. Christie, *Wilkes, Wyvill and Reform: The Parliamentary Reform Movement in British Politics 1760–1785* (London: Macmillan, 1962), 97.

[9] See Earl A. Reitan, *Politics, Finance, and the People: Economical Reform in England in the Age of the American Revolution, 1770–92* (Basingstoke, UK: Palgrave Macmillan, 2007), 32. The meeting was held on December 30. As F. P. Lock notes, Rockingham's political sway in Yorkshire was challenged by Wyvill's efforts (*Edmund Burke*, vol. I, 447).

[10] Langford, *Writings and Speeches*, III, 471.   [11] Langford, *Writings and Speeches*, III, 474.

was to "correct the present prodigal *constitution* of the civil executive government" of Britain.[12]

Burke tucked a compelling remark into *Speech on Public Expenses* that disclosed a self-conscious conception of his natural temper. He first noted that he had long been aware of the delinquencies of the British government and of the remedies necessary to combat them. Burke then said that he hesitated to publicly express his thoughts on reform, however, partially because his personal disposition resisted the rigid imperatives of public economy. "I am not naturally an œconomist," Burke admitted.[13] In this context, his use of "œconomist" did not denote the modern notion of an academic who undertakes research on microeconomic and macroeconomic trends, but suggested rather a person's instinctual attraction to frugality and unsentimental cost-benefit calculation. Burke is conveying that his habit of mind tended to repel against stinginess, an insinuation confirmed by his pattern of financially injudicious behavior, encouraged in part by his philanthropic generosity, throughout his private life.[14] He would later write in *Letter to a Noble Lord*, "I never could drive a hard bargain in my life, concerning any matter whatever; and least of all do I know how to haggle and huckster with merit."[15] Burke was not a tightfisted person by nature.

Speech on Economical Reform offers a dramatic expansion upon the principles set forth in *Speech on Public Expenses*, reflecting Burke's most exhaustive attempt to study the institutional infrastructure and public finances of the British government. As he said in *Speech on Economical Reform*, he "thought it necessary ... to take a comprehensive view of the state of this country; to make a sort of survey of its Jurisdictions, its Estates, and its Establishments."[16] In preparation for his plan of reform, which was to be embodied in a series of Civil Establishment bills, Burke received little input from his party's leaders and was responsible for almost all of the proposed measures drawn out in the speech.[17] Such exertions signaled Burke's growing leadership role in the Rockingham Whigs from 1774 to 1780, during which he spoke more than 400 times in Parliament.[18] One of the party's most influential authorities on financial matters, William Dowdeswell, had passed away in February 1775, leaving a void for an ambitious and industrious MP such as Burke to fill in the service of party and country.

Burke's review of British public administration that informed his Civil Establishment bills marks a penetration of mind and keen attention to detail. Burke plunged himself into the layered intricacies of the British government, consulting a stream of documents to examine and calculate the costs of offices,

---

[12] Langford, *Writings and Speeches*, III, 474.   [13] Langford, *Writings and Speeches*, III, 473.
[14] See "Labor, the Laboring Poor, and the Rich as Trustees," Chapter 3; and "The Roots of Burke's Interest in the Science of Political Economy," Chapter 1.
[15] Langford, *Writings and Speeches*, IX, 161.   [16] Langford, *Writings and Speeches*, III, 495.
[17] Langford, *Writings and Speeches*, III, 4.   [18] Langford, *Writings and Speeches*, III, 2.

the redundancies of departments, and the complex financial ecosystem of their operations.[19] See Figure 5.1 for one such document.

This point must be stressed. While Burke has achieved renown for his theoretical reflections on politics and society, he was also a rigorous student of empirical knowledge, and displayed a fascination with numbers and statistics in his engagement with political economy throughout his adult life. Such affinity for data divulged a high standard of judgment he treasured in his broader political philosophy: the truth of theoretical claims should be rooted in historically verifiable information. "Example," wrote Burke in *Thoughts on the Present Discontents*, is "the only argument of effect in civil life."[20] Abstract assertions cried out for concrete evidence.

Burke deployed this mode of reasoning with reference to the agricultural economy, including his own experiences as a farmer and dealer, in *Thoughts and Details*. His empirical observations also gave bite to the arguments he posed in his other writings and speeches on political economy, including the *Observations*; *Speech on Conciliation with America*; *Ninth Report of Select Committee*; and *Third Letter on a Regicide Peace*. Burke recognized the inherent limits in the quantification of human behavior, as indicated by his distrust of economic rationalism in *Thoughts and Details* and the *Reflections*; but his steady summoning of data to complement his method of research demonstrates a commitment to empirical study that continues to receive unwarranted neglect.

Burke's serious attention to public finance also clarifies his conception of a responsible statesman. There is an understandable temptation to become enchanted by the eloquence of his imaginative expressions of politics in his writings and speeches, yet we must remember that he was also a man of eminently practical inclinations. Burke grasped that judicious statesmanship demanded not simply grand flourishes of shimmering rhetoric in public forums but exacting inspection of government receipt and expense in private study. "Prudence, and a calm review of the financial powers of a country, were the first objects of a Statesman," Burke stated in *Speech on Army Estimates* on December 14, 1778.[21] Spanning back to 1752, when describing his first impressions of London, he wrote that while the House of Commons "not unfrequently exhibits explosions of eloquence that rise superior to those of Greece and Rome," an MP "will make more by the figures of arithmetic than the figures of rhetoric, unless he can get into the trade wind, and then he may sail secure over Pactolean sands."[22]

In fact, as demonstrated by *Speech on Economical Reform*, Burke showed that soaring eloquence and a fine attention to detail were not mutually exclusive. He presented the speech on February 11, 1780 to an unusually

---

[19] Langford, *Writings and Speeches*, III, 6–7. I thank Warren Elofson for his insights into this matter.

[20] Langford, *Writings and Speeches*, II, 296.   [21] Langford, *Writings and Speeches*, III, 396.

[22] Prior, *Life of Edmund Burke*, 34.

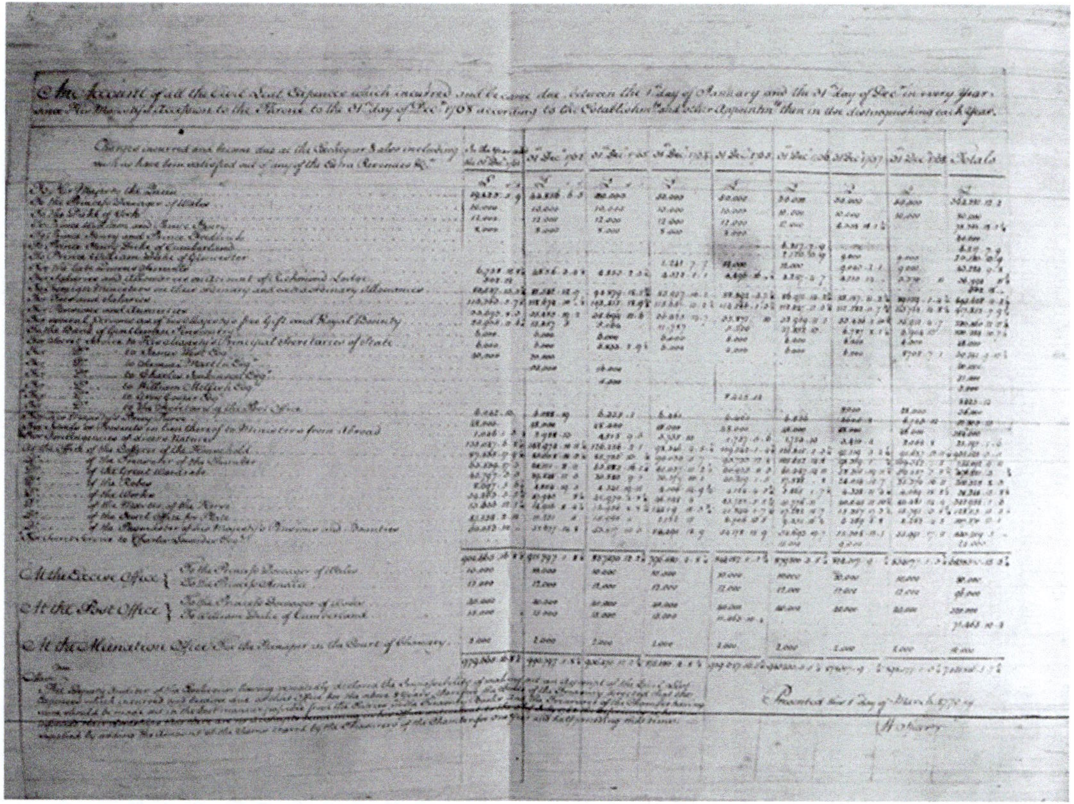

FIGURE 5.1 *An Account of All the Civil List Expences*, 1761–1768
Source: MSS. at Sheffield Archives, WWM/ R/18 (1–42)

crowded audience in the House of Commons. It was one of his most impressive oratorical attempts, spanning more than three hours. The speech weaves a beauty and richness of detail into a broader historical narrative about the Crown's subversion of constitutional equilibrium in the British government. It reflects an impressive breadth of knowledge about the internal affairs of the royal household and the expenses of state establishments that only laborious research on British public administration could produce.

In *Speech on Economical Reform*, Burke submits a range of measures for the principal object of tempering the malign influence of the king over MPs in Parliament in order to preserve the excellencies of the British constitution.[23] He aimed for the "reduction of that corrupt influence, which is itself the perennial spring of all prodigality, and of all disorder,"[24] with the expectation that this effort would recover the spirit of balanced constitutional government that had defined the character of British political order throughout the ages. Burke also intended to place the British state on a firmer financial substructure by controlling public expenditures and slicing off the bureaucratic flab of an overweening administrative apparatus, although he admitted late in his speech that "œconomy" was a "secondary view" of his plan.[25] In *Letter to a Noble Lord*, Burke stated that he acted, rather, on "state principles" in pursuing his plan for reform.[26] Burke's formal motion in support of his program in *Speech on Economical Reform* rang with the following words: "For the better regulation of his Majesty's civil establishments, and of certain public offices; for the limitation of pensions, and the suppression of sundry useless, expensive, and inconvenient places; and for applying the monies saved thereby to the public service."[27]

Burke proposes seven "fundamental rules"[28] for his program that by his estimation would lower expenditures by at least £200,000: (1) abolish expensive jurisdictions; (2) dispose of costly and corrupt landed estates of the Crown; (3) take away or consolidate unnecessary offices; (4) eliminate offices that obstruct the efficient administration of finance; (5) establish a consistent and impartial system for payments; (6) reduce establishments to "certainty"; and (7) dissolve subordinate treasuries.[29] In modern parlance, Burke believed that these seven rules would reduce waste, fraud, and abuse. The following sections will draw attention to the economic principles underlying this program by examining his beliefs on private land ownership, contracts, and the Board of

---

[23] See also a different speech of Burke on government reform, *Speech on Economical Reform Bill*, given on February 15, 1781, in Langford, *Writings and Speeches*, IV, 46–65, in particular pages 51–52: "what he valued more than all this saving, was the destruction of an undue influence over the minds of fifty members of Parliament in both Houses." This second speech does not delve into as much detail on Burke's proposals as his speech on February 11, 1780.

[24] Langford, *Writings and Speeches*, III, 483.   [25] Langford, *Writings and Speeches*, III, 546.
[26] Langford, *Writings and Speeches*, IX, 154.   [27] Langford, *Writings and Speeches*, III, 550.
[28] Langford, *Writings and Speeches*, III, 496.
[29] Langford, *Writings and Speeches*, III, 496–497.

Trade; and on pensions, costly public offices, and the Civil List. Keep in mind, however, that his deeper motivation was to constrain royal corruption, the glowing touchstone of the Rockingham Whigs' political resistance to the king.

5.3 SPEECH ON ECONOMICAL REFORM I: PRIVATE LAND, CONTRACTS, AND THE BOARD OF TRADE

Burke's fondness for markets and contracts emerges in *Speech on Economical Reform* in his discussion of the landed possessions of the Crown. While he defended ecclesiastical and aristocratic estates for serving as the stabilizing anchors of political communities, he did not believe the same principle obtained for all royal possessions. In the speech, Burke proposes to sell off Crown property to the private market because the landed estate of the king was "certainly the very worst which the crown can possess."[30] Government struggled to superintend vast amounts of land that required a heightened level of individual attention and stewardship. "All minute and dispersed possessions, possessions that are often of indeterminate value, and which require a continued personal attendance," Burke insists, "are of a nature more proper for private management, than public administration."[31]

Burke is identifying an inherent incentive structure in the private ownership of land recognized by a variety of thinkers ranging from classical philosophers such as Democritus and Aristotle to medieval theologians such as Thomas Aquinas to twentieth-century libertarians such as Milton Friedman: owners are more likely to tend to their personal property because they, unlike third parties, are directly responsible for its maintenance and cultivation. "[Landed estates] are fitter for the care of a frugal land steward, than of an office in the state," Burke says.[32] Even private estates that were dispersed and chargeable should be "sacrificed to the relief of estates more compact and better circumstanced."[33] In his view, the Crown did not manage its scattered estates with exceeding care and frugality, which is why he is so adamant in calling for the privatization of the king's land in *Speech on Economical Reform*.

Because men were more likely to be diligent stewards of private possessions than public estates, they could ameliorate the land with enough vigor to contribute to the public coffers. "The principal revenue which I propose to draw from these uncultivated wastes, is to spring from the improvement and population of the kingdom; which never can happen, without producing an improvement more advantageous to the revenues of the crown, than the rents of the best landed estate which it can hold," Burke explains.[34] Revenue should derive from the prosperity of cultivated estates. This belief contains a whiff of his more comprehensive argument on the same topic in his commentary on the

---

[30] Langford, *Writings and Speeches*, III, 505–506.
[31] Langford, *Writings and Speeches*, III, 506.   [32] Langford, *Writings and Speeches*, III, 506.
[33] Langford, *Writings and Speeches*, III, 506.   [34] Langford, *Writings and Speeches*, III, 507.

political economy of British India: the East India Company was able to raise revenue successfully when it had relaxed its political control over the Indian economy[35] – just as the British government, in Burke's judgment, would receive a steady amount of revenue from privately cultivated estates when released from the grip of the Crown. Burke also employs similar reasoning in his economic analysis of the French Revolution.

Burke connects his proposal to sell off royal property with a confidence in the interaction of supply and demand laws to determine the price of the estates. "If it be objected, that these lands at present would sell at a low market; this is answered, by shewing that money is at high price," he contends. "The one balances the other. Lands sell at the current rate, and nothing can sell for more."[36] The competitive price system communicates the market value of land to buyers and sellers with cool precision, reflecting shifting proportions of stock and want.

Regardless of the value of the estates, a transaction that moved land from indifferent stewards to attentive owners occasioned advantages for both:

[A] great object is always answered, whenever any property is transferr'd from hands that are not fit for that property, to those that are. The buyer and seller must mutually profit by such a bargain; and, what rarely happens in matters of revenue, the relief of the subject will go hand in hand with the profit of the exchequer.[37]

A unity of interest springs from the purchase of land. The seller will reap the profit of his sale, while the buyer will acquire new property for amelioration and cultivation, even if it is sold for a low price. Unlike the normal collection of revenue, which, Burke insinuates, hurts the taxed individuals, the sale of land will generate revenue for the treasury without harming the people. Burke's recognition of this merit of exchange sheds light on a recurrent theme that informed his conception of political economy throughout his entire public life, spanning all the way through *Thoughts and Details*: voluntary transactions galvanized by self-interest are led by a benevolent hand that spreads collective gifts to the contracting parties (even if, as in this case, one party happened to be the government).

Notice what Burke is, in effect, expressing: he is supporting the monetization of estates, an activity he roundly denounced in the *Reflections*. One key difference is that Burke in the *Reflections* assailed the French revolutionary government's violent expropriation of church land, while in *Speech on Economical Reform* he recommends to sell off royal land in a deliberate and voluntary manner. This contrast unveils Burke's deepest political convictions. Ecclesiastical property was not only a physical manifestation and foundation of Church activities, but also a sturdy intermediary institution that helped protect commoners from the ambitious designs of the Crown. In addition, *landed*

---

[35] See Chapters 9 and 10.   [36] Langford, *Writings and Speeches*, III, 506.
[37] Langford, *Writings and Speeches*, III, 506.

property itself, even if it was not held by the Church, was essential to preserving constitutional order, which is why Burke supported non-clerical private property rights over ecclesiastical claims to land during the Church *Nullum Tempus* bill debate.[38] In the case of *Speech on Economical Reform*, however, royal land was an extension of royal power, and royal power for Burke could be used as an instrument for despotism if not checked by the ballast of private landed property.

Another proposal Burke advertises in *Speech on Economical Reform* was the use of contracts to slice off the administrative lard of the royal household. He begins his commentary on this matter by discussing the conditions that made it possible for an economist to fulfill his responsibilities:

> It is impossible ... for any person to be an œconomist where no order in payments is established; it is impossible for a man to be an œconomist, who is not able to take a comparative view of his means, and of his expences, for the year which lies before him; it is impossible for a man to be an œconomist, under whom various officers in their several departments may spend, – even just what they please, – and often with an emulation of expence, as contributing to the importance, if not profit, of their several departments.[39]

Burke is describing the eighteenth-century conception of the term "œconomist" as an administrator concerned with frugal expense, with clear resonances of its traditional definition as the overseer of household management. The economist was one who carefully studied the system of payments and financial outlook of the state for the upcoming fiscal year through the dispassionate calculation of expense and receipt.

In light of these comments, recall Burke's remark that he was not an economist by nature. To suppress his displeasure for parsimony, then, Burke places the mask of an economist over his face in *Speech on Economical Reform* to guide his plan for reform of the royal household. He argues that the household had become "exceedingly abusive in its constitution."[40] Throughout its history, it had stubbornly retained its feudal offices and wielded its foreign powers to bring home plunder. "This inconvenient receipt produced an œconomy suited only to itself," Burke says. "It multiplied offices beyond all measure; buttery, pantry, and all that rabble of places, which, though profitable to the holders and expensive to the state, are almost too mean to mention."[41]

Yet even royal households were governed by larger forces of economic reality, the foremost being the great law of scarcity. "Frugality ... is founded

---

[38] See Langford, *Writings and Speeches*, II, 364–367.
[39] Langford, *Writings and Speeches*, III, 508. Burke says later in the speech, "In all dealings, where it is possible, the principles of radical œconomy prescribe three things; first, undertaking by the great; secondly, engaging with persons of skill in the subject matter; thirdly, engaging with those who shall have an immediate and direct interest in the proper execution of the business" (Langford, *Writings and Speeches*, III, 513).
[40] Langford, *Writings and Speeches*, III, 508.   [41] Langford, *Writings and Speeches*, III, 511.

on the principle, that all riches have limits," he asserts.[42] This insight is critical to his notion of public finance and to his comprehension of political economy and civilization in general: state expenditures are inherently constrained by finite resources. Society is not a utopia. A limiting principle must govern all things. The failure to come to terms with this reality, and to make appropriate institutional adjustments to wasteful practices, threatened the sound operation of public administration. "A royal household, grown enormous, even in the meanest departments, may weaken and perhaps destroy all energy in the highest offices of the state," Burke observes.[43] The bloated growth of government frustrates its capacity to fulfill its public duties and manage financial activities adequately, a message he emphasizes throughout *Speech on Economical Reform* with steadiness of purpose.

In Burke's judgment, one remedy to curb the royal household's abuses was to contract out the Crown's expenditures. "[T]he king's tables ... should be classed by the steward of the household, and should be contracted for, according to their rank, by the head or cover," he says.[44] More so, "[M]en should be contracted with only in their proper trade; and that no member of parliament should be capable of such contract."[45] Burke's endorsement of contracts illuminates a belief that transactions between the royal household and private vendors would be a more efficient, and less costly, vehicle to pay for services than the existing system of expenditures. The contracts would also diminish the patronage of the Crown by preventing MPs from receiving sinecures for their votes. They would thus accomplish two goals in Burke's judgment: lower the costs of the royal household and discipline the king's prodigality and influence.

When introducing his proposal for contracts in *Speech on Economical Reform*, Burke offers compelling remarks on their nature that exhibit his understanding of their merits and flaws in the greater market order. First he acknowledges the prospect of dishonest transactions. "No dealing is exempt from the possibility of fraud," he concedes.[46] This observation is similar to his recognition of the possibility of "force or fraud, collusion or combination"[47] in *Thoughts and Details*, although in both commentaries Burke does not tease out their specific conditions. At the very least, he is casting a ray of light on the imperfections of unregulated barter.

Even with such recognition, Burke's subsequent comments reflect an impassioned appreciation for voluntary exchange that permeates *Thoughts and Details* as well. In *Speech on Economical Reform*, Burke states:

[B]y a contract on a matter certain, you have this advantage – you are sure to know the utmost *extent* of the fraud to which you are subject. By a contract with a person in *his own trade*, you are sure you shall not suffer by *want of skill*. By a *short* contract you are

---

[42] Langford, *Writings and Speeches*, III, 512.   [43] Langford, *Writings and Speeches*, III, 512.
[44] Langford, *Writings and Speeches*, III, 514.   [45] Langford, *Writings and Speeches*, III, 514.
[46] Langford, *Writings and Speeches*, III, 514.   [47] Langford, *Writings and Speeches*, IX, 123.

sure of making it the *interest* of the contractor to exert that skill for the satisfaction of his employers.[48]

Transactions with clear and defined expectations between the state and the private party will expose the possibility of fraud. By contracting out a task to an individual with expertise in that service, the government will gain from that person's particular skills suited for the undertaking. The short duration of contracts will produce a strong incentive for the contractor to deploy his full effort in completing the service, which will further benefit the hirer. Burke spotlights Frederick the Great, king of Prussia at the time, as a pertinent example in which a distinguished monarch contracted out services to the private sphere to the advantage of the state.[49]

These conclusions illustrate a harmony with Burke's commentary on contracts in *Thoughts and Details*. While the historical circumstances of *Speech on Economical Reform* and the economic tract were dissimilar, in both instances his reflections placed emphasis on the mutual rewards that blossomed from voluntary agreements. The farmer would hopefully generate a profit with the help of his laborers, and his laborers would receive wages and good nutriment. The royal household would benefit from the service of the contractor, and the contractor would receive recompense for his skilled labor. (Burke does not explicitly make this last point in his comments quoted here, but it is implicit in this discussion.) Even with the potential for fraud, contracts were a means to public utility.

In *Speech on Economical Reform*, Burke's survey of Britain's Royal Mint, the institution responsible for making coins, reinforced his belief that contracts could serve as instruments for the common good. Although the Mint was not a department of the royal household, it was still a source of patronage and a costly encumbrance on the British government. The Mint once fulfilled a useful purpose as "the great center of money transactions and remittances for our own, and for other nations."[50] But after Charles I seized £130,000 of bullion in 1640,[51] mint never regained its full strength and was reduced simply to a manufacture. Therefore, Burke proposes in his speech that the Mint "ought to be undertaken upon the principles of a manufacture; that is, for the best and cheapest execution, by a contract, upon proper securities, and under proper regulations."[52] He does not stipulate these specific securities and regulations. But his proposition to reform the Mint guided by the economizing principles of a manufacture displays his attraction to contracts as mechanisms that could trim government costs and limit royal patronage.

---

[48] Langford, *Writings and Speeches*, III, 514.   [49] Langford, *Writings and Speeches*, III, 514.
[50] Langford, *Writings and Speeches*, III, 517.
[51] See William Robert Scott, *The Constitution and Finance of English, Scottish and Irish Joint-Stock Companies to 1720*, vol. I, *The General Development of the Joint-Stock System to 1720* (Cambridge: The University Press, 1912), 224.
[52] Langford, *Writings and Speeches*, III, 517.

Beyond his ideas to sell off royal property and contract out the Crown's services, Burke proposes to abolish two well-known state offices. The first was the American Secretary, or the Secretary of State for the Colonies, a post that oversaw British policy in the empire's North American colonies.[53] The second and more significant office was the Board of Trade, whose origins dated back to the early seventeenth century. The Board's modern iteration was created in 1696 under William III, and authorized by an Act of Parliament, for the purposes of advancing Britain's commercial interests and supervising the American plantations. The advisory body consisted of sixteen members, eight of whom sat regularly as salaried commissioners.[54]

Burke's heated plea to extinguish the Board of Trade is his most extended critique of any specific government office in *Speech on Economical Reform*, demonstrating both his aversion to its existence and his desire to promote the cause of liberal trade in the British Empire. Burke first alleges in this discussion that the Board "is of no use at all,"[55] a belief perhaps compounded by his experiences as an agent to the British colony of New York from 1770 to 1775, during which he would communicate with, and bear witness to the inefficiencies of, the advisory body.[56]

---

[53] See Arthur Herbert Basye, "The Secretary of State for the Colonies, 1768–1782," *The American Historical Review* 28 (1922): 13–23. The Secretary of State for the Colonies also served as President of the Board of Trade from 1768 to 1779. See Langford, *Writings and Speeches*, III, 554.

[54] For background on the Board of Trade, see Oliver Morton Dickerson, *American Colonial Government 1696–1765: A Study of the British Board of Trade in Its Relation to the American Colonies, Political, Industrial, Administrative* (Cleveland, OH: The Arthur H. Clark Company, 1912).

[55] Langford, *Writings and Speeches*, III, 535.

[56] See Hoffman, *New York Agent*, 103–125. Burke's time as agent, for which he received an annual salary, does not reveal much penetrating insight into his conception of political economy. Principal matters of concern during Burke's tenure involved controversies surrounding territory and property rights. During one dispute, he defended the property rights of New Yorkers against an attempt by Frenchmen to secure their claims to land near Lake Champlain, on the grounds that establishing the claims might be "an infringement of the right and jurisdiction of the Province of New York, and affect the properties of several who may have taken lands and made settlements in virtue of grants passed under the seal of your Colony" (108). Burke would argue that "our ancient limits should be settled according to the rights of Great Britain and not according to the pretensions of France" (115). Burke's worry was without foundation, however (108). New Yorkers were pleased by Burke's efforts on their behalf: "Your attention to the interests of the Colony in regard to the territorial rights, and to the private property of the Grantees under New York against the Canadian claims merits our warmest thanks" (116). Burke would later continue to defend the territorial integrity of New York during debate over the Quebec Act (142–150). In his final years as agent, Burke directed his attention to broader questions of Anglo-American imperial relations, seeking to illuminate the common interests between Britain and the colonies while pursuing a moderate solution to their conflict. In 1772 and 1773, Burke also discussed the relationship between the British government and the East India Company. (The Regulating Act of 1773 had been passed in this time.) See, for example, pages 220–223, 231. Ross J. S. Hoffman, the first writer to publish a complete account of Burke's

Burke's subsequent reasoning in opposition to the Board of Trade in *Speech on Economical Reform* is a summation of his arguments in favor of free intercourse that he expounded throughout his public life. He says it was "generally" true that commerce "flourishes most when it is left to itself. Interest, the great guide of commerce, is not a blind one. It is very well able to find its own way; and its necessities are its best laws."[57] Commerce thrives best when untangled from the thick web of public administration. The genius of interest lies in its powerful ability to channel the individual pursuit of material advantage in a way that induces prosperous trade for the many. The "necessities" of interest – Burke is most likely referring to supply and demand – replace the deadening effect of government regulation with opportunities for industry and ingenuity in the market. In other words, he is invoking the concept of his "benign and wise disposer" to seek the liberation of commerce from the Board of Trade twenty-five years prior to the publication of *Thoughts and Details*.

Yet the reign of Charles I was marred by gratuitous intervention in foreign intercourse, Burke contends in *Speech on Economical Reform*. In referring to the meddling of seventeenth-century committees of council tasked with investigating trade under the king's watch, he observes in the oration that "even where they had no ill intention (which was sometimes the case) trade and manufacture suffered infinitely from their injudicious tampering."[58] Burke is conveying his awareness of the intrinsic constraints of good intentions[59] by implying that commercial regulations aiming to benefit England were ultimately counterproductive. This conclusion explains Burke's critical remark that "all regulations are, in their nature, restrictive of some liberty."[60] His sympathy in support of free commerce makes its presence felt throughout *Speech on Economical Reform*.

The debate about the Board of Trade, however, surpassed considerations of economic doctrine by reaching into the deeper terrain of constitutional questions. For Burke, if commercial regulations should be implemented – he does not deny that sometimes they should – the locus of authority to determine the rules should reside in Parliament. "We want no instruction from boards of trade, or from any other board," he says.[61] The legislative body was quite capable of studying commercial matters: "Parliamentary enquiry is the only mode of obtaining parliamentary information."[62] Burke's diligent studies of

experience as agent, concludes that "[Burke's] employment by the New York Assembly was to him strictly a side-line activity that had little connection with his main interests, purposes, and conduct in public life" (189).

[57] Langford, *Writings and Speeches*, III, 535.   [58] Langford, *Writings and Speeches*, III, 535.

[59] In *Account*, the Burkes write that William Laud, Archbishop of Canterbury under Charles I who gained historical notoriety for his persecution of Puritans, was "one of those indiscreet men of good intentions, who are the people in the world that make the worst figure in politics" (141).

[60] Langford, *Writings and Speeches*, III, 535.   [61] Langford, *Writings and Speeches*, III, 535.

[62] Langford, *Writings and Speeches*, III, 535.

economic policy, as showcased by the Free Port Act and *Speech on Economical Reform*, among many efforts, testify to this statement.

Indeed, Burke argues that Parliament was far more effective in assessing the implications of trade regulations than the king and the beneficiaries of his patronage. "There is more real knowledge to be obtained, by attending the detail of business in the committees above stairs, than ever did come, or ever will come from any board in this kingdom, or from all of them together," he avows.[63] The delegation of authority in matters relating to foreign commerce should rest in a legislative chamber, not in an unaccountable advisory agency prone to the corrupting influence of the Crown's ministers.

Burke expands upon his reasoning about the inutility of the Board of Trade in *Speech on Economical Reform* by summoning an important empirical argument. He notes that "the flourishing settlements of New England, of Virginia, and of Maryland, and all our wealthy colonies in the West Indies"[64] all developed before an earlier form of the Board had operated under Charles II.[65] Burke explains that Pennsylvania and Carolina were settled after the extinction of the first board and prior to the creation of the second one. Then he contends that the two colonies that did owe their existence to the Board, Georgia and Nova Scotia, struggled to achieve commercial prosperity because they were hampered by a thicket of restrictions administered by the body. Until recently, Burke says, Georgia had made "a very slow progress."[66] And it "never did make any progress at all, until it had wholly got rid of all the regulations which the board of trade had moulded into its original constitution."[67] Burke's insinuation is difficult to ignore: the Georgian economy's emancipation from intrusive trade laws was the trigger for its commercial growth.

Burke's use of Georgia is a noteworthy example. Many Georgian industries that had received subsidies from Britain, including silk, olives, and wine, did not thrive. Consequently, Georgia had become a financial burden on the British government. "It always had, and it now has, an *establishment* paid by the public of England, for the sake of the influence of the crown; that colony having never been able or willing to take upon itself the expence of its proper government, or its own appropriated jobs," Burke observes.[68] In his view, British interference in the Georgian economy had discouraged the colony from assuming responsibility for its colonial administration. Rather than freeing it to prosper, the Board of Trade had condemned it to dependency.[69]

By contrast, other American colonies had been unshackled from imperial entanglements, which benefited them – and the British Empire. "[T]he colonies

[63] Langford, *Writings and Speeches*, III, 535.   [64] Langford, *Writings and Speeches*, III, 537.
[65] Burke made the same point in regard to Barbados. See *The Scots Magazine*, vol. 42 (Edinburgh: A. Murray and J. Cochran, 1780), 134.
[66] Langford, *Writings and Speeches*, III, 537.   [67] Langford, *Writings and Speeches*, III, 537.
[68] Langford, *Writings and Speeches*, III, 538.
[69] See a similar critique of the Georgian economy in *Account of the European Settlements*, in "*An Account of the European Settlements in America*," Chapter 6.

which have had the fortune of not being godfathered by the board of trade, never cost the nation a shilling, except what has been so properly spent in losing them," Burke states.[70] The absence of excessive commercial restrictions not only helped American plantations flourish, but they also relieved Britain of any possible encumbrances stemming from its colonial possessions. Such thinking mirrored Burke's view in *Speech on Conciliation with America* that Britain should grant American colonies the commercial freedom to develop and expand their industries, as we shall see in Chapter 7. Notice the consistency in his wider position on imperial economics: colonies unburdened by the weight of trade regulations supplied advantages both to Britain and its overseas subjects.

Burke applies this logic in *Speech on Economical Reform* to the case of the Acadian people in Nova Scotia. In this "one little neglected corner" of the Canadian province, it had "been shut out from the protection and regulation of councils of commerce, and of boards of trade."[71] Yet even "without assistance," the area had prospered "to a considerable degree," due in no small part to its "acquisitions of unregulated industry,"[72] before Britain extirpated the Acadians from the province.[73] What is the salient lesson for our study of Burke's political economy? He associates the expansion of commerce and industry with a paucity of imperial regulations. Thus, he concludes, "This board of trade and plantations has not been of any use to the colonies, as colonies."[74]

Burke also scolds the seeming laziness of the Board of Trade in order to strengthen his contention that liberal trade did not require state supervision. In *Speech on Economical Reform*, he cites two pending acts that would have lowered trade restrictions between England and Ireland. Burke praises these acts for "giving a free trade to Ireland in woollens and in all things else, with independent nations, and giving them an equal trade to our own colonies."[75] Such liberal trade reform was "great," as well as an "arduous and critical improvement of [the commercial] system."[76] In his judgment, the lackluster effort of the Board to examine the commercial implications of these new measures was glaring proof of its inutility.[77]

Burke believed that the abolition of the Board of Trade would save the British government "about £20,000 a year, besides seven members of parliament."[78]

---

[70] Langford, *Writings and Speeches*, III, 538.   [71] Langford, *Writings and Speeches*, III, 538.

[72] Langford, *Writings and Speeches*, III, 538.

[73] This event is known as the Expulsion of the Acadians, which started in 1755 during the French and Indian War.

[74] Langford, *Writings and Speeches*, III, 537.

[75] Langford, *Writings and Speeches*, III, 540. Consult "The Irish Trade Bills," Chapter 8.

[76] Langford, *Writings and Speeches*, III, 540.

[77] Langford, *Writings and Speeches*, III, 540–541.

[78] Charles William, Earl Fitzwilliam and Sir Richard Bourke, eds., *Correspondence of the Right Honourable Edmund Burke: Between the Year 1744, and the Period of His Decease, in 1797*, vol. II (London: Francis & John Rivington, 1844), 325.

Although the Board symbolized the royal abuse of sinecures, others suggested that its public value and activity might have been of greater consequence than he implied in the speech. For in a bid to defend the organization's efforts and wisdom, William Eden, an MP and Board member, had drawn attention to the litany of reports it had issued and to the distinguished economic thinkers that had comprised its membership over the years.[79]

Yet Burke showered ridicule on this point. In an additional parliamentary speech, he did admit in a mocking tone that the intellect of the Board's illustrious members, which included Eden and Edward Gibbon, was impressive: "Every department of literature, the solid and the entertaining, the instructive and the amusing, had its separate professor." Still, Burke insisted, the Board was "useless, idle, and expensive."[80] Therefore, as *Cobbett's Parliamentary History of England* reported him saying, "As an academy of Belles Lettres, he should hold them hallowed; as a board of trade he wished to abolish them."[81]

Burke is transmitting an idea he famously expressed in the *Reflections*: the engine of industry was not the scholar removed from the churn of the market but an individual who actually engaged in trade and husbandry by the sweat of his brow and the skill of his craft. In the *Reflections*, Burke notes that the "farmer" and "physician" procured food and medicine; the "professor of metaphysics" did not.[82] Similarly, in the debate over the Board of Trade, he argues that even though the body's members possessed distinguished credentials and exceptional intelligence, they still did not set in motion the wheels of commerce. The trader and laborer did. This conclusion is harmonious with Burke's broader political philosophy that emphasized the fatal limitations of speculative theory in encouraging productive human activity and fostering the growth of civilization.

In the end, the provision to ban the Board, which was part of one of Burke's Civil Establishment bills, passed by eight votes in a committee of the whole House.[83] This victory signified the apex of success for his proposed reforms, but the entire bill eventually withered away. Burke witnessed his efforts come to fruition in 1782, however, when the Board was disbanded by the Rockinghams. Yet a committee on trade with similar advisory functions was created in 1784 and made permanent in 1786.[84] Nevertheless, the body's ultimate triumph

[79] See Lock, *Edmund Burke*, vol. I, 457–458.

[80] *Cobbett's Parliamentary History of England*, vol. XXI, *Comprising the Period from the Eleventh of February 1780, to the Twenty-Fifth of March 1781* (London: T. C. Hansard, 1814), 237.

[81] *Cobbett's Parliamentary History of England*, vol. XXI, 238.

[82] Langford, *Writings and Speeches*, VIII, 111.

[83] *Cobbett's Parliamentary History of England*, vol. XXI, 278.

[84] See John E. Crowley, "Neo-Mercantilism and *The Wealth of Nations*: British Commercial Policy after the American Revolution," *The Historical Journal* 33 (1990): 341n8; and Dennis

should not obscure the important point relating to Burke's economic thought: his opposition to the Board was based, at least in part,[85] on his belief that it curbed the potential of the natural laws of commerce.

5.4 SPEECH ON ECONOMICAL REFORM II: PENSIONS, COSTLY OFFICES, AND THE CIVIL LIST

Burke examines a variety of other measures in *Speech on Economical Reform* that he thought would check royal patronage and lower the cost of government. One was his proposal to reform Britain's pension system. In March 1778, almost two years before Burke would present his program of economical reform, Thomas Gilbert, MP for Lichfield, had proposed to tax places and pensions by 25 percent during the American war. Burke registered his skepticism of the idea in *Speech on Economical Reform*, in turn unmasking clues about his conception of political economy that exceeded administrative considerations of pension reform.

Burke first admits in the speech that employments were a "proper subject of regulation."[86] But they were a "very ill-chosen subject for a tax."[87] While an equal tax on property is "reasonable" because "the object is of the same quality throughout," a uniform tax on salaries was unfair because the pay and nature of salaries were unequal: "[T]here can be no equality, and consequently no justice, in taxing them by the hundred, in the gross."[88] Burke's verdict illustrates a sparkling symmetry with his argument in *Thoughts and Details* that the enforcement of equal wage rates neglected to consider the complexity of labor conditions in England's agricultural economy. In *Speech on Economical Reform* Burke is referring to state pensions and in *Thoughts and Details* to private employment contracts. Yet the Aristotelian logic endures: equal taxation on unequal circumstances is unjust because it offends the principle of proportional equality.

Burke underlines this point by distinguishing between the holders of two government offices that pay £800 per year, the first man tasked with many responsibilities and the other with none. An equal tax of 25 percent would yield £200 for each office. But because the former office performed a real service, the tax would, in effect, be depriving the employee of £200 that he rightfully earned, while it would be rewarding the latter worker £600 for doing nothing. "The public robs the former, and the latter robs the public; and this

---

Stephen Klinge, "Edmund Burke, Economical Reform, and the Board of Trade, 1777–1780," *The Journal of Modern History* 51 (1979): 1186.

[85] See Klinge, "Edmund Burke, Economical Reform, and the Board of Trade," 1185–1200 for the view that Burke's opposition to the Board of Trade was driven by personal contempt as well as by Rockingham Whig principles.

[86] Langford, *Writings and Speeches*, III, 494.   [87] Langford, *Writings and Speeches*, III, 494.

[88] Langford, *Writings and Speeches*, III, 494.

mode of mutual robbery is the only way in which the office and the public can make up their accounts," Burke observes.[89]

Burke's related observation pertaining to Gilbert's tax captures the heart of his understanding of the elemental relation between industry and wages, which was the belief that hard work should be rewarded with a high salary. The tax, however, fostered the opposite effect; it was "a fine paid by industry and merit, for an indemnity to the idle and the worthless."[90] Laziness should not be compensated. In the case of economical reform in the late 1770s and early 1780s, this perverse incentive had a negative impact on the public in particular since it influenced the machinery of government finance. "[I]t is a fine paid by mismanagement, for the renewal of its lease," Burke says.[91] Consequently, the encouragement of indolence diminished the possibilities for institutional change. As he insists, "[S]uch a scheme is not calculated to produce, but to prevent reformation."[92] Burke's remarks on Gilbert's tax thus marry his wage theory with his conception of reform: remuneration should be given to diligent men and women working in private and public capacities; industry is the stimulant for improvement; and the incentive of reward helps spawn institutional and social progress. This frame of understanding about the cause and effect of incentives is essential to Burke's economic thought.

For Burke, therefore, the "double injustice" of Gilbert's tax militated against the interests of the state.[93] It would save £200 in one instance by taking that sum from the indolent employee. But the tax would burden the public with an additional debt three times that amount, since it would be seizing money from the assiduous employee who deserved recompense for his toil on behalf of the state. The odious consequences did not stop there: once that £600 reached the hands of government officials, they would use the spoils to advance their political self-interest. "[W]hilst you leave a supply of unsecured money behind, wholly at the discretion of ministers," Burke remarks with a heavy breath of cynicism, "they make up the tax to such places as they wish to favour, or in such new places as they may choose to create."[94] The Civil List would then bear the weight of even greater debt, surrendering the interests of the public to the designs of ministers: "[T]he public is obliged to repay, and to repay with an heavy interest, what it has taken by an injudicious tax."[95]

Burke is unveiling his grave apprehensions about the capacity of state officials to use public money with wisdom and discretion. In his judgment, a tax would simply funnel more riches to government administrators to disperse in accordance with their personal or political preferences. This revenue would not relieve the British government of debt but encumber it with greater financial obligations. "No revenue is large enough to provide

[89] Langford, *Writings and Speeches*, III, 494. [90] Langford, *Writings and Speeches*, III, 495.
[91] Langford, *Writings and Speeches*, III, 495. [92] Langford, *Writings and Speeches*, III, 495.
[93] Langford, *Writings and Speeches*, III, 494. [94] Langford, *Writings and Speeches*, III, 494.
[95] Langford, *Writings and Speeches*, III, 494.

both for the meritorious and undeserving; to provide for service which is, and for service which is not incurred," Burke stated in *Speech on Public Expenses*.[96] Political support for an improvident tax system failed to examine the unintended consequences that would arise from a surge in state lucre. The malign punishment of equal taxation on unequal offices spelled doom for sound public administration, and further put in jeopardy the financial welfare of the people.

Pension Reform

What, then, were Burke's proposals for the pension system in *Speech on Economical Reform*? He first calls to eliminate the Paymaster of Pensions, one of the various subordinate treasuries he wished to end, and to transfer the payment of service to the Exchequer. "The present course of diversifying the same object, can answer no good purpose," Burke notes,[97] indicating his preference to consolidate or abolish offices with redundant duties.

Burke then argues to lower pensions to £60,000 per annum, but leaves room for Parliament to exercise its judgment about whether to increase or decrease the amount slightly. Because the annual cost of pensions exceeded £100,000, his proposal, he calculates, would save the British government £40,000 per year. Rather than displacing the entirety of the pension system, Burke hoped his plan would gradually decrease its costs over time. These details offer little original insight into his economic thought, yet at their most basic level they demonstrate his proclivity for financial prudence and embrace of incremental change in the reform of public administration.

Burke did not go as far as Sir George Savile, however, in supporting the termination of all unmerited pensions. This decision, along with his refusal to advocate for the cancellation of sinecures, remained the two chief points of disharmony between Burke's initial program and the Yorkshire petitioners.[98] Even if all such allowances were eliminated, Burke reasons in *Speech on Economical Reform*, the power of the Crown would remain unchecked. Therefore, "[T]he very same undeserving persons might afterwards return to the very same list; or if they did not, other persons, meriting as little as they do, might be put upon it to an undefinable amount."[99] Any state allowance, moreover, that *might* serve a utility should be circumscribed, not eliminated. "In a plan of reformation, it would be one of my maxims, that when I know of an establishment which may be subservient to useful purposes, and which at the same time, from its discretionary nature, is liable to a very great perversion from those purposes," Burke proclaims, "*I would limit the quantity of the power that*

---

[96] Langford, *Writings and Speeches*, III, 472.   [97] Langford, *Writings and Speeches*, III, 523.
[98] See Ian R. Christie, "Sir George Savile, Edmund Burke, and the Yorkshire Reform Programme, February, 1780," *Yorkshire Archaeological Journal* 40 (1962): 205–208.
[99] Langford, *Writings and Speeches*, III, 525.

might be so abused."[100] Prudence converges with moderate thrift in his attempt to reform the pension system.

Burke's additional remarks on the patent offices in the Exchequer, which he considered to be the same as pensions in "reality and substance,"[101] lend deeper insight into his notion of political economy. His basic proposition was to lower the salary of the Auditor of the Receipt to £3,000 per year and the Auditor of the Imprests and other principal officers to £1,500 per year. Even though Burke concedes that the positions were "sinecures,"[102] he sought gradual rather than radical reform in this regard because the patent places, unlike pensions, were "held for life"[103]; thus they should be considered sacred property that warranted careful protection, not swift abolition. "They have been given as a provision for children; they have been the subject of family settlements; they have been the security of creditors," Burke insists.[104]

Accordingly, the patent places in the Exchequer were not simply remunerative offices but instruments that strengthened families and property throughout the generations. In Burke's view, the unleashing of arbitrary force on these settled offices would establish a foul precedent. "If the discretion of power is once let loose upon property, we can be at no loss to determine whose power, and what discretion it is that will prevail at last," he maintains.[105] Burke is announcing his firm objection to the exercise of arbitrary power over property, a stance that would animate his attack on the French Revolution a decade later.

Burke's comments in this section also display his most cherished convictions regarding the compatibility between property and law. "What the law respects shall be sacred to me," he avows.[106] Law should not be discarded simply based on the cold computation of utility: "If the barriers of law should be broken down, upon ideas of convenience, even of public convenience, we shall have no longer any thing certain among us."[107] Burke admits that public necessity sometimes superseded existing law, since law "being only made for the benefit of the community cannot in any one of its parts, resist a demand which may comprehend the total of the public interest."[108]

But Burke maintained that this prerogative did not prevail in the case of pensions because pensions engendered a public service. Therefore, since the allowances were secured by law, they deserved to be protected, if modified to fit changing circumstances. The principle inspiring Burke's defense of the pension system thus strikes the nerve of his philosophic creed: prescription confers authority on time-honored practices. Pensions were traditional payments, the source of reward for statesmen and their families and provision for their

---

[100] Langford, *Writings and Speeches*, III, 525.
[101] Langford, *Writings and Speeches*, III, 526.
[102] Langford, *Writings and Speeches*, III, 526.
[103] Langford, *Writings and Speeches*, III, 526.
[104] Langford, *Writings and Speeches*, III, 526.
[105] Langford, *Writings and Speeches*, III, 526.
[106] Langford, *Writings and Speeches*, III, 526.
[107] Langford, *Writings and Speeches*, III, 526.
[108] Langford, *Writings and Speeches*, III, 527.

children. They were a form of property, and property was the sturdiest manifestation of prescription in Burke's political theory.[109] Such insights demonstrate that his plan to reform the pension system was guided not simply by prudence and selective frugality but also by prescription.

Burke's defense of his proposal to assign fixed salaries to the patent places, then, was rooted in the idea that public service merited public reward. "There is a time, when the weather-beaten vessels of the state, ought to come into harbour," he insists, referring to hardworking government servants.[110] In praising the legal reasoning of Lord Somers,[111] Burke posits that a permanent reward not only honored officials for their labors but also produced social and economic advantages: it was "the origin of families; and the foundation of wealth as well as of honours."[112] Fixed salaries could nurture and fortify a distinguished aristocracy, as it was "the only genuine unadulterated origin of nobility"[113] and the indispensable guardian of constitutional government.

Burke certainly reaped the fruits of government reward by means of the pension system throughout his life. We recall that he had received an allowance starting in 1763 while working under William Gerard Hamilton, charged to the Irish Establishment. Burke would later receive one from the British government in 1794 – for £1,200 per year, the highest total authorized under the Civil List Act of 1782, the modified version of his original economic reform bill[114] – and was forced to defend the perquisite in 1796 after it had come under attack by MPs.[115] Taking into account such benefits, Burke's portrayal of the public-spirited government servant in *Speech on Economical Reform* in many ways reflected an image of himself – a diligent statesman who advanced the national interests of Great Britain and thereby warranted public recompense for his industry.

Burke's attempt to reward noble families for their service to the state breathed life into his conviction that a disciplined government payment system generated a salutary long-term impact in a commonwealth:

When men receive obligations from the crown through the pious hands of fathers, or of connections as venerable as the paternal, the dependences which arise from thence, are the obligations of gratitude, and not the fetters of servility. Such ties originate in virtue, and they promote it. They continue men in those habitudes of friendship, those political

---

[109] See "Property as a Constitutional Bulwark," Chapter 11.

[110] Langford, *Writings and Speeches*, III, 528.

[111] In 1696 Somers helped establish the constitutional principle that claimants could use a petition of right to recover arrears from the Crown if a contract was violated. See Theodore F. T. Plucknett, *A Concise History of the Common Law* (Indianapolis: Liberty Fund, 2010), 704.

[112] Langford, *Writings and Speeches*, III, 528.   [113] Langford, *Writings and Speeches*, III, 528.

[114] Langford, *Writings and Speeches*, IX, 8. Burke received two more pensions the following year, increasing the total amount of his government reward to £3,700.

[115] See "Letter to a Noble Lord," in Langford, *Writings and Speeches*, IX, 145–187.

connections, and those political principles in which they began life. They are antidotes against a corrupt levity, instead of causes of it.[116]

Fixed salaries should not be conceived as temporary payments but as lasting rewards that connected men of one generation to their ancestors who had served the state, stitching together a stable leadership class that could absorb the fluxes of day-to-day government operations.

Burke is claiming further that the royal power to dispense reward helped form bonds of affection with distinguished statesmen, which would prevent such men from acting in a servile manner toward the Crown, as long as this system did not slide into corruption. The son of an honorable minister who carried out exceptional service on behalf of the British Empire, for instance, should not have to beg the treasury for a pension.[117] Rather than cajoling the Crown for sinecures, state servants and their families would be assured a consistent source of income. Public reward conveyed a sense of gratitude from the Crown.

Is Burke's argument convincing? He is toeing an exceedingly fine line between denouncing royal corruption, on the one hand, and granting powers to the Crown to furnish sinecures to men, on the other. In theory, one could divide meritorious reward from venal patronage and argue that the security of pensions for true merit would protect against obsequious behavior. Yet it is harder to discern these differences in practice, and Burke does not sufficiently explain such distinctions in *Speech on Economical Reform*. The larger message he conveys, however, is that social attachments and sentiments did not just emerge from the organic nature of private associations and voluntary exchange; they could be strengthened in government as well through the state recognition of public service. The principles of association in government and those of society were not distinct.

In his discussion of the patent offices in the Exchequer, Burke expresses one of the most compelling insights of his entire corpus of statements on political economy. "An honourable and fair profit is the best security against avarice and rapacity; as in all things, a lawful and regulated enjoyment is the best security against debauchery and excess," Burke states.[118] His point is that a government salary – a "fair profit" regulated legally[119] – spawns the incentives necessary to promote good behavior, such as the expectation that a civil servant would be justly compensated for his toil on behalf of the state.

---

[116] Langford, *Writings and Speeches*, III, 528.
[117] Langford, *Writings and Speeches*, III, 528–529.
[118] Langford, *Writings and Speeches*, III, 531.
[119] Burke does not elaborate on what "lawful and regulated enjoyment" means. Would this also justify the regulation of wages? Clearly, based on his opposition to the idea in *Thoughts and Details*, it did not. But this remark does raise an ambiguity about his possible support for the regulation of other kinds of profit.

Burke is inverting a conventional pattern of thought on profit: rather than fueling greed and impropriety, individual reward could tame the savage human impulse to dominate others. There is an intriguing consonance between this line of thinking and Burke's thoughts on the East India Company and the Indian economy. In the case of the latter, Burke concluded that reviving the incentive for commercial profit would curtail, not exacerbate, the improprieties of Company servants in British India. His appraisal of honorable and fair profit in *Speech on Economical Reform* also anticipates his argument in *Thoughts and Details* that the pursuit of material gain could promote commercial virtue and ethical conduct. For Burke, even without the possibility of reaping compensatory profit, men working for no reward would still be attracted to the sparkle of riches, and thus would employ their public power in pursuit of private lucre. "For as wealth is power, so all power will infallibly draw wealth to itself by some means or other: and when men are left no way of ascertaining their profits but by their means of obtaining them, those means will be encreased to infinity," Burke remarks.[120] He was referring to a government allowance in *Speech on Economical Reform* and private reward in *Thoughts and Details*, but his principle in defense of profit remained constant: "This is true in all the parts of administration, as well as in the whole."[121]

Burke's argument captures his hesitancy to applaud statesmen who aspired to work in government without the prospect of remuneration. "[I]f men were willing to serve in such situations without salary, they ought not to be permitted to do it," he insists. "Ordinary service must be secured by the motives to ordinary integrity."[122] A British civil servant, like any man, harbored the reasonable expectation that he would receive equitable reward for his labor. A person who desired to work for the state with no opportunity for reward, however, posed a far more dangerous threat to the government. Burke observes, "[T]hat state which lays its foundation in rare and heroic virtues, will be sure to have its superstructure in the basest profligacy and corruption."[123] His apprehension of the limited nature of man blends here with his reform efforts: Burke is alerting listeners to the hollow professions of self-sacrifice by statesmen – flawed creatures like all human beings – who claimed to want to advance the public good without expecting approbation for their efforts. He suggests that such outward displays of heroism masked a sinister impulse for

---

[120] Langford, *Writings and Speeches*, III, 531. [121] Langford, *Writings and Speeches*, III, 531.

[122] Langford, *Writings and Speeches*, III, 530.

[123] Langford, *Writings and Speeches*, III, 530–531. In *Thoughts on the Present Discontents*, Burke warned readers to be on guard against men who claimed they had left their political party based on principle: "[W]hen a gentleman with great visible emoluments abandons the party in which he has long acted, and tells you, it is because he proceeds upon his own judgement; that he acts on the merits of the several measures as they arise; and that he is obliged to follow his own conscience, and not that of others; he gives reasons which it is impossible to controvert, and discovers a character which it is impossible to mistake" (Langford, *Writings and Speeches*, II, 318–319).

power and patronage. Burke's solution, then, was straightforward: supply an honest material reward for honest public service through the dispensation of fixed allowances.

Burke was not willing to destroy the "exorbitant emoluments"[124] of particular offices either, suggesting that the amount of public reward should not necessarily be determined by market value. "The service of the public is a thing which cannot be put to auction," he says, "and struck down to those who will agree to execute it the cheapest."[125] He does not explicitly reproach market laws in this discussion, but he insinuates that just reward for service to the state may transcend the dispassionate calculation of monetary cost and benefit. "When the proportion between reward and service, is our object, we must always consider of what nature the service is, and what sort of men they are that must perform it," Burke explains.[126]

Indeed, government value may mirror market value for these particular services. Yet his comments, integrated with his observations about the primacy of preserving a strong leadership class, hint at an intuition in Burke's thought that perceived public merit to hold value beyond strict financial considerations. As he would write later in defense of remuneration for public service in *Letter to a Noble Lord*, "Money is made for the comfort and convenience of animal life. It cannot be a reward for what, mere animal life must indeed sustain, but never can inspire."[127] The character of government, and of civil society, rests on more than the simple premise of transactional exchange. This belief holds vast implications for Burke's critique of the French Revolution.

In addition to these reforms, Burke in *Speech on Economical Reform* proposes to cleanse the British government of other weighty encumbrances. For example, he calls to eliminate subordinate jurisdictions that incurred high costs, struggled to raise revenue, and encouraged patronage and sinecures for MPs. One such jurisdiction was the duchy of Lancaster, whose estates were blemished by "pretensions" and "vexations" and "litigations."[128] According to Burke, they were "exchequers of unfrequent receipt, and constant charge,"[129] unworthy of being maintained. He also seeks to convert the functions of the Paymaster General of the Forces and the Treasury of the Navy, both lucrative positions, from treasuries into offices of administration.[130]

---

[124] Langford, *Writings and Speeches*, III, 530.   [125] Langford, *Writings and Speeches*, III, 530.
[126] Langford, *Writings and Speeches*, III, 531.   [127] Langford, *Writings and Speeches*, IX, 150.
[128] Langford, *Writings and Speeches*, III, 500.   [129] Langford, *Writings and Speeches*, III, 500.
[130] Langford, *Writings and Speeches*, III, 521. Lucy S. Sutherland and J. Binney note that the Paymaster had become "perhaps potentially the most lucrative [office] that a parliamentary career had to offer" in the eighteenth century. See Sutherland and Binney, "Henry Fox as Paymaster General of the Forces," *English Historical Review* 70 (1955): 230. Henry Fox, who had been Paymaster during the Seven Years War, exemplified the corrupting effects of the post, as he reaped conspicuous lucre during his tenure. Both the Paymaster and Treasurer of the Navy offices embodied the worst maladies of British public finance; they would brandish their power

Burke's name is frequently invoked as a defender of localism and community, and with ample justification. His stirring reference to the "little platoon[s]"[131] of society in the *Reflections* encapsulated his belief that immediate social associations were man's first sources of affection and the germs of his broader public allegiances. But Burke's petition to remove costly subordinate jurisdictions in *Speech on Economical Reform* communicated the view that policy should be pursuant to national aims rather than parochial desires. "It is exceedingly common," he asserts, "for men to contract their love to their country, into an attachment to its petty subdivisions; and they sometimes even cling to their provincial abuses, as if they were franchises, and local privileges."[132] Loving our closest family members and friends was a natural expression of sentiment, yet defending the profligacy of swollen jurisdictions was a selfish act of political expediency. Even more, asserting legal claims to franchises and privileges was a far more tenable endeavor than shielding political encumbrances from much-needed reform.

Burke is not advocating a policy of nationalism as the term is understood today, but he is drawing attention to the ways in which an excessive preoccupation with local offices could imperil sound public finance in national government. When outlining this argument, Burke presents striking insights into his beliefs about the financial self-interest of man:

[I]n places where there is much of this kind of estate, persons will be always found, who would rather trust to their talents in recommending themselves to power for the renewal of their interests, than to incumber their purses, though never so lightly, in order to transmit independence to their posterity. It is a great mistake, that the desire of securing property is universal among mankind. Gaming is a principle inherent in human nature. It belongs to us all. I would therefore break those tables; I would furnish no evil occupation for that spirit; I would make every man look every where, except to the intrigue of a court, for the improvement of his circumstances, or the security of his fortune.[133]

Man is more likely to secure and defend parochial advantage than to sacrifice his interests for the benefit of future generations. The instinct to use, and misuse, money for private gain – "gaming" – is sown in his natural constitution. For Burke, honorable reward stems from honorable initiative, which could be fostered if the British constitution discouraged the abuse of government offices and jurisdictions and established a fair pension system.

This point may appear to conflict with Burke's belief in *Thoughts and Details* that private interest leads to public advantage. The difference is that the pursuit of individual interest in *Thoughts and Details* generated broader collective benefit when pursued in an environment of market competition. The problem with gleaning benefits from swollen jurisdictions, Burke conveys, is that it

to extract abundant money from the Treasury and issue loans with interest, with the intent of making a quick profit. See Lock, *Edmund Burke*, vol. I, 451.
[131] Langford, *Writings and Speeches*, VIII, 97.   [132] Langford, *Writings and Speeches*, III, 501.
[133] Langford, *Writings and Speeches*, III, 501.

subverted the principle that men should seek to obtain and secure wealth absent royal favors – as he says, they should improve their condition "except to the intrigue of a court."

Burke's program thus abolished royal offices that, in his judgment, were useless and costly. As a result of the sale of the Crown's estates, the Surveyor General and two chief justices in Eyre – the latter presiding over the highest court of forest law in the Middle Ages[134] – would be eliminated.[135] (No doubt Burke remembered the baleful influence of the Surveyor General during the *Nullum Tempus* affair twelve years earlier that advantaged James Lowther.) Burke also lists anachronistic positions in the royal household that would be extinguished under his plan of reform, including: the Treasurer of the Household; the Comptroller of the Household; the Cofferer of the Household; the Treasurer of the Chamber; the Master of the Household; the Board of Green Cloth[136]; lower offices in the department of the Steward of the Household; the Great Wardrobe; the Removing Wardrobe; the Jewel Office; the Robes; the Board of Works; and almost all positions in the civil branch of the Board of Ordnance.[137] Please consult Table 5.1 for a review of Burke's plan of economical reform.

For Burke, these offices stunk of the feudal traces of the royal household and were gross examples of the Crown's exploitation of sinecures. The inert Board of Works captured the nub of the problem. It was cursed with the "grand radical fault, the original sin, that pervades and perverts all our establishments; the apparatus is not fitted to the object, nor the workmen to the work."[138] Society constantly evolved, and the demands of government frequently shifted, but the heavy weight of the royal household remained motionless.

Burke underscores in *Speech on Economical Reform* that his motivation was not to target the flesh-and-blood individuals who held these offices. In matters of economical reform, men should be careful to distinguish personal animosities from their rational capacity to identify the root of the institutional problem: "It is necessary, in all matters of public complaint, where men frequently feel right and argue wrong, to seperate prejudice from reason; and to be very sure, in attempting the redress of a grievance, that we hit upon its real seat, and its true nature."[139] The tribal instincts of human nature compel man to attack personnel, when in fact the flaws of the British government were driven by structural deficiencies. "Where there is an abuse in office, the first thing that

[134] See James Fitzjames Stephen, *A History of the Criminal Law of England*, vol. I (London: Macmillan, 1883), 136.

[135] Langford, *Writings and Speeches*, III, 507.

[136] Note that while Burke lists the Board of Green Cloth separately, many of the other offices on the list were headed by members who sat on the Board.

[137] Langford, *Writings and Speeches*, III, 518.   [138] Langford, *Writings and Speeches*, III, 516.

[139] Langford, *Writings and Speeches*, III, 519.

TABLE 5.1 *Burke's program of economical reform*

Sovereign jurisdictions to be abolished and united in the Crown

• Cornwall
• Duchy of Lancaster
• County palatine of Lancaster
• Wales
• Chester

Costly offices of jurisdictions to be abolished; vexatious titles extinguished by act of short limitation; sell estates that supported jurisdictions; turn tenant-right into a fee

Landed estates of the Crown to be reformed

• Sell off to private market
• Have particular manorial rights (regarding forest lands) valued on enclosure
 1. Exchange rights for portion of land to be sold
• Survey all timber lands
 1. Dispose of timber land useless to naval interest of Britain
 2. Enclose other timber lands that could furnish perpetual supply
 3. Terminate right of venison
• Extinguish forest rights
• Allot and compensate for commons
• Exceptions:
Houses, gardens, and parks of the Crown; one forest chosen by the Crown
• Offices eliminated:
Surveyor General
Two chief justices in Eyre

Services of royal household to contract out

• King's tables
• Great Wardrobe
• Mint

Reforms for Royal Artillery

• Subordinate civil functions to military functions
• Send military branch to army
• Send naval branch to Admiralty
• Create military commission of officers from army and navy to oversee reforms
• Contract out necessary services
• Methodize payments under inspection of minister of finance

(continued)

TABLE 5.1 *(continued)*

Offices to be abolished in the Royal Household
- Establishment of detail
- Treasurer of the Household
- Comptroller of the Household
- Cofferer of the Household
- Treasurer of the Chamber
- Master of the Household
- Board of Green Cloth
- Subordinate offices in the Steward of the Household
- Great Wardrobe
- Removing Wardrobe
- Jewel Office
- Robes
- Board of Works
- Almost all of the civil branch of the Board of Ordnance
- Master of the Buckhounds
- Master of the Staghounds
- Master of the Foxhounds
- Master of the Harriers

Banks/treasuries to be turned into offices of administration
- Paymaster of the Land Forces/Treasurer of the Army
- Treasurer of the Navy

Reforms for Bank of England
- Imprest money of pay offices (see above) to Bank of England
- Use money for charge of the Mint
- Use money for charge of remittance to troops abroad

Pension Reform
- Terminate Paymaster of the Pensions
- Transfer payment responsibilities to Exchequer
- Consolidate lists of pensions
- Reduce pensions from more than £100,000/yr to £60,000/yr (would save £40,000/yr)

(continued)

TABLE 5.1 (*continued*)

Patent offices in the Exchequer to be reduced to fixed salaries
• Auditor of the Receipt: £3,000/yr
• Auditor of the Imprest: £1,500/yr
• Rest of principal officers: £1,500/yr

Privileges retained under Crown
• Grant some pensions for exceptional public service

Offices/allowances to be preserved
• Pensions
• Exorbitant emoluments
• Offices of honor of king

State offices to abolish
• Secretary of State for the Colonies (American Secretary)
• Board of Trade

Order of offices to be prioritized for Civil List payments
• Judges
• Foreign ministers
• Government contractors
• Domestic servants of king and persons in efficient offices whose salaries are under £200/yr
• Pensions and allowances of royal family, including the queen, with stated allowance of Privy Purse
• Efficient offices of duty whose salaries may exceed £200/yr
• Whole pension list
• Office of honor (lords)
• First Lord of Treasury, Chancellor of Exchequer, and other treasury commissioners

---

occurs in heat is to censure the office," Burke says. "Our natural disposition leads all our enquiries rather to persons than to things."[140] In his speech, he targets things – offices – and not individual officeholders.

Burke also recommends the elimination of the royal sinecures of Master of the Buckhounds, Master of the Staghounds, Master of the Foxhounds, and Master of the Harriers.[141] In general, the sluggish character of the British government perpetuated a self-reinforcing cycle of redundancy, giving rise to

---

[140] Langford, *Writings and Speeches*, III, 519.   [141] Langford, *Writings and Speeches*, III, 532.

an endless chain of inefficacious and costly departments anathema to the common good. "In our establishments, we frequently see an office of account, of an hundred pounds a year expence, and another office, of an equal expence, to controul that office, and the whole upon a matter that is not worth twenty shillings," Burke utters with a mixture of derision and bemusement.[142] In modern vernacular, he is exposing the dangers of an enlarged and unaccountable administrative bureaucracy.

One specific pitfall of a swollen bureaucracy was the inefficiencies in banking and accounting practices, which invited the rise of unscrupulous profits. When explaining this feature of the British government in *Speech on Economical Reform*, Burke first provides brief comments that mark his comprehension of money and banking. "Money is a productive thing," he states.[143] Therefore, "[W]hen the usual time of its demand can be tolerably calculated, it may, with prudence, be safely laid out to the profit of the holder."[144] Such was the operating procedure of financial institutions. Thus "no profit can be derived from the use of money, which does not make it the interest of the holder to delay his account."[145] Making money off of money – interest – was an essential activity of banking.

In Burke's judgment, the problem was that this system had been corrupted by the Exchequer to produce "[t]he great and the invidious profits" for the Pay Office.[146] Treasury officials have "brought rigour and formalism to their ultimate perfection," obstructing the steady calculation of government expenses while producing windfall riches for themselves. The consequence laid bare the ignominious depths of bureaucratic incompetence: "[W]e have a long succession of pay-masters and their representatives, who have never been admitted to account, although perfectly ready to do so."[147] The paradox of formalism was that it bred delays and irregularities rather than efficiencies. "[T]he extreme of rigour in office (as usual in all human affairs) leads to the extreme of laxity," Burke laments.[148]

This defect was especially pronounced in the auditing procedures of the Exchequer, which, "more severe than the audit to which the accountants are gone, demands proofs which in the nature of things are difficult, sometimes impossible to be had."[149] Even the most powerful force that conquered man could not topple the national treasury. "Death ... domineers over every thing, but the forms of the exchequer," Burke observes wryly, reminding modern readers of Ronald Reagan's dictum that a "government bureau is the nearest thing to eternal life we'll ever see on this earth."[150] The imperfections of the Exchequer cried out

[142] Langford, *Writings and Speeches*, III, 513.   [143] Langford, *Writings and Speeches*, III, 519.
[144] Langford, *Writings and Speeches*, III, 519.   [145] Langford, *Writings and Speeches*, III, 519.
[146] Langford, *Writings and Speeches*, III, 519.   [147] Langford, *Writings and Speeches*, III, 520.
[148] Langford, *Writings and Speeches*, III, 519.   [149] Langford, *Writings and Speeches*, III, 520.
[150] Langford, *Writings and Speeches*, III, 520. For Reagan's quote, see H. W. Brands, *Reagan: The Life* (New York: Anchor Books, 2016), 4.

for reform, for the financial institution's stiffness of execution was fundamentally different from effectual but moderate administrative supervision.

We return to the royal offices. In *Speech on Economical Reform*, Burke thinks that their removal would "relieve the nation from a vast weight of influence," which would "forwar[d] every public service."[151] And British citizens would benefit: "When something of this kind is done, then the public may begin to breathe."[152] Burke is associating the elimination of costly offices with the advancement of the general welfare. More important, he argues that the eradication of useless royal offices characterized the British tendency to weigh variables in the cause of political reform that eclipsed considerations of public economy. "Under other governments, a question of expence is only a question of œconomy, and it is nothing more; with us in every question of expence, there is always a mixture of constitutional considerations," Burke observes.[153] Discriminating frugality should blend with constitutional principles to inform institutional reform.

This factor should be underlined. For Burke, economic questions were never divorced from constitutional, ethical, or political concerns. One of Burke's underlying messages in *Speech on Economical Reform*, and throughout his entire legislative campaign to promote his program, was that the House of Commons should reassert its constitutional authority over the decision-making procedures of public expenditure. "I am sure no man is more zealously attached than I am to the privileges of this house, particularly in regard to the exclusive management of money," he insists.[154] Reclaiming this duty would help restore the integrity of the British constitution and refresh the spirit of parliamentary independence.

Burke elaborated on this point one month later. When Lord North proposed on March 13, 1780 to form a commission, consisting of members unaffiliated with the House of Commons, to investigate the British government's public accounts, Burke leapt up in opposition. He believed that the officers would be unaccountable to the public because they would not be chosen from the Commons. The commission would be "composed of obscure individuals, men, picked out of corners, and huddled together no men knew how!"[155] North's measure would thus accelerate the pattern of royal corruption, for it would "increase the influence of the Crown, to create a new board, to create new dependents on the Minister, to create an unnecessary encrease of expence!"[156]

Instead, the House of Commons deserved to exercise its authority to examine government expenditures. "Who were so competent to inspect the public accounts as Members of Parliament?" Burke asks.[157] MPs were "men of high

---

[151] Langford, *Writings and Speeches*, III, 518.   [152] Langford, *Writings and Speeches*, III, 518.
[153] Langford, *Writings and Speeches*, III, 518.   [154] Langford, *Writings and Speeches*, III, 548.
[155] Langford, *Writings and Speeches*, III, 559.   [156] Langford, *Writings and Speeches*, III, 559.
[157] Langford, *Writings and Speeches*, III, 559.

character, whose names were known to the public and whose reputations were a bond of security and a seal of certainty."[158] And they would "honestly and faithfully discharge their duty as commissioners."[159] Unlike the democratic Commons, the growth[of a faceless independent agency unanswerable to the people would tilt the weight of the Constitution toward the executive branch. The members, who were "not authorized by the Constitution," would "possess a superseding power over members of Parliament."[160] This is precisely what Burke hoped his plan for economical reform would prevent.[161]

Essential Public Offices

In *Speech on Economical Reform*, Burke's sensitivity to the constitutional implications of reform applied no less to the Civil List, the list of money appropriated by the British government to fund the expenses of the royal household.[162] It served as a particular source of friction in English politics at the time because it raised fundamental questions about the balance of power between Parliament's authority over public finance and the independence of the Crown.[163] Opponents had attacked George III's exploitation of the Civil List as a corrupt instrument that purchased political allegiance from MPs through bribes and pensions.

Burke exhibits an awareness of the importance of sound public finance in his discussion of the Civil List by calling for the treasury to adopt a consistent and transparent process for payments. Burke's plan was for "a fixed and invariable order in all its payments, which it shall not be permitted to the first lord of the treasury ... to depart from."[164] He then proceeds to list the public offices that, in his judgment, warranted first priority in receiving the payments. This brief catalog tends to be overlooked in secondary commentaries on Burke. Yet it effectively distills his conception of the proper role of the state, and elucidates his definition of "public service," a term to which he refers frequently in his commentary on economical reform. In doing so, the list spotlights the government positions he believed were imperative for effectual public administration.

The list, in order of greatest-to-least importance, was as follows: judges; foreign ministers; tradesmen who contracted their services to the Crown; domestic servants of the monarch, and other persons of efficient offices whose

---

[158] Langford, *Writings and Speeches*, III, 559. [159] Langford, *Writings and Speeches*, III, 559.
[160] Langford, *Writings and Speeches*, III, 559.
[161] Note that Burke did propose to create a military commission consisting of officers from the army and navy. This was because military accounts became "too minute and complicated for legislature, and require[d] exact, official, military, and mechanical knowledge" (Langford, *Writings and Speeches*, III, 517).
[162] It was replaced by the Sovereign Grant in the Sovereign Grant Act of 2011.
[163] See Reitan, "Civil List in Eighteenth-Century British Politics," 318–337.
[164] Langford, *Writings and Speeches*, III, 542. Note that the First Lord of the Treasury was the head of the ministry.

salaries remained under £200 per year; allowances and payments of the royal family; efficient offices of duty for persons whose salary surpassed £200 per year; the whole pension list; "offices of honour" that courted the king; and the salaries and pensions of the First Lord of the Treasury and subordinate positions in the Treasury.[165]

These priorities are firmly compatible with Burke's later reflections on the responsibilities of government. Recall his statement in *Thoughts and Details* that the activities of the state should be confined "to every thing that is *truly and properly* public, to the public peace, to the public safety, to the public order, to the public prosperity."[166] Burke's list matches this description. Positions that preserved domestic order and defended Britain's interests abroad – judges and foreign ministers – commanded first priority. Judges held special importance in Burke's eyes; they "ought to be the very last to feel the necessities of the state" because "public justice ... holds the community together."[167] Since judges should maintain an air of independence from politics, and because they were responsible for securing the legal protections of citizens, they should not be forced to court others for payment. "They ought to be as *weak solicitors on their own demands*, as strenuous assertors of the rights and liberties of others," Burke avers.[168] The administration of justice was essential for the conservation of the state – and for liberty.

Somerset House and Additional State Investments in Public Projects

In light of Burke's views on the Civil List, it is worth mentioning a number of other government expenses he believed were worthy of their cost. In 1775, at a time when London lacked the type of grand public offices that populated European capitals, Burke supported a parliamentary resolution to increase funding for the conversion of Somerset House, a former royal palace whose upkeep had been neglected for decades,[169] into a national administrative building. Burke's argument, as captured in his parliamentary speech, *Speech on Somerset House*, was stirred by the conviction that public edifices should provoke awe among citizens and imbue in them a profound sense of attachment to their country. Citizens, Burke said, "pride themselves on the glory of their country possessing such" public works that are "elegant and magnificent."[170] He adopts a similar strand of reasoning in *Speech on Economical Reform* when condemning the Board of Works for the inconspicuous presence of the buildings it constructed: "[T]hough it is the perfection of charity to be concealed, it is ...

---

[165] Langford, *Writings and Speeches*, III, 542–543.
[166] Langford, *Writings and Speeches*, IX, 143. [167] Langford, *Writings and Speeches*, III, 542.
[168] Langford, *Writings and Speeches*, III, 542.
[169] See "History," Somerset House, accessed March 12, 2017, www.somersethouse.org.uk /history.
[170] Langford, *Writings and Speeches*, III, 170.

the property and glory of magnificence, to appear, and stand forward to the eye."[171] For Burke, the Board of Works did not promote the splendor of its constructions, to the extent that it had built any. In regard to Somerset House, Burke's efforts met with success; Parliament approved funding for the new building, and construction began the following year.[172]

Burke's advocacy of awe-inspiring public buildings in *Speech on Somerset House* conveyed a belief in the positive function of the state to advance the national welfare of the people. As he argued in the speech, government bore the responsibility to honor the eminence of its citizens, and of their country: "[A]s you must build – as there must be fronts and ornaments of some sort, let them be beautiful – let them really decorate this great capital – let them in some degree partake of the splendor of the people to whom they belong, and by whom they are raised."[173] The state could nourish sentiments of affection among the people and between the people and government, as long as public administration was selective in its investment of public money; this is what Burke called "laudable and useful expences."[174] Such investment must also advantage the people, because it was their money that was being spent in the first place. In this spirit, we must remember that radical parsimony was *not* an operating principle of Burke's approach to government expenditure.

Burke also supported investment in cultural and educational projects. He called for additional funding to the British Museum to advance "the liberal and polite arts."[175] The alternative, to discourage state support of the arts, would "forward the destruction"[176] of Britons and bring about civil strife. In addition, as discussed in Chapter 3, Burke inquired about obtaining government subsidies to support his school for children of French émigrés. These examples are supplementary evidence of his view that the state and the people were not natural antagonists, and that the former sometimes had a crucial role to play in promoting the well-being of the latter in a commonwealth.

Revenue, Public Finance, and Necker

We return to *Speech on Economical Reform*. A key theme in the speech is Burke's belief that the reduction of government expenditures would actually produce a *stronger* revenue stream for the state in the long run. This point is not emphasized in secondary accounts of Burke's oration, but it is essential to understanding his conception of the relation between public finance and revenue, not only in regard to his plan for economical reform but also to his

---

[171] Langford, *Writings and Speeches*, III, 516. Burke further notes that for all the heavy cost of maintaining the Board of Works, "[W]e do not see a building of the size and importance of a pigeon-house."

[172] Langford, *Writings and Speeches*, III, 171.   [173] Langford, *Writings and Speeches*, III, 171.

[174] Langford, *Writings and Speeches*, III, 171.   [175] Langford, *Writings and Speeches*, III, 336.

[176] Langford, *Writings and Speeches*, III, 336.

other writings and speeches on political economy. For Burke, sound public finance in general would not extinguish the collection of government receipts. On the contrary, it would create a firm system of revenue guided by regularity of form and predictability of payment. Once the landed estates of the Crown become privatized, Burke comments in *Speech on Economical Reform*, they would "come, through the course of circulation, and through the political secretions of the state, into our better understood and better ordered revenues."[177]

Similarly, Burke conjectures that his program would give rise to "two or three hundred thousand pounds a year."[178] If not, it would still provide a "system of œconomy, which is itself a great revenue."[179] A thread of logic connects this analysis to Burke's commentary on the political economy of Anglo-American and Anglo-Indian affairs. In his view, the easing of new commercial regulations in the North American colonies would produce greater public riches, a portion of which could then be collected by the British government as revenue. In British India, the East India Company's abuse of political authority harmed not only the Indian people but also its own financial interests, since the firm's intrusion into the industrious activities of natives thwarted the growth of the Indian economy, which, in consequence, generated less wealth for the Company to tax. Such reasoning helps explain why Burke, in *Speech on Public Expenses*, cited "that old and true lesson, *Magnum vectigal parsimonia*," meaning "Economy is a great revenue," from Cicero's *Paradoxa Stoicorum*.[180] And as Burke declares in *Speech on Economical Reform*, "No revenue, no not a royal revenue, can exist under the accumulated charge of antient establishment; modern luxury; and parliamentary political corruption."[181] The expansion of corrupt public administration causes the contraction of state revenue. The opulence of economy exposes the poverty of extravagance.

Burke lays an accent on this argument in *Speech on Economical Reform* by invoking the authority of Jacques Necker to demonstrate the salutary effects of sound public finance on the state. In October 1776, almost four years prior to Burke's speech, Necker had been appointed as directory of the royal treasury under Louis XVI, following Turgot's controversial tenure as France's Controller General of Finance. Not unlike the situation facing Britain, the disturbances of the American war had forced Necker to confront and attempt to remedy the precarious financial state of the French government. He proceeded to implement economical reform that aimed to resettle French finances on solid grounds and augment the power of the French navy.

[177] Langford, *Writings and Speeches*, III, 508.   [178] Langford, *Writings and Speeches*, III, 546.
[179] Langford, *Writings and Speeches*, III, 546.
[180] Langford, *Writings and Speeches*, III, 470, 470n2.
[181] Langford, *Writings and Speeches*, III, 511.

Burke was impressed by the seeming achievements of Necker's program. On December 14, 1778, in *Speech on Army Estimates*, Burke lauded "Monsieur Neckar" for asking for a modest loan to fund the French navy. "[I]t was evident" that France could raise the sum "with the greatest ease, and without imposing any new tax on her subjects."[182] Burke asserted that the strength of France's public finances surpassed that of Britain: he gave France "the credit and advantage greatly, both in point of power of finance, and wisdom of application of her resources."[183] One year later, in *Speech on Public Expenses*, Burke again praised Necker's program for financing France's modest war loans without introducing new taxes, and for reducing debt in the general budget while increasing government receipts. "The whole is funded on *œconomy*, and on improvement of the public revenue," he remarked with approval.[184]

Burke commends Necker in *Speech on Economical Reform* with an even greater measure of acclaim, calling him a "great man."[185] As a result of Necker's program, France had established a "regular, methodical system of public credit."[186] It was a "fabric laid on the natural and solid foundations of trust and confidence among men."[187] Necker's plan reflected "[p]rinciple, method, regularity, œconomy, frugality, justice to individuals, and care of the people."[188] France was able to achieve financial stability even during war, the same war Britain was fighting (albeit on the other side of the conflict). Burke saw "nothing of the character and genius of arbitrary finance; none of the bold frauds of bankrupt power . . . no robbery under the name of loan; no raising the value, no debasing the substance of the coin."[189] Instead, Necker's reforms stimulated a steady revenue stream, lowered national debt, and tamed the prodigality of the king's court.

In addition, Burke admired Necker's refusal to implement taxes to fill French coffers. Before referencing Necker, he opines in *Speech on Economical Reform* that taxes were a simplistic way to advance reform. "Taxing is an easy business," Burke states.[190] He continues: "Any projector can contrive new

---

[182] Langford, *Writings and Speeches*, III, 396.

[183] Langford, *Writings and Speeches*, III, 396. Burke further notes the irony in the different military priorities of France and Britain: while the former was augmenting the power of its navy, thereby resembling an island like Britain, Britain was trying to strengthen its armed forces, a greater imperative of a continental nation.

[184] Langford, *Writings and Speeches*, III, 469. Burke also indicated approval of Necker's program privately in October 1779. See Burke to the Duke of Portland, 16 October 1779, in John A. Woods, ed., *The Correspondence of Edmund Burke*, vol. IV, *July 1778–June 1782* (Cambridge: Cambridge University Press, 1963), 154.

[185] Langford, *Writings and Speeches*, III, 488. In a letter to Burke, Necker recognized Burke's praise of him in *Speech on Economical Reform*. See Necker to Burke, 5 May 1780, in *Correspondence of Edmund Burke*, vol. IV, 233.

[186] Langford, *Writings and Speeches*, III, 487.   [187] Langford, *Writings and Speeches*, III, 487.

[188] Langford, *Writings and Speeches*, III, 487.   [189] Langford, *Writings and Speeches*, III, 487.

[190] Langford, *Writings and Speeches*, III, 486.

impositions; any bungler can add to the old. But is it altogether wise to have no other bounds to your impositions, than the patience of those who are to bear them?"[191] Burke is questioning the wisdom of enacting intricate tax schemes to establish a system of sound public finance. Suggesting that the limits of such fiscal stratagems were preserved not by institutional checks but by the begrudging toleration of the people, he signals that a continuous cycle of taxation could lead to the exercise of arbitrary power. Burke is hinting at his deep-seated antipathy to "projector[s]" – or, in modern vocabulary, social engineers – eager to collect and redistribute wealth.

Burke then sheds light on Necker's effort to avoid taxation during the latter's attempt to restore the integrity of French public finance. Lord North "never could conceive it possible that the French minister of finance could go through [the previous] year with a loan of but seventeen hundred thousand pounds; and that he should be able to fund that loan without any tax."[192] Necker showed the same financial dexterity the following year: after France received a small loan, "No tax [was] raised to fund that debt; no tax [was] raised for the current services."[193] These comments display Burke's aversion to excessive taxation.

In hindsight, although Burke's high regard for Necker's program overestimated the long-term viability of its revenue streams,[194] his elaboration on its apparent qualities does offer a transparent window into his own priorities for economical reform.[195] Burke endeavored to produce frugality of expense, regularity of payment, and economy of administration. He wished to avoid passing new taxes. He was aware of the dangers of inflating the value of currency to mask corrupt financial deficiencies. And he resolved to diminish the undue influence of the Crown. Near the end of *Speech on Economical Reform*, Burke notes that the "principles of my proceedings are, in many respects, the very same with those which are now pursued in the plans of the French minister of finance."[196] Burke would later invoke Necker in the *Reflections* under vastly different circumstances.

5.5 AFTERMATH AND INFLUENCE

In Burke's view, other reform measures beyond those outlined in *Speech on Economical Reform* merited consideration, such as a bill to deprive customs officials of their vote and another to prevent contractors from serving as MPs in the House of Commons. Burke also applauded efforts to tighten the expenses of

---

[191] Langford, *Writings and Speeches*, III, 486.   [192] Langford, *Writings and Speeches*, III, 487.
[193] Langford, *Writings and Speeches*, III, 488.
[194] See *Correspondence of Edmund Burke*, vol. IV, 154n5. See also Robert D. Harris's summary of the "Necker question" in *Necker*, vii–viii.
[195] As F. P. Lock notes, Burke's appeal to Necker also served the purpose of cooling the impression that his plan carried anti-monarchical undertones (*Edmund Burke*, vol. I, 454).
[196] Langford, *Writings and Speeches*, III, 546.

elections and the military.[197] These ideas, he contended in the speech, would further revivify the spirit of independence in Parliament.

Burke himself recognized the imperfections of his own proposals. While the bills were politically palatable to reformers who were serious about curbing royal patronage and state expenditures, the measures, in his judgment, fell "infinitely short"[198] of the public's expectations for meaningful reform. They did not even fully satisfy his personal goals for altering the government's custom and excise tax system and other deformities of its financial administration.

Burke's reforms achieved limited immediate success. While a committee of the whole House voted to terminate the Board of Trade, it retained the American Secretary. Parliamentary oversight of public accounts was strengthened, but the idea to reduce the expenses of the royal household was rejected. Burke's bills were greeted with defeat once Parliament dissolved in September 1780, which further narrowed the opportunity for the Rockinghams to temper the more extreme voices of the reform movement.[199]

Even though Burke's program fell short of its stated aims, contemporary accounts lauded the substance and delivery of *Speech on Economical Reform*. The *London Evening Post* reported that "memory may supply the outlines of his plan, but it would require talents equal to his own to reach the beauties of his detail."[200] Lord North admitted that "there was not a man in England who could have made such a [speech], or treated so very difficult a matter with so much perspicuity, clearness, and ability."[201]

A more moderate version of Burke's Civil Establishment bills passed in 1782, when the Rockinghams were in power again for a brief time. The new bill, the Establishment Act, was a watered-down iteration of Burke's bold plan, yet it still achieved concrete successes. The act finally terminated the Board of Trade; eliminated 134 offices in the ministry and the royal household; and discontinued the American Secretary post. Furthermore, as Warren M. Elofson notes, it secured parliamentary authority over the Civil List. "If nothing else," he writes, "this program was a milestone in Rockingham constitutional thought."[202]

The larger resonances of Burke's efforts extended beyond the late 1770s and early 1780s. These years were a crucial period for the Whig party to establish

---

[197] Langford, *Writings and Speeches*, III, 547–548. Burke did not applaud all proposed reforms. He opposed the ideas emanating from petitioners in London and Yorkshire to enact universal male suffrage and to shorten the duration of Parliament, respectively (Langford, *Writings and Speeches*, IV, 49n2).

[198] Langford, *Writings and Speeches*, III, 547.

[199] When Burke proposed a bill in February 1781, modeled after the proposed reforms in his *Speech on Economical Reform* in 1780, it was also rejected (Langford, *Writings and Speeches*, IV, 65).

[200] Langford, *Writings and Speeches*, III, 481.   [201] *Scots Magazine*, vol. 42, 135.

[202] W, M. Elofson, *The Rockingham Connection and the Second Founding of the Whig Party, 1768–1773* (Montreal & Kingston: McGill-Queen's University Press, 1996), 8.

principles of parliamentary reform, for any attempt at institutional change carried the weight of influencing future arrangements of British constitutional government. "The years from 1778 to 1784 are of the greatest importance in the history of the British constitution, and of the greatest interest for the study of the theory of the constitution as expounded by Montesquieu," C. P. Courtney explains, citing a thinker Burke had once called the "greatest genius, which has enlightened this age."[203] Indeed, as Warren M. Elofson and John A. Woods explain, the program of Burke and the Rockingham Whigs laid the seeds for parliamentary reform achieved under Charles James Fox and later under Earl Grey and Lord John Russell in the nineteenth century.[204] While many of Burke's ideas for economical reform were not wholly original, in the end they represented some of the boldest efforts in the eighteenth century to subdue the corrupt influence of the Crown and revise Britain's system of public finance, forging a path for more fundamental political reform brought about by the Whig party in the following century.[205]

5.6   BURKE'S TRUSTEE THEORY OF REPRESENTATION AND HIS CONCEPTION OF REFORM

Burke's program of economical reform raises two additional matters that remain central to his notion of political economy. The first is his application of his trustee theory of representation to his reform efforts, which he famously articulated in *Speech at the Conclusion of the Poll*. He presented the speech to his electors – which included many politically active merchants – on November 3, 1774, the same day that he officially won a seat in Parliament representing Bristol, an entrepôt of England. In the speech, Burke argues that the connections between an elected legislator and his electors should be tightly woven by the thread of trust. The representative should "live in the strictest union, the closest correspondence, and the most unreserved communication with his constituents."[206] He should pay close attention to their inclinations: "Their wishes ought to have great weight with him; their opinion high respect; their business unremitted attention."[207]

For Burke, however, the lawmaker's attachment to the people did not demand that he blindly acquiesce to their instructions. Rather, the representative should exercise cool and independent discretion on legislative matters: "[H]is unbiassed opinion, his mature judgement, his enlightened

---

[203] C. P. Courtney, *Montesquieu and Burke* (Oxford: Basil Blackwell, 1963), 107. See Langford, *Writings and Speeches*, III, 6. For Burke's quotation, see *Writings and Speeches*, I, 445.

[204] See Langford, *Writings and Speeches*, III, 6.

[205] See Langford, *Writings and Speeches*, III, 482–483.

[206] Langford, *Writings and Speeches*, III, 68. Burke stated this point eight years earlier in *Speech on Enforcement of Stamp Act* (1766). "Nothing can hurt a popular assembly so much as the being unconnected with its constituents," he said (Langford, *Writings and Speeches*, II, 52).

[207] Langford, *Writings and Speeches*, III, 68–69.

conscience, he ought not to sacrifice to you."[208] Therefore, the moral obligation of a representative to his constituents included the duty to make sober decisions, even if this prerogative conflicted with the heated persuasions of public desire. "Your Representative owes you, not his industry only, but his judgement; and he betrays, instead of serving you, if he sacrifices it to your opinion," Burke declares.[209]

The implicit distinction in this formulation separates interest from opinion: what was in the best interest of constituents might not reflect their private wishes. The elected representative held the responsibility to pursue the former object, not the latter. Accordingly, the authority to exercise this responsibility emanated from "a trust from Providence" to act on behalf of his electors.[210] The lawmaker should not ignore the will of his constituents, but instead harness it, or even reject it if necessary, in order to arrive at a judicious political decision for the aim of advancing the public welfare.

Burke's trustee theory of representation inspired his efforts at economical reform. In *Speech on Economical Reform*, he stresses that he did not ignore popular appeals advocating for alterations to the British constitution but rather attended to them with an elevated seriousness of mind. "[It] is our duty when we have the desires of the people before us, to pursue them," Burke says.[211] He goes so far as to characterize the people, specifically those demanding government reform in 1780, as "the masters."[212] But the elected representative should not conform to their wishes "in the spirit of literal obedience."[213] Therefore, Burke insists, "I cannot indeed take upon me to say I have the honour *to follow* the sense of the people."[214] The art of responsible governance required fidelity to the imperatives of trust vested in lawmakers: "We are under infinite obligations to our constituents, who have raised us to so distinguished a trust, and have imparted such a degree of sanctity to common characters."[215]

Burke thus channeled the enthusiasms of the people into a coherent, if moderate, plan for economical reform. "The truth is, *I met it on the way*" he remarks, referring to public opinion.[216] Burke did not yield to the radical strands in Wyvill's movement calling for universal male suffrage or the expansion of parliamentary seats, but he did recognize that the political anxieties of the public warranted heightened consideration from lawmakers. "We are the expert artists; we are the skilful workmen, to shape their desires into perfect form, and to fit the utensil to the use," Burke utters when describing the governing responsibilities of MPs, embroidering his trustee theory with vivid imagery.[217] The people, on the other hand, "are the sufferers, they tell

---

[208] Langford, *Writings and Speeches*, III, 69.   [209] Langford, *Writings and Speeches*, III, 69.
[210] Langford, *Writings and Speeches*, III, 69.   [211] Langford, *Writings and Speeches*, III, 493.
[212] Langford, *Writings and Speeches*, III, 547.   [213] Langford, *Writings and Speeches*, III, 493.
[214] Langford, *Writings and Speeches*, III, 493.   [215] Langford, *Writings and Speeches*, III, 493.
[216] Langford, *Writings and Speeches*, III, 493.   [217] Langford, *Writings and Speeches*, III, 547.

the symptoms of the complaint; but we know the exact seat of the disease, and how to apply the remedy, according to the rules of art."[218]

Burke thereby pursued a policy of institutional modification that reflected the interests of petitioners, if not their desires. The alternate course of action, an unqualified submission to their demands, would have breached the trust that tied the duties of legislators to the welfare of the people. This was because elected representatives were bound by the sacred pledge to act pursuant to the general good, regardless of public sentiment, and because radical democratic changes would have upset the equipoise of British constitutional government – prospect Burke and the Rockinghams were keen on avoiding. Burke's trustee theory of representation, in short, guided his creative energies in the service of economical reform.

The Nature and Purpose of Reform

Burke's campaign to tame the insidious influence of the Crown introduces a second matter relevant to his science of political economy: the nexus between *Speech on Economical Reform* and his broader beliefs about the nature and purpose of reform. In this light, one conventional interpretation of Burke portrays him as the embodiment of a reactionary traditionalist, resisting the forces of change and clinging desperately to romantic relics of the past.[219] A more nuanced view draws attention to the element of gradualism in Burke's thought, emphasizing his sympathy for steady improvement through the retention and renewal of the best wisdom from prior generations.[220]

Speech on Economical Reform issues a fundamental challenge to the first view. Burke calls explicitly for the abolition of old offices and expenses of the royal households. He justifies these reforms by casting doubt on the perceived utility of medieval traditions and invoking the language of progress. The royal household is "formed upon manners and customs, that have long since expired," he says. "[I]t is formed, in many respects, upon *feudal principles*."[221] Burke proceeds to explain how the feudal structure of the royal household, including its corporate principles, might have served a necessary function in years past.

In Burke's judgment, however, the household failed to adapt to changing circumstances, thereby forfeiting its dignity while encouraging vainglorious luxury. "[T]he royal household has lost all that was stately and venerable in the antique manners, without retrenching any thing of the cumbrous charge of

---

[218] Langford, *Writings and Speeches*, III, 547.

[219] Strands of this interpretation are found most recently in Corey Robin, *The Reactionary Mind: Conservatism from Edmund Burke to Donald Trump* (Oxford: Oxford University Press, 2018); and Steven Pinker, *Enlightenment Now: The Case for Reason, Science, Humanism, and Progress* (New York: Penguin Books, 2019), 363.

[220] See, for example, Russell Kirk, *The Conservative Mind: From Burke to Eliot* (Washington, DC: Regnery Publishing, 2001), 45–47.

[221] Langford, *Writings and Speeches*, III, 508.

a Gothic establishment," he observes.[222] Hence maintaining tradition for the sake of tradition was nonsensical: "[W]hen the reason of old establishments is gone, it is absurd to preserve nothing but the burthen of them."[223] This rule obtained even if such establishments were governed by the principle of "*Body-corporate*,"[224] as in the case of the royal household and the Mint.[225]

Burke is known as an impassioned defender of corporate bodies and the corporate spirit.[226] But, as illustrated by his plan for economical reform, he was sensitive to their limits, or at least to their abuse, and did not hesitate to advocate for their termination or renovation when he believed they outlived their utility. Therefore, by inveighing against the lifeless encumbrances of ancestral customs and embracing institutional progress, Burke was appealing to a self-conscious conception of change. "[T]imes alter natures," he remarks in *Speech on Public Expenses* when describing how shifting circumstances influenced his disposition, an attitude that reflected the political temperament of the Whigs as a party keen on reforming outdated traditions.[227] Preserving the integrity of the British constitution required the shrewd fine-tuning of its malign practices.

Such thinking harmonizes with Burke's famous aphorism in the *Reflections* that a "state without the means of some change is without the means of its conservation."[228] Yet in *Speech on Economical Reform* he offers a more powerful attack on desperate clingers to the past:

If there is any one eminent criterion, which, above all the rest, distinguishes a wise government from an administration weak and improvident, it is this; "well to know the best time and manner of yielding, what it is impossible to keep." There have been Sir, and there are, many who chuse to chicane with their situation, rather than be instructed by it. Those gentlemen argue against every desire of reformation, upon the principles of a criminal prosecution. It is enough for them to justify their adherence to a pernicious system, that it is not of their contrivance; that it is an inheritance of absurdity, derived to them from their ancestors; that they can make out a long and unbroken pedigree of mismanagers that have gone before them. They are proud of the antiquity of their house; and they defend their errors, as if they were defending their inheritance: afraid of derogating from their nobility; and carefully avoiding a sort of blot in their scutcheon, which they think would degrade them for ever.[229]

Wise government derives from the facility to discern the appropriate time to reform. But the reflexive impulse to defend inherited practice can lead to the

---

[222] Langford, *Writings and Speeches*, III, 509.   [223] Langford, *Writings and Speeches*, III, 510.
[224] Langford, *Writings and Speeches*, III, 509.
[225] Langford, *Writings and Speeches*, III, 517. Burke writes that the Mint was "a sort of corporate body; and formerly was a body of great importance."
[226] See, for instance, Walter D. Love, "Edmund Burke's Idea of the Body Corporate: A Study in Imagery," *Review of Politics* 27 (1965): 184–197; and Stanlis, *Edmund Burke and the Natural Law*, 163–169.
[227] Langford, *Writings and Speeches*, III, 473.   [228] Langford, *Writings and Speeches*, VIII, 72.
[229] Langford, *Writings and Speeches*, III, 491.

cold tolerance of repeated human error, while blind reverence of the past revolts against the evolving character of English political institutions. Burke's program of economical reform displays a bitter repugnance to this type of reactionary behavior.

The second interpretation of Burke's idea of reform – of gradualist change, steered by the wisdom of the past – also requires elucidation. Burke did hold that change should occur steadily rather than at once. It is in the public interest that reform should be temperate, Burke states in *Speech on Economical Reform*, because "a temperate reform is permanent; and because it has a principle of growth."[230] Even more, he explains that a "great part" of his idea of reform was to "operate gradually; some benefits will come at a nearer, some at a more remote period."[231] In his *Speech on Civil Establishment Bill*, given on March 8, 1780, which concerned his proposal to eliminate the Secretary of State for the Colonies, Burke conceded that terminating the one position would reduce government expenses only slightly. But, he continued, "[E]very plan must have a beginning, and every great plan must unavoidably exist of many small parts."[232] Burke's economical program embodied this ethic of noble caution.

Burke's conception of reform penetrated deeper, however, by distinguishing between incremental change that occurred without a mindful purpose with steady change that was steered by a coherent set of teleological principles. In *Speech on Economical Reform Bill*, his 1781 speech that addressed similar economical reforms, the *Parliamentary Register* reported Burke's remarks as follows:

This reform he endeavoured to effect, not arbitrarily, piece-meal, and at random, but upon certain principles by which the different particulars, in which he endeavoured to effect a reformation, would be connected into one system, which should grow up by degrees to greater perfection, and be productive of still increasing benefits.[233]

And in his *Speech on Economical Reform* in 1780, Burke proclaimed that his goal was to "*œconomize by principle*," meaning that he was motivated "to put affairs into that train, which experience points out as the most effectual, from the nature of things, and from the constitution of the human mind."[234] He further exhorted Parliament to "proceed in reformation on the principles of reason."[235]

We may take such comments to show that Burke's self-understanding of reform did not indicate a deference to the tides of meliorism independent of human will. It underscored, rather, the conscious effort by flesh-and-blood human beings to adapt government to shifting political circumstances based on a structure of principles seeking to fulfill a definable aim. In other words, the

---

[230] Langford, *Writings and Speeches*, III, 492.
[231] Langford, *Writings and Speeches*, III, 492–493.
[232] Langford, *Writings and Speeches*, III, 557.   [233] Langford, *Writings and Speeches*, IV, 51.
[234] Langford, *Writings and Speeches*, III, 513.   [235] Langford, *Writings and Speeches*, III, 521.

principle of reform was not simply process-driven but goal-oriented. Principle gave change the coherence to grow with purpose. And, Burke adds, principled reform should be informed by fairness: "If I cannot reform with equity, I will not reform at all."[236] While the political invocation of "principle" in the eighteenth century could indeed slide into sanctimonious pietism, Burke's application of the word to his economical program appears to have reflected an earnest vision of unity in pursuit of a lofty aspiration: restore the constitutional independence of Parliament.

Burke's idea of reform, nevertheless, has been interpreted by Russell Kirk and Leo Strauss in a way that leaves a false impression about the British philosopher-statesman. "By and large, change is a process independent of conscious human endeavor, if it is beneficial change," Kirk writes in summarizing Burke's outlook on historical development.[237] Similarly, Leo Strauss insists that "the sound political order for [Burke], in the last analysis, is the unintended outcome of accidental causation."[238]

Without a doubt, Burke certainly believed that the growth of civilization was not the product of individual human design. Yet Kirk's and Strauss's portrayal of him in this context communicates a popular but misguided representation of Burke as someone who, because of his opposition to radical change, advocated letting history take its course, believing that man should defer to the larger currents of society outside his control to dictate the horizons of progress.

In assessing *Speech on Economical Reform*, the *Reflections*, and his many other public writings and speeches, however, let us make a key distinction in Burke's philosophy of reform that offers greater clarity to his notion of progress: human beings did not possess the individual intellect necessary to refashion the entire structure of civil society – nor should they try to – but they did harbor the capacity to consciously reform the ways in which institutions were managed and policies were carried out for posterity. As Burke realized, these changes helped set the direction for social progress or decay. If reform was informed by a unified collection of principles and pursued in a steady manner, then men and women did possess sufficient power to change the course of society and of history.

This general conception of reform was the compass for Burke's specific notion of commercial improvement. He recognized that his efforts in advancing liberty of trade – regarding, for example, the Free Port Act of 1766, the Irish trade bills, the repeal of middlemen trading practices, and the opposition to the government regulation of wages – were all steps in the grander process of placing England on firmer commercial principles. Consistent with Burke's remarks, these efforts were not "arbitrar[y]" or "random" but rather exemplified a synthesis of thought on the merits of liberal intercourse. His idea

---

[236] Langford, *Writings and Speeches*, III, 522.   [237] Kirk, *Conservative Mind*, 45.
[238] Strauss, *Natural Right and History*, 314–315.

of commercial reform was characterized not only by gradual change but by principled practical reason.

Burke's notion of reform in *Speech on Economical Reform* contains an additional insight that presages some of his most poignant remarks in the *Reflections* on the limits of abstract theory. In response to the suggestion to place the patent offices in the Exchequer under the normal pension system, Burke claims that to do so in this case would be unwise. "If I should take away the present establishment, the burthen of proof rests upon me, that so many pensions, and no more, and to such an amount each, and no more, are necessary for the public service," he says.[239] Burke continues: "This is what I can never prove; for it is a thing incapable of definition."[240] Measuring the value of "public service" escaped strict numerical quantification. Now recall his aforementioned comment that public service "cannot be put to auction."[241] One could indeed calculate the expenses of offices and establishments, as Burke did with impressive rigor in his study of British public finance, but the overall worth of human behavior and toil on behalf of the state could not be reduced to statements of aprioristic rationalism embodied in abstract numbers or theories. The political resonance of this insight would fully emerge in Burke's critique of the French Revolution.

Furthermore, the wisdom of reform counseled against sweeping change based on such speculative logic. "I do not like to take away an object that I think answers my purpose, in hopes of getting it back again in a better shape," Burke contends. "People will bear an old establishment when its excess is corrected, who will revolt at a new one."[242] The wholesale and sudden rearrangement of institutions risks producing counterproductive effects. And the temperament of a people is more conditioned to accept revisions and modifications than radical alterations, the latter of which could induce widespread distempers. In essence, Burke unites his embrace of prudence and principle with his distrust of rigid calculation in *Speech on Economical Reform* in his attempt to champion his program of economical reform.

The Connection between *Speech on Economical Reform* and Burke's Economic Thought

It is evident how *Speech on Economical Reform* relates to Burke's grasp of political economy consistent with its narrow definition, the study of public finance and government expenditure. But how does the oration connect to Burke's economic thought on markets and commerce? Scholars have offered an assortment of answers to this question. Isaac Kramnick writes that the speech "reveals the glaring bourgeois face of Burke" and the capitalist

---

[239] Langford, *Writings and Speeches*, III, 529. [240] Langford, *Writings and Speeches*, III, 529.
[241] Langford, *Writings and Speeches*, III, 530. [242] Langford, *Writings and Speeches*, III, 529.

sympathies in his thought.[243] Rod Preece disputes Kramnick's portrayal, insisting that he was unable to find "one passage, not even one sentence" in the speech "suggestive of laissez faire, of state withdrawal from economic intervention."[244] This observation is challenged by the most glaring example in *Speech on Economical Reform*: Burke's discussion of the inutility of the Board of Trade was informed by the idea that colonies achieved commercial prosperity when their trade was not regulated by the Board's meddling hands.

Still, the spirit of Preece's larger point remains accurate: *Speech on Economical Reform* was not a manifesto for government restraint in the marketplace, nor was it a defense of capitalism. (This is conceptually and historically true, since the term "capitalism" had not yet arrived in England.) One did not need to be a robust advocate of market liberty at the time to support restraining royal patronage and limiting government expenditure. Preece himself portrays the speech as an argument for "rationalization, efficiency and impartiality."[245] Yet he goes on to write, in describing the message of the speech, "Rather than leaving to Providence, to the 'invisible hand,' the task of correcting disabilities, it is the responsibility of government to correct them."[246] Nevertheless, Preece accepts similar presuppositions as Kramnick by framing *Speech on Economical Reform* in binary categories of modern economic thinking as a statement either for or against government intervention in the market.

The best way to comprehend *Speech on Economical Reform*, however, is to view it as a lucid expression of Burke's opposition to the concentration of power in the Crown, and of his commitment to renew the balance of power in British constitutional government in general. In the speech, and throughout his parliamentary career, Burke did not advocate toppling the monarchy; not only did this radical idea lie far beyond his toleration for change, but the institution was also an essential instrument in preserving the political stability and permanency in the British government, and it also served as a symbol of Britain's rich constitutional heritage. Yet Burke did seek to constrain the Crown, not only by limiting its public expenses but also by softening its corrupt influence over MPs in Parliament, his two stated aims in his reform bill.

Given such considerations, even if one cannot characterize *Speech on Economical Reform* as a robust statement of economic doctrine, the speech does relate to Burke's thoughts on political economy in important ways, as this chapter has outlined. His proposal to sell off royal estates demonstrated his belief that the private stewardship of property, rather than public ownership, occasioned the productive cultivation of land. Burke's favorable assessment of contracts revealed his judgment that voluntary consent produced collective

---

[243] Kramnick, *Rage of Edmund Burke*, 162.
[244] Preece, "Political Economy of Edmund Burke," 269.
[245] Preece, "Political Economy of Edmund Burke," 270.
[246] Preece, "Political Economy of Edmund Burke," 270.

benefits to the transacting parties. His attack on the Board of Trade underscored his conviction that foreign trade released from chains of regulations generated industry and opulence. Most important, his resistance to the concentration of royal power was rooted in a steadfast commitment to protecting liberty. While *Speech on Economical Reform*, on its surface, does not announce an explicit position on bourgeois capitalism, the speech does suggest harmonious cooperation between Burke's dedication to constitutional government and the principles of market exchange.

5.7 CONCLUSION

When immersing oneself in the details flowing out of *Speech on Economical Reform*, it is easy to lose sight of the larger picture that slowly emerges throughout the speech: in championing the systematic reformation of government, Burke is issuing a resolute defense *of* the state as a necessary, and noble, ornament of civil society. Although he was a proponent of a free domestic grain trade and liberal foreign intercourse, Burke did not seek to strip government bare of all offices and narrow its scope to the most trifling extent possible. In his judgment, government performed an integral function in creating, administering, and enforcing fair rules. The state was imperative for political order.

Even more, Burke's conception of an effective state rests on an important distinction he drew between the necessary functions of government and excessive offices and allowances. There was a crucial difference between enabling public officials such as judges and foreign ministers to fulfill their government duties, on the one hand, and pouring lavish perquisites and privileges on lazy servants, on the other. "The power of distributing places, pensions, and honours ... by many was confounded with the idea of government itself," Burke states in *Speech on Economical Reform Bill*, given in 1781, a year after *Speech on Economical Reform*, "and it was thought the one could not subsist without the other, consequently that the power of the state was weakened by a diminution of such instruments."[247] The notion that extravagant allowances constituted the anatomy of the state was based on sheer illusion: "They mistook the emoluments of government for government itself."[248] Hence the reduction of improvident expenditure would not condemn the government to want. "[A] system of frugality will not *lessen* your riches," Burke contends in *Speech on Economical Reform*.[249]

The opposite was the case: a system of frugality would confine the sloth and invigorate the springs of public management. "An œconomical constitution is a necessary basis for an œconomical administration," Burke remarks in the speech.[250] A firm, if lean, state governed by constancy of integrity and purpose would be able to meet the responsibilities necessary to preserve the

---

[247] Langford, *Writings and Speeches*, IV, 63.   [248] Langford, *Writings and Speeches*, IV, 63.
[249] Langford, *Writings and Speeches*, III, 487.   [250] Langford, *Writings and Speeches*, III, 497.

constitutional liberties of the people. "Government ought to have force enough for its functions; but it ought to have no more," Burke affirms. "It ought not to have force enough to support itself in the neglect, or the abuse of them."[251] The successful functioning of a state did not require wasteful remuneration and sinecures; it simply demanded the consistent, regular enforcement of justice and protection from foreign and domestic enemies; the dispensation of reward to true public servants; and selective investment in administrative buildings, museums, and other structures of national reverence.

Accordingly, the broader desideratum in Burke's plan for economical reform was to restore the just proportions of the British constitution in a way that could enhance its capacity to serve as an honorable and efficacious institution of the British people. Economical reform would not simply provide material benefits to the British sown by the privatization of land and the liberation of foreign commerce from the Board of Trade. Its most significant achievement, rather, would be to revive the strength of an institution essential to constitutional order and indispensable to the shaping of a collective political identity.

This point can be underscored by the offices and perquisites Burke did not seek to eliminate in *Speech on Economical Reform*. Sir George Savile preferred to strike all unmerited pensions, while Lord George Gordon and William Jolliffe called to expunge exorbitant emoluments and sinecure places.[252] Burke, however, desired to reform the pension system – not end it. He demanded that judges be paid first, and aimed to change the functions of the Paymaster of the Forces and the Treasury of the Navy, rather than outright extinguish the offices. Burke defended the idea of fixed salaries for the patent offices in the Exchequer. He did not call to reduce "exorbitant emoluments" to efficient offices. Burke admitted in the speech that he retained at least some of these honors, rather than offer more drastic measures, for considerations of prudence rather than principle.[253] Yet his hesitation to dismantle government offices reflected an endorsement of the state and a spirit of moderation, distinct not only from the radical political proposals emanating from Wyvill's movement but also from parliamentary pleas to lessen the expenses of government, such as those from Savile, Gordon, and Jolliffe.

Burke's reform measures, then, articulated a higher purpose of the state beyond the administration of justice: it served as a pillar of constancy that provided stability for the rhythmic circulation of individuals rotating in and out of government. In his defense of paying fixed salaries to the patent offices in the Exchequer, Burke noted that "[i]ndividuals pass like shadows; but the commonwealth is fixed and stable."[254] This utterance marked his conception of the *institutional* primacy of a steady state. Men and women come and go, but the backbone of firm public administration endures: "The difference therefore

---

[251] Langford, *Writings and Speeches*, III, 472.
[252] *Cobbett's Parliamentary History*, vol. XXI, 171–172.
[253] Langford, *Writings and Speeches*, III, 529.   [254] Langford, *Writings and Speeches*, III, 527.

of to-day and to-morrow, which to private people is immense, to the state is nothing."[255]

Such was one chief reason why Burke supported government funding for the conversion of Somerset House into a new public edifice. The molding of national unity and memory through the construction of majestic buildings fostered an element of permanency amid the constant churn of society. For Burke, the importance of the state transcended the perpetuation of the rule of law; the state itself helped produce the cement that bound generations together and maintained the order of the ages.

Furthermore, it helped maintain the vitality of the British Empire. From Burke's perspective, the Empire was defined by more than the extension of its power across the globe; it was the fitness of the British government's public administration and the regularity of its accounting practices that empowered Englishmen to invest energy and resources in distant lands. This is why Burke praised Necker's program of economical reform in the late 1770s. The (attempted) rehabilitation of France's financial solvency encouraged the nation to fortify its navy, and, consequently, its overall influence around the globe. Burke's campaign to reform the British government was moved by the idea that the sinews of public finance amplified the power of the state.

Burke and Classical Liberalism

The deeper dimensions to Burke's defense of the state lay bare a core philosophical difference between his economic thought and that of classical liberals and libertarians. Both Burke and the latter groups championed the great advantages of market liberty. But classical liberals and libertarians, and even some conservatives, tend to describe the theoretical coexistence between the people and the government either as an adversarial relationship, pitting the individual against the state, or as a transactional relationship, in which persons consent to civil government in order to secure their preexisting natural rights.[256] According to the lines of this reasoning, the chief aims of government are to protect private citizens' right to property and to enforce the rule of law. To be sure, many policies desired by classical liberals and libertarians in modernity contain echoes of Burke's advocacy of voluntary exchange in the eighteenth

---

[255] Langford, *Writings and Speeches*, III, 527.
[256] Hobbes's *Leviathan* and Locke's *Two Treatises of Government* are most famous in this regard. See also, among many, Robert Nozick, *Anarchy, State, and Utopia* (New York: Basic Books, 1974); Hayek, *Road to Serfdom*; Richard A. Epstein, *The Classical Liberal Constitution: The Uncertain Quest for Limited Government* (Cambridge, MA and London: Harvard University Press, 2014); Roger Kimball, ed., *The New Leviathan: The State versus the Individual in the 21st Century* (New York and London: Encounter Books, 2012); the libertarian essays in Frank S. Meyer, ed., *What Is Conservatism?* (Wilmington, DE: ISI Books, 2015); and Albert Jay Nock, *Our Enemy, The State* (Caldwell, ID: The Caxton Printers, 1950). Consult the writings and novels of Ayn Rand as well.

century. And moderate forms of classical liberalism and libertarianism do not in themselves advance a doctrine of radical individualism.

But a deep-rooted conceptual difference between Burke and classical liberals and libertarians slowly emerges in *Speech on Economical Reform*. For Burke, government did not stand in direct opposition to the citizen, and its purpose was not simply to limit the exercise of arbitrary power and establish the legal conditions for the private maximization of wealth. The state and the citizen were not self-contained entities but integrated expressions of a country's structure, heartbeat, and character. The government, most notably the House of Commons, was comprised of people, and people comprised the government. "Let the commons in parliament assembled, be one and the same thing with the commons at large," Burke exhorts in *Speech on Economical Reform*.[257] MPs should emphasize their connection to the people as partners in the pursuit of a common welfare. Let us pledge, Burke says, that "we *belong* to them; that we are their auxiliaries, and not their task-masters; the fellow-labourers in the same vineyard, not lording over their rights, but helpers of their joy."[258]

The intrinsic nature of government did not militate against the autonomy of private associations; government itself was an association of public and private groups, illuminating the human instinct to forge social relations with others in a political community for a purpose beyond individual need. Burke was not an orthodox Aristotelian or Thomist, but in this spirit he embraced Aristotle's and Aquinas's conception of the state as a natural reflection of the human character rather than a necessary evil of it.

Not unlike many libertarians and classical liberals, Robert Nisbet, a traditional conservative who called Burke "the prophet"[259] of conservatism, erected a looming wall between the state and society. In his landmark book *The Quest for Community*, Nisbet declared that "[s]tate and society must be sharply distinguished."[260] An irrepressible chasm prevailed between government force and the human associations that comprised society: "The conflict between the central power of the political State and the whole set of functions and authorities contained in church, family, guild, and local community has been, I believe, the main source of those dislocations of social structure and uprootings of status which lie behind the problem of community in our age," Nisbet stated, writing in 1953.[261] In his view, the state posed a menacing threat to civil society.

Compared with Nisbet, Burke depicts a stronger symbiotic relationship between government and the people in *Speech on Economical Reform* and his

[257] Langford, *Writings and Speeches*, III, 549.   [258] Langford, *Writings and Speeches*, III, 550.

[259] Robert Nisbet, *Conservatism: Dream and Reality* (New Brunswick, NJ and London: Transaction Publishers, 2008), 18.

[260] Robert Nisbet, *The Quest for Community: A Study in the Ethics of Order and Freedom* (Wilmington, DE: ISI Books, 2010), 92.

[261] Nisbet, *Quest for Community*, 91.

other speeches and writings. Because the state and society were not distinct entities, public administrators and elected representatives shared similar goals as the public writ large, and thus should execute positive functions of the state, such as the erection of public buildings and the preservation of remunerative pensions, in order to advance their welfare. Furthermore, the people should recognize that government could, and should, serve as a source of national pride, since government was administered in the image of themselves. In Burke's judgment, the best way to breed an effectual state was not to display unbridled antagonism toward it. Instead, it was to offer substantive institutional reform of its malign practices in order to strengthen its rightful authority over matters truly related to public management, thereby instilling a sense of confidence in the people and deepening their healthy – though not blind – attachment to government.

How can one square Burke's affirmative conception of the state in *Speech on Economical Reform* with his conclusion in *Thoughts and Details* that government can "do very little positive good" in providing necessities, or "perhaps in any thing else"?[262] The answer lies in the context of each writing. *Thoughts and Details* did not put forth a comprehensive view on Burke's theory of the state but confronted and addressed a particular historical circumstance. Burke presents his most lucid grasp of supply and demand laws and the competitive price system in the memorial, but he does not elaborate on broader issues that were inextricably linked with the proper functioning of public administration, such as national agencies, pensions, and royal offices. Because *Speech on Economical Reform* discusses these issues in greater depth, and because it discloses clues about Burke's fondness for markets, the speech is a smooth complement to *Thoughts and Details*, revealing serious reflections on the place of the state in civil society that the economic tract does not.

Burke's refusal to stress natural dichotomies between the government and the individual is not the only theoretical difference between his conception of the state and that of classical liberals and libertarians. Throughout *Speech on Economical Reform*, he hints that the that did not exist authority of government did not simply rest on consent, and that public service should not necessarily be determined by strict monetary considerations. This is why Burke remarks in *Speech on Economical Reform* that such noble service "cannot be put to auction."[263]

The implication for Burke's political and economic thought is profound. If, in his view, the authority of the state exceeded the satisfaction of popular agreement, and if it could not be put to auction, then the relationship between government and the people should not be conceived as a simple medium of transactional exchange like the market. This belief guided Burke to the conclusion that the ultimate significance of the state was its enduring character: it was a stable vessel of public administration and civil society that

[262] Langford, *Writings and Speeches*, IX, 120.   [263] Langford, *Writings and Speeches*, III, 530.

lasted throughout the generations and helped perpetuate the conditions for the flourishing of civilization. Burke famously argued in the *Reflections* that the state – which, in the context of the phrase in the writing, included the wider social order – was more than "a partnership agreement."[264] *Speech on Economical Reform* conveys a similar point in regard to economical reform.

Therefore, unlike strands of classical liberal and libertarian thought, Burke maintained that the state should be fortified by an element of public *reverence*, a sentiment that could be dissolved by the unbounded extravagance and wastefulness of government. "[I]t is for the sake of Government, for the sake of restoring to it that reverence, which is its foundation, that I wish to restrain the exorbitance of its influence," he uttered in *Speech on Public Expenses*.[265] Reverence was the silent underpinning of legitimate government. In this speech and in *Speech on Economical Reform*, Burke's contention was that the state carried the weighty obligation to advance the interests of its citizens; it could do so not only when it performed functions within its proper scope of responsibility and authority, but also when it was capable of preserving its existence in the first place. "The first duty of a State is to provide for its own conservation," Burke asserted in 1796.[266] Only when self-preservation coexisted with the exercise of responsible authority could government earn the just reverence from the people necessary to sustain it from generation to generation.

The *Reflections* places an even sharper accent on the importance of reverence in the perpetuation of political order. The state should be "looked on with other reverence" distinct from qualities associated with social partnerships of a transactional nature.[267] Reverence reflected collective recognition of the lasting wisdom and utility of time-honored establishments. "We procure reverence to our civil institutions on the principle upon which nature teaches us to revere individual men; on account of their age; and on account of those from whom they are descended," Burke asserts in describing the British people's appreciation for tradition.[268] Reverence minted the rule of law with a degree of heightened esteem that shielded constitutional liberty from radical innovation: "To be enabled to acquire, the people, without being servile, must be tractable and obedient. The magistrate must have his reverence, the laws their authority."[269]

Burke's position is that for any society to exist, there must be *some* authority that warrants enough admiration so that citizens are willing to abide by its established laws. Otherwise, social disorder would persist. Burke is not justifying popular submission to despotism: as he expresses in *Speech on*

---

[264] Langford, *Writings and Speeches*, VIII, 147.   [265] Langford, *Writings and Speeches*, III, 472.
[266] Burke to the Rev. Thomas Hussey, [*post* 9 December 1796], in *Correspondence of Edmund Burke*, vol. IX, 168.
[267] Langford, *Writings and Speeches*, VIII, 147.
[268] Langford, *Writings and Speeches*, VIII, 85.
[269] Langford, *Writings and Speeches*, VIII, 290.

Economical Reform, the state must earn reverence from the people, and if it violates their trust, the people have the right to petition for meaningful alterations to its underlying substructure. At worst, the state can sow the seeds of its own destruction, and society's destruction, if it does not properly exercise its lawful authority. "[W]henever Government abandons law, it proclaims Anarchy," Burke wrote in 1796, excepting cases of war.[270]

Additionally, reverence for established authority protected institutions from the consequences of abstract political theory, a hallmark of Burke's political philosophy. As Burke declaimed in the *Reflections*, theoretical visions of society that could not be implemented in reality should be cast away. He conveys a similar attitude in *Speech on Economical Reform*. "Those things which are not practicable, are not desirable," he states.[271] In this section of the speech, Burke was trying to convince MPs that the moderation of his economical program was not a vice but a virtue. The anticipated merit of reform, relating to public administration or life in general, sprung from the likelihood that it could be achieved in concrete circumstances.

Burke was not a pessimist in this regard, for he held that real change was an eminent possibility because God made it so. "There is nothing in the world really beneficial, that does not lie within the reach of an informed understanding, and a well directed pursuit," Burke remarks in the oration. "There is nothing that God has judged good for us, that he has not given us the means to accomplish, both in the natural and the moral world. If we cry, like children for the moon, like children we must cry on."[272] God gifted man with the faculty for reform.

Burke, in his reference to "beneficial" things that could be improved upon, also lets slip a hint of his predilection for utility in his political thought. For Burke, human beings possessed the skills necessary to refresh institutions and traditions that were sliding into decay. But they must acknowledge the constraints of their current situation before marching forth to change existing practices. "We must follow the nature of our affairs, and conform ourselves to our situation," he cautions.[273] Burke's rhetorical purpose in *Speech on Economical Reform* was to assuage critics that his economical reform did, in fact, go far enough to subdue royal corruption and reduce public expenditure. Yet the theoretic substance of his remarks strikes the heart of his philosophic thought: principled prudence should steer the path to human improvement.

Burke's conception of political economy can now be filled in with greater detail. He defended the natural laws of commerce as instruments of prosperity and argued that internal grain markets should generally be left to their own course, free from the grasping hands of regulators. He endorsed the competitive

---

[270] Burke to the Rev. Thomas Hussey, [*post* 9 December 1796], in *Correspondence of Edmund Burke*, vol. IX, 169.

[271] Langford, *Writings and Speeches*, III, 546.   [272] Langford, *Writings and Speeches*, III, 546.

[273] Langford, *Writings and Speeches*, III, 546.

price system for circulating goods to needy areas in a responsible yet vibrant manner. Burke contended that the useless expenditures of the British government should be disciplined or eliminated; that the British constitution should be purified of the Crown's insidious influence; and that some administrative offices, such as the Board of Trade, compromised the possibilities for commercial growth. Such positions illustrated his resolute belief that a strong and effectual state was a trim and selective one. Besides the Board of Trade, however, these considerations of his political economy primarily addressed matters that remained within the geographical confines of Britain proper. Which begs the question: did Burke recalibrate his support for trade if goods moved beyond the edge of English shores?

PART IV

FOREIGN TRADE

6

Account of the European Settlements in America, the British West Indies, and the Free Port Act of 1766

[I]t is found in nations as it is in the fortunes of private men, that what does not arise from labour, but is acquired by other means, is never lasting. Such acquisitions extinguish industry, which is alone the parent of any solid riches.[1]

Account of the European Settlements in America, 1760

Jamaica is nothing like fully cultivated. The Bahamas, our undisputed right, where it is highly probable sugars might be cultivated to advantage, remain at present utterly neglected, as if unworthy of all notice, though they are many in number, large in extent, fruitful in their soil, situated in a very happy climate, and are in a manner the keys of the West-India navigation.[2]

Account of the European Settlements in America, 1760

6.1 INTRODUCTION

Although Burke did express vigorous support for free market activity in *Thoughts and Details on Scarcity,* he was discoursing primarily on the employment arrangements between farmers and laborers in the domestic grain market, not on the relationship between nations in the international commercial arena. Did Burke, then, apply the lessons in *Thoughts and Details* about the merits of voluntary exchange to foreign trade? Did the laws of supply and demand grant similar benefits to nations as they did to farmers and laborers? How *should* a nation measure its wealth? In bullion? In exports? In both? In neither? The following three chapters seek to explain Burke's answers to these questions.

---

[1] *Account of the European Settlements,* vol. II, 293.
[2] *Account of the European Settlements,* vol. II, 24.

Interpreting Burke's commentary on foreign commerce is a more difficult task than examining his beliefs on the internal grain industry because the former subject cast bright light on the many dimensions and complexities of statecraft in the wider global order. A stream of geopolitical considerations shaped his thought in this regard: English manufactures reached peoples outside the jurisdiction of the British Empire; control of the sea trade was intimately related to a country's naval strength; the wealth of a nation in many ways steered the course of its military and territorial ambitions; many British traders – who were also constituents of elected representatives in Parliament – harbored prejudices against the reduction of prohibitions and duties; adjustments to commercial policy influenced colonial behavior in British dependencies; trade regulations were not theoretical propositions but historically established traditions; and debate over free trade, in general, intersected with concerns about national security and imperial honor. The study of foreign intercourse demanded careful reflection not only on supply and demand and wealth and expense, then, but also on the status of Britain in the world, and on the broader political and economic activities of trade competitors such as the French, the Dutch, and the Irish.

In addition, the use of modern classifications such as "free trade" or "protectionism" to describe attitudes on commercial policy in the eighteenth century is problematic in itself. In Burke's day, "free trade" had not yet hardened into the categorical concept it has today, and remained somewhat of a radical idea into the late 1700s and early 1800s: as Dugald Stewart observed during that period, the "doctrine of a Free Trade was itself represented as of a revolutionary tendency."[3] And "free trade" could connote a variety of meanings held by different people in disparate historical contexts. Did a belief in free trade support the swift nullification of all commercial barriers between nations? Was such a belief compatible with a defense of imperial possessions in distant lands?[4] How free should "free" trade be?

To relate these questions to Burke, could one rationalize empire but also advocate free trade at the same time? Could one balance an allegiance to his home country with a fondness for intercourse with other nations? Could one endorse free trade in times of peace but oppose it in times of war? With such considerations in mind, we may take "free trade" in this chapter to mean the general easing of commercial restrictions between nations. Note, however, that this idea is not necessarily synonymous with a belief in the immediate abolition of all trade barriers.

Given the great difficulty in evaluating Burke's beliefs on foreign trade, scholars have translated his views on this subject in a multitude of ways. One

---

[3] Sir William Hamilton, ed., *The Collected Works of Dugald Stewart*, vol. X (Edinburgh: Thomas Constable and Co., 1858), 87.

[4] For an intellectual history of free trade, see Douglas A. Irwin, *Against the Tide: An Intellectual History of Free Trade* (Princeton: Princeton University Press, 1996).

school characterizes his early economic thought as a species of mercantilism, arguing that Burke gradually adopted the doctrine of free trade later in his career. "It was probably only as Burke's mercantilist views moderated with the passage of time" that Adam Smith could connect Burke's economic principles with his own, David Stevens argues, capturing a common perspective.[5]

The second interpretation portrays Burke as a sturdy advocate of free trade. C. B. Macpherson, exemplifying this tendency, writes that Burke's commercial preferences were "always for free trade"[6] (Macpherson does allow for exceptions in the service of the national interest, such as Burke's support for the Navigation Acts). Alfred Cobban claims that Burke was "one of the first prophets of free trade."[7]

These two interpretations, while touching the truth, require clarification and elucidation. As this chapter will demonstrate, Burke was not what we today would consider to be a champion of "free trade" absolutism because of his defense of the British Empire and the political constraints imposed on him as an elected legislator. Yet this does not mean that Burke held neutral positions in debates concerning commercial policy, or that his economic thought is best framed through a lens of mercantilism or capitalism.

Instead, historical evidence illustrates that Burke leaned strongly, though not wholly, in favor of liberal commercial intercourse between nations – particularly those within the British Empire – throughout his adult life, even prior to his entry into Parliament in 1766. His body of arguments in defense of free trade bears a telling resemblance to *Thoughts and Details* in many respects,

---

[5] David Stevens, "Adam Smith and the Colonial Disturbances," in *Essays on Adam Smith*, eds. Andrew S. Skinner and Thomas Wilson (Oxford: Clarendon Press, 1975), 204. In a similar vein, Carl B. Cone writes that the intellectual compatibility between Burke and Smith would be firmer if "one could find Burke attacking the protectionist system of the [British] Empire as vigorously as Smith" (Cone, *Age of the American Revolution*, 326). Francis Canavan claims that Burke was "not an absolute free-trader" but an "enlightened imperialist" whose "imperialism included imperial protectionism" (Canavan, *Political Economy of Edmund Burke*, 119). James Conniff describes Burke as a "moderate" regarding the struggle between mercantilism and free trade (*Useful Cobbler*, 116). Bernard Semmel insists that "in the seventies and eighties, Burke had not freed himself from the fundamental presuppositions of the old commercial system" (Semmel, *The Rise of Free Trade Imperialism: Classical Political Economy the Empire of Free Trade and Imperialism 1750–1850* (Cambridge: Cambridge University Press, 1970), 21). F. P. Lock writes, "In the 1770s, [Burke] still held to the mercantilist belief that exclusive or preferential trade with its colonies benefits the home country" (*Edmund Burke*, vol. I, 388).

[6] Macpherson, *Burke*, 53.

[7] Cobban, *Edmund Burke and the Revolt against the Eighteenth Century*, 193. Yuval Levin takes note of Burke's "ardent capitalism" (Levin, *The Great Debate: Edmund Burke, Thomas Paine, and the Birth of Right and Left* (New York: Basic Books, 2014), 120). See also Renee Prendergast, "The Political Economy of Edmund Burke," in *Contributions to the History of Economic Thought: Essays in Honour of R. D. C. Black*, eds. Antoin E. Murphy and Renee Prendergast (London and New York: Routledge, 2000), 251–271. Prendergast takes a nuanced approach; she notes Burke's support for free trade but writes that he did not see it as "some sort of absolute ideal" (256).

placing steady emphasis on the material and social advantages that arose from voluntary exchange and the diffusion of commerce. Even more, while Burke's defense of empire would appear to overlap with the mercantilist attraction to colonial expansion, in other ways he disagreed with conventional tenets of mercantilism.

This point is important because it reveals the friction Burke encountered as an MP between economic principle and political prudence. The following three chapters will attempt to draw out such friction by explaining how he oftentimes accepted the watered-down nature of particular free trade measures in Parliament with grim reservation. Rather than pursuing moderation in free trade as a predetermined policy goal, Burke frequently yielded to the reality that existing political circumstances constrained any additional action at the time to further promote the spirit of commercial liberty in the foreign arena.

Finally, and most important, Burke's reflections on foreign trade must be understood in the context of his imperial political thought. Burke believed that the British Empire possessed the authority to govern its subordinate colonial dependencies, replete with all their political and social diversity. Yet with this belief came at least two key qualifications that informed his theory of imperial political economy. First, the Empire was bound by the moral law to rule with gentle beneficence over its subjects. Second, the Empire should not regulate all of their commercial activities; in Burke's judgment, one effectual strategy for the soothing of political tensions and enhancement of social relations was to promote – not restrict – foreign trade. His thought and action on this subject disclose a strong-willed attempt to balance his commitment to the Empire with his endorsement of liberal commercial activity.

The additional layer of Burke's imperial political thought was his awareness that the power of the British Empire derived not simply from its commerce and navigation but also from deeper sources of authority that could not be measured in tonnage. As will be shown, Burke at times made considerations of trade subservient to the wider imperatives of British imperial order, the foremost being its security and integrity. By taking into account such complex dimensions of politics and policy, Burke's economic statesmanship reflected a compelling approach to foreign trade in the eighteenth century worthy of attention.

The next three chapters will examine this approach. This chapter will discuss Burke's thoughts on commerce relating to the British West Indies, as communicated in *An Account of the European Settlements in America* and by the Free Port Act of 1766. The following chapter will elaborate on his reflections on commerce in *Observations on a Late State of the Nation* and probe his views of the political economy of Anglo-American imperial relations in *Speech on American Taxation* and *Speech on Conciliation*. The third chapter in this sequence will examine Burke's reflections on Anglo-Irish trade, including the Irish trade bills; the connection between nature and the right to industry; and, in two of the most conspicuous instances in which he violated his belief in free commerce, William Pitt's commercial propositions and the Anglo-French

Commercial Treaty of 1786. But first we must briefly survey the history of foreign trade in the British Empire in order set the historical context for Burke's actions in Parliament on the question of foreign intercourse.

6.2   BRITISH COMMERCIAL POLICY AND THE NAVIGATION ACTS

England's prevailing tariff system was somewhat limited in scope at the time William III assumed the throne in 1689.[8] A 5 percent tax existed on most import and export articles in 1689.[9] Specific import bans persisted in the Middle Ages and early modern period, but the only levy of real consequence was on woolen cloth. In general, the traditional purpose of English prohibitions and duties was to raise public revenue rather than to enact a self-conscious and systematic program of commercial protectionism.

It was in the fifteen years following the accession of William III,[10] however, that this relatively tame tariff system transformed into an expanding cage of trade restrictions. Its chief purpose was to underwrite military expeditions. In order to finance its war with France in the 1690s, for instance, the British government erected additional duties, sometimes reaching up to 20 percent, on a wide variety of imported goods.[11] The financial impact of the duties affected approximately two-thirds of the aggregate worth of the commodities.[12] Almost all significant manufactured goods were saddled with even more duties. Seizing the opportunity for private advantage, merchants increasingly lobbied government to establish regulations that would obstruct foreign competition in their industries, as Burke would learn in his first session in Parliament, and while serving as an elected representative to the port city of Bristol.

This precedent set in motion a pattern in which tariff rates were imposed progressively higher for more than a century to fund wars. As the 5 percent duty on all ordinary imports increased to 10 percent in 1697 and 15 percent in 1704–1705, England's tariff system was signaling that the protectionist sympathies of British traders were merging and settling into an unavoidable political force. After William III took the throne, Ralph Davis writes, "the English tariff structure was transformed from a generally low-level, fiscal system into a moderately high-level system which, though still fiscal in its

---

[8] This section's analysis of the history of British trade will rely on the following sources: Deane and Cole, *British Economic Growth*, 40–97; Thomas and McCloskey, "Overseas Trade and Empire," 87–102; Ralph Davis, "The Rise of Protection in England, 1689–1786," *The Economic History Review* 19 (1966): 306–317; Mokyr, *Enlightened Economy*, 145–170; and H. F. Kearney, "The Political Background to English Mercantilism, 1695–1700," *The Economic History Review* 11 (1959): 484–496.

[9] See Davis, "Rise of Protection," 307.   [10] Queen Anne would assume the throne in 1702.

[11] The other purpose of the taxes was to further subjugate Ireland. See Davis, "Rise of Protection," 310.

[12] Davis, "Rise of Protection," 310.

purposes, had become in practice protective."[13] The currents of mercantilism, in short, gained speed as a consequence of the expansion of state power for the prosecution of war.

Sugar became the most prominent import good in the eighteenth century. Other productive imports included rice, tobacco, and coffee. A significant portion of customs revenue came from tobacco, food, drink, and wine.[14] The linen and silk industries grew favorably as well under protectionism, reflecting policies intended to strangle French trade.[15]

This summary is intended to show that protectionist measures, rather than reflecting a uniform economic theory, were driven by an overlapping yet discordant mixture of commercial desires, the political pull of mercantile lobbying groups, and geopolitical rivalries. Indeed the British Empire, as did other European powers, frequently utilized prohibitions and duties as instruments to drain the political and military strength of other countries, in addition to funding wars. The British government's imposition of prohibitive tariffs on French products marked the quintessential example of this strategy.[16] Burke took into account all of these considerations in his practice of economic statecraft.

Navigation Acts

The Navigation Acts illustrated England's most vigorous attempt to exploit trade regulations for political and economic purposes, serving as the core of the British Empire's imperial commercial policy in the seventeenth and eighteenth centuries. The modern Acts[17] were a series of regulations first passed by the British Parliament in the mid-seventeenth century under Oliver Cromwell to assist English traders in competing with Dutch merchants, whose commercial activity was thriving at the time following the lifting of the trade embargo between the Spanish Empire and the Dutch Republic in 1647. The laws would also target France and Spain.

The foremost object of the Navigation Acts was to encourage the flow of trade to remain within the British Empire. This was done in order to enhance the trading privileges of English merchants and ensure that the riches of the flourishing American colonies would reach Britain. The Acts also served the broader political aspiration of strengthening its imperial posture in the face of European rivals seeking to weaken Britain's influence around the globe.

The laws generally mandated four kinds of regulations concerning: the destination of colonial trade goods; import and export bounties, rebates,

---

[13] Davis, "Rise of Protection," 307.   [14] Davis, "Rise of Protection," 315.
[15] Davis, "Rise of Protection," 316.   [16] Davis, "Rise of Protection," 309.
[17] Earlier forms of the Navigation Acts dated back to the fourteenth century. See Eli F. Heckscher, *Mercantilism*, vol. II, trans. Mendel Shapiro, ed. E. F. Söderlund (London: George Allen & Unwin Ltd., 1962), 36.

drawbacks, and export taxes; preferences for particular domestic manufactures; and the ownership of the ships, and the nationality of the ships' crews, that transported the goods.[18] In regard to British North America, the Acts permitted goods to be trafficked to the American colonies only if they were transported in British-made vessels and manned by British crews.[19] Products from other European powers could not reach American shores unless they passed through English ports. The Acts, which were repealed in 1849, two hundred years after their modern form was introduced, have been called the "heart" of British mercantilism.[20]

Warfare underwritten by the proceeds of mercantilist regulations bred sharp colonial disturbances. Americans became most upset by the first type of regulation establishing a list of enumerated products that could be exported only to Britain, thereby placing many European and Caribbean trade markets beyond the fingertips of colonial traders. The cost of this trade was further aggravated by the mandate that foreign goods entering the American colonies had to go through British ports and be subject to their customs duties. In addition, the Americans were not allowed to produce hats, iron, wool, and other enumerated goods. Britain also provided export bounties to domestic manufacturers of silks, other non-woolen textiles, linen, and gunpowder to sweeten their competitive edge against foreign traders dealing (albeit with restrictions) in the English colonies.[21]

Robert Walpole, recognized as the first prime minister of Britain, carried out reforms in 1722 that consolidated and simplified the tariff system, ended almost all export duties, and eased import restrictions on some minor materials. The rates of import duties instituted under William III and Anne remained the same, however. More important for our purposes, England implemented a wave of protectionist laws from 1763 to 1776, overlapping with the time that Smith was preparing his draft of the *Wealth of Nations*,[22] and with the start of Burke's parliamentary service. New import bans were imposed against silk products, leather gloves, and stockings, while duties were elevated on linens and paper products. As Davis writes, "At the time [Smith] was writing his great work the system [of mercantilist protectionism] was well developed, was extending and – still primarily under fiscal influences – was to be strengthened further in the war years at the end of the eighteenth century."[23]

---

[18] See Thomas and McCloskey, "Overseas Trade and Empire," 94.
[19] For a short introduction, see James S. Olson, ed., *Historical Dictionary of European Imperialism* (New York: Greenwood Press, 1991), 424.
[20] Edward Mead Earle, "Adam Smith, Alexander Hamilton, Friedrich List: The Economic Foundations of Military Power," in *Makers of Modern Strategy from Machiavelli to the Nuclear Age*, ed. Peter Parent (Princeton: Princeton University Press, 1986), 223.
[21] Thomas and McCloskey, "Overseas Trade and Empire," 94.
[22] See Campbell and Skinner, *Adam Smith*, 145–150.
[23] Davis, "Rise of Protection," 314. Davis does note that duties were reduced on some raw materials such as raw silk and beaver skins.

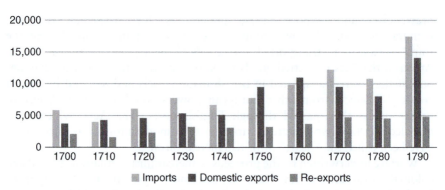

FIGURE 6.1 External trade of England and Wales in the eighteenth century, by decade (in £ thousand)
Source: Mitchell (1988)

There has been much debate about the influence of the Navigation Acts in stimulating or hampering the economic growth of Britain and America in the early modern period. Nevertheless, it is evident that Britain witnessed a blossoming of overseas trade in the eighteenth century, which performed a vital role in fueling its Industrial Revolution and spreading the empire's public prosperity around the globe. The last half of the century in particular experienced a noticeable ascent in foreign trade that greatly exceeded the nation's commercial growth in the first half. See Figure 6.1.

In addition, the sources animating the British expansion of trade changed dramatically in the eighteenth century. At the beginning of the 1700s, almost 62 percent of English imports were drawn from Europe (not including the British Islands), but this figure plummeted to 30 percent by the end of the century.[24] One principal cause for this decline was the swift emergence of British colonial possessions in North America and the West Indies as bountiful reservoirs of trade,[25] as Burke keenly recognized in some of his earliest published thoughts on commerce. In essence, British traders increasingly shifted their restless mercantile eyes from European markets to Atlantic and Caribbean colonial ports in Burke's age.

The important factor to remember about such trading activity in our study of his economic thought, however, was that it developed under the commanding purview of the British Empire, which harbored its own geopolitical and military aims beyond the enlargement of commerce. Strictly speaking, English and American merchants never enjoyed complete laissez-faire trade in the

---

[24] Calculations based on figures in Deane and Cole, *British Economic Growth*, 87. Deane and Cole label English imports in 1797–1798 as "British." Calculations for 1797–1798 include the Fisheries.

[25] Consult Deane and Cole, *British Economic Growth*, 86–88.

eighteenth century. And at the time Burke entered Parliament in 1766, the tides of history were not moving in the direction of free trade; as mentioned, that year was part of an era in which England was enacting more, not fewer, commercial restrictions that confined trade to British ports. The question Burke confronted in his economic thought and as an MP was whether these laws enhanced or diminished the wealth of nations, and the honor of empire.

6.3 AN ACCOUNT OF THE EUROPEAN SETTLEMENTS IN AMERICA

The intellectual roots of Burke's thought on foreign trade were cast wide and deep in *An Account of the European Settlements in America*, a work he coauthored with Will Burke and published anonymously in 1757. Following the outbreak of the Seven Years War in the mid-1750s, questions of conquest and commerce had been thrust to the forefront of England's public consciousness at the time, providing an opportunity for the Burkes to expound the implications of empire on foreign affairs.

Written in this historical backdrop, the *Account* furnishes a muscular defense of Britain's colonial possessions as a means to opulence and a sturdy check against French imperial ambitions. It offers intricate descriptions of many topics of global significance that reflected an impressive, if unoriginal, breadth of knowledge for the time period, such as the history of European colonization (including a complimentary portrayal of Christopher Columbus), the political economy of empire, the quality of soil and production of crops in colonies, and the utility of navigable waterways.[26] Burke himself provided conflicting accounts on whether he or Will was primarily responsible for the work, but most likely Burke wrote some passages, amended others, and delivered its more penetrating philosophic remarks. The *Account*, we can safely say, is representative of Burke's frame of mind on the subject of imperial political economy in the embryonic stages of his intellectual development.[27]

The *Account* is often overlooked in the study of Burke's thought. As this section aspires to demonstrate, such neglect is unfortunate. The writing supplies specific economic insight into the role of regulations in colonial settlements, the influence of accidental causation on history, French expansionism, human nature, slavery, exclusive trading companies, the acquisition of gold, the enduring sources of public prosperity, the hazards of paper money, and the influence of a people's character on their commercial and colonial destinies. The writing also broaches questions about the merits and demerits of free trade and mercantilism that remain essential to understanding Burke's reflections on foreign commerce. The legacy of the *Account* for our purposes,

---

[26] As F. P. Lock notes, the *Account* was indebted to *Navigantium atque iterantium bibliotheca, or A Complete Collection of Voyages and Travels*, a large work published in the 1740s under the editorial direction of John Campbell.

[27] See Lock, *Edmund Burke*, vol. I, 125–130 for background on the composition of the work.

then, is significant: it illuminates general principles of political economy that would serve as durable guideposts to Burke's economic thought throughout the rest of his public and private life.

Commercial Regulations, Empire, and the Virtues of Vice

We begin with one such general principle: European powers held the right to conquest, but excess entanglements in the flow of trade, and unbounded fascination with the acquisition of precious metal, discouraged public opulence in their colonies and in their own mother nation. The *Account* employs the Spanish Empire as a case study. The Burkes blast Spain for imposing unnecessary regulations on the circulation of commerce, arguing that the Empire's envious impulses spawned policies that suppressed the growth of riches:

Jealousy is the glaring character of the court of Spain, in whatever regards their American empire; and they often sacrifice the prosperity to an excessive regard to the security of their possessions. They attend in this trade principally to two objects; the exclusion of all strangers from any share in it, and the keeping up the market for such goods as they send; and they think both these ends best answered by sending out only one annual fleet, and that from one only port in Spain, and to one port only in Mexico.[28]

Trade restrictions and distortions – the confinement of the market; the artificial enhancement of price; and the limitation of ports – clog channels of commerce and thwart public prosperity. The Burkes therefore ask "how they shall get the greatest returns upon the smallest quantity of goods."[29]

The Spanish Empire's control of trade between two ports generated further consequences: "[T]hey discourage in the old world all their towns from that emulation, which would not only enable them to traffic in foreign commodities, but in time to set up fabrics of their own ... [and] they cannot carry their produce directly to the best market." Given such considerations, the Burkes write, "[I]t is very certain, that even trifling discouragements operate very powerfully where the commercial spirit is weak, and the trade in its infancy."[30] In these comments, we can detect underlying economic maxims that Burke would later elucidate and amplify in Parliament: restricting commerce to a select number of ports squeezes the enterprising capacities of a people (in this case, the Spaniards); regulations prevent dealers from reaching vibrant markets; and any limitation on trade had an exceedingly negative impact on underdeveloped markets. The extension of commerce to broader shores, the *Account* suggests, would remedy these defects.

---

[28] *Account of the European Settlements*, vol. I, 234.
[29] *Account of the European Settlements*, vol. I, 234.
[30] *Account of the European Settlements*, vol. I, 235. The Burkes also note in this passage that the confinement of trade encouraged illicit trade.

In addition, the Burkes shrewdly observe that the Spanish Empire had accumulated many valuable metals from its vast colonial possessions – yet such acquisitions in themselves did not occasion national affluence. Up until recently, "[T]he tide of wealth, that constantly flowed from America into Spain, ran through that kingdom like a hasty torrent, which, far from enriching the country, hurried away with it all the wealth which it found in its passage." The *Account* underlines the delicious irony: "No country in Europe receives such vast treasures as Spain. In no country in Europe is seen so little money."[31]

This pronouncement is more significant than it first appears. An influential pattern of thought at the time associated with mercantilism argued that an imperial power's stockpile of bullion through conquest was the avenue to national riches. The Burkes are challenging this prevailing opinion through empirical observation: Spain was not affluent by virtue of its collection of gold and silver as a result of military conflict. The false splendor of metals masked the true poverty of nations.

Even more, the Spanish Empire's intemperate territorial ambitions came "at a vast expence of blood and treasure." Its wars "were a continual drain, which carried off their people, and destroyed all industry in those who remained." Acquisition in one area led to weakness in another: "The treasure which flowed in every year from the new world, found them in debt to every part of the old."[32] The Empire's extensive possessions thus bred commercial decay, not to mention political despotism and religious intolerance. "In government, tyranny; in religion, bigotry; in trade, monopoly," the Burkes state in their description of Spanish imperial dominion.[33] The *Account* insinuates that a source other than sparkling metal or brute conquest offered a more promising means to public prosperity, a consideration central to Burke's notion of imperial political economy.

This passage in the *Account* also imparts a subtle insight that would come to inspire Burke's reflections on public finance. The Burkes write that "œconomy," referring to the revenue streams of the Spanish Empire, was "a great revenue itself, and the great support of all the others."[34] This seeming paradox revealed a principle that animated Burke's plan for economical reform, and that informed his vision of imperial economics in general: the confinement of government to carefully defined tasks sets the preconditions for a vigorous flow of public receipts, rather than gratuitous intervention in the activities of its subjects. The reduction of state powers sharpened the efficacy of public administration.

The *Account* submits other examples in which imprudent entanglements discouraged trade and industry. Particular regulations of the Navigation Acts

---

[31] *Account of the European Settlements*, vol. I, 296.
[32] *Account of the European Settlements*, vol. I, 297.
[33] *Account of the European Settlements*, vol. I, 296–297.
[34] *Account of the European Settlements*, vol. I, 297.

increased the cost of the foreign trade in rice exports from Carolina; but the relaxation of such laws "again revived the rice trade."[35] Carolina's planters "raise now above double the quantity of what they raised some years ago."[36] The Burkes in these comments are endorsing the axiom that a flourishing trade is encouraged by soft and selective regulations.

The *Account*'s examination of Britain's Georgian settlement discloses even greater sympathy for this principle. The Burkes criticize the trustees of Georgia for spinning a vast web of regulations over its economy: banning the importation of slaves; circumscribing the amount of property families were permitted to hold; forbidding the inheritance law of fee simple[37]; and proscribing the importation of rum.[38]

Such laws carried benevolent intentions, but they ignored the specific weather conditions of Georgia and the temper of the Georgian people. "These regulations, though well intended, and meant to bring about very excellent purposes," the *Account* states, "yet it might at first, as it did afterwards appear, that they were made without sufficiently consulting the nature of the country, or the disposition of the people which they regarded."[39] The climate was hot, farming was especially laborious, and some Georgians lacked experience in working in such an environment, leading to inactivity and want. The Burkes suggest that the importation of slaves could have provided additional labor to mitigate these effects.

In this section, the *Account* judiciously integrates analysis of the Georgian settlement with deeper reflections on political matters that are enlivened by metaphor. "A levelling scheme in a new colony is a thing extremely unadviseable," the book declares, conveying Burke's distaste for attempts by government to redistribute property, a belief he would most forcefully express in the *Reflections*.[40] In the case of colonies, because the majority of mankind "must always be indigent," especially those in a new settlement, there must be some encouragement to industry, similar to the "strong beams and joists" of buildings[41]; but there must not be discouragements to industry, such as limitations on property. Besides, as the book observes, one such limitation – the allotment of only twenty-five acres of land – was established without considering the quality of the land, thereby diminishing its value in certain

---

[35] *Account of the European Settlements*, vol. II, 247.

[36] *Account of the European Settlements*, vol. II, 247.

[37] Fee simple was the absolute and unlimited freehold of land, the highest form of ownership of an estate.

[38] *Account of the European Settlements*, vol. II, 265–266. As we have seen in Chapter 5, Burke, in *Speech in Economical Reform*, would later highlight the regulatory encumbrances that hindered the growth of the Georgian economy in 1780.

[39] *Account of the European Settlements*, vol. II, 266.

[40] *Account of the European Settlements*, vol. II, 267.

[41] *Account of the European Settlements*, vol. II, 267.

areas. These limitations were further saddled by the quitrent, a type of land tax with feudal origins.[42]

It is on the subject of quitrents that the *Account* draws attention to the inverse relation between taxes and revenue. "When you have a flourishing colony, with extensive settlements, from the smallest quit-rents the crown receives a large revenue; but in an ill-settled province, the greatest rents make but a poor return, and yet are sufficient to burden and impoverish the people," the Burkes write.[43] Quitrents collected in a selective manner in a prosperous settlement produced a healthy flow of receipts for the public coffers, yet those imposed on an underdeveloped colony hindered revenue and deprived settlers of wealth. This observation, not unlike the *Account*'s critical survey of the Spanish Empire, would come to settle as a guiding principle of Burke's conception of public finance throughout his entire political life. The enactment of a taxing system, narrow in scope yet forceful in execution, generated great income for the state; but excess taxes curbed public prosperity, for both the people and the government.

The *Account*'s comments on the manufacture of silk and vines in Georgia reiterated the Burkes' awareness of the limits of good intentions, in turn revealing some of Burke's cherished beliefs about human nature. The encouragements for silk and vines illustrated a misjudgment of economic priority on the part of Georgian trustees, since settlers in a new province would first have to concentrate their energies on the production of necessities, such as corn, rather than on the manufacture of items of luxury. In addition, the manufacture of silk and vines would require additional employment if traders were to retain any hope of selling the goods at a reasonable price, with sufficient quantity, in the market. It came as little surprise, then, that the silk and vines markets foundered. The *Account* remarks:

We are apt suddenly to change our measures upon any failure; without sufficiently considering whether the failure has been owing to a fault in the scheme itself; this does not arise from any defect peculiar to our people, for it is the fault of mankind in general, if left to themselves. What is done by us is generally done by the spirit of the people; as far as that can go we advance, but no farther. We want political regulations, and a steady plan in government, to remedy the defects that must be in all things, which depend merely on the character and disposition of the people.[44]

The failure of the silk and vines industries did not derive from the Georgian people's particular shortcomings but rather weakness in the encouragements themselves, and the flaws of man in general. Men tend to alter laws when the laws do not meet their expectations; but, as these remarks imply, sometimes the defect is the very scheme in the first place. A people's industrious capacities thus

---

[42] See Beverley W. Bond, Jr., "The Quit-Rent System in the American Colonies," *The American Historical Review* 17 (1912): 496–516.
[43] *Account of the European Settlements*, vol. II, 268.
[44] *Account of the European Settlements*, vol. II, 271–272.

determine the scale of cultivation and production, not government intervention. Any imperfections in a community's agricultural or manufactural activities simply reflected the temperament and nature of man. Man is a fallible creature.

Although it denounces the meddling of the state into Georgian affairs, however, the *Account* does not argue for the abolition of trade laws. The Burkes recognize in the book that prudent and well-executed regulations were a means to promote the enterprising capacities of British subjects and enhance the wealth of the British Empire. The initial sluggishness of industry in North Carolina, they write, should not "make us neglect all future efforts, or hinder us from forming very reasonable expectations of seeing the trade of this country, with proper management, become a flourishing and fruitful branch of the British American commerce."[45]

The *Account* observes similarly that the "natural advantages" of South Carolina, a wealthier colony, "if properly managed," would continue to spur its economic growth.[46] And perhaps the cotton imported into Jamaica should receive encouragement from a "moderate premium," the Burkes suggest.[47] In general, the writing argues not for the complete absence of imperial regulation but for wise and judicious management of dependencies, as the authors conceive it, based on considerations of the different economic environments of the British Empire's various colonial possessions.

The Accidents of History

Continuing our discussion of the Burkes' remarks on human fallibility, the *Account* argues that even the weakness of man permitted opportunities for wealth, if tempered and channeled in a productive direction. The *Account* observes it is a "great happiness" that "unfortunate men, whom unavoidable accidents, the frowns of the world, or the cruelty of creditors, would have rendered miserable to themselves, and useless to the public," could find asylum in Britain's West Indian settlements.[48] There, "[w]ith the advantage of an experience acquired by their mistakes, they are free from the ill reputation which attended them; and they prove a vast service to their country, to which they could be of no advantage whilst they remained in it."[49] Accordingly, they would return to their mother country "in opulence and credit."[50] New colonies offered a sanctuary for flawed men, beset by hardship, to transform their lives for the better, to the benefit of themselves and their nation. The same principle that applied to cultivation, then, applied to man's temper: "Since experience has

---

[45] *Account of the European Settlements*, vol. II, 256.
[46] *Account of the European Settlements*, vol. II, 259.
[47] *Account of the European Settlements*, vol. II, 122.
[48] *Account of the European Settlements*, vol. II, 107.
[49] *Account of the European Settlements*, vol. II, 108.
[50] *Account of the European Settlements*, vol. II, 107.

taught us, that as there is no soil or climate which will not shew itself grateful to culture, so that there is no disposition, no character in mankind, which may not be turned with dextrous management to the public advantage."[51]

The *Account*'s deeper philosophic lesson on this matter is that initial vices of society, and the accidents of history, may end up generating public good in the long run unforeseen by man, encumbered by his limited epistemological horizons. The Burkes write:

[W]e [have] drawn from the rashness of hot and visionary men; the imprudence of youth; the corruption of bad morals; and even from the wretchedness and misery of persons destitute and undone, the great source of our wealth, our strength and our power. And though this was neither the effect of our wisdom, nor the consequence of our foresight; yet having happened, it may tend to give us more wisdom and a better foresight; for it will undoubtedly be a standing monitor to us, how much we ought to cherish the colonies we have already established, by every encouragement in our power, and by every reasonable indulgence; and it will be an additional spur to make us active in the acquisition of new ones.[52]

Human imperfections retain untapped sources for man's capacity for refinement and improvement, giving rise to new possibilities for growth. Yet these possibilities are realized not through the conscious design of man's individual intellect, but, the Burkes insinuate, through the mysterious forces of history, which man can only understand in part. The *Account* is not removing the element of human agency from history – indeed, the Burkes more or less affirm it in this chapter by acknowledging man's potential to elevate his vices into virtues – but the writing is hinting that man's inherent fallibility limits his capacity to fully predict and comprehend the fate of human affairs. Such intuitions in Burke's thought would come to shape his beliefs on the French Revolution and on politics as a whole.

The additional implication of these remarks is that the Burkes accept the right to colonization throughout the *Account*. "We derive our rights in America from the discovery of Sebastian Cabot, who first made the Northern continent in 1497," they write. "The fact is sufficiently certain to establish a right to our settlements in North America."[53] And conquest exposed an indelible principle of man's constitution: the Greek notion that "barbarians were naturally designed to be their slaves" (an idea Aristotle accepted, the Burkes note) has "its principle in human nature" because "the generality of mankind very readily slide from what they conceive a fitness for government, to a right of governing; and they do not so readily agree, that those who are superior in endowments should only be equal in condition."[54] The spirit of conquest evinced man's natural tendency to rule over others.

---

[51] *Account of the European Settlements*, vol. II, 109.
[52] *Account of the European Settlements*, vol. II, 108–109.
[53] *Account of the European Settlements*, vol. II, 138.
[54] *Account of the European Settlements*, vol. I, 32.

Slavery

One cruel manifestation of man's desire to rule over his fellow brethren at the time the *Account* was published was chattel slavery, a practice the Burkes discuss multiple times throughout the book. They remark that the enlargement of the East Africa trade might be a cheaper source of slaves than the West African coast; in turn, the *Account* grants a measure of credibility to the trade, and to the British Empire's role in supporting it, as a means to augment British commerce and power.[55] The Burkes further acknowledge that slaves "must be ruled with a rod of iron. I would have them ruled, but not crushed with it."[56] From a modern perspective, this comment, and the *Account*'s implicit stamp of legitimacy to the African trade – even if the writing merely reflected the temper of the times that accepted slavery's existence – are repugnant.

The distinctive feature of the *Account*, however, was that it moved beyond these considerations to convey noticeable liberal sentiments toward slaves that were somewhat uncommon in Burke's age. As noted by Richard B. Sheridan, an authority on the political economy of the British West Indies, and Thomas Clarkson, a prominent English abolitionist, the *Account* was one of the first English publications in the eighteenth century to voice specific criticisms of slavery.[57] "The negroes in our colonies endure a slavery more compleat, and attended with far worse circumstances," the Burkes state, "than what any people in their condition suffer in any other part of the world, or have suffered in any other period of time."[58] Such comments in the writing predated Britain's mainstream abolitionist movement by decades.

This humane attitude, relative to the general views of Englishmen in the mid-eighteenth century, inspired the *Account* to offer proposals to alleviate the harsh condition of slaves. The Burkes recommend granting slaves plots of land and employment opportunities, and having them pay rent, in order to promote their potential for industry and give them a stake in their community.[59] The *Account* further calls for slaves to be allowed to attend church on Sundays and to receive instruction in morals, and also to have time for recreational activities.[60] The Burkes believed that such reforms, which anticipated Burke's plan for gradual abolition twenty-three years later, *Sketch of a Negro Code*, would encourage masters to see slaves as their fellow human beings: "Such methods would by degrees habituate their masters, not to think them a sort of beasts, and without

---

[55] *Account of the European Settlements*, vol. I, 309–310.
[56] *Account of the European Settlements*, vol. II, 128.
[57] See Richard B. Sheridan, *Sugar and Slavery: An Economic History of the British West Indies, 1623–1775* (Kingston, Jamaica: Canoe Press, 2007), 481; and Clarkson, *History of the Rise, Progress, and Accomplishment*, vol. I, 55–56.
[58] *Account of the European Settlements*, vol. II, 124.
[59] *Account of the European Settlements*, vol. II, 131.
[60] *Account of the European Settlements*, vol. II, 129.

souls, as some of them do at present, who treat them accordingly."[61] The relevance of the *Account*'s discussion of slavery to Burke's economic thought, then, can be captured in a contradiction that the writing does not resolve: he understood that the expansion of the African trade would advance the commercial interests of the British Empire; but he also maintained that men, regardless of race, should be afforded the opportunity for industry.[62]

Exclusive Trading Companies

The Burkes' attraction to foreign commerce in the *Account* is underscored by their commentary on the utility of exclusive trading companies, institutions that received government charters to enjoy monopolistic trading privileges in certain regions of the globe. These remarks presaged Burke's ruminations later in his political life on the credibility of Britain's East India Company. In the *Account*'s discussion of reform of the French trade in the West Indies in the late seventeenth century, the Burkes state, "Exclusive companies may probably be useful to nourish an infant trade. They may be useful too for a very distant one, where the market is to be nicely managed, and where it is under the dominion of foreign and barbarous princes."[63] But the Burkes go on to insist that exclusive companies that trade in dominions "of the same prince, under the protection of his laws, carried on by his own subjects, and with goods wrought in his own country" are "equally absurd in their nature, and ruinous in their consequences to the trade."[64]

The *Account* uses the example of Hudson's Bay Company to support this argument. Ever since the company received an exclusive charter for trade in Hudson's Bay, it had provided "great benefit" to its proprietors, but comparatively "little advantage" to Britain. The Burkes acknowledge the Company's promotion of trade, but disparage it for its small capital, its insufficient enthusiasm to expand its commerce to the fullest extent possible, and its harboring of jealous impulses, which were common in all walks of society with men "endued with peculiar privileges."[65] Burke is illustrating his awareness of the limits in gifting exclusive trading rights to companies.

The *Account*'s next comments display sympathy for free trade principles. If the trade in Hudson's Bay "were laid open," the Burkes write, three "capital advantages" would ensue. First, it would produce greater competition, which would excite demand for manufactures; increase employment opportunities and shipping; and encourage fur imports to Britain, which in itself would decrease its price, thereby making British fur more competitive in foreign

---

[61] *Account of the European Settlements*, vol. II, 129.
[62] Consult Collins, "Edmund Burke on Slavery and the Slave Trade."
[63] *Account of the European Settlements*, vol. II, 8.
[64] *Account of the European Settlements*, vol. II, 8–9.
[65] *Account of the European Settlements*, vol. II, 288.

markets. The expansion of this trade could further attract new "species of fur," which would "open new channels of trade, which in commerce is a matter of great consideration."[66]

Second, the enlargement of commerce in Hudson's Bay would make it "better known," which would prompt migration to the area. Population growth could possibly lead to the establishment of an English colony at the location, thereby stimulating the fur trade and English manufactures with greater celerity. Third, the extension of trade at Hudson's Bay would enable the English to better assess the promise and constraints of using the Northwest Passage as a trade route.[67] The *Account*'s examination of the political economy of Hudson's Bay marks Burke's view that liberty of trade in the inlet would generate many benefits to the British Empire, and anticipates his later commentary on the complex imperial effects of market activities that carried influence beyond particular industries or traders.

Gold, Industry, and the Peopling of Colonies

Building on its commentary on the Spanish Empire, the *Account* yields an additional insight into Burke's economic thought that would acquire sharper expression in his parliamentary activities: the true wealth of a nation did not stem from metal. "I do not in the least hesitate to say that we derive more advantage, and of a better kind, from our colonies, than the Spaniards and Portuguese have from theirs," the Burkes write, "abounding as they are with gold and silver and precious stones; although in ours there is no appearance at all of such dazzling and delusive wealth."[68] They proceed to argue that the British received greater benefits from their brand of trade than they would have from their metals:

Our present intercourse with them is an emulation in industry; they have nothing that does not arise from theirs, and what we receive enters into our manufactures, excites our industry, and increases our commerce; whereas gold is the measure or account, but not the means of trade. And it is found in nations as it is in the fortunes of private men, that what does not arise from labour, but is acquired by other means, is never lasting. Such acquisitions extinguish industry, which is alone the parent of any solid riches.[69]

These are some of the most significant comments in the *Account* for our purposes. While gold can serve as the measure of wealth, commercial intercourse – not the possession of metal – is the trigger for national opulence. Accordingly, even if it was not accumulating metals with the same frequency as

---

[66] *Account of the European Settlements*, vol. II, 289.
[67] *Account of the European Settlements*, vol. II, 289–290.
[68] *Account of the European Settlements*, vol. II, 293.
[69] *Account of the European Settlements*, vol. II, 293.

Spain and Portugal, Britain was not relinquishing any advantage to them, but was in fact profiting greatly from the extension of its trade.

The final two sentences in this quotation are perhaps even more important in grasping the intellectual roots of Burke's economic thought. The Burkes are declaring that wealth that endures over time was not the product of arbitrary extraction but of toil. Fortunes gained by means other than labor – conquest, war, despotic government – had a perishable quality, for they were not built up through the slow, arduous process of industry. Quick fortune thus lacked the stable foundations that would allow men to retain and expand it in future generations. This chain of reasoning on the question of imperial economics would come to shape Burke's understanding of wealth, and of public administration, throughout his public and private life.

The Burkes do admit, however, that the swift acquisition of gold served as the initial spark for European colonization: the "insatiable thirst of gold" had been "a thousand times extremely prejudicial" to the affairs of Spanish and Portuguese adventurers.[70] Nevertheless, if it were not for the incentive of gold, "which kindled the spirit of discovery and colonization first in Spain and Portugal, and afterwards in all parts of Europe, America had never been in the state it now is; nor would those nations ever have had the beneficial colonies, which are now established in every part of that country."[71]

Framed differently, the prospect of trade was too faint in itself to motivate explorers to venture into unchartered and potentially dangerous territories. "It was necessary there should be something of an immediate and uncommon [gain], fitted to strike the imaginations of men forcibly, to tempt them to such hazardous designs," the *Account* states.[72] Therefore, "[T]here must be some strong active principle to give life and energy to all designs, or they will languish, let them be ever so wisely concerted."[73] Even though the procurement of metal did not furnish solid grounds for long-term prosperity, the Burkes conclude that it did perform a crucial function in provoking Europeans to explore distant lands.

Still, according to the *Account*, because flesh-and-blood *people* – not gold and silver – were ultimately responsible for the exercise of industry and diligence, the migration of Englishmen from their mother country to British colonies was a sign of prosperity both for the country and its dependencies. Indeed, England itself gained population in the long run, even when it was peopling its settlements: "The barbarism of our ancestors could not comprehend how a nation could grow more populous by sending out a part of its people." Consequently,

[70] *Account of the European Settlements*, vol. I, 47.
[71] *Account of the European Settlements*, vol. I, 47.
[72] *Account of the European Settlements*, vol. I, 47–48.
[73] *Account of the European Settlements*, vol. I, 49.

That a rich, trading and manufacturing nation should be long in want of people, is a most absurd supposition; for besides that the people within themselves multiply the most where the means of subsistence are most certain, it is as natural for people to flock into a busy and wealthy country, that by any accident may be thin of people, as it is for the dense air to rush into those parts where it is rarified.[74]

Traders and manufacturers, farmers and laborers, were energizing resources for the growth of commerce. The enrichment of an imperial power derived in large part from the diffusion of its people.

The *Account*'s political argument in this context was that the North American colonies offered profitable opportunities for Britain to develop its trade as a check against French aggrandizement: "The great point of our regard in America, ought therefore to be the effectual peopling, employment, and strength of our possessions there; in a subordinate degree the management of our interests with regard to the French and Spaniards." England could withstand the Spaniards, whose empire was deteriorating; the French, on the other hand, posed a formidable threat to the British Empire. Hence, the Burkes conclude, "[W]e ought to use every method to repress them, to prevent them from extending their territories, their trade, or their influence, and above all to connive at not the least encroachment."[75]

Britain's soundest strategy to exploit its colonies was to encourage their capacities for growth through sound and selective regulation:

America is our great resource; this will remain to us when other branches of our trade are decayed, or exist no more; and therefore we ought to grudge no expense that may enable them to answer this end so effectually, as one day to supply the many losses we have already had, and the many more we have but too much reason to apprehend in our commerce. These expences are not like the expences of war, heavy in their nature, and precarious in their effects; but when judiciously ordered, the certain and infallible means of rich and successive harvests of gain to the latest posterity, at the momentary charge of a comparatively small quantity of seed, and of a moderate husbandry to the present generation.[76]

The North American colonies were abundant sources of commerce and industry, and would serve as the spring for British imperial wealth even if some English industries withered away. Unlike the uncertain effects of a costly war on commerce, the relatively inexpensive charge of preserving the dependencies would spawn many advantages for Britain. Such glowing depictions of the American colonies in the *Account* foreshadow Burke's rapturous depiction of them in *Speech on Conciliation*.

Even though (or because) France was Britain's rival, the *Account*'s detailed examination of French colonies emits a heightened sense of esteem. While the

---

[74] *Account of the European Settlements*, vol. II, 294.
[75] *Account of the European Settlements*, vol. II, 295.
[76] *Account of the European Settlements*, vol. II, 262–263.

French were among the last European powers to establish settlements in the West Indies, they "made ample amends by the vigour with which they pursued them, and by that chain of judicious and admirable measures which they used in drawing from them every advantage, which the nature of the climate would yield; and in contending against the difficulties which it threw in their way."[77] Burke's fascination with the political economy of France would endure for the remainder of his life.

The Burkes, then, implore the English to strengthen their own advantages during the French and Indian War, rather than impugn France, in order to match the latter's imperial and commercial prowess. After remarking that a man of one nation can both oppose and admire his nation's enemy, the Burkes summarize England's competition with France this way:

We have been engaged for above a century with France in a noble contention for the superiority in arms, in politics, in learning, and in commerce; and there never was a time, perhaps, when this struggle was more critical. If we succeed in the war, even our success, unless managed with prudence, will be like some former successes, of little benefit to us; if we should fail, which God forbid, even then, prudence may make our misfortunes of more use to us, than an ill-managed success; if they teach us to avoid our former errors; if they make us less careless; if they make us cultivate the advantages we have with care and judgment: this, and not our opinion of the enemy, must decide the long contest between us.[78]

The Burkes' point strikes the page: the fate of the British Empire in its imperial rivalry with France and the wider global order resided in its own hands, not in those of its enemy. Commerce and industry were a means to wealth and power.

Paper Money

Beyond its reflections on the imperial politics of European trade, the *Account* also communicates Burke's grave unease over paper money. In a discussion on the romantic yearnings of Juan Ponce de León to discover the Fountain of Youth in Florida, the Burkes write that if a spring had indeed been found there, "it would undoubtedly be the best commodity the country could yield, both for domestic consumption, and for the foreign markets, and would be a far better basis for stocks and funds than the richest mines of gold or silver."[79] This comment buttresses the book's

---

[77] *Account of the European Settlements*, vol. II, 3. Dating back to 1747, Burke was struck by the power of French commercial activity. During a meeting of his debating club, Burke noted that "the Dutch interests and the English closely united, that the Dutch were the barrier between us and the Continent & if the French overrun them they'd overspread Europe, and be the destruction of our trade" (Samuels, *Early Life Correspondence and Writings*, 243).

[78] *Account of the European Settlements*, vol. II, 49.

[79] *Account of the European Settlements*, vol. II, 37.

argument that the true sources of wealth stemmed from industry and trade, not metal.

The Burkes continue:

Yet, without this, an idea, altogether as romantic, of a trade hither, opperated so strongly upon a very wise nation, as to serve for the instrument of one of those dangerous masterstrokes in politics, by which nations are sometimes saved, individuals undone, and an entire change and reversement brought about, not only in the common ways of thinking of mankind, but of all that seemed most fixed and permanent in a state.[80]

The Burkes then connect such disorder to John Law's investment scheme in French Louisiana in the early eighteenth century, in which the rapid issuance of paper money, fueled by Law's overstatement of the wealth in the territory and inspired by a similar hint of romanticism, led to the Mississippi Bubble.[81] The *Account* calls this scheme "that remarkable delusion."[82] Burke is conveying a discerning awareness of the hazards of speculative enterprise driven feverishly by paper currency, an observation that would motivate some of his most vicious attacks on the French Revolution in the *Reflections*.

Imperial Commercial Policy and Free Trade

In their description of Britain's North American colonies, the Burkes offer a summary of their blueprint for imperial commercial policy guided by selection and wisdom:

The general plan of our management with regard to the trade of our colonies, methinks, ought to be, to encourage in every one of them some separate and distinct articles, such as not interfering, might enable them to trade with each other, and all to trade to advantage with their mother country. And then, where we have rivals in any branch of the trade carried on by our colonies, to enable them to send their goods to the foreign market directly; using at the same time the wise precaution which the French put in practice, to make the ships so employed take the English ports in their way home; for our great danger is, that they should in that case make their returns in foreign manufactures, against which we cannot guard too carefully. This, and that they should not go largely into manufactures interfering with ours, ought to be the only points at which our restrictions should aim.[83]

They continue:

These purposes ought not to be compassed by absolute prohibitions and penalties, which would be unpolitical and unjust, but by the way of diversion, by encouraging them to fall into such things as find a demand with ourselves at home. By this means Great Britain and all its dependencies will have a common interest, they will mutually play into each

---

[80] *Account of the European Settlements*, vol. II, 37.
[81] See "The Political Economy of the Ancien Régime," Chapter 11.
[82] *Account of the European Settlements*, vol. II, 36.
[83] *Account of the European Settlements*, vol. II, 182.

other's hands, and the trade so dispersed, will be of infinitely more advantage to us, than if all its several articles were produced and manufactured within ourselves.[84]

Britain's imperial regulations should promote trade within and among its colonial possessions that cultivate unique industries; and when similar goods are produced by rival nations, Britain should permit its subjects to trade their own goods on the foreign market, provided that the vessels carrying the articles pass through English ports upon returning home. The British government should also be open to restricting colonial and foreign manufactures if they provided competition to English wares.

In general, colonial prosperity would advantage Britain as a nation, for it would be a "mistake of the most fatal consequence" to assume that the "shipping, seamen, commodities, or wealth of the British colonies, were not effectively the shipping, seamen, and wealth of Great Britain herself."[85] Encouragement and diversion, not prohibition and punishment, were the guiding principles behind the Burkes' belief that wise policy could shower many commercial advantages on the British Empire.

Even when British merchants traded with the French, however, the British Empire did not necessarily suffer losses. "The French, in permitting us to supply them [with lumber and other ship-building commodities], it is true, give us a proof that they have advantages from this trade; but this is no proof at all that we derive none from it; for on that supposition no trade could be mutually beneficial," the Burkes state.[86] The *Account* is drawing out a key insight into foreign commerce that would imbue Burke's reflections on Irish trade, and define Adam Smith's economic thought in the *Wealth of Nations*: because liberal trade was not a zero-sum contest, commercial relations between two nations generated could benefit for both. One trading partner did not necessarily gain at the expense of the other.

F. P. Lock argues that the *Account* "offers little support" for the view that Burke was an "advocate of free trade."[87] As suggested by the comments quoted earlier, however, classifying a work such as the *Account* through modern frameworks of "free trade" or "anti-free trade" imposes a binary choice on the Burkes that they themselves did not establish in their discourse on colonial policy. Certainly the writing's vindication of European colonialism would not accord with strict free market doctrine, or most strands of economic thought for that matter, today. Nevertheless, the pertinent question the *Account* addressed was not whether "mercantilism" or "free trade" was a desirable commercial policy, but rather whether a defense of colonization could accommodate support for a light regulatory presence in imperial dependencies.

The Burkes believed it could: the steady circulation of goods within the broad reach of the British Empire could strengthen both its economic prosperity and

[84] *Account of the European Settlements*, vol. II, 182–183.
[85] *Account of the European Settlements*, vol. II, 181–182.
[86] *Account of the European Settlements*, vol. II, 180.   [87] Lock, *Edmund Burke*, vol. I, 133.

global prestige in an era when European rivals threatened its integrity and honor. In this context, it must be reiterated that the *Account* weighed considerations of politics, national defense, history, and geography, as well as commerce, in its examination of European colonization. They did not view the study of international politics simply through the lens of wealth maximization and the expansion of commercial freedom. To the extent that the Empire could promote trade throughout the globe without sacrificing its security and colonial interests, we may take the *Account* to offer a firm yet prudent stance in favor of liberal commerce as one instrument – but by no means the only instrument – in the art of imperial statecraft.

General Principles of *Account of the European Settlements* and the Primacy of Temper

With the *Account*'s survey of European colonization in mind, we can summarize some general lessons in the book that would come to inform Burke's conception of political economy for the next forty years: the incentive of gold was a stimulant to colonization, but industry and trade were lasting sources of wealth creation; the accumulation of metals and the assertion of military might offered but fleeting riches; wise and selective regulations formed the fertile conditions for colonial affluence; the efforts of private men were the catalysts of enterprise; meddlesome trade laws discouraged the circulation of foreign commerce; exclusive trading privileges were tenable if used to launch a nascent trade; and a regular but modest system of taxation generated strong revenue for the imperial power.

Perhaps the most important principle in the *Account* underlying these precepts is illustrated in the book's discussion of the wars between England and France. The Burkes argue that such nations could recover with relative ease from the ravages of conflict because they retained a particular ethos resistant to adversity. "While the spirit of trade subsists, trade itself can never be destroyed," the *Account* declares.[88] Even in the depths of turmoil, nations that preserve their character could withstand temporary difficulties. "Wherever the vital principle subsists in full vigour, wounds are soon healed," the Burkes state. "Disorders themselves are a species of remedies; and every new loss not only shows how it may be repaired, but by the vigour it inspires, makes new advantages known." They continue: "Such losses renew the spirit of industry and enterprise; they reduce things to their first principles; they keep alive motion, and make the appetites of traders sharp and keen."[89] Temper and character sustain commercial activity.

Informed by this maxim of Burke's political wisdom, the *Account* stresses that the British Empire must rely on its own capacities and energies, rather than

---

[88] *Account of the European Settlements*, vol. II, 17.
[89] *Account of the European Settlements*, vol. II, 17.

on raw military power, for the promotion of imperial riches. "We must not therefore place our dependence for keeping ourselves on a par of power with France, upon the prejudice which we can do its trade in time of war," the Burkes argue, "but upon the vigour, œconomy, and wisdom of the measures which we take to secure and advance our own, both in war and in peace."[90] The fortunes of England's commercial prosperity ultimately derived from the success of its industry, not from hostilities with rival nations.

It was this genius of the English people that distinguished Britain from other European powers in America. As the Burkes write, the Spaniards benefited from the collection of gold, but they were indolent; the Portuguese were enterprising but not industrious (they did, however, use precious metals in a less extravagant manner than the Spaniards); the French were active and eager but tended to be "obedient to rules and laws which bridle[d] these dispositions"; and the Dutch were diligent and frugal.[91]

The English temper, on the other hand, blended its instinct for business with a sober disposition and skill in agriculture, all moved by a knack for economy of energy and a love of liberty:

The English, of a reasoning disposition, thoughtful and cool, and men of business rather than of great industry, impatient of much fruitless labour, abhorrent of constraint, and lovers of a country life, have a lot which indeed produces neither gold nor silver; but they have a large tract of a fine continent; a noble field for the exercise of agriculture, and sufficient to furnish their trade without laying them under great difficulties. Intolerant as they are of the most useful restraints, their commerce flourishes from the freedom every man has of pursuing it according to his own ideas, and directing his life after his own fashion.[92]

The English did not extract much gold or silver, but their flair for enterprise induced great advantages for their colonial possessions. Because England's success against France, according to the Burkes, depended on its own agency, such vigilant attachment to liberty would serve an essential function in strengthening and enhancing the power of the British Empire. Once again, the constitution and character of a people determined their commercial and political destinies.

Therefore, some European nations established settlements with "a vast ambition supported by surprizing feats of a romantic courage mixed with an insatiable thirst of gold."[93] In other settlements, a body of rules governed the cultivation of territory; such colonies were "the regular product of a systematic

---

[90] *Account of the European Settlements*, vol. II, 18.

[91] *Account of the European Settlements*, vol. II, 57–58.

[92] *Account of the European Settlements*, vol. II, 57–58. The Burkes shower particular praise on the yeomanry of New England: "[t]he people by their being generally freeholders, and by their form of government, have a very free, bold, and republican spirit. In no part of the world are the ordinary sort so independent, or possess so many of the conveniencies of life" (167).

[93] *Account of the European Settlements*, vol. II, 60.

policy tempering and guiding an active industry."[94] But in the case of the English, "we are to display the effects of liberty; the work of a people guided by her own genius, and following the directions of their own natural temper in a proper path."[95]

This is why the British Empire's American colonies have "a most flourishing trade with their mother country," and communicate with trading nations from around the globe.[96] Britain was the "heart and spring" of this "lively circulation of trade" from "whence it takes its rise, and to which it all returns in the end."[97] The triumphalist tone Burke conveys throughout his life in support of English commerce makes an early appearance in the *Account*.

Yet the basic reason that colonies were gifted with the salutary conditions for growth stemmed from England's ability to strike a balance between preserving local liberties and preventing political disorder. "The settlement of our colonies was never pursued upon any regular plan; but they were formed, grew, and flourished, as accidents, the nature of the climate, or the dispositions of private men happened to operate," the Burkes explain.[98] They continue: "We ought not therefore to be surprised to find in the several constitutions and governments of our colonies, so little of any thing like uniformity."[99] England's hesitation to encourage economic development based on hardened conformity of design promoted the cause of colonial prosperity.

The *Account* goes on to note, however, that although the "unbounded freedom" of chartered governments "contributed in some degree" to the flourishing of the settlements, their democratic foundations provided more precarious value to Britain than a more orderly political system.[100] Hence the ideal relations between a new settlement and its imperial power were characterized as thus:

Here the ends to be answered, are to make the new establishment as useful as possible to the trade of the mother country; to secure its dependence; to provide for the ease, safety, and happiness of the settlers; to protect them from their enemies, and to make an easy and effectual provision to preserve them from the tyranny and avarice of their governors, or the ill consequences of their own licentiousness; that they should not, by growing into an unbounded liberty, forget that they were subjects, or lying under a base servitude have no reason to think themselves British subjects. This is all that colonies, according to the present and best ideas of them, can or ought to be.[101]

---

[94] *Account of the European Settlements*, vol. II, 60.
[95] *Account of the European Settlements*, vol. II, 60.
[96] *Account of the European Settlements*, vol. II, 59–60.
[97] *Account of the European Settlements*, vol. II, 60.
[98] *Account of the European Settlements*, vol. II, 296.
[99] *Account of the European Settlements*, vol. II, 296.
[100] *Account of the European Settlements*, vol. II, 300.
[101] *Account of the European Settlements*, vol. II, 301.

New colonies could procure advantages to the mother country while profiting themselves from its protection. This principle of collective benefit would come to wield a profound impact on Burke's views of the political economy of empire.

Conclusion

Early in the *Account*, with reference to the early adventures of Spanish and Portuguese explorers in the late fifteenth and early sixteenth centuries, the Burkes write:

The speculative knowledge of trade, made no part of the study of the elevated or thinking part of mankind, at that time. Now it may be justly reckoned amongst the liberal sciences; and it makes one of the most considerable branches of political knowledge. Commerce was then in the hands of a few, great in its profits, but confined in its nature. What we call the ballance of trade, was far from being well understood; all the laws relative to commerce were every where but so many clogs upon it. The imposts and duties charged on goods, were laid on without distinction or judgment. Even amongst ourselves, the most trading and reasoning people in Europe, right notions of these matters began late, and advanced slowly.[102]

Economics is a familiar discipline to modern ears; but, as these comments suggest, we should continue to remind ourselves throughout this book that man's understanding of the complexities of foreign trade was only beginning to emerge in Burke's age. For the "ballance of trade," as the *Account* states, was "far from being well understood," and pursued by imposing "many clogs" – trade restrictions – upon the flow of goods. Burke exerted a powerful, though largely overlooked, influence in unclogging this flow, and in clarifying and advancing the principles of liberal trade in British politics, throughout his public life, beginning in his very first session in the House of Commons.

6.4 THE BRITISH WEST INDIES AND THE FREE PORT ACT OF 1766

The West Indies was an object of lasting fascination for Burke. In the *Account*, the Burkes keenly observed that particular underdeveloped islands possessed the bountiful resources necessary for British prosperity in the region. "Jamaica is nothing like fully cultivated. The Bahamas, our undisputed right, where it is highly probable sugars might be cultivated to advantage, remain at present utterly neglected, as if unworthy of all notice," they write, "though they are many in number, large in extent, fruitful in their soil, situated in a very happy climate, and are in a manner the keys of

---

[102] *Account of the European Settlements*, vol. I, 48.

the West-India navigation."[103] The authors emphasize that unwise commercial policy could threaten Britain's potential for commercial gain in the West Indies.

Mindful of this consideration, the Burkes, in one of the more intriguing chapters in the *Account*, provide a hypothetical statement written from the perspective of a West Indian merchant concerned about the negative effects of the British Empire's imperial trade laws in the region. The merchant first establishes two general precepts of foreign trade: "The whole secret of managing a foreign market, is contained in two words, to have the commodity of a good kind, and to sell it cheap; and the whole domestic policy of trade consists in contriving to answer these two ends, and principally the latter."[104]

Yet the West Indian dealer argues that the British Empire's excessive duties on sugar inhibited the capacities of merchants to compete with the French in foreign trade. He asks, "Now, by what magic can we effect to sell as cheap as the French at any foreign market, when our planters pay four and a half per cent. duty upon all the sugars … ?", among various costs imposed on the sugar trade.[105] For any encumbrances on the circulation of commerce in the British West Indies aggravated the price of wares in Britain itself. "[W]hat you charge, or suffer to be charged on the islands, is only the price of your own goods enhanced so much at the foreign market," the West Indian merchant contends.[106]

He explains further that while French colonies also supported their empire's military establishment, France's management of their affairs was wise, not meddling. The French "know that a little judicious expence is often the best œconomy in the world."[107] Although they learned "many of their maxims of trade, as well as many of the fabrics which supply it, from us," the West Indian dealer urges the English to learn from them as well.[108] In an environment of heightened trade costs, "[W]e do not feel all the benefit which we might expect from a more general and better regulated liberty."[109] The reduction of arbitrary entanglements would excite the commercial energies of merchants in the British West Indies.

On this note, in the midst of their survey of Britain's West Indian colonies in the *Account*, the Burkes make a point to note the tantalizing fertility of the English colony of Jamaica. "None of our islands produce so fine sugars," they write of the island.[110] It was "the largest and best of our islands, where there are

---

[103] *Account of the European Settlements*, vol. II, 24.
[104] *Account of the European Settlements*, vol. II, 112.
[105] *Account of the European Settlements*, vol. II, 112.
[106] *Account of the European Settlements*, vol. II, 113.
[107] *Account of the European Settlements*, vol. II, 115.
[108] *Account of the European Settlements*, vol. II, 115.
[109] *Account of the European Settlements*, vol. II, 115.
[110] *Account of the European Settlements*, vol. II, 62.

prodigious tracts of uncultivated land."[111] Yet the Burkes observe that the area was in decay: "It appears at present, that Jamaica is rather upon the decline; a point this that deserves the most attentive consideration."[112] Regardless of the causes of the island's mismanagement, the Burkes insist, "they deserve a speedy and effectual remedy from those, in whose power it is to apply it."[113]

Burke seized this opportunity in his first session in Parliament by helping draft the Free Port Act of 1766. Although this episode did not appear to yield any comprehensive speech of Burke available to scholars discussing the principles of his political economy, it does illustrate his embrace of market liberty almost three decades prior to the composition of *Thoughts and Details*, and exhibits his strong attention to the subject of imperial commerce early in his political life.

The Act was one of Burke's first major legislative initiatives in Parliament, serving as a key part of the Rockingham ministry's broader effort in revising Britain's imperial system of commercial regulations in favor of liberal trade following the mercantilist policies of George Grenville's ministry. Under Grenville, Britain's prime minister from 1763 to 1765, the Sugar Act and Stamp Act had limited foreign imports and European rights of navigation in the British West Indies and North America. The laws also aimed to preserve West Indian monopolies and narrowly confine the use of trade ports. Grenville claimed these policies were merely an effort to extinguish illicit trafficking in the West Indies.[114] While the Acts certainly injured colonial trade, it is unclear whether the policies can be indicted as the principal source of American commercial decay in 1765 and 1766.[115]

The Rockingham ministry of 1765–1766, of which Burke was emerging as a prominent member, pledged to reform this intrusive economic framework. In private, in fact, Burke conveyed that the Rockinghams were attempting to transcend the boundaries of incremental change: "We are, it is true, demolishing the whole Grenvillian Fabrick" of unnecessary mercantile restrictions, he admitted to Charles O'Hara, his Irish friend and correspondent, in late April 1766.[116] Even more, the Burkes had anticipated the futility in Grenville's attempt to reduce fraud through stiff regulatory decrees: as they wrote in the *Account*, "[W]e may know by experience … how insufficient all regulations are to prevent a contraband."[117]

---

[111] *Account of the European Settlements*, vol. II, 121.
[112] *Account of the European Settlements*, vol. II, 69.
[113] *Account of the European Settlements*, vol. II, 70.
[114] See Paul Langford, *The First Rockingham Administration 1765–1766* (London: Oxford University Press, 1973), 113; and Allan Christelow, "Contraband Trade between Jamaica and the Spanish Main, and the Free Port Act of 1766," *The Hispanic American Historical Review* 22 (1942): 335.
[115] See Langford, *First Rockingham Administration*, 186–188.
[116] Burke to Charles O'Hara, 23, 24 [*April* 1766], in *Correspondence of Edmund Burke*, vol. I, 252.
[117] See *Account of the European Settlements*, vol. II, 181.

Consequently, the Rockinghams first repealed the Stamp Act[118] and passed the Declaratory Act, both receiving royal assent on March 18, 1766. Yet the culminating achievement of the ministry's trade reform efforts in the session was the Free Port Act, passed on June 6, 1766. The Act established four free ports in Jamaica: Kingston, Savannah la Mar, Montego Bay, and Santa Lucea; and two additional free ports in Dominica, in Prince Rupert's Bay and Roseau. The legislation loosened trade regulations between British colonial posts in the North American colonies and the West Indian markets, including Spanish and French colonies as well as British possessions.[119]

Such reform provided sweeteners to placate the demands of both the American colonists and British West Indian traders while also attempting to revive the Spanish trade. For example, the Act lowered the cost of sugar imports into North American ports. Foreign bottoms with a maximum of one deck traveling from the American colonies could trade all goods of non-British origin, besides tobacco, with merchants in Dominica. Duties in general were set relatively low.[120] To appease the sugar interest in Jamaica, the legislation prohibited particular foreign imports into Jamaica of goods that were produced on the island, including sugar, molasses, and tobacco.[121]

The Free Port Act was not a flawless act of statesmanship, nor were free ports in the West Indies a novel idea.[122] It was a compromise measure and passed hastily without rigorous deliberation. Rockingham lawmakers sacrificed a measure of legislative independence by permitting merchants to heavily influence the crafting of the bills, particularly early on in the process.[123] Paul Langford writes, "[A]t no time in the eighteenth century were Administration and Parliament more at the command of the commercial interests than in the spring of 1766."[124] In addition, the Act was not able to stem the flow of all smuggled goods; it is not clear whether the free ports were shining commercial successes; and the restoration of Spanish trade did not achieve the vibrancy for which many had hoped.[125]

---

[118] Two of Burke's speeches in favor of repealing the Stamp Act "filled the town with wonder," according to Samuel Johnson. There are scant parliamentary records of these speeches, however. See the introductory remarks before Richard Burke, Sr.'s letter to James Barry, 11 February 1766, in *Correspondence of Edmund Burke*, vol. I, 237.

[119] See Frances Armytage, *The Free Port System in the British West Indies: A Study in Commercial Policy, 1766–1822* (London: Longmans, Green and Co., 1953); and Bourke, *Empire & Revolution*, 309–314. See also P. J. Marshall, *Edmund Burke & the British Empire in the West Indies: Wealth, Power, & Slavery* (Oxford: Oxford University Press, 2019).

[120] Christelow, "Contraband Trade," 338.   [121] Armytage, *Free Port System*, 42.

[122] See Christelow, "Contraband Trade," 334–335.

[123] Grenville noted the "overbearing and delegation of administration to a Club of North America merchants at the King's Arms Tavern." See L. Stuart Sutherland, "Edmund Burke and the First Rockingham Ministry," *The English Historical Review* 47 (1932): 66.

[124] Langford, *First Rockingham Administration*, 200.

[125] Consult Langford, *First Rockingham Administration*, 206–207; and Christelow, "Contraband Trade," 339.

But the Free Port Act did represent conscious movement in the direction of freer commercial intercourse by the very fact that it established six new free trade ports. This breakthrough was particularly acute because the conventional pattern of the British government at the time was to preserve its prohibitions and duties in the West Indies with unthinking reflex. The law further conveyed the British government's awareness – and Burke's awareness – that French imperial commerce presented a competitive threat to English merchants, a concern outlined in the *Account*.[126] The Rockinghams, moreover, provided a jolt of encouragement to traders in North American colonies who had been remonstrating in support of liberal trade relations with West Indian merchants.

While not all the demands of traffickers were satisfied, then, the Act did fulfill some of their wishes. As the London North American Merchants stated at the time, "We consider [the commercial reforms] as the basis of an extensive System of Trade between Great Britain and her Colonies framed on liberal principles of reciprocal Advantage."[127] Nancy F. Koehn describes the legislation in a similar way: "Some ten years before Adam Smith would take the doctrines of mercantilism to task and half a century before David Ricardo would articulate the theory of comparative advantage, MPs decided that the prosperity of the imperial economy was best promoted by *not* regulating all aspects of colonial exchange."[128] The free port system, even with its many imperfections, endured until 1822.

Burke, along with Charles Townshend and William Dowdeswell, Chancellor of the Exchequer at the time, were the principal champions of the Free Port Act.[129] At the time, Burke represented Wendover, a modest borough in contrast to the bustling commercial hub of Bristol, the city he would later represent from 1774 to 1780. In the spring of 1766, Burke helped engineer the Rockinghamite campaign in studying the intricacies of British imperial commerce and their implications for Britain's national interests; he had wielded so much influence throughout the process that by the culmination of the legislative session, his reputation switched from being Rockingham's "Right hand" man to being "both his hands," as Richard Bourke notes.[130]

Burke confessed thirty years later, in *Letter to a Noble Lord*, that his tireless efforts during the session threatened his physical condition. "Then in the vigour of my manhood, my constitution sunk under my labour," he wrote.[131] Burke claimed he thought he was "very near death."[132] (Remember also that Burke and Rockingham Whigs at this time were laying the groundwork for the repeal of the Stamp Act and passage of the Declaratory Act.) Burke admitted he

---

[126] See *Account of the European Settlements*, vol. II, 176–177.

[127] Quoted in Langford, *First Rockingham Administration*, 206.

[128] Nancy F. Koehn, *The Power of Commerce: Economy and Governance in the First British Empire* (Ithaca and London: Cornell University Press, 1994), 199.

[129] Armytage, *Free Port System*, 40.

[130] Burke to Grenville, 11 June 1766, in Bourke, *Empire & Revolution*, 310.

[131] Langford, *Writings and Speeches*, IX, 159.   [132] Langford, *Writings and Speeches*, IX, 159.

enjoyed inquiring into and discussing the trade provisions more so than the Stamp Act. "[I]t is a business I like," he wrote to O'Hara in early March 1766.[133]

As we have seen in the *Account*, Burke devoted himself to the vigorous inspection of commerce even prior to the start of his parliamentary service in 1766. Additional evidence points to his study of trade early in his rise to power. Serving as the secretary to Rockingham, who was also prime minister at the time, Burke received remuneration from him "for obtaining various Informations and Materials relative to the Trades and Manufacturers," according to a note dated 25 November 1765 from one of Rockingham's private notebooks.[134] Another entry, dated 19 April 1766, discloses that Burke, then in Parliament, was paid "for obtaining various informations and materials to Trade &c."[135] That this note was posted in late April, soon before the Free Port Act was passed into law, strengthens the claim from contemporaries, not to mention from Burke himself, that he examined the complexities of West Indian commerce and helped craft the bill with uncommon care and diligence.

Burke's activity at this juncture also included receiving petitions, consulting merchants, and preparing arguments for the Rockingham ministry's attempt to repeal the Stamp Act. In late 1765 and early 1766, when British merchants were amplifying their opposition to the Act because of its negative impact on trade, he displayed elevated attention to their concerns. Burke received a letter from Archibald Henderson, a prominent Glasgow merchant, who enclosed in the document a copy of a memorial from Glasgow merchants revealing "the alarming situation they are reduced to, in consequence of the Stamp-act."[136] As Henderson wrote, "[T]he merchants of Glasgow do not exceed the bounds of truth, when they assert the debts due to them, from those provinces [of Virginia and Maryland] alone, to be above half a million sterling."[137] Burke convened a breakfast meeting with a group of Glasgow merchants to discuss the Act's impact on trade.[138] And he received a letter from Abraham Rawlinson, a merchant of Lancaster, and seventy other traders to thank Burke for the "great Attention" he gave to "the Commercial Int'rest of Great Britain and her Colonies, during the last long & laborious Session of Parliament."[139] Such letters offer additional proof of Burke's active engagement with commercial

---

[133] Burke to Charles O'Hara, I, 4 March 1766, in *Correspondence of Edmund Burke*, vol. I, 240.

[134] *Correspondence of Edmund Burke*, vol. I, 211n1.

[135] *Correspondence of Edmund Burke*, vol. I, 211n1.

[136] Archibald Henderson to Edmund Burke, 9 February 1766, in William and Bourke, *Correspondence of the Right Honourable Edmund Burke*, vol. I, 99.

[137] Archibald Henderson to Edmund Burke, 9 February 1766, in William and Bourke, *Correspondence of the Right Honourable Edmund Burke*, vol. I, 100.

[138] Burke to the Marquess of Rockingham, [January 1766], in *Correspondence of Edmund Burke*, vol. I, 235.

[139] Lock, *Edmund Burke*, vol. I, 217.

matters early in his parliamentary career, fortifying the notion that he acquired a well-earned reputation in Parliament as an authority on the topic of political economy.

Burke grasped that the aspirations of the Rockinghams in reforming the Navigation Acts exceeded the pursuit of piecemeal measures. In his letter to O'Hara in early March 1766, a week before the North American and West Indian interests settled on a tentative agreement over the trade provisions, Burke remarked, "We now prepare for a compleat revision of all the Commercial Laws, which regard our own or the foreign Plantations, from the act of Navigation downwards."[140] In *Short Account of a Late Short Administration* (1766), Burke submitted the claim that the Rockingham ministry was the first administration to actively consult and act on the opinions of merchants throughout the British colonies when deliberating the provisions.[141]

The *Short Account*, while sanitized from the abusive rhetoric that characterized political journalism in Burke's day, was not a meditation on philosophy but a tract intended to defend the Rockingham ministry's political achievements.[142] Burke thus may have exaggerated when he insisted that the Rockingham ministry was the first administration to consult merchants. Still, the ministry's commitment to organizing meetings of merchants to solicit their counsel on trade was a novel way to develop new commercial laws at the time. Paul Langford writes that such activity exemplified "an extraordinary break with precedent" in seeking the wisdom of those outside the King's Cabinet, and even Parliament, in the formation of national policy.[143]

Without a doubt, the mercantile influence in shaping the drafting of the bill was powerful, and critics of the Rockinghamite initiative actually agreed with Burke's assertion about the ministry's pioneering outreach to merchants, even when lamenting this development.[144] Burke wrote of the Free Port Act in the *Short Account*, "The trade of *America* was set free from injudicious and ruinous Impositions – Its Revenue was improved, and settled upon a rational Foundation – Its Commerce extended with foreign Countries; while all the Advantages were secured to Great Britain."[145] Fifteen years after the passage of the Act, Burke would say, in *Speech on St Eustatius*, that the British had "thrown open Dominica upon the same principle [of free trade]" as a result of the legislation.[146]

---

[140] Burke to Charles O'Hara, I, 4 March 1766, in *Correspondence of Edmund Burke*, vol. I, 239–240.
[141] See Langford, *Writings and Speeches*, II, 55.
[142] See Langford, *Writings and Speeches*, II, 54.   [143] Langford, *Writings and Speeches*, II, 250.
[144] See Armytage, *Free Port System*, 28–29.
[145] Langford, *Writings and Speeches*, II, 55. Burke also listed other achievements of the Rockingham administration in the *Short Account*. He included the Stamp Act and Declaratory Act but also the repeal of the cider tax, an effort led by Dowdeswell. See also Langford, *First Rockingham Administration*, 214.
[146] Langford, *Writings and Speeches*, IV, 82.

In the *Short Account*, Burke described the commercial relations between West Indian traders, who traditionally opposed foreign competition, and North American merchants, who favored free trade with foreign sugar colonies, this way:

[T]he Interests of our Northern and Southern Colonies, before that Time jarring and dissonant, were understood, compared, adjusted, and perfectly reconciled. The Passions and Animosities of the Colonies, by judicious and lenient Measures, were allayed and composed, and the Foundation laid for a lasting Agreement amongst them.[147]

Burke was inflating the achievement of the Act when he wrote the traders' respective interests were "perfectly reconciled," since the legislation did not produce the vigorous commercial activity for which its backers had wished.

But the first and last parts of his statement did mirror the truth. Both the West Indian and North American interests were represented fairly and prominently during the drafting of the bill in the House of Commons, and in merchants' meetings.[148] More significant is that Burke's remarks here present a dimension of his economic thought that would attain greater prominence in his commentary on the Irish trade bills: the relaxation of commercial entanglements could soothe political relations between antagonistic parties and advance the cause of public prosperity.

The Free Port Act and the Power of Political Constraints

If the Free Port Act did not end all trade regulations, and if it did introduce others to appease the interests of West Indian traders, do such considerations suggest that Burke embraced the principles of mercantilist protectionism at this early stage in his parliamentary career? Does the limited nature of the legislation hint that he possessed a neutral, moderate attitude toward liberal commerce? Indeed, Burke's private views on the matter illuminate the friction he encountered between his desire to promote additional free trade measures and the weight of political exigencies. In his letter to O'Hara, Burke indicated a preference to enlarge the orbit of the Act by incorporating Ireland into the new free trade program. "Could not Ireland be somehow *hooked* into this System?" he asked hypothetically.[149] Yet Burke admitted later that month, in another letter to O'Hara, that Anglo-Irish commercial relations would need to be addressed as a separate question. "The Irish affairs are a System by themselves, and will I hope one day or another undergo a thorough scrutiny" he wrote, presaging his legislative activity in the late 1770s on the question of Irish trade.[150]

---

[147] Langford, *Writings and Speeches*, II, 55–56.   [148] See Armytage, *Free Port System*, 34–42.
[149] Burke to Charles O'Hara, I, 4 March 1766, in *Correspondence of Edmund Burke*, vol. I, 240.
[150] Burke to Charles O'Hara, 29 March [1766], in *Correspondence of Edmund Burke*, vol. I, 247.

While Burke's correspondence to O'Hara in March 1766 exhibits his support for a more robust system of free trade, then, it also demonstrates his awareness that contemporary circumstances had tempered movement toward the fulfillment of this aim. In a letter dated 27 March, Burke rejected O'Hara's proposals to soften trade restrictions on camblets, a woven fabric, and cotton because they "cross British manufactures, at least in prejudice and things are not ripe for it."[151] Burke was acutely conscious of the political might of British merchants who harbored protectionist opposition to the easing of commercial regulations. Two days later, Burke told O'Hara that while he had given serious consideration to O'Hara's trade reform proposals, he thought "every one of them impracticable; because they all stand directly in the way of some predominant prejudice, and some real interest or supposed, of this Country."[152] Burke continued that those ideas "require time and leisure to make their way by the slow progression of reason into the minds of people here, who just now seem shut against them."[153] Note that he is associating support for protectionism with the defiance of reason, as he understood the word.

Burke's impatience with protectionist sympathies was further displayed by his expression of regret over the limited nature of commercial reform in 1766, which explains why he targeted his ire toward the watered-down bill in late April 1766, a few weeks before the Free Port Act was formally introduced in the House on May 15. The bill became "half a measure; the most odious thing, I am sure to my Temper and opinions that can be conceived," Burke wrote in another letter to O'Hara.[154] He continued: "However, even this miserable remnant is better than nothing."[155] Burke remarked in the letter that his frustrations with mercantile sentiment in favor of protectionism reached a pitch with William Pitt the Elder, or Lord Chatham,[156] who harbored an initial resistance to the idea of liberating trade from unnecessary entanglements, and who was wary of Burke's commercial persuasions.[157]

---

[151] Burke to Charles O'Hara, [27 March 1766], in *Correspondence of Edmund Burke*, vol. I, 246.

[152] Burke to Charles O'Hara, 29 March [1766], in *Correspondence of Edmund Burke*, vol. I, 246.

[153] Burke to Charles O'Hara, 29 March [1766], in *Correspondence of Edmund Burke*, vol. I, 246–247.

[154] Burke to Charles O'Hara, 23, 24 [April 1766], in *Correspondence of Edmund Burke*, vol. I, 251.

[155] Burke to Charles O'Hara, 23, 24 [April 1766], in *Correspondence of Edmund Burke*, vol. I, 251.

[156] Pitt the Elder, the 1st Earl of Chatham, was the father of William Pitt the Younger, the future prime minister and Chancellor of the Exchequer to whom Burke would send *Thoughts and Details*.

[157] Burke wrote in the letter, "I went down to Hayes with a very respectable Merchant of Lancaster, to talk [Pitt], if possible, out of his peevish and perverse opposition to so salutary and unexceptionable a measure. But on this point, I found so great a man utterly unprovided with any better arms than a few rusty prejudices. So we returned as we went, after some hours [of]

Burke reinforced this mix of bitterness and regret thirty years later in *Letter to a Noble Lord*, when he indicated he would have pushed for greater trade reform if not for extenuating political conditions. After stating that he surveyed the "whole commercial, financial, constitutional and foreign interests" of the British Empire, he went on to assert, "A great deal was then done; and more, far more would have been done, if more had been permitted by events."[158] In addition, Burke's outreach to the merchants confirms the strength of his previous assertion about the Rockingham ministry's efforts to consider the advice of traders in the drafting of the bill. It exhibits Burke's practical and immediate engagement with questions of commerce in his parliamentary career, and underscores the fraught tension he faced in balancing his personal policy convictions in support of liberal foreign trade with the spirited tribunal of mercantile opinion.

We can begin to understand how the Free Port Act embodies the difficulty in describing Burke's parliamentary activities regarding foreign commerce as expressions of either "free trade" or "mercantilism." The law did establish new commercial ports, but it also retained a selection of protectionist measures to mollify the prejudices of West Indian planters. This difficulty is further illustrated by considering Richard B. Sheridan's analysis of the British West Indies. Sheridan, who has written one of the definitive histories of the political economy of the region,[159] distinguishes between the colonial position of Burke, who contended that the West Indian sugar colonies did benefit the Britain homeland, and Adam Smith, who criticized this notion. Hence their colonial positions "stood at opposite poles."[160]

Yet Sheridan goes on to note the growing anxieties of North American merchants who believed their trade was suffering under the weight of West Indian monopolies. "From the North came appeals for free trade in Caribbean waters," he writes[161] – appeals that were satisfied by the Free Port Act. As Sheridan's rendering of the Act demonstrates, Burke helped orchestrate parliamentary efforts in 1766 to translate these entreaties for free trade into concrete legislation, even though he was not as wary as Smith of the perceived utility of Britain's Caribbean colonial possessions. We may conclude, then, that the Act was an early example of Burke's conception of economic statecraft, seeking to move the British Empire in the direction of freer trade while retaining

---

fruitless conference" (Burke to Charles O'Hara, 23, 24 [April 1766], in *Correspondence of Edmund Burke*, vol. I, 251–252). Chatham was flummoxed by Burke's views on commerce. "As to his notions and maxims of trade, they can never be mine," he wrote in October 1766. "Nothing can be more unsound and more repugnant to every true principle of manufacture and commerce, than the rendering so noble a branch as the Cottons, dependant for the first material upon the produce of French and Danish Islands, instead of British." See Sir William R. Anson, ed., *Autobiography and Political Correspondence of Augustus Henry Third Duke of Grafton* (London: John Murray, 1898), 108.

[158] Langford, *Writings and Speeches*, IX, 159.   [159] Sheridan, *Sugar and Slavery*.
[160] Sheridan, *Sugar and Slavery*, 6.   [161] Sheridan, *Sugar and Slavery*, 10.

a healthy degree of sensitivity to existing prejudices suspicious about the liberal movement of commerce.

6.5 CONCLUSION

In the end, *Account of the European Settlements in America* catches a flavor of Burke's thoughts on imperial political economy at the initial stages of his mature intellectual life. The writing does not provide doctrinaire precepts in favor of either mercantilism or "free trade," as those phrases are understood in modernity, but rather communicates a nuanced attempt to identify the underlying sources of commercial prosperity in a fluid imperial environment. These sources, the Burkes emphasize, included not simply the presence of natural resources but also the particular character of a people – a character that could not be measured by the false splendor of bullion. They maintained the hope that the potent combination of the British people's love of liberty and genius for industry would make France, and other rival nations, tremble at the power of English commerce.

The Free Port Act was a budding attempt to breathe life into this power. The Act carries lasting importance for our study of Burke's economic thought because it denoted his great influence behind the Rockingham administration's attempt to loosen the rigid system of imperial protectionism that had defined the British Empire's commercial policy starting in the late seventeenth century. The substance of the Act was limited; the symbolic meaning of the bill, however, was significant, for it laid dents into the hardening steel of the Navigation Acts in the British West Indies, thereby unclogging the flow of traffic within West Indian islands, and between the islands and North America. As Paul Langford writes, "In the last analysis [the commercial reforms] represented the first significant attempt to launch an experiment in free trade and a portentous, if small, breach in the old imperial system."[162]

The Act further illuminated Burke's concern that the French Empire posed a threat to Britain throughout the globe, including in the West Indies, as outlined in the *Account*.[163] Pledging support to English traders in the region would not only enhance the commercial prowess of Britain, then, but also foster their competitive advantages against French traders. Burke's close attention to the Anglo-French rivalry would persist through the age of the French Revolution.[164]

Additionally, the Free Port Act was an early embodiment of Burke's attitude toward the American colonies that would attain greater prominence in the

---

[162] Langford, *First Rockingham Administration*, 207.
[163] See *Account of the European Settlements*, vol. II, 176–177. Burke would retain his concern for the influence of France in the West Indies during the age of the French Revolution. See Langford, *Writings and Speeches*, IX, 96–99, 274–275.
[164] See Langford, *Writings and Speeches*, IX, 96–97.

1770s: Britain possessed the imperial right to rule over the dependencies, but it should relieve them of burdensome taxing schemes in order to encourage their economic development and promote the commercial interests of the British Empire as a whole.

Yet Burke's influence in the drafting of the Free Port Act has been minimized by Lucy S. Sutherland. She writes that Burke was "of far too slight consequence to be a deciding factor" in the commercial policy of the Rockinghams," and could "claim no credit as a commercial reformer."[165] Instead Sutherland emphasizes his practical efforts in organizing mercantile support for policy reform of Grenville's program. Burke indeed demonstrated an indisputable element of pragmatism by lending an ear to the worries of traders in the development of the Act. Sutherland's portrayal, however, gives short shrift to Burke's serious study of imperial commercial policy before his entry into Parliament, and during his first legislative session in the body, that informed his efforts in helping to draft the Act. One should not underestimate the heightened consideration Burke gave to questions of political economy as a thinker and lawmaker in the 1750s and 1760s.

Burke's reflections in the *Account* and his industrious parliamentary activity in support of the Free Port Act helps us begin to understand the constancy of his economic thought throughout his life. His prominent role in the Rockingham ministry's push for the legislation marks a fidelity to liberal trade early in his political life. Burke did not call for the abolition of all trade regulations in the 1760s, but his objection to the surfeit of commercial privileges within the British Empire signaled a discontent with the excesses of protectionism that foreshadowed later attacks on the mercantile system in England. In other words, Burke was sympathetic to the cause of economic liberty when he entered the House of Commons in 1766, and conveyed significant interest in the ideal even prior to the commencement of his parliamentary service.

The Free Port Act also was a tribute to the commercial principles that came to inspire the Rockingham party's approach to imperial policy. Four years after the Act, in *Thoughts on the Present Discontents*, Burke issued his seminal vindication of party government (and of the Rockingham party in particular), based on the premise that coalitions of individuals united on common principle provided an invaluable service to government, and thus to political society:

Party is a body of men united, for promoting by their joint endeavours the national interest, upon some particular principle in which they are all agreed. For my part, I find it impossible to conceive, that any one believes in his own politicks, or thinks them to be of any weight, who refuses to adopt the means of having them reduced into practice.[166]

The Free Port Act exemplified this ethic of party. The law was the product of a group of legislators, stirred by the notion that the power of liberal commerce

---

[165] Sutherland, "Edmund Burke and the First Rockingham Ministry," 59.
[166] Langford, *Writings and Speeches*, II, 317.

could advance national and imperial (and political) aims, who joined together in government to reduce the superfluities of trade laws in the British West Indies. Party could serve as a noble and efficacious association in the pursuit of wise economic policy.

Burke's following comments in *Thoughts on the Present Discontents* integrated this defense of party with a conception of just statesmanship. He writes:

It is the business of the speculative philosopher to mark the proper ends of Government. It is the business of the politician, who is the philosopher in action, to find out proper means towards those ends, and to employ them with effect. Therefore every honourable connexion will avow it as their first purpose, to pursue every just method to put the men who hold their opinions into such a condition as may enable them to carry their common plans into execution, with all the power and authority of the State.[167]

Such remarks capture Burke's state of mind, and the substance of his legislative activities, in his support of the Free Port Act. Because Burke was aware that existing political realities under the Rockingham administration would inhibit greater progress in favor of liberal commercial relations,[168] his labor in advancing the Act was an early display of his political temperament of prudence. This prudence was defined by a purposeful attempt to move toward the realization of a principle and yet tolerate, however regrettably, the policy results that followed given the constraints of political circumstances.

Finally, although there is limited historical evidence of Burke's intellectual commentary on the Free Port Act, Burke's remarks in the *Short Account* about the reconciliation of competing trading interests imparted his lasting belief that exchange relations could transform perceived antagonists into commercial partners. In the 1760s, Burke discerned that free trade spread advantages to the many, serving as a much-needed corrective to zero-sum mercantilist regulations in which one gained at the expense of another. This insight was famously propounded by Adam Smith in the *Wealth of Nations* – a text published a decade after the enactment of the Free Port Act.[169]

---

[167] Langford, *Writings and Speeches*, II, 317–318.

[168] Burke's description in the *Short Account* of the benefits generated by the free ports illustrates his political attempt to assuage the British merchants and persuade them that the new commercial laws advanced their trading interests. "Materials were provided and insured to our Manufactures – The Sale of these Manufactures was encreased – The *African* Trade preserved and extended – The Principles of the Act of Navigation pursued, and the Plan improved – And the Trade for Bullion rendered free, secure, and permanent," Burke wrote (Langford, *Writings and Speeches*, II, 55).

[169] Smith would remark in the *Wealth of Nations*, "The most perfect freedom of trade is permitted between the British colonies of America and the West Indies, both in the enumerated and non-enumerated commodities. Those colonies are now becoming so populous and thriving, that each of them finds in some of the others a great and extensive market for every part of its produce. All of them taken together, they make a great internal market for the produce of one another" (vol. II, 580).

7

Observations on a Late State of the Nation and the Political Economy of Anglo-American Imperial Relations

> Tyranny is a poor provider. It knows neither how to accumulate, nor how to extract.[1]
>
> Edmund Burke, *Speech on American Taxation*, 1774

7.1 BRITISH IMPERIAL POLICY AND THE AMERICAN COLONIES

The British government's approach to commercial policy in Burke's age projected considerable influence not only in the West Indies but also in North America. For its mismanagement of the fraught Anglo-American relationship during the decade following Burke's entry into Parliament in 1766 sparked among the most defining events in the histories of Great Britain and the United States, and in Burke's own life. In the views of American colonists, the British Empire had hardened into an oppressive force in British North America by imposing a progressive series of political and tax mandates without seeking their counsel.

Britain at this moment was saddled with excessive national debt from the Seven Years War, and retained additional financial encumbrances that derived from its maintenance of a standing army in America. Taking into account such fiscal challenges, the British government eyed the colonies as a bountiful economic resource from which it could generate revenue to help pay for the costs of preserving its empire overseas, which in consequence would further subordinate the growth of colonial commerce to British national interests. The British impetus to extract money from the colonies was particularly strong in the mid-1760s because the empire struggled to enforce existing trade restrictions on the colonies in the first half of the eighteenth century, leading to a rise in illicit colonial trade.[2]

---

[1] Langford, *Writings and Speeches*, II, 461.
[2] See Thomas C. Barrow, "Background to the Grenville Program, 1757–1763," *The William and Mary Quarterly* 22 (1965): 93–104.

The political and commercial program of the Grenville ministry aspired to reassert the strength of the British Empire to meet these financial burdens. The Sugar Act of 1764, for instance, reduced the rate of taxation on molasses in half and expanded enforcement measures to collect greater revenue for Britain's imperial commitments.[3] Duties were imposed on imported wares such as wine, coffee, and linen.[4] And Grenville's Stamp Act, which passed in March 1765, levied taxes on official paper documents circulated in the colonies, including newspapers and legal writings.[5]

The Stamp Act was the first internal direct tax on colonists, as Grenville's other taxes consisted of restrictions on external trade goods. It was the catalyst for colonial protests, boycotts against British products, and intimidation tactics against stamp collectors. Furthermore, the Act triggered a debate over whether Britain held the lawful authority to tax the colonists without their consent. The colonists argued that only their representative assemblies were vested with the legitimate power to tax the people.[6] The Rockingham ministry of 1765–1766 repealed the Stamp Act in March 1766.

Following the first Rockingham administration, the Chatham ministry took power and passed the Townshend Acts in 1767, which set import duties on more goods, such as tea, paper, and glass. In a draft to a speech on the proposed duties, Burke admitted that they were "well chosen," noting, in shorthand, that "the foreign [taxes were] grafted on Benefits given and Commerce [was] enlarged."[7] The levies on fruits and wine actually originated from restrictions envisioned by the Rockingham party,[8] which perhaps explains Burke's support for Townshend's specific measures here.

Nevertheless, Burke opposed the Townshend Acts overall for their imprudent nature. He maintained that a colonial dependency could not be expected to accept additional imperial taxation when they were already bound by existing trade laws, such as the Navigation Acts. "It is impossible

---

[3] This measure updated the Molasses Act of 1733, which taxed imports on molasses but was continually evaded by colonists and set to expire in 1763.

[4] For historical background on the Sugar Act, consult, among many, Edmund S. Morgan, ed., *Prologue to Revolution: Sources and Documents on the Stamp Act Crisis, 1764–1766* (Chapel Hill: The University of North Carolina Press, 1959), 3–23; and John Phillip Reid, *Constitutional History of the American Revolution*, vol. II, *The Authority to Tax* (Madison: The University of Wisconsin Press, 1987), 194–207.

[5] For historical background on the Stamp Act, consult, among many, Morgan, *Prologue to Revolution*, 24–43; and Reid, *Constitutional History of the American Revolution*, vol. II, 208–216. See also Jean-Yves Michel Le Saux, "Commerce and Consent: Edmund Burke and the Imperial Problem during the American Revolution, 1757–1775" (PhD thesis, Princeton University, 1992).

[6] A related debate concerned the distinction, if any, between "internal" versus "external" taxation. See Helen Henry Hodge, "The Repeal of the Stamp Act," *Political Science Quarterly* 19 (1904): 252–276.

[7] Langford, *Writings and Speeches*, II, 62.

[8] See Langford, *Writings and Speeches*, II, 62–63n6; and Bourke, *Empire & Revolution*, 309.

that the Same Country could be at once subservient to your Commerce and your Revenues," Burke wrote in his draft speech on the Townshend Acts.[9] This insight was part of Burke's broader view of imperial economics: schemes of excessive taxation would clog the flow of commerce, which would injure both imperial and colonial trade, diminish public revenue, and provoke colonial unrest. Besides, Burke observed, the Acts were bad economics for Britain because it harmed English producers as well as the Americans. The Townshend duties were "intended to distress the Manufacturers of Great Britain," he insisted in a speech in November 1768.[10]

Colonists reacted with rage following the implementation of the Townshend Acts, legislation which confirmed their growing suspicions that Britain was intent on abusing its political might for imperial advantage. All Townshend duties on goods except for tea were repealed in 1770, which created a de facto truce between the two powers until 1772. The Tea Act of 1773 followed, then the Boston Tea Party uprising, and then the Intolerable Acts of 1774 to punish Tea Party participants. America's Second Continental Congress voted to declare independence on July 2, 1776, and formally ratified the Declaration of Independence's text on July 4.

What significance did these events hold for Burke? First, questions of political economy – the right to tax, the benefits and drawbacks of trade restrictions, the history of the Navigation Acts, and the relationship between regulations and commerce, and commerce and power – were central to grasping the imperial relationship between Britain and America. Second, they illuminated the sharp tensions the British government faced in attempting to preserve the commercial vitality of its empire while cooling the disturbances of its colonial subjects, an issue that was immediately relevant to Britain's relationship with Ireland as well. Third, these events drew attention to the eighteenth-century debate over the efficacy of commercial regulations in strengthening social connections between two peoples.

Burke's principal belief concerning the American question was that the political authority of the British Empire over the colonies rested on wholly legitimate grounds. But he also maintained that imperial rule demanded morally responsible governance. Burke thus argued that the British government should ease its regulatory control over the Americans in order to placate their fractious tendencies, respect their thirst for liberty, and promote their economic prosperity, which in turn would advance the commercial interests of the Empire.

This is why Burke and the Rockingham Whigs pushed forth the repeal of the Stamp Act and the passage of the Declaratory Act, or the American Colonies Act, of 1766. The Declaratory Act reasserted Britain's power to tax the colonies

[9] Langford, *Writings and Speeches*, II, 62.   [10] Langford, *Writings and Speeches*, II, 97.

"in all cases whatsoever,"[11] but it was more a symbolic law than a specific policy prescription. Burke thought this Act would reinforce the authority of Westminster, and, at the same time, recognize the colonists' awakened instinct for freedom while safeguarding their desire to control matters relating to internal taxation. Such a careful balance would, ostensibly, permit the colonies to govern themselves in practice while preserving the integrity of the British Empire. Before inspecting Burke's commentary on Anglo-American and Anglo-Irish commercial relations, however, we must confront an important, though overlooked, writing in Burke's early parliamentary career that in many ways connected his activities in support of the Free Port Act with his later reflections on imperial politics and the American war.

7.2   OBSERVATIONS ON A LATE STATE OF THE NATION

The dissolution of the Rockingham ministry in the summer of 1766 did not halt debate about the merits of its commercial policy, nor did it relax tensions between the Rockinghamite and Grenvillian factions in British politics. In response to an attack on the former in 1768 by William Knox, an enterprising acolyte of Grenville, Burke wrote *Observations on a Late State of the Nation*. Published in February 1769, the writing was his first extended party defense of the Rockingham ministry. The *Observations* is not a comprehensive statement on Burke's economic or political thought, and its partisan nature drains the writing of philosophic depth. Unsurprisingly, it is typically given cursory treatment in the study of Burke's political and economic theory.

Nevertheless, the *Observations* is crucial to understanding the development of Burke's earliest intellectual reflections on the role of commerce in the British Empire, and offers insights into his broader conception of political economy that he would sharpen in his later writings and speeches. The *Observations* is also a smooth analytic complement to Burke's activities in support of the Free Port Act of 1766; it elucidates his own cast of mind in his campaign to help orchestrate the Act's passage, and provides a clearer window into his perspective on the achievements and motivations behind the Rockinghams' commercial policy that he touched upon briefly in the *Short Account*. Even more, the *Observations* is significant for representing Burke's first major undertaking in his public life to deploy statistical data as a tool to supplement his method of reasoning and discredit the empirical arguments of his opponent.

Burke's primary opponent in this instance was Knox. Published in October 1768, the *State of the Nation* was Knox's attempt to deliver a partisan defense of Grenville's record in the aftermath of the Seven Years

---

[11] Langford, *Writings and Speeches*, II, 46. See pages 46–51 for Burke's notes for his "Speech on Declaratory Resolution" in which he sketches this argument.

War, which had ended in 1763.[12] In Knox's telling, the war had incurred immense financial costs on the British government and crippled Britain's stature in the world, leaving France to seize political momentum in the Anglo-French imperial rivalry. Following the war, Grenville had pursued commercial and financial policies that aimed to solidify the grounds of British public finance. Grenville's measures included the notorious Stamp Act of 1765, the direct tax on the use of printed paper in the American colonies that had been repealed by the Rockinghams in 1766.

Knox's argument hinged on his dark, overcast portrayal of the weak state of British commerce in the aftermath of the Seven Years War. "[T]he most successful enterprise could not compensate to the nation for the waste of its people, by carrying on a war in unhealthy climates, and the perpetual burdens laid upon its manufactures for payment of the excessive rate of interest at which money was to be borrowed," Knox claimed.[13] He armed the pamphlet with a wealth of data in an attempt to demonstrate that the British economy suffered tremendous hardship from the war.

The pamphlet's rekindling of conflict between the Grenville and Rockingham political wings arrived at an inopportune moment. Both parties, in fact, had an interest at the time to unite together to oppose the seemingly haphazard colonial policies of the Grafton administration, which had assumed power following the Chatham ministry in October 1768. The Rockinghams, however, refused to ignore what they perceived as an unjustified attack on their commercial policy, and felt compelled to issue a stark rejoinder.

Burke was enlisted to craft the Rockinghams' response. He wrote the vast majority of the *Observations*, although evidence suggests he received some assistance in drafting particular sections of the pamphlet. Burke most likely utilized the knowledge of William Dowdeswell in the earlier parts of the writing on questions relating to financial matters. Sir George Macartney, an envoy to St. Petersburg from 1764 to 1767 who had been a principal architect of the Anglo-Russian Treaty of 1765–1766, may have originally written the passage in the *Observations* defending the treaty. The *Observations*, then, was not only a statement communicating Burke's views on Knox's pamphlet, but also the product of his judicious collection and organization of information furnished by Rockingham's allies.

Knox's *State of the Nation* was influential in its own right. Its forlorn picture of the British economy tapped into the popular anxieties of the English people reeling from the political instabilities of the aftermath of the Seven Years War.

---

[12] See Langford, *Writings and Speeches*, II, 102–109 for the historical backdrop of *Observations*, from which this account borrows.

[13] William Knox, *The Present State of the Nation: Particularly with Respect to Its Trade, Finances, &c. &c.* (London: J. Almon, 1768), 7–8.

The writing garnered widespread acclaim from the press and from political and literary leaders.[14]

But the force of argument in Burke's response was even more impressive, particularly in his attempted refutation of Knox's assertions relating to public economy. The *Observations* received immediate praise upon its publication.[15] Horace Walpole remarked that the writing "solidly confuted Grenville, exposed him and exploded his pretensions to skill in finance."[16] (Knox's pamphlet mirrored the formal views of Grenville's party; Grenville had examined the draft before publication, and was thought at first to be its author.[17]) Yet the *Observations*' fate has proven to be anticlimactic. Its initial popularity sunk over the years, confining the pamphlet to a neglected domain of Burke's intellectual corpus far removed from his more celebrated early works such as *Thoughts on the Present Discontents*.

Two main themes divide the composition of the *Observations* and guide the direction of the tract's argument. First, Burke strives to rebut Knox's melancholy description of English trade and optimistic account of French public finance, and in doing so reveals his attraction to empirical knowledge that he would later display in his writings on economical reform and the Indian economy. This exposition takes up around the first three-quarters of writing. Second, in the final quarter, Burke describes the Rockinghams' prior efforts to ease and simplify Grenville's colonial tax policy while providing deeper elaboration on the party's efforts in drafting the Free Port Act of 1766. In his discussion of these two subjects, Burke presents underdeveloped observations on the balance of trade, the political economy of commerce, and schemes of wealth redistribution that acquired greater conceptual clarity in his subsequent political commentary spanning the 1770s to the 1790s.

One of Burke's first extended arguments in the *Observations* casts doubt on the idea that a favorable balance of trade advantaged the home country, a line of reasoning espoused by Knox in the *State of the Nation* and by proponents of mercantilism in the eighteenth century.[18] After Britain relinquished the French colonies of Guadeloupe and Martinique back to France in 1763, Burke explains, imports from the islands continued to flourish. He marshals empirical data to validate this claim, as reproduced in Figures 7.1 and 7.2.[19]

---

[14] Langford, *Writings and Speeches*, II, 107.

[15] Five editions of *Observations* were published. The third edition made slight changes to the previous editions. The fourth and fifth editions made no revisions. See Langford, *Writings and Speeches*, II, 108n3.

[16] Horace Walpole, *Memoirs of the Reign of King George the Third*, vol. II, ed. Denis Le Marchant (Philadelphia: Lea & Blanchard, 1845), 164. Walpole would go on to criticize Burke: he "had far more shining abilities than solid conduct, and, being dazzled by his own wit and eloquence, expected that those talents would have the same effect on others."

[17] Langford, *Writings and Speeches*, II, 103.   [18] See Heckscher, *Mercantilism*, vol. II, 248–259.

[19] Langford, *Writings and Speeches*, II, 119–120. Figures were drawn from the Inspector General's compilation of customs statistics and can be found in Sir Charles Whitworth, *State of the Trade*

In 1761, there was no entry of goods from any of the conquered places but
    Guadaloupe; in that year, it stood thus:

Imports from Guadaloupe,	value, £482,179
In 1762, when we had not yet delivered up our conquests, the account was,	
Guadaloupe,	513,244
Martinico,	288,425
Total imports in 1762,	value, £801,669

FIGURE 7.1 British imports from Guadeloupe and Martinique in 1761
and 1762
Source: Burke, *Observations on a Late State of the Nation*, in Langford,
Writings and Speeches, II, 119

In 1763, after we had delivered up the sovereignty of these
    islands, but kept open a communication with them, the imports were,

Guadaloupe,	412,303
Martinico,	344,161
Havannah,	249,386
Total imports in 1763,	value, £1,005,850

FIGURE 7.2 British imports from Guadeloupe, Martinique, and
Havana in 1763
Source: Burke, *Observations on a Late State of the Nation*, in
Langford, *Writings and Speeches*, II, 120

In Burke's judgment, the worth of Britain's investment in the West Indies
stemmed from these imports. "I take the imports from, and not the exports to,
these conquests, as the measure of the advantages which we derived from
them," he insists.[20] Therefore, "I choose the import article, as the best, and
indeed the only standard we can have, of the value of the West India trade."[21]
Notice Burke's comment in Figure 7.2 that Britain, even though it gave up such
possessions, still retained a "communication" with them, indicating that the
kingdom preserved an enduring commercial connection with its former
territories.

*of Great Britain in Its Imports and Exports, Progressively from the Year 1697: Also of the Trade
to Each Particular Country, during the above Period, Distinguishing Each Year* (London:
G. Robinson et al., 1776).
[20] Langford, *Writings and Speeches*, II, 120.
[21] Langford, *Writings and Speeches*, II, 120. Burke does not note that while imports from
Martinique increased in 1763, imports from Guadeloupe decreased.

In this section, Burke transitions from the French colonies to British possessions in the West Indies in his survey of trade imbalances, and sticks to his reasoning that an excess of imports yielded a net benefit to Britain. "We know that the West Indians are always indebted to our merchants, and that the value of every shilling of West-India produce is English property," he writes.[22] Accordingly, "[O]ur import from them, and not our export, ought always to be considered as their true value; and this corrective ought to be applied to all general balances of our trade, which are formed on the ordinary principles."[23] The products manufactured in the West Indies originated from British colonial investment in the region in the first place; their importation into Britain would be augmenting – not draining – the commercial value of its empire. Therefore, seeking to correct trade imbalances was "quite ridiculous."[24]

Burke appears to counter his own argument by stating elsewhere in this section that fostering a balance of trade in "most foreign branches" was "on the whole, the best method."[25] He does not elaborate on this remark, however, leaving the listener puzzled by such a claim in light of his broader opposition to balance of trade theory. (Perhaps he had in mind Britain's trade balances with nations outside the British Empire.) Later in the *Observations*, Burke reinforces his original point that trade deficits presented an illusory picture of the wealth of nations with reference to British intercourse with Ireland, America,[26] and Newfoundland.

Burke's reflections on Newfoundland, which nursed a vibrant fishing trade,[27] are a noticeable example underlining his distrust of balance of trade theory. From his perspective, even though Britain imported commodities from Newfoundland, the imports were no less valuable in providing nutriment than if they were produced by the British in their home country. "[Y]our exports to Newfoundland are your own goods," Burke begins.[28] His comments proceed to a higher pitch: "Your import is your own food; as much your own, as that you

---

[22] Langford, *Writings and Speeches*, II, 120.   [23] Langford, *Writings and Speeches*, II, 121.

[24] Langford, *Writings and Speeches*, II, 120. See the starred footnote in which Burke provides empirical data on this imbalance. Burke also mentions that export data did not include the sale of African slaves, remittances, and "the payment of part of the balance of the North American trade."

[25] Langford, *Writings and Speeches*, II, 120.

[26] Burke writes, "The whole import from Ireland and America, and from the West Indies, is set against us in the ordinary way of striking a balance of imports and exports; whereas the import and export are both our own. This is just as ridiculous, as to put against the general balance of the nation, how much more goods Cheshire receives from London, than London from Cheshire" (Langford, *Writings and Speeches*, II, 144).

[27] France ceded the sovereignty of Newfoundland to Britain under the Treaty of Utrecht in 1713 but maintained certain fishing privileges. The treaty prompted the great expansion of the British fishery. See Olaf U. Janzen, *War and Trade in Eighteenth-Century Newfoundland* (Liverpool: Liverpool University Press, 2013), 21, 157.

[28] Langford, *Writings and Speeches*, II, 144.

raise with your ploughs out of your own soil; and not your loss, but your gain; your riches, not your poverty."[29]

Then Burke's disgust with balance of trade doctrine reaches a crescendo:

To state the whole of the foreign import *as loss*, is exceedingly absurd. All the iron, hemp, flax, cotton, Spanish wool, raw silk, woolen and linen yarn, which we import, are by no means to be considered as the matter of a merely luxurious consumption; which is the idea too generally and loosely annexed to our import article. These above-mentioned are materials of industry, not of luxury, which are wrought up here, in many instances, to ten times, and more, of their original value. Even where they are not subservient to our exports, they still add to our internal wealth, which consists in the stock of useful commodities, as much as in gold and silver. In looking over the specific articles of our export and import, I have often been astonished to see for how small a part of the supply of our consumption, either luxurious or convenient, we are indebted to nations properly foreign to us.[30]

Burke's commentary on Anglo-Newfoundland trade thus outlines a collection of arguments in favor of liberal commerce intended to calm mercantilist suspicions of trade imbalances, such as: British imports are products of industry; their value in Britain can rise through increased investment; commercial intercourse is not a zero-sum contest but an avenue for reciprocity; and, therefore, the circulation of goods from a colony to its mother country disseminates advantages to all British parties. Burke invokes this latter principle later in the *Observations* when he explains that the British government and the East India Company negotiated on the "true principle of credit" as "equal dealers, on the footing of mutual advantage."[31] Burke further challenges mercantilist thinking in his remarks quoted here by insisting that the value of goods derived not from the physical source of its creation but from the demands of the market, and that "useful commodities" contributed to public opulence as much as bullion. The wealth of nations was not built up by positive trade balances but by the radiance of commerce.

We must be cautious before asserting that Burke was a rigid advocate of free trade in the modern sense, however. Remember that these comments were made in the larger context of his qualified defense of the British Empire. For Burke, the diffusion of goods benefited Britain not only because of the principle of mutual exchange, but because Britain's trading partners carried on a unique relationship with their mother country in the first place. With regard to English trade with Ireland and America, "The whole revolves and circulates through this kingdom, and is, so far as it regards our profit, in the nature of home trade, as much as if the several countries of America and Ireland were all pieced to Cornwall," Burke observes. "The course of exchange with all these places is fully sufficient to demonstrate that this kingdom has the whole

[29] Langford, *Writings and Speeches*, II, 144–145. [30] Langford, *Writings and Speeches*, II, 145.
[31] Langford, *Writings and Speeches*, II, 171–172. Of course, the Company was a chartered corporation with a trading monopoly in the East Indies.

advantage of their commerce."[32] Striking a trade balance was an effectual exercise in redundancy, if not disadvantage, since the benefits flowing from the dispersal of goods throughout British colonial possessions would eventually reach English merchants anyway.

The Function of Empirical Information

Burke's deployment of British import data in the *Observations* to challenge the presumptions of balance of trade theory illustrated a procedure of practical logic central to his thought. In his view, general claims about political economy, and political life overall, should be verified by the sanction of historical experience. One instructive way to corroborate this experience relating to commerce was through the timely and judicious use of statistical knowledge. Burke was keen on utilizing deploy data with care and discretion, however, for he was quite aware that their real truths could often be lost in the mists of political propaganda and statistical sleight-of-hand, as he attempted to show in his response to Knox's pamphlet.

An additional example in the *Observations* beyond his study of the import data of Guadeloupe, Martinique, and Havana will suffice to showcase Burke's deftness in using empirical information to his advantage. In the appendix to the *Observations*, Burke attempts to discredit Knox's claim that the Rockinghams were responsible for the plunge in trade in 1765 because they permitted Spanish vessels to traffic in British ports in the West Indies, particularly in Jamaica, starting in August 1765. Burke first identifies a basic error in Knox's argument: the order to allow Spanish access to colonial ports was signed by the treasury board on November 15, 1765. Because this date was so close to the end of the year, it would be grossly misleading to attribute the reduced state of British exports in 1765 to this order.

Next, Burke lambastes Knox's further assertion that the passage of the Free Port Act in the spring of 1766, by relaxing the laws of trade in the West Indies, had compounded the supposed depression of British exports in the region. Burke notes that, once again, Knox should check his facts: the regulation to open Jamaican ports did not go into effect until November 1766. Therefore, data on British exports for the year 1766 would be largely useless. The important data point, Burke emphasizes, is the measurement of British exports in the year 1767, more than one full year after the relaxation of trade restrictions in Jamaica. He then brandishes a telling chart, which can be viewed below as Figure 7.3.

Based on these figures, Burke concludes that British exports in 1767, following the enactment of the Free Port Act, exceeded exports in each of the previous two years by more than £52,000 and in 1764 by more than £11,000. Burke thus insists, "Nothing but the thickest ignorance of the Jamaica trade could have made any one entertain a fancy, that the least ill effect on our commerce could follow

---

[32] Langford, *Writings and Speeches*, II, 144.

1764 Exports to Jamaica	£456,528
1765	415,624
1766	415,544
1767 (first year of the Free-port act)	467,681

FIGURE 7.3 British exports to Jamaica, 1764–1767
Source: Burke, *Observations on a Late State of the
Nation*, in Langford, *Writings and Speeches*, II, 217

from this opening of the ports."[33] As Frances Armytage has documented, the salutary long-term effect of the Free Port Act was dubious. Indeed, Burke does not engage the broader counterfactual: might there have been greater trade in Jamaica, and the West Indies, over time if Britain had not established colonies there in the first place? Nevertheless, Burke's examination of export figures in this example captures his readiness to use empirical data to fortify his mode of reasoning on subjects relating to political economy.

The strength of Burke's empirical argumentation in the *Observations* lies in its accuracy of detail, reflecting a fluency in the language of statistics and public finance exceptional for a lawmaker in his time. After the publication of the *Observations*, Knox penned a response, titled *An Appendix to the Present State of the Nation*, in which he leveled ad hominem attacks against Burke.[34] The conspicuous feature of Knox's new tract was its revelation that, in Knox's review, only one factual inaccuracy existed in the entirety of Burke's pamphlet – and that error was regarding an inconsequential misstatement in a footnote relating to the percent of a premium increase. Burke wrote it was 1 percent, when in reality it was one-half of 1 percent.[35] Ironically, he added the note in a section of the *Observations* in which he (accurately) showed that Knox's estimation of the British government's expenditures in peacetime was off by £878,544.[36] To be sure, both Burke and Knox were guilty of petty remarks in their dispute; in his note, Burke accused Knox of violating "the first rule of arithmetick,"[37] while Knox, in *Appendix*, insinuated that Burke violated the "second rule of arithmetic."[38]

[33] Langford, *Writings and Speeches*, II, 217.
[34] Knox, referring to Burke, writes, "Exploring the devices of a malignant heart, and exposing its machinations, detecting its misrepresentations and wiping off its calumnies, are, to a man of humanity, the most painful occupations." See William Knox, *An Appendix to* The Present State of the Nation. *Containing a Reply to the Observations on that Pamphlet* (London: J. Almon, 1769), 59.
[35] See Langford, *Writings and Speeches*, II, 108, 136, 136n1. There was at least one other factual error presented by Burke. See Langford, *Writings and Speeches*, II, 123n1.
[36] Langford, *Writings and Speeches*, II, 133–136.
[37] See the starred footnote in Langford, *Writings and Speeches*, II, 136.
[38] Knox, *Appendix to* The Present State of the Nation, 42.

Burke exposed the inaccuracies and distortions of Knox's survey of finances in a myriad of other ways in the *Observations*. For instance, Knox alleged in the *State of the Nation* that France raised more than £50,000,000 from 1756 to 1762 by taxation. Burke clarified that such money derived from loans, not taxes.[39] This explanation was part of his larger argument in the pamphlet that Knox overstated the vitality of the French economy, and that France, seemingly unbeknownst to Knox, had levied a wide variety of taxes on its people, unrelated to the £50,000,000 it received from loans.[40] Knox conceded the mistake in the *Appendix* but intimated that he noticed it himself.[41] Yet even Knox admitted his description of the French financial scheme "said more than the truth."[42] Additionally, when the fourth edition of the *State of the Nation* was published in 1769 (the same year as Knox's *Appendix*), it was revised to reflect Burke's criticisms of Knox's factual imprecision.[43] Knox acknowledged the "many errors and mistakes" of his first edition, both "of the printer and author."[44]

Burke's refutation of Knox's sunny appraisal of France in this context included broader remarks on French public finance and taxation that exemplified his abiding interest in the country's political economy that emerged prior to the publication of the *Observations*. One decade before the pamphlet was released, Burke's *Annual Register* for 1759 observed the growing discrepancy between the sound public administration of England and the teetering finances of France during the Seven Years War. While the latter was becoming "bankrupt," England was able to borrow money on favorable terms, and had only enacted a single tax, on malt, to fund the interest on the loan.[45]

Burke continues this criticism of French administration in the *Observations*. He begins by writing, "There are three standards to judge of the good condition of a nation with regard to its finances. 1st, The relief of the people. 2d, The equality of supplies to establishments. 3d, The state of public credit."[46] Burke believed the French government failed on all three accounts, going so far as to suggest in the pamphlet that the weight of France's unpaid expenses might provoke "some extraordinary convulsion in that whole system; the effect of

---

[39] Langford, *Writings and Speeches*, II, 148–149. See Langford, *Writings and Speeches*, II, 108.

[40] Langford, *Writings and* Speeches, II, 152–153. To reinforce his point that Knox was overstating the strength of the French economy, Burke employs a chart comparing French and English stock prices. As Burke shows, English stock prices far exceeded French prices at the time.

[41] Burke's critical assessment of Knox's discussion of French wartime finance, Knox writes, was "most fortunately for him published before the correct edition [of the *State of the Nation*], which I had advertised could be brought out" (Knox, *Appendix to* The Present State of the Nation, 17).

[42] Knox, *Appendix to* The Present State of the Nation, 17.

[43] See Langford, *Writings and Speeches*, II, 108.

[44] Knox, *The Present State of the Nation: Particularly with Respect to Its Trade, Finances, &c. &c.*, 4th ed. (London: J. Almon, 1769), iii.

[45] *The Annual Register, of the Year 1759* (London: R. and J. Dodsley, 1762), 56.

[46] Langford, *Writings and Speeches*, II, 151.

which on France, and even on all Europe, it is difficult to conjecture," an uncanny prophetic remark twenty years prior to the French Revolution.[47]

Soon thereafter, Burke asks Knox whether he was aware that the French nobility suffered "under the load of the greater part of the old feudal charges, from which the gentry of England have been relieved for upwards of 100 years, and which were in kind, as well as burthen, much worse than our modern land tax?"[48] In *Speech on Economical Reform*, Burke reprimanded the feudal relics of the royal household; here he is blasting the malign residue of feudal taxes on the French aristocracy, an order that continued to be deprived of liberties that England's propertied men enjoyed in the eighteenth century. The decrepit conditions of the French state did not end there: was Knox not mindful of France's salt monopoly, which forced "the people to take a certain quantity of it, and at a certain rate, both rate and quantity fixed at the arbitrary pleasure of the imposer?"[49] Burke is summing up a key lesson of *Thoughts and Details* more than twenty-five years prior to the memorial's publication: meddling with the flow of trade and tinkering with the competitive price system impairs the health of an economy.

Even more, Burke condemns the *taille*, the harshest direct tax of prerevolutionary France that was abolished during the French Revolution, as "an arbitrary imposition on presumed property."[50] And taxes on industry added to the overweening weight of the French government on the country's economic activity. "There is not a single article of provision for man or beast, which enters that great city [of Paris], and is not excised; corn, hay, meal, butchers meat, fish, fowls, every thing," he asserts.[51] The ironic tinge of his comments is difficult to ignore: Burke is giving expression to some of the same concerns that French revolutionaries voiced twenty years later in their attack on the ancien régime.

We return to Burke's attempt to disclose the sloppiness in Knox's handling of statistics. Knox had declared in the *State of the Nation* that neutral nations engrossed British navigation during six years of the Seven Years War, a belief that validated Knox's judgment about the grave impact of the war on British commerce. Burke attacks Knox's reasoning in the *Observations* by parsing his deceptive use of "average" in his attempt to provide an empirical basis for his claim. Burke observes that Knox's contention was based on averaging the first three years of the war, when the unpredictable perils of military conflict upset the regular churn of navigation. But, Burke continues, British traders had adjusted to the conflict,[52] so that in the following three years tonnage actually increased dramatically.

---

[47] Langford, *Writings and Speeches*, II, 151.   [48] Langford, *Writings and Speeches*, II, 152.
[49] Langford, *Writings and Speeches*, II, 152.   [50] Langford, *Writings and Speeches*, II, 153.
[51] Langford, *Writings and Speeches*, II, 153. Burke does admit that he did not intend to rebuke consumption taxes in luxurious cities in France.
[52] This point illustrates Burke's awareness of the fluid modifications of economic behavior. "[B]y degrees, as the war continued, the terror wore off; the danger came to be better appreciated, and better provided against; our trade was carried on in large fleets, under regular convoys, and with

Burke's principle of methodology in this case was thus:

[A]n average estimate of an object in a steady course of rising or of falling, must in its nature be an unfair one; more particularly if the cause of the rise or fall be visible, and its continuance in any degree probable. Average estimates are never just but when the object fluctuates, and no reason can be assigned why it should not continue still to fluctuate.[53]

Averages are misleading if the pattern of the activity it calibrates is steadily heading in one direction, such as the ascent of British navigation. In other words, averages can minimize signs of progress.

Knox's attacks notwithstanding, Burke himself was not completely immune from statistical imprecision; at one point he cites the aggregate amount of tonnage from 1756 to 1761 rather than the medium, an error ultimately inconsequential to his overall argument about the potentially illusory effect of employing averages as an empirical benchmark.[54] The broader point in relation to Burke's economic thought, however, is that his critical assessment of Knox's claim signaled his alertness to the possible deceptions latent in the use of statistical data stripped of historical context. "If we had lost something in the beginning, we had then recovered, and more than recovered, all our losses," Burke concludes in describing the impressive reinvigoration of English commerce during the war.[55]

In addition, Burke wielded an extensive amount of customs data on imports and exports to unmask Knox's limited understanding of trade balances, and to show that such imbalances were not necessarily injurious to the British economy.[56] Burke most likely began to acquire this knowledge while serving as secretary to William Gerard Hamilton in the late 1750s and early to mid-1760s. Hamilton's tenure as commissioner on the Board of Trade, Irish Chancellor of the Exchequer, and Chief Secretary for Ireland overlapped in part with Burke's employment,[57] which unlocked opportunities for Burke to strengthen his command of commercial subjects. In a private letter written in July 1763, for example, Burke mentioned that he "examin[ed] the Custom House books" when describing duty rates on traded goods.[58]

In fact, Hamilton reportedly confessed to a friend that, upon meeting and discussing commercial matters with Burke for the first time, he recognized "his own inferiority, much as he had endeavoured to inform

---

great safety. The freighting business revived. The ships were fewer, but much larger; and though the number decreased, the tonnage was vastly augmented" (Langford, *Writings and Speeches*, II, 124).

[53] Langford, *Writings and Speeches*, II, 124.   [54] Langford, *Writings and Speeches*, II, 123n1.

[55] Langford, *Writings and Speeches*, II, 124.   [56] Langford, *Writings and Speeches*, II, 143–145.

[57] For background on Hamilton, consult his entry in Sir Lewis Namier and John Brooke, eds., *The History of Parliament: The House of Commons 1754–1790*, vol. II, *Members A-J* (London: Her Majesty's Stationery Office, 1964), 572–574.

[58] Burke to Mrs. Elizabeth Montagu, 29 July [1763], in *Correspondence of Edmund Burke*, vol. I, 172.

himself, and aided as he was by official documents, inaccessible to any private person" – an especially glowing remark considering that Hamilton was then on the Board of Trade.[59] As we have learned, Burke continued his engagement with the study of the British commercial system as secretary to the Marquess of Rockingham and in the crafting of the Free Port Act of 1766. Lord Chatham, in October 1766, even made an oblique reference to Burke's name being broached as a possible candidate for England's Board of Trade.[60]

In general, the richness of empirical detail furnished by Burke's flowing pen in the *Observations* does not overwhelm his argument but supplements it, reflecting both an agility of mind and discretion of judgment. The writing consults at least twenty-two charts, including those in footnotes and the appendix, many of which were used to advertise the healthy state of the British economy in order to disprove Knox's gloomy portrayal of its fitness for commercial growth. The charts, some of which have been cited, touch upon subjects spanning: imports of Guadeloupe, Martinique, and Havana; British imports from the West Indies; British exports to the West Indies; trade balances; foreign and domestic British tonnage; government expenditures in peacetime; debt interest during war; the cloth trade; revenue from consumption taxes; interest paid by France and England; French and English stock prices; anticipated projections of government expenditure; and the produce of duties on soap, candles, and animal hides. As mentioned, some of these charts most likely derived from the hand of Dowdeswell. Yet Burke's skillful integration of the data into the *Observations* indicates his early taste for statistical information and his shrewd attention to detail, two faculties of his mind that remain largely overlooked in the study of his intellectual development.

Burke's harnessing of charts to buttress his argument about consumption taxes is especially noteworthy because it raises an intriguing question about his commitment to free market principles. In response to Knox's contention that wartime tax hikes had depressed British manufacturing and consumption, Burke introduces empirical evidence about the cloth industry to demonstrate that its manufactures had actually increased since the end of the war, and had even exceeded levels before the war on average.[61] Similarly, he presents data illustrating that consumption taxes, including those on beer and malt, had not sunk consumption – and revenue

---

[59] Burke, *Thoughts and Details*, vi.

[60] "My engagement to Lord Lisburne for the next opening at the Board of Trade is already known to your Grace; nor is it a thing possible to wave for Mr. Burke" (Anson, *Autobiography and Political Correspondence*, 108).

[61] Langford, *Writings and Speeches*, II, 138–139.

from consumption taxes – to the extent that Knox claimed it had, and in fact had grown since their enactment.[62]

Was Burke abandoning his sympathy for free markets in his use of such information? He moves toward answering this question in the *Observations* when he remarks, in regard to the taxes, "[Knox] sees nothing but the burthen. I can perceive the burthen as well as he; but I cannot avoid contemplating also the strength that supports it.[63] Burke continues: "From thence I draw the most comfortable assurances of the future vigour, and the ample resources, of this great misrepresented country."[64] He is conceding that taxes are a strain – a "burthen" – on people. But Burke's larger message from these remarks, and in this section in the *Observations* overall, is that the spirit of industry emanating from the British people helped them overcome temporary wartime encumbrances on their capacity for commercial activity. Burke is not making the abstract normative claim that consumption taxes should be implemented regardless of circumstance, but that the aftermath of the Seven Years War did not bring about the violent depression of commerce as Knox had insisted. Keep in mind as well that the *Observations* was a political tract intended to defend the trade policy and public economy of the Rockingham administration; hence Burke was intent on showing that the reign of his party did not permanently injure English commerce.

Burke does make a compelling remark in this discussion that, at the very least, should give us pause before we assert that he was an ardent opponent of all taxes. He contends that even though many English taxes had been enacted starting in the early 1700s, the British economy continued to ascend. "A very great part of our taxes, if not the greatest, has been imposed since the beginning of this century," Burke observes.[65] But English exports, he notes, had doubled in that time period. The thrust of Burke's contention is that English prosperity was not confined to a particular time period, for it had grown throughout the century even with the implementation of a modern system of taxation. "Yet England was then [in the early eighteenth century] a rich and flourishing nation," Burke writes with a heavy dose of sarcasm, mocking the Knoxian presumption that tax increases portended the decline of British industry.[66] Burke is not necessarily arguing that taxes were the immediate cause of English prosperity, but that the steady promulgation of taxes did not sentence England to poverty in the 1700s.

---

[62] See Langford, *Writings and Speeches*, II, 140–141.
[63] Langford, *Writings and Speeches*, II, 142. [64] Langford, *Writings and Speeches*, II, 142.
[65] Langford, *Writings and Speeches*, II, 143. [66] Langford, *Writings and Speeches*, II, 143.

Wealth Redistribution, Standards of Living, and Supply and Demand Principles

The first half of the *Observations* also includes tinctures of Burke's broader philosophy of political economy that transcend the partisan context of the tract. These comments are not fully developed, but they do provide an early glimpse into his thoughts on wealth redistribution, material standards of living, and supply and demand laws that would receive greater amplification later in his life.

First, Burke volunteers fascinating remarks on the merits of wealth redistribution that prefigure his commentary on the subject in the *Reflections* and *Thoughts and Details*. In the *Observations*, he ridicules the speculative proposal of Knox in the *State of the Nation* to tax a public fund consisting of revenue from the East India Company. Early in his public career, Burke was keenly sensitive to any attempt by Parliament to intervene in the financial affairs of the Company; he thought that such government encroachment would threaten the firm's chartered liberties and usurp its propertied possessions overseas.

The gist of Burke's remarks in this context was that the principle of uniform taxation inherent in Knox's scheme ignored the sheer diversity of establishments that provided support, financial or otherwise, for the management of the British Empire. Different institutions and possessions – including monied companies, trading companies, and colonies – all contributed to Britain's public coffers in many ways. Marry the impulse to decree inflexible policy with high assertions of the parliamentary right to tax, however, and one would occasion not only the disruption of British public finance but the collapse of commercial and political order. "[I]n the complicated oeconomy of great kingdoms, and immense revenues, which in a length of time, and by a variety of accidents, have coalesced into a sort of body," Burke explains, "an attempt towards a compulsory equality in all circumstances, and an exact practical definition of the supreme rights in every case, is the most dangerous and chimerical of all enterprizes."[67]

One could thread this remark into any section in the *Reflections* with seamless effort. The particular contexts were different, but two underlying principles remained constant: first, forced equality generates political distempers; and second, claims of abstract right endanger settled property rights. "The old building stands well enough, though part Gothic, part Grecian, and part Chinese, until an attempt is made to square it into uniformity," Burke laments. "Then it may come down upon our heads all together in much uniformity of ruin; and great will be the fall thereof."[68] The imposition of rigid policy on a variety of social and political institutions, with the aim of establishing a uniformity of wealth, produces an equality of poverty.[69]

---

[67] Langford, *Writings and Speeches*, II, 175.   [68] Langford, *Writings and Speeches*, II, 175.
[69] Burke also stresses the diversity of colonial possessions of the British Empire when assailing Knox's proposal to permit Americans to sit in Parliament. "He appears not to have troubled his head with the infinite difficulty of fettling that representation on a fair balance of wealth and

Additionally, Burke offers brief but intriguing comments on the notion that British manufacturers were fleeing to France. He first denies the charge. Even if this were the case, Burke continues, the lower cost of living translated into lower wages. "If living is cheaper in France, that is, to be had for less specie, wages are proportionately lower," he writes.[70] And the prospect of lower remuneration discouraged producers from seeking commercial opportunity in that country: "No manufacturer, let the living be what it will, was ever known to fly for refuge to low wages" because "[m]oney is the first thing which attracts him."[71] It came as no surprise, then, the sparkle of gain fixed the eyes of producers to Britain. "[O]ur wages attract artificers from all parts of the world," Burke observes.[72]

Even more, a lower cost of living did not indicate a heightened standard of living. In the case of England and France, it was quite the opposite in fact: "[I]t will be hard to prove, that a French artificer is better fed, cloathed, lodged, and warmed, than one in England; for that is the sense, and the only sense, of living cheaper."[73] The merit of a nation's economy did not derive from low living costs; it stemmed from access to high-quality goods and services that met man's basic needs for food and shelter. Burke is endorsing a view he expressed in *Thoughts and Details* and elsewhere: high wages in market economies were signs of commercial strength, not weakness.

Besides, Burke insists, the relative cost of living in Britain was actually lower than Knox let on. When issuing this claim, Burke displays his awareness of the complexity of supply and demand phenomena that he would articulate in *Thoughts and Details* almost thirty years later. The price of meat, he explains, was somewhat moderate; and even during the temporary moments when it was dear, this aggravated cost did not originate from wartime taxes but from the increase in consumption and the money supply. Reduce the amount of money in the hands of consumers, Burke explains, and the price would drop – but the purchasing power of consumers would plummet as well. "Diminish [money], and meat in your markets will be sufficiently cheap in account, but much dearer in effect; because fewer will be in a condition to buy. Thus your apparent plenty will be real indigence."[74] Designs to manipulate the money supply for the purpose of making meat accessible would occasion extreme want.

These insights into supply and demand may appear basic to the twenty-first-century student of economics, but they illustrated careful reflection on the inner mysteries of markets at a time when the discipline was still an emerging science in Europe. In this light, Burke's remarks demonstrate impressive comprehension of the intricate forces that set fluid market prices in vibrant economies. They also exhibit his serious attention to the unintended effects of

numbers throughout the several provinces of America and the West-Indies, under such an infinite variety of circumstances" (Langford, *Writings and Speeches*, II, 178–179).

[70] Langford, *Writings and Speeches*, II, 138.   [71] Langford, *Writings and Speeches*, II, 138.
[72] Langford, *Writings and Speeches*, II, 138.   [73] Langford, *Writings and Speeches*, II, 138.
[74] Langford, *Writings and Speeches*, II, 147.

seemingly innocuous interventions in market activities endeavoring to lower the cost of provisions. One can thus connect a straight line from Burke's description of supply and demand sensations in the *Observations* to his commentary in *Thoughts and Details*: markets are delicate creatures, and attempts to disturb them could generate destructive consequences for producers and consumers.

Before proceeding, one must reiterate that Burke's message in the *Observations*, at face value, appears conflicted at times. Throughout the writing, he argues that wartime taxes did not depress consumption nor hinder Britain's economy, at least to the depth that Knox avowed it had, thereby suggesting that war could be used as an instrument to stimulate commercial activity. Yet here and elsewhere, Burke submits a firm, if not fully developed, endorsement of free market principles. Then consider that in the same tract he disseminates robust statements in support of commercial liberty, Burke inveighs against Knox's desire to simplify the colonial regulations as embodied in the Navigation Acts, and in doing so defends the Acts as a necessary system of selective restrictions.[75] These apparent contradictions expose the partisan specks of the writing's ad hoc nature, creating difficulties in drawing out the overall economic message behind the tract.

We may attempt to untangle such confusions. First, Burke strongly indicates in the *Observations* that he was *not* arguing that war provided an ideal environment for vigorous commercial activity. "War is a time of inconvenience to trade; in general it must be straitened, and must find its way as it can," he writes.[76] Burke conveyed a similar point two years earlier, noting that the "War" – ostensibly the Seven Years War – "made an appearance of Wealth in the Colonies fallacious to them and to us."[77] In the *Observations*, he describes the economic consequences of war: war requires expense, expense requires money; therefore, the belligerent nation is compelled to borrow money to fund its war, which leads to debt. And the greater the desire for money to finance war, the more difficult it will be to obtain it.[78] Mindful of these inescapable facts of wartime expense, Burke alerts readers to a fundamental reality about limited resources that informed his writings and speeches on political economy: "[T]he scarcity of the commodity will enhance the price."[79] For Burke, then, Knox's seemingly revelatory insights into the high borrowing costs for war loans confirmed a basic truth about military conflict: "[W]ar is expensive, and peace desirable."[80]

---

[75] Langford, *Writings and Speeches*, II, 181–182; and Knox, *State of the Nation*, 80–81.
[76] Langford, *Writings and Speeches*, II, 123.   [77] Langford, *Writings and Speeches*, II, 62.
[78] High premiums for war loans merely shows that "the more expence is incurred by a nation, the more money will be required to defray it; that, in proportion to the continuance of that expence, will be the continuance of borrowing; that the encrease of borrowing and the encrease of debt will go hand in hand; and lastly, that the more money you want, the harder it will be to get it" (Langford, *Writings and Speeches*, II, 125–126).
[79] Langford, *Writings and Speeches*, II, 126.   [80] Langford, *Writings and Speeches*, II, 126.

Second, Burke's treatment of the Navigation Acts in the *Observations*, and in his speeches on America, imparts his belief that the trade regulations must have played *some* role in setting the conditions for British prosperity, since the blooming of English commerce in the seventeenth and eighteenth centuries coexisted with the laws. Ironically, the Free Port Act, which Burke helped to pass in Parliament, made significant alterations to the Acts in the West Indies. Burke's suggestion in the *Observations* is that the concomitant rise of British commerce with the Acts suggested that political prudence should dictate reform of the laws, rather than wreaking a "strange havock" on them.[81] Therefore, in his view, "The regulations for the colony trade ought not to be more nor fewer, nor more or less complex, than the occasion requires. And, as that trade is in a great measure a system of art and restriction, they can neither be few nor simple."[82]

Burke's argument is weak and unconvincing in this case. What distinguished Knox's proposal from the Free Port Act? Was it simply prudence? The reality is that the political nature of both the *Observations* and Knox's pamphlets makes it difficult, though not impossible, to identify common patterns of thought in Burke's commentary. Accordingly, one should keep in mind the following considerations when reading the tract: (1) the economic argument in the *Observations* is a *relative* one – the strength of the British economy was greater than Grenville and Knox had led the public to believe; (2) on a similarly comparative scale, the *Observations* intended to show that Britain's industrious capacities and resources remained more potent than France's; and (3) most important, Burke, like many of his other writings, did not draft the *Observations* to be a treatise on the normative foundations of his economic theory. He addressed a pressing historical circumstance, the aftermath of the Seven Years War, and employed specific empirical data unique to the particular time period.

Principles of Political Economy in the *Observations*

Even with such qualifications, small rays of Burke's notion of political economy do poke through the partisan scaffolding of the *Observations*. For Burke, the imperatives of *public* economy – the prudential management of government resources – should not target the military as its first object of policy experimentation in order to diminish costs. "Of all the public services, that of the navy is the one in which tampering may be of the greatest danger," he insists, suggesting its indispensability to the national security of the British Empire.[83] The Navy should be funded on sound financial principles; yet Knox's proposals for the reduction of expense signified the opposite approach. Burke's distaste for

---

[81] Langford, *Writings and Speeches*, II, 182.   [82] Langford, *Writings and Speeches*, II, 182.
[83] Langford, *Writings and Speeches*, II, 161.

arbitrary public economy that he communicates in *Speech on Economical Reform* is passionately expressed in the *Observations* as well:

[Some politicians] first propose savings, which they well know cannot be made, in order to get a reputation for oeconomy. In due time they assume another, but a different merit, by providing for the service they had before cut off or straitened, and which they can then very easily prove to be necessary. In the same spirit, they raise magnificent ideas of revenue on funds which they know to be insufficient. Afterwards, who can blame them, if they do not satisfy the public desires? They are great artificers; but they cannot work without materials.[84]

These comments show that Burke's meditations on political economy not only confronted private market activity but also drew attention to a profound challenge of statesmanship: how to create a sound revenue stream for the state without engaging in bureaucratic legerdemain. In the *Observations*, as in *Speech on Economical Reform*, Burke indicates that revenue *was* necessary for effective government. Yet, in his judgment, deceptive accounting practices, such as those put forth by Knox, subverted the state's capacities to procure revenue with regularity of design.

Burke's admonition of Knox's schemes to raise revenue provides additional outlines of his economic thought, and also anticipates his later commentary on Anglo-Irish relations. In the *Observations*, Burke condemns Knox's idea to require America and Ireland to make annual payments of £200,000 and £100,000, respectively, to Britain. He first asks, why stop at that amount? Why not seek £600,000?[85] For Burke, a limiting principle must govern systems of taxation. Next, he disputes Knox's presumption that the reason for national indigence, such as poverty in Ireland, was largely due to a "*want* of judicious taxes" such as a land tax.[86] Burke's stress on "want" hints at his subtle incredulity over Knox's reasoning: how could taxing a resource occasion prosperity?

After criticizing the unserious character of Knox's inquiry into Irish trade, Burke contends that the imposition of a land tax would provoke convulsions in Ireland. Knox's sweetener for the Irish, ending the ban on the Irish export of wool, would trigger corresponding tumults in Britain, even if the idea in principle was a "very right idea," Burke admits.[87] This censure of Knox's revenue scheme lays bare Burke's antipathy to new taxes, specifically the land tax, with no vision of purpose; and it illustrates his belief that Irish trade should be liberated from trade restrictions, but only if executed in a systematic fashion that would not induce political unrest. Burke's remark further exposes his general hesitation to impose regulations on British subjects and draw them closer to the seat of empire for fear of suffocating their liberties.

In an echo of his observations on the many circumstances characterizing Britain's colonial possessions, Burke goes on to note that the Americans lived

---

[84] Langford, *Writings and Speeches*, II, 163.   [85] Langford, *Writings and Speeches*, II, 164.
[86] Langford, *Writings and Speeches*, II, 164.   [87] Langford, *Writings and Speeches*, II, 165.

under a variety of jurisdictions. "They have different methods of taxation in the different provinces, agreeable to their several local circumstances," he writes.[88] The authority to raise revenue should remain in the governing hands of those closest to the particular geographical area. Besides, an increase in taxes paid by the acre depresses the incentive for industry: it "would be the most effectual means of preventing that cultivation they are intended to promote."[89] Excessive taxation diminishes opportunities for economic growth.

Even though Burke's insights on political economy in the *Observations* are not fully developed, they mark an expansive mind sensitive to the changing nature of commercial activity. It was not unusual, he argues in the pamphlet, for a perceived decline in a branch of trade to show its face in a different shape. Burke gives the example of wool. Britain previously exported coarse wool to Russia. Once Russia began to supply herself with the commodity, British exports in this industry declined. But a new related industry sprung up for British merchants: the trade of "finer cloths."[90] Accordingly, "Objects like trade and manufacture, which the very attempt to confine would certainly destroy, frequently change their place; and thereby, far from being lost, are often highly improved."[91] Manufactures that languish in some geographical regions may emerge with a brighter glow in different areas. Burke stresses, for instance, that the growing prosperity of the Scottish trade was a net benefit to the British economy. Hence, in his judgment, "A trade sometimes seems to perish when it only assumes a different form."[92]

Allow us to place this statement in the context of Burke's broader political philosophy as expressed in the *Reflections* and elsewhere. Civil order requires the careful retention and adaptation of past traditions to present circumstances; and weakness in one instance is a source of strength in another, as the *Account* observed. The same principles guide Burke's economic thought. The preservation of thriving economies entails that different industries adjust to the shifting preferences and demands of the market. The decline in some regulations and customs does not necessarily portend ruin, but in fact may give rise to new possibilities, commercial and otherwise, that encourage progress and prosperity. This theme, in the context of Burke's political and economic thought, unveils the versatile capacities of his analytic disposition: he possessed an uncommon ability to sift through intricate details of seemingly unconnected events, and then thread them together into a unified fabric that disclosed his deepest philosophical convictions.

There remains another important argument in the *Observations* that connects Burke's economic thought to the *Reflections*. In his view, painting

---

[88] Langford, *Writings and Speeches*, II, 167.
[89] Langford, *Writings and Speeches*, II, 167. Burke criticizes these taxes while also hinting at "the secret virtues of a land tax," but he does not specify these virtues.
[90] Langford, *Writings and Speeches*, II, 139.   [91] Langford, *Writings and Speeches*, II, 139.
[92] Langford, *Writings and Speeches*, II, 139.

a dismal picture of public well-being in order to arouse popular sentiment, of which he believed Knox was guilty in the *State of the Nation*, betrayed a sinister campaign of self-interest. Burke's imaginative expression of this lesson is worth quoting in full:

> The same sun which gilds all nature, and exhilarates the whole creation, does not shine upon disappointed ambition. It is something that rays out of darkness, and inspires nothing but gloom and melancholy. Men, in this deplorable state of mind, find a comfort in spreading the contagion of their spleen, They find an advantage too; for it is a general popular error to imagine the loudest complainers for the publick to be the most anxious for its welfare. If such persons can answer the ends of relief and profit to themselves, they are apt to be careless enough about either the means or the consequences.[93]

Beware of those who spread utterances of doom throughout the public mind, for men who ignite the energies of the people may be secretly trying to gratify their personal ambitions for political power and social control. The drive to relieve public misery *and* advance themselves compels no restraint on the exercise of force. The *State of the Nation* was certainly not Abbé Sieyès's *What Is the Third Estate?*, one of the most influential French political pamphlets leading up to the French Revolution. But Burke here is displaying a shrewd awareness of a fundamental danger of radical democratic politics that remains a source of great apprehension in his writings and speeches spanning from the *Observations* to the *Reflections*: the potential threat to political order lurking in the recesses of popular agitation.

The *Observations* and the Free Port Act

The final fourth of the *Observations* issues a steadfast defense of the policy program of the Rockingham ministry, which included the repeal of the Stamp Act, the passage of the Declaratory Act, and the enactment of the Free Port Act. This section offers Burke's elaborations on the political backdrop of the Free Port Act, marking a fidelity to commercial principles that guided the legislative efforts of Burke and the Rockinghams in their mission to enlarge trade in the British West Indies.

Before the Rockingham ministry, the Grenville administration had imposed an "innumerable multitude of commercial regulations" on British merchants, Burke pronounces with contempt.[94] Its members equated restrictions with sagacity and dismissed concerns from dealers that the laws inflicted heavy hardship on their trade. Grenvillians "talk[ed] of these regulations as prodigies of wisdom; and, instead of appealing to those who are most affected and the best judges, they turn round in a perpetual circle of their own reasonings and pretences."[95] The ministry's repeated self-rationalizations of its own

---

[93] Langford, *Writings and Speeches*, II, 154.   [94] Langford, *Writings and Speeches*, II, 200.
[95] Langford, *Writings and Speeches*, II, 200.

policies shunned the opinions of those who were impacted most powerfully by the weight of onerous commercial entanglements.

Burke notes, by contrast, that the commercial policy of the Rockingham administration was informed by two kinds of regulations: the first of a "mixed nature" of trade and revenue, and the second concerning trade specifically.[96] In applying the first category to the American colonies, the desire of the Rockinghams was to favor trade: "Where trade was likely to suffer, they did not hesitate for an instant to prefer it to taxes."[97] In regard to the second type of regulation, the ministry aimed to "suit the revenue to the object."[98] The Rockinghams thus endeavored to reduce smuggling by "keeping the duties as nearly as they could on a balance with the risque."[99] A prudent course in pursuit of greater commercial freedom defined Rockinghamite economic policy.

Accordingly, the Rockinghams, unlike the Grenvillians, lent a tactful ear to the trepidations of merchants, particularly those from Bristol, Liverpool, and Manchester, who had voiced their sharp displeasure over the perceived disturbance of trade in the West Indies. The Rockinghams enabled dealers "to bring the matter home to the feeling of the house."[100] Moreover, Burke explains, "[O]ur then ministers were not ashamed to say, that they sympathized with the feelings of our merchants."[101] Mercantile apprehensions were further provoked by the rise in contraband trafficking in the West Indies, not to mention by traders' general anxieties over the depression of commercial activity in the region.

Burke then recounts the Rockinghams' laborious exertions in organizing meetings with merchants and manufacturers, an initiative that granted these latter groups an open forum to express their concerns. "[T]he meetings of merchants upon the business of trade were numerous and public," he recalls.[102] They were held at houses "always open to every deliberation favourable to the liberty or the commerce of his country."[103] These efforts were proof of the Rockinghams' sensitivity to the interests of English traders: "The universal desire of that body will always have great weight with them in every consideration connected with commerce; neither ought the opinion of that body to be slighted . . . in any consideration whatsoever of revenue."[104]

Let us pause and take in the significance of Burke's account of the drafting of the Free Port Act: in his very first session in Parliament, he immediately established himself as a lawmaker alert to the advantages of commerce and to the interests of traders. This is not Burke acting in the character of the propertied traditionalist, defending the great landed estates of the hereditary aristocracy against the enterprising activities of unscrupulous dealers. Instead,

---

[96] Langford, *Writings and Speeches*, II, 199.   [97] Langford, *Writings and Speeches*, II, 199.
[98] Langford, *Writings and Speeches*, II, 199.   [99] Langford, *Writings and Speeches*, II, 199.
[100] Langford, *Writings and Speeches*, II, 198.   [101] Langford, *Writings and Speeches*, II, 191.
[102] Langford, *Writings and Speeches*, II, 201.   [103] Langford, *Writings and Speeches*, II, 201.
[104] Langford, *Writings and Speeches*, II, 191.

the Act exposed a side of Burke rarely discussed with the consideration it warrants: a man who was eminently active in encouraging, defending, and crafting into law measures that afforded the gift of commercial liberty to profit-seeking men. Burke, in many ways, was a man of commerce from the instant he set foot in the House of Commons. As Will Burke had written in March 1766, Edmund "is full of real business, intent upon doing real good to his country, as much as if he was to receive twenty per cent. from the commerce of the whole empire, which he labours to improve and extend."[105]

Being a man of commerce, however, required mining the wisdom of a broad range of merchants, rather than a select few, in the formation of government policy. In the *Observations*, Burke stresses that the Rockinghams were careful not to rely upon a limited number of traders in the drafting of the Free Port Act. "All administrations" have been "directed by the opinion of one or two merchants, who were to merit in flatteries, and to be paid in contracts."[106] This was because the judgments of individual traders might advance their own interests by proposing trade regulations that would subvert the welfare of the many. They "frequently advised, not for the general good of trade, but for their private advantage."[107] In the *Wealth of Nations*, as part of his wider attack on the mercantile system, Adam Smith famously pilloried traders who lobbied governments to enact regulations that would promote their specific enterprise and strangle market competition.[108] Burke is delivering the same message here, seven years prior to the publication of Smith's text: be on watchful guard against powerful traders who advise governments on commercial policy.

A just program of trade regulations, then, should not succumb to the centripetal force of narrow commercial prejudice. Burke is known for defending a salutary conception of prejudice in the *Reflections* that reflected the distilled wisdom of the past. But he also harbored negative conceptions of the word, and his notion in regard to political economy is no exception. For Burke, traders who championed favorable restrictions to obstruct competition exhibited local commercial prejudice. Government submission to this form of prejudice offended the principle of fairness by sacrificing the public good to private gratification. Burke, then, makes a point in the *Observations* to underscore the Rockinghams' refusal to capitulate to local prejudices. "No private views, no local interests prevailed," he insists.[109] Instead, the party

---

[105] James Barry, *The Works of James Barry, Esq. Historical Painter*, vol. I (London: T. Cadell and W. Davies, 1809), 42.

[106] Langford, *Writings and Speeches*, II, 201.   [107] Langford, *Writings and Speeches*, II, 201.

[108] Smith, *Wealth of Nations*, vol. I, p. 267.

[109] Langford, *Writings and Speeches*, II, 201. Burke does not use the word "prejudice" here, but this is the idea he is conveying in his reference to "no private views" and "no local interests." He does make specific references to prejudice in his letters to O'Hara on the Free Port Act (see "The British West Indies and the Free Port Act of 1766," Chapter 6) and in his discussion of the Irish trade bills (see Chapter 8).

crafted the Free Port Act with enlarged minds: "Never were points in trade settled upon a larger scale of information."[110]

From an objective viewpoint, Burke's claim was not entirely accurate. By preserving various protectionist duties in the British West Indies, the Free Port Act privileged British interests over those of other rival imperial powers. Burke admitted as much: "[W]e have the advantage in every essential article of [the West Indian trade]."[111] Once again, his defense of free trade was not inviolable. As demonstrated in the previous section, this position was motivated in large part by his recognition that the local prejudices of West Indian traders prevented the creation of a more vigorous trade in the region – and by the realization that the French Empire posed a formidable threat to British imperial interests there as well.

Therefore, even though Burke's political thought is rightly synonymous with a defense of local associations, he also recognized that a preoccupation with our closest attachments sometimes threatened the comprehension of national aims, such as balanced reform of constitutional government and vibrant commercial activity. Burke's attack on reflexive defenders of costly jurisdictions in *Speech on Economical Reform* was one such example, while his caution against surrendering to local commercial biases in the *Observations* was another. Rigid economic localism stymied the expansion of public prosperity.

In describing the political milieu of the Free Port Act, Burke weaves in an important argument central to his conception of imperial economics – one that he and Will Burke broached in the *Account* – that would come to animate *Speech on American Taxation* and *Speech on Conciliation with America*: Britain held the imperial right to rule over its North American colonies, but the suppression of Americans' industrious faculties would injure both them and the English. When developing this position in the *Observations*, Burke first acknowledges that the colonies were "founded in subservience to the commerce of Great Britain."[112] Colonial imports must derive from Britain, and colonial exports must be sent to Britain, consisting of a "double monopoly."[113] The novelty of new colonial possessions, therefore, must occasion a way of thinking dependent not upon "mere abstract principles of government" but upon "actual circumstances."[114] Thinking must change with the times, and speculation must not dictate reality. Such were two essential maxims of Burke's theory of progress.

The actual circumstances to which Burke refers were the imperatives of empire: a global power possessed the authority to govern its foreign territories, including the territories' economic activity. Consequently, "[A] principle of commerce, of artificial commerce, must predominate," Burke states. "This commerce must be secured by a multitude of restraints

---

[110] Langford, *Writings and Speeches*, II, 201.   [111] Langford, *Writings and Speeches*, II, 201.
[112] Langford, *Writings and Speeches*, II, 192.   [113] Langford, *Writings and Speeches*, II, 192.
[114] Langford, *Writings and Speeches*, II, 193–194.

very alien from the spirit of liberty; and a powerful authority must reside in the principal state, in order to enforce them."[115] This is why trade "is a creature of law and institution."[116] These comments confirm the notion that Burke did not subscribe to an inflexible theory of free trade, for the responsibilities of imperial dominion inevitably called for the regulations of the sovereign's subjects in some manner.

Burke does not stop there, however. He remarks that the men and women of the American colonies were rooted in a familiar heritage that conditioned their orientation to support the blessings of freedom: "[T]he people who are to be the subjects of these restraints are descendants of Englishmen; and of an high and free spirit. To hold over them a government made up of nothing but restraints and penalties, and taxes in the granting of which they can have no share, will neither be wise, nor long practicable."[117] This is the crux of Burke's imperial conception of political economy: subjects, especially those inclined toward liberty, should not be regulated into servitude. Instead they should be afforded the freedoms to cultivate, produce, and trade, released from the thick net of arbitrary imperial entanglements.

According to Burke's narrative, the Grenville administration renounced the spirit of this principle. In its attempt to stamp out illicit trafficking through stricter naval enforcement, the American trade sunk under the weight of cumbersome commercial restrictions. "Regulation was added to regulation; and the strictest and most unreserved orders were given, for a prevention of all contraband trade [in the West Indies], and in every part of America," he observes. "A teazing custom-house, and a multiplicity of perplexing regulations, ever have, and ever will appear, the master-piece of finance to people of narrow views."[118] By strangling the industrious capacities of Americans, the empire had further aroused their anxieties and discouraged the steady flow of Anglo-American commerce.

This discussion also transmits Burke's grave suspicion of abstract theory in the settlement of practical political and commercial disputes. According to Burke, the Stamp Act epitomized the Grenville ministry's attempt to secure a consistent revenue stream from the American colonists. The imperial right to do so was not in question, but because it was exercised with such infrequency, the Americans did not protest its existence. Indeed, they cheerfully administered their local governments, which had met "all the purposes necessary to the internal oeconomy of a free people."[119]

---

[115] Langford, *Writings and Speeches*, II, 194.   [116] Langford, *Writings and Speeches*, II, 193.

[117] Langford, *Writings and Speeches*, II, 194.

[118] Langford, *Writings and Speeches*, II, 186. Burke further mentions the political unrest caused by the rejection in the House of Lords of the Silk Bill of 1765, which aimed to enhance regulations of the silk industry to protect English manufacturers (Langford, *Writings and Speeches*, II, 189, 189n2).

[119] Langford, *Writings and Speeches*, II, 187.

The happiness of the Americans rendered imperial questions of right immaterial before Grenville's Stamp Act triggered a wave of protest, bringing to the fore unnecessary theoretical debates about the scope of rights:

[T]he two very difficult points, superiority in the presiding state, and freedom in the subordinate, were on the whole sufficiently, that is, practically, reconciled; without agitating those vexatious questions, which in truth rather belong to metaphysicks than politicks, and which can never be moved without shaking the foundations of the best governments that have ever been constituted by human wisdom.[120]

Abstract claims of right lead to conflict that unsettles the stability of imperial order, a political condition that, as modeled by the relatively free state of the American colonists at the time, was certainly not incompatible with liberty. The intrusion of exploded metaphysics into politics gives rise to mayhem. The seed for Burke's attack on the French Revolution is planted in the *Observations*.

An alternative path to Grenville's program was forged by the Rockingham Whigs, in Burke's judgment. The Rockinghams maintained that Britain should balance the unlimited, though largely unexercised, right of imperial authority over the American colonies, as asserted in the Declaratory Act, with the practical wisdom of limited regulation. Extinguish the general imperial right, and the legitimacy of empire will be vitiated. But recalibrate that right's powerful tendencies into soft and selective policy, and the ruler will be governed by a high sense of prudence, avoiding theoretical debates about the precise start and end of its imperial authority. "[P]oliticks ought to be adjusted, not to human reasonings, but to human nature; of which the reason is but a part, and by no means the greatest part," Burke states in the *Observations*.[121] It followed that equitable commercial policy should conform to the constitution of the people. "People must be governed in a manner agreeable to their temper and disposition," he remarks.[122] Just as might did not make right for Burke, right sometimes did not make might.

7.3 THE AMERICAN WAR AND THE NAVIGATION ACTS: SPEECH ON AMERICAN TAXATION AND SPEECH ON CONCILIATION WITH AMERICA

Burke's vision of imperial commercial policy attains a sharper outline in his two celebrated speeches on Anglo-American relations in the mid-1770s, *Speech on American Taxation* and *Speech on Conciliation with America*, during a time when the disturbances in the North American colonies were reaching a political crescendo, as exemplified by the Boston Tea Party of 1773. The speeches reveal the most fundamental premise of Burke's beliefs on foreign trade that he hinted at in the *Observations*: questions of commerce beyond the shores of Britain

---

[120] Langford, *Writings and Speeches*, II, 188.   [121] Langford, *Writings and Speeches*, II, 196.
[122] Langford, *Writings and Speeches*, II, 194.

were not mere speculative exercises in economic philosophy but concrete applications of commercial principles to geopolitical realities. For Burke, foreign trade could not be separated from larger considerations of imperial authority, competition with rival nations, and Anglo-American history.

Speech on American Taxation is a case in point. Burke gave the speech on April 19, 1774 in support of Rose Fuller's motion to debate and repeal the duty on tea that had been established by the Townshend Acts of 1767. In order to reposition the East India Company on a firmer substructure of financial stability, the Tea Act of 1773 granted the Company monopoly rights to control the sales and import trade of tea in the American colonies. Passed in May 1773, the Act reduced, but retained, the Townshend duty on tea, which rekindled the anxieties of colonists resistant to the progressive regulation of colonial trade by the British government. The Boston Tea Party commenced in December 1773.

Fuller's motion provided a political opportunity for Burke to condemn the increasingly coercive policies of the North ministry and articulate his own integrated perspective on the proper role of imperial authority in the American colonies. In many ways *Speech on American Taxation*, while more famous than the *Observations*, offers fewer insights into Burke's economic thought. The import of *Speech on American Taxation* for our purposes, however, is drawn from its fuller elaborations on the history of the Navigation Acts and the imperial exercise of English regulatory power in British colonies. Burke's speech lasted more than two hours, displaying the ringing eloquence that he would later showcase in *Speech on Conciliation*. The *London Evening Post* called it "the most excellent speech that has perhaps been ever uttered in a public Assembly."[123]

Burke begins his oration by defending the repeal of the Stamp Act in 1766 and attacking the perpetuation of the tea duty. But his deeper commentary on the imperial implications of political economy emerges around one-third of the way through the speech. It is in this section that he provides a firm defense of the traditional system of the Navigation Acts before the advent of Grenville's Sugar Act of 1764. Burke first asserts that the original act of navigation was the "corner-stone" of British policy toward the American colonies.[124] He explains that this system was "purely commercial" from its infancy.[125] Yet Burke does not distinguish "commercial" from regulation. In fact, they overlapped: "[T]he commercial system was wholly restrictive."[126] Indeed, "It was the system of a monopoly"[127] – a British monopoly.

This system of monopoly did permit the colonies to trade elsewhere if Britain could not benefit. "No trade was let loose from the constraint, but merely to enable the Colonists to dispose of what, in the course of your trade, you could

[123] Langford, *Writings and Speeches*, II, 407.   [124] Langford, *Writings and Speeches*, II, 426.
[125] Langford, *Writings and Speeches*, II, 426.   [126] Langford, *Writings and Speeches*, II, 426.
[127] Langford, *Writings and Speeches*, II, 426.

not take; or to enable them to dispose of such articles as we forced upon them, and for which, without some degree of liberty, they could not pay," Burke utters.[128] The genius of the Navigation Acts allowed for the discriminatory channeling of American goods to British purchasers while permitting exceptions to this general principle. The Acts constituted an "infinite variety of paper chains by which you bind together this complicated system of the Colonies."[129]

In a larger sense, the Navigation Acts embodied the basic imperial right of Great Britain to rule over its colonial subjects. Burke emphasizes later in *Speech on American Taxation* the "*imperial character*" of Britain, in which, "as from the throne of heaven, she superintends all the several inferior legislatures, and guides, and controls them all without annihilating any."[130] Burke's striking metaphor of the throne of heaven underscored his unflinching belief in the authority of the British Empire to rule over its vast territories. It comes as no surprise in this section, then, that he avows that provincial assemblies in the colonies should all be "subordinate" to the British Parliament, and that the legislature's powers "must be boundless."[131]

But the authority of the British Empire did not lead to the suppression of its colonial subjects; instead, it brought them a great deal of public advantages. In *Speech on American Taxation*, Burke lays a sharp accent on the close union between the American colonies and the Navigation Acts to demonstrate that the emergence of the former as a commercial power coincided with the existence of the latter. "The act of navigation attended the Colonies from their infancy, grew with their growth, and strengthened with their strength," Burke insists.[132] This statement captures the heart of his argument about the relation between the colonies and the Navigation Acts, and can be classified under two headings, one of commerce and the other of prudence.

First, if the commercial prestige of the colonies had expanded under the Acts, then could one not reasonably assume that the attachment of the colonies to the seat of the British Empire had *something* to do with their success? "By [Britain's] immense capital" Burke claims, "[the colonies] were enabled to proceed with their fisheries, their agriculture, their ship-building (and their trade too within the limits), in such a manner as get far the start of the slow languid operations of unassisted nature."[133] And the commercial might of Britain certainly helped colonial industry: the American colonies' "monopolist happened to be one of the richest men in the world."[134]

Burke speaks in lavish terms of the historic progress of the American colonies:

---

[128] Langford, *Writings and Speeches*, II, 426.   [129] Langford, *Writings and Speeches*, II, 427.
[130] Langford, *Writings and Speeches*, II, 460.   [131] Langford, *Writings and Speeches*, II, 460.
[132] Langford, *Writings and Speeches*, II, 428.
[133] Langford, *Writings and Speeches*, II, 428–429.
[134] Langford, *Writings and Speeches*, II, 428.

This capital was a hot-bed to them. Nothing in the history of mankind is like their progress. For my part, I never cast an eye on their flourishing commerce, and their cultivated and commodious life, but they seem to me rather antient nations grown to perfection through a long series of fortunate events, and a train of successful industry, accumulating wealth in many centuries, than the Colonies of yesterday; than a set of miserable out-casts, a few years ago, not so much sent as thrown out, on the bleak and barren shore of a desolate wilderness three thousand miles from all civilized intercourse.[135]

Burke's soft imaginative vocabulary is merging with his hard analytic point in *Speech on American Taxation*: the commercial synthesis of Britain and the American colonies facilitated a rise in prosperity in a short burst of time.

Second, the imperatives of prudence also cautioned Burke to defend the older incarnation of the Navigation Acts. He remarks that supporters of the newer forms of regulation claimed that the traditional Acts in themselves were an ossified system, which Burke himself acknowledges. Nevertheless, that the Acts coexisted with the colonies from the latter's "infancy," as Burke notes, suggests that the Americans had grown accustomed to the system of commercial restrictions. They "bore it" from the first Navigation Act.[136] Burke then affixes this insight to a bedrock of his political thought: "[M]en do bear the inevitable constitution of their original nature with all its infirmities."[137] Over time, the initial imperfections of institutional beginnings settle into predictable, and possibly useful, traditions. According to Burke, such was the case with the Acts and the colonies: the latter "were confirmed in obedience to it, even more by usage than by law. They scarcely had remembered a time when they were not subject to such restraint."[138] A fundamental alteration to the Acts would be a fundamental alteration to the prosperous commercial anatomy of the American colonies and to the imperial constitution.

This was not to say the Navigation Acts should remain unchanged. Recall that Burke helped arrange efforts to reform the newer species of the Acts under the first Rockingham administration in order to promote greater free trade in the British West Indies, an initiative that culminated in the Free Port Act of 1766. And in *Speech on American Taxation*, Burke admits that America, "if left uncompensated" by the Acts, would live under "a condition of as rigorous servitude as men can be subject to."[139] For Burke, a defense of the Acts did not signify blind adherence to theories praising the merits of commercial regulation; it signaled, instead, a practical recognition that the colonies had bloomed under their direction.

In Burke's judgment, the real problem was a shift in the priorities of the Navigation Acts. Their original purpose was to steer colonial trade to Britain, rather than issue a cascade of regulations to generate money for British public

---

[135] Langford, *Writings and Speeches*, II, 429.   [136] Langford, *Writings and Speeches*, II, 428.
[137] Langford, *Writings and Speeches*, II, 428.   [138] Langford, *Writings and Speeches*, II, 428.
[139] Langford, *Writings and Speeches*, II, 428.

coffers. "England pursued trade, and forgot revenue," Burke explains.[140] But this system was reversed in the 1760s and 1770s, as encouraged by the likes of Charles Townshend and George Grenville. The Acts were transformed from a negative system of trade restrictions into a positive, and meddling, scheme of raising revenue. In *Speech on American Taxation*, Burke recounts a "brilliant harangue" of Townshend, probably given in March 1763, that put forth "the image of a revenue to be raised in America."[141]

Such was the "first glimmerings of this new Colony system,"[142] in which Britain began to regulate its American possessions into submission to extract greater revenue for its government. The flash point was the Sugar Act of 1764. It absorbed these glimmerings, hardened them, and cast out a "new principle" far and wide that attempted to establish a "regular plantation parliamentary revenue."[143] The Act thus compounded trade restrictions with a labyrinthine system of taxation: it created a "revenue not substituted in the place of, but superadded to, a monopoly," enforced by the military.[144] The burdens of "unlimited monopoly" and "unlimited revenue" signified "*legal* slavery."[145]

In this part of the speech, Burke delivers his own harangue at Grenville for pushing forward this policy of colonial servitude: "[Grenville] conceived, and many conceived along with him, that the flourishing trade of this country was greatly owing to law and institution, and not quite so much to liberty; for but too many are apt to believe regulation to be commerce, and taxes to be revenue."[146] These important remarks embody a central tenet of Burke's conception of political economy in regard to both foreign and domestic commerce: prosperity derives from liberty of commerce, not from a cage of restrictive policies. Grenville's regulations aiming to reduce contraband trade militated against this principle, for they dampened both licit and illicit commerce. As a result, this newer form of the Navigation Acts ended up "strangling" the Americans.[147]

Burke's insights also illustrate his views on sound public finance. Similar to his commentary in *Speech on Economical Reform* and in the *Observations*, Burke here is conveying that an arbitrary system of taxation spawns not a steady revenue stream but a long train of political distempers. "Your scheme yields no revenue; it yields nothing but discontent, disorder, disobedience; and such is the state of America, that after wading up to your eyes in blood you could only end just where you begun; that is, to tax where no revenue is to be found," he declaims near the end of *Speech on American Taxation*.[148] Burke would apply this same principle to his commentary on the East India Company in British

[140] Langford, *Writings and Speeches*, II, 429.   [141] Langford, *Writings and Speeches*, II, 431.
[142] Langford, *Writings and Speeches*, II, 431.   [143] Langford, *Writings and Speeches*, II, 434.
[144] Langford, *Writings and Speeches*, II, 434.   [145] Langford, *Writings and Speeches*, II, 458.
[146] Langford, *Writings and Speeches*, II, 432.   [147] Langford, *Writings and Speeches*, II, 433.
[148] Langford, *Writings and Speeches*, II, 459.

India: regulating subjects into coerced acquiescence produces depressed revenue and volatile tumults, not consistent receipts for the government purse.

Burke concludes his argument in *Speech on American Taxation* by urging the North ministry to reclaim the traditional spirit of the Navigation Acts. In this section of the oration, he exudes his reservations over abstract claims of right:

[R]evert to your old principles – seek peace and ensure it – leave America, if she has taxable matter in her, to tax herself. I am not here going into the distinctions of rights, nor attempting to mark their boundaries. I do not enter into these metaphysical distinctions; I hate the very sound of them. Leave the Americans as they antiently stood, and these distinctions, born of our unhappy contest, will die along with it.[149]

And:

Be content to bind America by laws of trade; you have always done it. Let this be your reason for binding their trade. Do not burthen them by taxes; you were not used to do so from the beginning. Let this be your reason for not taxing. These are the arguments of states and kingdoms. Leave the rest to the schools; for there only they may be discussed with safety.[150]

Britain should retain the authority to set foreign trade regulations steering colonial goods to British ports, but it should let America regulate the course of its own internal affairs. Debates over the abstract right to tax internal or foreign commerce will not calm colonial disturbances nor improve British relations with its imperial subjects. Metaphysical assertions of right in theory, more fit for intellectual "schools," sow political instability in reality, an insight Burke would repeat with unremitting force in the *Reflections*.

These comments underscore Burke's verdict that controversies over imperial commerce, generally speaking, were not speculative enterprises but eminently practical policy questions linked to geopolitical considerations. He did not view the debate over trade laws as a rigid division between free trade and mercantilism, as modern perspectives on eighteenth-century political economy tend to do.[151] Rather, *Speech on American Taxation* rests on a careful integration of Burke's economic thought with the demands of prudential statesmanship sensitive to the particular historical context of the 1770s. This is why his interpretation of the "constitution of the British Empire," as opposed to the British constitution, held a nuanced position on the imperial authority to tax. "I consider the power of taxing in parliament as an instrument of empire, and not as a means of supply," Burke opines.[152]

[149] Langford, *Writings and Speeches*, II, 458.   [150] Langford, *Writings and Speeches*, II, 458.

[151] See, among many, Murray N. Rothbard, "Free Market," in David R. Henderson, ed., *The Concise Encyclopedia of Economics* (Indianapolis: Liberty Fund, 2008), 200–202; Laura LaHaye, "Mercantilism," in Henderson, *Concise Encyclopedia of Economics*, 340–343; Chi-Yuen Wu, "Mercantilism vs. Free Trade: The Early Years," *Mises Institute*, September 14, 2013, accessed January 31, 2018, https://mises.org/library/mercantilism-vs-free-trade-early-years; and Mokyr, *Enlightened Economy*, 64–65.

[152] Langford, *Writings and Speeches*, II, 460.

If one does seek to illuminate the abiding economic principle from the speech, however, this remark moves closer to its core. The broad theme of Burke's political economy in *Speech on American Taxation* is that sovereigns cannot tax their way to commercial opulence. Taxation stifles industry, discourages trade, sparks political turbulence, and diminishes revenue in the long run. "Tyranny is a poor provider," Burke declares in the speech. "It knows neither how to accumulate, nor how to extract."[153] The new system of taxation produced "the loss not only of peace, of union, and of commerce, but even of revenue."[154] The accumulation of national wealth was encouraged by select regulations, not arbitrary taxation. Accordingly, in Burke's judgment, the British "drew more from the Colonies than all the impotent violence of despotism ever could extort from them."[155]

Burke, at least at a cursory glance, appears to contradict himself in *Speech on American Taxation*. He issues a firm defense of the old iteration of the Navigation Acts, but he also attacks them for regulating the colonies into submission. Indeed, among all the regulations supported by Grenville, the Acts, Burke states, "stood first in reputation" as his "idol."[156] We may attempt to harmonize this apparent conflict by approaching the issue from Burke's own perspective: he was not arguing for the abolition of the Acts but merely for the confinement of their regulations to objects of trade, not revenue enhancement, unlike Grenville's new schemes of taxation. Burke's defense of the older trade restrictions, then, was actually an endorsement of a freer but moderated system of commercial liberty. While the Sugar Act and its kin were formed on *political* principles, the proper imperial relationship between Britain and America should rest on a solid foundation of *commercial* principles, which he believed were consistent with the prevailing trade regulations of the Acts prior to Grenville.

In fact, Burke intimates in *Speech on American Taxation* that he would be willing to ease these older trade restrictions. "[I]f the act be suffered to run the full length of its principle, and is not changed and modified according to the change of times and the fluctuation of circumstances, it must do great mischief, and frequently even defeat its own purpose," he admits.[157] Such remarks confirm the primacy of prudence in Burke's estimation of the Acts. Clearly he harbored various apprehensions over the trade laws. Nevertheless, his primary purpose in defending them in the speech was to acknowledge their practical efficacy while maintaining, at the same time, that extending their scope to schemes of revenue would corrupt its original spirit, thereby exciting unnecessary political divisions between Britain and the Americans.

---

[153] Langford, *Writings and Speeches*, II, 461. [154] Langford, *Writings and Speeches*, II, 461.
[155] Langford, *Writings and Speeches*, II, 461. [156] Langford, *Writings and Speeches*, II, 432.
[157] Langford, *Writings and Speeches*, II, 432.

Speech on Conciliation with America

Admittedly, such a nuanced conclusion may leave the reader unsatisfied in our attempt to uncover lasting principles of Burke's imperial political economy. For could not Burke be characterized as a proponent of mercantilism, as well as an advocate of free trade, in his defense of the Navigation Acts? Even if he criticized the Grenville and North ministries' novel schemes of taxation, did not Burke also suggest, if not outright insist, that the Acts played a pivotal role in unleashing the burst of commercial prosperity in the American colonies?

Speech on Conciliation with America helps clarify such ambiguities. Presented on March 22, 1775, it denotes Burke's evolving conception of Britain's relation with the American colonies. While *Speech on American Taxation* was largely a defense of the Rockingham ministry's program of 1765–1766, and a condemnation of the North administration, *Speech on Conciliation* furnishes a more robust vision for British imperial policy moving forward.

Burke gave *Speech on Conciliation* at a fraught moment in British imperial history. A flood of proposals had been presented in the press and in Parliament in the months leading up to the oration that addressed the American question. Burke himself had been pondering a durable remedy for the colonial tumults for some time. *Speech on Conciliation* provides his most authoritative statement on the affair, arguing that Britain should revert back to the old system of the Navigation Acts while recognizing the spirit of liberty emanating from the American people – who, in Burke's judgment, cherished the gift of their inherited freedom just as strongly as their English brethren.[158] To complement his speech, Burke introduced a bill of moderate reform measures that he hoped would temper the American disturbances while preserving Britain's imperial authority in the colonies.

Speech on Conciliation captured Burke at the peak of his rhetorical and intellectual powers. It received glowing acclaim from people of a wide variety of political backgrounds, moving the imaginations of MPs and sealing Burke's reputation as a silver-tongued orator.[159] The speech was also recognized for its thorough survey of the political economy of Anglo-American relations. *St. James's Chronicle* described Burke's effort as a "most masterly and comprehensive Investigation and general View of the Trade and Commerce" of the North American colonies.[160] It demonstrated the "clearest and most extensive and familiar Knowledge of the Subject in every possible Light of Commerce, Policy, and Finance."[161] *Speech on Conciliation* is an essential oration for understanding Burke's notion of imperial economics, and his economic thought in general.

---

[158] See Langford, *Writings and Speeches*, III, 102–103 for the historical background of *Speech on Conciliation*.

[159] Langford, *Writings and Speeches*, III, 103–104.

[160] *St. James's Chronicle*, issue 2201, 23–25 March 1775.

[161] *St. James's Chronicle*, issue 2201, 23–25 March 1775.

The analytic depth of *Speech on Conciliation*, however, stems from its attempt to integrate such conceptions of political economy with an examination of the wider cultural and historical roots of the Anglo-American connection. Burke's remarks combine a vividness of detail with the powers of generalization. They incorporate empirical study of Anglo-American exports, reminiscent of his use of data in the *Observations*, with the broad range of his intellectual and imaginative mind. The speech glitters with philosophical, literary, and legal references spanning Aristotle, Horace, Hyginus, Juvenal, Milton, Ovid, Shakespeare, and Virgil, not to mention biblical citations, such as to the books of Genesis, Matthew, and Psalms. The agility of his intellectual range, as exhibited here and elsewhere, reflects a comfort in summoning both statistical information and literary authorities that was rare in his day, and ours. Most important for our purposes, the speech's relevance for Burke's conception of political economy derives from its patient elaboration on the Anglo-American commercial link, the Navigation Acts, and the historical and cultural forces behind the growth of American industry.

The early part of *Speech on Conciliation* reaffirms Burke's commitment to surveying Anglo-American relations with a heightened application of mind. Upon entering the House, at a time when the Stamp Act was a source of controversy, Burke noted that he found himself as a "partaker in a very high trust" in the debate over imperial authority in the colonies.[162] He then draws attention to the unusual diligence with which he studied the colonial policy of the British Empire. Rather than relying on his "natural abilities," Burke says he was "obliged to take more than common pains, to instruct myself in every thing which relates to our Colonies."[163] These efforts included the investigation of commercial matters, as shown not only by Burke's prominent effort in the Rockingham ministry's repeal of the Stamp Act but also by his assiduous toil on behalf of the Free Port Act of 1766.

The next section in the speech emphasizes Burke's plea for a conciliatory settlement between Britain and the American colonies. It is here that Burke plunges into a comprehensive survey of the history, culture, and economy of the colonies. After remarking that they were inhabited by at least two million people – and "of our own European blood and colour" at that[164] – he deploys export data to highlight the sparkling commercial nexus between England and the Americans that emerged in the eighteenth century. Please consult Figure 7.4[165] and Figure 7.5.[166]

---

[162] Langford, *Writings and Speeches*, III, 106. [163] Langford, *Writings and Speeches*, III, 106.

[164] Langford, *Writings and Speeches*, III, 111.

[165] Langford, *Writings and Speeches*, III, 113. Burke notes that he gathered this information from a manuscript of Charles Davenant, a former Inspector General (112).

[166] Langford, *Writings and Speeches*, III, 113. Burke remarks that he collected this information from accounts reviewed by Parliament (112). He includes the slave trade in the export statistics (113).

Exports
    To North America, and the West Indies, £483,265
    To Africa,   86,665
                                     569,930

FIGURE 7.4 English exports to North America, the West Indies, and Africa in 1704
Source: Edmund Burke, *Speech on Conciliation with America*

[Exports]
    To North America, and the West Indies,   £4,791,734
    To Africa,   866,398
    To which if you add the export trade from Scotland,   364,000
        which had in 1704 no existence,*

                                                     6,022,132

---

* Scotland and England were united by the Act of Union in 1707.
FIGURE 7.5 English exports to North America, the West Indies, and Africa in 1772
Source: Edmund Burke, *Speech on Conciliation with America*

Burke then furnishes data showing that the export trade to the colonies alone in 1772 was only £486,868 less than the entire export trade of England, including trade to the colonies, in 1704.[167]

Burke submits such information to provide an empirical basis for one of his main arguments in *Speech on Conciliation*: the interests of Britain and those of the Americans were connected together by the harmonizing chords of commerce. He rests this position on his belief, as discoursed in *Thoughts and Details* and demonstrated by the Free Port Act of 1766, that the exchange of goods generated mutual benefits for the transacting parties. Burke states:

[I]s not this American trade an unnatural protuberance, that has drawn the juices from the rest of the body? The reverse. It is the very food that has nourished every other part into its present magnitude. Our general trade has been greatly augmented; and augmented more or less in almost every part to which it ever extended.[168]

Burke is seeking to refute the zero-sum orthodoxy of observers suspicious of intercourse between England and America. In his view, the growth in colonial

---

[167] Langford, *Writings and Speeches*, III, 114. Burke miscalculates the difference in the speech; he said it was £487,868.
[168] Langford, *Writings and Speeches*, III, 114.

trade did not lead to the correspondent reduction in British commerce; rather, it coexisted with the latter's attendant rise as a global economic power. Remember, of course, that the operation of the Navigation Acts persisted in the eighteenth century, indicating that this commercial burst did not operate in an environment stripped of all trade restrictions. In the historical context of *Speech on Conciliation*, however, Burke's larger point is directed at those ministries and legislators intent on advocating schemes of taxation in order to extract greater revenue from the colonies: concessions to the Americans would not sanction the destruction of British trade, for the economic vibrancy of the former smoothly complemented and accented the commercial spirit of the latter.

Burke's description of American agriculture in the speech augments this view. In the eighteenth century, Britain was not immune from the possibility of scarcity, and by the 1760s had become a net importer of grain.[169] Yet the energies of colonial husbandry relieved the British from any harsher consequences caused by depressions in farming. "For some time past, the old world has been fed from the new," Burke explains. "The scarcity which you have felt would have been a desolating famine; if this child of your old age, with a true filial piety, with a Roman charity, had not put the full breast of its youthful exuberance to the mouth of its exhausted parent."[170] He is invoking the commercial principle of a harmony of interest: the achievements of colonial agriculture did not crush the British economy, but rather supplemented and fortified it in a way that engendered advantages to both.

Such economic codependency meant that any attempt to injure the colonies would bring hazardous effects upon Britain itself. Later in *Speech on Conciliation*, Burke argues that a tax on the tobacco of Virginia would "give its death-wound to your English revenue at home, and to one of the very greatest articles of your own foreign trade."[171] Therefore, "If you tax the import of that rebellious Colony, what do you tax but your own manufactures, or the goods of some other obedient, and already well-taxed Colony?"[172] Excessive taxation of one's trading partner would diminish the taxing power's own opportunities to reap a profit and collect receipts for the treasury.

In addition to American agriculture, Burke portrays the American fishery trade in a laudatory fashion:

Whilst we follow them among the tumbling mountains of ice, and behold them penetrating into the deepest frozen recesses of Hudson's Bay, and Davis's Streights, whilst we are looking for them beneath the Arctic circle, we hear that they have pierced into the opposite region of polar cold, that they are at the Antipodes, and engaged under the frozen serpent of the south.[173]

[169] Mitchell, *British Historical Statistics*, 221. [170] Langford, *Writings and Speeches*, III, 117.
[171] Langford, *Writings and Speeches*, III, 160. [172] Langford, *Writings and Speeches*, III, 160.
[173] Langford, *Writings and Speeches*, III, 117.

Burke here illumines his sketch of the New England whale fishery with a flash of his imaginative rhetoric. According to his narrative, the Americans' remarkable facility for trade reached the farthest shores of the Atlantic Ocean and North America (and the South Pacific). Their fortitude animated their ingenuity in opening up new avenues for commerce previously dismissed as impractical: "Falkland Island, which seemed too remote and romantic an object for the grasp of national ambition, is but a stage and resting place in the progress of their victorious industry."[174] Hot climates did not discourage American vigor, either.[175] Burke goes so far as to state, without qualification, that the enterprising diligence of American colonists exceeded the capacities of traditional European powers. "Neither the perseverance of Holland, nor the activity of France, nor the dextrous and firm sagacity of English enterprize, ever carried this most perilous mode of hardy industry to the extent to which it has been pushed by this recent people," he declares.[176]

In this section of *Speech on Conciliation*, Burke's broad message is that colonial prosperity stemmed not from the cold hand of imperial regulation, the older Navigation Acts notwithstanding, but from the creative energies of a people trading in a free economic environment. The "Colonies in general owe little or nothing to any care of ours, and that they are not squeezed into this happy form by the constraints of watchful and suspicious government," Burke observes, "but that through a wise and salutary neglect, a generous nature has been suffered to take her own way to perfection."[177] A deluge of commercial restrictions and schemes of taxation – "watchful and suspicious government" – did not occasion the rise in American trade. Instead, the British Empire's implicit authorization of commercial liberties through lenient regulatory enforcement – a key premise of "salutary neglect," one of Burke's most celebrated phrases – set the conditions for public opulence in the colonies. Freedom is the parent of prosperity.

Burke insists that the British should applaud, rather than regret, the growth in American wealth. The fruits drawn from acquisitions in the colonial fishery trade "seemed even to excite your envy; and yet the spirit, by which that enterprizing employment has been exercised, ought rather, in my opinion, to have raised your esteem and admiration."[178] Blend this insight with Burke's conclusion about the mutual benefits of trade: Britain should recognize the industry and perseverance that propelled the circulation of American commerce, not only for their value as virtues in themselves, but also for their pivotal role in the diffusion of trade that benefited the British Empire as a whole.

---

[174] Langford, *Writings and Speeches*, III, 117.
[175] Burke writes, "Nor is the equinoctial heat more discouraging to them, than the accumulated winter of both the poles. We know that whilst some of them draw the line and strike the harpoon on the coast of Africa, others run the longitude, and pursue their gigantic game along the coast of Brazil" (Langford, *Writings and Speeches*, III, 117).
[176] Langford, *Writings and Speeches*, III, 118.   [177] Langford, *Writings and Speeches*, III, 118.
[178] Langford, *Writings and Speeches*, III, 117.

In the next section of *Speech on Conciliation*, in which he urges for an imperial policy of prudent management, not coercive force, Burke puts forth his celebrated description of the English roots of American liberty. For the purposes of understanding Burke's conception of political economy, the salient point in these passages is that the commercial spirit of the Americans reflected a temper that transcended a mere attraction to material acquisition. "In this Character of the Americans, a love of Freedom is the predominating feature, which marks and distinguishes the whole," Burke proclaims.[179] American colonists were ever on watchful guard against attempts to seize it. Thus "this fierce spirit of Liberty is stronger in the English Colonies probably than in any other people of the earth."[180]

From which source did the Americans' instinct for liberty derive? From their English heritage. The "people of the Colonies are descendents of Englishmen."[181] The Americans "are therefore not only devoted to Liberty, but to Liberty according to English ideas, and on English principles."[182] They were not, however, dedicated to metaphysical conceptions of freedom: "Abstract Liberty, like other mere abstractions, is not to be found."[183] The freedoms of the Americans were the product of a specific historical inheritance, that of England's rich constitutional traditions in circumscribing the exercise of arbitrary power and securing the private property and legal rights of citizens. According to Burke, the Americans' cry for liberty was not an exhortation to break free from their English past, but was rather a reassertion of their rights of Englishmen that had been suppressed by the designs of British imperial power in the 1760s and 1770s.[184]

Burke's comments following these statements are not as well-known, but they supply additional insight into his conception of political economy in the context of his broader political thought. What distinguished political struggles in England from those in ancient republics was debate "upon the question of Taxing."[185] The "question of money was not with them so immediate," Burke says, referring to the republics.[186] He describes how English writers from time immemorial argued over the authority of the House of Commons to tax the people:

They took infinite pains to inculcate, as a fundamental principle, that, in all monarchies, the people must in effect themselves mediately or immediately possess the power of granting their own money, or no shadow of liberty could subsist. The Colonies draw

---

[179] Langford, *Writings and Speeches*, III, 119.

[180] Langford, *Writings and Speeches*, III, 119–120.

[181] Langford, *Writings and Speeches*, III, 120.   [182] Langford, *Writings and Speeches*, III, 120.

[183] Langford, *Writings and Speeches*, III, 120.

[184] In 1797, Burke would remark in *Third Letter on a Regicide Peace* that America was of "European origin" and had "not yet, like France, destroyed all traces of manners, laws, opinions, and usages which she drew from Europe" (Langford, *Writings and Speeches*, IX, 325).

[185] Langford, *Writings and Speeches*, III, 120.   [186] Langford, *Writings and Speeches*, III, 120.

from you as with their life-blood, these ideas and principles. Their love of liberty, as with you, fixed and attached on this specific point of taxing.[187]

Notice the unfolding progression of Burke's argument about liberty in *Speech on Conciliation*: first, colonial prosperity marked a capacity for material industry that illustrated the merit of light imperial regulation. But this attraction to commerce was rooted in a deeper tradition of English liberty. English liberty in itself was not an abstract concept, but rather emerged in a historical struggle throughout the generations that rested on an exceedingly practical question: which English body, if any, possessed the rightful authority to tax the people? Because the Americans shared the same heritage as England, colonial resistance to the British Empire was inspired by a similar dispute.

Consider the significant implications this argument holds for Burke's science of political economy. We have established that his economic thought praised the natural laws of commerce for spreading goods to the many in an effectual fashion. Yet this is not the heart of Burke's narrative of English liberty in this specific passage in *Speech on Conciliation*. Instead, its crux is his sharp emphasis on the question of the *authority* to tax, rather than on supply and demand laws. Traditions of English liberty, at their deepest level, were defined not by competitive price systems but by repeated human effort to delimit the exercise of arbitrary power.

Of course, for Burke, these two elements of political economy – the authority to tax and the wisdom of free markets – were not mutually exclusive. In *Thoughts and Details*, he argues that the artificial creation of wage rates by magistrates was an arbitrary imposition of power on private farmers and laborers. The illuminative feature of Burke's survey of English liberty in *Speech on Conciliation*, however, is his notion that the use of arbitrary force did not simply impact the flow of commerce; it cut off the very roots of representative government. Accordingly, colonial legislatures are "popular in an high degree; some are merely popular; in all, the popular representative is the most weighty; and this share of the people in their ordinary government never fails to inspire them with lofty sentiments, and with a strong aversion from whatever tends to deprive them of their chief importance."[188] Popular representation is antithetical to arbitrary might. Meld this principle with their shared English past, and the colonies exemplified a fundamental maxim of freedom: the character of a people determines the enduring strength of their liberty – a lesson the *Account* affirmed as well.

The colonists' attachment to liberty was further enlivened by the powerful impetus of religion. Because political economy did not operate in isolation for Burke, he recognized the centrality of this force in breathing a spirit of enlightened vigor into the American soul. "Religion" is "always a principle of

---

[187] Langford, *Writings and Speeches*, III, 120–121.
[188] Langford, *Writings and Speeches*, III, 121.

energy in this new people," he remarks.[189] In particular, the imperatives of Protestantism occasioned awakened vigilance from colonists resistant to any possible encroachments upon their treasured freedoms. The distinct brand of Protestantism the Americans practice, Burke insists, "is the most adverse to all implicit submission of mind and opinion."[190] Indeed, "This is a persuasion not only favourable to liberty, but built upon it."[191] Burke places religion in a political and historical context: he characterizes Protestantism as a "sort of dissent" that secured the "natural liberty" of its adherents against "all the ordinary powers of the world."[192]

It is in this passage that Burke famously depicts the religion of the northern American colonies as "the dissidence of dissent; and the protestantism of the protestant religion."[193] The northern denominations of Protestantism were bound in "the communion of the spirit of liberty."[194] Let us not overlook the importance of such remarks in the context of his theory of political economy: for Burke, discourses on liberty inevitably blended with more profound questions of faith. In the case of the colonists, American liberty was moved by a unique form of religion particularly suited to recognize and combat the imperious schemes of arbitrary force.

Burke observed another salient feature of American culture that helped condition colonial aptitudes for liberty. "In no country perhaps in the world is the law so general a study," he explains.[195] The proliferation of Blackstone's *Commentaries* in the colonies testified to this gravitational attraction. The study of law, Burke comments, "renders men acute, inquisitive, dextrous, prompt in attack, ready in defence, full of resources."[196] While citizens in other nations reacted to the deformation of political principles only when manifested in concrete wrongs, in America "they anticipate the evil, and judge of the pressure of the grievance by the badness of the principle."[197] They "augur misgovernment at a distance; and snuff the approach of tyranny in every tainted breeze."[198] The Americans were armed with a magazine of legal wisdom, ready to brandish at a moment's notice at any sign of despotism.

Slavery in *Speech on Conciliation*

In this section in *Speech on Conciliation*, Burke inserts remarks on slavery that warrant brief consideration. He poses the hypothetical objection that even though a spirit of dissidence emanated from the northern colonies, this spirit was nullified by the presence of the Church of England in the southern colonies.

---

[189] Langford, *Writings and Speeches*, III, 121. [190] Langford, *Writings and Speeches*, III, 121.
[191] Langford, *Writings and Speeches*, III, 121. [192] Langford, *Writings and Speeches*, III, 121.
[193] Langford, *Writings and Speeches*, III, 122. [194] Langford, *Writings and Speeches*, III, 122.
[195] Langford, *Writings and Speeches*, III, 123. [196] Langford, *Writings and Speeches*, III, 124.
[197] Langford, *Writings and Speeches*, III, 124. [198] Langford, *Writings and Speeches*, III, 124.

Burke was not convinced by such reasoning, however, because the southern colonies were guided by a liberty "more high and haughty" than that in the North.[199] This difference could be attributed to the institution of slavery, such as that practiced in Virginia and the Carolinas. When men own slaves, Burke notes, "[T]hose who are free, are by far the most proud and jealous of their freedom."[200] Moreover, "Freedom is to them not only an enjoyment, but a kind of rank and privilege."[201] Southerners think their freedom is "more noble and liberal" than the liberty of the northern colonies.[202] Burke does strain to deny the moral rectitude of this freedom, for it had "at least as much pride as virtue in it."[203]

Yet Burke stresses that he is simply observing a constitutive element of human nature. And, he continues, "I cannot alter the nature of man."[204] Therefore, the people in the southern colonies "are much more strongly, and with an higher and more stubborn spirit, attached to liberty than those" in the north.[205] In many ways, Burke in these remarks is outlining the classical conception of hierarchical freedom: the free man was the citizen who did not have to perform labor in order to survive because this task was the responsibility of women and slaves. Moreover, freedom from the enslavement of the passions was the true mark of liberty. If one could not control his passions – as masters believed slaves could not – he was not free.[206]

As we have learned, Burke drafted one of the first English plans to abolish the British slave trade. The question in this passage in *Speech on Conciliation*, nevertheless, is whether he hints at any conflict between a landowner's love of liberty and his enslavement of others. Southerners, he remarks, do not see that freedom "may be united with much abject toil, with great misery, with all the exterior of servitude."[207] For slave owners, "[T]he haughtiness of domination combines with the spirit of freedom, fortifies it, and renders it invincible."[208] Burke is indeed spreading intimations about the cruel contradiction between freedom and slavery. Later in the speech he describes slavery as "that inhuman traffick."[209] The politically sensitive nature of the institution at the time, however, explains Burke's somewhat awkward articulation of it in *Speech on Conciliation*.

---

[199] Langford, *Writings and Speeches*, III, 122.   [200] Langford, *Writings and Speeches*, III, 122.
[201] Langford, *Writings and Speeches*, III, 122.
[202] Langford, *Writings and Speeches*, III, 122. See Michael E. Woods, *Emotional and Sectional Conflict in the Antebellum United States* (Cambridge: Cambridge University Press, 2014), 109.
[203] Langford, *Writings and Speeches*, III, 122.   [204] Langford, *Writings and Speeches*, III, 122.
[205] Langford, *Writings and Speeches*, III, 122.
[206] Aristotle, *Politics*, 63–75; see also Arendt, *Human Condition*, for discussion on enslavement by biological necessity, 79–93.
[207] Langford, *Writings and Speeches*, III, 122.   [208] Langford, *Writings and Speeches*, III, 123.
[209] Langford, *Writings and Speeches*, III, 131.

The Spirit of Liberty and the Navigation Acts

Allow us to summarize. For Burke, the genius of colonial disobedience could be traced back to six principal sources: a shared English heritage; popular forms of government; a peculiar brand of Protestantism in the north; "manners" in the south (Burke is ostensibly connecting this source to the southern spirit of hierarchical liberty); Americans' education in the law; and finally, the vast ocean separating the colonies and Britain. This portrait of American liberty displays the versatility and depth of Burke's intellectual disposition, taking in and molding a variety of seemingly disparate subjects – history, religion, geography, culture, law – into a picture of analytic coherence.

Burke proceeds to argue that among the three options facing the British, the first two – alter the spirit of American liberty by removing its causes, and criminally prosecute American resisters – were impractical and unwise. To the first, Burke supplies two compelling remarks on general principles of political economy, one that relates to the law of scarcity and the other to the subject of unintended consequences. One proposed remedy to change the American spirit was for the Crown to halt grants of land to the colonists in order to stem population growth. For Burke, however, this policy would simply enlarge the powers of wealthy landowners since they already possessed large tracts of unsettled property. "[T]he only effect of this avarice of desolation, this hoarding of a royal wilderness, would be to raise the value of the possessions in the hands of the great private monopolists, without any adequate check to the growing and alarming mischief of population," Burke states.[210] Scarcity in itself creates and enhances value; further limitations on the amount of colonial property would escalate prices even more, to the benefit of the affluent propertied classes.

Next, even if the Crown terminated the grants, this action would not smother the Americans' flair for industry. "If you drive the people from one place," Burke explains, "they will carry on their annual Tillage, and remove with their flocks and herds to another."[211] Attempts to trap the colonists would be ineffectual, for they would merely encourage Americans to adjust to the restrictions by pursuing new agricultural opportunities elsewhere. Burke's insinuation is hard to ignore: the stated intentions of one policy may engender consequences unforeseen by its advocates. Accordingly, the third option Burke proposes for the British – comply with the American spirit while reconciling it to the interests of their empire – was the far more desirable option.

Burke does admit that obstructing the course of American commerce would be easier. But, returning to his earlier theme of political economy, he observes that this policy was premised on the sinister myth of zero-sum economics. We see "ourselves as rivals to our Colonies, and persuaded that of course we must

---

[210] Langford, *Writings and Speeches*, III, 128.
[211] Langford, *Writings and Speeches*, III, 128–129.

gain all that they shall lose."[212] Burke is repelled by such thinking: "Much mischief we may certainly do."[213] In general, a man imbued with a spirit of liberty would be the least appropriate person to coax another freedom-living man into servitude: "An Englishman is the unfittest person on earth, to argue another Englishman into slavery."[214] That is why Burke highlights the impractical nature of plans to condemn the Americans to imperial subjugation.

After Burke rejects the second option, criminal prosecution, for being too narrow to comprehend the infinite complexities of imperial authority, he explains that compliance with the American spirit would be the most sensible course of action for Britain. It is in this section that Burke adumbrates his thoughts on the Navigation Acts. Before beginning this discussion, however, he conveys his famous antipathy to theoretical debates over the right to tax. The Americans insisted that taxation without representation was unjust. Yet for Burke, "I put it totally out of the question."[215] It was immensely difficult to finely thread the answers to these questions into a dense blueprint for government. "I do not examine, whether the giving away a man's money be a power excepted and reserved out of the general trust of Government; and how far all mankind, in all forms of Polity, are intitled to an exercise of that Right by the Charter of Nature," he declares. "Or whether, on the contrary, a Right of Taxation is necessarily involved in the general principle of Legislation, and inseparable from the ordinary Supreme Power?"[216]

Burke may be guilty of slightly inconsistent logic; recall his earlier point that traditions of English liberty were guided by the belief that the people possessed the direct or indirect authority to dispense with their own money. But in the case of the Americans, disputes about rights would never resolve themselves; instead, the British should bring about the conditions that would satisfy the colonists' interests, thereby quelling political tumults and stabilizing the imperial authority of the British Empire. "The question with me is, not whether you have a right to render your people miserable; but whether it is not your interest to make them happy?" he utters. "It is not, what a lawyer tells me, I *may* do; but what humanity, reason, and justice, tell me, I ought to do."[217] Justice and utility should serve as the moral criteria for colonial policy.

Burke's succeeding comments on the Navigation Acts embolden his stance in *Speech on American Taxation* that a return to the older commercial system would disarm colonial unease. In *Speech on Conciliation*, he remarks how the trade laws were invoked either to spotlight their inefficacy or to justify new schemes of taxation as security for the restrictions. On this last point, Burke channels his ire at the contradictions of Lord North: "[Y]ou keep up revenue laws which are mischievous, in order to preserve trade laws that are useless."[218]

[212] Langford, *Writings and Speeches*, III, 129. [213] Langford, *Writings and Speeches*, III, 129.
[214] Langford, *Writings and Speeches*, III, 130. [215] Langford, *Writings and Speeches*, III, 135.
[216] Langford, *Writings and Speeches*, III, 135. [217] Langford, *Writings and Speeches*, III, 135.
[218] Langford, *Writings and Speeches*, III, 137.

He then provides a qualified endorsement of the Acts. Burke says he could not go as far as North "concerning the inutility of the trade laws," ascribing North's views to the possible influence of Josiah Tucker's *Four Tracts on Political and Commercial Subjects*, which assailed the Acts.[219] Burke, however, believed the trade restrictions contributed in some manner to the public prosperity of the British Empire. "For without idolizing them," he avers, "I am sure they are still, in many ways, of great use to us; and in former times, they have been of the greatest."[220]

Burke does concede that the Navigation Acts "do confine, and they do greatly narrow, the market for the Americans."[221] But the thrust of his argument is not the theoretical proposition that the laws were good in themselves. Instead, Burke puts forth three claims: the schemes to raise revenue from the colonies did not strengthen the basis of the existing commercial restrictions; the traditional system of the Acts was not the source of colonial disobedience; and concession to the Americans' demands to relieve their tax burden would not necessarily lead to the relinquishing of all imperial authority.[222]

On the second point, it should be noted that Burke's argument was not an inaccurate portrayal of the colonial perspective on the older Navigation Acts. In 1774, the First Continental Congress adopted a statement insisting that while colonies possessed the legislative authority over their internal affairs, they "cheerfully" consented to "such acts of the British parliament, as are bona fide, restrained to the regulation of our external commerce, for the purpose of securing the commercial advantages of the whole empire to the mother country, and the commercial benefits of its respective members."[223] This admission conveyed formal colonial assent to the Acts, recognizing the laws to be tenable measures of imperial policy connecting American goods to the seat of empire.

What, then, are the implications for Burke's theory of political economy? First, his description of the Navigation Acts confirms his view expressed in *Speech on American Taxation* that the trade laws must have furnished *some* advantage to the Anglo-American connection, as displayed by the sparkling growth of British and American commerce in the eighteenth century. Second, our inquiry into Burke's remarks on commerce, revenue, and taxation, particularly in the 1770s, requires elevated attention to the historical and political contexts in which he introduced his arguments, without merely reducing his commentary to the time period in which he lived. Third, characterizing Burke's economic thought through stiff frames of either free

---

[219] Langford, *Writings and Speeches*, III, 137–138; and 138n1.
[220] Langford, *Writings and Speeches*, III, 138. [221] Langford, *Writings and Speeches*, III, 138.
[222] Langford, *Writings and Speeches*, III, 138.
[223] Worthington C. Ford, ed., *Journals of the Continental Congress 1774–1789*, vol. I (Washington, DC: Government Printing Office, 1904–1937), 68–69.

trade or mercantilism overlooks the complexities of commercial policy he and his fellow legislators were forced to confront and weigh in Parliament in the 1700s.

Burke's Plan for Reform of the Anglo-American Imperial Relationship

Speech on Conciliation concludes by presenting Burke's substantive plan for reform. He premises his plan by briefly outlining England's political relationship with Ireland, Wales, and Chester, with the purpose of demonstrating that an imperial power need not coerce its subjects into servitude. According to Burke, Britain maintained its authority over these possessions, but also granted their people a large amount of internal freedom. The British government "never altered" the constitution of Ireland, which "made Ireland the great and flourishing kingdom that it is."[224]

Burke goes further: "This country cannot be said to have ever formally taxed her."[225] The prosperity of Ireland, and of the Anglo-Irish relationship, was made possible by the light presence of imperial authority, not the brawny hand of imperial might. Once again, Burke also underscores that a state could not tax its way to opulence: "Your Irish pensioners would starve, if they had no other fund to live on than taxes granted by English authority."[226] Similarly, once Wales and Chester received internal liberties from England, they flourished. These successes reflected the "eternal law" that "Providence had decreed vexation to violence; and poverty to rapine."[227] The control of a people's political and economic energies set the conditions for impoverishment, not affluence. Therefore, "[F]reedom and not servitude is the cure of anarchy."[228]

Burke transitions into his plan for reform by introducing "six fundamental propositions."[229] These resolutions called for the enactment of certain duties in the colonies; a reduction of customs duties on the British export of cocoa beans produced by the colonies; the termination of drawbacks discouraging Chinese earthenware exported to the colonies; a more robust effort to limit the trafficking of clandestine goods in the colonies; a repeal of the duty on tea; the nullification of the Intolerable Acts, excepting the Quebec Act; and a revision of a treason statute[230] that would strengthen the impartial enforcement of justice in the Province of Massachusetts Bay.[231]

Burke also recommended the repeal of the Boston Port Bill, one of the Intolerable Acts established following the Boston Tea Party that had closed the Port of Boston until colonists repaid the Crown for their destruction of

---

[224] Langford, *Writings and Speeches*, III, 140.   [225] Langford, *Writings and Speeches*, III, 140.
[226] Langford, *Writings and Speeches*, III, 141.   [227] Langford, *Writings and Speeches*, III, 142.
[228] Langford, *Writings and Speeches*, III, 144. Burke completes this sentence with his famous remark about religion: "religion, and not atheism, is the true remedy for superstition."
[229] Langford, *Writings and Speeches*, III, 146.   [230] 35 Hen. VIII, c.2.
[231] Langford, *Writings and Speeches*, III, 153; and 153n1.

British commerce; the continuation of the charters of Rhode Island and Connecticut; the restoration of the charter of Massachusetts Bay, which had been changed in 1774 by the Massachusetts Government Act, another part of the Intolerable Acts that had enhanced the powers of the Crown over the colony's internal affairs; the preservation of judicial independence in colonial governments; and the regulation of the Courts of Admiralty to promote a fairer administration of justice.[232]

Burke's proposals strike the essence of his attitude toward political and economic reform. They were substantive in nature but not radical in practice. The measures were motivated by a vision of imperial principle, the idea that Britain should lighten its regulatory presence in its dependencies. Furthermore, the recommendations promoted the cause of colonial freedom, with the understanding that such liberty would be cushioned by the authority of Britain's imperial constitution. As we have learned, these precepts also informed Burke's vision for the Free Port Act of 1766 and his economical program in the early 1780s, not to mention his thoughts in *Account of the European Settlements in America*. The steady advance of ordered liberty was the glowing touchstone of Burke's science of political economy.

Additional Reflections on Market Liberty in *Speech on Conciliation*

The underlying creed governing Burke's proposed measures in *Speech on Conciliation* contains similarities with *Thoughts and Details*. In the latter tract, Burke stressed that private employment contracts reflected a synthesis of compromise between the farmer and laborer. In *Speech on Conciliation*, he applies the same general principle to the relationship between government and the people, two entities he did not believe were in inherent conflict with one another. "All government, indeed every human benefit and enjoyment" – such as wealth – "every virtue, and every prudent act, is founded on compromise and barter," he says.[233] Burke even migrates toward a Lockean conception of natural rights in this discussion: "As we must give away some natural liberty, to enjoy civil advantages; so we must sacrifice some civil liberties, for the advantages to be derived from the communion and fellowship of a great empire."[234] Men relinquish some freedom in order to enjoy the benefits of civil society.

Burke's grander theoretical point connects his praise of compromise with his heavy skepticism of abstract theory in guiding human affairs. Ordered liberty under the eye of the British Empire was not established by engaging in metaphysical debate about right and morality. "Aristotle, the great master of reasoning, cautions us, and with great weight and propriety, against this species of delusive geometrical accuracy in moral judgments, as the most fallacious of

[232] Langford, *Writings and Speeches*, III, 153–155.
[233] Langford, *Writings and Speeches*, III, 157.   [234] Langford, *Writings and Speeches*, III, 157.

all sophistry," Burke declares.[235] Instead, ordered liberty in imperial dominions was achieved through the gentleness of compromise and mediation, of give and take, of intuitive understandings and unspoken sympathies. Inflexible assertions of right roused the anxieties of the disputing parties, yet pragmatic settlements and concessions merged their competing interests into a delicate and symbiotic unity.

This is Burke's philosophical argument in *Speech on Conciliation*, and it shaped his conception of voluntary exchange in *Thoughts and Details* two decades later as a reconciling medium for the satisfaction of practical wants. Consider another remark by Burke in the speech:

> In every arduous enterprize, we consider what we are to lose, as well as what we are to gain; and the more and better stake of liberty every people possess, the less they will hazard in a vain attempt to make it more. These are *the cords of man*. Man acts from adequate motives relative to his interest; and not on metaphysical speculations.[236]

Even though *Speech on Conciliation* addresses Anglo-American relations and not strict considerations of political economy, these comments catch the heart of Burke's psychological understanding of man in his economic thought. Man is conditioned to assess his enlightened self-interest in the fulfillment of any significant undertaking. In the process of barter, he does not consider whether the purchase of some good reflects the speculative principles of an economic doctrine, but rather whether accessing a concrete service will promote his well-being. The churn of markets, and of human relations, oftentimes rests on practical considerations. For Burke, a precise delineation of the start and end of liberty ignores this ethic of practicality, undercutting the basis for compromise and kindling unnecessary social discord.

Revenue in *Speech on Conciliation*

One final argument deserves attention for our purpose of studying Burke's political economy in *Speech on Conciliation*. Burke avowed in *Speech on American Taxation* that attempts to raise revenue through excessive taxation actually obstructed the steady collection of receipts. He reinforces this argument in *Speech on Conciliation*. The "first of all Revenues" is "the power of REFUSAL."[237] Because the creation of wealth depends on human enterprise, governments that limit their control of the people's industrious energies build a stronger revenue stream, since there will be a greater pot of money from which to extract. "Most may be taken where most is accumulated," Burke says.[238] Indeed, "[W]hat is the soil or climate where experience has not uniformly proved, that the voluntary flow of heaped-up plenty, bursting from the weight of its own rich luxuriance, has ever run with a more copious stream of revenue,

---

[235] Langford, *Writings and Speeches*, III, 157.   [236] Langford, *Writings and Speeches*, III, 157.
[237] Langford, *Writings and Speeches*, III, 162.   [238] Langford, *Writings and Speeches*, III, 163.

than could be squeezed from the dry husks of oppressed indigence, by the straining of all the politic machinery in the world."[239]

One is impressed by Burke's attempt to adorn the discussion of such a dry subject with such vivid imagery; has the dullness of tax policy ever been beautified in this way before? His analytic point is that the commercial potentialities of the people were the true sources of state revenue. This message fits neatly into his broader understanding that no intrinsic antagonism existed between the state and the people because, among many reasons, the prosperity of the latter generated advantages for the former, such as income for the Exchequer. In a larger sense, there was no friction between an imperial authority and its subjects that could not be seasoned with reconciling principles. The preservation of colonial liberty would benefit the Americans and the British, while the relaxation of taxes would produce fortunes for both. The protection of industry would allow seemingly discordant interests to arrange themselves into a mosaic of unity. Ordered liberty would beget harmonious flourishing.

7.4 CONCLUSION

Burke's approach to Anglo-American foreign trade was inspired by the maxims of his economic thought in favor of commercial exchange – and by his mindful recognition of the broader implications of British imperial policy in North America and the British West Indies. Commerce was a means for opulence and an instrument for power: Burke knew that the strengthening of Britain's economic relationship with the Americans, a vibrant, industrious people, would not only swell its public riches but also fortify its stature in the wider global order against European rivals. Because Burke did not perceive foreign trade to produce zero-sum effects, an increase in affluence for the Americans promised an increase in affluence for the British.

Furthermore, the inflexible classification of Burke's thought on foreign commerce in *Speech on American Taxation* and *Speech on Conciliation* as either "pro-free trade" or "pro-mercantilism" disregards the complicated nature of British imperial commercial policy in the eighteenth century. The enlargement or reduction of the Navigation Acts was not simply an exercise in commercial reform; it was an exercise in *imperial* reform and *national security* reform and *social* reform as well, all of which carried serious consequences for the imperial constitution that had governed the British Empire for over a century. Proposed revisions of trade regulations, then, were naturally attached to questions of politics, foreign policy, religion, culture, and English history. Resistance to the swift abolition of all trade laws, in itself, did not necessarily indicate a deeper philosophical position in support of, or in opposition to, free trade.

---

[239] Langford, *Writings and Speeches*, III, 163.

For Burke, however, the weight of English history was no excuse to avoid discussion about modifying existing regulations. On the contrary, the avenues to substantive reform required a discerning awareness of the trade laws that had bound the Americans to the British for years, as exemplified by Burke's own quest to soften trade restrictions that inhibited commercial freedom – through the crafting of the Free Port Act; the recovery of the older (and less onerous) system of the Navigation Acts; and the expression of liberal economic principles in general. "[A] sovereign who, instead of fighting the rebels in a province, lays a dead hand on the trade of his subjects, is no better than a madman," he wrote in notes for a speech on the American war.[240] Burke's economic statesmanship reflected a vision of Anglo-American imperial order animated by lightness of touch.

---

[240] William and Bourke, *Correspondence of the Right Honourable Edmund Burke*, vol. IV, 471.

8

Anglo-Irish Commercial Relations, *Two Letters on the Trade of Ireland*, and the Politics of Free Trade

[J]ustice to others is not always folly to ourselves.[1]

Edmund Burke, *Two Letters on the Trade of Ireland*, 1778

8.1 INTRODUCTION

Was it possible that Burke supported laws that advanced the cause of commercial liberty for the purpose of political convenience rather than on the grounds of economic principle? Consider the Free Port Act. While Burke and the Rockinghams may have retained sympathies toward free ports, they also recognized the political opportunity that lay before them in 1765 to ostracize George Grenville and win over disaffected merchants hurt by the feeble trade market under his ministry.[2] For Burke himself, it is also plausible that he saw this moment as an occasion early in his parliamentary career to curry favor with English merchants and gratify his incipient political ambitions for power. Interpreted in the worst light, then, Burke's support for the Act could be understood as the clever exploitation of mercantile discontent in the service of private advancement and not as an expression of authentic economic conviction.

Furthermore, consider Burke's commentary in the *Observations*, *Speech on American Taxation*, and *Speech on Conciliation*. Even if Burke expressed support in the speeches for the reduction of arbitrary imperial regulations, might he have employed this position as a vehicle to soothe the discontents of the Americans in any way possible? If the enlargement of colonial freedoms

---

[1] Langford, *Writings and Speeches*, IX, 507.
[2] See Langford's discussion of this political dynamic in *First Rockingham Administration*, 113–114.

could bring about political reconciliation, then why not harness the power of trade to achieve Anglo-American concord? To be sure, Burke's reflections on the American question do provide substantive statements on the merits of commercial intercourse; but, as discussed, they also confronted a wide variety of other matters relating to culture, religion, history, European geopolitics, and morality, leading to the challenging task of extracting the essence of Burke's remarks on free trade from these additional considerations.

The possibility that Burke promoted the spirit of liberal commerce for politically expedient ends encounters a sturdy challenge, however, when studying his commentary on Anglo-Irish trade relations. As for the first narrative, the notion that Burke's support for the Free Port Act was merely an attempt to bend to the demands of merchants does not explain his later campaign to advocate Irish free trade measures when his constituents, many of whom were also influential merchants, *opposed* the easing of protectionist restrictions. As for the second line of reasoning, Burke's support for Irish trade, similar to his remarks on Anglo-American relations, indeed cannot be read without an awareness of British imperial politics. Nevertheless, his statements on Irish commerce draw a sharper picture of the principles inspiring his sympathy for free trade in comparison to his remarks on the American question. For Burke, the material wealth of nations derived from the glitter of commerce.

8.2   THE COMMERCIAL TENSIONS BETWEEN ENGLAND AND IRELAND

Anglo-Irish trade relations were fraught with distrust and jealousy in Burke's time. The British Empire's commercial policy toward Ireland was designed to favor England and discourage Irish mercantile capacities by imposing regulations on the flow of Irish traffic that persisted well into the eighteenth century. This trend began before Burke was born, however. Under Charles II, Parliament established a series of commercial restrictions, such as those impacting the cattle industry,[3] which were intended to suppress competition from Irish traders and privilege English economic interests.

England's desire to strangle Irish trade continued under William III, as exemplified by the Irish Woollen Act of 1699, which banned the exportation of Irish woolen products to foreign ports. Although the law did not proscribe exports to England, existing duties on wool remained excessively high.[4] One source of the political movement behind this protectionist legislation was a vocal group of merchants in Bristol – the same city Burke represented in the 1770s, and one whose mercantile constituency would object to his proposals for

[3] Carolyn A. Edie, "The Irish Cattle Bills: A Study in Restoration Politics," *Translations of the American Philosophical Society* 60 (1970): 1–66.
[4] L. M. Cullen, *Anglo-Irish Trade 1660–1800* (Manchester: Manchester University Press, 1968), 2n1.

free trade. According to H. F. Kearney, in fact, the economist attributed with spearheading the campaign against the Irish woolen industry, John Cary, was from Bristol.[5]

Ireland did receive particular advantages from the trading system. It could trade with the British colonies, for instance, even though duties were set on different types of linens. Yet the Navigation Act of 1671 forbade Ireland from directly importing items from English colonies, making the country even more reliant on England to furnish supplies of goods.[6] Consequently, Ireland could not take in colonial products like tobacco and sugar unless they were transferred "round-about" through Britain.

In general, the composition of Parliament at the time of these trade restrictions was disproportionately represented by members from districts whose industries manufactured wool and bred cattle.[7] Therefore, rather than reflecting a defined and coherent mercantilist doctrine, England's protectionist policies in this context were largely the consequence of active interest groups seeking to carve out trading privileges for their particular industries, a development Adam Smith would condemn in the *Wealth of Nations*. As Oliver M. Dickerson writes, "No greater error can be made than to assume that the system [of the Navigation Acts] in operation at a given time corresponded even roughly to the mercantilist theories expounded by the well-known writers."[8]

Burke was conscious of the harmful effects spurred on by these trade wars. In 1778, he remarked upon the state of the woolen manufacture in Ireland, saddled by the burdensome duties and prohibitions established by both the Irish Parliament, under the influence of England, and the British Parliament:

[T]he whole Woollen Manufacture of Ireland, the most extensive and profitable of any, and the natural Staple of that Kingdom, has been in a manner so destroyed by restrictive Laws of *ours*, and (at our persuasion, and on our promises) by restrictive Laws of *their own*, that in a few years, it is probable, they will not be able to wear a Coat of their own Fabrick?[9]

We should also note that Burke's library included a copy of John Lord Sheffield's *Observations on the Manufactures, Trade, and Present State of Ireland*, from which Burke most likely gleaned additional insight into the state of Irish trade.[10]

Even though such constant friction between England and Ireland prevailed throughout the 1700s, their commercial relationship grew closer during Burke's

---

[5] Kearney, "Political Background to English Mercantilism," 484.
[6] See Cullen, *Anglo-Irish Trade*, 37–38.   [7] Cullen, *Anglo-Irish Trade*, 2.
[8] Oliver M. Dickerson, *The Navigation Acts and the American Revolution* (New York: A. S. Barnes & Company, 1963), 6.
[9] Langford, *Writings and Speeches*, IX, 516; 516n1.
[10] Listed as "Sheffield on the Trade of Ireland," in *Catalogue of the Library of Burke*, 20, 21, 33.

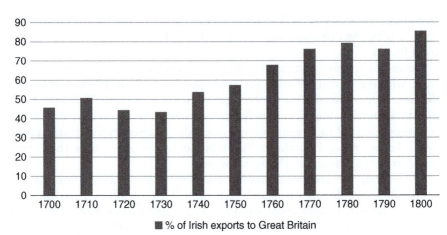

FIGURE 8.1 Percentage of total exports from Ireland traded to Great Britain, by decade
Source: Cullen (1968, 45)

time. Irish imports from Britain increased from around 54 percent of total imports at the beginning of the eighteenth century to more than 78 percent by 1800.[11] Britain progressively became the destination of Irish exports as well. "The most striking feature of Irish overseas trade in the eighteenth century is therefore the growing dependence on England," explains L. M. Cullen, "which provided a much bigger outlet for Irish exports than the limited markets on the European mainland."[12] Please consult Figure 8.1 for the percentage of exports from Ireland that reached Great Britain from 1700 to 1800.

Furthermore, consider the general growth of Anglo-Irish trade in the decades in which Burke emerged as a leading public figure, as captured in Figure 8.2. In essence, commercial relations between England and Ireland sprouted in Burke's day in the eighteenth century, even as industry interest groups persisted in lobbying the English and Irish parliaments to erect protectionist roadblocks to frustrate the ambitions of rival merchants.

Burke was keenly aware that the ascent of Anglo-Irish trade relations could be stunted by the pressures of mercantilism. As Richard Bourke has noted, the 1762 edition of the *Annual Register*, then under Burke's editorial direction, published a letter that presented both a vigorous statement in favor of free trade and a fierce attack on the mercantile system. "[T]he removal of obstacles is all that is necessary to the success of trade," the writer stated.[13] He praised the virtues of market freedom and chastised the idea that the study of economics could be reduced to the simplicities of an exact science. The context of the letter is important: the writer was responding to a 1750 work by Girolamo Belloni,

[11] Cullen, *Anglo-Irish Trade*, 46.   [12] Cullen, *Anglo-Irish Trade*, 46.
[13] *The Annual Register, of the Year 1762* (London: R. and J. Dodsley, 1763), 177.

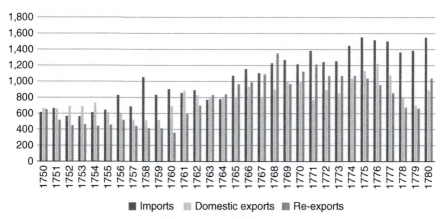

FIGURE 8.2 External trade of England and Wales with Ireland, 1750–1780 (in £ thousand)
Source: Mitchell (1988)

Del commercio dissertazione,[14] which reflected the mercantilist school of political economy. Belloni's dissertation had been published by the *Annual Register* in a previous issue. While every writing in the *Annual Register* did not necessarily match Burke's private beliefs, the publication of these two pieces in the journal suggests his attentiveness to the growing importance of questions relating to trade and commerce even before his entry into Parliament.[15]

Burke and Trade Early in the 1760s

Not only was Burke alert to the controversy over free trade in the 1760s, but he was also active in addressing Irish trade disputes prior to the start of his career in the House of Commons. On March 22, 1765, the body agreed to craft a bill restricting the number of Irish trade ports that could legally export wool and the number of English ports that could import it.[16] In a letter written to Henry Flood[17] in mid-May 1765, around eight months before he was seated in Parliament, Burke suggested that he aided Charles Townshend's efforts in Parliament to defeat the bill.

In his letter, Burke first criticized English traders who "rashly attributed"[18] the decline of English wool imports from Ireland to the illicit wool trade between Ireland and France. He then wrote:

[14] See Bourke, *Empire & Revolution*, 479.
[15] The 1764 edition of the *Annual Register* also reviewed Adam Anderson's *An Historical and Chronological Deduction of the Origin of Commerce* (London: A. Millar et al., 1764). See "Manners and Ethics as Preconditions for Commerce and the Scottish Enlightenment," Chapter 12.
[16] *Correspondence of Edmund Burke*, vol. I, 193n1.   [17] Flood was an Irish politician.
[18] Burke to Henry Flood, 18 May [1765], in *Correspondence of Edmund Burke*, vol. I, 193.

This Idea founded in an Ignorance of the Nature of the Irish Trade had weight with some persons; but the decreased import of Irish Wool and Yarn being accounted for, upon true and rational principles, in a Short memorial delivered to Mr Townshend; he saw at once into it with his usual Sagacity; and he has silenced this complaint at least for this Session.[19]

Burke may have written the "Short memorial" for Townshend himself. By referencing "Nature," he was insinuating that the decline in Irish wool exports to Britain could be attributed to the natural adjustments and readjustments of market forces. Notice also that Burke associated proponents of the illicit trade argument with ignorance and irrationality, while suggesting that his position opposing additional restrictions on Irish trade was grounded in truth and rationality. Such intimations about the moral basis of free trade will become more relevant later in this chapter in our discussion of the role of nature in Burke's economic thought.

In the end, the bill to limit the number of Irish trade ports was reconsidered by the House in March 1766, when Burke was seated in Parliament. He had an influential hand in defeating this second measure: Lord Charlemont reported to Flood that Burke "supported the cause of Ireland in the most masterly manner, and the bill was rejected."[20] Burke's reputation as an authority on matters of political economy – not to mention his knack for industry and attention to administrative detail – early in his political life illustrates why he was considered by a contemporary to be a "man of business" who was "deeply immersed in public affairs, commercial and political" upon entering Parliament.[21]

In his first parliamentary session in 1766, in addition to the Free Port Act, Burke endorsed additional measures that aimed to promote the commercial liberties of Ireland within the British Empire. One proposal would have encouraged the sugar trade by allowing Ireland to import the commodity directly from the West Indies. The second reform would have permitted Irish soap manufactures to be imported into Britain's settlements in America.[22] In light of the first measure, Burke asked O'Hara, in a letter sent in early March, to send him "some Arguments from those who are most intelligent relative to the direct import of English W. India Sugars into Ireland."[23]

Burke then conveyed to O'Hara his impatient disdain for undue commercial regulations. "The late regulations here were to shut out in a Civil way the Portuguese; but I think they have hurt the whole Trade," he claimed. "Cannot

---

[19] Burke to Henry Flood, 18 May [1765], in *Correspondence of Edmund Burke*, vol. I, 193.

[20] Thomas Rodd, ed., *Original Letters, Principally from Lord Charlemont, the Right Honorable Edmund Burke, William Pitt, Earl of Chatham, and Many Other Distinguished Noblemen and Gentlemen, to the Right Hon. Henry Flood* (London: J. Compton, 1820), 40.

[21] The Rev. Dr. Leland to Edmund Burke, 9 January 1766, in William and Bourke, *Correspondence of the Right Honourable Edmund Burke*, vol. I, 95.

[22] See *Journals of the House of Commons*, vol. 30 (London: H.M. Stationery Office, 1803), 825.

[23] Burke to Charles O'Hara, I, 4 March 1766, in *Correspondence of Edmund Burke*, vol. I, 240.

the good be kept and the bad part be rejected? The principles I remember, the details have passed away from my memory."[24] (Burke was most likely alluding to British legislation in 1765 that attempted to reduce fraud in the sugar trade.) This latter remark – "Cannot the good be kept and the bad part be rejected?" – bears an intriguing resemblance to his famous aphorism in the *Reflections* that a "state without the means of some change is without the means of its conservation."[25] Both quotations mark Burke's belief that selective modification of past practice could facilitate progress while preserving social order. In his engagement with commercial policy in the 1760s, however, Burke soon encountered the political potency of protectionist sympathies in England. He learned that English merchants engaged in the sugar trade to Ireland were intent on resisting the sugar measures, which would have stimulated market competition in their industry.

Burke turned his creative energies to the soap measure, a policy that did not command widespread backing in the House of Commons. In a letter he wrote to O'Hara on May 24, 1766, Burke said he made a "stren[u]ous, though an unsuccessfull one, for the Irish Sope Bill" on May 15.[26] He recognized that the brisk winds of political sentiment were blowing against him: "I debated *alone* for near an hour, with some sharp antagonists; I grew warm; and had a mind to divide the house on it."[27] Once Burke realized the strength of parliamentary opposition and the prospect of immediate defeat, he agreed to withdraw the motion until the next session.

Even in this single, seemingly insignificant instance, Burke's recounting of his legislative efforts unveils lessons about his approach to political economy that would become more transparent in his speeches over the Irish trade bills. In his fight in support of soap exports, Burke exhibited a willingness to advance the principle of free trade with Ireland even in the sharp teeth of acute parliamentary resistance – enough so that he was willing to split the House on the issue, as he admitted. In the letter to O'Hara, moreover, Burke claimed that House members told him that the soap export proposal was "new and serious."[28] This comment suggests not only that Burke was a chief advocate of the relaxation of commercial restrictions early in his parliamentary career, but that he was also recognized by his peers as an MP who proposed novel and substantive legislative measures on economic matters. Burke's entire engagement with questions of Irish political economy throughout his political life explains why he insisted, in 1785, that he had "endeavoured to make himself master of the nature, extent and produce of the Irish commerce, expenditure and revenue."[29]

[24] Burke to Charles O'Hara, I, 4 March 1766, in *Correspondence of Edmund Burke*, vol. I, 240.
[25] Langford, *Writings and Speeches*, VIII, 72.
[26] Burke to Charles O'Hara, 24 [May 1766], in *Correspondence of Edmund Burke*, vol. I, 254.
[27] Burke to Charles O'Hara, 24 [May 1766], in *Correspondence of Edmund Burke*, vol. I, 254.
[28] Burke to Charles O'Hara, 24 [May 1766], in *Correspondence of Edmund Burke*, vol. I, 254.
[29] Langford, *Writings and Speeches*, IX, 586.

8.3   THE IRISH TRADE BILLS AND TWO LETTERS ON THE TRADE
      OF IRELAND

These two considerations – Burke's quest to pursue free trade policies, even in
the face of bitter opposition, and his prominent role in doing so – acquired
visible form in his parliamentary activity during the Irish trade bill debates in the
late 1770s. At this time, the American war was inflicting serious harm on the
Irish economy, a consequence that stemmed from British limitations on
Americans' access to Irish exports and from Irish emigration. Irish
manufacturers were further banned from exporting woolen and glass
products and faced prohibitive duties on other goods, which diminished their
commercial opportunities to access British markets. In effect, the imperial might
of cumbersome regulations prevented Ireland from fully engaging in trade with
the American colonies, thereby shaking the confidence of Irish merchants and
escalating the nation's wrath toward Britain in the late 1770s. In this fraught
milieu, Irish merchants issued progressively vocal exhortations urging England
to ease the commercial restrictions in order to provide a jolt to Anglo-Irish and
American-Irish trade.

There remains another consideration of the time period that is essential for
understanding Burke's views and political activities on Irish trade. From 1774
to 1780 Burke represented Bristol, a lively center of trading activity inhabited
by prominent English merchants, who had built up a vast network of
commercial connections across North America and the West Indies
throughout the 1700s. At the start of the eighteenth century, Bristol had
emerged as the second-largest trading hub in England. Its population rose
from 20,000 in 1700 to more than 60,000 by 1801.[30] At the time of Burke's
tenure as representative, the city's electorate included approximately 5,000
freeholders and freemen.[31]

Although the city's stature declined relative to other English cities
throughout the century, it still retained formidable commercial power at the
time Burke served as its representative. Yet in the 1770s, Bristol merchants, like
Irish dealers, were not immune from the negative impact of the American war
on English commerce. Their anxieties were further roused by the prospect of
relaxing trade laws, which, in their judgment, would threaten their competitive
market advantages, a belief shared by other English dealers as well. It came as
no surprise, then, that Bristol merchants supported the preservation of the
commercial restrictions limiting the scope of Irish manufactures.

---

[30] W. E. Minchinton, ed., *The Trade of Bristol in the Eighteenth Century*, vol. 20 (Bristol: Bristol
Record Society, 1966), ix. In the mid-eighteen century, the population hovered between 43,000
and 44,000. See John Latimer, *The Annals of Bristol in the Eighteenth Century* (Bristol: Butler &
Tanner, 1893), 292. Cone puts the figure at 75,000 during Burke's service as elected representative of the city (*Age of the American Revolution*, 268).

[31] P. T. Underdown, "Edmund Burke, the Commissary of His Bristol Constituents, 1774–1780,"
The English Historical Review 73 (1958): 252.

"Throughout the 18th century Bristol merchants were as determined as the nation at large that Ireland should be kept in a subordinate position," W. E. Minchinton writes.[32]

Burke did not surrender to such mercantile desires for protectionism. In Parliament, he was an early supporter of the proposal from Lord Nugent, an Irish landlord, on April 2, 1778 to form a committee to discuss the question of Anglo-Irish trade relations.[33] Burke "spoke for some time"[34] in support of Nugent's proposal. He maintained that "it particularly behoved this country to admit the Irish nation to the privileges of British citizens."[35] Because Ireland was the "chief dependency"[36] of the British monarchy, he said, it would benefit Britain to grant the nation similar advantages. Such comments were early signs during the Irish trade bill debates of Burke's attempt to demonstrate that freer commercial intercourse would promote a synthesis of interest between Ireland and Britain.

Burke did not stop there in his campaign for the emancipation of commerce in the spring of 1778. During a House debate on April 7 that discussed Irish trade, Burke, according to the *London Evening Post*, "took a much more enlarged view of the subject than the motion included: he wished to give Ireland a substantial, and not a seeming good, by giving them at once a free manufacture and export of every thing."[37] By calling for "substantial" commercial reform, Burke was indicating that his ultimate aim during deliberation over the trade bills was not piecemeal modification but bold action in the pursuit of liberal commerce.

Two days later, on April 9, in the midst of House negotiations over five resolutions tendered by the Committee on Irish Trade, Burke proposed an important amendment to the first resolution. It would have enabled Ireland to export goods directly to the colonies that had initially been purchased legally from Britain and foreign countries.[38] After Burke offered the amendment, Benjamin Allen "cast an oblique reflection" on him "for his hurry in this business," according to the *London Evening Post*.[39] Burke's response to Allen's gesture supplies an additional clue about the reasons behind his avid support for free trade during parliamentary deliberation: "The stirring of interest could alone produce the harmony he wished, and if he could not play successfully on that, he despaired of his end."[40] In his reference to a "stirring of interest," Burke was intimating that his strategy of political persuasion during the Irish trade debate was to tap into the self-interest of both Irish and British traders in order to show

[32] W. E. Minchinton, ed., *Politics and the Port of Bristol in the Eighteenth Century: The Petitions of the Society of Merchant Venturers 1698–1803*, vol. 23 (Bristol: Bristol Record Society, 1963), xxxii.

[33] Langford, *Writings and Speeches*, IX, 504.   [34] Langford, *Writings and Speeches*, IX, 504.

[35] Langford, *Writings and Speeches*, IX, 504.   [36] Langford, *Writings and Speeches*, IX, 504.

[37] Langford, *Writings and Speeches*, IX, 504–505.

[38] Langford, *Writings and Speeches*, IX, 505–506.

[39] Langford, *Writings and Speeches*, IX, 506n2.   [40] Langford, *Writings and Speeches*, IX, 506.

that free trade would benefit both parties and occasion a self-perpetuating unity. Put differently, Burke was summoning the principle of cooperative reciprocity in the context of foreign commerce, the same idea that would later inspire his discussion of farmer-laborer relations in *Thoughts and Details*.

Two Letters on the Trade of Ireland

Burke elaborated on the theme of reciprocity in *Two Letters on the Trade of Ireland*, which was published on May 12, 1778. He wrote *Two Letters* in response to Bristol merchants who objected to the reduction of commercial restrictions between Ireland and England. Samuel Span, acting as the representative of the Society of Merchant Adventurers of Bristol, an organization of prominent traders in the city, had written Burke four days after Burke's amendment on April 9 to express his displeasure over the parliamentary resolutions calling for the trade concessions. On April 27, Harford, Cowles & Co., a group of iron manufacturers, also wrote Burke to voice their staunch opposition to the bills.[41] These groups believed that the relaxation of Irish trade regulations would introduce unwelcome competition into transatlantic commerce, in turn draining the power of English merchants.

Two Letters contains Burke's most comprehensive remarks on free trade. The writings do not come close to matching the breadth and depth of Adam Smith's *Wealth of Nations*, but they do construct a sturdy theoretical frame for Burke's legislative activities in support of liberal commerce that had remained underdeveloped in his prior speeches and writings on the Free Port Act of 1766 and Anglo-American relations. The letters lie at the bountiful convergence of Burke's economic thought and his trustee theory of representation, reflecting a blend of commercial principle and prudential statesmanship that came to define a core dimension of Burke's political life.

In addition, even though *Two Letters* addresses foreign trade, its arguments reflect underlying maxims that Burke would later convey in *Thoughts and Details* in his discourse on the internal grain industry: a harmony of interest arises from the individual pursuit of commerce; voluntary exchange is not a zero-sum activity; and mutual trade can infuse a spirit of political conciliation and social communion into all its participants. These themes will now be examined.

First, Burke's argument in favor of trade reductions in *Two Letters* is based on the virtue of a collective identity of interest between two trading parties – an idea similar to his response to Benjamin Allen, and to his argument in *Thoughts and Details*, that consensual market exchange is the trigger for mutual advantage between the farmer and the laborer. "[J]ustice to others is not

---

[41] See Langford, *Writings and Speeches*, IX, 506–507.

always folly to ourselves," he writes to Span.[42] Even more, "[Y]ou trade very largely where you are met by the goods of all nations."[43] Burke stresses this point: "We cannot be insensible of the calamities which have been brought upon this nation by an obstinate adherence to narrow and restrictive plans of government,"[44] referring to the regulations limiting commercial intercourse between Ireland and England. As Burke wrote in a letter to Span two weeks before the publication of *Two Letters*, "The prosperity arising from an enlarged and liberal system improves all its objects: and the participation of a trade with flourishing Countries is much better than the monopoly of want and penury."[45]

Burke's idea of a unity of interest illuminates a cornerstone of his economic thought: voluntary trade relations do not spawn zero-sum transactions but instead spread gifts to both parties. He writes in *Two Letters*, "[It] is but too natural for us to see our own *certain* ruin, in the *possible* prosperity of other people. It is hard to persuade us, that every thing which is *got* by another is not *taken* from ourselves."[46] He continues: "Trade is not a limited thing; as if the objects of mutual demand and consumption, could not stretch beyond the bounds of our Jealousies."[47] As Burke explains,

[I]f Ireland is beneficial to you, it is so, not from the parts in which it is restrained; but from those in which it is left free, though not unrivalled. The greater its freedom, the greater must be your advantage. If you should lose in one way, you will gain in twenty.[48]

Irish liberties exercised in a trial of market competition will produce advantages for England as well as for Ireland. Burke here is trying to invert the argument posed by Span and Bristol merchants that English traders would be harmed by the appearance of Irish goods in English markets. In Burke's view, such traders would profit from additional mercantile activity, because what would be gained by one party would not be lost by the other.

Before proceeding, we should note that Burke's refutation of zero-sum thinking applied to commercial enterprise beyond Anglo-Irish and Anglo-American trade relations. In *Speech on St Eustatius*, given three years after *Two Letters*, he insisted that the trading activities of the Dutch island of St. Eustatius, a cosmopolitan merchant community, advantaged all dealers.[49] In the speech, he first asserted a principle of free trade: "The merchant does not

---

[42] Langford, *Writings and Speeches*, IX, 507.   [43] Langford, *Writings and Speeches*, IX, 511.

[44] Langford, *Writings and Speeches*, IX, 508.

[45] Burke to Samuel Span, [9] April 1778, in George H. Guttridge, ed., *The Correspondence of Edmund Burke*, vol. III, *July 1774–June 1778* (Cambridge: Cambridge University Press, 1961), 426.

[46] Langford, *Writings and Speeches*, IX, 514.

[47] Langford, *Writings and Speeches*, IX, 514–515.

[48] Langford, *Writings and Speeches*, IX, 517.

[49] The *Account of the European Settlements* discusses how the Dutch turned the island into an area of industry and commerce. See vol. II, 54–55.

carry his goods to a place to lay them up, but to sell them."[50] St. Eustatius in particular was a shining model in promoting trade. "[I]t was the known, established, and admired principle of St Eustatius to be a mart for all the world, and consequently equally advantageous to us as to the enemy," he observed.[51] Foreign merchants, including those from Britain and its economic rivals, the Dutch, profited from the global vibrancy of undisturbed commerce. Yet to Burke's dismay, Britain had waged war on the island in February 1781, which offended the principle of neutral trade and unsettled the flow of goods and naval stores.[52]

In the case of the Irish trade bills, Burke suggests that the trade concessions were also equitable because, rather than granting individual benefits to Ireland, they were simply removing arbitrary commercial entanglements. "Do we in these resolutions *bestow* any thing upon Ireland? Not a shilling," Burke avers. "We only consent to *leave* to them, in two or three instances, the use of the natural faculties which God has given to them, and to all mankind."[53] The reduction of trade barriers secured the conditions for a fair playing field. Establishing free commercial intercourse did not require the dispensation of financial rewards to Ireland, but rather the prohibition of instruments that squeezed the country's capacities to produce goods.

The Relation between Free Trade and Politics

At its most basic level, Burke's contention that free trade created mutual advantages was an economic argument. There remains a deeper philosophical implication to this claim, however, that casts light on an essential theoretical question motivating this book: how does Burke understand the connection between politics and economics? In the case of free trade, Burke attempts to explain in *Two Letters* how political relations between parties, such as England and Ireland, could improve by the encouragement of free economic activity.

Burke conveys this point by showing how the softening of commercial restrictions would remove the need for the British government to exercise its raw power over Ireland. "God forbid, that our conduct should demonstrate to the world, that Great Britain can, in no instance whatsoever, be brought to a sense of rational and equitable policy, but by coercion and force of arms!" he writes.[54] The thick breath of Britain in Ireland suffocated the industrious talents of the Irish, paving a sinister path for their unpitied oppression. "The Military force, which shall be kept up in order to cramp the natural faculties of a people, and to prevent their arrival to their utmost prosperity," Burke writes, "is the instrument of their Servitude, not the means of their protection."[55] Commercial

---

[50] Langford, *Writings and Speeches*, IV, 82.   [51] Langford, *Writings and Speeches*, IV, 82.
[52] Consult Marshall, *Edmund Burke & the British Empire in the West Indies*, 140–154.
[53] Langford, *Writings and Speeches*, IX, 509.   [54] Langford, *Writings and Speeches*, IX, 509.
[55] Langford, *Writings and Speeches*, IX, 515.

trafficking could diminish this reliance on military muscle and help sustain Anglo-Irish political relations on a more reciprocal and less coercive basis.

Free trade, in Burke's view, would also relax the charged feelings of jealousy and envy springing from the hearts of traders. Recall his earlier comment that laid doubt on the idea that commerce "could not stretch beyond the bounds of our Jealousies."[56] And remember his remark in the *Short Account* that the Free Port Act "allayed and composed" the "Passions and Animosities" of North American and West Indian colonial traders.[57] He repeats this point multiple times in *Two Letters*. Burke outlines the salutary impact of Scotland's trading activities in the British Empire to disclose the mediating power of free commercial relations. In presenting this argument in the letters, he first underscores his repudiation of zero-sum economic thinking: "[I]f Scotland, instead of paying little [into Britain's public coffers], had paid nothing at all, we should be gainers, not losers by acquiring the hearty co-operation of an active intelligent people, towards the increase of the common stock."[58]

Burke then remarks that such cooperation was a far better option than another scenario in which a zero-sum commercial brawl would be provoked by mercantile envy. This alternative would be "our being employed in watching and counteracting them, and their being employed in watching and counteracting us, with the peevish and churlish jealousy of rivals and enemies on both sides."[59] In his concluding thoughts in his letter on May 2, Burke draws attention to similar apprehensions behind the campaign to frustrate Irish competition: "[I]f our Jealousies were to be converted into Politicks as systematically as some would have them, the Trade of Ireland would vanish out of the System of Commerce."[60]

According to Burke, then, one fundamental connection between politics and economics was that the impact of commercial exchange extended beyond the boundaries of material gain; trade held a *social* purpose as well, converting envious rivals into communal partners serving the greater good. Burke summons this principle even when questioning the idea at the time for union between Great Britain and Ireland: "Until it can be matured into a feasible and desirable scheme, I wish to have as close an union of interest and affection with Ireland, as I can have."[61] In regard to the two nations, Burke regrets that it "is very unfortunate, that we should consider those as Rivals, whom we ought to regard as fellow labourers in a common Cause."[62]

One year later, a measure – originally drafted by Lord Camden but amended significantly by Burke – introduced by Rockingham in the House of Lords in May 1779 called for the king to consider the grievances of the Irish and to plan trade measures that "may enable the National Wisdom to pursue effectual

---

[56] Langford, *Writings and Speeches*, IX, 514–515.
[57] Langford, *Writings and Speeches*, II, 55–56.   [58] Langford, *Writings and Speeches*, IX, 511.
[59] Langford, *Writings and Speeches*, IX, 511.   [60] Langford, *Writings and Speeches*, IX, 517.
[61] Langford, *Writings and Speeches*, IX, 510.   [62] Langford, *Writings and Speeches*, IX, 517.

methods for promoting the common strength, wealth and commerce of his Majesties Subjects in both Kingdoms."[63] Voluntary trade builds up common affections and interests that give rise to imperial unity.

In this context, Burke's approach to Anglo-Irish trade veers toward the Scottish Enlightenment's irenic view on commerce,[64] captured famously by Montesquieu's *doux commerce* (gentle trade) thesis,[65] and is a forerunner to Hayek's notion of catallaxy.[66] This pattern of thought posited that economic exchange guided competing trading interests toward social harmony. As Hayek observed, one meaning of the ancient Greek word of *katallattein*, or *katallassein*, the etymological basis for catallaxy, was "to change from enemy into friend."[67]

As we shall learn, Burke was quite aware of the limits of the *doux commerce* thesis; and we should also note the growing body of literature that has explored the Scottish thinkers' and Montesquieu's nuanced understanding of the concept as well.[68] In addition, taken in its fullest dimensions, Burke's economic thought was not identical to the Scots' and Hayek's attitudes toward commerce.[69] At the very least, however, we may conclude that Burke's reasoning specific to *Two Letters* rests on a notion similar to Hayek's idea of catallaxy and the Scots' embrace of trade: the invigoration of commerce can be a tool to reduce social tensions and build new attachments between peoples and nations.

Two Letters and History

The idea that commerce, and not coercive force, could serve as a reconciling instrument between political competitors was especially pertinent in the late 1770s, as Irish sentiments at the time were stirred by the resistance of American

---

[63] Langford, *Writings and Speeches*, III, 437.
[64] Consult Christopher J. Berry, *The Idea of Commercial Society in the Scottish Enlightenment* (Edinburgh: Edinburgh University Press, 2015).
[65] Albert O. Hirschman, *The Passions and the Interests: Political Arguments for Capitalism before Its Triumph* (Princeton and Oxford: Princeton University Press, 2013).
[66] F. A. Hayek, *Law, Legislation, and Liberty*, vol. II, *The Mirage of Social Justice* (Chicago: The University of Chicago Press, 1976), 107–132.
[67] Hayek, *Mirage of Social Justice*, 108.
[68] See, e.g., Andrew Wyatt-Walter, "Adam Smith and the Liberal Tradition in International Relations," *Review of International Studies* 22 (1996): 5–28; Maria Pia Paganelli and Reinhard Schumacher, "Do Not Take Peace for Granted: Adam Smith's Warning on the Relation between Commerce and War," *Cambridge Journal of Economics* 43 (2019): 785–797; Rob Goodman, "*Doux Commerce*, Jew Commerce: Intolerance and Tolerance in Voltaire and Montesquieu," *History of Political Thought* 37 (2016): 530–555; and Samuel Gregg, "Trade, Nations, and War in an Enlightened Age," *Law & Liberty*, November 15, 2018, www.lawliberty.org/2018/11/15/trade-nations-and-war-in-an-enlightened-age/.
[69] See "Manners and Ethics as Preconditions for Commerce and the Scottish Enlightenment," Chapter 12.

colonists to the British Empire. In addition, since the early 1600s, when large numbers of Irish settlers started emigrating to the North American colonies, a growing transatlantic connection had emerged between the Americans and the Irish.[70] Mindful of these extenuating considerations as well, Burke hoped that the Irish trade concessions would cool Irish attitudes desiring greater political independence, and, hopefully, limit the prospect of Irish rebellion.

These historical contingencies should alert us to the broader political context of *Two Letters*. Even though they represent Burke's most complete statement on his conception of free trade, and even though he harbored genuine sympathy toward Ireland, they also reflected his mission to advance the national interests of the British Empire. This is the case for a number of reasons. First, as noted, Burke endeavors to stress in *Two Letters* that vibrant commercial intercourse between England and Ireland would serve the aims of English citizens. As he tells Span and other Bristol merchants, "It is *for* you, and *for* your Interest, as a dear, cherished, and respected part, of a valuable whole, that I have taken my share in this question"[71] of Irish free trade. By appealing to the power of self-interest, Burke was deploying a clever rhetorical strategy to disarm Bristol traders resistant to the contraction of trade regulations.

Second, the British Empire was facing an emerging geopolitical threat at the time Burke drafted *Two Letters*: the ascendant alliance between France and the United States. The two countries had signed the Treaty of Alliance and Treaty of Amity and Commerce on February 6, 1778, only two months before Burke would direct his attention to the Irish trade bills. The latter treaty implicitly recognized the independence of the United States and formed a new commercial pact to compete with Britain's Navigation Acts.[72] (The former treaty pledged mutual military assistance.) Securing the strength of the British Empire, then, acquired even greater urgency in the backdrop of such fluid historical circumstances that offered possible advantages to English rivals at the expense of British imperial influence.

Practical Arguments

Beyond these wider considerations, Burke submits more practical arguments in *Two Letters* and his Irish trade bill speeches that address the specific concerns put forward by critics of the legislation. One such objection was that Ireland did not deserve to reap the benefits of commercial trade because it did not contribute its fair share of taxes to the Exchequer. Burke responds by first claiming that Ireland paid as many taxes as it could afford. Then he writes that Ireland should be granted the gift of greater commercial freedom before it should be expected to pay more taxes to the Exchequer. "Ireland pays as many

---

[70] See Bourke, *Empire & Revolution*, 390–391.   [71] Langford, *Writings and Speeches*, IX, 514.
[72] See Richard Dean Burns, Joseph M. Siracusa, and Jason C. Flanagan, *American Foreign Relations since Independence* (Santa Barbara, CA: ABC-CLIO, 2013), 4–5.

taxes, as those who are the best judges of her powers, are of opinion she can bear," he states. "To bear more she must have more ability; and in the order of nature, the advantage must *precede* the charge."[73]

Burke reinforced this argument in his May 6 speech on Irish trade. Ireland, he observes in the speech, was taxed disproportionately more than England, even though Ireland was poorer than England. Using the measure of "internal opulence and external advantage" and not population size, Ireland "is taxed in a quadruple proportion more than England."[74] Thus "[s]he is taxed, without enjoying the means of payment."[75] Ireland is "restricted from trading," thereby having "no opportunity of acquiring wealth to defray and discharge the taxes imposed upon her."[76] Latent in these remarks is Burke's belief that a people with confined liberties could, and should, not be expected to fully meet their political responsibilities when they did not possess sufficient autonomy to do so.

Burke further attempted to assuage the unease of English manufacturers concerned about the perceived danger of cheap Irish labor to the British economy. Until the price of labor was equal, he contends in his May 6 speech, England would retain its superior manufacturing advantages, because high-wage labor signaled that the condition of manufacturing capacities was healthy and vibrant. "The price of labour rises with the growth of manufacture, and is highest when the manufacture is best," Burke says.[77] A telling constancy weaves together this position and his reflections on British and French economies in the *Observations* and on farmer-laborer relations in *Thoughts and Details*: high wages correspond with industry, not indolence, an insight that remained at odds with contemporary strands of mercantilist thinking.[78] As noted in Chapter 2, Burke also declares in his May 6 speech that "where the price of labour is highest, the manufacture is able to sell his commodity at the lowest price."[79] Growing wages spell the reduction of costs and the expansion of commerce.

Burke presents another rationalization of the Irish trade bills by arguing that the anxieties of British merchants about the sailcloth trade were unfounded. Two days after he wrote his letter to the merchants of Harford, Cowles & Co., Burke proposed in Parliament to remove British import duties on Irish cordage and sailcloth.[80] This was the fifth resolution offered by the Committee on Irish Trade. Somerset merchants involved in the sailcloth industry feared that the measure would squeeze their commercial activities because it would awaken the energies of Irish competitors. English traders

---

[73] Langford, *Writings and Speeches*, IX, 510.   [74] Langford, *Writings and Speeches*, IX, 521.
[75] Langford, *Writings and Speeches*, IX, 521.   [76] Langford, *Writings and Speeches*, IX, 521.
[77] Langford, *Writings and Speeches*, IX, 522.
[78] See "The Laws of Supply and Demand, Wages, and Price Theory," Chapter 2.
[79] Langford, *Writings and Speeches*, IX, 522.   [80] Langford, *Writings and Speeches*, IX, 518.

would be forced to sacrifice "this important branch of trade," according to a petition drafted by the Somerset activists.[81]

Yet the free duties already existed. Perhaps Burke already knew this when he proposed the fifth resolution; perhaps not.[82] Once the sailcloth privilege was discovered, however, Burke pointed out that the fears of the Somerset petitioners had not come to fruition. In a May 4 speech, Burke proclaimed that their "preposterous apprehension" was "founded merely on the basis of imagination, and not the ground plot of reality."[83] Additionally, "[I]t was facetious to see that they felt occasion for fear at the idea, though they had not been injured by the reality."[84]

Burke sharpened this line of reasoning two days later in regard to sailcloth and iron. British merchants feared that the free exportation of iron would threaten their iron trade. English traders "had not felt from the reality, what they dreaded from the idea, for an act existed at this time permitting the free exportation of manufactured iron, which, however, had not been prosecuted, because of the advantages enjoyed by the English."[85] Burke here attempts to draw attention to the gap between the apprehensions of English traders and the benign consequences of a free sailcloth and iron trade, demonstrating that theoretical propositions did not necessarily reflect unfolding historical realities. This insight anticipates his more famous commentary in the *Reflections* that highlighted the vast gulf between abstract ideology and experience in shaping the growth of civilization.

The crux of Burke's reform efforts was to establish a system of commercial intercourse that would benefit Anglo-Irish welfare, and England in particular. Two years after the trade bill debates, he confided to Thomas Burgh:

[T]hat to which I attached myself the most particularly was, to fix the principle of a free trade in all the parts of these islands, as founded in justice, and beneficial to the whole, but principally to this seat of the supreme power; and this I laboured to the utmost of my might, upon general principles, illustrated by all the commercial detail with which my little enquiries in life were able to furnish me.[86]

Notice that Burke associates free trade with the diffusion of fruits to the many. England would obtain advantages, not disadvantages, from the relaxation of commercial restrictions impacting its imperial subjects, suggesting that the promotion of free commerce was rooted in a sense of justice. (And we should not ignore his subtle affirmation in these remarks of

---

[81] Langford, *Writings and Speeches*, IX, 518.

[82] Thomas H. D. Mahoney conjectures that Burke set a trap for his trading constituents who opposed free trade. See Mahoney, *Edmund Burke and Ireland* (Cambridge, MA: Harvard University Press, 1960), 77–78. F. P. Lock is skeptical of this interpretation. See Lock, *Edmund Burke*, vol. I, 428–429n92.

[83] Langford, *Writings and Speeches*, IX, 518.   [84] Langford, *Writings and Speeches*, IX, 518.

[85] Langford, *Writings and Speeches*, IX, 522.

[86] Langford, *Writings and Speeches*, IX, 549–550.

his engagement with economic matters: his "little enquiries" provided "commercial detail.")

Burke appeared to project some influence in his support for the bill permitting Ireland to import colonial goods. The legislation achieved a second reading by a vote of 126 to 77. Overall, however, the Irish trade resolutions were watered down by compromise measures. Ireland gained permission to directly export goods to the colonies, with specific articles excluded, and to trade Irish cotton yarn to Britain without duties.[87] The resolutions led to slightly more commercial freedom in the West Indian and African trades and in the linen industry, especially in the checked linen trade.[88]

Burke's reasoning on behalf of the Irish trade bills attracted the ears of other MPs. Henry Dundas conceded that, after first opposing them, he had been convinced by Burke of the merits of the bills:

[A]fter attending for several days to the subject [of Irish trade], he had been converted in the course of the last session, by the solid reasonings of the hon. gentleman who had spoke some time since (Mr. Burke) and from thence forward, he could safely affirm, he never uttered a sentence, nor gave a single vote contrary to what fell on that occasion, from the hon. gentleman.[89]

According to Burke, at least twenty other MPs told him they were similarly moved by his arguments in support of the resolutions.[90]

Ironically, although Burke holds a reputation as a prudent statesman, he may have acted imprudently in his quest in the House of Commons to help pass the Irish trade bills. He and other MPs failed to accurately assess the mood of public (or at least mercantile) opinion in Bristol and other trading cities in the late 1770s, which regarded the commercial concessions to Ireland with deep suspicion. English merchants were still burdened by the American war. Perhaps if Burke, at the start of discussion over the bills in April 1778, had pushed the Committee on Irish Trade to introduce a more limited series of resolutions, instead of five resolutions, English traders might have displayed a greater willingness to support the slow expansion of commercial liberties in Ireland. Mercantile opposition to the bills was fierce, however, so it was unlikely dealers would have firmly embraced any significant trade concession, plus Burke himself despised haphazard legislative proposals unguided by regularity of form. Still, the swift movement by Burke and other free trade advocates in the House to advance the resolutions lacked a measure of tactical wisdom. Furthermore, while Burke's zealous support for the Irish trade bills

---

[87] Langford, *Writings and Speeches*, IX, 401.
[88] "The History of Europe," *The Annual Register, For the Year 1778* (London: J. Dodsley, 1779), 192. See also Mahoney, *Edmund Burke and Ireland*, 75–92.
[89] *Cobbett's Parliamentary History of England*, vol. XX, *Comprising the Period from the Seventh of December 1778, to the Tenth of February 1780* (London: T. C. Hansard, 1814), 1215.
[90] Langford, *Writings and Speeches*, IX, 550.

was not the sole reason why he decided to terminate his reelection campaign for Bristol in 1780, it most likely did not help his cause.[91]

Two Letters and Bristol Trade

One principal weakness of *Two Letters* is that Burke does not seriously engage possible objections to his assertions about the advantages of free trade. Would particular industries witness a reduction in employment in the trades that were hurt by the commercial concessions? What psychological effect would such job losses have on unemployed manufacturers? Would Burke convey the same degree of sympathy for free trade if he were a Bristol trader and faced the prospect of Irish competition? Did not the business community's argument that its trade would be injured have *some* merit?[92] He does not offer satisfying answers to these questions.

The reality is that Burke understated the difficulties of Bristol trade following the closure of the North American markets during the American war in the 1770s. There was almost a 42 percent reduction in the annual volume of transatlantic shipping received in Bristol from 1773–1777 to 1778–1780. (Please see Figure 8.3.) This was the lowest such volume since the War of the Austrian Succession more than two decades prior. Even though Bristol traders continued to trade modestly with merchants in Philadelphia, Charleston, and New York City, only fifteen American colonial ships entered Bristol ports between 1776 and 1780.[93]

Given Burke's insistence that he was a shrewd student of political economy, surely he could have acknowledged these developing empirical realities, if only to attempt to rebut them. In fact, this recognition might have occasioned an opportunity for him to articulate a larger persuasive argument about free trade in the eighteenth century that he hints at but does not fully explicate: even with short-term commercial fluctuations, vigorous trade tended to advantage most dealers in the *long run*. Indeed, the annual volume of ship cargo entering Bristol surpassed the city's yearly amount before the American war by the late 1780s at the latest, as evidenced by Figure 8.3.

We should be careful not to cast an unreasonable measure of critical judgment upon historical figures for particular imperfections in their

---

[91] Burke withdrew from the Bristol electoral contest in 1780 after six years as the city's MP. Intraparty Whig rivalries and other factors, rather than simply Burke's controversial position on free trade, may have ultimately contributed to his loss of political support. See I. R. Christie, "Henry Cruger and the End of Edmund Burke's Connection with Bristol," *Transactions of the Bristol and Gloucestershire Archaeological Society* 74 (1955): 153–170.

[92] In a 1780 letter to Thomas Burgh, an MP in the Irish Parliament, Burke does briefly acknowledge that MPs who opposed the Irish trade bills because of political pressures stemmed from constituents' "ideas, which, though I do not always follow, I can never blame" (Langford, *Writings and Speeches*, IX, 551).

[93] Kenneth Morgan, *Bristol and the Atlantic Trade in the Eighteenth Century* (Cambridge: Cambridge University Press, 1993), 25.

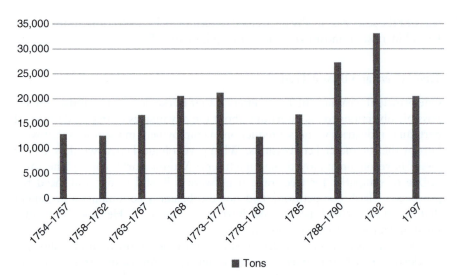

FIGURE 8.3 Ships entering Bristol from transatlantic destinations, 1754–1797 (annual averages, in tons)
Source: Morgan (1993, 14)

arguments. But it is somewhat surprising that for someone so serious about the study of political economy, Burke did not lay sharper emphasis in *Two Letters* on the probable triumph of long-term gains over short-term losses as a salutary effect of the trade concessions.

Burke as a "Disciple" of Smith

Burke's *Two Letters* were written only two years after Adam Smith published the *Wealth of Nations*, the most famous discourse written in the eighteenth century – and perhaps ever – on the malign effects of mercantilism in the wider commercial order. In this light, it is tempting to ascribe Burke's economic views in part to the influence of Smith's advocacy of free trade in the text, as scholars have done in tracing the free trade sympathies of Lord Shelburne and William Pitt the Younger in the eighteenth century to Smith's work.[94]

Scholars have thus attributed Burke's views on political economy to Smith as well. "[T]here is little doubt that Burke regarded himself, and was regarded by others, as a disciple of Smith, a proponent of free trade and a free market

---

[94] For Shelburne, see Rae, *Life of Adam Smith*, 153–154. For Pitt, see Jennifer Mori, "The Political Theory of William Pitt the Younger," *History* 83 (1998): 234–248; and Eric J. Evans, *William Pitt the Younger* (London and New York: Routledge, 1999), 28. See also Kirk Willis, "The Role in Parliament of the Economic Ideas of Adam Smith, 1776–1800," *History of Political Economy* 11 (1979): 505–544.

economy," Gertrude Himmelfarb writes, typifying a view stated often by others.[95] This trend dates all the way back to the initial publication of *Thoughts and Details* in 1800. In its brief review of the economic tract that year, *The Gentleman's Magazine* asserted that Burke "proceed[ed] on the principles of Dr. Adam Smith, that all trade should be free; and that government should not interfere by compulsory acts and regulations, particularly in grain and agriculture."[96]

The assumption that Burke was a disciple of Smith requires serious revision, however. Donal Barrington has provided the strongest rebuttal to this argument to date, and other scholars have made remarks questioning the influence of Smith on Burke, but allow us to review the evidence in greater detail.[97] As this book has demonstrated, Burke communicated a belief in the virtues of commercial liberty prior to the publication of the *Wealth of Nations* in 1776, as exemplified by *An Account of the European Settlements*; his efforts working for Charles Townshend and in his first parliamentary session promoting Irish free trade in 1765 and 1766; his advocacy on behalf of the Free Port Act in 1766, in which he asserted (with slight exaggeration) that the North American and West Indian trading interests were "perfectly reconciled"[98]; and his arguments in the *Observations*, *Speech on American Taxation*, and *Speech on Conciliation* that called for limited and selective economic regulations.[99] In these writings and legislative activities, Burke presented themes that the *Wealth of Nations* would later elucidate and amplify: commerce promotes a unity of interest between seeming adversaries; a balance of trade does not necessarily favor the home country; an excess of trade entanglements hampers public opulence; the disturbance of the natural laws of commerce obstructs the smooth allocation of scarce resources; national policy should not be dictated by the parochial

---

[95] Gertrude Himmelfarb, *The Roads to Modernity: The British, French, and American Enlightenments* (New York: Alfred A. Knopf, 2005), 73. Frank Petrella, Jr. argues that their relationship was one of "master and disciple" – Smith being the master and Burke the disciple (Petrella, "Edmund Burke and Classical Economics," 4). Elie Halévy contends that Burke, along with Jeremy Bentham, were among the "chief" disciples of Smith (Halévy, *The Growth of Philosophic Radicalism*, trans. Mary Morris (New York: The Macmillan Company, 1928), 230). Alfred Cobban maintains that the "theories of Adam Smith and the Physiocrats," as well as other influences, helped "dictate his economic modes of thought" (*Edmund Burke and the Revolt against the Eighteenth Century*, 196). William Clyde Dunn claims, "There is much of Smithian economics in Edmund Burke" ("Adam Smith and Edmund Burke," 343).

[96] *The Gentleman's Magazine*, vol. 70 (London: Nichols and Son, 1800), 1270.

[97] For Donal Barrington, see his article "Edmund Burke as an Economist," *Economica* 21 (1954): 252–258. Also see Winch, "Burke-Smith Problem," 238; and Robert H. Murray, *Edmund Burke: A Biography* (Oxford: Oxford University Press, 1931), 258. Barrington, however, does not address much of the material I outline in this book as evidence of Burke's support for market economies prior to his direct exposure to Smith, including Burke's influential role in promoting the Free Port Act and the 1772 repeal of middlemen trading practices.

[98] Langford, *Writings and Speeches*, II, 55.

[99] Admittedly, Burke's position on Anglo-American relations was not the same as Smith's. Smith expressed a greater desire for Britain to relinquish its American dependencies.

interests of select merchants; wealth redistribution is harmful and counterproductive; high wages are evidence of industry and vigor; and market economies constantly shift in accord with the changing nature of supply and demand.

Even more, Burke's concept of the Invisible Hand[100] – his "benign and wise disposer of all things"[101] – made a distinctive appearance in his writings and legislative activities years before his first reported contact with Smith. In *Tracts relating to Popery Laws*, which Burke most likely drafted in the early to mid-1760s, he praised "laudable avarice" for serving as the stimulus of human effort for the long-term amelioration of land, a remark made over a decade prior to the publication of the *Wealth of Nations*.[102] Similarly, in 1772, Burke promoted the spirit of laudable avarice by orchestrating the repeal of bans against middlemen trading practices, an endeavor that predated Smith's attack on the prohibitions in the *Wealth of Nations* by four years.

These insights were by no means unique to Burke in the first three quarters of the eighteenth century. The general idea that private initiative could promote the common good was famously captured by Bernard Mandeville in *The Fable of the Bees* in the early eighteenth century (although Mandeville's conception was not synonymous with Burke's and Smith's notion of an Invisible Hand-type phenomenon).[103] And, of course, neither Burke nor Smith were the only thinkers to discuss the merits of liberal trade in the eighteenth century.

Yet historical evidence does not suggest that Burke initially accessed such wisdom into the science of political economy from Smith's *Wealth of Nations*. The earliest known letter between Burke and Smith is dated 10 September 1759, in which Burke praised the *Theory of Moral Sentiments*.[104] Smith did refer to an "invisible hand" in the *Theory*,[105] so it is possible Burke adopted this concept from him, although there is no indication on Burke's part that he did so. In addition, no surviving letter remains between the two thinkers that examines economic principles in depth. Burke's library did include the *Wealth of Nations*,[106] and many of the ideas in the text had been discussed by Smith in his lectures on jurisprudence in the 1760s, but there is no available proof

---

[100] In the *Wealth of Nations*, Smith famously writes, "It is not from the benevolence of the butcher, the brewer, or the baker, that we expect our dinner, but from their regard to their own interest" (vol. I, 26–27).

[101] Langford, *Writings and Speeches*, IX, 125.   [102] Langford, *Writings and Speeches*, IX, 477.

[103] See Bernard Mandeville, *The Fable of the Bees* (London: J. Tonson, 1724). Consult also Henry C. Clark, *Commerce, Culture, & Liberty: Readings on Capitalism before Adam Smith* (Indianapolis: Liberty Fund, 2003).

[104] Mossner and Ross, *Correspondence of Adam Smith*, 46–47. Hume also noted in a letter to Smith on July 28, 1759 that Burke enjoyed the *Theory of Moral Sentiments* (42). Years later, Burke became more critical of the book. See Stewart, *Memoir Written on a Visit to Lord Lauderdale with Mr Burke and Adam Smith*.

[105] Smith, *Theory of Moral Sentiments*, 184.   [106] *Catalogue of the Library of Burke*, 20, 29.

showing that he exchanged remarks with Burke on them in that decade.[107] We should also note that Smith was nominated to the Club, the distinguished literary club of which Burke was a member, in 1775, but they most likely did not meet for the first time until 1777.[108]

This is not to say that Burke did not read and learn from Smith and the *Wealth of Nations*. As mentioned, Burke called Smith's book an "excellent digest" in 1784.[109] In *Letter to a Noble Lord*, Burke insinuated that he discussed commercial matters with Smith throughout the years (ostensibly starting in or after 1777).[110] And recall Robert Bisset's anecdote that Smith, according to Burke, thought "exactly" the same way as Burke had on subjects relating to political economy.[111] These facts are also not to suggest that Smith was directly influenced by Burke's thought (although, as discussed in Chapter 4, fragmentary evidence conveys some, if limited, influence).

Yet the idea that Burke was a "disciple" of Smith rests on dubious footing, for he embraced key tenets of economic freedom prior to his engagement with Smith, as this book has documented. Additionally, notice the subtle intimation in Burke's characterization of the *Wealth of Nations* as an "excellent digest": he did not describe it as a text that consisted of wholly new information, but as a "digest" – that is, a compilation and amplification of existing and disparate knowledge. Surely this was a lofty compliment coming from a distinguished thinker like Burke, but it perhaps also hinted at his underlying belief that the *Wealth of Nations* endorsed the same spirit of commercial liberty that he had advanced in the previous decade.

It remains beyond a doubt that the *Wealth of Nations* is a far more rigorous inquiry into the commercial system than the sum of Burke's writings and speeches on the topic. Furthermore, Burke's political and economic thought was not the same as Smith's; Smith, for example, expressed a stronger desire for Britain to relinquish its American dependencies, and displayed greater pessimism about the sustainability of the imperial project in general.[112] Burke, we should add, may have deepened his understanding of the science of political economy early in his intellectual life from reading Hume's *Essays*, which he possessed in his library, and other writings on the subject.[113]

The important point for our purposes, however, is that Burke – much as he did so in regard to other political affairs he confronted in his life – exhibited independent and prescient thinking on matters relating to commerce and trade before they were understood with great clarity in Parliament in the eighteenth

---

[107] We should also note that while Burke had Hume's writings in his library (*Catalogue of the Library of Burke*, 30), there are no extant letters between him and Hume discussing commerce and trade.
[108] *Correspondence of Adam Smith*, 47n4.
[109] Stewart, *Memoir Written on a Visit to Lord Lauderdale with Mr Burke and Adam Smith*.
[110] Langford, *Writings and Speeches*, IX, 160.   [111] Bisset, *Life of Edmund Burke*, 429.
[112] Smith, *Wealth of Nations*, vol. II, 946–947.
[113] See "Burke as a Political Economist," Chapter 1.

century; and that he was one of the most prominent lawmakers during that time to raise the idea of free market exchange to a tenable position in British politics prior to the publication of the *Wealth of Nations* in 1776.[114] We may end on a harmonizing note: rather than seeking to elevate one thinker over the other, we should appreciate Burke's and Smith's mutual dedication to advancing the cause of economic liberty in an age that, while gradually becoming more tolerant of trade, still remained suspicious of liberating commercial activity from the hands of government.

8.4   IRISH TRADE, NATURE, PRINCIPLE, AND PRUDENCE

The final theme in *Two Letters* that deserves elaboration is Burke's conception of nature in relation to trade. In the letters, he contends that England should not inhibit the natural capacity of the Irish to pursue commercial opportunities, thereby granting an implicit measure of approval to the Lockean notion that individuals possessed pre-political rights that warranted protection from state regulation. In doing so, Burke adopts comparable language he summons later in *Thoughts and Details* when connecting the general principles of economics to the immutable laws of nature.

First, recall Burke's comment in *Two Letters* that supporters of the Irish trade bills were simply seeking to permit the Irish to employ their "natural faculties which God has given to them, and to all mankind."[115] Because these "natural" abilities of man were gifts from God, Burke indicates in the letters that England should not arbitrarily obstruct Ireland's ingenious capacities to produce goods. Later in the paragraph Burke writes, "Ireland is a country, in the same climate, and of the same natural qualities and productions"[116] as England. In this instance he is not referring specifically to the natural abilities of man but to the natural environment and manufacturing capabilities of the Irish. But the salient lesson is that Burke in both cases is calling attention to the authority of nature, not to custom, tradition, and prescription,[117] in order to vindicate his position that greater commercial liberty should be afforded to Ireland.

Burke then issues a powerful statement outlining the symbiotic relationship between nature and industry in *Two Letters*. Beautifying his argument by invoking the steady movement of water, he declares:

I believe it will be found, that if men are suffered freely to cultivate their natural advantages, a virtual equality of contribution will come in its own time, and will flow by an easy descent, through its own proper and natural channels. An attempt to disturb

---

[114] Of course, other thinkers, merchants, and statesmen besides Burke also endorsed the principles of commercial liberty prior to the 1770s. See Clark, *Commerce, Culture, & Liberty*.

[115] Langford, *Writings and Speeches*, IX, 509.   [116] Langford, *Writings and Speeches*, IX, 509.

[117] Burke does blend prescription with ideas of natural law. See "Property as a Constitutional Bulwark," Chapter 11.

that course, and to force nature, will only bring on universal discontent, distress and confusion.[118]

Burke underlines this idea near the end of the first letter. He writes that he wished the Irish Parliament would, "in its own wisdom, remove these impediments, and put their country in a condition to avail itself of its natural advantages. If they do not, the fault is with them, and not with us."[119]

In these comments, Burke is appealing to nature to justify the expansion of commercial freedom, an argument similar to his reference to man's "natural faculties" and "natural qualities." Based on the context of *Two Letters*, in which he defends free trade, the "natural advantages" to which Burke most likely is referring were the climate and natural environment of Ireland, and the natural productive abilities of Irishmen to create and sell goods. He is associating the free circulation of commerce with "natural" movement and the interruption of this activity with unnatural forces.

Burke confirms the pivotal role of nature in informing his beliefs about free trade when he offers a specific reference to natural rights in his discussion of France in *Two Letters*:

France, and indeed most extensive empires, which by various designs and fortunes have grown into one great mass, contain many Provinces that are very different from each other in privileges and modes of government; and they raise their supplies in different ways; in different proportions; and under different authorities; yet none of them are for this reason, curtailed of their *natural rights*; but they carry on trade and manufactures with perfect equality [italics added].[120]

Although he is known as a foe of natural rights doctrine, here in *Two Letters* Burke supplies an unequivocal reference to "natural rights" – a concept he derides in the *Reflections* according to his understanding of the abstract natural rights theories of French revolutionaries. How, then, can one understand Burke's notion of natural rights in the letters?

First we must clarify Burke's message to Span. For Burke, even though imperial authorities superintended different commercial dependencies under a large empire like France, such variety of circumstance did not mean natural rights should be restricted for particular people in a confined area. Burke, then, is referring to natural rights in a wholly positive and cosmopolitan light here. He intimates that the preservation of natural rights was the spring for commercial productivity and economic growth; that these rights should not be circumscribed; and that the exercise of natural rights trended toward equality. (Burke does not specify which type of equality, whether it be economic, social, or political.[121])

---

[118] Langford, *Writings and Speeches*, IX, 510.   [119] Langford, *Writings and Speeches*, IX, 512.
[120] Langford, *Writings and Speeches*, IX, 510–511.
[121] See "Wealth Redistribution and Equality in *Thoughts and Details*," Chapter 3 for Burke's reflections on economic equality.

Burke's notion of natural rights in *Two Letters* becomes clearer and sharper in the second letter:

God has given the Earth to the Children of Man; and he has undoubtedly, in giving it to them, given them what is abundantly sufficient for all their Exigencies; not a scanty, but a most liberal provision for them all. The author of our Nature has written it strongly in that Nature, and has promulgated the same Law in his written Word, that Man shall eat his Bread by his Labour; and I am persuaded, that no man, and no combination of Men, for their own Ideas of their particular profit, can, without great impiety, undertake to say, that he *shall not* do so; that they have no sort of right, either to prevent the Labour, or to withhold the Bread.[122]

These comments are Burke's most fully developed statements on the subject of natural rights in *Two Letters*. Even though he does not directly reference the term, it is clear, based on the specific remark about "right" and his description of the argument he is endeavoring to make, Burke is presenting a form of natural rights reasoning: the individual has at least some right to produce, and he has the right to consume the rewards of his toil.

In these reflections, Burke goes beyond his earlier gestures to nature by elaborating on the connections among the fruits of nature, the authority of God, and the sanction of the Bible. Burke, in claiming that God bestowed the gift of nature upon human beings, is echoing Psalms 115:16, which teaches, "The heavens, *even* the heavens, *are* the LORD's: but the earth hath he given to the children of men."[123] Nature provides bountiful opportunities for man to take advantage of for the procurement of food and supplies. In addition, the "author of our Nature" created the law that man eats by his labor, a statement reflecting Genesis 3:19, which reads, "In the sweat of thy face shalt thou eat bread, till thou return unto the ground."[124] The right to labor, Burke suggests, stems from God's granting of the gift of nature for all to use. Such comments imply a firm, if rudimentary, notion of natural rights in *Two Letters*, and hint that the authority of natural rights derived from the will of God.

Burke not only argues in the letters that God gave nature to man to exploit. He also invokes God when advancing his argument about Irish taxation. The entire quotation is:

To that argument of equal taxation, I can only say, that Ireland pays as many taxes, as those who are the best judges of her powers, are of opinion she can bear. To bear more she must have more ability; and in the order of nature, the advantage must *precede* the charge. This disposition of things, being the law of God, neither you nor I *can* alter it.[125]

---

[122] Langford, *Writings and Speeches*, IX, 515.
[123] "Psalms: Chapter 115." *King James Bible*, www.kingjamesbibleonline.org/Psalms-Chapter -115/.
[124] "Genesis: Chapter 3," *King James Bible*, www.kingjamesbibleonline.org/Genesis-Chapter-3/.
[125] Langford, *Writings and Speeches*, IX, 510.

The "law of God," expressed in the "order of nature," is that the market actor must be provided with the freedom to produce before he should be expected to pay more in taxes.

Burke further insists in the second letter "we" – those who believed trade produced zero-sum effects, such as his mercantile constituents – should "form to ourselves a way of thinking, more rational, more just, and more religious"[126] in order to grasp that commercial exchange benefited both parties. Burke is insinuating that unhindered commercial activity was a reflection of nature and should be defended on grounds of rationality and justice, and even piety.

Notice what Burke does not argue in *Two Letters* in support of free trade and natural right. He does not claim that the right to labor and produce was a prescriptive right, drawn from the wisdom of tradition and custom, nor that the Irish trade bills were simply a manifestation of the recovery of ancient Irish economic rights.[127] One can explain the absence of these arguments by discerning Burke's clever mode of rhetoric suffusing *Two Letters*: his summoning of nature suggested a recognition of the common humanity between England and Ireland that existed beyond the reach of a particular political or economic tradition, such as English mercantilism.

Guided by this manner of thinking, Burke was aware that an appeal to nature could stir the consciences of Bristol traders to relate to the Irish in the spirit of brotherly communion. Beckoning the authority of history, on the other hand, would draw attention to the chain of commercial deprivation imposed by Britain on Ireland throughout the seventeenth and eighteenth centuries. Therefore, while his political philosophy did retain meaningful space for natural law,[128] we must be aware that Burke also called forth nature in *Two Letters* to persuade his mercantile audience, particularly Span and other Bristol merchants, that the reduction in trade regulations would promote their commercial interests. Blending timely rhetoric with a species of natural rights theory, Burke in *Two Letters* displays an appreciation for the natural roots of commercial freedom that is integral to understanding his economic thought.

Bristol and Burke's Trustee Theory of Representation

Burke's support for the Irish trade bills introduces broader implications for his conception of statesmanship by exemplifying the application of his trustee theory of representation to a concrete policy question. This theory, as discussed in Chapter 5, is famous for advancing the idea that an elected

---

[126] Langford, *Writings and Speeches*, IX, 514.
[127] Burke could have made a plausible argument in *Two Letters* by insisting that the bills were recovering Irish commercial rights prior to the mercantilist policies of William III. He does use this form of argumentation in his May 6 bill on Irish trade. The trade measures, Burke said, "were no more than restorations of what the wisdom of a British Parliament had, on a former occasion, thought proper to invest Ireland with" (Langford, *Writings and Speeches*, IX, 519).
[128] See Stanlis, *Edmund Burke and the Natural Law*.

representative should make independent judgments on legislative matters in pursuit of the national interest, even if these judgments conflicted with the political persuasions of his constituents. This governing imperative did not mean that the representative should ignore public sentiment, however. In Burke's view, if public opinion aligned with the common good, the lawmaker *should* channel its enthusiasms into legislative proposals, as shown by his own efforts in promoting his economical program in *Speech on Economical Reform*.

Before elaborating on Burke's trustee theory of representation in the context of his advocacy of the trade bills, let us first discuss an additional example of the second approach – channeling popular opinion, rather than rejecting it – during his tenure as an elected representative of Bristol. In the mid-1770s, the city's mercantile interest had conveyed its thick displeasure over the plundering of shipwrecks, which deprived traffickers of their commercial property for trade. Burke was sympathetic to their concerns, and thus introduced a Shipwreck Bill in 1775 (and later a modified version in 1776) that required local officials to return the property from shipwrecks that had washed ashore to their lawful owners. The legislation enacted punitive measures against those who obstructed this recovery process. Yet Burke's measure encountered opposition from those who thought that remuneration for damaged goods, especially in coastal cities, would be far more expensive than traditional practices of compensation.[129]

The significance of Burke's legislative efforts in this context emerges from his attempt to reflect, rather than defy, an influential voice of his electorate, since his belief in preserving the integrity of commercial property converged with the interests of Bristol traders. "[C]ommercial Countries, particularly this, which prided itself on its national Honour, should take Care to do every Thing possible in its Power, to discourage and punish such outrageous Proceedings," Burke declaimed in Parliament when introducing his bill on March 27, 1776.[130] The legislation was defeated in late April, even after Burke insisted in an additional speech that France's compensatory system for shipwrecks was more effectual than England's laws.[131] Burke's attempt, even in defeat, illuminated a dimension of his trustee theory of representation that calls for greater attention in the study of his parliamentary activity: while Burke did maintain that a legislator should not necessarily follow public opinion, he also thought, as evidenced by the Shipwreck Bill, that the lawmaker *should* echo the wishes of constituents if their desires achieved symmetry with the common good.

---

[129] See Langford, *Writings and Speeches*, III, 225–226 for background on Burke's Shipwreck Bill.
[130] Langford, *Writings and Speeches*, III, 226.
[131] "He then entered into a View of the French Laws, and shewed, in a Variety of Instances, what great Advantages they had over ours, in Respect of Ships wrecked on their Coasts" (Langford, *Writings and Speeches*, III, 227).

Beyond its connection to Burke's trustee theory of representation, the Shipwreck Bill marked his attention to the important role of compensation in securing private property. Undeterred by the bill's defeat, Burke, in a parliamentary speech on May 1, 1776, continued to press the matter of remuneration for the plunder of commerce. According to *St. James's Chronicle*, "He observed that the Principle being once established it would follow that the atrocious disgraceful Custom of plundering Wrecks came within the Description of the general Law of Compensation."[132] Burke also recommended that three other statutes relating to legal compensation be read in the House of Commons. The first addressed compensation for owners of property damaged by rioters; the second regarded compensation for owners of trees that were unlawfully cut down; and the third stipulated penalties for those who attacked owners' cattle, trees, houses, and barns.[133]

Burke's speeches on the Shipwreck Bill lie at the intersection of his conception of statesmanship and political economy. Burke was acting on behalf of the preferences of his constituents; and, in the process, he affirmed his belief that national honor derived, in part, from the vigorous protection of commerce (particularly in light of the threat represented by foreign competitors like France). Burke further registered his commitment to the security of personal property in general, and to just notions of recompense, when he moved for the House of Commons to read statutes relating to the destruction of private land and goods. Fidelity to sound principles of political economy demanded the resilient defense of lawful possessions.

Burke fulfilled the interests of his Bristol constituents in other ways. In a letter written in March 1775, in addition to citing his legislative activities pushing the Shipwrecks Bill, he also made note of his parliamentary effort calling for the importation of Irish potatoes and pulses as part of an English trade bill. The prior iteration of the bill, which became law, had permitted imports of beef and other salted provisions, a privilege that technically expired at the end of February 1775.[134] The collector of customs in Bristol evidently refused to admit particular provisions after that time.

Burke was annoyed by the punctilio of such behavior: from his perspective, adhering to the "*strict* Letter of the Law" in this case was "injurious" not only to the "Commerce" of Bristol but also to "the supply of the poor."[135] The consequences of trade restrictions surpassed the discouragement of mercantile profit; excess regulations also suppressed the flow of provisions to the lower classes. Burke's labor on behalf of Bristol dealers embodied his view that the promotion of trade was one principal duty of an elected lawmaker representing an entrepôt like Bristol. "[T]he Interest of Bristol ever shall be dear to me, and

---

[132] Langford, *Writings and Speeches*, III, 228.
[133] Langford, *Writings and Speeches*, III, 228n4.
[134] See *Correspondence of Edmund Burke*, vol. III, 141; 141n7; 132n4.
[135] Burke to Robert Smith, 24 March 1775, in *Correspondence of Edmund Burke*, vol. III, 141.

the preservation and encrease of her commerce one of the fir[st] Objects of my attention," he insisted in the letter.[136]

It was this aim that motivated Burke to champion the Irish trade bills, even though vocal Bristol merchants tenaciously opposed them. Burke's zealous effort in support of the measures was a serious test for the most audacious maxim of his trustee theory of representation – the judgments and actions of elected representatives should not be dictated by the weight of public sentiment. The certitude of Burke's embrace of the bills was not in doubt: in denying in *Two Letters* that the initial Irish trade measures sprung from his mind, he writes, "[W]hen things are so right in themselves, I hold it my duty, not to enquire from what hands they come."[137] "So right in themselves" – this is not a statement of prudence but a declaration of a self-evident truth, as Burke understood it.

Burke underlined this conclusion in a speech on Irish trade on May 5, three days after he wrote his second letter to the iron manufacturers. On that day, thirty-five petitions opposing the bills were recognized in Parliament.[138] In the snarl of such opposition, Burke, according to the *General Evening Post*, "acknowledged that he did look all of one side; for there was but one side to look at, as the question for our consideration was simply this, whether or not we should suffer a country to enjoy that to which she had a natural right."[139] Here Burke musters an expression of unequivocal certainty – "one side to look at" – and integrates it with his conception of natural right. Once again, this is not the prudential, cautious Burke about which we are accustomed to reading.

One day later, on May 6, when the bill allowing the direct importation of colonial products into Ireland was approved, Burke revivified the spirit of his pro-trade convictions. In a speech in the House of Commons, he "differed in opinion from [his constituents] on the noblest principle, namely, from the conviction of his being in the right."[140] Furthermore:

[I]f, from his conduct in this business, he should be deprived of his seat in that honourable House, it would stand on record, an example to future representatives of the Commons of England, that one man, at least, had dared to oppose his constituents when his judgment assured him they were in the wrong.[141]

---

[136] Burke to Robert Smith, 24 March 1775, in *Correspondence of Edmund Burke*, vol. III, 142. For deeper insight into Burke's service as a representative of Bristol, see George Edward Weare, *Edmund Burke's Connection with Bristol, from 1774 till 1780; with a Prefatory Memoir of Burke* (Bristol: William Bennett, 1894). Burke also acted on behalf of his Bristol constituents by pledging to fight a proposal, opposed by Michael Miller, a prominent merchant, to turn the Company of Merchants Trading to Africa into a joint-stock company. The measure would have reduced market competition in the African trade. Burke stated that the idea reflected "the grossest ignorance of every commercial principle." See Burke to Michael Miller, 17 April 1779, in *Correspondence of Edmund Burke*, vol. IV, 60.
[137] Langford, *Writings and Speeches*, IX, 508.   [138] Langford, *Writings and Speeches*, IX, 518.
[139] Langford, *Writings and Speeches*, IX, 519.   [140] Langford, *Writings and Speeches*, IX, 523.
[141] Langford, *Writings and Speeches*, IX, 523.

Such is not a statement of prudence or utility or calculation. Burke is asserting that he was willing to lose his seat in Parliament in the pursuit of free commerce by shunning political opposition to the trade concessions that had mounted in late April and early May, a period in which around sixty petitions reprimanding the Irish trade bills were sent to the House of Commons.[142]

Let us be blunt: Burke is not channeling the popular views of dissatisfied Bristol merchants; he is outright rebuffing them.[143] In these comments, then, Burke is presenting a taste of his trustee theory of representation that he outlined in *Speech at the Conclusion of the Poll*, which he presented almost four years prior to his May 6 speech. "If the local Constituent should have an Interest, or should form an hasty Opinion, evidently opposite to the real good of the rest of the Community," Burke insisted in *Speech at the Conclusion of the Poll*, "the Member for that place ought to be as far, as any other, from any endeavour to give it Effect."[144] While an elected representative should mold public opinion into policy reform if it accorded with the national interest, he also held the weighty responsibility to repudiate the views of his constituents if, in his sober judgment, they undermined the pursuit of the common good. Burke determined that mercantile attitudes in favor of existing commercial restrictions did indeed militate against the general welfare. Therefore, it was his duty to oppose them.

In a letter to Thomas Burgh in January 1780, Burke laid stress on this guiding principle of his statesmanship when describing his parliamentary exertions on behalf of Irish trade: "I acted then, as I act now, and I hope I shall act always, from a strong impulse of right, and from motives in which popularity, either here, or there, has but a very little part."[145] Right warranted priority over popularity in the practice of statesmanship.

Burke's decision to act on economic principle, regardless of the negative consequences it might have held for his future in Parliament, calls into question Leo Strauss's critical assessment of Burke in *Natural Right and History*. In this influential book, Strauss claimed that Burke flirted with suggesting that "to oppose a thoroughly evil current in human affairs is perverse if that current is sufficiently powerful" and that Burke was "oblivious of the nobility of last-ditch resistance."[146] Burke's unpopular activities promoting free trade in the 1770s, and his broader efforts advancing the cause of Irish Catholics throughout his entire political life – not to mention his advocacy on behalf of Indians and his principled opposition to the French Revolution – represent a bold challenge to Strauss's statements.[147] Regardless

---

[142] Langford, *Writings and Speeches*, IX, 549n3.
[143] Of course, "popular" opinion in Bristol reflected the loudest wishes of affluent merchants.
[144] Langford, *Writings and Speeches*, III, 69–70.
[145] Langford, *Writings and Speeches*, IX, 544.   [146] Strauss, *Natural Right and History*, 318.
[147] For further discussion on Strauss's interpretation of Burke, see Gregory M. Collins, "Edmund Burke, Strauss, and the Straussians," *Perspectives on Political Science* 48 (2019): 192–209.

of the merits of his pro-trade arguments, Burke here is clearly engaged in a proverbial struggle of last-ditch resistance against mercantile sentiments partial to trade restrictions.

Burke's written communication in *Two Letters* is marked by a more delicate tone than in *Thoughts and Details*, most likely reflecting the variation in the readership of each writing. The former was a statement intended to assuage the opinions of constituents suspicious of the Irish trade bills, while the latter was written for government officials at a time when Burke had already retired from Parliament, removed from the demands of electoral politics.

We may thus attribute Burke's careful articulations in *Two Letters* to his continual struggle in Parliament in balancing his support for free commerce with the heavy burden of political realities. He was keenly aware that Span, and the merchants he represented, objected to his free trade positions. Yet even in this light, it is striking that Burke does not conceal his beliefs in the letters. How many elected representatives today would have the gall to tell their constituents, without qualification, that they should tame their envy of the commercial prosperity of others and support free trade legislation?

Burke's gentle yet firm treatment of the Irish trade bills, similar to his orchestration of the Shipwreck Bill, provides a glimpse into his understanding of the relation between economic doctrine and statesmanship. In the case of the trade bills, Burke, not unlike his critical opinion about the limitations of the Free Port Act, expressed regret that the proposed Irish trade measures did not extend the principles of market liberty even further. "The fault I find in the scheme is, – that it falls extremely short of that liberality in the commercial system," Burke writes in *Two Letters*, "which, I trust, will one day be adopted."[148] He insists that the Irish trade resolutions "aim, however imperfectly, at a right principle."[149] Consequently, "I voted for [the Irish trade bills], not as doing compleat Justice to Ireland; but as being something less unjust, than the general prohibition which has hitherto prevailed."[150]

Burke conveyed a similar fondness for the trade measures in statements independent of *Two Letters*. In a 1778 letter to Edmund Sexton Pery, the Speaker of the Irish House of Commons and a representative for Limerick City, Burke asserted that it was "a great deal to have broken up the frozen Ground,"[151] the frozen ground signifying the rigid system of commercial restrictions between Ireland and England. And Burke hoped, as he wrote to Thomas Burgh two years later, that "we might obtain gradually, and by parts, what we might attempt at once, and in the whole, without success."[152] That attempt was to "fix the principle of a free trade"

---

[148] Langford, *Writings and Speeches*, IX, 507.   [149] Langford, *Writings and Speeches*, IX, 507.
[150] Langford, *Writings and Speeches*, IX, 516.
[151] Burke to Edmund Sexton Pery, 19 May 1778, in *Correspondence of Edmund Burke*, vol. III, 448. I thank F. P. Lock for alerting me to this source.
[152] Langford, *Writings and Speeches*, IX, 549.

throughout Britain's colonial possessions.[153] Once again, Burke here is communicating his support for free trade. Keeping in mind the imperatives of statesmanship, however, he is also exhibiting an understanding that principles sometimes have to be cooled temporarily because of the constraints of political exigencies. As he was quite aware, circumstance dictated compromise out of legislative necessity in the case of the Irish trade bills, much as it did regarding the Free Port Act of 1766.

Burke's Suspension of Commercial Principle in the Interest of Long-Term Benefit

In fact, Burke was willing to sacrifice particular provisions of free trade policy in the short term during the debates over the Irish trade bills, in the hope that broader advantages would be gained in the future from these concessions. When the House was discussing the bill to allow Ireland to directly export its goods to the colonies, Bamber Gascoyne offered an amendment on May 19, 1778 that would have banned particular Irish items from being exported. Sir Thomas Egerton then moved that the bill should not take effect until Ireland eliminated the duty on linen yarn exports to Britain.[154]

Burke supported Gascoyne's amendment. Contemporary accounts of his speech suggest he did so because, in his view, the overall bill to allow direct exportation to the colonies would have still enlarged the sphere of Irish commercial activity. He reasoned that thus far, "[T]he bill would appear to the people of Ireland a very considerable acquisition."[155] Even more, Burke "confirmed the principle of extending the Irish trade, upon principles of prudence, policy, and justice."[156] His principal message was that the bill, even with Gascoyne's amendment, signified a concrete step in the direction of freer trade:

[B]y granting a bill, to show our inclination to give whatever could be safely granted, we would prove to Ireland that we wished to give them encouragement, so on the other hand, in the course of the next session, as would be fully prepared and informed to discuss the question at large, and be enabled to form a judgment that would or would not be fit to give to Ireland, by way of indulgence.[157]

Gascoyne's amendment passed the committee.

Burke's position on Egerton's proposal, which he opposed, is similarly complicated. The essence of his argument was that the British textile industry did not deserve to have primacy access to the Irish linen industry since Ireland retained the right to produce and regulate linen according to its own preferences, as recognized by traditional English trade law. At the time,

---

[153] Langford, *Writings and Speeches*, IX, 550.   [154] Langford, *Writings and Speeches*, IX, 523.
[155] Langford, *Writings and Speeches*, IX, 524.   [156] Langford, *Writings and Speeches*, IX, 524.
[157] Langford, *Writings and Speeches*, IX, 524.

Manchester was the epicenter of the textile industry, and had proposed to raise and fund its own regiment upon hearing news about the Battle of Saratoga in 1777, the inflection point in the American war that tilted the conflict in favor of the colonists. Burke claimed that Manchester wrongly believed that it had "an exclusive right to [the British government's] favours and indulgences, and demand[ed] the oppression of others for the aggrandisement of themselves."[158] Notice that Burke associates the free export of linen yarn to Britain with hurting the Irish and helping the English. In other words, he is suggesting that Ireland's linen industry would benefit from being protected from the English textile trade, a position that conceivably revolted against his general belief that limited commercial regulations would bring advantages to both the Irish and the English.

Britain's textile industry, on the other hand, supported Egerton's measure because it created more opportunities for English manufacturers to compete with Irish traders in the linen check industry. The linen yarn was also useful to Britain's textile industry since it could furnish the warp used in cotton cloth products.[159] Moreover, Burke observed that Britain "preserves to itself the exportation of cottons in their mixed and unmixed states by which alone the article of checks can be rendered valuable, and wishes at the same time to have an exclusive right to the exportation of linen checks."[160] He then offered the more practical point that, in his estimation, the linen check industry in Britain was not worth more than £1,500 per year, while in Ireland the export duty on linen created £7,500 in annual revenue.[161]

Burke's argument in this case does not rest on the abstract principle of free trade. Rather, it suggests that if Britain was going to benefit from its exclusive exportation of cotton, then Ireland should be allowed to exercise the same right to glean advantages from its linen industry – and through punitive measures if necessary. The Irish "have a right to retaliate, as they may retaliate upon us, our injustice."[162] While England originally recognized Ireland's exclusive right to the linen manufacture, its government had corrupted the spirit of this allowance in 1711 by prohibiting the Irish export of checked linen, under the reasoning that dyed linen was no longer linen.[163] In essence, one party should not be prevented from protecting its industry if the other party, in this case England, was already doing so, and especially if this latter party had twisted the original understanding of trade restrictions in the first place to benefit itself at the expense of the other. Of course, Burke could have proposed a compromise proposal as an alternative to the measures of Gascoyne and Egerton: Ireland

---

[158] Langford, *Writings and Speeches*, IX, 525.   [159] Langford, *Writings and Speeches*, IX, 523.
[160] Langford, *Writings and Speeches*, IX, 526.   [161] Langford, *Writings and Speeches*, IX, 527.
[162] Langford, *Writings and Speeches*, IX, 526.
[163] See Langford, *Writings and Speeches*, IX, 526; and Langford, *Writings and Speeches*, IX, 526n3.

should lower its duties on linen yarn, and England should relax its grip on the cotton export industry.

Nevertheless, Burke, in his discussion of Egerton's amendment, was insistent that Ireland harbored the right to economic liberty. In an argument reminiscent of his invocations of nature in *Two Letters*, Burke declared that England should not deny Ireland its natural rights and natural advantages to produce. Members of Manchester's textile industry, because it offered to raise and fund a regiment following the Battle of Saratoga, thought that gesture would "induce Government to deprive Ireland of the rights of nature to enrich them." Burke stressed the primacy of Ireland's natural economic environment conducive to the linen industry: "The linen manufacture of Ireland is its natural and staple commodity." The compact between England and Ireland "gives them the free, unqualified, unlimited, and unspecified right to the linen manufacture."[164] This is not an expression of moderation but a stirring proclamation of economic principle.

In addition, from Burke's account in the speech, Ireland claimed authority over the linen trade according to "all the laws of equity, and by the right of inheritance." Irish traders "do not come requesting it as a favour, but demanding it as justice."[165] Notice that in Burke's telling, the Irish, not Burke, were calling attention to the authority of inheritance in asserting their claim over the linen industry. Yet he repeatedly summons the language of natural rights to defend the capacities of Ireland to control the trade, blending his aptitude for rhetorical suasion with his belief in nature as a foundation for the right to industry.

The question of Irish grievances concerning free trade was revived again in Parliament in February 1779. On February 15, Lord Newhaven proposed that the House consider the pending legislation on Irish trade in ten days. Burke picked up on his argument from the 1778 debates that the British government's efforts to expand its imperial power over its colonies resulted in the diminution of its authority and a sharp increase in political instability. In the 1779 debate, he said that "every measure for some years past, particularly such as had led us into the American war, were avowedly adopted under the idea of *rendering government* powerful and paramount over the several dependencies of the British empire; yet what was the consequence?"[166]

Burke continued: "We had lost already *one third* of the empire past redemption; Ireland was ruined and bankrupt; the reins of government were become so loose, that tumults and insurrections were daily feared."[167] He also asserted in his speech that Britain "had *no right to bind Ireland*, and that such a control so exercised, was no better than arbitrary and tyrannical."[168] Burke's remarks in his February 1779 speech draw out two themes of his commentary

---

[164] Langford, *Writings and Speeches*, IX, 526.   [165] Langford, *Writings and Speeches*, IX, 526.
[166] Langford, *Writings and Speeches*, IX, 527.   [167] Langford, *Writings and Speeches*, IX, 527.
[168] Langford, *Writings and Speeches*, IX, 528.

on Irish trade: first, the enlargement of political power could undermine its own authority; and second, Burke's advocacy of commercial freedom was rooted in notions of right and justice.

Burke's correspondence with Thomas Burgh in January 1780 sheds further insight into his frame of mind during parliamentary discussion over Irish trade in 1779. In the letter to Burgh, Burke expressed disappointment over the strategic method by which the proposition to permit Ireland to import colonial sugar had been carried out. He criticized the initiative for its lack of outreach to representatives of the "country party"[169]; the absence of planning to anticipate political opposition; and the disorganized nature in which it was presented. Still, Burke wrote, "I supported the principle of enlargement which [supporters of the bill] aimed at, though short and somewhat wide of the mark, giving as my sole reason, that the more frequently those matters came into discussion, the more it would tend to dispel fears and to eradicate prejudices."[170] Burke was willing to lend his support to severely flawed pieces of commercial legislation because, in his judgment, it would have quickened the process of convincing skeptics that free trade would produce timely advantages to the public welfare.

In the letter to Burgh, Burke disclosed his opposition to two additional measures that had created government incentives for particular industries. The first provided an incentive to grow tobacco, and the second granted an export bounty on hemp from Ireland. He disapproved of the reforms because "the cultivation of those weeds (if one of them could be at all cultivated to profit) was adverse to the introduction of a good course of agriculture."[171] Burke also objected to them because "the encouragement given to them, tended to establish that mischievous policy of considering Ireland as a country of staple, and a producer of raw materials."[172] Although he did not elaborate on this remark, Burke was suggesting that the measures established a forced incentive structure compelling the misallocation of goods. From his perspective, Irish industry was best left to its natural course.

8.5 PITT'S COMMERCIAL PROPOSITIONS

There is one glaring instance in Burke's engagement with Anglo-Irish commercial questions, however, in which he did not support free trade measures in a meaningful sense. In 1784 and 1785, William Pitt the Younger, prime minister at the time, proposed a series of eleven commercial propositions that called for the easing of trade restrictions between Ireland and England, with the expectation that Ireland would make heavier financial contributions from

---

[169] Langford, *Writings and Speeches*, IX, 552.   [170] Langford, *Writings and Speeches*, IX, 553.
[171] Langford, *Writings and Speeches*, IX, 554.
[172] Langford, *Writings and Speeches*, IX, 554–555.

its hereditary fund to Britain's imperial defense.[173] Ireland's House of Commons approved the measures on February 12, 1785.[174] Yet Burke, following the example of opposition leader Charles James Fox, gave two speeches in February and May 1785 disapproving of Pitt's measures, in effect embracing the protectionist sentiments that he resisted in the previous decade over the Irish trade bills.[175]

A flurry of political considerations influenced the debate concerning Pitt's commercial propositions, leading scholars to attribute Burke's position to a number of factors: Burke succumbed to factionist impulses, lending "himself to the party cry that Pitt was taking his first measures for the re-enslavement of Ireland," as John Morley wrote[176]; his mind was preoccupied with India at the time; he thought the resolutions were a backhand way to take revenue from Ireland (not unlike Britain's strategy with the American colonies), thereby swelling the financial burdens of the Irish; he was doubtful that Ireland would be able to provide sufficient revenue to the Crown in any event; he had not made a full recovery from the political bedlam of the previous session, in which he faced sharp political hostility following the demise of the Fox-North coalition in 1783 and the ascent of Pitt; or he was worried that further concessions to Ireland would have paved the way toward either unrestricted Anglo-Irish union or full Irish independence.[177]

There is no single unifying theory to explain Burke's motives. An adherence to factionalism, combined with a focus on Indian affairs at the time, perhaps best explains Burke's behavior. Burke was exceedingly distrustful of Pitt, who was backed by King George, following the downfall of the Fox-North coalition. And Burke thought Pitt's measures lacked systematic inquiry into Ireland's ability to furnish sufficient surplus revenue for Britain's imperial defense.[178] Burke was not the only MP to contradict his free trade principles in favor of devotion to party: William Eden, an adherent of Adam Smith's science of political economy, also opposed Pitt's propositions.[179]

We must also not underestimate Burke's commitment to retaining the integrity of the British Empire, which demanded the preservation of its imperial authority over Ireland. In both speeches on Pitt's commercial propositions, Burke asserted that Ireland was a "co-ordinate" state because it had been afforded an independent legislature[180] as a result of the repeal of the

---

[173] See Mahoney, *Edmund Burke and Ireland*, 136–151; and Langford, *Writings and Speeches*, IX, 405–406.

[174] Langford, *Writings and Speeches*, IX, 585.

[175] See Semmel, *Rise of Free Trade Imperialism*, 35.   [176] Morley, *Burke*, 126.

[177] See Langford, *Writings and Speeches*, vol. IX, 585–593; Mahoney, *Edmund Burke and Ireland*, 149–150; Morley, *Burke*, 125–127; and Bourke, *Empire & Revolution*, 404–406.

[178] See Langford, *Writings and Speeches*, vol. IX, 588.

[179] See Semmel, *Rise of Free Trade Imperialism*, 35–36.

[180] Langford, *Writings and Speeches*, vol. IX, 591. See also Langford, *Writings and Speeches*, IX, 586. Burke was never comfortable with the idea of an independent legislature, lacking

Declaratory Act of 1719 in 1782. Nevertheless, he continued, "Independence of legislature had been granted to Ireland; but no other independence could Great Britain give her without reversing the order and decree of nature: Ireland could not be separated from England; she could not exist without her; she must for ever remain under the protection of England, her guardian angel."[181]

The promotion of a joint interest did not mean Britain should set the conditions for permanent Irish independence. Besides, Burke thought, the Irish remained unappreciative of British parliamentary attempts to grant them greater commercial freedom, as F. P. Lock notes.[182] On the other hand, Burke was also hesitant to establish formal union between Britain and its dependencies, not only in the case of Ireland but also America, for fear of encouraging a centripetal imperial force that would impose oppressive taxing schemes on British subjects and swallow up their liberties.

Burke's speeches on Pitt's commercial propositions offer limited philosophic insight into his conception of political economy. They do, however, provide clarification to his idea of reciprocity. While the very nature of voluntary commercial exchange enabled advantages to reach both market participants, as Burke emphasized in *Two Letters* and *Thoughts and Details*, there was no natural force of reciprocity in political relations, such as those between Britain and its colonies. A political concession from one party did not in itself occasion a political concession from the other, since this interaction was not governed by the necessities of supply and demand.

Therefore, Burke suggested in his speech on Pitt's commercial propositions in February 1785 that MPs should undertake serious study of the measures' financial implications to determine whether they would actually bestow advantages on England. "[I]t would be necessary that the Members should have before them all the information that wou'd be wanted to enable them to form a judgment, whether the propositions which the Chancellor of the Exchequer [Pitt] intended shortly to move, would be really for the mutual advantage of both kingdoms," he declared.[183] Harmony in exchange economies naturally rises from a structure of market incentives; but harmony in politics demands conscious deliberation between two parties motivated by considerations beyond the gratification of commercial desire.

Burke's speech on Pitt's commercial propositions in May also reveals a possible contradiction in his thoughts on free trade. In *Two Letters*, Burke insisted to Bristol merchants that the relaxation of trade regulations would spread benefits to England and Ireland. Yet in his May speech, Burke insinuated that Pitt's measures would injure the commercial trade of English

---

confidence that the body would act in accord with the public welfare of Ireland. See Burke to Earl Fitzwilliam, 20 November 1796, in *Correspondence of Edmund Burke*, vol. IX, 122–123.

[181] Langford, *Writings and Speeches*, IX, 591.   [182] Lock, *Edmund Burke*, vol. II, 17.

[183] Langford, *Writings and Speeches*, IX, 588.

merchants. This consequence, compounded by the weight of financial encumbrances, would harm English prosperity. England

was loaded with an enormous weight of debt and taxes; however she had in her trade and manufactures the most astonishing resources; but should these be once taken from her, the immense load of debt would crush her to atoms; at least it would throw her from her rank among the nations round her, and not leave her wherewithal to defend either Ireland or herself.[184]

Burke then summoned zero-sum logic, undercutting his statements in *Two Letters* that praised the mutual advantages of free trade: "To take from her the manufactures would be to deprive her of her resources, and to effect the ruin of the two kingdoms at once."[185] Because the interests of both countries were bound tightly, the commercial decline of one would induce the economic deterioration of the other.

As someone who was keenly aware of the contradictions in the thought of others, surely Burke was conscious of the seeming reversal in his argument in contrast to *Two Letters*. Perhaps he was enlisting such logic as an instrumental weapon of rhetoric to mask his deeper reservations against Pitt. Or maybe Burke thought his rationale aligned with his broader point that trade concessions demanded true reciprocity from both parties, a responsibility he believed Ireland was not meeting, or could not meet. He also suspected that the Protestant Ascendancy, which heavily shaped the politics of the Irish Parliament, would be eager to foist more oppressive taxes upon Irish Catholics.[186] In the end, Pitt's propositions, which expanded to nineteen measures by the end, were supported by the House of Commons and the House of Lords. The Irish Parliament approved them as well, but afterwards the propositions were removed from consideration.[187]

8.6 THE ANGLO-FRENCH COMMERCIAL TREATY OF 1786

An additional exception to Burke's embrace of free trade beyond Anglo-Irish relations was his suspicion of Britain's commercial relations with France, as exemplified by the Anglo-French Commercial Treaty or Eden Treaty, of 1786. Beginning in 1713, the Treaty of Utrecht had attempted to govern trade between the two nations on the principle of collective advantage. Nevertheless, Britain chose not to ratify two articles of the agreement, which prompted France to revive the series of high duties and trade regulations that had traditionally characterized its commercial policy. Britain also retained laws that discouraged French imports. The new treaty of 1786, which was signed in September of that year, attempted to ease these commercial tensions by

[184] Langford, *Writings and Speeches*, IX, 592.   [185] Langford, *Writings and Speeches*, IX, 592.
[186] See Lock, *Edmund Burke*, vol. II, 20.   [187] Langford, *Writings and Speeches*, IX, 593.

ending particular prohibitions and lowering tariffs. The agreement was sent to Parliament for approval in January 1787.[188]

Burke, communicating long-lasting Whig apprehensions over promoting commercial ties with France, registered firm objections to the treaty. As he explained in a speech on February 21, 1787, free trade was a worthy object to pursue with Ireland because Ireland was within the British Empire and shared a common tongue and mutual interests. France, however, was a different species. Burke was convinced that the long-term intent of the French government, which encouraged Britain to enter into the treaty negotiations in the first place, was to ruin British commerce and establish itself as Britain's imperial, naval, and economic superior, even if the treaty might hurt French manufactures in the immediate future. "The advantages [France] is to gain are political, naval and commercial; ours will consist only in the sale of manufactures," he insisted in the speech.[189]

By implication, Burke's argument rested on granting priority to English commerce over English manufactures, thereby reflecting general Whig attitudes at the time.[190] Accordingly, Burke explained that British capital maintained its clear dominance over French capital throughout the eighteenth century; he went so far as to state that the former had "tyrranized" the global market as a consequence of the powerful partnership among British merchants, bankers, and manufacturers.[191] Yet the Anglo-French Commercial Treaty would allow France "to insinuate herself into the partnership, and, in the end, come in for a share of the capital."[192]

By enabling France to penetrate its markets and possessions, the treaty would diminish the integrity of the British Empire, in Burke's judgment. The enjoyment of short-term trade advantages would not make up for this loss. "If [a nation] has ever lost its character, all is gone, and nothing remains but gaudy trappings to conceal its misery," he proclaimed.[193] Britain, in fact, did appear to gain from the treaty, at least until the start of the Anglo-French wars in the 1790s.[194] Burke's deeper message was that a country was defined by more than the sum of its material goods and public riches. A nation's prosperity was enhanced by commerce and capital, but its essence was ultimately locked and secured by the principle of honor – a principle Burke believed would be sacrificed under the Anglo-French Commercial Treaty.

---

[188] For additional information on the Anglo-French Commercial Treaty, see W. O. Henderson, "The Anglo-French Commercial Treaty of 1786," *The Economic History Review* 10 (1957): 104–112; J. Holland Rose, "The Franco-British Commercial Treaty of 1786," *The English Historical Review* 23 (1908): 709–724; and Langford, *Writings and Speeches*, IV, 235–236.

[189] Langford, *Writings and Speeches*, IV, 239.

[190] See Semmel, *Rise of Free Trade Imperialism*, 41–42.

[191] Langford, *Writings and Speeches*, IV, 237.   [192] Langford, *Writings and Speeches*, IV, 237.

[193] Langford, *Writings and Speeches*, IV, 240.

[194] Consult Evans, *William Pitt the Younger*, 29.

8.7 THE QUESTION OF MERCANTILISM REVISITED

After considering Burke's thought and political activity on the question of foreign commercial intercourse outlined in the previous three chapters, can we say that Burke did indeed endorse mercantilism, at least early in his parliamentary career? Before proceeding, we must reiterate that "mercantilism" did not rest on a uniform set of doctrinal propositions. Nevertheless, some general principles did slowly emerge from connotations of the phrase in the eighteenth century, including the following ideas: cheap wages were desirable in order to help domestic producers undersell foreign traders and preserve profit for themselves; import regulations were beneficial in order to create an export surplus; wealth should be measured in bullion; a nation should produce goods at home rather than purchase them abroad; imperialism and slavery were possible means to the pursuit of wealth; and trade was a zero-sum competitive enterprise.[195]

One line of reasoning holds that Burke embraced these tenets. According to this interpretation, while Burke supported small channels of free commerce in the wider expanse of the British Empire, he envisioned a mercantile system governed by the selective exploitation of trade laws that steered commerce to the seat of Great Britain. Burke defended the Navigation Acts; he did not call for the elimination of all commercial restrictions; and was a committed proponent of Britain's imperial right of conquest. He thus advocated mercantilism.[196]

This argument contains a degree of truth but also encounters a number of problems on a practical and theoretical level. First, reconsider the historical context for one of Burke's first major legislative achievements in Parliament, the Free Port Act of 1766. The Grenville ministry had implemented the Sugar Act and Stamp Act in order to extract greater revenue from the colonies and benefit the manufacturing interest in the British West Indies. As Thomas Whately[197] explained, Grenville's commercial regulations in the Caribbean had engendered a "Preference" for "the Produce of our *West-Indian* Colonies" by taxing heavily "Indigo, Coffee, Sugar, and Melasses of the foreign Islands imported into *North America*, while the same Commodities raised in our own, were lightly charged at the most, and some of them entirely free."[198] In other words, the Grenvillian restrictions endeavored to advantage British West Indian planters at the expense of French and American competitors.

---

[195] See Thomas Sowell, *On Classical Economics* (New Haven and London: Yale University Press, 2006), 5–6. See also Wiles, "Theory of Wages in Later English Mercantilism," 113–126; and Gary M. Anderson and Robert D. Tollison, "Sir James Steuart as the Apotheosis of Mercantilism and His Relation to Adam Smith," *Southern Economic Journal* 51 (1984): 456–468.

[196] See "British Commercial Policy and the Navigation Acts," Chapter 6.

[197] Whately was an MP and a writer on imperial political economy.

[198] Thomas Whately, *Considerations on the Trade and Finances of This Kingdom* (London: J. Wilkie, 1766), 70.

The Rockingham administration, however, loosened the chains of these trade regulations. Their actions were galvanized by the belief that the enlargement of commercial intercourse in the West Indies, and between the West Indies and the colonies, produced greater benefits to the British Empire. The Free Port Act did retain protectionist measures for West Indian traders, but it also established six new free ports, spawned commercial freedoms for the Americans, and opened up competition to French and Spanish vessels. Furthermore, recall Burke's expressions of frustration to Charles O'Hara at the time that the bill had been watered down, and that the prejudices of British merchants inhibited the advancement of additional free trade measures in the legislation. And remember Paul Langford's remark that the Act embodied "the first significant attempt to launch an experiment in free trade and a portentous, if small, breach in the old imperial system."[199] The Act's attempt to relax the British stranglehold on colonial and foreign markets illustrated Burke's notion that colonies should not be regulated into submission and that competition was a net benefit to trading partners.

Even more, Burke's comments in *Speech on American Taxation* and *Speech on Conciliation* were not intended to expound his deepest philosophical convictions on political economy. They certainly incorporated elements of Burke's economic thought, but the broader political realities of the time period awakened Burke's instinct for prudence in his assessment of Anglo-American relations. His objects were the reduction of colonial agitation and the reclamation of the sacred connection between Britain and the Americans, on both political and commercial principles. Indeed, the overall mood of *Speech on Conciliation* was a conciliatory attitude toward the Americans that emphasized the alignment of interests, including the synthesizing bonds of liberal trade, between England and its colonies.

But Burke believed that the abolition of the Navigation Acts would be nonsensical and intemperate: there was no strong evidence that the source of colonial disturbances was rooted in the traditional system of trade regulations, and the Acts helped strengthen the commercial attachments between Britain and the colonists throughout the eighteenth century. And yet Burke still admitted that, unless Britain desired to further instigate the Americans, they should be "changed and modified" according to shifting circumstances.[200]

Burke's more theoretical positions on foreign trade also veered away from mercantilist persuasions. As indicated, Burke rejected the premise of zero-sum reasoning in political economy by maintaining that trade generated mutual advantages and a spirit of cooperative reconciliation between parties. The prosperity of one merchant, or country, did not drain other market participants of wealth. Even this was not a mere theoretical claim; Burke marshaled a wealth of data to expose the empirical fruits of commercial vigor,

[199] Langford, *First Rockingham Administration*, 207.
[200] Langford, *Writings and Speeches*, II, 432.

such as surges in imports and exports for trading partners. In addition, as shown in the *Observations*, he was highly skeptical of the argument that the balance of trade favored the home country. And in draft notes for a speech on the American war, Burke wrote, "The balance of trade ... is a mischievous principle; the effect of which is to accumulate a debt, and the more it inclines in your favour, the greater the debt."[201]

The real vehicle of public prosperity, then, was liberal intercourse – not favorable trade balances, or the accumulation of bullion, or military conquest. A "Free Trade," Burke wrote in his private notes regarding Anglo-Irish relations and the history and sources of Irish poverty, "is in Truth the only scource of wealth."[202] This is Burke's most categorical statement in favor of free trade throughout his entire life. Hence, he goes on to remark in the notes, the "obvious" remedy for the poor was "to obtain the means of Wealth."[203] Poverty could be diminished by the soft release of industrious activity from the watchful eye of government. In contrast, war created the pretense of lucre but was actually a prelude to strains on commerce, as Burke observed in *Speech on Townshend Duties*[204] and the *Observations*.[205] On principle, Burke challenged cardinal orthodoxies of mercantilism.

But do these thoughts not contradict Burke's defense of the Navigation Acts and the project of empire in general? One can begin to discern the great difficulty in classifying eighteenth-century economic thought through a modern binary framework of either "free trade" or "mercantilism." To add to the confusion, Adam Smith, perhaps the most celebrated advocate of free trade in modernity also supplied a conditional defense of the Acts – specifically, the Act of Navigation of 1660 – for the purposes of national security, even while acknowledging they did not create the perfect conditions for his system of natural liberty.[206]

If Burke embraced mercantilism because he supported the Acts, then did Smith also endorse mercantilism because he approved of them? The lesson is that Burke's qualified endorsement of the Navigation Acts did not necessarily indicate a strict allegiance to or refutation of mercantilist orthodoxy. In the judgment of Burke (and Smith), commercial activity operated in a deeper political context, and at times should be subordinate to and guided by broader considerations of the national interest.

In the end, can we accurately argue that Burke embraced free trade? The answer is a firm yes – with the qualifications that "free trade" in the eighteenth century did not necessarily denote the same concept as inflexible notions of the

---

[201] William and Bourke, *Correspondence of the Right Honourable Edmund Burke,* vol. IV, 477.
[202] MSS. at Sheffield, Bk. 8–173. [203] MSS. at Sheffield, Bk. 8–173.
[204] Langford, *Writings and Speeches,* II, 62.
[205] Langford, *Writings and Speeches,* II, 123. Remember, of course, that Burke argued in the *Observations* that war had not harmed the English economy to the extent Knox had claimed, not that war was the best means to promote commerce.
[206] Smith, *Wealth of Nations,* vol. I, 464–465.

term do today; that his understanding of the idea was reconcilable with a defense of empire; and that he was quite aware of the limits of trade in the practice of statecraft.[207] Burke did not call for the complete and immediate eradication of all commercial restrictions between nations,[208] but he did support the steady, systematic relaxation of trade regulations within the British Empire, and at times beyond the empire, as far as existing political exigencies and security concerns would permit. This approach perhaps explains why John Rae, the biographer of Adam Smith, claimed that Lord Shelburne "was the first English statesman, except perhaps Burke, who grasped and advocated free trade as a broad political principle."[209]

8.8 CONCLUSION

Burke's campaign on behalf of the Irish trade bills in the late 1770s marked his most determined attempt in Parliament to convince skeptics that the expansion of commerce could integrate and reconcile seeming market adversaries into a partnership of social communion. Free trade could serve as a unifying thread of human relations, reducing tensions and allaying jealousies in a manner that bred social and economic order. It substituted transactional exchange in place of coercion as a mediating bond between nations. The advantages derived from the diffusion of goods were not confined to one particular people, but rather reached a mixed mass of traders and communities. Trade was a dynamic stimulant for public opulence, while excess state entanglements clipped the wings of commercial prosperity. Such insights illuminated the more fundamental political and moral dimension of free trade in Burke's political economy: economic activity could encourage social concord between nations – particularly those within the British Empire.

As mentioned, Burke's reflections on the salutary economic and social benefits of commerce were not unique to the eighteenth century. Beyond Adam Smith, other thinkers in the Scottish Enlightenment tradition, such as David Hume and William Robertson, as well as French political theorists like Montesquieu, noticed that intercourse between nations brought about a rise in

---

[207] See also the discussion of Burke's views on the Traitorous Correspondence Bill in Chapter 12.
[208] Here I qualify my claim in my article, "Edmund Burke on Commercial Intercourse in the Eighteenth Century," *Review of Politics* 79 (2017): 565–595, that Burke was a "resolute, consistent advocate of market liberalization between and within nations" (595). As discussed, he did indeed declare in *Two Letters* that "you trade very largely where you are met by the goods of all nations," but we should stress that he was more cautious about establishing free trade relations with nations outside the orbit of the British Empire, particularly those that were enemies or rivals of Britain. See "The Anglo-French Commercial Treaty of 1786" in this chapter; and my discussion of Burke's *Speech on Traitorous Correspondence Bill* in "The Limits of Voluntary Contracts and Transactional Exchange," Chapter 12.
[209] Rae, *Life of Adam Smith*, 153–154.

mutual prosperity and tended to orient adversaries toward peaceful relations.[210] As this book will examine later, Burke's economic thought in this regard deviated from the Scots and other proponents of market liberty with respect to the lasting effect of commercial transactions in perpetuating social order, but for now we can offer the provisional conclusion that both schools praised free trade as a possible catalyst for collective opulence and political repose.

Nevertheless, we must not underestimate the political audacity of Burke's challenge to the protectionist sentiments of his age: remember that the shadow of mercantilism loomed menacingly over English trade policy at the time he wrote his letters, for the 1760s and 1770s had witnessed a spike in new protectionist laws designed to empower England at the expense of its mercantile competitors. Yet Burke mustered an uncommon strength of conviction at the time in support of greater commercial intercourse, seeking to emancipate trade from the labyrinths of meddlesome policy. Therefore, while Adam Smith provided a more robust intellectual defense of free trade in the eighteenth century, Burke was one of the most influential British *legislators* to bestow a degree of dignity on foreign, and domestic, commercial exchange prior to the publication of the *Wealth of Nations* in 1776.

We must remember, however, that free trade was not an isolated object of study in Burke's economic thought. As the previous three chapters have demonstrated, he approached questions of commerce in the wider context of the British Empire, taking into account its history, international rivals, colonies, and mercantile prejudices. From his perspective, commerce was not simply a means to prosperity but an instrument for imperial strength throughout the globe. Burke's careful attention to these additional factors – which, it is safe to say, was also motivated by the fact that he was an elected representative as well as an intellectual thinker – help explain his attempt to defend commercial intercourse *within* an imperial framework. Burke's integration of commercial liberty with empire thus exhibited his tendency to combine a variety of considerations into a unified conception of political economy.

We may also conclude that Burke was keener on establishing commercial relations with the Irish and other British subjects than with the French because the former group held a shared language and overlapping defense interests. The implicit message in Burke's thoughts on foreign trade is that intercourse was more likely to lead to peaceful relations if the two transacting parties already

---

[210] See Montesquieu, *The Spirit of the Laws*, trans. and ed. Anne M. Cohler, Basia Carolyn Miller, and Harold Samuel Stone (Cambridge: Cambridge University Press, 1994), 338; and Hirschman, *Passions and the Interests*, 60–63. For David Hume, see his *Essays: Moral, Political, and Literary*, ed. Eugene F. Miller (Indianapolis: Liberty Fund, 1994), 253–267, 327–331. For William Robertson, see Robertson, *The Works of Wm. Robertson, D.D.*, vol. III (London: W. Pickering, 1825), 74.

possessed similar social attitudes and national security concerns, even given the differences between English and Irish cultures. (Of course, in the case of the American colonists, the breakout of the American war destroyed this hope.)

For Burke, then, an enlightened assessment of free trade required sharp comprehension of geopolitical developments in Europe and domestic political interests in Britain. This is why he moderated his commitment to the principle of free trade at times in the spirit of prudence, as exemplified by the Free Port Act, or because of weightier matters such as national reputation and security, as displayed by his objection to the Anglo-French Commercial Treaty. In the end, Burke's legislative activities reflect a delicate balance among his endorsement of commercial liberty, his exercise of political moderation, and his awareness of the imperative of national defense, demonstrating that practitioners of statesmanship must recognize and harmonize these competing priorities in the service of the common good. Free trade was a noble aim, but sometimes the wealth of nations must surrender to the honor and integrity of empire.

PART V

INDIA

9

Britain's East India Company, Indian Markets, and Monopoly

> The Spirit of all these Regulations naturally tended to weaken, in the very original Constitution of the Company, the main Spring of the Commercial Machine, the *Principles of Profit and Loss.*[1]
>
> *Ninth Report of Select Committee, 1783*

9.1 INTRODUCTION

We have concluded thus far that Burke supported liberty of commerce in European markets spanning Britain, Ireland, the British West Indies, and the American colonies. But did he apply his defense of private property and voluntary exchange to the activities of non-European peoples? Burke's penetrating treatment of British India presents an opportunity to answer this question. In the context of Anglo-Indian relations, Burke is most famous for his vicious attack on the oppressive rule of Warren Hastings over Indian natives, which raised vital questions about the improprieties of the British Empire in the late eighteenth century that continue to shape discussion on the legacies of European colonialism to this day.[2] Yet Burke's

---

[1] Langford, *Writings and Speeches*, V, 241.
[2] See, among many, Frederick G. Whelan, *Edmund Burke and India: Political Morality and Empire* (Pittsburgh: University of Pittsburgh Press, 1996); Pitts, *Turn to Empire*; P. J. Marshall, *"A Free though Conquering People": Eighteenth-Century Britain and Its Empire* (Burlington, VT: Ashgate, 2003); Sunil M. Agnani, *Hating Empire Properly: The Two Indies and the Limits of European Anticolonialism* (New York: Fordham University Press, 2013); Daniel I. O'Neill, *Edmund Burke and the Conservative Logic of Empire* (Oakland: University of California Press, 2016); and Sankar Muthu, *Enlightenment against Empire* (Princeton and Oxford: Princeton University Press, 2003).

particular thoughts on the economic ties between Britain and India – the focus of this chapter – warrant greater discussion and amplification.

Burke's study of Anglo-Indian commercial relations offers a conception of political economy distinct from his other reflections on the subject because it grappled with an institution that powerfully captured the contradictions and ambiguities of the British Empire: the East India Company. The Company was a chartered company founded in 1600 that enjoyed a commercial monopoly on trade between England and the East Indies for much of its history. It was a creation and a subject of the British government but an institution that steadily acquired sovereign powers – those of war and peace and law enforcement – throughout its history in India. By the end of the seventeenth century, the Company, according to Burke, had become "a subordinate sovereign power; that is, sovereign with regard to the objects which it touched, subordinate with regard to the power from whence this great trust was derived."[3]

The purpose of the Company was to advance British trading interests in the Indian subcontinent, but the firm ended up compromising its own commercial integrity, and placed in peril the livelihoods of native Indians in the process. In addition, while the firm achieved a reputation for its meticulous accounting and record-keeping practices, it fueled financial fraud and political extortion. Such contradictions inspired Adam Smith to portray the firm's institutional composition as a "strange absurdity,"[4] a sovereign enigma enveloping a commercial riddle, neither of which was held to serious account by the British government.

We must not underestimate the historical significance of the East India Company. It was a chief energizing source for the extension of British commerce across the globe from the early seventeenth century through to the mid-nineteenth century, and for the integration of vast trading networks during a period in which trafficking in distant lands remained a hazardous endeavor. The Company pioneered the modern concept of "civil service" as a distinct administrative unit separate from military and ecclesiastical offices; even more, the actual term derived from the institution, according to Richard A. Chapman.[5] The firm was one of the first companies to offer a kind of limited liability protection for its investors,[6] and it served as an important institutional medium for the exposure of the British people to different cultural traditions and foreign goods. Even though we cannot trace a direct

---

[3] Langford, *Writings and Speeches*, VI, 283.

[4] Smith, *Wealth of Nations*, vol. II, 637. The Company also raised compelling legal questions about the role of English law in India and the firm's status as a corporate body. See Philip J. Stern, "The English East India Company and the Modern Corporation: Legacies, Lessons, and Limitations," *Seattle University Law Review* 39 (2016): 423–445.

[5] See Richard A. Chapman, *The Higher Civil Service in Britain* (London: Constable, 1970), 9.

[6] Ron Harris, *Industrializing English Law: Entrepreneurship and Business Organization, 1720–1844* (Cambridge: Cambridge University Press, 2000), 128n38.

line from the Company to modern corporations, in many ways the firm anticipated their emergence as powerful commercial institutions that benefited from the legal establishment and protection of corporate property rights. Most important, the rampant decline of the Company's conduct in India gave rise to a host of questions in Britain about the promise and peril of imperial dominion at the same time Burke served in Parliament. This moment afforded him a special opportunity to meditate deeply on the role of the British Empire in the world.

Accordingly, Burke's inquiry into the political economy of India exceeded questions relating to chartered monopolies and supply and demand laws, for it formed part of his broader conception of the possibilities and limits of commercial empire in late eighteenth-century England. Commerce was not simply a matter of voluntary exchange between trading partners. It was also a means to increase and fortify British influence in foreign affairs; to gain access to untapped material resources that could ostensibly advantage the British people; and to promote the honor and integrity of the British Empire. In short, our grasp of Burke's analysis of the political economy of India requires comprehension of his wider beliefs about imperial politics as well as his commentary on free trade.[7]

Burke's general attitude toward the imperial relationship between Britain and India was consistent with his position on the American question. He held that the right of war and the right of conquest, as well as treaty concessions from the Moghul Empire and local rulers, granted Britain the authority to govern and acquire wealth in Asian territories. Nevertheless, similar to his view of British relations with the North American colonies, he contended that the just exercise of these rights required the moral obligation to rule over subjects with a benevolent hand – and a modest one.

On this note, more than twenty years prior to Burke's sustained engagement with the Anglo-Indian question, he and Will Burke provided the following comments in *Account of the European Settlements in America*:

[I]gnorant country people and barbarous nations, are better observers of times and seasons, and draw better rules from them, than more civilized and reasoning people, for they rely more upon experience than theories, they are more careful of traditionary observations, and living more in the open air at all times, and not so occupied but they have leisure to observe every change, though minute, in that element, they come to have great treasures of useful matter, though, as it might be expected, mixed with many superstitious and idle notions as to the causes. These make their observations to be

---

[7] In his analysis of Anglo-Indian relations, Burke discussed many events that carried economic implications. Due to the extensive scope of this material, however, the following two chapters will highlight specific speeches and reports of his on the subject that draw out his underlying beliefs on political economy. Consult Whelan, *Edmund Burke and India*, for additional commentary on Burke's engagement with Indian affairs.

rejected as chimerical in the gross by many literati, who are not near so nice and circumspect as they ought to be in distinguishing what this sort of people may be very competent judges of, and what not.[8]

The *Account* is suggesting that Europeans should check their tendency to assume that non-European peoples, such as natives of the British West Indies, lacked knowledge and insight into the climatic conditions of their own environment. Because indigenous populations' understanding of their local circumstances might surpass the refined wisdom of their seemingly civilized betters, European imperial dominion should be governed by a sense of humility.

This belief informed Burke's public and private reflections on Anglo-Indian relations decades later. Burke defended the East India Company as a legitimate institution, backed by the authority of its royal charter, that carried the prescriptive right to operate and trade in India. The Company should confer advantages on the British Empire, he maintained, but it should also respect the local customs and tempers of native Indians – including their spirit of commercial enterprise.

9.2 THE POLITICS OF THE EAST INDIA COMPANY

England's East India Company[9] was a joint-stock company that had obtained its royal charter in 1600 under Queen Elizabeth I for the purpose of competing with the Dutch spice trade in the Spice Islands of the East Indies (in present-day Indonesia).[10] It held an exclusive commercial monopoly within the British Empire between Britain and the Far East. After struggling to compete with Dutch traders in the first few decades of the seventeenth century, however, the Company began to expand its trade with India and China. The firm was typically seen as a safe investment, offering a regular dividend of 6 percent to

---

[8] *Account of the European Settlements*, vol. II, 98.

[9] The following sources were used for the historical background of the Company: Lucy S. Sutherland, *The East India Company in Eighteenth-Century Politics* (Oxford: Clarendon Press, 1952); Whelan, *Edmund Burke and India*; Emily Erikson, *Between Monopoly and Free Trade: The English East India Company, 1600–1757* (Princeton and Oxford: Princeton University Press, 2014); Langford, *Writings and Speeches*, V, 1–27; Philip Lawson, *The East India Company: A History* (London and New York: Longman, 1993); H. V. Bowen, Margarette Lincoln, and Nigel Rigby, eds., *The Worlds of the East India Company* (Suffolk, UK: The Boydell Press, 2006); H. V. Bowen, *The Business of Empire: The East India Company and Imperial Britain, 1756–1833* (Cambridge: Cambridge University Press, 2006); Bowen, "The 'Little Parliament': The General Court of the East India Company, 1750–1784," *The Historical Journal* 34 (1991): 857–872; Bourke, *Empire & Revolution*, 334–338; Lock, *Edmund Burke*, vol. I, 235–236; Lock, *Edmund Burke*, vol. II, 31; and Smith, *Wealth of Nations*, vol. II, 746–758.

[10] One company enjoyed trading privileges until 1698, when a competitor was formed by charter. In 1709 they were officially consolidated to form the *United Company of Merchants of England Trading to the East Indies*. The firm initiated its first joint-stock venture in 1614, and became a "genuine joint-stock endeavour" in 1657, writes Philip Lawson (*East India Company*, 21).

shareholders.[11] The institution's executive body was the Court of Directors, which consisted of twenty-four members. They were elected by, and from, the Court of Proprietors, the group of the company's prominent shareholders.

The Company controlled small territories in the seventeenth and early eighteenth centuries, but the orbit of its political and military activities was constrained by the narrow mission of its charter to foster and enhance trade. In 1757, however, Colonel Robert Clive and the Company defeated Siraj-ad-daula, the Nawab[12] of Bengal, and his French allies in the Battle of Plassey during the Seven Years War, which led to the dramatic expansion of the institution's political and territorial power in Bengal, the eastern region in the Indian subcontinent.

The Treaty of Allahabad, signed in August 1765, entrenched the East India Company's bureaucratic footing in Bengal. The treaty formally recognized the Company as the authority responsible for revenue administration, or *diwani*, in Bengal, whose lucrative receipts ranged from £2 million to £4 million annually.[13] "[A]lthough the East India Company's regime had quickly become corrupt and abusive," explains Frederick G. Whelan, who has written the definitive book on Burke's engagement with India, "its title to rule in Bengal was sound, arising as it did from a combination of conquest in justifiable wars and formal grants of authority from the Mogul emperor."[14]

The Company thus acquired the power and territory to be a domineering force in the region: upon winning the Battle of Plassey and receiving *diwani* privileges, it wielded authority over an area of land whose size and population were considerably larger than England's. The Company's swift political ascent was matched by its widening military footprint, which was employed to safeguard its possessions in India. The total number of regular troops under the corporation's rule in India climbed from 3,000 in 1749 to 26,000 by 1763. By 1778, its military commanded more servicemen than the British army in peacetime.[15]

Extending into the early 1760s, the British government and the East India Company had forged a relatively placid relationship, with the former issuing the continual renewal of the firm's charter and the latter trading in India to promote British commercial interests. Because the Seven Years War that ended in 1763 had produced a rapid increase in Britain's national debt, however, Lord Chatham shifted his acquisitive eye toward the coffers of the corporation, in the hope that an investigation by Parliament into its financial practices would result in the Company contributing to the British treasury.

---

[11] Lock, *Edmund Burke*, vol. I, 235.
[12] A nawab was the honorific title granted by the Mughal emperor to quasi-independent Muslim governors in India.
[13] Bowen, *Business of Empire*, 3. [14] Whelan, *Edmund Burke and India*, 7.
[15] Gerald Bryant, "Officers of the East India Company's Army in the Days of Clive and Hastings," *The Journal of Imperial and Commonwealth History* 6 (1978): 203.

Chatham was mindful that such a proposal was politically attractive to MPs who were concerned about the growing presence of "nabobs" in British politics. Nabobs, affluent East India Company servants suspected of obtaining their wealth in India through nefarious means, returned from the subcontinent and brandished their new riches to expand their electoral and social influence in England. Robert Clive was only one of the more conspicuous nabobs in this environment; in the twenty years after 1760, between 200 and 300 of them[16] arrived in Britain, suggesting that Britain's involvement in Indian affairs rested on increasingly suspicious commercial and ethical grounds.

Burke and India

Burke had been an observer of India even before he entered Parliament in 1766. In 1758, he was confident enough to disagree with Samuel Johnson on a question concerning the region.[17] By 1772, Burke had acquired enough of a reputation on commercial and imperial matters that he received an offer to serve on a supervisory commission in Bengal tasked with investigating the institutional delinquencies of the East India Company.[18] Burke turned down the opportunity, yet he continued to deepen his reservoir of knowledge about the cultural ethos and commercial environment of India while serving in the House of Commons.

The pull of Indian affairs on Burke's mind reflected his uncommon thirst for the consumption of historical and empirical knowledge. We have witnessed this quality in its most expressive form so far in his thorough background research for his economical reform plan and for his writings and speeches on British commercial interests in the West Indies and the American colonies. Burke absorbed an even more prodigious body of knowledge in the case of India, blending and synthesizing commercial, cultural, political, historical, and legal information in a manner that furnished a comprehension of the subcontinent broader than that of many of his peers. By 1785, P. J. Marshall writes, he "almost certainly knew more about India than did any other man in public life who had not actually been there."[19]

Burke's beliefs about the institutional and moral integrity of the East India Company evolved over time. In the late 1760s and early 1770s, as additional reports from India of the corporation's activities reached London, the British government became more conscious of the Company's growing mismanagement on the subcontinent. The institution had further plunged into

---

[16] Philip Lawson and Jim Phillips, "'Our Execrable Banditti': Perceptions of Nabobs in Mid-Eighteenth Century Britain," *Albion* 16 (1984): 227.

[17] Langford, *Writings and Speeches*, V, 2.

[18] Langford, *Writings and Speeches*, V, 2. As P. J. Marshall notes, however, this offer did not necessarily stem from recognition of Burke's heightened attraction to India per se but rather his general reputation as a "man of business."

[19] Langford, *Writings and Speeches*, V, 1.

severe financial difficulty, which prompted Chatham's interest in using the firm's wealth to pay down the national debt. Yet Burke during this time was dedicated to protecting the property of the firm from parliamentary temptations to acquire its riches.

When Parliament was considering new regulations that would have levied an effectual tax of £400,000 on the East India Company and restricted its dividend to 10 percent or lower,[20] Burke drafted notes for a speech opposing the idea of legislative intrusion into its affairs. In his draft, *Speech on East India Dividend Bill*,[21] Burke asserted his cherished principle that property should be secured from the creeping designs of government. The legislation was "going to restrict by a positive arbitrary Regulation the enjoyment of the profits which should be made in Commerce."[22] Parliament should not wield its capricious power to seize the wealth of a trading firm, even if the firm had received a government charter in the first place to operate in foreign lands.

Burke's attempt to shield the commercial profit of the East India Company from the British government typified his stern effort to defend mobile and landed property throughout his parliamentary career. "I always took it to be an invariable rule and what distinguished Law and Freedom from Violence and Slavery is, that the property vested in the Subject by a known Law – and forfeited by no delinquency defined by a known [law] could be taken away from him by any power or authority whatsoever," Burke stated in his notes.[23] The rule of law was the guardian of property rights.

Burke was also suspicious of men who claimed to be acting pursuant to the common welfare, such as those who supported extracting wealth from the East India Company to reduce the national debt: "I would much sooner listen to an interested man crying out injustice – than to another crying out publick good – because I never knew any man that was not willing to be publick spirited at another mans expence know property of certain Birds where their Nest lies."[24] He proceeded to insist that the difference between the 10 percent dividend desired by the legislation and the 12.5 percent dividend sought by proprietors would lead to a reduction of an additional £80,000 in Company revenue, which, in his view, could cripple its financial solvency.[25] As such examples attest, Burke demonstrated a steadfast commitment to sheltering the property of the corporation from parliamentary schemes starting at the outset of his service in the House of Commons.

Burke continued his defense of the East India Company during debate over Lord North's Regulating Bill of 1773, which aimed to tighten ministerial control over the Company's administration. The bill, which passed into law in

[20] Company proprietors desired 12.5 percent (Langford, *Writings and Speeches*, II, 65).
[21] There is no evidence that he presented the speech in Parliament, however (Langford, *Writings and Speeches*, II, 64).
[22] Langford, *Writings and Speeches*, II, 65.   [23] Langford, *Writings and Speeches*, II, 65.
[24] Langford, *Writings and Speeches*, II, 66.   [25] Langford, *Writings and Speeches*, II, 66.

June of that year as the Regulating Act of 1773, installed Warren Hastings as the Governor General of Bengal, granted him political authority over the presidencies of Madras and Bombay, and established a Supreme Court in Calcutta. Burke opposed North's bill. He argued, with streaks of exaggeration, that the reform effort would fuel ministerial corruption and aggrandize royal power. And he defended the Company on its individual merits, claiming that it should simply reassert its independent privileges and recover its chartered liberties. That Burke was in the parliamentary opposition most likely also influenced his resistance to the legislation.

Following the bill's passage, however, Burke became progressively aware of the Company's hardening lawlessness in the East Indies. He realized that the institution would not be able to carry out the reforms necessary to ameliorate its financial difficulties and halt its political oppression of Indian natives. In the end, Burke turned out to be one of the corporation's most strident antagonists in Parliament.

Burke was presented with an opportunity to influence Indian affairs when he was appointed to a Select Committee in the House of Commons in 1781. The task of the Committee was to clarify the role of the Supreme Court in Calcutta, in light of petitions from the East India Company and British inhabitants of Calcutta that the Court had abused its powers. The Committee's recommendations were included in a bill written primarily by Burke (and changed substantially by the House of Lords), called the Bengal Judicature Bill of 1781, that defined the constraints of the Court's authority and, in turn, signified a commitment to respecting the local political and legal traditions of Indians.[26] Not only did the bill mark one of Burke's lawmaking triumphs, but his place on the Select Committee also positioned him to deepen his investigation into British maladministration in India. The committee's reports confirmed allegations of the widespread misconduct of the Company over natives.[27]

The Select Committee was recreated in December 1781, filing eleven reports from February 1782 to November 1783 on British imperial rule in South Asia.[28] Burke emerged as its most knowledgeable and passionate student of Indian affairs. It was in this committee that some of his most perceptive and captivating insights into the political economy of India gained formal expression, as articulated in *Ninth Report of Select Committee* (1783) and *Eleventh Report of Select Committee* (1783). In addition to these reports, Burke presented keen commentary on Anglo-Indian relations in *Speech on Fox's India Bill* (1783) and

---

[26] See Langford, *Writings and Speeches*, V, 140–144.

[27] Burke was further convinced of the need to reform the East India Company after Haidar Ali, the ruler of Mysore in southern India, invaded the Carnatic. To address this development, North created another Select Committee, headed by Henry Dundas, which called for additional ministerial oversight of the Company. See Lock, *Edmund Burke*, vol. II, 35.

[28] Lock, *Edmund Burke*, vol. II, 35.

Speech on Nabob of Arcot's Debts (1785), and in his various speeches on Hastings's impeachment proceedings. These writings and speeches will be examined later in this chapter.

Burke's study of the East India Company and British India coincided with possible financial conflicts of interest. In late 1766, when Burke was arguing in Parliament that the Company should be protected from ministerial intervention, he was, at the same time, implicated in a financial arrangement devised by Lord Verney[29] and Will Burke that speculated heavily in East India Company stock. Both Verney and Will suffered heavy losses after the market crashed in 1769, in turn compromising Burke's finances due to the overlapping pool of resources between Burke and Will.[30] Following this financial calamity, Will sought to recover his losses by serving as an agent for the Raja of Tanjore in the late 1770s and early 1780s. He most likely received an annual salary of £8,000 for his service.[31] Burke's financial ties to Will raised a cloud of suspicion that Burke himself was a paid agent of the Raja.[32]

Burke's fortunes became directly linked to the success of the East India Company in October 1780, when he bought £1,000 worth of Company stock.[33] His investment permitted him to participate in Company proceedings and vote in the Court of Proprietors. Burke sold his stake in the corporation in February 1782.[34] Note also that he served as Paymaster of the Forces, the position responsible for funding the British army using expenditures authorized by Parliament, two separate times under the second Rockingham administration and the Fox-North coalition in the early 1780s.

Although one must be alert to these possible conflicts of interest when probing Burke's assessment of Anglo-Indian relations, it would be misguided to impute sinister motives behind his shifting positions on the East India Company throughout his political life. Even with his financial connections, it is far from clear that Burke stood to gain substantially from Will Burke's agency, as P. J. Marshall observes.[35] More important, Burke, in his commentary on India, displays a command of knowledge on political

---

[29] Verney helped secure Burke's seat for Wendover in Parliament in late 1765.

[30] See Dixon Wecter, "Edmund Burke and His Kinsmen: A Study of the Statesman's Financial Integrity and Private Relationships," in *The University of Colorado Studies*, vol. I, Series B, Studies in the Humanities, eds. Francis Ramaley, Irene P. McKeehan, and Hugo G. Rodeck (Boulder: University of Colorado, 1939), 27–33, 107.

[31] Langford, *Writings and Speeches*, V, 10. Tanjore was a fertile, quasi-independent state that had been occupied by the East India Company and transferred to the Nawab of the Carnatic in 1773. London directors ordered Lord Pigot, the newly installed governor of Madras, to return Tanjore to the Raja. Pigot fulfilled this task. The Madras Council, however, removed his authority, motivated by the underlying hope that placing Tanjore under the Nawab's control would make it easier for him to pay off his debts to the Company. See Langford, *Writings and Speeches*, V, 11–13; Whelan, *Edmund Burke and India*, 111–112; Bourke, *Empire & Revolution*, 516; and Lock, *Edmund Burke*, vol. II, 38.

[32] Langford, *Writings and Speeches*, V, 10.   [33] Lock, *Edmund Burke*, vol. I, 485.

[34] Lock, *Edmund Burke*, vol. I, 485.   [35] See Langford, *Writings and Speeches*, V, 10.

economy that reflected his earlier and later statements on the virtues of market exchange that were unrelated to the Company, suggesting that his effort to restore the corporation on a firmer financial substructure was impelled by considerations of economic principle and wisdom, not pecuniary self-interest. Furthermore, Burke's remarks on the Company offer new glimpses into his thinking on commercial monopoly and merchants that cannot be attributed to underlying motivations of individual need, as we shall learn in this chapter.

9.3   BURKE'S GENERAL PRINCIPLES OF TRADING MONOPOLIES

Before proceeding, let us pause and review the general principles of Burke's conception of monopoly and apply them to his commentary on the East India Company. In appended notes to the 1844 edition of his correspondence, he defined monopoly as "the power, in one man, of exclusive dealing in a commodity or commodities, which others might supply if not prevented by that power." He laid a sharp accent on the moral implication of this definition: because monopoly obstructed the activities of others, it was "contrary to common right" and to "Natural Right." Monopoly was legitimate only if it were based on the legal assent of the parties involved.[36]

Burke did not always oppose monopolies in practice. He defended them when they secured intellectual property rights, as exemplified by his approval of the Booksellers Bill, which protected copyright privileges for authors,[37] and by his support for Richard Champion's attempt to renew a patent on a china clay manufactory.[38] He also expressed approval of monopolies when they safeguarded corporate property rights, as demonstrated by his opposition to a parliamentary proposal to build a new waterway, the Selby-Leeds Canal, which would have threatened the Aire & Calder Navigation's prosperous monopoly on traffic flow linking Leeds to Selby.[39] Accordingly, Burke's notes in the 1844 edition of his correspondence proffered two rules for awarding monopolies. The first encouraged men to "employ themselves in useful

---

[36] William and Bourke, *Correspondence of the Right Honourable Edmund Burke*, vol. IV, 459.

[37] See W. Forbes Gray, "Alexander Donaldson and His Fight For Cheap Books," *Juridical Review* 38 (1926): 180–202.

[38] See Hugh Owen, *Two Centuries of Ceramic Art in Bristol: Being a History of the Manufacture of "The True Porcelain" by Richard Champion* (London: Bell and Daldy, 1873), 143. At the same time Burke supported Champion's bid, however, he opposed the extension of James Watt's fire-engine invention, leading to various interpretations of his motives. See Eric Robinson, "Matthew Boulton and the Art of Parliamentary Lobbying," *The Historical Journal* 7 (1964): 209–229; B. D. Bargar, "Matthew Boulton and the Birmingham Petition of 1775," *The William and Mary Quarterly* 13 (1956): 26–39; and Phillip Johnson, "The Myth of Mr Burke and Mr Watt: For Want of a Champion!" *Queen Mary Journal of Intellectual Property* 6 (2016): 370–379.

[39] See Burke's speech on the proposal in Osborn Files 2242, "Speech on the Selby Canal: manuscript copy of an extract / n.d," Beinecke Library. For background on the canal, see Baron F. Duckham, "Selby and the Aire & Calder Navigation 1774–1826," *The Journal of Transport History* 7 (1965): 87–95.

inventions," like books; and the second inspired men to pursue "great risks in useful undertakings."[40]

It was this second principle that most likely informed Burke's defense of the East India Company. Granting a monopoly to such firms was worthy because commercial enterprise in distant regions carried the burden of attendant uncertainties and hazards. "The beginnings of many useful undertakings may be full of risk and danger of all kinds; the following of them safe," Burke stated in the notes.[41] While domestic merchants in England operated in familiar market environments, dealers in foreign commerce faced a profusion of challenges trading in remote lands. The state authorization of a monopoly for a trading institution, then, conveyed formal recognition that the beneficiary's commercial endeavors bore heightened risk far beyond the vagaries of internal markets, suggesting that the government held the responsibility to support such perilous undertakings for the benefit of its people.

According to Burke, this trading institution deserved to enjoy privileges for as long as it pursued hazardous trade. He stressed in his notes that "the duration of the monopoly ought not, in equity, to be continued longer than till the undertaker is compensated the full value of the risk." Risk should be determined based on "the supposed loss of the capital, and the ordinary *simple* interest of the money, or the current value of insurance." Even more, "If he has gained his capital with *compound* interest, this ought to be the very utmost; it seems, indeed, rather too much."[42] Overseas commercial investment with exceptional financial costs merited the selective sanction of monopoly.

Not only did the initial explorer of new trade routes deserve trading privileges, but a trading company's enlargement of existing commercial opportunities also carried risk; consequently, this company warranted protection as well. The new dealer "runs a risk for a beneficial purpose, as much as the first dealer does; for to *extend* trade is beneficial as well as to *discover* it; and risks are run in extending as well as discovering." Burke explained further that there "will be some difference where, in the original grant of the monopoly, a price has been limited."[43]

A monopoly for a trading firm, however, was not the same privilege as a monopoly for an author. Burke contends that the former, unlike the latter,[44] could be circumscribed by the imperatives of utility. Monopolies of useful undertakings may "have limits; in most cases they *ought* to have limits; else they will transgress the purposes of their establishment, which was to discover a benefit for the most beneficial, that is, the most generally beneficial,

[40] William and Bourke, *Correspondence of the Right Honourable Edmund Burke*, vol. IV, 460.

[41] William and Bourke, *Correspondence of the Right Honourable Edmund Burke*, vol. IV, 460.

[42] William and Bourke, *Correspondence of the Right Honourable Edmund Burke*, vol. IV, 461.

[43] William and Bourke, *Correspondence of the Right Honourable Edmund Burke*, vol. IV, 462.

[44] William and Bourke, *Correspondence of the Right Honourable Edmund Burke*, vol. IV, 460. Burke writes, "I know of no dealing, except in books of the author's own invention, wherein a perpetual monopoly can be reasonable."

purposes."[45] For Burke, providing a perpetual copyright for an author's own invention was a more tenable exercise of government authority than giving a perpetual monopoly to a trading company. Once the chartered institution stopped generating advantages for the public (or once those advantages could be created without bearing the burden of high risk), Burke indicates, the justification for its charter withered away.

We can draw a provisional conclusion about Burke's larger conception of political economy that derives from his reflections on monopoly: his defense of the state licensing of trading privileges for risky adventures signaled his belief in a positive role for the state to advance the national welfare. *Thoughts and Details* announced Burke's conviction that government should not regulate the domestic flow of goods. Yet recall in the economic tract that he briefly mentioned the protection of trading companies – "the corporations that owe their existence to its fiat"[46] – as a proper function of government.

Burke's notes on a trade monopoly in the 1844 edition of his correspondence give support to this point. In his judgment, even though the state should not regulate internal markets, it harbored a responsibility to encourage commercial investment in distant parts of the world. This did not mean that the British government possessed a mandate to regulate all mercantile activities of the trading company, however. Instead, once the company received the charter, it should be free to pursue trade independent of intrusive meddling from the state – as long as the firm did not abuse its delicate authority.

9.4   NINTH REPORT OF SELECT COMMITTEE I: MARKETS AND THE CORRUPTION OF SUPPLY AND DEMAND LAWS

Burke navigates the terrain of Indian economic affairs with the confidence of a policy expert and the sensitivity of a local observer of Indian culture in the *Ninth Report*, of which he was widely acknowledged by contemporaries to be its primary author.[47] Brimming with historical data and empirical information, the report provides a sweeping political analysis of Britain's public administration in India. Yet the *Ninth Report*'s most important feature for our purposes is its penetrating study of the economic impact of the East India Company on Indian trading markets. As the report notes, the Company's "Commerce," as well as the British governing presence over natives, were the "Two great links" that maintained the connection between Britain and India.[48] Burke recognized that shedding light on the inner workings of the commercial link was essential to comprehending the nature of their political relationship.

The *Ninth Report* furnishes interpretive advantages that *Thoughts and Details* and some of Burke's other statements on political economy do not. Although the

[45] William and Bourke, *Correspondence of the Right Honourable Edmund Burke*, vol. IV, 462.
[46] Langford, *Writings and Speeches*, IX, 143.   [47] See Langford, *Writings and Speeches*, V, 194.
[48] Langford, *Writings and Speeches*, V, 222.

report, like his other economic writings, addresses a particular historical circumstance, its large scope appears to have required long reflection and careful preparation. In addition, Burke hoped the report would be accessible for public consumption; as he explained, the Committee attempted to write it in "plain and popular Language."[49] These reasons perhaps explain why the *Ninth Report* displays a more dispassionate tone than the *Reflections*; the former was an official government report intended to be referenced for objective commentary and empirical data on British India, while the latter was a perceptive but highly charged letter denouncing the French Revolution. The *Ninth Report* also weighs profound questions beyond supply and demand laws, such as the geopolitical relationship between an imperial power and its native subjects, that in significant ways offers an intellectual depth unmatched by *Thoughts and Details*. In short, the report is one of Burke's most wide-ranging statements on the subject of political economy, and yet his specific arguments about the nexus between market principles and the local conditions of Indian society tend to be underappreciated in the study of his imperial and economic thought.

The *Ninth Report* demonstrates a command of the principles of supply and demand early in its discussion on British India. Prior to the East India Company's assumption of *diwani* responsibilities in 1765, the report notes, intercourse between India and Europe was governed by the natural rhythm and flow of market laws. The "trade with India was carried on upon the common Principles of Commerce, namely, by sending out such Commodities as found a Demand in the India Market; and where that Demand was not adequate to the reciprocal Call of the European Market for Indian Goods, by a large annual Exportation of Treasure, chiefly in Silver."[50] Other European companies also sold silver to traders in India. Such vibrant commercial relations were unimpeachable evidence of Europe's high regard for the Indian economy; and their reciprocal flavor further fostered economic development in native lands. "This Influx of Money poured into India by an Emulation of all the Commercial Nations of Europe, encouraged Industry, and promoted Cultivation in a high Degree," the report states, even while acknowledging the wars fought on Indian soil and the corruption of local governance.[51]

Yet Mir Kasim Ali Khan,[52] the second nawab of Bengal, noticed that Indians were still being "excluded as Aliens"[53] from their trade, and that the revenue of princes was discouraged by the domineering commercial activities of the British. Khan then annulled all duties on trade, thereby placing natives on the same level playing field as Europeans. The *Ninth Report*'s response to this measure evinces Burke's disgust of monopoly and endorsement of markets: "Never was a Method of defeating the Oppressions of Monopoly more forcible, more

---

[49] Langford, *Writings and Speeches*, V, 197.   [50] Langford, *Writings and Speeches*, V, 222.
[51] Langford, *Writings and Speeches*, V, 222–223.
[52] *Ninth Report* spells his name Cossim Ali Khan.
[53] Langford, *Writings and Speeches*, V, 245.

simple, or more equitable."[54] This comment hints at Burke's later discussion in the *Ninth Report* about the economic measures necessary to relieve Indians of their misery.

The natural circulation of goods was corrupted by the East India Company's arbitrary exercise of authority over territorial revenue in Bengal. Previously the Company had imported bullion from Europe to invest in its Indian trade. But in the years following the Battle of Plassey, and fueled by the imperious prerogatives of *diwani* in 1765, the Company, facing a sharp credit crisis in East India, progressively exploited its political power to use surplus revenue as investments into its commercial enterprise.[55] As the *Ninth Report* explains, "A new Way of supplying the Market of Europe, by means of the British Power and Influence, was invented."[56] Rather than seeing free trade as a source to create revenue, the firm identified revenue as a means to stimulate trade. This scheme upset the settled supply and demand principles of the Indian economy. While goods traded from Europe to India benefited the Europeans in Bengal, "no Sort of Merchandize" – beyond commodities with low value, like copper utensils – was "sent from England that is in Demand for the Wants or Desires of the Native Inhabitants."[57] Supply did not meet demand, for there was scant demand for the supply to begin with.

One "pernicious"[58] effect of the East India Company's revenue-for-investment scheme was the erosion of market reciprocity. Because the firm controlled the Indian trade through coercion, natives did not receive advantages from the corporation's use of their goods for export. "[T]he whole exported Produce of the Country (so far as the Company is concerned) is not exchanged in the Course of Barter; but is taken away without any Return or Payment whatsoever," the *Ninth Report* states.[59] It continues: "In a Commercial Light therefore, England becomes Annually Bankrupt to Bengal, to the Amount nearly of its whole Dealing; or rather, the Country has suffered what is tantamount to an Annual Plunder of its Manufactures and its Produce to the Value of Twelve hundred thousand pounds."[60] The *Ninth Report* makes a point to deny that this economic relationship resembled the free circulation of goods: it was "Intercourse (for it is not Commerce),"[61] the report states, deploying a parenthetical. For Burke, voluntary barter allowed both dealers to gain advantages from the transaction. Because Indians did not have the freedom to negotiate recompense for their goods, they were deprived of the bountiful fruits of their trade.

[54] Langford, *Writings and Speeches*, V, 245.
[55] See C. A. Bayly, *The New Cambridge History of India*, vol. II, *Indian Society and the Making of the British Empire* (Cambridge: Cambridge University Press, 2002), 53.
[56] Langford, *Writings and Speeches*, V, 223.   [57] Langford, *Writings and Speeches*, V, 226.
[58] Langford, *Writings and Speeches*, V, 226.   [59] Langford, *Writings and Speeches*, V, 226.
[60] Langford, *Writings and Speeches*, V, 226.   [61] Langford, *Writings and Speeches*, V, 226.

The East India Company's use of revenue to purchase goods to export to England created the comforting mirage in Britain of a prosperous corporation and an affluent India. The bitter reality, however, was that the Company was draining wealth from natives, a conclusion that would strongly influence succeeding analyses of Anglo-Indian relations.[62] Referring to the firm's revenue-for-investment scheme, Burke writes that "this main Cause of the Impoverishment of India has been generally taken as a Measure of its Wealth and Prosperity."[63] Exceeding confidence in the Company led to inflated stock prices, contributing to the bubble that occasioned the Company's financial crash of 1769 from which Will Burke and Lord Verney (and, by implication, Burke) had suffered.

Burke's beliefs about the virtues of free markets already begin to emerge with an intensifying glow in these early comments in the *Ninth Report*: free exchange produces benefits to both parties involved in the deal. Supply and demand laws reconcile a diversity of market wants into a symmetry of interest. Traders from different social and economic and cultural backgrounds can all glean benefits from market liberty. Such insights mark a telling harmony with Burke's additional writings, speeches, and legislative activities on the science and practice of political economy, as we have learned thus far. In the case of British India, the East India Company's attempt to stimulate investment through revenue flattened all of these energizing principles.

The *Ninth Report* even acknowledges that the East India Company, before it assumed the political authority to collect territorial revenue in Bengal, did not operate in a pristine free market environment *in Britain.* "[T]he System of the Company's Commerce was not formed upon Principles the most favourable to its Prosperity," the report avers. Although it received sanction from royal and parliamentary charters, the Company was met with an "invidious Jealousy" that apparently threatened Britain's national interest. Hence the country attempted to frustrate the movement of the corporation's most lucrative trade items; under William III and George I, the British government banned foreign imports of silk stuffs and stained and painted cottons. "The British Market was in a great Measure interdicted to the British Trader," the *Ninth Report* states. Consequently, the East Indian interest was "undoubtedly injured"[64] by the restrictions.

Price controls and export regulations also prevented the East India Company from trading in a truly free market prior to 1765. The corporation was "obliged to furnish the Ordnance with a Quantity of Saltpetre at a certain Price, without any Reference to the Standard of the Markets either of Purchase or of Sale." And the Company was "obliged to export annually a certain Proportion of British Manufactures, even though they should find for them in India none, or but an unprofitable Want."[65] The report observes that this situation might have been worse than a tax; while a tax typically harmed the consumer more than the

---

[62] See "Conclusion," Chapter 10.   [63] Langford, *Writings and Speeches*, V, 223.
[64] Langford, *Writings and Speeches*, V, 241.   [65] Langford, *Writings and Speeches*, V, 241.

vendor, in this case the vendor – the East India Company – was burdened by the weight of the export mandate.[66]

The significance of this analysis is that, much like its investigation into the Company after 1765, the standard by which the *Ninth Report* assessed desirable economic conditions before 1765 was the degree of market freedom that existed. The more the free market permitted the East India Company to benefit from supply and demand laws, the better; the less the free market operated, the worse. The fingerprints of Burke's support for voluntary exchange mark the pages of the *Ninth Report*.

Burke thoroughly examines the laws of profit and loss in his survey of Anglo-Indian commercial relations. In the *Ninth Report*, he explains that these laws were subverted by Britain's trade restrictions, which undermined the incentive to deal. "The Spirit of all these Regulations naturally tended to weaken, in the very original Constitution of the Company, the main Spring of the Commercial Machine, the *Principles of Profit and Loss*," Burke writes.[67] A "Mischief" that unfolded from the rejection of those economic principles continued to rise "with the Increase of [the firm's] Power."[68] Burke is connecting the dissolution of free markets with the augmentation of the East India Company's power. Commercial freedom afforded the Company the opportunity to reap material advantages from the operation of market principles, but this environment conducive to trade did not inject the corporation with the political might to oppress. Only when the Company gained sovereign power did such commercial principles decay, according to Burke.

Notice also that Burke associates commercial freedom with both profit *and* loss. This is more suggestive than it first appears: he is exhibiting an awareness that market activity involved the potential for gain and the possibility of risk. Not all traders earn a lucrative profit. Markets are delicate creatures, for the opportunity to earn money also entails the prospect of squandering it.

These realities were especially pertinent in the case of the East India Company. In the four-year span it studied, the *Ninth Report* discusses how the firm suffered a substantial financial loss from its revenue investment in Bengal, while its trading activity in other regions was more lucrative. Once again, Burke apprehends an inverse relationship between commercial success and political control. "[A]s the Power and Dominion of the Company was less, their Profit on the Goods was greater," he states in describing the experiences of traders in jurisdictions other than Bengal.[69] The insinuation is that the preservation of market principles enabled trade outside Bengal to flourish.

According to the *Ninth Report*, once the East India Company assumed sovereign rights in Bengal, the institution did not face the inherent incentives and constraints of a typical market economy. "[I]t was not to be expected that

---

[66] Langford, *Writings and Speeches*, V, 241.   [67] Langford, *Writings and Speeches*, V, 241.
[68] Langford, *Writings and Speeches*, V, 241–242.   [69] Langford, *Writings and Speeches*, V, 243.

the Attention to Profit and Loss would have increased," Burke writes.[70] He continues:

The idea of remitting Tribute in Goods, naturally produced an Indifference to their Price and Quality; the Goods themselves appearing little else than a Sort of Package to the Tribute. Merchandize, taken as Tribute, or bought in lieu of it, can never long be of a Kind, or of a Price fitted to a Market, which stands solely on its Commercial Reputation. The Indifference of the Mercantile Sovereign to his Trading Advantages, naturally relaxed the Diligence of his subordinate Factor-Magistrates, through all their Gradations and in all their Functions; it gave Rise, at least so far as the Principal was concerned, to much Neglect of Price and of Goodness, in their Purchases.[71]

The East India Company's use of surplus revenue to buy Indian products at artificial prices (or through tribute) to export, an activity that operated outside of traditional supply and demand laws, fostered a British attitude indifferent to the real market value of the acquired goods. The Company's political and commercial monopoly diminished the incentive for English traders to be attentive to the quality of products. Commercial reputation could not remedy this gross distortion of the natural laws of commerce.

Who ultimately benefited from this economic arrangement? "The Company might suffer above, the Natives might suffer below; the intermediate Party must profit to the Prejudice of both," the *Ninth Report* states.[72] This intermediate party, Burke suggests, was the collection of factor-magistrates, trading agents who sold goods on behalf of the Company.[73] If they did, in fact, show "Accuracy and Selection" in trading the goods, their decisions would "naturally be in Favour of that Interest to which they could not be indifferent" – themselves.[74] Neither the Company nor the local Indian population ultimately obtained advantages from such a trading environment that corrupted supply and demand principles.

The *Ninth Report*'s criticism of the East India Company's disturbance of Indian markets is expressed in two noteworthy examples: the market for raw silk and the market for piece goods, or textiles. While the Company did not impose formal monopolies on these trades, its manipulation of the competitive price system strangled their manufacturing potentialities in Bengal. The corporation fixed prices, raised the cost of textile production for natives, and forced natives to work in the textile industry, all to the unpitied detriment of the local Indian artisan and merchant.

The raw silk trade was a particularly egregious example of Britain's exploitation of markets. Meager demand existed in England for the indigenous wrought silk made in India, so the East India Company concentrated on encouraging the production of raw silk. In brandishing the

---

[70] Langford, *Writings and Speeches*, V, 242.   [71] Langford, *Writings and Speeches*, V, 242.
[72] Langford, *Writings and Speeches*, V, 242.
[73] A factor-magistrate was distinct from the classification of "merchant."
[74] Langford, *Writings and Speeches*, V, 242.

powers of the Bengali presidency, the corporation harnessed the incentive of high wages to compel existing wrought silk producers to leave their jobs and work for the Company's raw silk manufacturers. Additionally, it increased the prices of the manufacturing materials in order to restrict competition from other merchants and European competitors. "A double Bounty was thus given against the Manufactures, both in the Labour and in the Materials," the *Ninth Report* states.[75]

The East India Company's heavy investment in the raw silk trade generated high prices and a decline in quality of Indian manufactures, leading to their painful demise: "By the Increase of the Price of this and other Materials, Manufactures, formerly the most flourishing, gradually disappeared under the protection of Great Britain."[76] Forced to abandon their manufacturing businesses, natives were hired to work for the Company. Ostensibly they were to receive higher wages paid from territorial revenue, but in reality they suffered under suffocating labor conditions without enjoying fair recompense for their toil. "The manufacturing Hands were to be seduced from their Looms by high Wages, in order to prepare a raw Produce for our Market; they were to be locked up in the Factories," the *Ninth Report* states.[77] The commodity would then be "carried out of the Country, whilst its Looms would be left without any Material but the debased Refuse of a Market enhanced in its price, and scanted in its Supply."[78]

The new commercial impulse of the East India Company, then, was to choke the flow of market competition. Beyond the previously-mentioned evidence, the corporation compelled the Presidency of Madras to raise prices on goods to discourage foreign trade, and restricted the weavers of Culladore from producing cloths of the same kind that the East India Company employed in its own trade. These measures enabled rapacious servants of the Company "to buy at an advanced Price," which "did of Necessity furnish Means and Excuses for every sort of Fraud in their Purchases."[79] The servant could overbid the market or deliver goods to his superior, who would then exchange them for a loss overseas.[80] The rise of such artificial prices, the report notes, will fuel speculation, an especially odious consequence for markets that were distant from one another.[81]

Burke explains that this corruption of market order in India deprived the East India Company itself, as well as the indigenous population, of commercial advantages. By disrupting the private silk industry, the Company undermined its administrative capacities to raise and collect revenue from taxes: "Whatsoever, by Bounties or Immunities, is encouraged out of a Landed Revenue, has certainly some Tendency to lessen the net Amount of that

---

[75] Langford, *Writings and Speeches*, V, 253.   [76] Langford, *Writings and Speeches*, V, 254.
[77] Langford, *Writings and Speeches*, V, 254.   [78] Langford, *Writings and Speeches*, V, 254.
[79] Langford, *Writings and Speeches*, V, 255.   [80] Langford, *Writings and Speeches*, V, 256.
[81] Langford, *Writings and Speeches*, V, 256.

Revenue, and to forward a Produce which does not yield to the gross Collection rather than one that does."[82] The Company continued to incur losses, finally recognizing its raw silk enterprise to be self-defeating, and then relinquished it into private hands. In outlining this process, Burke is showing his characteristic attention to the dangers of unintended consequences, as exemplified by the Company's counterproductive investment in raw silk.

The *Ninth Report*'s discussion of the oppressed state of native middlemen dealers in Dhaka underscores the writing's attack on the East India Company's perversion of local markets. These middlemen, called *dalals*, had helped build up the flourishing cotton goods industry in the city prior to the firm's augmentation of power in the area. The Company, however, accused *dalals* of charging high prices for the items. Subsequently, Richard Barwell, the head of the Dhaka trading post for the Company, imposed a policy in 1774 that tightened control over weavers in order to effectively extinguish *dalals*, a repercussion that would also hurt European merchants unaffiliated with the Company.[83]

Similar to its inquiry into the Bengali economy, the *Ninth Report* observes that trade in Dhaka had prospered in the past. It was a city "once full of opulent Merchants and Dealers of all Descriptions."[84] Yet Barwell's policy led to price fixing and command of the cotton trade, unleashing a "most violent and arbitrary Power over the Whole."[85] The East India Company would force weavers to assume high levels of debt, in turn making them subservient to the capricious demands of Company agents; then the agents would seize their goods and imprison them.[86] The additional economic concern was that Barwell's measure offended the imperatives of competition: "Where there is not a vigorous Rivalship, not only tolerated but encouraged, it is impossible ever to redeem the Manufactures from the Servitude induced by those unpaid Balances."[87] Competition drove commercial production, which could have aided Indians in relieving themselves of debt.

The themes of Burke's political economy suffusing the *Ninth Report*'s treatment of Barwell's policy align with his other reflections in praise of market exchange. A free market in cotton goods generated commercial prosperity not just for middlemen but for Dhaka as a whole. Indian traders should not be pilloried for seeking their self-interest in market economies. Competition was not an insidious force for individual evil but a salutary instrument for general affluence. These currents in Burke's economic thought anticipate his stress in *Thoughts and Details* on the merits of a free circulation of provisions. The *Ninth Report*'s defense of Dhaka traders is also compatible with his vindication of English middlemen in *Thoughts and Details* as a group

---

[82] Langford, *Writings and Speeches*, V, 254.
[83] See Langford, *Writings and Speeches*, V, 259n1.
[84] Langford, *Writings and Speeches*, V, 259.   [85] Langford, *Writings and Speeches*, V, 259.
[86] Langford, *Writings and Speeches*, V, 259–260.   [87] Langford, *Writings and Speeches*, V, 268.

that performed a crucial role in the allocation of scarce resources. Material acquisition was a defensible, indeed praiseworthy, aim when pursued in a climate of market competition.

The *Ninth Report*'s proposal to remedy the situation in Dhaka marries Burke's embrace of market freedom with his instinct for prudence. "To make a sudden Change ... might destroy the few Advantages which attend any Trade," the report states, "without securing those which must flow from one established upon sound Mercantile Principles, whenever such a Trade can be established."[88] Therefore, Indian trade should be released from the cold grasp of the East India Company, but in a gradual manner. "The Revival of Trade in the Native Hands is of absolute Necessity; but ... it will rather be the Effect of a regular progressive Course of Endeavours for that Purpose, than of any one Regulation, however wisely conceived," the *Ninth Report* insists.[89] Burke's argument is sealed: the return of commercial freedom to Indian dealers should be guided by clarity of purpose and steadiness of execution.

9.5   NINTH REPORT OF SELECT COMMITTEE II: MONOPOLY

Building on its description of the deformation of supply and demand laws in British India, the *Ninth Report* proceeds to draw greater attention to the menace of monopoly that plagued Indian markets in the latter half of the eighteenth century. Because the East India Company enjoyed political sovereignty, Burke notes, it was granted the false license to abuse the native Indian population with little consequence. Yet the corporation's political monopoly also imposed a *commercial* monopoly on domestic Indian markets through its sweeping control over the local supply of goods in Bengal. For Burke, this latter form of monopoly inflicted heavy punishment on natives by injuring Indian trade and thwarting the commercial prosperity of the region.

In the *Ninth Report*'s discussion of this phenomenon, it first explains that even prior to the Treaty of Allahabad in 1765, when the East India Company assumed complete responsibility for revenue administration, Indian trade was marred by British interference in local free markets. After the Battle of Plassey in 1757, the Company's servants "obtained a mighty Ascendant over the Native Princes of Bengal."[90] The servants abused their exemption to customs; then such "Immunity began to cover all the Merchandize of the Country."[91] As a result, local Indian traders were excluded from dealing in their own economies, while Company traders controlled the buying and selling of goods.

---

[88] Langford, *Writings and Speeches*, V, 269.

[89] Langford, *Writings and Speeches*, V, 269. This insight is reminiscent of Burke's statement to Adam Smith regarding the repeal of middlemen trading practices that "legislators must proceed by slow degrees" to achieve economic freedom. See "The 1772 Repeal of Statutes Banning Forestalling, Regrating, and Engrossing," Chapter 2.

[90] Langford, *Writings and Speeches*, V, 244.   [91] Langford, *Writings and Speeches*, V, 244–245.

The *Ninth Report*, then, lambastes the East India Company for cementing de facto monopolistic practices in Indian industries:

The Servants therefore, for themselves, or for their Employers, monopolized every Article of Trade, Foreign and Domestic; not only the raw Merchantable Commodities, but the Manufactures; and not only these, but the Necessaries of Life, or what, in these Countries, Habit has confounded with them; not only Silk, Cotton, Piece Goods, Opium, Saltpetre, but not unfrequently Salt, Tobacco, Betel Nut, and the Grain of most ordinary Consumption. In the name of the Country Government they laid on or took off, and at their Pleasure heightened or lowered, all Duties upon Goods.[92]

The Company was able to dictate the price and circulation of commodities and to determine their level of taxation according to the indulgent preferences of the firm's servants. Competition was destroyed, supply and demand laws corrupted. The effect was commercial ruin: the "whole Trade of the Country was either destroyed, or in Shackles."[93] As the *Ninth Report* remarks, the Treaty of Allahabad in 1765 tightened this commercial stranglehold over native traders with even greater force. Such comments illustrate Burke's hatred of monopoly in internal markets.

By emphasizing the dangers of monopoly, Burke anticipates his later condemnation of the practice in *Thoughts and Details*. Recall that in the economic tract, Burke cautions that the new government-mandated positions of miller or mealman could extinguish the private grain trade. "[U]nder the appearance of a monopoly of capital," Burke writes in the memorial, those positions "will, in reality, be a monopoly of authority, and will ruin whatever it touches."[94] The centralization of political authority was bound to discourage commercial vibrancy and enhance the state's capacity to suppress trade – in England, and in India.

Beyond its investigation into raw silk and piece goods, the *Ninth Report* offers an elaborate investigation into the industries of opium, saltpeter, and salt, three commodities that were formally authorized monopolies under the East India Company. Philip Francis, who had fought – figuratively and literally[95] – with Warren Hastings when both were members of the Supreme Council in Bengal, had remarked that while Burke was the author of most sections of the *Ninth Report*, Francis himself was responsible for writing the sections on the salt and opium monopolies, as well as on other unspecified articles. Francis said he drafted these for Burke at Burke's "own desire."[96] Being that Burke was a firm opponent of domestic monopolies and an advocate of commercial liberty

---

[92] Langford, *Writings and Speeches*, V, 246.   [93] Langford, *Writings and Speeches*, V, 246.
[94] Langford, *Writings and Speeches*, IX, 135.
[95] Francis participated in a duel with Hastings in 1780. Francis returned to England in 1781.
[96] Langford, *Writings and Speeches*, V, 194. Starting in 1782, Burke came to rely more heavily on Francis as a source of information about India. Even though Francis held a personal rivalry with Hastings, he still proved to offer valuable insights into the country (Langford, *Writings and Speeches*, V, 19).

throughout his career, we may take these sections to reflect his own beliefs on the consequences stemming from the political control of economic resources.

Consider the *Ninth Report*'s survey of the opium industry. It describes how the East India Company's command of the trade was designed under a variety of pretenses, such as reducing exorbitant consumption at home, preventing an oversupply of goods, and securing the trade against adulteration. The odious effect of this policy, however, was that it obstructed the local producer from enjoying reward for his toil. "[I]t seems to be a Part of the Policy of this Monopoly to prevent the Cultivator from obtaining the natural Fruits of his Labour," the *Ninth Report* states. "Dealing with a private Merchant he could not get *Money in Abundance*, unless his Commodity could procure *an abundant Profit*."[97] This comment illuminates a core precept of Burke's economic thought, as suggested in *Thoughts and Details* as well: individuals should be secured the opportunity to pursue profit. Moneymaking could be an instrument for good in civil society, providing the incentive for labor and the means by which men purchase products in the mart.

The problem was when market actors who pursued profit prevented others from doing the same, regardless of the benevolent intentions of the monopolists. "Upon whatever Reasons or Pretences the Monopoly of Opium was supposed," the *Ninth Report* continues, "the real Motive appears to be the Profit of those who were in Hopes to be concerned in it."[98] For Burke, the East India Company became the wicked embodiment of this reality: it set out to acquire lucre by curbing the market freedoms of local Indians, a campaign that generated endless financial misadventures.

Francis's additional details on the opium monopoly in the *Ninth Report* mirror Burke's concerns about the danger of controlling property and resources. Francis discusses corrupt contracts offered to the highest English bidder; the cultivation of a low quality of opium; the usurpation of Indians' private land to compel the growth of poppies; the imprisonment of natives on fraudulent pretenses; and the reckless attempt to trade contraband opium with China, which had proscribed the importation of the commodity. The contracts in particular abandoned any pretense of fidelity to the laws of supply and demand because East India Company contractors coerced native cultivators into selling the commodity on the contractors' own terms. In addition, the contractors were rewarded an advance sum of money for their efforts; this payment removed the incentive for them to be judicious in their transactions, while Indians did not receive market value for their crops.[99] Accordingly, contractors with the Company enriched themselves in the opium trade at the expense of native cultivators and consumers.

The salt monopoly produced similarly destructive consequences. The *Ninth Report* argues that the artificial management of the supply and demand for salt

[97] Langford, *Writings and Speeches*, V, 270.   [98] Langford, *Writings and Speeches*, V, 271.
[99] Langford, *Writings and Speeches*, V, 276.

would "raise the Price on the Consumer beyond its just Level."[100] Francis's insight is similar to Burke's contention in *Thoughts and Details* that government intrusion into the grain market would "instantly raise the market upon itself."[101] The state control of a good aggravates the costs of purchasing it. The *Ninth Report* notes that embezzlement and the importation of salt would ensue, which, in the end, meant that government would "probably be undersold, and beaten down to a losing Price."[102] Burke's description of the financial mismanagement of the East India Company following its political takeover of Bengal served as a powerful example of this consequence.

The *Ninth Report*'s criticism of the saltpeter monopoly, particularly in the province of Bahar, further communicates Burke's worries about the perils of corrupting natural market order. The East India Company dictated the price and production of saltpeter, and persecuted manufacturers who were unable to complete the orders of the Company and who were saddled with heavy debt. Instead of imprisoning debtors, the Company would deduct the balance from their current production. The report notes that this entire process of economic control created a perverse incentive by dissuading natives from producing high-quality goods in an effectual manner. "People must be discouraged from entering into a Business, when the Commodity being fixed to one invariable Standard, and confined to one Market, the best Success can be attended only with a limited Advantage," the *Ninth Report* explains, "whilst a defective Produce can never be compensated by an augmented Price."[103]

In essence, fixing prices and confining trade to a single market drained any motivation to be industrious and aim for profit, since enterprising Indians would not receive a commensurate reward for their efforts. "[T]here can be no Life and Vigour in any Business under a Monopoly so constituted; nor can the true productive Resources of the Country, in so large an Article of its Commerce, ever come to be fully known," the *Ninth Report* declares.[104] The commercial possibilities for natives were inhibited by the dead weight of government monopoly. The *Ninth Report*'s commentary on the opium, salt, and saltpeter monopolies also shows how the firm's control of markets was the precursor to intimidation and extortion, property violations and imprisonment. It converted the debt of natives into a razor-edged weapon for political and economic oppression, condemning Indians to servitude and Britain to dishonor.

9.6 CONCLUSION

The *Ninth Report* emphasizes that the antidote to the abuse of native merchants was to infuse competition into Indian markets. "This Competition, the Operation of which they endeavour to prevent, is the natural Corrective of

---

[100] Langford, *Writings and Speeches*, V, 289.   [101] Langford, *Writings and Speeches*, IX, 135.
[102] Langford, *Writings and Speeches*, V, 289.   [103] Langford, *Writings and Speeches*, V, 305.
[104] Langford, *Writings and Speeches*, V, 305.

the Abuse, and the best Remedy which could be applied to the Disorder," the report insists.[105] Moreover, "The Prosperity of the Natives must be previously secured, before any Profit from them whatsoever is attempted."[106] Burke maintains that the stimulation of local trade should occur before Britain make any attempts to extract revenue from the Indians.

These ideas firmly align with Burke's appraisal of market competition throughout his life. In *Thoughts and Details* he remarks that farmers might not suffer from government intervention in the mart – but only "as long as there is a tolerable market of competition."[107] Burke's parliamentary activities demonstrate a steady commitment to injecting doses of competition into regulated markets: advocating for the Free Port Act; fighting to overturn the bans on forestalling, regrating, and engrossing; supporting the Poor Removals Bill; promoting the Irish free trade bills; and resisting state interference in the domestic grain trade. As indicated by such efforts, Burke thought that competition permitted enterprising men, regardless of background, to engage in the pursuit of profit, goods, and labor, which spawned prosperity not only for themselves but also for the general welfare.

In the end, the *Ninth Report*'s attack on monopoly displays a noticeable consistency with Burke's approach to politics. In both cases, Burke abhorred the concentration of decision-making authority in the hands of a single entity. In the realm of politics, constitutional government required subduing the ambitions of the Crown. In the realm of economics, vibrant commercial enterprise demanded that the means of production be released from the control of one trader. For Burke, the perpetuation of political and commercial liberty relied on the diffusion of power.

---

[105] Langford, *Writings and Speeches*, V, 271.   [106] Langford, *Writings and Speeches*, V, 221.
[107] Langford, *Writings and Speeches*, IX, 135.

10

Speech on Fox's India Bill, Six Mercantile Principles, and the Danger of Political Commerce

[The East India Company] became that thing which was supposed by the Roman Law so unsuitable, the same power was a Trader, the same power was a Lord.[1]
Edmund Burke, *Opening of Impeachment*, 1788

10.1 THE EAST INDIA COMPANY, ELEVENTH REPORT OF SELECT COMMITTEE, AND SPEECH ON FOX'S INDIA BILL

British lawmakers were mindful that Lord North's Regulating Act of 1773 did not achieve its goal of taming the maladministration of the East India Company. The institution continued to suffer financial losses, and the Governor General, Warren Hastings, continued to perpetrate or condone the Company's abuse of natives. In the light of these growing political realities, North's ministry made slight amendments to the Regulating Act in 1781, but it was not until the Fox-North coalition assumed power in April 1783 that the prospect for substantive reform gained parliamentary traction.

Burke took a leading role in orchestrating these reform efforts. Historical evidence suggests that he was heavily involved in the drafting of two bills that aspired to change the management structure of the East India Company. The second bill established a regulatory framework to govern the Company's administration in India. The first bill offered a more controversial proposal: it proposed two commissions, with four-year terms for good behavior, to oversee the Company's shareholders and directors. The first commission, consisting of seven allies of the Fox-North coalition, would be responsible for the Company's administration and disciplining of misbehaving servants, and the second would oversee the Company's commercial activity.[2]

[1] Langford, *Writings and Speeches*, VI, 283.   [2] See Langford, *Writings and Speeches*, V, 379.

This bill, known as Fox's India Bill, was greeted with political hostility from opposition MPs. By giving more power to special commissions, they argued, the bill would increase the power of the Crown; rob East India Company shareholders of their chartered rights; aggrandize the influence of party ministers; and damage national credit.[3] In effect, the bill shifted the locus of the Company's power base from Calcutta, its headquarters at the time, to London. There was, of course, a tinge of irony in the fact that Burke had originally resisted efforts to reform the Company through stronger ministerial oversight, as illustrated by his opposition to the Regulating Act of 1773.

Before Burke delivered his eloquent defense of Fox's bill in December, the Select Committee on India released another report, *Eleventh Report of Select Committee*, to chronicle the delinquencies of Hastings's rule. Attributed to Burke, the report was released strategically on the same day the two bills were introduced.[4] Its level of comprehension does not match that in the *Eleventh Report*, and the writing conveys little original insight into Burke's economic thought, but it does provide additional details into his frame of mind on the cruel manner in which the Company oppressed natives. The *Eleventh Report* focuses primarily on the dishonest ways in which Hastings acquired financial resources through the extortion of Indians, resources he then used to fund diplomatic and financial misadventures.[5]

In the report, Burke highlights how Hastings had acquired money by receiving "pretended Free Gifts"[6] from natives in violation of the law. In reality, Burke argues, British administrators intimidated Indians into giving them lucre for the Company's benefit, thereby taking advantage of natives' basic desire for security. The Indians' "Generosity is found in Proportion, not to the Opulence they possess, or to the Favours they receive, but to the Indigence they feel, and the Insults they are exposed to."[7]

The fraudulence of Hastings's forced payments supplied the incentive for the natives to engage in corrupt practices as well: "The very Nature of such Transactions has a Tendency to teach the Natives to pay a corrupt Court to the Servants of the Company."[8] Yet Indians were more willing to engage in business with the firm if financial deals were carried out with integrity. "If the Transaction was fair and honest," Burke observes, "every Native must have been desirous of making Merit with the great governing Power."[9] The *Eleventh Report* lays blame squarely on Hastings for encouraging this environment of financial corruption, which had the effect of eroding the bond of trust between the British and native Indians.

On December 1, 1783, less than six months after the *Ninth Report* was published, Burke articulated his main defense of Fox's bill in *Speech on Fox's*

---

[3] Langford, *Writings and Speeches*, V, 383.   [4] Lock, *Edmund Burke*, vol. I, 529.
[5] See Langford, *Writings and Speeches*, V, 335n2.   [6] Langford, *Writings and Speeches*, V, 334.
[7] Langford, *Writings and Speeches*, V, 350–351.   [8] Langford, *Writings and Speeches*, V, 359.
[9] Langford, *Writings and Speeches*, V, 359.

India Bill. The speech is an elaborate survey of British India characterized by his sweet flair for rhetoric and imagery. Burke paints a romanticized view of India, summoning a picture of a flourishing culture before the East India Company began to persecute natives. The portions of the oration relevant to his political economy include shrewd insights into the important functions of merchants in markets. *Speech on Fox's India Bill* also shines light on Burke's beliefs regarding Indian land tenure that evoke his commentary on landed property rights expressed in his other writings and speeches.

Six Mercantile Principles

In *Speech on Fox's India Bill*, Burke offers the fullest statement in his political life on the necessary standards of conduct for a trader in market economies. He proposes a list of six mercantile qualities he believed should serve as a guiding framework for dealing and financial activities, carving out sharp distinctions between his vision of an ethical trader and the nefarious misbehavior of East India Company servants.

The first quality reveals Burke's fondness for the integrity of supply and demand laws: the "principle of buying cheap and selling dear is the first, the great foundation of mercantile dealing."[10] A trader was successful when he purchased inexpensive goods and sold them off at a higher price. Yet the Company violated this principle: "[F]or years have they not actually authorized in their servants a total indifference as to the prices they were to pay?"[11] Similar to the *Ninth Report*, Burke here is underlining his fierce disapproval of the firm's ignorance of the price mechanism as a tool to promote efficient trade.

The second, third, and fourth criteria were matters of financial discipline, prudence, and oversight: good trading men must show a "great deal of strictness in driving bargains for whatever we contract"[12]; and they must "see that their clerks do not divert the dealings of the master to their own benefit."[13] The fourth quality of a merchant was "to be exact in his accounts."[14] The East India Company abandoned any pretense of ethics in its accounting practices: in referring to the shady contractual agreement of James Auriol, a Company civil servant, to supply rice to other jurisdictions, Burke writes, "A new principle of account upon honour seems to be regularly established in their dealings and their treasury, which in reality amounts to an entire annihilation of the principle of all accounts."[15]

Burke's fifth quality of a good merchant was the commitment to "calculate his probable profits upon the money he takes up to vest in business."[16] He "does

[10] Langford, *Writings and Speeches*, V, 431. [11] Langford, *Writings and Speeches*, V, 431.
[12] Langford, *Writings and Speeches*, V, 431. [13] Langford, *Writings and Speeches*, V, 431.
[14] Langford, *Writings and Speeches*, V, 432. [15] Langford, *Writings and Speeches*, V, 432.
[16] Langford, *Writings and Speeches*, V, 432.

not meditate a fraudulent bankruptcy."[17] The judicious dealer did not invest with a brazen lack of discipline, discarding careful consideration of the prospect for profit. The final characteristic of Burke's merchant was "the taking care to be properly prepared, in cash or goods, in the ordinary course of sale, for the bills which are drawn on them."[18] Burke lambastes the Company for failing to assess whether their sales would be sufficient to cover interest payments owed to Company servants, from whom the corporation borrowed money in order to fund its investment in trade exports. Such recklessness was particularly imprudent at a time when the institution's financial resources were devoted to funding military campaigns. "Has the Company ever troubled themselves to enquire whether their sales can bear the payment of that interest, and at that rate of exchange?" he asks derisively.[19]

Burke's description of these six qualities uncovers an underlying ethical structure that, in his view, should have governed the merchant's financial activities, as opposed to the unscrupulous practices instigated by East India Company traders. Accordingly, Burke's elevation of the merchant to a respectable position in civil society, here and elsewhere in his writings such as *Thoughts and Details*, was conditioned on the premise that the trader exhibit probity and discipline in his market activities. The flourishing of commercial and financial enterprise depended on the integrity of those who bought and sold goods. A vibrant trade required commercial virtue.

Yet the corruption of traders stripped markets of the moral core necessary to ensure honest transactions. Both commerce and morality would then suffer. As Burke insists in *Speech on Fox's India Bill*, "Indeed no trace of equitable government is found in their politics; not one trace of commercial principle in their mercantile dealing," which is why the British Parliament must "restore the countries destroyed by the misconduct of the Company, and to restore the Company itself, ruined by the consequences of their plans for destroying what they were bound to preserve."[20] Rehabilitate the Company on sound mercantile principles, which were governed by deeper ethical principles, and the Indian economy – not to mention the Company itself – would be reinvigorated on solid grounds.

Burke's image of the ideal trader integrates smoothly with an earlier comment he had made in *Speech on Fox's India Bill*. In defending the legitimacy of the East India Company as a long-lasting institution, Burke claims, "I have known merchants with the sentiments and the abilities of great statesmen; and I have seen persons in the rank of statesmen, with the conceptions and character of pedlars."[21] This comment was most likely a jab at the belief, embraced by thinkers such as Adam Smith, that merchants did not possess the qualifications to rule the company, and that the structural incentives

---

[17] Langford, *Writings and Speeches*, V, 432.   [18] Langford, *Writings and Speeches*, V, 432.
[19] Langford, *Writings and Speeches*, V, 432.   [20] Langford, *Writings and Speeches*, V, 432–433.
[21] Langford, *Writings and Speeches*, V, 387.

of the firm discouraged wise administration in any event.[22] Burke continues by insisting that nothing would disqualify men from carrying out the functions of government except that "by which the power of exercising those functions is very frequently obtained, I mean, a spirit and habits of low cabal and intrigue; which I have never, in one instance, seen united with a capacity for sound and manly policy."[23] In essence, merchants were capable of performing the traditional duties of statesmen.

Burke's discussion of a merchant's qualifications to rule requires critical assessment for a number of reasons, however. First, Burke's faith in the capacity of mercantile administrators to govern responsibly militated against existing widespread evidence to the contrary. Second, although he praises traders in *Speech on Fox's India Bill*, he famously assailed French revolutionaries in the *Reflections* for believing that those who were employed as a "hair-dresser" or "tallow-chandler" were qualified to rule.[24] Indeed, the occupation of a hairdresser was not equivalent to a trader for the East India Company. But is Burke still guilty of inconsistency in praising merchants in *Speech on Fox's India Bill* for their capacities to govern, but denouncing the qualifications of dealers and artisans in menial occupations in the *Reflections* to do so as well? In the former, he knows merchants with the "sentiments and abilities" of distinguished statesmen. In the latter he does not.

At an elemental level, Burke did believe, as he states in the *Reflections*, that the two qualifications to govern were "virtue and wisdom, actual or presumptive."[25] Individual merit, whether earned through toil or inherited from one's ancestral lineage, sanctioned the exercise of political authority. But his inclination to support the landed aristocracy in Parliament marked his conviction that members of that class were less likely to threaten the liberties of the people: they possessed wealth, so they were not keen on taking it from others; they pursued the common good, not self-interest; and they exhibited a moderate cast of mind resistant to the spell of radicalism.

We may *attempt* to trace harmony in Burke's views. As he notes in *Speech on Fox's India Bill*, the trait that most disqualified a person from government was the tendency to pursue cabal and intrigue. French revolutionaries acted upon this tendency with deadly force, exposing their utter incapacity to govern with prudence. In the judgment of Burke, landed aristocracies did not seek to combine together to subvert the public welfare, and thus were qualified to rule. In essence, the common standard linking Burke's assessment of the qualifications to rule was the individual's ability to withstand the temptation to design political schemes that imperiled the liberties of the government's subjects. If traders tamed this impulse, they were just as qualified to govern as the landed nobility.

---

[22] See Collins, "The Limits of Mercantile Administration."
[23] Langford, *Writings and Speeches*, V, 387.   [24] Langford, *Writings and Speeches*, VIII, 100.
[25] Langford, *Writings and Speeches*, VIII, 101.

Such reasoning is theoretically possible but ultimately unpersuasive, for the *Reflections* is a great deal more categorical in its attack on the governing abilities of undistinguished artisans and dealers. "[T]he state suffers oppression, if such as they, either individually or collectively, are permitted to rule," Burke insists. "In this you think you are combating prejudice, but you are at war with nature."[26] Although this book has argued that a broad consistency threads together Burke's remarks on market economies, such uniformity is not so transparent in his assessment of the necessary qualifications to rule. Burke even weakens his claim in the *Reflections* by declaring, in the next paragraph, that "virtue and wisdom" could be found in any "profession or trade."[27] *Were* tradesmen qualified to rule, or were they not? In the context of the East India Company, Burke contends they are. In the *Reflections*, he contends they are not. Which one was it? Was Burke's argument based on cultural and political differences – were the lower orders of French artisans and dealers unequipped to rule, but affluent and noble British merchants of the Company were? He never makes such distinction, showing that his comments on mercantile rulers denote a tension in his economic thought that he struggles to resolve throughout his public life.

Burke, Rights, and Trust

Burke assesses the governing capacities of merchants in the larger context of his institutional defense of the East India Company in *Speech on Fox's India Bill*. In response to the accusation leveled by critics that Fox's bill would destroy the "chartered rights of men,"[28] he argues that the corporation carried a heightened sense of legitimacy. Burke's reflections on this matter in the speech offer compelling insights into chartered firms, natural rights, and the relationship between political authority and its subjects, which we shall discuss here.

These insights are best understood by tracing Burke's beliefs about the East India Company back to November 1766, when he gave his first speech about India in the House of Commons. It was around this time that Lord Chatham was seeking to inquire about the state of the Company's finances, with the intention of using a portion of its increased wealth to pay down the debt from the Seven Years War. Burke "jumped up instantly,"[29] in opposition to the Duke of Bedford's motion to establish a committee of inquiry consistent with Chatham's wishes. His resistance to the inquiry, and to subsequent attempts seeking to regulate the Company's dividend, stemmed from a firm commitment to protect the chartered rights and private property of the Company from the

---

[26] Langford, *Writings and Speeches*, VIII, 100–101.
[27] Langford, *Writings and Speeches*, VIII, 101.   [28] Langford, *Writings and Speeches*, V, 383.
[29] Burke to Charles O'Hara, 27 [November 1766], in *Correspondence of Edmund Burke*, vol. I, 281.

stratagems of the British government.[30] Burke, as a member of the Rockingham Whigs, the party that relinquished power once Chatham took over, claimed that this belief did not derive from "principles of factious opposition."[31]

Burke realized that the East India Company's property rights were the fulcrum of political debate over the corporation's mismanagement in India. At the time of *Speech on Fox's India Bill*, when he knew that reform of the Company was necessary, Burke strongly countered the objection that Fox's bill placed in danger the chartered rights of the corporation. In the speech, he begins by insisting that there *were* such things as natural rights that warranted sacrosanct protection. "The rights of *men*, that is to say, the natural rights of mankind, are indeed sacred things," he claims.[32] He elaborates:

If these natural rights are further affirmed and declared by express covenants, if they are clearly defined and secured against chicane, against power, and authority, by written instruments and positive engagements, they are in a still better condition: they partake not only of the sanctity of the object so secured, but of that solemn public faith itself, which secures an object of such importance.[33]

Although Burke has acquired a reputation for opposing the abstract natural rights doctrine of the French Revolution, here he extols his own conception of a properly construed natural rights theory. This notion achieves an eminent harmony with his beliefs about property, as exemplified by his commentary on the *Nullum Tempus* affair[34] and elsewhere: natural rights and property rights were rooted in nature, and acquired greater authority through time as expressed in prescriptive titles, formal agreements, and statutory acts. For Burke, natural rights most likely did indeed exist, but their realization could best be manifested and fortified in a community that protected them through a long train of institutional and historical processes. Because man was a social being, the perpetual security of rights demanded legal recognition from other human beings. In his speech, Burke references King John's assent to Magna Carta and Henry III's[35] confirmation of the charter in 1265 as worthy examples of public declarations of natural rights.

For Burke, however, Fox's bill did not threaten these real chartered rights of men because the charter of the East India Company was formed on diametric principles. Magna Carta was a document limiting the power of the king and the concentration of political authority, while the purpose of the Company charter was to grant the firm institutional privileges. As Burke says, "*Magna charta* is a charter to restrain power, and to destroy monopoly. The East India charter is

---

[30] Burke did not convey sympathy toward oppressed Indian natives at this time, although this absence could be explained by his growing awareness of the Company's abuses in the mid-to-late 1770s.

[31] Burke to Charles O'Hara, 27 [November 1766], in *Correspondence of Edmund Burke*, vol. I, 281.

[32] Langford, *Writings and Speeches*, V, 383.   [33] Langford, *Writings and Speeches*, V, 383–384.

[34] See "Property as a Constitutional Bulwark," Chapter 11.   [35] 1207–1272.

a charter to establish monopoly, and to create power."[36] Therefore, unbridled authority was not a natural right: "Political power and commercial monopoly are *not* the rights of men; and the rights to them derived from charters, it is fallacious and sophistical to call 'the chartered rights of men.'"[37]

If anything, they "at least suspend the natural rights of mankind at large" and may even "fall into direct violation of them."[38] These remarks illustrate that Burke does not slouch toward political positivism in believing that the genesis of rights only derived from social assent. In his view, there remained an underlying moral component to natural rights that determined whether chartered liberties were grounded in just or unjust principles. Just principles include those that limited the concentration of power, while unjust ones included those that augmented it.

Even though Burke acknowledges that the East India Company charter did not express the real natural rights of man, he avows that the firm did possess the authority to exercise their political and trading privileges. Burke says in *Speech on Fox's India Bill*, "I . . . freely admit to the East India Company their claim to exclude their fellow-subjects from the commerce of half the globe."[39] This was because these privileges were granted by "charter and acts of parliament," and "without a shadow of controversy" at that.[40] Burke's reasoning merges with his defense of prescription in his broader political philosophy, one that consecrated long-lasting bodies because of the authority of time and the utility of their existence. As he states in the speech, "I feel an insuperable reluctance in giving my hand to destroy any established institution of government, upon a theory, however plausible it may be."[41] The Company was a legitimate institution; it enjoyed chartered privileges; and its enduring authority protected itself from pleas to terminate its charter.

If in fact a charter conferred privileges on an institution that narrowed the natural rights of mankind, that charter should provide advantages to the subjects over whom the institution ruled. "[A]ll political power which is set over men, and that all privilege claimed or exercised in exclusion of them, being wholly artificial, and for so much," Burke writes, "a derogation from the natural equality of mankind at large, ought to be in some way or other exercised ultimately for their benefit."[42] Burke was not a utilitarian, but he did recognize the importance of utility in political communities: if natural rights were delimited by political prerogative – nay, especially if natural rights were delimited by political prerogative – individuals should receive benefits from this governing arrangement. Accordingly, the East India Company's chartered liberties should produce commercial gifts for the English people. This argument further demonstrates that Burke did not hold natural rights to be

---

[36] Langford, *Writings and Speeches*, V, 384.   [37] Langford, *Writings and Speeches*, V, 384.
[38] Langford, *Writings and Speeches*, V, 384.   [39] Langford, *Writings and Speeches*, V, 384.
[40] Langford, *Writings and Speeches*, V, 385.   [41] Langford, *Writings and Speeches*, V, 387.
[42] Langford, *Writings and Speeches*, V, 385.

inviolable. He hints that the limitation on natural rights might be justified if the action that curbed them – in this case, the Company charter – engendered some reward to those subjects whose rights were constrained.

In Burke's judgment, the problem was not the chartered existence of the East India Company but the unrepentant abuse of its authority. It broke treaties, restricted the liberties of Indian traders, seized property, extorted local rulers, and launched military campaigns. This point is representative of a larger, more important theme in his political and economic theory: there existed a sacred covenant between the ruler and the ruled. An institution's legal exercise of political or commercial authority did not mean it could disregard the ethical responsibilities of governance; indeed, political rule demanded that it meet these weighty responsibilities. As Burke wrote in *Thoughts on the Present Discontents* in 1770, "Before men are put forward into the great trusts of the State, they ought by their conduct to have obtained such a degree of estimation in their country, as may be some sort of pledge and security to the publick, that they will not abuse those trusts."[43]

Such a belief governed Burke's thoughts on statesmanship throughout his entire adult life, spanning from the Free Port Act of 1766; *Speech on American Taxation* and *Speech on Conciliation*; *Speech on Economical Reform*; the Irish trade bill debates; and here in *Speech on Fox's India Bill*. In the case of the East India Company in *Speech on Fox's India Bill*, Burke explains that the British government's authorization of commercial privileges to the Company conveyed an elevated level of confidence in the corporation's ability to use those privileges wisely. The firm failed this moral test, dissolving the bonds of trust between the political authority that granted the charter and the institution that benefited from it. Burke writes that if

every description of commercial privilege, none of which can be original self-derived rights, or grants from the mere private benefit of the holders, then such rights, or privileges, or whatever you choose to call them, are all in the strictest sense a *trust*; and it is of the very essence of every trust to be rendered *accountable*; and ever totally to *cease*, when it substantially varies from the purposes for which alone it could have a lawful existence.[44]

A trust connects not only the ruler to the ruled but the ruler to the political authority – in this case, Parliament and the Crown – that authorized the charter. This was the case not simply in regard to politics, however, but also in regard to the trading arena: the "commercial trust," Burke argued in *Speech on Fox's India Bill*, demanded that East India Company merchants act consistent with the ethical principles he outlined in the speech.[45] Privilege is a gift, not a right. And because privilege is a gift,

---

[43] Langford, *Writings and Speeches*, II, 279.   [44] Langford, *Writings and Speeches*, V, 385.
[45] Langford, *Writings and Speeches*, V, 431.

there prevails an even greater moral imperative to exercise it with exceeding care and caution.[46] But if the institution violates this implicit pledge of trust, it loses its right to maintain its privileges.

To Burke, Fox's India Bill was a legitimate attempt to remedy this breach of trust and charter. If the British government was the source of the Company's odious behavior, it bore the heavy responsibility to correct it. "[I]f we are the very cause of the evil, we are in a special manner engaged to the redress," he states.[47] In Burke's view, then, the bill did not put in jeopardy the chartered liberties of men but aimed to reform the chartered privileges of the East India Company.[48]

Even more, the British government was morally obligated to reform the East India Company because of the firm's contravention of trust: "I ground myself therefore on this principle – that if the abuse is proved, the contract is broken; and we re-enter into all our rights; that is, into the exercise of all our duties."[49] These comments are a revealing window into Burke's conception of the relationship between rights and duties. While Burke was a vigorous supporter of the right to produce and trade, his comments here imply another notion of rights that were inseparable from duties. Legislators in Parliament possessed the right to grant privileges to the Company, but once the organization frayed the government's trust, they also held the right to reform the institution. "Our own authority is indeed as much a trust originally, as the Company's authority is a trust derivatively," he says.[50] The relationship among the ruler, the privileged, and the ruled drew its strength ultimately from the moral chord of trust rather than from the conditional instrument of commercial contracts.

Consider the deeper implication of Burke's argument. If the East India Company's violation of political and commercial trust demanded that men satisfy their prior duty to reform the institution, then the natural state of mankind was governed by a code of ethics. The natural right to live – to produce, to trade, to rule – did not release one from the imperative to live virtuously, just as the chartered privilege to exist, in the case of the East India Company, did not free it from the obligation to rule ethically. Burke's state of nature, insofar as it can be called that, was a state of social interaction – and moral responsibility.

---

[46] Of course, Burke also believed that natural rights should be enjoyed responsibly.

[47] Langford, *Writings and Speeches*, V, 385.

[48] The bill ended up being defeated in the House of Lords on December 17, 1783, leading to the dismissal of the Fox-North coalition the next day. A ministry directed by Pitt assumed power. See Langford, *Writings and Speeches*, V, 451; and the entry for Pitt in Sir Lewis Namier and John Brooke, eds., *The History of Parliament: The House of Commons 1754–1790*, vol. III, *Members K-Y* (London: Her Majesty's Stationery Office, 1964), 299–301.

[49] Langford, *Writings and Speeches*, V, 386.   [50] Langford, *Writings and Speeches*, V, 386.

Burke's Defense of the Institutional Credibility of the East India Company

In general, Burke's attempt to revive the spirit of the East India Company's charter exposes possible limitations of his political philosophy. His inclination to support returning an institution to its original state displays insufficient attention to the possibility that there might be something defective in the original state itself that was the fundamental problem. Did Burke not consider that a state-backed company, armed with exclusive trading privileges in a distant part of the world, might transform into a domineering political institution? Were the events of 1757 and 1765 – the years of the Battle of Plassey and the firm's acquisition of *diwani*, respectively – not unpredictable?

Burke was clearly aware that the East India Company's presence spread a noxious commercial influence prior to 1765. In his February 16 speech on Hastings's impeachment, he observed that Company servants had abused their privilege of trading goods duty free in India, a gift given to them by the Mughal emperor in 1717. They used the *dastak*, the permit relieving them of paying duties, so often that "it was more like robbery than trade."[51] This abuse impaired the operation of supply and demand laws: "They sold at their own prices and forced the people to sell to them at their own prices."[52] Therefore, "It appeared more like an army going to pillage the people under pretence of Commerce than any thing else."[53] Burke even emphasized in his speech on Hastings's impeachment a day earlier that, by the sanction of the Company's charters in the seventeenth century, the firm had steadily aggrandized its military presence and expanded the scope of its civil and criminal jurisdiction.[54]

Was this territorial acquisition not the logical outgrowth of granting a trading company vast amounts of commercial leverage? Was it not inevitable that a trader working for such a powerful company would undermine the principles of free commerce and persecute its subjects? Was it not naive to think that a chartered company operating in a remote land with limited oversight would not abuse its authority? Burke's critical examination of the East India Company in his speeches and the Select Committee reports demonstrates an impressive penetration of mind, but his reflections on the corporation leave such questions unanswered.

Does Burke's support for the Company contradict his other statements on political economy in praise of free trade? This question raises the difficulty, once again, in defining "free trade" in the eighteenth century. As we have learned, the phrase in Burke's age had not hardened into the rigid concept that it has today, and held different meanings to different people in the 1700s.

The important point to remember is that Burke always calibrated his support for trade within larger constitutional, prescriptive, and imperial contexts. At

---

[51] Langford, *Writings and Speeches*, VI, 335. [52] Langford, *Writings and Speeches*, VI, 335.
[53] Langford, *Writings and Speeches*, VI, 335.
[54] Langford, *Writings and Speeches*, VI, 282–283.

times, these factors encouraged him to approve of policies that imposed restrictions on the free movement of goods, such as his endorsement of the Company and the Navigation Acts. Indeed, his defense of the firm's charter in the 1760s and 1770s was driven by constitutional and property considerations, as well as commercial ones – Burke believed that royal or parliamentary intrusion into the Company's commercial affairs would threaten the corporation's property rights and unsettle the balance of British constitutional government. Yet Burke maintained that the chartered monopoly of the Company was not antithetical to the flow of goods, and in fact facilitated their growth. Because trade in distant lands was rife with risk and danger, government support for trading companies did not discourage commerce but opened up new avenues for the trafficking of foreign commodities, which, Burke believed, created and enhanced the wealth of the British Empire.

Allow us to elaborate on these, and other, factors that motivated Burke's defense of the East India Company beyond strict considerations of trade. As mentioned, Burke says in *Speech on Fox's India Bill* that he was reluctant to overthrow "any established institution of government" rooted in an abstract theory. This reasoning conformed powerfully to his political defense of prescription[55]: ancestral institutions that provided a public utility obtained an authority through the test of time, and therefore should not be destroyed simply because theoretical reason aimed to discredit their legitimacy.

In this spirit, the credibility of the Company stemmed largely from repeated constitutional sanction from the Crown and Parliament. The firm's chartered rights were "secured to that body by every sort of public sanction," Burke insists in *Speech on Fox's India Bill.*[56] They were "stamped by the faith of the King" and by "the faith of Parliament."[57] Burke's point here is not that the Company carried a presumption of legitimacy because of its territorial expansion in India in the seventeenth and eighteenth centuries, but because the British government affirmed its credibility throughout the years by the continual renewal of its charter, bestowing a seal of public faith on the institution.

This is not to say that Burke opposed reforming long-lasting institutions, particularly if their activities veered away from the original purpose of their existence. As this book has shown, one constant theme of his political and economic thought *was* the importance of reform through conservation and refinement. Burke's treatment of the East India Company applied this belief to imperial policy: the Company, in his view, should remain in existence because of the time-tested authority of its Elizabethan charter and the history of its role

---

[55] Burke's idea of prescription will be discussed more fully in Chapter 11.

[56] Langford, *Writings and Speeches*, V, 384.

[57] Langford, *Writings and Speeches*, V, 384. In his first speech on the impeachment of Warren Hastings, Burke underscored the same point. He stated that the Company was granted "several grants and Charters," including the authorization of *diwani*, from the Mughal emperor (Langford, *Writings and Speeches*, VI, 280; see also 133).

in the British Empire. Yet it should reform because its political and commercial monopolies flouted the boundaries of its charter and corrupted the integrity of its trading practices. Even in his comments on preserving the Company in *Speech on Fox's India Bill*, Burke hints that the firm warranted more criticism than it had received: "I know much is, and much more may be said against such a system" as the Company.[58] Burke was a defender of the commercial institution, but not a blind one.

An additional consideration closely related to Burke's notion of prescription, time-tested utility,[59] was also a key factor in his defense of the East India Company. According to Burke, the trading company did in fact provide a utility to Britain by unlocking new commercial possibilities for its empire in foreign lands, which benefited British subjects in the mother country as well. Prior to the firm's acquisition of *diwani*, the *Ninth Report* states, England "was considerably benefitted both in Trade and in Revenue."[60] In his notes on monopoly in the 1844 edition of his correspondence, Burke argued that exclusive privileges were just if they were conferred for "the good of the whole," which, we recall, included supporting men to pursue "great risks in useful undertakings."[61] Commercial enterprise in a distant land was a perilous adventure; but if the firm enlarged the scope of trade in the region, this effect signaled that it generated concrete advantages for the British people.

Burke also saw the East India Company as an emblem of imperial honor, reflecting an implied mandate derived from its charter to advance the commerce *and* glory of the British Empire throughout the globe. In his speech on the opening of Hastings's impeachment in February 1788, Burke stated that the Company "had its origin about the latter end of the reign of Elizabeth" and was tasked with "increasing the commerce and the honour" of Britain.[62] Even more, "For to increase its commerce without increasing its honour and reputation would have been thought at that time, and will be thought now, a bad bargain for the Country."[63] Taming the Company's political misconduct, while preserving the original commercial spirit of its charter, was the avenue to imperial prestige.

Other practical concerns influenced Burke's endorsement of the charter. First, it was unlikely that any other collection of merchants could achieve the same level of commercial activity in the East Indies as the Company. "[W]ith all their connections, all their stock, all their powers of continuing the trade, it was absurd to suppose any other description of persons could so well pursue the same line of traffick," he said in 1781.[64] Hence he "ridiculed" the idea of "not

---

[58] Langford, *Writings and Speeches*, V, 386.
[59] See "Property as a Constitutional Bulwark," Chapter 11.
[60] Langford, *Writings and Speeches*, V, 223.
[61] William and Bourke, *Correspondence of the Right Honourable Edmund Burke*, vol. IV, 460.
[62] Langford, *Writings and Speeches*, VI, 282.   [63] Langford, *Writings and Speeches*, VI, 282.
[64] Langford, *Writings and Speeches*, V, 133.

continuing to sanctify the exclusive right to a commerce with India to the East-India Company."[65] Furthermore, removing the entire presence of the British Empire from India, Burke contended the following year, "would be impracticable" and would "leave the miserable natives in a worse situation than before."[66]

Besides, Burke says in *Speech on Fox's India Bill*, Englishmen must acknowledge the realities of Britain's entrenched historical footprint in India, which constrained the range of options for reform of the Company. "All these circumstances are not, I confess, very favourable to the idea of our attempting to govern India at all," he admits. "But there we are; there we are placed by the Sovereign Disposer."[67] Therefore, "[W]e must do the best we can in our situation. The situation of man is the preceptor of his duty."[68] Burke here recognizes the imperfect state of Anglo-Indian imperial relations, but appears resigned to the fact that Britain would remain in India for the foreseeable future, and thus believed Parliament should carry out reforms mindful of this inescapable political circumstance.

We must also not forget that Burke's position as an elected representative demanded heightened vigilance of any possible design by the Crown to increase its powers. The concentration of royal power necessarily led to the reduction in corporate liberties; because the Whig party in particular was keenly alert to attempts by the monarchy to limit the authority of corporate bodies, Burke demonstrated firm resistance to the British government's temptation to usurp the corporate privileges of trading institutions like the Company. A defense of corporate privilege was a defense of property – and of constitutional balance.

Indeed Burke believed that safeguarding property, including corporate property, was necessary for commercial liberty. "'Free-Trade' is the same thing as 'Use of Property,'" he wrote in his notes on monopoly published in 1844.[69] In short, Burke's accommodation of chartered trading companies unmasked a deeper dimension to his economic thought that integrated his constitutional and imperial commitments with a sensitivity to the hazards of trading in foreign lands. Commerce was part of empire, and empire was fraught with risk.

10.2 SPEECH ON FOX'S INDIA BILL AND THE DESTRUCTION OF THE LOCAL ECONOMY AND CULTURE

In addition to arguing for the perpetuation and reformation of the East India Company, *Speech on Fox's India Bill* highlights the destructive consequences of

---

[65] Langford, *Writings and Speeches*, V, 133.
[66] "Committee on the Reports of the Secret Committee for East-India Affairs," *The Gazetteer*, 16 April 1782.
[67] Langford, *Writings and Speeches*, V, 404.   [68] Langford, *Writings and Speeches*, V, 404.
[69] William and Bourke, *Correspondence of the Right Honourable Edmund Burke*, vol. IV, 459.

the institution's reign over the native population. At face value, these sections of the speech appear to address matters of political power rather than political economy. We must remember, however, that Burke's capacious understanding of economics encompassed considerations that transcended supply and demand laws, such as the harmony between commercial activity and landed property, which, in his judgment, was indispensable for the flourishing of civilization, including Indian civilization.

We begin with Burke's observation that the Company's dominion over a vast amount of land deprived the natives of their independent capacity to produce and feed themselves. "Through all that vast extent of country there is not a man who eats a mouthful of rice but by permission of the East India Company," Burke says in the speech.[70] The Company's monopoly forced locals to become wholly reliant upon the corporation for sustenance, thereby reinforcing their subservient status to the imperial power.

Depending on an external source for provisions was perilous if that source was ravenous. "When they extirpate the shepherd and the shepherd's dogs, they piously recommend the helpless flock to the mercy, and even to the *tenderest care*, of the wolf," Burke remarks with a tone of hostile sarcasm.[71] This comment was made in regard to the East India Company's attempt to diminish the influence of poligars, de facto feudal governors in southern India, while feigning to preserve the autonomy of weavers and manufacturers. Burke's point was to illuminate the danger behind the Company's benevolent claim that it was acting in the best interests of natives. The corporation's self-declared charitable aims – its "anxious cares"[72] – sanctioned persecution. The gap between its theoretical overtures and actual conduct exposed the limits of good intentions.

At the center of Burke's discussion was how the East India Company's failure to protect the independent spirit of natives bore a negative impact on the Indian nobility and Indian commercial activity. It is in this section in *Speech on Fox's India Bill* that he famously limns an idyllic picture of the Indians. They were not "gangs of savages" but a people "for ages civilized and cultivated."[73] Among the Indian inhabitants there was "to be found an antient and venerable priesthood, the depository of their laws, learning, and history," as well as "a nobility of great antiquity and renown."[74] Beyond recognizing the dignity of the natives and attempting to evoke a deep sense of empathy, these comments carry an important purpose for Burke's survey of Indian political economy: they were part of his wider portrait of Indian civilization that, from his perspective, was prospering prior to the Company's abuse of its commercial authority. India possessed a

---

[70] Langford, *Writings and Speeches*, V, 389. [71] Langford, *Writings and Speeches*, V, 424.
[72] Langford, *Writings and Speeches*, V, 424. [73] Langford, *Writings and Speeches*, V, 389.
[74] Langford, *Writings and Speeches*, V, 389–390.

multitude of cities, not exceeded in population and trade by those of the first class in Europe; merchants and bankers; individual houses of whom have once vied in capital with the Bank of England; whose credit had often supported a tottering state, and preserved their governments in the midst of war and desolation; millions of ingenious manufacturers and mechanicks; millions of the most diligent, and not the least intelligent, tillers of the earth.[75]

Burke's romanticized imagery notwithstanding, his core message is that the natives were quite capable of sustaining a flourishing culture – including an economically vibrant culture – without requiring meddlesome interventions from Britain. The implication of these observations is that the Company destroyed such prosperity by upsetting the supply and demand laws of local markets and corrupting Indians' economic, social, and political institutions. Such remarks also underline Burke's belief, as articulated in the *Reflections*, that land and commerce were not natural enemies but mutually reinforcing elements of a thriving civilization.

Burke's sensitivity to the Indian economy shaped his understanding of Indian society in general. He emphasizes in *Speech on Fox's India Bill* that India was a complex country, consisting of a multiplicity of peoples and subcultures. "All this vast mass, composed of so many orders and classes of men, is again infinitely diversified by manners, by religion, by hereditary employment, through all their possible combinations," Burke states.[76] India is of a "complicated nature."[77] These measured insights draw attention to the inherent difficulty for an imperial power to govern a society inhabited by great varieties of people in a uniform manner.

Recall that Burke in *Thoughts and Details* focuses readers' attention on the complex nature of social and economic activities, stressing that government regulations failed to reflect the diversity of labor and experience in the agricultural economy. *Speech on Fox's India Bill* extends such reasoning: Indian culture, including but not limited to its economy, was a heterogeneous society. Ruling such a society based on conformity of design was bound to disturb local customs and inhibit fluid voluntary exchange. Therefore, Burke maintains that the imperial government must be exceedingly careful before implementing commercial policy, because doing so too rashly or without considering the weight of practical circumstance might uproot local order. The infinite diversity of the subcontinent, Burke argues in *Speech on Fox's India Bill*, "renders the handling of India a matter in an high degree critical and delicate."[78] The complicated nature of Indian civilization demands that rulers act with prudence.

For Burke, the East India Company disrupted Indian society even further by converting the land of rulers in Indian into weapons of monetary exchange. The first example Burke provides in this section in *Speech on Fox's India Bill* is Shah

---

[75] Langford, *Writings and Speeches*, V, 390.   [76] Langford, *Writings and Speeches*, V, 390.
[77] Langford, *Writings and Speeches*, V, 390.   [78] Langford, *Writings and Speeches*, V, 390.

Alam II, emperor of the Mughal Empire, who was the "first potentate sold by the Company for money."[79] Following the Treaty of Allahabad, Shah Alam granted the Company the responsibility of revenue administration in exchange for tribute from the corporation. "Money is coined in his name; In his name justice is administered; He is prayed for in every temple through the countries we possess – But he was sold," Burke explains.[80]

Subsequently, the Company reneged on its obligations by refusing to pay tribute. Instead Warren Hastings sold the Mughal districts of Kora and Allahabad to Shujah al-Daula, Wazir of Oudh.[81] This was simply one instance in a litany of unscrupulous land sales Burke exposes and condemns in *Speech on Fox's India Bill*. He concludes by denouncing the transformation of native territory into instruments for profit, at the ultimate expense of Indian society: "All these bargains and sales were regularly attended with the waste and havoc of the country, always by the buyer, and sometimes by the object of the sale."[82]

The East India Company's targeting of natives' landed property is a recurring motif in *Speech on Fox's India Bill*. Burke describes how the Company destroyed *zamindars*, aristocratic landowners under the Mughal Empire responsible for collecting taxes, among other public duties, in order to shore up its revenue streams. This campaign resulted in the usurpation of land: "[T]hey seized upon the estates of every person of eminence in the country, and, under the name of *resumption*, confiscated their property."[83] Burke continues, "I wish … to be understood universally and literally, when I assert, that there is not left one man of property and substance for his rank, in the whole of these provinces, in provinces which are nearly the extent of England and Wales taken together."[84] He casts light on the demise of both landed and commercial activity: "Not one landholder, not one banker, not one merchant, not one even of those who usually perish last, the *ultimum moriens*[85] in a ruined state, no one farmer of revenue."[86]

In Burke's view, the East India Company's exploitation of the territory of Faizullah Khan, the first Nawab of Rampur, represented the deviant ways in which the corporation's expropriation of land injured the local economy and culture. Following the First Rohilla War in 1774, Khan was able to retain control over feudal land at Rampur. Burke notes that even enemies of Khan acknowledged his effective stewardship of the land. In his paraphrase of their viewpoint, Burke says they admitted that "the whole of his country *is* what the whole country of the Rohillas *was*, cultivated like a garden,

[79] Langford, *Writings and Speeches*, V, 391.   [80] Langford, *Writings and Speeches*, V, 392.
[81] Langford, *Writings and Speeches*, V, 392n3.   [82] Langford, *Writings and Speeches*, V, 394.
[83] Langford, *Writings and Speeches*, V, 408.   [84] Langford, *Writings and Speeches*, V, 408.
[85] "*ultimum moriens*": last one dying.   [86] Langford, *Writings and Speeches*, V, 408.

without one neglected spot in it."[87] The critics further conceded that he doubled the population and revenue of the territory.

But the East India Company had attacked Khan for allowing peasant asylum seekers into his land. Burke conveys a thick air of disgust over the Company's treatment of him, insisting that Khan warranted praise, not least for helping mankind by cultivating his land. Burke transmits this message by citing Jonathan Swift in *Gulliver's Travels*, who "somewhere says, that he who could make two blades of grass grow where but one grew before, was a greater benefactor to the human race than all the politicians that ever existed."[88] Burke's approval of Swift's quotation evokes a theme of his political economy that he articulated in his criticism of England's Board of Trade, when he praised its members as an "academy of Belles Lettres" but still wished for the body to be abolished,[89] and in the *Reflections*, when he said that he would rather ask for the help of "the farmer and the physician, rather than the professor of metaphysics"[90] to obtain food or medicine. For Burke, the farmer, merchant, and manufacturer generated greater practical advantages to man than the abstract philosopher, ruler, and administrator. Tilling and trading put food on people's tables. Theorizing and orating did not.

Burke apprehended a similar pattern of destruction in the Carnatic region in southern India. "It may be affirmed universally, that not one person of substance or property, landed, commercial, or monied, excepting two or three bankers ... is left in all that region," he observes.[91] Burke's insights into the agricultural economy of the Carnatic illuminate an appreciation for Indian enterprise, for he stresses that the knowledge of the natives – "Gentûs" – enabled them to use natural resources to the advantage of industry, and with spiritual sanction at that. "[T]he moisture, the bounty of Heaven, is given but at a certain season," he states.[92] "Before the aera of our influence, the industry of man carefully husbanded that gift of God."[93] Such was an echo of his belief expressed in *Two Letters* that nature was supplied by God for man's use.

Burke's esteem for the sagacity of the natives becomes even clearer in his discussion of their conservation of rain for their irrigation system. "The Gentûs preserved, with a provident and religious care, the previous deposit of the periodical rain in reservoirs, many of them works of royal grandeur; and from these, as occasion demanded, they fructified the whole country," he explains.[94] Moreover, "To maintain these reservoirs, and to keep up an annual advance to the cultivators, for seed and cattle, formed a principal object of the piety and policy of the priests and rulers of the Gentû religion."[95]

---

[87] Langford, *Writings and Speeches*, V, 408.   [88] Langford, *Writings and Speeches*, V, 408.
[89] See "*Speech on Economical Reform* I: Private Land, Contracts, and the Board of Trade," Chapter 5.
[90] Langford, *Writings and Speeches*, VIII, 111.   [91] Langford, *Writings and Speeches*, V, 422.
[92] Langford, *Writings and Speeches*, V, 422.   [93] Langford, *Writings and Speeches*, V, 422.
[94] Langford, *Writings and Speeches*, V, 422.   [95] Langford, *Writings and Speeches*, V, 422.

Once again, Burke is displaying his inclination to commend the local knowledge and shrewdness of natives who made efficient use of natural resources. Recall the quotation cited in *Account of the European Settlements in America* in the previous chapter: "[I]gnorant country people and barbarous nations, are better observers of times and seasons, and draw better rules from them, than more civilized and reasoning people." In his judgment, the East India Company's mismanagement of the local Indian economy negated the wisdom of natives, thereby upending their entire process of cultivation and throwing landowners, merchants, and farmers into ruin.

The settled estates of Indians were thus seized and converted into instruments for personal financial gain under the dreadful influence of British imperial power. In *Speech on Fox's India Bill*, Burke favorably compares the *zamindars* of Bengal with France's landed aristocracy at the time. Bengal and its provinces "once contained, as France does contain, a great and independent landed interest, composed of princes, of great lords, of a numerous nobility and gentry, of freeholders, of lower tenants, of religious communities, and public foundations."[96] Yet after Warren Hastings became president of Bengal, these lands were auctioned off for five-year leases. Hastings set up "the whole nobility, gentry, and freeholders, to the highest bidder."[97]

This process exhibited no respect for the ancestral possessions of Indian land, the sting of exploded avarice infecting the settled traditions of Bengal's past. "No preference was given to the ancient proprietors," Burke says. "They must bid against every usurer, every temporary adventurer, every jobber and schemer."[98] There is an intriguing analogue between this description and his attack on French revolutionaries in the *Reflections*: in both cases, traditional landowners were threatened by monied enthusiasts scheming to make a profit off the ruling power. While Burke's comparison between the French aristocracy and Bengali landowners was simplistic, he was correct in calling attention to the East India Company's impairment of the *zamindars*, who were uprooted from their land following Hastings's scheme, at least for a limited time.[99]

In addition to assailing the East India Company for displacing Indian landed proprietors, Burke provides an interesting comment on middlemen that was a precursor to his defense of traders in *Thoughts and Details*. British administrators in Bengal "adopted, as a fixed plan of policy, the destruction of all intermediate dealers between the Company and the manufacturer."[100] Consequently, "[N]ative merchants have disappeared of course."[101] Burke conveys in *Thoughts and Details* that middlemen performed an important role in market economies by helping distribute resources in an effectual manner to a variety of communities. He is putting forth the same observation

---

[96] Langford, *Writings and Speeches*, V, 425.   [97] Langford, *Writings and Speeches*, V, 426.
[98] Langford, *Writings and Speeches*, V, 426.   [99] Langford, *Writings and Speeches*, V, 426n3.
[100] Langford, *Writings and Speeches*, V, 427.   [101] Langford, *Writings and Speeches*, V, 427.

in *Speech on Fox's India Bill*: Indian middlemen exercised a critical function in the circulation of goods, and yet the East India Company's monopoly crushed them.

10.3 POLITICAL COMMERCE, AVARICE, AND ARBITRARY RULE

Political Commerce and Revenue

The additional question Burke confronts about the improper mixing between politics and economics in regard to the Indian economy was whether commerce should be the source of revenue, or revenue for commerce. Put another way, should commercial growth be the genesis for revenue collection – through, say, moderate taxation on goods – or should the distribution of revenues through high taxation be relied on to stimulate commerce? In his commentary on British India, and in his writings and speeches addressing other topics, Burke communicates sympathy for the former view; an economic environment that allowed commerce to flourish provided a sufficient amount of revenue for the state, in his judgment. This is what Burke calls a "Commercial"[102] principle: first establish commerce, then revenue will follow.

Burke appeals to this commercial principle throughout the *Ninth Report*. In the previous chapter we discussed his criticism in the report of the East India Company's revenue-for-investment scheme. Later in the *Ninth Report* Burke applies this criticism to other European chartered companies trading in India: "[T]he whole Foreign Maritime Trade, whether English, French, Dutch, or Danish, arises from the Revenues; and these are carried out of the Country, without producing any Thing to compensate so heavy a Loss."[103] The companies in turn rejected "a Principle merely Commercial."[104] The revenue in other countries, however, "following the natural Course and Order of Things, arises out of their Commerce."[105] Rulers would have ample opportunity to extract revenue from an economy that generated wealth from vigorous commercial activity.

That the East India Company implemented the opposite policy – collect as much revenue as possible to drive its investment in trade – penetrates to the core of Burke's critique of the Company: by improperly mixing political and economic power, it transformed from a commercial enterprise into a despotic government. "The constitution of the Company began in commerce and ended in Empire," Burke declaimed in his speech on Hastings's impeachment on February 15, 1788.[106] The corporation's chartered purpose to pursue trade in India for the advantage of Britain collapsed into a license to rule maliciously over natives. Its autocratic governance shredded the tender bonds of trust with

---

[102] Langford, *Writings and Speeches*, V, 227.   [103] Langford, *Writings and Speeches*, V, 227.
[104] Langford, *Writings and Speeches*, V, 227.   [105] Langford, *Writings and Speeches*, V, 227.
[106] Langford, *Writings and Speeches*, VI, 283.

Indians and, by defeating supply and demand principles, subverted its own mandate to traffic on behalf of the English people. In short, the Company slid from a commercial monopoly to a political monopoly.

The politicization of commerce is a theme that informed Burke's commentary on the East India Company prior to the 1780s. In April 1775, at a time when American commerce was providing shocks of competition to British merchants, Parliament considered a bill that called for the Company to export a selected amount of English manufactures. Burke noted that Britain's simultaneous attempt to discourage American exports and encourage English exports, the latter through the medium of the Company, was a gross affront to the principles of commerce. "Thus is the present a measure of political commerce, and not of commercial intelligence," he averred.[107] Burke highlighted the illogic of political commerce perpetrated by Parliament: the legislative body had furnished the Company with a loan, but before the firm started to repay it, Parliament then asked to enact what was in effect a tax on the corporation. Was this process "consonant with the ideas either of commerce or of finance?"[108] Burke answered with an emphatic no, and opposed the measure.

Burke's additional comments in opposition to the bill confirmed his seething dislike for the arbitrary control of commerce. He observed in his speech that haphazard regulations reduced the value of commodities. "[T]he principles of this Bill are false and rotten, every view of it will tell us; it depreciates our most valuable products and manufactures," Burke professed. And forced commerce did not mitigate the cold reality that the British misjudged the potential for the industries of plum pudding and broad cloth. "I now find all our English ideas are very erroneous, and that instead of being good things, they go a begging for a market," he said in regard to those industries.[109]

Even so, Burke blasted the assumption that British manufactures held *no* value. This premise justified the notion that their "exportation must be enforced at all events, or they will lie a dead weight on the hands of the manufacturers."[110] He proposed rather that Britain should "clothe the numberless poor" in the country and charge the Company with the bill.[111] Notice the middle ground Burke is taking: he did not hesitate to reckon that the measure corrupted the principles of supply and demand, but he also acknowledged that manufactures with little demand still retained some value, and thus could be used for the benefit of the British people.

One might counter: political institutions were responsible for the creation of the East India Company's charter in the first place. Was this fact not

---

[107] *Cobbett's Parliamentary History of England*, vol. XVIII, *1744–1777* (London: T. C. Hansard, 1813), 617.
[108] *Cobbett's Parliamentary History of England*, vol. XVIII, 617.
[109] *Cobbett's Parliamentary History of England*, vol. XVIII, 618.
[110] *Cobbett's Parliamentary History of England*, vol. XVIII, 617.
[111] *Cobbett's Parliamentary History of England*, vol. XVIII, 618.

evidence that the firm carried an inherently political character anyway? Further clarification is required on this matter. In his speech on the opening of Hastings's impeachment proceedings, which lasted almost three hours,[112] Burke indeed emphasizes that the political authority of the Company was rooted in its original royal charter and subsequent parliamentary approval, which started in 1698.[113] In this case, then, political sanction preceded commercial activity. But, Burke contends, once the Crown and Parliament had approved its charter, the Company should have confined its activities to the enlargement of commerce in the East Indies, thereby fulfilling its institutional purpose to advance the trading interests of the British Empire.

Instead, it was authorized by subsequent royal charters in the seventeenth century to extend its military presence, expand its civil and criminal jurisdiction over natives, and adopt the powers of a sovereign, particularly those of war and peace. By the end of the reign of Charles II, Burke says in his February 15 speech, the Company "did not seem to be merely a Company formed for the extension of the British commerce, but in reality a delegation of the whole power and sovereignty of this kingdom sent into the East."[114] By venturing far beyond its commercial objective, the Company assumed the political role of serving as the supreme ruler over native Indians, in effect transgressing the constraints of its original charter. In this case, then, it prioritized the political dimension of ruling over its original commercial aim of trading.

For Burke, this frightful convergence of political and economic activity augmented the East India Company with a power that was anathema to ancient jurisprudence. "It became that thing which was supposed by the Roman Law so unsuitable, the same power was a Trader, the same power was a Lord," he says in the speech.[115] Such clout allowed the Company to set price controls, usurp property, regulate the cultivation of crops, and carry out an unending chain of autocratic edicts that hardened into imperial domination over Indians. Of course, as Burke underscores in his study of India, these despotic measures were self-defeating, for compulsion bred the decline of the firm's revenue and commerce.

Burke's reflections on India also examine the related consequences stemming from the combination of political and economic monopoly, such as extortion, bribery, and collusion, not only among East India Company traders but also between British and Indian rulers. His assault on Warren Hastings highlighted this systemic pattern of financial subterfuge. Hastings, Burke declared on February 18, 1788, "formed Plans and Systems of Government for the very purpose of accumulating bribes and presents to himself."[116] Burke's acute

---

[112] Langford, *Writings and Speeches*, VI, 266.   [113] Langford, *Writings and Speeches*, VI, 280.
[114] Langford, *Writings and Speeches*, VI, 283.   [115] Langford, *Writings and Speeches*, VI, 283.
[116] Langford, *Writings and Speeches*, VI, 376.

suspicion of the Nabob of Arcot's debts[117] reinforced his abiding awareness of Company delinquencies. "[T]he Nabob of Arcot and his creditors are not adversaries, but collusive parties, and that the whole transaction is under a false colour and false names," he insists in *Speech on Nabob of Arcot's Debts.*[118]

Furthermore, crooked political deals damaged the "public revenues" and hurt "the miserable inhabitants of a ruined country."[119] Burke, blending imaginative rhetoric with doses of sharp criticism, continues: "It is therefore not from treasuries and mines, but from the food of your unpaid armies, from the blood withheld from the veins, and whipt out of the backs of the most miserable of men, that we are to pamper extortion, usury, and peculation, under the false names of debtors and creditors of state."[120] Contaminating economic activity with political monopoly crippled the financial health of a state and harmed those who were most vulnerable: ordinary people untouched by political and commercial corruption – such as the many native Indians Burke gave voice to in his writings and speeches on British India.

Avarice

Burke's treatment of the East India Company's fusion of political and commercial capacities indicates a possible contradiction in his economic thought. As discussed, he endorsed the virtue of "laudable avarice"[121] in *Tracts relating to Popery Laws* for sparking the human capacity for industry and accumulation; and he defended the "excessively avaricious"[122] farmer in *Thoughts and Details* for his pursuit of profit. Laudable avarice stimulated the smooth coordination of market activities and gave rise to public prosperity.

Yet, in his speeches on the impeachment of Hastings, Burke reprobates Hastings for spreading toxins of avarice throughout India. "There is

---

[117] The Nawab of Arcot had waged military campaigns with financial backing from the East India Company in order to widen his territorial base. The British government recognized the need to formally acknowledge and authorize repayment of the debts under the management of the Company. In 1784, the Court of Directors proposed to use the revenue of the Carnatic to pay the debts, upon careful examination of the fund in which the revenue would be deposited. The Board of Control took out the requirement for examination and called for the full repayment of the debts of the nawab, which had been consolidated by European creditors. In *Speech on Nabob of Arcot's Debts*, Burke contends that the vast majority of the debts was the product of fraudulent dealing between Europeans and the Nawab. (Burke exaggerated the extent of the seeming fictitious debt.) He also posits that the acceptance of debt repayments stunk of corruption between creditors who had backed Pitt in the 1784 election and the Pitt ministry. See Langford, *Writings and Speeches*, V, 478–479.

[118] Langford, *Writings and Speeches*, V, 496. Remember that Burke most likely exaggerated the fraudulent nature of these debts.

[119] Langford, *Writings and Speeches*, V, 496.   [120] Langford, *Writings and Speeches*, V, 496.

[121] See Langford, *Writings and Speeches*, IX, 477.

[122] See Langford, *Writings and Speeches*, IX, 126.

a pollution in the touch, in the principle of that Governor who makes nothing but money his object," he utters, referring to Hastings.[123] His "great ruling principle" was "money."[124] Moreover, "It is the vice of base avarice, which never is, nor ever looks to the prejudices of mankind, to be any thing like a virtue."[125]

Burke's seemingly incongruous positions on avarice can be reconciled in the following sense: avarice in the context of exchange economies was tenable, even praiseworthy, because the structure of incentives connected the pursuit of self-interest with the well-being of other market participants. As he observes in *Thoughts and Details* in regard to the "excessively avaricious" farmer, "the more he desires to increase his gains, the more interested is he in the good condition of those, upon whose labour his gains must principally depend."[126]

In *Speech on Fox's India Bill*, Burke goes so far as to defend the avarice of Tartary invaders into India. Even while acknowledging their rapacity, he admits that "with few political checks upon power, Nature had still fair play; the sources of acquisition were not dried up; and therefore the trade, the manufactures, and the commerce of the country flourished."[127] Indians still retained the freedom to acquire and produce in equitable market economies guided by the hand of nature. And the impulse to acquire was the trigger for the growth of riches: "Even avarice and usury itself operated, both for the preservation and the employment of national wealth."[128] Avarice in a climate conducive to commerce spread benefits to members of the community.

Yet avarice in an environment of political and economic monopoly fueled corruption and peculation, in turn destroying the local economy of Indians to the benefit of its greedy rulers. Hastings "squeezed more money out of the inhabitants of the Country than other persons could have done, money got by oppression, violence, extortion of the poor, or the heavy hand of power upon the rich and great."[129] The Company's monopoly fed an avarice that felt no commercial or moral pull to reciprocate natives for the corporation's plunder of their fruits: "England has erected no churches, no hospitals,[130] no palaces, no schools; England has built no bridges, made no high roads, cut no navigations, dug out no reservoirs," Burke says.[131] The failure to build any charitable institutions or supervise public construction projects symbolized how avarice eroded the trust between the Company and India and sabotaged the common welfare.

---

[123] Langford, *Writings and Speeches*, VI, 376.   [124] Langford, *Writings and Speeches*, VI, 377.
[125] Langford, *Writings and Speeches*, VI, 377.   [126] Langford, *Writings and Speeches*, IX, 126.
[127] Langford, *Writings and Speeches*, V, 401–402.
[128] Langford, *Writings and Speeches*, V, 402.
[129] Langford, *Writings and Speeches*, VI, 376–377.
[130] The published version of Burke's speech includes a footnote with reference to hospitals: "[t]he paltry foundation at Calcutta is scarcely worth naming as an exception" (Langford, *Writings and Speeches*, V, 402).
[131] Langford, *Writings and Speeches*, V, 402.

The contrast between this type of avarice and Burke's "laudable avarice" now emerges with clearer distinction: political avarice unchecked by market constraints, and renouncing any moral obligations to the people, undermined the public good and established clearly defined winners (the beneficiaries of political bribery) and losers (the local producer and consumer). Avarice manifested in market economies, however, conferred benefits to traders because of the element of reciprocity; an individual could be as greedy as he wants, but he would struggle to obtain private reward unless he furnished a service to others. The further implication, Burke suggests, was that the power of market reciprocity diminished the likelihood for plunder and extortion, while the absence of reciprocity increased the chances for corruption encouraged by imperious rulers such as Hastings.

Spanning back to his early writings, we should also note Burke's suggestion in *A Vindication of Natural Society* that the temptation of avarice was inherent in man. Natural society was founded in "natural Appetites and Instincts," the Noble Writer declared in the letter.[132] But "Man would go farther." For the "great Error of our Nature is, not to know where to stop, not to be satisfied with any reasonable Acquirement; not to compound with our Condition; but to lose all we have gained by an insatiable Pursuit after more."[133] The formation of civil society reflected man's attraction to gain. Because the *Vindication* was a parody of Lord Bolingbroke's judgment of the virtues of natural society, we may interpret these comments to convey Burke's belief that the creation of artificial institutions did not transform human appetite into avarice. The desire for advantage was sown in the constitution of man – which made it an even greater necessity for market economies to channel the energies of avarice toward the public good.[134]

In the case of India, Britain's political monopoly over the local economy produced the scourge of stable commonwealths and vibrant markets: the exercise of arbitrary rule. The "principles upon which Mr Hastings governed his conduct in India, and upon which he grounds his defence" can be "reduced to one short word, *Arbitrary Power*."[135] Most important for our inquiry into Burke's political economy, arbitrary power shook the foundations of property. "Law and arbitrary power are at eternal enmity," Burke says in his February 16 speech on Hastings's impeachment. "Name me a Magistrate, and I will name property."[136] Burke is suggesting that the steady, regular enforcement of law built a shield around the citizen's landed possessions. This remark also indicates his sharp consciousness of the distinction between liberal political economy and

---

[132] Langford, *Writings and Speeches*, I, 138.

[133] Langford, *Writings and Speeches*, I, 138–139.

[134] In notes for a speech on amending the Marriage Act, Burke noted in 1781 that legal protections for property would naturally encourage greed. "The same laws, which secure property, encourage avarice; and the fences made about honest acquisition are the strong bars, which secure the hoards of the miser" (Langford, *Writings and Speeches*, IV, 97).

[135] Langford, *Writings and Speeches*, VI, 374.   [136] Langford, *Writings and Speeches*, VI, 351.

anarchy: the former required the state – government officials – to use its legal authority to safeguard land, while the latter denoted the absence of law. Here, then, does the nexus between law and economics in Burke's political economy correspond to his thoughts on property articulated elsewhere throughout his public career: the consistent enforcement of law protects a commonwealth from the despotism of arbitrary rule, thereby sustaining the right to private property.

The origin of law, moreover, derived not from statutes or legal decisions but from nature and God:

> We are all born in subjection, all born equally, high and low, governors and governed, in subjection to one great, immutable, pre-existent law, prior to all our devices, and prior to all our contrivances, paramount to our very belief itself, by which we are knit and connected in the eternal frame of the universe, out of which we cannot stir.
>
> This great law does not arise from our conventions or compacts. On the contrary, it gives to our conventions and compacts all the force and sanction they can have. It does not arise from our vain institutions. Every good gift is of God; all power is of God; and He who has given the power and from whom it alone originates, will never suffer the exercise of it to be practised upon any less solid foundation than the power itself.[137]

Protections for property could be traced back to preexisting moral law and the divine creator of man. Arbitrary government violates property, and thus violates natural law and the law of God. "[N]o man can succeed to fraud, rapine and violence; neither by compact, covenant or submission, nor by any other means can arbitrary power be conveyed to any man," he pronounces in his February 16 speech.[138] No man has a lawful right to contravene the will of God.

These comments signal Burke's flirtation with Lockean notions on the right to resist oppressive government. At face value, the moral implication of Burke's remarks is unambiguous: because arbitrary rule offended natural law and the law of God, men were commanded by the ethical imperative to resist despotism. Burke almost admits as much in his February 16 speech on the opening of Hastings's impeachment: "Those who give and those who receive arbitrary power are alike criminal, and there is no man but is bound to resist it to the best of his power wherever it shall shew its face to the world." In addition, "Nothing but absolute impotence can justify men in not resisting it to the best of their power."[139] Unless they are impotent, Burke suggests, men possess an unassailable duty to fight arbitrary rule.

Because Burke was not a systematic philosopher, he does not, in his speeches on the Hastings impeachment or elsewhere, tease out the specific conditions under which the persecuted people should resist their government. Furthermore, Burke's remarks in his February 16 speech place a heavier accent on natural law compared to his comments on prescription in the *Reflections*, and in the *Nullum Tempus* affair. His reflections on property,

---

[137] Langford, *Writings and Speeches*, VI, 350. [138] Langford, *Writings and Speeches*, VI, 351.
[139] Langford, *Writings and Speeches*, VI, 351.

however, retain the consistent argument that the genesis of property rights ultimately resided in nature, not convention, and that individuals were bound by the moral law to challenge arbitrary rule, whether in an incremental or immediate fashion.

10.4 CONCLUSION

Burke's struggle to alter the institutional structure of the East India Company fell short. Fox's India Bill met defeat in the House of Lords, presaging the downfall of the Fox-North coalition. A subsequent attempt at reform, William Pitt's India Act of 1784, preserved the commercial privileges of the Company and provided government oversight of the firm, yet such oversight was weaker than the proposals recommended by Fox's India Bill. Burke was critical of the India Act, but later conceded it rested on similar principles as Fox's bill.[140] Starting in the mid-1780s, he turned his attention to preparing the prosecution's case against Warren Hastings, who had arrived back in England in 1785. (The House of Lords acquitted Hastings on all counts in 1795.) The changes established by the India Act generally endured until the Company was nationalized by the British government in 1858. The firm was dissolved in 1874.

Burke's investigation into Anglo-Indian relations was marred at times by hyperbole, distortion, and oversimplification. Burke had never been to India, and therefore was forced to rely on secondhand reports of British officials returning from the subcontinent, such as Philip Francis, some of whom (including Francis) may have carried personal agendas or subjective viewpoints. In addition, Burke's Manichean picture of a ruthless British institution exploiting helpless Indian natives has not fully held up in light of later historical research that has drawn a more nuanced picture of Anglo-Indian relations. For example, P. J. Marshall has argued that Bengal achieved greater prosperity relative to other Indian territories at the time, contrary to the impression Burke paints in his writings and speeches on the subject; and that portraying the British takeover of India in 1757 and 1765 as the start of the empire's pillage of the subcontinent, as Burke had, may have exaggerated the negative impact of the Company's rule on the natives beginning in those years.[141] We must also remind ourselves that Burke's committee reports and speeches were articulated in a tense political environment rather than in a university classroom.

Even with these limitations, Burke's commentary on Indian affairs was exhaustive at the time. His arguments on India were not necessarily original, but the penetration of detail and coherence of thought that animated his

---

[140] Burke to Lord Loughborough, [*circa* 17 March 1796], in *Correspondence of Edmund Burke*, vol. VIII, 427–428.
[141] P. J. Marshall, *East Indian Fortunes: The British in Bengal in the Eighteenth Century* (Oxford: Clarendon Press, 1976), 257–271. See also Lawson, *The East India Company*, 70.

committee reports and speeches would be impressive in any era – particularly for someone with no real incentive or institutional obligation to acquire it. "For any major political figure to become an expert on India in the 1770s was unusual; for a man in opposition without any direct administrative responsibility to do so was wholly unprecedented," Marshall writes.[142]

In fact, the *Ninth Report*'s "drain of wealth" thesis – the idea that Britain was responsible for the sudden transfer of wealth from India to London in the late eighteenth century through its revenue-for-investment scheme – was perhaps the first systematic explanation of this phenomenon in British history. Alexander Dow made note of this pattern in the early 1770s, and a number of other East India Company administrators followed suit. Burke's analysis, however, with the help of Francis, put forth a rigorous and coherent exposition of the economic consequences of British oppression in India that was exceptional for its time, and that has continued to shape interpretations of British India into the nineteenth and twentieth centuries.[143]

Let us now weave together the threads of Burke's commentary on the East India Company with his other reflections on political economy. Consider one of the most significant arguments Burke conveys in *Thoughts and Details*: the liberal circulation of goods tends to benefit the trading parties involved. As we have seen, he applied this principle not only to England's domestic grain trade but also to his examination of British trade relations with America, Ireland, and the European powers in the West Indies.

Similarly, for Burke, if Indian natives were allowed to trade freely according to the natural laws of supply and demand, an identity of interest would blossom from mutual commercial agreements between English and native traders. Burke illustrates this reasoning by explaining how the gross intrusion of the East India Company into internal Indian markets generated zero-sum consequences: what was gained by British officials was taken away from the natives. "Every rupee of profit made by an Englishman is lost for ever to India," Burke says in *Speech on Fox's India Bill*.[144] The firm's corruption of market principles extinguished the element of reciprocity in voluntary exchange, which choked the abilities of Indians to reap rewards for their labor, condemning them to poverty.

Burke observed that this system was ultimately counterproductive, since the zero-sum struggle between British and native traders in India actually

---

[142] Langford, *Writings and Speeches*, V, 3.

[143] See Rama Dev Roy, "Some Aspects of the Economic Drain from India during the British Rule," *Social Scientist* 15 (1987): 39–47; Vijay K. Seth, *The Story of Indian Manufacturing: Encounters with the Mughal and British Empires (1498–1947)* (London: Palgrave Macmillan, 2018), 122; Romesh Chunder Dutt, *The Economic History of India Under Early British Rule: From the Rise of the British Power in 1757 to the Accession of Queen Victoria in 1837* (London: Kegan Paul, Trench, Trübner & Co., 1906), 48–50. See also Onur Ulas Inca, *Colonial Capitalism and the Dilemmas of Liberalism* (New York: Oxford University Press, 2018).

[144] Langford, *Writings and Speeches*, V, 402.

compromised the integrity of British public finance and hindered the advancement of the empire's commercial prosperity. According to Burke, the fortunes of the Company were bound up with the fortunes of the natives, and the suffering of the latter would necessarily affect the state of the former. "The Whole of this History will serve to demonstrate," the *Ninth Report* states, regarding the Company's flawed investment in the raw silk trade, "that all Attempts, which in their Original System, or in their necessary Consequences, tend to the Distress of India, must, and in a very short Time will, make themselves felt, even by those in whose Favour such Attempts have been made."[145] The negative impact of monopolistic practices on Indian merchants would hit British traders hard as well.

This is why Burke insists that the recovery of the East India Company's lawful powers and the relaxation of its control of trade would benefit both Britain and India, rather than serve as a prelude to the Company's downfall. In *First Report Select Committee:* "Observations,"[146] the first report issued by the Select Committee on India after it had reconvened for the 1782 session of Parliament, he writes, "There is nothing which can strengthen the just Authority of Great Britain in India, which does not nearly, if not altogether, in the same Proportion, tend to the Relief of the People."[147] Removing the Company's capacity to exercise arbitrary power would recover to Indians the freedom they had once possessed. The interests between an imperial power and its subjects need not be antagonistic if their self-interests could be relaxed and reconciled through mediums of reciprocal advantage, such as commercial exchange. Furthermore, there is "nothing, which renders those, who exercise the subordinate Trusts of Power, less responsible, or less obedient to the Government from whence that Power is derived ... which does not tend to depress the Minds, and destroy the Prosperity, of the Natives," he writes.[148] Hence commercial freedom could help transform market actors from different cultural backgrounds into social partners.

This last point is essential to understanding the multiple dimensions of Burke's economic thought. On a surface level, as this book has shown, Burke defended supply and demand principles, freedom of contract, liberal trade,

---

[145] Langford, *Writings and Speeches*, V, 258.

[146] The report was published on February 5, 1782. It addresses the new civil court in Calcutta, the *Sadr Diwani Adalat*, which had been formed in October 1780. The East India Company held the responsibility to reform the civil court system in Bengal, so Hastings had selected Sir Elijah Impey to be the judge of the *Sadr Diwani Adalat*. This raised concerns about a conflict of interest: how would Impey be able to exercise independent judgment on legal matters relating to the Company if he was being paid by the corporation to serve on one of its established courts? Hastings's squabbles with Impey regarding the jurisdiction of the Supreme Court, on which Impey served as Chief Justice, raised questions of impropriety. Impey's conflicting judicial responsibilities as both head of the new civil court and as Chief Justice also drew concern. See Langford, *Writings and Speeches*, V, 144–145; and Bourke, *Empire & Revolution*, 550–551.

[147] Langford, *Writings and Speeches*, V, 179.   [148] Langford, *Writings and Speeches*, V, 179.

limited government regulations, the competitive price system, and a market for wages. But Burke also intimates in his discussion on Anglo-Indian relations that commercial exchange did not harbor inherent biases against one culture or another; voluntary trade carried out in accord with the natural laws of commerce conferred fruits on traders regardless of racial, ethnic, or religious background. Indians were not Europeans, and yet Burke argues vociferously that they, as well as the British, stood to benefit from market competition.

We can connect Burke's distrust of zero-sum thinking to the broader cosmopolitan inclinations of his economic thought that gained expression during the Irish trade bill debates in the late 1770s. As noted, Burke was cautious about extending commercial overtures to hostile foes of Britain. But his parliamentary activity promoting trade beyond English shores also hinted at an intuition that market exchange could complement cultural difference by providing a joint mechanism for barter under a shared imperial umbrella. The pursuit of self-interest was a common human instinct; liberal markets could tame and redirect this impulse in a way that advanced the greater good through the dispensation of material reward to people from a variety of political and religious communities throughout the British Empire. This gift of reciprocity was part of Burke's conception of "that law of common justice which cements them to us and us to them,"[149] with reference to Anglo-Indian affairs.

Burke's moderate cosmopolitan sympathies in the context of political economy shed light on his idea of the link between natural rights and market freedom. Although Burke was not an orthodox natural law thinker, he did not repudiate the role of nature in matters of commerce and markets. In his view, people regardless of lineage held the natural right to produce and reap what they sowed. As discussed, he invoked this thinking to justify his defense of commercial freedom, ranging from the rights of Irish Catholics to the rights of English middlemen to the rights of Indian traders. According to Burke, this natural right was not inviolable, but it was the starting point at which all subsequent discussion of market regulations should begin. "When, indeed, the smallest rights of the poorest people in the kingdom are in question," Burke wrote in 1781, "I would set my face against any act of pride and power countenanced by the highest that are in it; and if it should come to the last extremity and to a contest of blood – God forbid! God forbid! – my part is taken, I would take my fate with the poor, and low and feeble."[150] This declaration was pronounced in a different setting,[151] but its principle may be applied with equal force here: oppressed Indians – just like struggling Irishmen, and enslaved Africans, and industrious Americans, and enterprising individuals of all stripes – possessed just as much of a right to labor and deal and earn a profit as affluent Englishmen.

---

[149] Langford, *Writings and Speeches*, VI, 279.   [150] Langford, *Writings and Speeches*, IV, 97.
[151] Burke apparently made this comment during a speech in 1781 when he opposed efforts to reform the Marriage Act.

Government for Profit

But the most important lesson of Burke's commentary on the political economy of British India was his ominous warning about the destructive effects originating from the transformation of government into a market for profit. This may seem paradoxical at first: as discussed in this chapter, Burke contended that the East India Company should restore sound market principles in the Indian economy.

But Burke's larger argument is that the ruler's pursuit of mercantile profit *acting as a political sovereign* dissolved the ethical and institutional roots necessary for just government. In the case of the East India Company, its servants used the institution's wealth to bribe and extort Indian rulers for pecuniary self-gratification. Without reforming the Company, Burke declares in *Speech on Fox's India Bill*, it would be thought that the British would have "sold the blood of millions of men, for the base consideration of money."[152] Thus, "We had not a right to make a market of our duties."[153] Accordingly, Burke condemns in his speech the Company's widespread selling of districts, peoples, and rulers to potentates under the Moghul Empire. Markets could channel self-interest toward the common good; a monopoly on power could not.

Warren Hastings was the guiltiest culprit of this delinquent pattern of corruption. After he became Governor General of Bengal, Burke noted with emphasis, "the landed interest" of the territory was "set up to public auction!"[154] Established Indian traditions were unsettled by a spirit of greed fueled by British servants. The pursuit of profit in a market of wants was a tenable, indeed laudatory, endeavor. Yet the application of this principle to civil society as a whole threatened to undermine the moral and cultural foundations of a political community, for the reduction of social relations to the imperatives of financial advantage laid the seeds for its own self-destruction. Such a lesson did not merely pertain to India, however. Burke communicated this message with unmatched eloquence in response to the most calamitous political event of his age, one that forced him to seriously confront the limits of that which he defended throughout his entire life: transactional exchange.

[152] Langford, *Writings and Speeches*, V, 386.   [153] Langford, *Writings and Speeches*, V, 386.
[154] Langford, *Writings and Speeches*, V, 426.

PART VI

THE FRENCH REVOLUTION

Reflections on the Revolution in France: Property, the Monied Interest, and the *Assignats*

> Your legislators, in every thing new, are the very first who have founded a commonwealth upon gaming, and infused this spirit into it as its vital breath. The great object in these politics is to metamorphose France, from a great kingdom into one great play-table; to turn its inhabitants into a nation of gamesters.[1]
>
> Edmund Burke, *Reflections on the Revolution in France*, 1790

11.1 INTRODUCTION

The integrity of Burke's beliefs about the relationship between commerce and virtue comes into full form in his commentary on the French Revolution. We have discussed his steady confidence in the virtues of free intercourse to bring about public opulence; but what happens when the spirit of voluntary exchange escapes the moral boundaries of markets? Burke's famous condemnation of the Revolution, *Reflections on the Revolution in France*, helps answer this question, as do his other writings and speeches that address the historical event, such as *Speech on the Army Estimates* (1790); *Appeal from the New to the Old Whigs* (1791); and *Letters on a Regicide Peace* (1795–1797). The following analysis of Burke's conception of political economy will be steered by the *Reflections*, but it will also weave in his observations from these other sources in order to paint a fuller picture of his economic thought as it related to the Revolution.

Before proceeding, we must summarize the general strands of Burke's blistering critique of the French Revolution.[2] Burke was the first noteworthy

---

[1] Langford, *Writings and Speeches*, VIII, 240.

[2] For overviews of the French Revolution, see, among many sources, Simon Schama, *Citizens*; William Doyle, *The Oxford History of the French Revolution* (Oxford: Oxford University Press, 2002); and P. M. Jones, *Reform and Revolution in France: The Politics of Transition, 1774–1791* (Cambridge: Cambridge University Press, 1995).

public figure to attack its political developments,[3] lashing out at revolutionaries for seeking to engineer a new conception of man through the complete transformation of French politics and society. Desiring swift revolution over incremental reform, French ideologues, in Burke's judgment, sought to: abolish the monarchy; strike at the Gallican Church; eradicate social hierarchies and ancient privileges; suppress the hereditary aristocracy; inject secularism and atheism into the public sphere; establish democratic political institutions; and spread radical egalitarian sentiment throughout the nation and Europe. These objects were inspired by a regimented form of abstract reason captured by one of the Revolution's most famous slogans, *liberté, egalité, fraternité* – liberty, equality, fraternity. Such was a theory divorced from the weight of historical wisdom that Burke treasured in his political thought.

In *Speech on the Army Estimates*, his first public commentary on the French Revolution, Burke observed with horror that the French had "completely pulled down to the ground, their monarchy; their church; their nobility; their law; their revenue; their army; their navy; their commerce; their arts; and their manufactures."[4] As indicated by his reference to the decline in revenue, commerce, and manufactures, Burke here associates the advent of the revolution with the descent of the French economy. Such destruction, in his view, reflected the ghastliest impulse of the French Revolution: the attempt to remodel man in order to bring about a utopian state of human perfection.

Accordingly, secondary studies on Burke's broadside against the French Revolution have drawn attention to his stinging rebuke of the revolutionaries' idea of abstract reason; their campaign to radically overthrow existing institutions; and their rejection of the ancestral traditions that built up French political order throughout the ages. The following examination, however, will focus on Burke's observations on the connection between the French Revolution and political economy.

This area continues to be a neglected aspect of Burke's remarks on the French Revolution, and yet it remains one of the most significant parts of his commentary in the *Reflections*. We cannot truly comprehend the many dimensions of Burke's philosophy of political economy, nor his general attack on the Revolution in the *Reflections* and in his other writings, unless we understand his criticism of the event's impact on commerce, revenue, and property. His analysis stretched beyond considerations of supply and demand laws and fiscal policy, however, for the *Reflections* illuminated the broader ethical implications of his economic thought that shaped his understanding of the role of markets in the wider growth of European civilization. While *Thoughts and Details* is the beginning of Burke's intellectual conception of political economy, the *Reflections* is the conclusion of it.

---

[3] Steven Blakemore, ed., *Burke and the French Revolution: Bicentennial Essays* (Athens and London: The University of Georgia Press, 1992), ix.

[4] Langford, *Writings and Speeches*, IV, 285.

11.2 THE POLITICAL ECONOMY OF THE ANCIEN RÉGIME

A brief background on the state of France leading up to the French Revolution, with particular emphasis on economic trends relevant to Burke's thoughts in the *Reflections*,[5] will allow us to better grasp his critique of the political economy of the affair.[6] The chief problems of the ancien régime prior to 1789 were the inequalities and inefficiencies of its commercial and revenue structures, as exemplified by its complicated system of taxation that tended to privilege the higher orders of the clergy and the nobility over the commoners.[7] Hence the French government struggled to procure and spend revenue with any regularity of form. As Florin Aftalion notes, the ancien régime effectively had no state budget.[8] Long-term loans of the government tended to be paid through a system of annuities, such as life annuities, financed by moneylenders – a group Burke would later characterize disparagingly in the *Reflections* as the "monied interest."

The *taille*, the direct land tax Burke had criticized in the *Observations* in 1769, was the most notorious and onerous levy and exerted a disproportionate impact on peasants. Indirect taxes were also enacted under the ancien régime that aggravated the cost of the free movement of goods and hurt the poor, such as the *gabelle*, the tax on salt. By 1789, there were 1,600 toll-houses in France. Jacques Necker, the financier and finance minister Burke praised multiple times in various writings and speeches for his fiscal prudence, described this entire fiscal system as a "real monstrosity in the eyes of reason."[9]

The clergy carried the lightest tax burden among the three orders of French society and would choose the amount of money it contributed to the Royal Treasury. Even more, the tithe faced increasing resentment, deepening public animosities toward the Gallican Church, the Catholic Church of France, which owned around one-tenth of the land surface in the country.[10]

The Royal Treasury never was able to extricate itself from the morass of financial difficulties that had plagued the nation starting in the late seventeenth century. France had accrued a huge debt stemming from European wars in the final decades of the reign of Louis XIV. Aftalion notes that government outlays

---

[5] This is not to suggest that this chapter will examine Burke's political economy from a Marxian perspective, but rather to narrow the scope of the French Revolution – an event that has produced an enormous amount of secondary literature – to the focus of this book, Burke's economic thought.

[6] This section is indebted to the scholarship of Florin Aftalion. See Aftalion, *Economic Interpretation*, 11–47. See also Henry C. Clark, *Compass of Society: Commerce and Absolutism in Old-Regime France* (Lanham, MD: Lexington Books, 2007).

[7] Gerri Chanel argues that scholars have exaggerated the burdensome nature of the ancien régime's tax system. She emphasizes that French taxpayers were most disgusted by the arbitrary nature of the system, rather than its sheer weight. See Chanel, "Taxation as a Cause of the French Revolution: Setting the Record Straight," *Studia Historica Gedanensia* TOM 6 (2015): 65–81.

[8] Aftalion, *Economic Interpretation*, 18.   [9] Aftalion, *Economic Interpretation*, 15.

[10] Jones, *Reform and Revolution in France*, 53.

spiked twofold, from 1689 to 1697 and from 1701 to 1714, and that the state deficit at the time of the king's death in 1715 was larger on a proportional basis than it would be in 1789.[11] National credit became crippled, and Treasury finances sunk into dire peril.

Various measures of expediency in the 1700s aspired to settle France on a stronger financial base, yet few reforms achieved lasting success. The Mississippi Bubble was one such attempt that offered a cautionary tale for posterity. John Law, a Scottish economist who was appointed Controller General of France in 1720, engineered a failed investment scheme in French Louisiana by overstating the territory's wealth, which sparked speculative delirium and the issuance of a flood of banknotes to meet investor demand. The bubble finally burst, causing panic to sweep over the public and provoking a bank run and riots. It was one of the first financial bubbles in modernity,[12] and would leave a residual scar on the French psyche.[13]

The Royal Treasury continued to rest on an unsteady foundation throughout the eighteenth century. Louis XVI took the throne in 1774 and ruled France through the start of the French Revolution until the monarchy was abolished in 1792, but he failed to improve the nation's fiscal predicament. Turgot, who served as the Controller-General from 1774 to 1776, had plans for a uniform land tax and a policy of economic liberalization. In 1775, Burke, referring to France under Turgot's leadership, observed that a "certain System d'oeconomie politique," as well as a certain tenor of "Philosophy," had "passed from the closet of {Learned} men to the Cabinets of Princes" and had "humanized perhaps too relaxed the minds of" the French people.[14] Turgot's plan for free trade, however, gave rise to riots. (Poor harvests during his tenure did not help matters.) The Parlements thwarted Turgot's plans to suppress powerful guilds and the *corvée*, the system of forced labor for commoners that had contributed substantially to the construction of France's roads. Turgot was dismissed in 1776.

The tenure of Jacques Necker as France's director of finances[15] from 1777 to 1781 encountered the added financial burden of French involvement in the American war. Still, Necker declined to raise taxes. "[F]or the first time ever, a French king waged a war without demanding new contributions from his

---

[11] Aftalion, *Economic Interpretation*, 18.

[12] See Peter M. Garber, *Famous First Bubbles: The Fundamentals of Early Manias* (Cambridge, MA and London: The MIT Press, 2001).

[13] For additional information on Law, see Antoin E. Murphy, *John Law: Economic Theorist and Policy-Maker* (Oxford: Clarendon Press, 1997); and François R. Velde, "John Law's System," *American Economic Review* 97 (2007): 276–279.

[14] Langford, *Writings and Speeches*, III, 212.

[15] Because Necker was a Protestant, he could not receive the title of Controller-General in France, a Catholic nation. For additional background on Necker, consult Robert D. Harris, *Necker: Reform Statesman of the Ancien Régime* (Berkeley: University of California Press, 1979).

subjects," Aftalion writes.[16] Necker did not end France's financial difficulties, but his skill and knowledge of public finance shaped a fiscal program that mitigated their worst effects. Necker in general wielded stronger influence than prior ministers and achieved a reputation as a practical and disinterested official dedicated to securing French credit on solid grounds, which helps explain Burke's attraction to his reform efforts.

Necker, though, was not immune from clever accounting methods. And his published summary of the finances of the Royal Treasury, *Compte rendu au roi* in 1781 – a project significant in itself, for it represented the first time that France's finances had been outlined extensively for public consumption – painted an inaccurate picture of the receipts and expenditures of the French government.[17]

Prerevolutionary reforms under subsequent Controller-Generals (including Necker, who later returned to the office) failed to reinvigorate the health of the French government's finances. Even with the litany of defects afflicting the ancien régime's system of taxation, however, France in general witnessed a steady expansion of its economy in the eighteenth century. After a sluggish start in the century's first few decades, due in no small part to the accumulation of debt under Louis XIV and John Law's financial scheme, France gradually enhanced its productive activities. According to Aftalion, the nation's economy grew at an annual rate of 0.5 percent.[18] Although regulatory constraints remained in place, foreign trade bloomed as well, in many ways meeting or exceeding Britain's performance in international markets.[19] As Jan Marczewski observed in 1961, "[S]ince the beginning of the eighteenth century, the economic growth of France has been following a continuously rising curve, with some alternative periods of acceleration and deceleration."[20]

While it did attain modest growth throughout the eighteenth century, French agriculture was prone to wild swings. The vagaries of the weather and the undeveloped state of farming technology would occasion spurts of famine and scarcity, leading to unemployment and spikes in corn prices, which took its steepest toll on peasants. We must not underestimate the impact of price increases: by the late 1700s, the French people – more than three-fourths of whom still lived outside of cities in 1789[21] – typically used 50 percent of their

---

[16] Aftalion, *Economic Interpretation*, 23.
[17] Aftalion, *Economic Interpretation*, 24–25. See also Robert D. Harris, "Necker's *Compte Rendu* of 1781: A Reconsideration," *The Journal of Modern History* 42 (1970): 161–183.
[18] Aftalion, *Economic Interpretation*, 32.
[19] See, among many, David Parker, *Class and State in Ancien Régime France: The Road to Modernity?* (London and New York: Routledge, 1996), 209–210; and Silvia Marzagalli, "Commerce," in *The Oxford Handbook of the Ancien Régime*, ed. William Doyle (Oxford: Oxford University Press, 2012), 252–266.
[20] Jan Marczewski, "Some Aspects of the Economic Growth of France, 1660–1958," *Economic Development and Cultural Change* 9 (1961): 386.
[21] S. E. Harris, *The Assignats* (Cambridge, MA: Harvard University Press, 1930), 3.

income on bread purchases.[22] Poor workers would thus convey deeper anxieties over their ability to access bread than over the level of wages.

Riots would break out in times of extreme deprivation, a phenomenon not unique to France in the latter part of the eighteenth century. Social disorder was accompanied by cries to fix bread prices, a proposal Louis XVI had obliged, contradicting the free market beliefs of Turgot. Such problems were exacerbated by the rapid increase in population and the blossoming of urban hubs in eighteenth-century France, not to mention the emergence of paupers as a conspicuous presence of the French population.

After Necker returned as France's finance minister, he carried out interventionist policies that aggravated the consequences of the modest harvest of 1788. People hoarded grain; shortages occurred; grain costs shot up; and riots intensified. The cost of bread and corn would reach its highest level ever on July 14, 1789, the same day revolutionaries stormed the Bastille, the medieval fortress and prison. It remains a bitter historical irony that Necker – the man whom Burke had praised for promoting sound financial policies – was responsible, at least in part, for provoking the distempers that inspired the political event Burke believed spelled the decline of European civilization.

The unresolved fiscal crisis of France, then, was one significant cause of the convening of the Estates General in May 1789, the first major step in the path toward the overthrow of the ancien régime. The additional events leading up to the French Revolution have become etched in our consciousness: in June 1789, the third estate transformed itself into the National Assembly; in July 1789, rebels charged the Bastille; the next month, the National Constituent Assembly, the second iteration of the National Assembly, eliminated feudalism. Later in August, the legislative body enacted the *Declaration of the Rights of Man and of the Citizen*, a defining statement of modernity that proclaimed a belief in the universality of natural rights and the equality of man. In November 1789, the French government nationalized the property of the Gallican Church. The Civil Constitution of the Clergy, which subordinated the church to the state, was enacted in July 1790. The French were well on their way to transforming their society through the manufacture of man.

Burke and the French Revolution

It was most likely by September 1789, before the nationalization of church property, that Burke's positions on the French Revolution in the *Reflections* crystallized.[23] In his reply to a letter from William Windham, Burke observed that the French people had "thrown off the Yoke of Laws and morals."[24] He

---

[22] Aftalion, *Economic Interpretation*, 39.   [23] Langford, *Writings and Speeches*, VIII, 13.
[24] Burke to William Windham, 27 September 1789, in Alfred Cobban and Robert A. Smith, eds., *The Correspondence of Edmund Burke*, vol. VI, *July 1789–December 1791* (Cambridge: Cambridge University Press, 1967), 25.

perceived that property was under grave threat, remarking that his son had received a letter from France that described the "miserable and precarious situation of all people of property in dreadful colours."[25] On November 4 of that year, Burke was asked by Charles-Jean-François Depont, a young Frenchman whose family Burke had hosted in its trip to England in 1785, to offer his thoughts on the political developments in France. Burke replied by condemning the revolutionary activities. He sent a second letter to Depont, which was the *Reflections*.[26]

Burke's thoughts on the French Revolution in the *Reflections* and elsewhere are central to understanding his economic thought. Burke threads discerning remarks on commerce, manufactures, supply and demand laws, and public finance into his commentary on the Revolution, revealing a strong command of market principles that he displayed in the three previous decades. But the real strength of his critique of the Revolution is drawn from its meditation on the role of commerce in the wider growth of civil order and decay. Burke's comments on this matter illustrate a depth of thought on the harmonizing integration of political economy and political philosophy that distinguished his economic reflections from many of his contemporaries in the eighteenth century – and that distinguishes them from many thinkers today. We begin by exploring one indispensable aspect of Burke's political economy he believed was under dire attack during the Revolution: landed property.

11.3   PROPERTY AS A CONSTITUTIONAL BULWARK

Burke on Property Prior to the French Revolution

A brief discussion of Burke's support for property rights prior to the *Reflections* will enrich our understanding of the intellectual roots of his economic critique of the French Revolution. We begin by observing that Burke championed property rights with unbending resolve throughout his life. In 1747, when he was still a student at Trinity College, a member of the debating club in which he participated argued that a person found guilty of sheep stealing should not face the punishment of death. Burke objected to this opinion with unusual vehemence:

When we are to repeal a standing law we are not to do it lightly; our Ancestors saw the wisdom of this Law, or they would not enact it; when then is it less good? Has all the benefits our Ancestors have receiv'd rendered it now useless? No, a man's property's his life. The Law of Nature gives a man power to kill offenders. Now he that seizes my property would seize my life. The Law cannot be cruel, for rich men might thro' a love of

---

[25] Burke to William Windham, 27 September 1789, in *Correspondence of Edmund Burke*, vol. VI, 26.

[26] See Langford, *Writings and Speeches*, VIII, 5.

rapine plunder the poor past reparation. When Murder was made Death, so was Theft, & justly, since it destroys bad men who by their wantonness wou'd ruin Society.[27]

Beyond his familiar conveyance of respect for the wisdom of the past, Burke here displays a steadfast belief in the inviolability of property. The usurpation of property was not a mere taking of goods but an attack on the owner's very life. This kind of violation warranted death – not leniency. Burke was not even twenty years of age when he gave these remarks, but they testify to a commitment in support of property rights that would remain constant throughout his entire adult life.

Burke endorsed landed property rights in particular as the pillar of civil stability. It is difficult to overstate this important dimension of his political thought, which also carried immediate relevance for his conception of political economy. Burke seized an opportunity to defend property rights in the late 1760s during the *Nullum Tempus* affair. This episode arose when Sir James Lowther attempted to employ the common law principle of *nullum tempus occurrit regi*, "no time runs against the king,"[28] – meaning that the statute of limitations did not apply to land claims of the Crown – to argue that he had a right to parts of the third Duke of Portland's estates under dispute.

In a series of highly charged letters written to the *Public Advertiser*,[29] Burke led efforts by the Rockingham Whigs in striking back against Lowther's argument while, at the same time, promoting a conception of private property rights as a sturdy check against royal prerogative. As Burke communicated in these writings, landed estates tamed the designs of monarchical and ministerial ambition, because property was the cornerstone of constitutional liberty. Yet the application of *nullum tempus* on behalf of Lowther attempted to upend this principle; it was a "practical Menace to all Landed Property."[30]

Property acquired authority through the trial of prescription, a key concept in Burke's political and social thought that remains prominent throughout the *Reflections*. Distinct from traditional laws of inheritance such as primogeniture entail, prescription, in his view, was the idea that undisturbed and settled possession over time sanctioned a measure of legitimacy upon existing property holdings, thereby granting to the possessor a specific title to property.[31] It also recognized the importance of utility in political communities: that particular institutions had lasted throughout time, and had

---

[27] Samuels, *Early Life Correspondence and Writings*, 289.

[28] For background on the *Nullum Tempus* affair, see Langford, *Writings and Speeches*, II, 75–76; R. B. Levis, "Sir James Lowther and the Political Tactics of the Cumberland Election of 1768," *Northern History* 19 (1983): 108–127; Bourke, *Empire & Revolution*, 246–251; Lock, *Edmund Burke*, vol. I, 244–247; and Cone, *Age of the American Revolution*, 162, 164–165. See also Burke's advocacy of property rights during the Church *Nullum Tempus* bill debate in Langford, *Writings and Speeches*, II, 364–367.

[29] Langford, *Writings and Speeches*, II, 75–86. One remains unpublished.

[30] Langford, *Writings and Speeches*, II, 78.   [31] Langford, *Writings and Speeches*, II, 85.

been explicitly or implicitly acknowledged repeatedly by the people, suggested it had conferred a benefit on the public, and thus should not be swiftly eliminated at the first perceived sign of inefficiency or inequity. Hence settled institutions should enjoy a presumption of credible authority against schemes of radical innovation.[32] Even more, prescription was grounded in nature as well as history: for Burke, securing the prescriptive basis of property rights through legislation was "the Law of Nature, not made, but only explained & inforced by positive statute," as Richard Bourke notes.[33]

Prescription and utility would sometimes be in conflict. Burke's notion of prescription, however, accommodated the reformation of practices and institutions if they ceased to provide advantages to the commonwealth, as exemplified by his plan of economical reform in the late 1770s and early 1780s. Prescription, then, was not antithetical to change but served as a necessary support for it; by granting layers of authority upon the ancient possession of land and time-honored institutions, it allowed men to reform established practices while protecting against social engineering and civil instability. According to Harvey C. Mansfield, "Prescription states neither the natural *end* of society ... nor the natural *origin* of society" but rather the "natural *manner of growth* of society."[34]

Such possession of property could never remain on solid grounds if it was the constant subject of legal wrangling, excessive litigation, and speculative claims of right. Therefore, while prescription was not the only basis for property and social order, it was their most resilient safeguard from Burke's perspective. He would later comment in 1784, in defending the ancient traditions of the British constitution against radical attempts to reform it, that prescription was "the most solid of all titles, not only to property, but, which is to secure that property, to Government."[35] Burke's efforts during the *Nullum Tempus*

---

[32] See, for example, Burke's defense of the prescriptive authority of the British constitution in *Speech on Parliamentary Reform* (Langford, *Writings and Speeches*, IV, 219–220), and his defense of Britain's East India Company on prescriptive grounds, as discussed in Chapter 10. On Burke's conception of prescription, see Paul Lucas, "On Edmund Burke's Doctrine of Prescription; Or, an Appeal from the New to the Old Lawyers," *The Historical Journal* 11 (1968): 35–63; Francis Canavan, "Burke on Prescription of Government," *The Review of Politics* 35 (1973): 454–474; Canavan, *Political Economy of Edmund Burke*, 61–69; J. G. A. Pocock, "Burke and the Ancient Constitution: A Problem in the History of Ideas," *The Historical Journal* 3 (1960): 125–143; Pocock, *The Ancient Constitution and the Feudal Law: A Study of English Historical Thought in the Seventeenth Century* (Cambridge: Cambridge University Press, 1987), 379–384; and Harvey C. Mansfield, *Statesmanship and Party Government: A Study of Burke and Bolingbroke* (Chicago and London: The University of Chicago Press, 2013), 221–222. See also George Fasel, "'The Soul That Animated': The Role of Property in Burke's Thought," *Studies in Burke and His Time* 17 (1976): 27–41. And see Burke's speech on the Church *Nullum Tempus* bill in Langford, *Writings and Speeches*, II, 364–367.

[33] Bourke, *Empire & Revolution*, 249n164.

[34] Mansfield, *Statesmanship and Party Government*, 222.

[35] Langford, *Writings and Speeches*, IV, 219.

affair, and consistent defense of prescription throughout his life, helped elevate the idea to a theoretically coherent and tenable doctrine central to the Whig vision of the British constitution in the latter part of the eighteenth century.[36]

Burke's awareness of the political function of property gained sharper expression in *Thoughts on the Present Discontents* (1770), when he argued that propertied men, joined together by party and motivated by a genuine concern for the common good, was a far stronger ballast of constitutional stability than a government of court favoritism exploited by the King's friends. In the *Thoughts*, Burke declares that it is the business of men – specifically men of property – to "bring the dispositions that are lovely in private life into the service and conduct of the commonwealth; so to be patriots, as not to forget we are gentlemen ... To model our principles to our duties and our situation."[37] A lofty sense of public-spiritedness channeled by party, combined with the awareness that a defense of country need not sacrifice the practice of virtue, animated just government. And just government preserved political balance. "Our constitution stands on a nice equipoise, with steep precipices, and deep waters upon all sides of it," Burke writes, providing one of the most beautiful metaphors ever expressed on the institutional anatomy of political order.[38]

The spirit of the nobility – and, Burke suggests in the *Thoughts*, the spirit of distinguished men of new wealth – provided a counterweight to the private ambitions of Court politics. "This method therefore of governing, by men of great natural interest or great acquired consideration, was viewed in a very invidious light by the true lovers of absolute monarchy," Burke remarks, describing English politics following the Glorious Revolution.[39] Independent men of weight checked the aggrandizement of the Crown, thereby providing security to the people and protecting against the rise of political tyranny. In order for the Crown to expand its political influence, it served its interest to deprive the landed nobility of their power – and of their property. This insight would hold much sway over Burke's commentary in the *Reflections*.

The security of landed property also provided a foundation for commerce and industry. In *Tracts relating to Popery Laws*, in which Burke attacked the penal codes for depriving Irish Catholics of opportunities to own and inherit property, he contended that landed property was the incubator of material improvement because the extended length of possession enabled owners to ameliorate the estate through repeated acts of industry over time. A short land tenure of thirty years, he writes in *Tracts*,

is evidently no tenure upon which to build; to plant; to raise enclosures; to change the nature of the ground; to make any new experiment which might improve agriculture; or

---

[36] See Lucas, "On Edmund Burke's Doctrine of Prescription," 59.
[37] Langford, *Writings and Speeches*, II, 320.   [38] Langford, *Writings and Speeches*, II, 311.
[39] Langford, *Writings and Speeches*, II, 259.

to do any thing more than what may answer the immediate and momentary calls of rent to the landlord and leave subsistence to the tenant and his family.[40]

Securing the possession of land for extended periods allowed for refinements and adjustments to agricultural practices. Such changes were gradual accretions, forming slowly but steadily throughout the ages. Therefore, the penal codes' collection of stringent restrictions on Catholic land possession was "one of the most capital discouragements to all that industry which may be employed on the lasting improvement of the soil, or is any way conversant about land."[41]

Burke was not simply referring to the stewardship of land in his discussion in the *Tracts* of the long-term consequences of the penal laws' limitations on Catholic property ownership. The regulations also brought about the depression of commercial improvement by choking the opportunities of Catholics to possess the fruits of their industry and trade. "[Industry] is further discouraged by the limitation of its own direct object, profit," Burke writes. "This is a regulation extremely worthy of our attention, as it is not a consequential, but a direct discouragement to melioration; as directly as if the Law had said in express terms, 'Thou shalt not improve.'"[42] Scholars have rightly noted Burke's preference for incremental reform over radical change, but we should also recognize his application of this conception of reform to the realm of economic improvement, as seen in the *Tracts*.

The penal laws also disabled traders from employing their knowledge and resources to help better the condition of land. This was an "evil effect"[43] of the laws, Burke states in the *Tracts*. As he writes:

They must have observed very little who have not remarked the bold and liberal spirit of improvement, which persons bred to trade have often exerted on their land purchases; that they usually come to them with a more abundant command of ready money than most landed men possess; and that they have in general a much better idea, by long habits of calculative dealings, of the propriety of expending in order to acquire.[44]

Traders possess a bountiful repository of knowledge about the function of money in the process of amelioration. They have the experience – "long habits" – crucial to determining whether specific financial investments and trades were worth the risk. In Burke's view, men accustomed to trading activities held these advantages over the archetypal landed gentleman, who was more suspicious of commercial exchange and thus did not carry the stock of accumulated knowledge and experience necessary to make sound investments that would improve the landed estate.

Burke is especially insistent on this point. He continues:

---

[40] Langford, *Writings and Speeches*, IX, 476–477.
[41] Langford, *Writings and Speeches*, IX, 476.   [42] Langford, *Writings and Speeches*, IX, 477.
[43] Langford, *Writings and Speeches*, IX, 478.   [44] Langford, *Writings and Speeches*, IX, 478.

Besides, such men often bring their spirit of commerce into their estates with them, and make manufactures take a root where the mere landed gentry had perhaps no capital, perhaps no inclination, and most frequently not sufficient knowledge to effect any thing of the kind. By these means what beautiful and useful spots have there not been made about trading and manufacturing towns, and how has agriculture had reason to bless that happy alliance with commerce; and how miserable must that nation be whose frame of polity has disjoined the landing and the trading interests.[45]

Once again, the landed gentry did not harbor the "sufficient knowledge" that traders carried. Burke is known as an uncompromising defender of the landed aristocracy, but it is noteworthy in the two previous quotations that he downgrades that class and elevates the role of the trader to a tenable position of dignity. Similar to his sympathetic appraisal of middlemen in *Thoughts and Details*, Burke here unmasks an underappreciated strain of his thought that identified and praised the integral role of commercial traders in commonwealths.

Burke, then, recognized a harmonious connection between possessors of immobile and mobile property in the *Tracts*: "For a Law against property, is a Law against industry," he states, "the latter having always the former, and nothing else, for its object."[46] The flourishing of political communities depended on the healthy symbiosis between the permanence of land and the energy of commerce. The former provided the steady foundations for the protection of liberty by furnishing stability and moderation; the latter used such freedoms to generate material advantages and improvements for the people. Burke's understanding of this relationship would heavily influence his economic interpretation of the French Revolution.

Burke and Property during the French Revolution

The political and commercial functions of the landed interest that Burke discussed in his writings and speeches prior to 1789 play a prominent role in his thoughts on the French Revolution. In light of the Revolution's campaign to eliminate the remnants of feudalism and uproot settled claims to property, Burke recognized the urgent political necessity in renewing and strengthening a broader theoretical defense of landed estates in the 1790s. Similar to his treatment of estates in the *Tracts*, he argued in the context of the Revolution that they provided firmness and constancy in civil society, both of which were preconditions for the preservation of ordered liberty and constitutional balance. In *Third Letter on a Regicide Peace* Burke writes that landed property was "in it's nature the firm base of every stable government."[47] He invokes the authority

---

[45] Langford, *Writings and Speeches*, IX, 478.   [46] Langford, *Writings and Speeches*, IX, 476.
[47] Langford, *Writings and Speeches*, IX, 374.

of Aristotle,[48] who, according to Burke, "observes that the agricultural class of all others is the least inclined to sedition."[49]

Burke is marking his belief, reflective of British and classical notions of property, that the intrinsic characteristic of the landed aristocracy was its stabilizing presence. Its members did not combine together to threaten the foundations of political tranquility, but instead dedicated themselves to furthering the good of the community and serving as patrons of high culture. Such commitments were guided by a disposition inclined toward virtue and prudence, not radicalism.

Modern notions of freedom, particularly in the West, identify individual liberty with the flourishing of commercial enterprise in metropolitan areas inhabited by powerful bankers, traders, and businessmen. Nonetheless, the telling feature of Burke's conception of the relationship between property and liberty is his view that freedom was maintained not because of the activities or intellectual pursuits of urban elites but because of the anchor of landed property. If there had been one factor that contributed to England's "steady resistance, the fortunate issue, and sober settlement, of all our struggles for liberty," Burke insists in *Third Letter on a Regicide Peace*, it was that the landed interest had been "in close connexion and union with the other great interests of the country."[50] Therefore, it had been "spontaneously allowed to lead and direct, and moderate all the rest."[51]

The landed interest preserved the crucial element of continuity in a commonwealth, as Burke emphasizes in the *Reflections* with regard to families of hereditary wealth:

The power of perpetuating our property in our families is one of the most valuable and interesting circumstances belonging to it, and that which tends the most to the perpetuation of society itself. It makes our weakness subservient to our virtue; it grafts benevolence even upon avarice. The possessors of family wealth, and of the distinction which attends hereditary possession (as most concerned in it) are the natural securities for this transmission.[52]

A smooth consistency aligns these insights with Burke's commentary on the penal laws that oppressed the Irish Catholics.[53] By supplying the virtue of stability, private property becomes the backbone of an enduring political

---

[48] Burke refers to Aristotle as "the Stagyrite," named after the classical Greek city, Stagira, in which Aristotle was born.

[49] Langford, *Writings and Speeches*, IX, 374. Burke also mentions Cicero as a thinker who, "above all" classical writers, also reflected this understanding of property.

[50] Langford, *Writings and Speeches*, IX, 374.

[51] Langford, *Writings and Speeches*, IX, 374–375.

[52] Langford, *Writings and Speeches*, VIII, 102.

[53] See "Address and Petition of the Irish Catholics," in Langford, *Writings and Speeches*, IX, 429–434; and "Tracts relating to Popery Laws," in Langford, *Writings and Speeches*, IX, 434–482.

order. Stewardship of land tames man's basest passions and elevates his capacity for moral and temperate action. Even more, families are the social units responsible for tending to their estates. The inherited property rights of families throughout the ages generate a principle of constancy amid the fluid shifts and motions of mundane human activities. Families that possess land are the deep roots of stable political communities.

Admittedly, Burke displays a tendency in the *Reflections* to glorify families of the hereditary aristocracy, providing textual ammunition to his critics who assailed him for overlooking the hardships of French commoners under Louis XVI. Yet in this particular section of the *Reflections*, he offers some context for his praise of hereditary aristocrats, and implicitly suggests their negative qualities. "Let those large proprietors be what they will," Burke states, "and they have their chance of being amongst the best, they are at the very worst, the ballast in the vessel of the commonwealth."[54] Illustrating his gift for metaphor, Burke validates his belief that even if propertied families were sluggish, they still provided the stability – the "ballast" – necessary for social order.

Burke then admits that hereditary wealth, and hereditary aristocrats, were "too much idolized by creeping sycophants, and the blind abject admirers of power."[55] The existence of large wealth encouraged jealous fawners to desire it with licentious impropriety. Burke, however, retains his conviction that such aristocrats warranted special entitlements. "Some decent regulated pre-eminence, some preference (not exclusive appropriation) given to birth, is neither unnatural, nor unjust, nor impolitic," he writes.[56] Because possessors of landed property fulfill an indispensable function in fostering social and political moderation, the state should bestow explicit privileges on the propertied classes.

Burke's beliefs about property align comfortably with his broader political philosophy. The growth of political order required maintaining the best traditions created and perpetuated by previous generations, including the customary protection of the landed aristocracy. As we recall from this book's Introduction, Burke notes in the *Reflections* that Britain had an "inheritable crown; an inheritable peerage; and an house of commons and a people inheriting privileges, franchises, and liberties, from a long line of ancestors."[57] The security of property was an emblem of Britain's rich constitutional heritage, standing as the unswaying edifice of political tranquility.

The enduring role of private property in a commonwealth also sheds light on Burke's epistemology underlying his political theory. Britain's constitutional traditions in support of property rights reflected the distilled wisdom of many generations, preserving and fortifying the long chain of chartered English liberties. He writes in the *Reflections*:

[54] Langford, *Writings and Speeches*, VIII, 102.   [55] Langford, *Writings and Speeches*, VIII, 103.
[56] Langford, *Writings and Speeches*, VIII, 103.   [57] Langford, *Writings and Speeches*, VIII, 83.

You will observe, that from Magna Charta to the Declaration of Right, it has been the uniform policy of our constitution to claim and assert our liberties, as an *entailed inheritance* derived to us from our forefathers, and to be transmitted to our posterity; as an estate specially belonging to the people of this kingdom without any reference whatever to any other more general or prior right.[58]

To Burke, the security of English property rights did not derive from an abstract claim to liberty – a "general or prior right" – conceived by a single thinker. Instead, such protection reflected the delicate embodiment of inherited laws, customs, and institutions that were adjusted to fit contemporary circumstances. England's Magna Carta and Declaration of Right, both of which safeguarded the rights of Englishmen against the king, exemplified this proud tradition of English liberty. They were not theoretical treatises written by a brilliant philosopher dedicated to laying out a vision for a perfect world, but rather practical documents granting shelter to English property. England's conventions protecting property rights, then, were the result of collective wisdom, not individual ingenuity. And if property could not be secured, the roots of commonwealth would be dissolved. As Burke writes in the *Reflections*, "[I]t is to the property of the citizen, and not to the demands of the creditor of the state, that the first and original faith of civil society is pledged."[59] He put the matter even more succinctly in *First Letter on a Regicide Peace*: "The property of the nation is the nation."[60]

11.4 THE FRENCH REVOLUTION'S ATTACK ON CHURCH PROPERTY

The French Revolution threatened entirely to undermine Burke's cherished beliefs about property. In his judgment, ambitious revolutionaries wished to transform property from a foundation of constancy into a weapon for radical social change. Any possible good-faith efforts to remedy the abuses of the ancien régime collapsed into a ruthless quest to destroy the private right to possess land. This point is essential to understanding Burke's treatment of the Revolution: while he has attained a reputation for blasting abstract reason and lamenting the loss of chivalry in his commentary in the *Reflections*, the concrete object Burke believed to be under threat during the Revolution was the *landed property* of ecclesiastical and secular authorities.

Even more, because considerations of property were essential to Burke's thought, French revolutionaries' assault on property delivered a shock to his deepest convictions on political economy. This is not to say Burke's defense of property rested on his apprehension of supply and demand laws, but that the seizure of landed property necessarily posed grave implications for his understanding of the relation between land and commerce.

---

[58] Langford, *Writings and Speeches*, VIII, 83.   [59] Langford, *Writings and Speeches*, VIII, 157.
[60] Langford, *Writings and Speeches*, IX, 252.

In October 1789, five months after the convening of France's Estates General, Burke wrote in a letter that he would welcome the anticipated changes in France as long as he was assured that each of its citizens would be "in a perfect state of legal security, with regard to his life, – to his property, – to the uncontrolled disposal of his person, – to the free use of his industry and his faculties," among various stipulations.[61]

As Burke predicted, these hopes quickly vanished. Jacobinism, he writes in *First Letter on a Regicide Peace*, was "the revolt of the enterprising talents of a country against it's property."[62] Such men of "enterprising talents" Burke has in mind were not merchants qua merchants, but combinations of individuals intent on seizing power for the aim of radical innovation. He continues:

When private men form themselves into associations for the purpose of destroying the pre-existing laws and institutions of their country; when they secure to themselves an army by dividing amongst the people of no property, the estates of the ancient and lawful proprietors; when a state recognizes those acts; when it does not make confiscations for crimes, but makes crimes for confiscations; when it has it's principal strength, and all it's resources in such a violation of property; when it stands chiefly upon such a violation; massacring by judgments, or otherwise, those who make any struggle for their old legal government, and their legal, hereditary, or acquired possessions – I call this *Jacobinism by Establishment*.[63]

In *Second Letter on a Regicide Peace*, Burke observes that property was "in complete subjection" to the revolutionary government.[64] In *Third Letter on a Regicide Peace*, Burke states that the "present war is, above all others, (of which we have heard or read) a war against landed property."[65] The French Revolution placed private property in the crosshairs.

Burke identified the French war on the landed property of the Gallican Church as the primary trigger for the Revolution.[66] The Church, prior to the Revolution, was "the most powerful organisation inside the kingdom, with a physical presence to match," writes Nigel Aston.[67] The institution was symbolic of everything revolutionaries despised about the ancien régime: the size of its landed wealth, the special privileges afforded to it, the smell of its feudal background – not to mention its seemingly dogmatic religiosity. In

[61] Burke to Mons. Dupont, October 1789, in Charles William, Earl Fitzwilliam and Sir Richard Bourke, *The Works and Correspondence of the Right Honourable Edmund Burke* (London: Francis & John Rivington, 1852), vol. I, 559.

[62] Langford, *Writings and Speeches*, IX, 241.   [63] Langford, *Writings and Speeches*, IX, 241.

[64] Langford, *Writings and Speeches*, IX, 289.   [65] Langford, *Writings and Speeches*, IX, 374.

[66] Indeed, Schama writes that with "the momentous exception of the expropriation of the Church, between 1789 and 1792 the Revolution produced no significant transfer of social power. It merely accelerated trends that had been taking place over a longer period of time" (Schama, *Citizens*, 520).

[67] Nigel Aston, *Religion and Revolution in France, 1780–1804* (Washington, DC: The Catholic University of America Press, 2000), 3.

addition to owning around one-tenth of the land surface in France, the Church collected approximately 250,000,000 livres in revenue every year from tithes and land rents. The Church was generally exempt from taxation, and thus contributed only a minuscule percentage of its revenue to the state.[68]

Even before French revolutionaries confiscated church property, they had agreed upon a notorious series of decrees that struck at the heart of the ancien régime, including the abolition of feudal privileges of the landed nobility. For Burke, however, the most abhorrent decision carried out by the new French government was the gross seizure of church property. After the Estates General had dissolved and transformed into the democratic National Assembly, and then the Constituent Assembly,[69] Burke noted in *Speech on the Army Estimates* that the French

instantly, with the most atrocious perfidy and breach of all faith among men, laid the axe to the root of all property, and consequently of all national prosperity, by the principles they established, and the example they set, in confiscating all the possessions of the church.[70]

Burke gave this speech on February 9, 1790. Three months earlier, on November 2, 1789, the Constituent Assembly voted to place the property of clergymen at the "disposal of the nation."[71] The idea, originating with Talleyrand, a French bishop no less, and formally proposed by Mirabeau, was raised for the ostensible purpose of refilling France's treasury to pay down the national debt and stave off financial calamity.[72] The measure turned the private possessions of the clergy into *biens nationaux*, or national goods, in effect nationalizing the Gallican Church. (Royal estates had also been declared the property of the state.[73]) Because the Church was the shining ornament of French tradition, the confiscation of church lands for revolutionaries signified the end of feudal oppression and the dawn of a new era of enlightenment.

This was a perilous first step, Burke believed. As he indicates, the expropriation of church property established principles that could justify the state usurpation of all private property. Furthermore, the decision violated the sacred trust – the "faith among men" – between government and its subjects that Burke thought was fundamental to political order. And it is telling that he

---

[68] See Jones, *Reform and Revolution in France*, 53–54; and Doyle, *Oxford History of the French Revolution*, 33–34. As Doyle notes, the Church did provide periodic "free gifts" that came from a tax on clerical income, and also paid interest on loans. Note further that the percentage of clergy relative to the entire French population decreased significantly in the eighteenth century leading up to the Revolution.

[69] The National Assembly lasted from June 17, 1789 to July 9, 1789; the National Constituent Assembly lasted from July 9, 1789 to September 30, 1791; and its replacement, the National Legislative Assembly, lasted from October 1, 1791 to September 20, 1792.

[70] Langford, *Writings and Speeches*, IV, 289. [71] Aftalion, *Economic Interpretation*, 62.

[72] See Schama, *Citizens*, 482–483.

[73] See E. Levasseur, "The Assignats: A Study in the Finances of the French Revolution," *The Journal of Political Economy* 2 (1894): 180.

connects the destruction of landed property with the steep decline of France's "national prosperity," hinting that he did not perceive an irreconcilable tension between land and commerce. The Constituent Assembly's confiscation of ecclesiastical estates, Burke concludes, showed that the "service of the state was made a pretext to destroy the church."[74] The Church was now subordinate to the whims of revolutionaries in power. Religion became subservient to the state.

The confiscation of church lands marked a rebellion against Burke's legal conception of property rights. Recall Burke's conviction from the *Nullum Tempus* affair that the right to private property was rooted in the law of nature and acquired thick layers of authority through prescription. The French Revolution repudiated this idea. "With the national assembly of France," he writes in the *Reflections*, "possession is nothing; law and usage are nothing."[75] The assembly "openly reprobate[s] the doctrine of prescription,"[76] Burke later observed in a letter to Adrien-Jean-François Duport, a French lawyer and politician, that a people

who thirst for blood and confiscation in the bosom of Peace, who could endure even to hear of a maxim that the goods of any one Citizen possessed by a long acknowledged legal title belong to the State, and that those who assume the exercise of sovereign Authority are free to take it from him and to make such a distribution of it as they please, such a People are not fit to sit in a seat of Judgment, or for any other function, because they despise the very foundation of social Union.[77]

The French revolutionary impulse to discard the doctrine of prescription in favor of property confiscation and redistribution shredded the roots of "social Union" – that is, civil society.[78]

Burke makes an effort in the *Reflections* to emphasize that natural law was the genesis of the prescriptive right to property. He remarks that Jean Domat, the distinguished French lawyer, said "with great truth" the doctrine of prescription was a "part of the law of nature."[79] Burke writes that the National Assembly's naked contempt for the legal doctrine rejected "this great fundamental part of natural law."[80] Although the *Reflections* is most famous for praising the authority of history and decrying the dictatorship of abstract reason of the French Revolution, it is significant that Burke retains his cautious approval of natural law – one that informed his beliefs in the *Nullum Tempus* affair and in his commentary on the penal laws – in his defense of prescription in the writing. This conception of nature in the *Reflections* is

---

[74] Langford, *Writings and Speeches*, VIII, 170.   [75] Langford, *Writings and Speeches*, VIII, 200.
[76] Langford, *Writings and Speeches*, VIII, 200.
[77] Burke to Adrien-Jean-François Duport, [*post* March 1790], in *Correspondence of Edmund Burke*, vol. VI, 108.
[78] See also Burke's comments on the French Revolution's war on prescription in *Appeal from the New to the Old Whigs* in Langford, *Writings and Speeches*, IV, 447.
[79] Langford, *Writings and Speeches*, VIII, 200.   [80] Langford, *Writings and Speeches*, VIII, 200.

underdeveloped and unclear at times, and perhaps reflects an attempt to reinterpret traditional notions of natural law,[81] but Burke's gesture to it indicates a conscious attempt to anchor the historical primacy of prescription in a firmer philosophical foundation.

Burke argues that the protection of private property was a principal reason for the formation of civil society in the first place – an insight not unlike Locke's theory of civil society. Domat, according to Burke, taught that "the positive ascertainment of [the doctrine of prescription]'s limits, and its security from invasion, were among the causes for which civil society itself has been instituted."[82] Private property was not simply a function of prescription rooted in natural law but a possession that demanded security. The only way to furnish such protection was to create a political community in which the rights of property owners would be respected, honored, and safeguarded by law.

For Burke, then, French radicals' war on private property militated against notions of justice, thereby unleashing a war on civil society. He writes, in referring to France's confiscation of church lands, that "it is in the principle of injustice that the danger lies."[83] Again appealing to France, Burke states, "I see, in a country very near us, a course of policy pursued, which sets justice, the common concern of mankind, at defiance."[84] In addition, "Justice is itself the great standing policy of civil society; and any eminent departure from it, under any circumstances, lies under the suspicion of being no policy at all."[85] Civil society should pursue justice. France's war on property was unjust. Therefore, French revolutionaries had failed to fulfill the ethical imperatives of civil society, and instead waged a mutinous campaign targeting its very foundations.

Because the French Revolution failed to protect the private property of religious authorities and the landed aristocracy, it compromised the hierarchical character of the social order that Burke believed was essential for the preservation of a state. The transformation of the Estates General from a division of three social classes into one democratic assembly further perverted this order. The French "first destroyed all the balances and counterpoises which serve to fix the state; and to give it a steady direction; and which furnish sure correctives to any violent spirit which may prevail in any of the orders," Burke says in *Speech on the Army Estimates*.[86] The separate powers and functions of different social classes congealed into one undifferentiated mass in the French government, in turn removing that trait in a community – moderation – that could soothe the enthusiasms of political faction and check the concentration of power.

---

[81] Paul Lucas argues that Domat's conception of natural law differed from Burke's. See Lucas, "On Edmund Burke's Doctrine of Prescription," 42–44.
[82] Langford, *Writings and Speeches*, VIII, 200.   [83] Langford, *Writings and Speeches*, VIII, 200.
[84] Langford, *Writings and Speeches*, VIII, 200.   [85] Langford, *Writings and Speeches*, VIII, 205.
[86] Langford, *Writings and Speeches*, IV, 288–289.

In the *Reflections*, Burke also signals that the French Revolution's assault on property destroyed the capacity of monastic orders to make important contributions to French civil society. His argument on this topic attempts to rebut the criticism that monasteries were inhabited by superstitious monks inclined to idleness and lacking in productive utility. Burke remarks that even if monks were "lazy"[87] in the sense of shunning labor typically associated with the modern economy, they still performed important rituals such as "singing in the choir."[88] Burke here hints that spiritual ritual was as meaningful to civil society as material production. He goes so far as to say that he would favor relieving common laborers of their "miserable industry"[89] – manual work – rather than upsetting the repose of monasteries.

Before proceeding to discuss his further comments on monasteries, it must be noted that Burke qualifies this statement about "miserable industry," and in doing so exposes a significant insight into his theory of political economy in the *Reflections*. He allows that he would be more willing to protect laborers from their degrading occupation – but only "[i]f it were not generally pernicious to disturb the natural course of things, and to impede, in any degree, the great wheel of circulation which is turned by the strangely directed labour of these unhappy people."[90] Burke is tracing the connection between private labor and the public good by praising industry for its important role in the production and distribution of goods, and by affirming the correspondence between such liberty and natural order, two tenets of his economic thought that he expressed before and after the French Revolution as well. Burke does make an implicit concession that the advantages that flow from market exchange take precedence over the conditions of laborers. He then qualifies this concession by remarking that "[h]umanity, and perhaps policy, might better justify me in the one than in the other."[91] Nevertheless, Burke's comments highlight his endorsement of private initiative as the parent of "the great wheel of circulation," as noted.

Burke is now poised to attack the heart of the revolutionary logic that monasteries did not contribute advantages to the public weal. In the *Reflections*, he praises the religious institutions not simply for providing stability and carrying out spiritual rituals but for generating tangible goods for public consumption:

Why should the expenditure of a great landed property, which is a dispersion of the surplus product of the soil, appear intolerable to you or to me, when it takes its course through the accumulation of vast libraries, which are the history of the force and weakness of the human mind; through great collections of antient records, medals, and coins, which attest and explain laws and customs; through paintings and statues, that, by imitating nature, seem to extend the limits of creation; through grand monuments of the dead, which continue the regards and connexions of life beyond the grave; through

---

[87] Langford, *Writings and Speeches*, VIII, 209.   [88] Langford, *Writings and Speeches*, VIII, 209.
[89] Langford, *Writings and Speeches*, VIII, 209.   [90] Langford, *Writings and Speeches*, VIII, 209.
[91] Langford, *Writings and Speeches*, VIII, 209.

collections of the specimens of nature, which become a representative assembly of all the classes and families of the world, that by disposition facilitate, and, by exciting curiosity, open the avenues to science?[92]

The wealth from monasteries is channeled into gifts for common benefit: libraries, archives, medals, coins, artwork, monuments, and scientific advancements. Monkish institutions of seeming indolence in French revolutionary myth are lively provenances of ingenuity and progress in concrete reality. And the labor that built up such institutions was useful: "Does not the sweat of the mason and carpenter, who toil in order to partake the sweat of the peasant, flow as pleasantly and as salubriously, in the construction and repair of the majestic edifices of religion, as in the painted booths and sordid sties of vice and luxury ... ?"[93] The crux of Burke's argument is that landed property owned by religious authorities contributed no less to the public good than the commercial wealth of movable property.[94] In confiscating lands that were supposedly inert, French revolutionaries undermined their aim of advancing the social welfare.[95]

Burke integrates this defense of monks with an additional consideration: how could one be certain that the new purchaser of the confiscated church property would be a better proprietor of land than the religious authority? Burke begins this line of reasoning by illuminating the productive activities of a landed estate. "In every prosperous community," he writes, "something more is produced than goes to the immediate support of the producer."[96] This surplus makes up the income of the "landed capitalist," which is then spent by a "proprietor who does not labour."[97] The proprietor is the facilitator of, rather than a hindrance to, commercial prosperity because he uses his income wisely in the service of improving the land. The "only" concern of government, then, was that the "capital taken in rent from the land, should be returned again to the industry from whence it came; and that its expenditure should be with the least possible detriment to the morals of those who expend it, and to those of the people to whom it is returned."[98] The responsibility of the state was to secure the conditions for the efficient use of capital in the industry in which it originated, and to do so without corrupting the morals of the people.

Burke applies his argument to the Constituent Assembly's expropriation of church lands. Before transferring authority to the confiscators, "[W]e ought to have some rational assurance that the purchasers of the confiscated property will be in a considerable degree more laborious, more virtuous, more sober" than the ecclesiastical possessors of property.[99] It must be ensured that the new

---

[92] Langford, *Writings and Speeches*, VIII, 210.   [93] Langford, *Writings and Speeches*, VIII, 210.
[94] Of course, as will be demonstrated, Burke thought that the two types of property were not mutually exclusive.
[95] See Derek Beales, "Edmund Burke and the Monasteries of France," *The Historical Journal* 48 (2005): 415–436 for a broader analysis of Burke's bold defense of monasteries in the *Reflections*.
[96] Langford, *Writings and Speeches*, VIII, 209.   [97] Langford, *Writings and Speeches*, VIII, 209.
[98] Langford, *Writings and Speeches*, VIII, 209.   [99] Langford, *Writings and Speeches*, VIII, 209.

proprietors will be "less disposed to extort an unreasonable proportion of the gains of the labourer, or to consume on themselves a larger share than is fit for the measure of an individual, or that they should be qualified to dispense the surplus in a more steady and equal mode, so as to answer the purposes of a politic expenditure."[100] It was by no means guaranteed that buyers of the land would be more conscientious stewards and improvers of property than the supposedly ignorant monks. Burke associates the management of church lands with labor, virtue, and sobriety, and intimates that religious authorities were less likely than new purchasers to exploit laborers and more likely to distribute income in an equitable manner.

Overall, although the Constituent Assembly's decision to seize church lands alerted Burke to the democratic despotism emerging within France, his apprehensions were also roused by the possibility that the revolutionary contagion could spread to Britain. "I see the confiscators begin with bishops, and chapters, and monasteries; but I do not see them end there," Burke insists in the *Reflections*.[101] This dark precedent of expropriation could penetrate English minds, leading to the subversion of English property rights:

It is not the confiscation of our church property from this example in France that I dread, though I think this would be no trifling evil. The great source of my solicitude is, lest it should ever be considered in England as the policy of a state, to seek a resource in confiscations of any kind; or that any one description of citizens should be brought to regard any of the others, as their proper prey.[102]

Aspirations to confiscate church property could explode into a sanction to usurp all kinds of property, ecclesiastical and secular. Burke's comment about citizens seeing each other as "proper prey" further exposes his fear that the seizure of property would lead not simply to a war on property but to a war on one's fellow man.

Who, then, were the French revolutionaries Burke assailed as the perpetrators behind the dissolution of property rights in France? They included the members of the Third Estate, who dominated the National Assembly after incorporating the clergy and the nobility into the body. These members were practitioners of law, who were of "the inferior, unlearned, mechanical, merely instrumental members of the profession."[103] Undistinguished lawyers were joined by similarly inept doctors, illiterate "country clowns,"[104] and narrow-minded traders.

In Burke's judgment, the principal defect of these members' incapacity to rule was their failure to seriously consider and advance the common good of the state. He acknowledges in the *Reflections* that many members possessed individual merit.

---

[100] Langford, *Writings and Speeches*, VIII, 209.
[101] Langford, *Writings and Speeches*, VIII, 200–201.
[102] Langford, *Writings and Speeches*, VIII, 203.
[103] Langford, *Writings and Speeches*, VIII, 93.   [104] Langford, *Writings and Speeches*, VIII, 94.

Because of their inexperience in ruling, however, they became intoxicated by their rapid acquisition of political power. Since many were the product of new wealth, moreover, they displayed a grave inattentiveness to the requirements necessary to sustain political stability in France. In other words, Burke is deriding the new French legislature for being vastly underrepresented in the ancient landed interest – a class which, in his view, was eminently qualified to rule because of its commitment to promoting the public welfare through the steady hand of moderation. For Burke, however, the underrepresentation of the landed nobility was only one of the frightful signs of economic disorder fomented by France's revolutionary impulses.

11.5   THE MONIED INTEREST AND THE ASSIGNATS

Burke's devastating criticism of the political economy of the French Revolution in the *Reflections* was driven by his attack on the monied interest. Before exploring his rebuke of this interest, it should be stressed that Burke was not an opponent of money and investment. We have seen throughout this book that he was a vocal supporter of the right to pursue profit, as illustrated by his advocacy of commercial liberty spanning his adult life. Furthermore, Burke had endorsed the free circulation of money and the rights of investors during the French Revolution in *Third Letter on a Regicide Peace*, which he had begun drafting in late 1796, when the Revolution was being waged under the French Directory. The value of money, Burke insists in the letter, "must be judged like every thing else from it's rate at market."[105] And to "force that market, or any market, is of all things the most dangerous."[106] The former statement unites strongly with Burke's embrace of supply and demand principles in *Thoughts and Details*; and the latter is reminiscent of the tract's declaration that out of all regulatory innovations, an "indiscreet tampering with the trade of provisions is the most dangerous."[107] The strength of Burke's support for market liberty did not recede during the age of the French Revolution.

In *Third Letter*, Burke also provides a firm defense of the liberty to pursue financial opportunities, particularly investment in government loans. "The monied men have a right to look to advantage in the investment of their property," Burke writes.[108] His subsequent comments cast light on his understanding that investment involves uncertainty, which helped explain its heightened cost: "To advance their money, they risk it; and the risk is to be included in the price."[109] In pinpointing the element of risk, Burke is displaying his grasp of the fragile nature of financial investment. He supports speculative investment here on the basis that the potential rewards for successful projects

---

[105] Langford, *Writings and Speeches*, IX, 346.
[106] Langford, *Writings and Speeches*, IX, 346–347.
[107] Langford, *Writings and Speeches*, IX, 120.   [108] Langford, *Writings and Speeches*, IX, 347.
[109] Langford, *Writings and Speeches*, IX, 347.

might be lucrative, but the losses might also be substantial, which, Burke writes, "would amount to a tax on that peculiar species of property."[110] In essence, Burke was championing the right of investors to garner profit around the same time he was attacking French revolutionaries for their full embrace of the monied interest.

Burke also did not despise the idea of national debt, and in fact had affirmed its utility after the publication of the *Reflections*. In *First Letter on a Regicide Peace*, published in 1796, he writes that public credit, with reference to England, was a "great but ambiguous principle" that "has so often been predicted as the cause of our certain ruin, but which for a century has been the constant companion, and often the means, of our prosperity and greatness" following the Glorious Revolution.[111] The existence of state debt did not portend financial calamity but instead nourished England's economy with the plentiful means necessary for commercial opulence. Burke extended and fortified this point in *First Letter* by describing the harmonizing coexistence of British debt with the enlargement of English trade, the reduction in navigation costs, the surge of private credit, and the (uneven) development of English naval superiority, all of which exemplified Britain's growing leadership role in Europe in the eighteenth century.[112] Indeed, "[g]overnment gave the impulse" for the cultivation of English honor and preeminence.[113]

Who, then, constituted the "monied interest" that exhausted the energies of Burke in the *Reflections*? As its name suggests, the monied interest was not a class of abstract philosophers but a group of financiers. Under the ancien régime, a "financier" was "a person with a private fortune who contracted with the government to perform some task in which he handled the government's money," Robert D. Harris writes.[114] These tasks included the collection of taxes; the provisioning of bread to the army; and the supervision of trade for France's East India Company.[115] Beyond its collection of taxes, financiers – armed with privileges gifted to them by the ancien régime – would assume quasi-military and judicial functions as well. Their influence grew as the regime's weak credit in the eighteenth century plunged the government into increasingly desperate financial straits. Financiers "served as de facto bankers to the king," Gail Bossenga explains.[116] Burke was quite aware of the powerful, and insidious,

---

[110] Langford, *Writings and Speeches*, IX, 347.   [111] Langford, *Writings and Speeches*, IX, 230.
[112] Langford, *Writings and Speeches*, IX, 231–232.
[113] Langford, *Writings and Speeches*, IX, 236.   [114] Harris, *Necker*, 138.
[115] Gail Bossenga, "A Divided Nobility: Status, Markets, and the Patrimonial State in the Old Regime," in *The French Nobility in the Eighteenth Century: Reassessments and New Approaches*, ed. Jay M. Smith (University Park: The Pennsylvania State University Press, 2006), 69.
[116] Bossenga, "Divided Nobility," 69.

impact that creditors could project in politics, as illustrated by his philippics against Paul Benfield throughout the 1780s in the case of India.[117]

In the *Reflections*, Burke portrays the monied interest as a ravenous concoction of French speculators, stockjobbers, and investors in government debt intent on wielding the cudgel of public credit to accelerate its pursuit for profit and court influence. He intended "monied interest" to be a pejorative term,[118] radiating an image of unbridled rapacity and self-aggrandizement antithetical to the common good. The monied interest remains an obscure subject in the *Reflections*, especially compared to Burke's more famous attacks on the rights of man, abstract reason, and the displacement of tradition, but it is central to his critique of the Revolution. For it epitomized the danger of combining state power with mobile property and unbounded avarice, a convergence of great anxiety for Burke in his economic and political thought.

Why did Burke direct his inflamed outbursts toward the "monied interest" in the *Reflections*? First recall that the confiscation of Gallican Church property was initially justified in order to ensure stability in France's system of public finance. The French government's plan was to sell off expropriated church lands, with the hope that the funds would be able to pay down the state's debt in order to restore public credit. Sound state credit carried profound geopolitical implications because it was a means to fund military expeditions, enabling rulers to pursue their imperial ambitions with wider access to capital and with the ostensible backing of the people.

Burke's concern in the case of France was that the monied interest had exploited public credit to exert disproportionate political influence on the conduct of government operations, a trend that began prior to the French Revolution. "By the vast debt of France a great monied interest had insensibly grown up, and with it a great power," he writes in the *Reflections*.[119] By referencing that the interest had "grown up," Burke insinuates that the monied interest did not, in fact, signify a thunderbolt to French society in the late 1780s and early 1790s, but rather had emerged concomitantly with the growth of the country's debt obligations under the ancien régime. This interest had steered the trajectory of national policy, provided the financial credit necessary for France to wage wars, and drained power from the landed interest. Such phenomena, Burke had noticed years before, shaped the development of English politics in the eighteenth century as well.[120]

---

[117] Consult "Head of Objections to Benfield," in Langford, *Writings and Speeches*, V, 124–132; and "Speech on Nabob of Arcot's Debts," in Langford, *Writings and Speeches*, V, 478–552.

[118] This book acknowledges the partisan nature of the term but will use it frequently for the sake of clarifying Burke's condemnation of the *assignats*.

[119] Langford, *Writings and Speeches*, VIII, 158.

[120] Describing the growth of power under George III after his accession (which had occurred in the middle of the Seven Years War) in *Thoughts on the Present Discontents*, Burke writes, "His influence, by additions from conquest, by an augmentation of debt, by an increase of military

Burke most likely acquired, or deepened, his knowledge of the influence of financiers on the ancien régime from Jacques Necker's *De l'Administration des Finances de la France* (1784), the French edition of which Burke references multiple times in the *Reflections*.[121] Necker had written in the text, "Public credit is one of the most notable attributes of government, when that confidence is due to its conduct and good faith; but it is a degradation of this noble idea, when the strength of an empire is left to depend on a few individuals grown wealthy through its carelessness."[122] The monied interest swayed the legislative process and public administration through nefarious means: "[S]ometimes they have even imperiously dictated laws, and demanded the removal of a minister, as one condition for the continuation of their services."[123] Their political imprint expanded during the exigencies of military conflict. The "power of these finance agents is increased and fortified only, in the midst of the horrors of war, and of the confusions of the state."[124]

These themes saturate Burke's reflections on the French Revolution: from his perspective, the monied interest helped give rise to the expansion of the French state. In the case of the Revolution, the union between this monied interest and the "Men of Letters," a "literary cabal"[125] of *philosophes* who spread revolutionary ideology, Burke insists in the *Reflections*, was responsible for the assault on church property and the subversion of the Gallican Church.

In *Second Letter on a Regicide Peace*, Burke mentions a third noxious influence: the "spirit of ambition"[126] of the new French middle class, including merchants, which "had swelled far beyond their former proportion."[127] Burke did not dismiss the function of ambition in civil society: as he wrote in the *Philosophical Enquiry*, "there never could be any improvement" among men without ambition.[128] Otherwise, men would merely

---

and naval establishment, much strengthened and extended" (Langford, *Writings and Speeches*, II, 262–263). This led to the "aggrandisement of a Court Faction" (263). England also faced questions about the solvency of its own national debt at the time Burke wrote the *Reflections*. See Langford, *Writings and Speeches*, VIII, 10–11. For historical background on the growth of British debt, see John Brewer, *The Sinews of Power: War, Money and the English State, 1688–1783* (Cambridge, MA: Harvard University Press, 1990), 88–134. See also P. G. M. Dickson, *The Financial Revolution in England: A Study in the Development of Public Credit, 1688–1756* (London: Macmillan, 1967).

[121] Jacques Necker, *De l'Administration des Finances de la France* (Lausanne: J.-P. Heubach, 1784). Burke quite possibly was also attracted to Necker's aversion to abstract theories of government, and to his appreciation for the settled customs of a nation (Harris, *Necker*, 96).

[122] Jacques Necker, *A Treatise on the Administration of the Finances of France*, vol. III (London: J. Walter 1785), 130.

[123] Necker, *Treatise on the Administration*, 131.

[124] Necker, *Treatise on the Administration*, 135. Late in this chapter of his book, Necker does recognize the "good qualities of the principal finance officers," which "moderate the inconveniences attached to the recent veneration I have seen them treated with" (136).

[125] Langford, *Writings and Speeches*, VIII, 160.

[126] Langford, *Writings and Speeches*, IX, 292.   [127] Langford, *Writings and Speeches*, IX, 291.

[128] Langford, *Writings and Speeches*, I, 225.

imitate one another. The problem in the case of eighteenth-century France, however, was that the monied interest combined with the mercantile interest, which enabled "the spirit of ambition" to become "connected with spirit of speculation," Burke writes in *Second Letter*.[129] The new middle class became "impatient of the place which settled society prescribes to them,"[130] and acquired a disproportionate amount of political power.

Financiers, fueled by this dreadful combination, provoked revolutionary France's speculative credit boom; the political men of letters (and the press) condoned their behavior – the same writers who, like the financiers, were attracted to the sparkle of innovation. Collectively, the two groups' actions, Burke writes in the *Reflections*, were a "*cause*, for the general fury with which all the landed property of ecclesiastical corporations has been attacked."[131] Later in the writing, he asks hypothetically, "Who but the most desperate adventurers in philosophy and finance could at all have thought of destroying the settled revenue of the state, the sole security for the public credit, in the hope of rebuilding it with the materials of confiscated property?"[132]

The associations of these different groups formed a dangerous alliance. "The correspondence of the monied and the mercantile world, the literary intercourse of academies; but, above all, the press, of which they had in a manner, entire possession, made a kind of electrick communication every where," Burke explains in *Second Letter*.[133] Encouraged by such communication, financial speculators had gained undue influence over French political affairs in many ways, including, most conspicuously, by granting a stamp of legitimacy upon the seizure of church land.

This malicious trend invited serious political risks. In Burke's view, while the landed interest was committed to advancing the common good, the monied interest was devoted to selfish endeavors, promoting risky financial opportunities for individual gain at the expense of the public welfare. Its disposition was characterized by an untamed eagerness, rather than by the steadiness and moderation of the landed aristocrat. The monied interest "is in its nature more ready for any adventure; and its possessors more disposed to new enterprizes of any kind," Burke writes.[134] The monied interest had no concrete stake in the community, such as inherited land, and therefore dismissed any consideration of fostering its political well-being.

The monied interest's commitment to speculative enterprise thereby required the defeat of the propertied classes, which could be achieved by attacking the monarchy and the Gallican Church. Burke remarks in the *Reflections* that the monied interest "struck at the nobility through the crown and the church." And

---

[129] Langford, *Writings and Speeches*, IX, 292.   [130] Langford, *Writings and Speeches*, IX, 291.
[131] Langford, *Writings and Speeches*, VIII, 162.
[132] Langford, *Writings and Speeches*, VIII, 281.
[133] Langford, *Writings and Speeches*, IX, 292.
[134] Langford, *Writings and Speeches*, VIII, 159.

it "attacked them particularly on the side on which they thought them the most vulnerable, that is, the possessions of the church, which, through the patronage of the crown, generally devolved upon the nobility." While membership in the hereditary nobility required a pedigree dating back generations, the monied interest did not hail from a long line of distinguished ancestors. It was, rather, a novel group of pretentious profit-seekers whose members came from "unendowed pedigrees and naked titles of several among the nobility."[135]

Thus the "pride of the wealthy men, not noble or newly noble, increased with its cause."[136] The appearance of the monied interest posed a menace to the landed interest that had governed France for centuries. Because Burke endorsed the idea that the landed interest should command disproportionate influence in ruling a country, the emergence of monied men, lacking in the temperament and wisdom necessary to promote the general welfare, marked a provocative defiance of Burke's treasured beliefs about the proper qualifications to lead.[137]

The *Assignats*

The primary way the monied interest spread a noxious influence throughout revolutionary France was its heavy investment in *assignats*, a kind of bond that soon became legally recognized paper money throughout the country.[138] The roots of Burke's hostility to *assignats* can be detected in *An Account of the European Settlements in America*, published more than thirty years before the *Reflections*; indeed, the *Account*'s very conclusion discusses public finance, suggesting that the Burkes assigned great weight to the subject in their study of imperial policy and political economy. As they remarked in the writing, even though British provinces in America had experienced a flourishing of trade, "[v]ery little money" was observed among them.[139] This was because paper currency was employed by unscrupulous sources for credit schemes: "This money is not created for the conveniency of traffic, but by the exigencies of the government, and often by the frauds and artifices of private men for their particular profit."[140] The growing burdens of government, driven in no small part by "the execution of projects too vast for [the colonies'] strength," demanded access to credit.[141]

---

[135] Langford, *Writings and Speeches*, VIII, 159.
[136] Langford, *Writings and Speeches*, VIII, 159.
[137] For additional insight into Burke's analysis of the influence of the monied interest on the French Revolution, see J. G. A. Pocock's introduction to the Hackett edition of the *Reflections* (Indianapolis/Cambridge: Hackett Publishing Company, 1987), xxviii–xxxi.
[138] See Rebecca L. Spang, *Stuff and Money in the Time of the French Revolution* (Cambridge, MA: Harvard University Press, 2015), 107–109 for a detailed description of the different conceptions of the *assignats* after they were first issued.
[139] *Account of the European Settlements*, vol. II, 305.
[140] *Account of the European Settlements*, vol. II, 305.
[141] *Account of the European Settlements*, vol. II, 305.

The *Account* explained that colonial governments were thus compelled to impose taxes, offer land securities, and issue paper currency to relieve them of their piling financial obligations. Yet the taxes could not pay down the debt, the land securities were often based on fraud, and the currency lost much of its value. Nevertheless, the governments remain undeterred, continuing to issue more bills in order to gain additional credit for the aim of discharging their debt.[142]

The caprices of these public finance schemes shocked the stability of British settlements. The Burkes wrote:

It is easy to perceive how much the intercourse of business must suffer by this uncertainty in the value of money, when a man receives that in payment this day for ten shillings, which to-morrow he will not find received from him for five, or perhaps for three. Real money can hardly ever multiply too much in any country, because it will always as it increases be the certain sign of the increase of trade, of which it is the measure, and consequently of the soundness and vigour of the whole body. But this paper money may, and does increase, without any increase of trade, nay often when it greatly declines, for it is not the measure of the trade of the nation, but of the necessity of its government; and it is absurd, and must be ruinous, that the same cause which naturally exhausts the wealth of a nation, should likewise be the only productive cause of money.[143]

The zealous issuance of paper currency created odious uncertainties and volatilities in colonial economies. Their widespread diffusion led not to the enlargement of trade but to the depletion of wealth, for paper money did not ultimately determine the value of commercial activity but simply measured the desires and needs of government. The Burkes emphasized that these vulgar effects wielded a profound influence not only on the health of economies but on the perpetuation of civil order: "Laws themselves are hardly more the cement of societies than money; and societies flourish or decay according to the condition of either of these."[144] Such insights into monetary policy would come to inspire Burke's economic critique of the French Revolution more than three decades later.

In the 1790s, the French remained aware of these dangers to some extent, since the political residue of John Law's failed financial scheme continued to raise lingering suspicions throughout France about the perils of uninhibited paper-backed currency. Yet such apprehensions were muted in the Constituent Assembly. Deputies reasoned that while Law's system was based on gold mines that did not exist, *assignats* were backed by actual property.[145] Subsequently, the Assembly authorized the sale of *assignats* to creditors in order to pay off the national debt, with the expectation that the future sale of the seized church and

---

[142] *Account of the European Settlements*, vol. II, 306–307.
[143] *Account of the European Settlements*, vol. II, 307.
[144] *Account of the European Settlements*, vol. II, 305.
[145] See Aftalion, *Economic Interpretation*, 73.

royal estates would provide the necessary collateral for the government's debtor obligations.[146]

The *assignats* may have been the first comprehensive attempt by a Western state to impose on its people a monetary policy defined by fiat money, a currency decreed by the government that cannot be converted into a physical commodity.[147] In a foreword to Andrew Dickson White's *Fiat Money Inflation in France*, which describes the policy in great detail, John Mackay, writing in 1914, argued that it was "the most gigantic attempt ever made in the history of the world by a government to create an inconvertible paper currency, and to maintain its circulation at various levels of value." White's book also outlined "perhaps the greatest of all governmental efforts – with the possible exception of Diocletian's – to enact and enforce a legal limit of commodity prices."[148]

A brief chronology is necessary to illustrate the French revolutionaries' insatiable devotion to *assignats*.[149] First, on December 19, 1789, the Constituent Assembly proposed to auction off the property, valued at 400 million francs, and to issue the *assignats* in the domination of 1,000 livres at 5 percent interest in order to reimburse the debt of the Caisse d'Escompte, the quasi-bank of France. Although this plan was not implemented, the principle of issuing *assignats* became entrenched in the consciousness of deputies of the Assembly. The body then considered on March 17, 1790 to sell and transfer over properties worth 400 million to the municipality of Paris. On April 17, 1790, the state voted to issue *assignats* at 3 percent interest, and the official sale started on May 14, 1790. By early September the 400 million had been used up, as there was no additional revenue from taxes at that point.

The Constituent Assembly was not discouraged: on September 29, 1790, it sold an additional amount of 800 million worth of *assignats*, this time with no interest. Following a clarifying decree on December 13, *assignats* became

---

[146] See the following sources for information on *assignats* during the French Revolution: Harris, *Assignats*; Spang, *Stuff and Money*; Levasseur, "Assignats," 179–202; Aftalion, *Economic Interpretation*, 68–85; and Elise S. Brezis and François H. Crouzet, "The Role of Assignats during the French Revolution: An Evil or a Rescuer?" *The Journal of European Economic History* (1995): 7–40.

[147] See Ralph T. Foster, *Fiat Paper Money: The History and Evolution of Our Currency*, ed. Paul J. Myslin (Berkeley, CA: Ralph T. Foster, 2010). Paper money first emerged in China in the eleventh century. See pages 7–9. The Bank of Sweden – not formally the Swedish government – issued bank notes for the first time in the West in 1661 (58–59). Note also that, according to Milton Friedman, the "earliest episodes" of hyperinflation in the West were the "U.S. Revolution, with its Continental currency, and the French Revolution, with its *assignats*." (The United States had not yet formed when the Continental Congress began to issue paper money in 1775.) See Friedman, *Money Mischief: Episodes in Monetary History* (New York: Harcourt Brace Jovanovich, 1992), 189.

[148] John Mackay, "Foreword," in Andrew Dickson White, *Fiat Money Inflation in France: How It Came, What It Brought, and How It Ended* (New York and London: D. Appleton-Century Company, 1933).

[149] This chronology is indebted to Levasseur, "Assignats."

FIGURE 11.1 *Assignat* issued during the French Revolution
Source: Division of Work and Industry, National Museum of American History,
Smithsonian Institution

official legal tender in France. All of these actions besides the final decree had occurred by the time Burke made his final edits to the *Reflections* in October 1790,[150] and before the letter was published on November 1, 1790. *Assignats* continued to be issued after its publication. They were abolished in February 1796. Please consult Figure 11.1 for an image of an *assignat* issued during the French Revolution.

The injection of *assignats* into France's economy, combined with the rash political leadership of revolutionaries and a variety of other factors, bred or exacerbated perilous economic consequences, such as the dramatic depreciation of the currency and hyperinflation (particularly following the 1790–1791 period). After the initial sale of the paper money, its value dropped by 5 percent. By September 1791, the *assignats* had declined between 18 and 20 percent.[151] In the meantime, gold and silver became scarce; they "disappeared and hid themselves in the earth from whence they came," as Burke observed in the *Reflections*.[152] When the National Convention assumed power in September 1792, the currency's value had diminished by 44 percent.[153] By the end of the Convention three years later, the *assignats* had plummeted

---

[150] See Lock, *Edmund Burke*, vol. II, 283–284. Burke did not correct some out-of-date information before the *Reflections* was sent off to be published.
[151] Levasseur, "Assignats," 185. [152] Langford, *Writings and Speeches*, VIII, 90.
[153] Levasseur, "Assignats," 187.

98 percent.[154] Between August 1794 and March 1796, France experienced "spectacular depreciation," S. E. Harris writes.[155]

As Elise S. Brezis and François H. Crouzet argue, "[T]here is no doubt that the huge increase in *assignats* from 1792 onwards is correlated with the inflation starting then."[156] This steep rise in inflation benefited an enlarged debtor class, comforted by the fact that they were repaying their financial obligations in depreciated paper money. In addition, the printing of *assignats* provided much-needed succor to the French government in financing the nation's wars against Austria and Prussia, which began in the spring of 1792.[157] At the time the *assignats* were eliminated in early 1796, their value barely exceeded the paper on which they were printed.[158]

The proliferation of *assignats* caused the price of goods, including grain, to spike, while vendors and contractors refused to accept the *assignats* as payment. Food shortages enraged the *sans-culottes*, the radical commoners of the French Revolution. The National Convention attempted to alleviate these difficulties in May 1793 by implementing regulations inspired by the doctrine of *dirigisme*, the state control of economic resources. The government mandated a maximum price ceiling, and decreed the punishment of death for merchants found selling goods at higher prices than those stipulated by law.[159] It was such reckless policies that partially motivated Burke to berate state interference in the internal grain market in *Thoughts and Details*.

Revolutionary France's initial regulations, first affecting grain and then other commodities, failed horribly. The price ceiling inhibited scrupulous trading practices, promoted fraud, and created a shortage of goods.[160] Such corruption of supply and demand laws hurt industry and manufactures because producers were not able to reap profits under this oppressive system of price controls.[161] And farmers did not want to sell their crops at state-mandated prices. This hoarding led the French government to start seizing private goods to help supply its army.[162] The price ceiling mandates were repealed in December 1794.[163]

Burke abhorred the invasion of *assignats* into the domain of French public finance, an abstruse subject at the time – even for deputies – that, nevertheless, dominated national debate in France, particularly in the early years of the

---

[154] Levasseur, "Assignats," 189.   [155] Harris, *Assignats*, 186.

[156] Brezis and Crouzet, "Role of Assignats," 27.

[157] Brezis and Crouzet, "Role of Assignats," 16.

[158] Aftalion, *Economic Interpretation*, 173. Overall, the real value of *assignats* swung up and down due to the instability of the French Revolution.

[159] Levasseur, "Assignats," 189–190.   [160] Levasseur, "Assignats," 190.

[161] Brezis and Crouzet, "Role of Assignats," 34.

[162] Brezis and Crouzet, "Role of Assignats," 17.

[163] Note, again, that many of these economic developments occurred after Burke wrote the *Reflections*.

French Revolution.[164] In the *Reflections*, he registers sharp opposition to the French government's plan to melt the sturdy edifice of Church property into commercial instruments for the ostensible purpose of financial solvency. He first scorns the initial idea to sell church lands directly because such auctions would diminish their worth. To auction off ecclesiastical and royal property through market exchange was "obviously to defeat the profits proposed by the confiscation, by depreciating the value of those lands, and indeed of all the landed estates throughout France."[165]

Burke then critically summarizes the Constituent Assembly's multiple decisions to sell *assignats*. The Assembly "proposed to take stock in exchange for the church lands," he writes.[166] Consequently, once municipalities heard of the plan to transfer property to the "stock-holders"[167] of Paris to be sold off, they pleaded for paper currency with the intention of reviving "their perishing industry."[168] The Assembly's decision to sell more *assignats* at 3 percent interest confirmed the Revolution's idolatry of paper money.[169]

The fatal effect of this policy was the transformation of the Church from an institution of worship into an instrument for material gain and revolutionary coercion. "The spoil of the church was now become the only resource of all their operations in finance; the vital principle of all their politics; the sole security for the existence of their power," Burke avers.[170] Ironically, even though the Constituent Assembly expropriated church lands for the seeming aim of advancing the interests of the state, the legislative body became wholly reliant on the church as its financial lifeblood, Burke observes.

Here, then, is an example in which Burke's confidence in markets did not translate into support for the conversion of church property into a conduit of exchange. If he opposed the creation of markets out of ecclesiastical property, can we say that this view indicates an acute skepticism of the salutary effects of commercial enterprise?

There is a soundness, however, behind Burke's reasoning that retains consistency with his embrace of market liberty. In his judgment, the state should preserve the conditions for a vibrant provisions market in the internal trade and liberal intercourse in foreign trade, particularly among British dependencies and allies. Yet the government confiscation of church land, even if it did lead to the creation of new bond markets, violated the right to private property authorized by prescription and rooted in the law of nature. The ethic of state restraint that Burke advocated in *Thoughts and Details* was defied brazenly by the Constituent Assembly's decision to confiscate church land

---

[164] Consult Spang, *Stuff and Money*, 57–61.　　[165] Langford, *Writings and Speeches*, VIII, 170.
[166] Langford, *Writings and Speeches*, VIII, 170.
[167] Langford, *Writings and Speeches*, VIII, 171.
[168] Langford, *Writings and Speeches*, VIII, 171.
[169] Langford, *Writings and Speeches*, VIII, 171.
[170] Langford, *Writings and Speeches*, VIII, 171.

holdings. More important, as we shall learn, Burke held the steadfast belief that some institutions in civil society, such as the church, should remain beyond the grasp of supply and demand laws.

Burke suggests further that the selling off of church property through the circulation of paper money *shook the foundation* of market principles by weakening the value of the property. As mentioned, Burke highlights that bringing the landed estates to the financial market was to "defeat the profits proposed by the confiscation" by "depreciating the value of those lands and, indeed, of all the landed estates throughout France."[171] Confiscating property as security against the national debt crippled efforts to optimize the value of land.

Such financial legerdemain, of course, was only one source of Burke's antipathy to the expropriation of church lands. The savagery of trespass against sentiments attached to private possessions; the offense to the complexity of society permitting a variety of forms of possession; and the entrapment of state policy to questions of material gain, combined with the auctioning off of ecclesiastical estates, stirred Burke's outrage against French radicals' infringement of property rights.

Hence Burke condemns revolutionaries for their "fanatical confidence in the omnipotence of church plunder,"[172] reiterating his unflinching opposition to the seizure of Gallican Church properties.[173] Then he writes, with a zeal that leaps off the page:

Is there a debt which presses them – Issue *assignats*. – Are compensations to be made, or a maintenance decreed to those whom they have robbed of their freehold in their office, or expelled from their profession – *Assignats*. Is a fleet to be fitted out – *Assignats*. If sixteen millions sterling of these *assignats*, forced on the people, leave the wants of the state as urgent as ever – issue, says one, thirty millions sterling of *assignats* – says another, issue fourscore millions more of *assignats*.[174]

Although hyperinflation had not yet occurred, Burke notices the inflationary trajectory of the paper money: "Are the old *assignats* depreciated at market? What is the remedy? Issue new *assignats*."[175]

Burke's mocking repetition of "*assignats*" has a striking effect on the reader, laying bare his animus toward revolutionaries' consecration of paper money as the new saving grace of their political economy. French politicians and

---

[171] Langford, *Writings and Speeches*, VIII, 170.
[172] Langford, *Writings and Speeches*, VIII, 280.
[173] On this note, Burke considers, for the sake of argument, that even if the initial idea to sell the lands was sound, the Constituent Assembly still failed to accurately assess the value of the lands in a transparent and candid manner. The legislative body and the Revolution's financial managers were also not prepared for the rapid fluctuation of the properties' value in response to political vicissitudes. See Langford, *Writings and Speeches*, VIII, 282–283, including 282n1.
[174] Langford, *Writings and Speeches*, VIII, 280.
[175] Langford, *Writings and Speeches*, VIII, 280.

managers were all "philosophic financiers" and "professors of *assignats*,"[176] retaining an irrational hope that the notes would magically cure France's economic maladies.[177] According to Burke, however, such fanatical attraction to paper money exposed radicals' utter lack of self-control and prudence.

Burke's foresight about the inflationary effects of the *assignats* was accurate but not original. French members of the Assembly, not to mention Necker, conveyed similar trepidations about how the unchecked spread of paper money would depreciate its value, hurt creditors, and increase the price of goods.[178] Abbé Maury, Jacques Antoine Marie de Cazalès, and Jean Raymond de Cucé de Boisgelin, Archbishop of Aix believed that the *assignats* "were necessarily going to depreciate, thus occasioning a rise in price of basic commodities, the ruin of the state's creditors and the impoverishment of the workers," Florin Aftalion writes.[179] The hazards of this policy were evident not only to conservative members of the Assembly but also to Condorcet,[180] the famous revolutionary whose philosophy of abstract rationalism offended the principle of prudence in Burke's political thought.

Nonetheless, such observations by the French should not diminish our appreciation of the intellectual foundations of Burke's thought on public finance and monetary policy. His stinging comments about the *assignats* testified to his belief that a strong currency, protected from the menace of devaluation, was essential for a flourishing and stable economy. In addition to the comments just quoted, Burke remarks critically in the *Reflections* that after the Constituent Assembly had started to issue paper notes earlier in 1790, "This paper also felt an almost immediate depreciation of five per cent. which in little time came to about seven."[181] He then extols the wisdom of Jacques Necker for drawing attention to the importance of metal in providing balance to financial artifice. Necker believed that France "could not live upon *assignats* alone; that some real silver was necessary."[182]

This was the case "particularly for the satisfaction of those, who having iron in their hands, were not likely to distinguish themselves for patience, when they should perceive that whilst an increase of pay was held out to them in real money, it was again to be fraudulently drawn back by depreciated paper."[183]

---

[176] Langford, *Writings and Speeches*, VIII, 280.
[177] Burke further decried the revolutionary proposition to transform church bells into currency. The "project for coining into money the bells of the suppressed churches" was the revolutionaries' "alchymy" (Langford, *Writings and Speeches*, VIII, 288).
[178] See Aftalion, *Economic Interpretation*, 74–79.   [179] Aftalion, *Economic Interpretation*, 74.
[180] Aftalion, *Economic Interpretation*, 79.   [181] Langford, *Writings and Speeches*, VIII, 286.
[182] Langford, *Writings and Speeches*, VIII, 286. Earlier in the *Reflections*, Burke had cited Necker's *De l'Administration des Finances de la France* to demonstrate that France had witnessed a growth in wealth. See Langford, *Writings and Speeches*, VIII, 178–179. For Burke's other thoughts on Necker, see "*Speech on Economical Reform* II: Pensions, Costly Offices, and the Civil List," Chapter 5.
[183] Langford, *Writings and Speeches*, VIII, 286.

Burke criticizes French legislators for asserting that there was "no difference in value between metallic money and their *assignats*."[184] Revolutionaries, their mad rush to sell off church land compromising their judgment, "took their fictions for currencies."[185] An economy stands on unsteady ground if not augmented by the backbone of metal.

An intriguing harmony emerges from Burke's evaluation of metallic money and his defense of the landed aristocracy. In his view, they both provided the virtue of stability in human affairs – metal in the case of markets, and propertied men in the case of politics. Both were proof against the vicissitudes of political fortune and party stratagems, furnishing the principle of constancy beneath the tempestuous fluxes of civil society. The role performed by metallic money and the landed nobility also reflected Burke's broader recognition throughout his writings of the relation between stability and change, preservation and reform. Civil society required a careful balancing between these two imperatives of social order. Metal provided the former in exchange economies, for it steadied the swift ascent of financial prosperity and tempered the inflationary excesses of paper money.[186]

Burke's condemnation of the currency illustrates his searing judgment that the marriage between the monied interest and the profusion of *assignats* in the French economy created the monster of paper-money despotism. *Assignats* were "those tickets of despotism," he writes in *Second Letter on a Regicide Peace*.[187] Paper-money despotism did not simply devalue the currency, however. For Burke, it also represented a dereliction of political obligation, a psychological escape from confronting and meeting the sober responsibilities of wise public administration. The purpose of popular leaders in the French legislature, Burke writes in the *Reflections*, "seems to have been to evade and slip aside from *difficulty*."[188] Yet difficulty generates advantage: it "is a severe instructor ... He that wrestles with us strengthens our nerves, and sharpens our skills. Our antagonist is our helper. This amicable conflict with difficulty obliges us to an intimate acquaintance with our object, and compels us to consider it in all its relations."[189] These comments bear a similarity to the *Account*'s argument more than three decades prior that a principle of strength lies within the weakness of man.

The *assignats* represented the antithesis of wrestling with difficulty: they did not instruct but corrupt, trapping the mind to promote licentious paper-money despotism rather than enlarging it to consider sustainable fiscal and monetary

[184] Langford, *Writings and Speeches*, VIII, 287.
[185] Langford, *Writings and Speeches*, VIII, 285.
[186] According to Burke, however, the belief that the accumulation of bullion was the surest means to wealth rested on faulty premises, as did balance of trade theory in general. See "*Observations on a Late State of the Nation*," Chapter 7.
[187] Langford, *Writings and Speeches*, IX, 288.
[188] Langford, *Writings and Speeches*, VIII, 215.
[189] Langford, *Writings and Speeches*, VIII, 215.

policies. According to Burke, "[I]t is the degenerate fondness for tricking short-cuts, and little fallacious facilities, that has in so many parts of the world created governments with arbitrary powers."[190] This evasion of duty marked the curse of the French nation under the reckless leadership of revolutionaries: "It is this inability to wrestle with difficulty which has obliged the arbitrary assembly of France to commence their schemes of reform with abolition and total destruction."[191] The allure of *assignats* had so entranced the minds of legislators that their slavish devotion to the currency removed their capacity for independent judgment. Paper money had achieved the power of hypnosis.

Revenue and the French Revolution

Paper-money despotism and the expansion of public credit bred additional deformities of the French economy. First, it disrupted existing revenue streams. Burke asks in the *Reflections*, "Who but the most desperate adventurers in philosophy and finance could at all have thought of destroying the settled revenue of the state, the sole security for the public credit, in the hope of rebuilding it with the materials of confiscated property?"[192] Unlike his more celebrated attack on abstract ideology, Burke's commentary on public revenue in the *Reflections* has not struck a resonant chord among readers, but it remained at the center of his critique of French revolutionary fiscal policy and illuminated his broader conception of responsible statesmanship.

Allow us, then, to elaborate on Burke's thoughts on revenue in the *Reflections*. For Burke, the "state," at its most elemental level, was comprised of institutions that were braced by the support of public revenue. "The revenue of the state is the state," Burke flatly asserts. "In effect all depends upon it, whether for support or for reformation."[193] His fondness for market economies did not lead him to the conclusion that government must be consigned to the shadows of civil society. Instead, civil society required public administration – and public administration had to be funded, up to some point, by wealth derived from the citizens of the commonwealth.

But the function of revenue transcended the financing of government offices. It conferred power and authority, and was a vehicle for public morality. On this point, Burke presents in the *Reflections* the most important comments in his entire life on the relation between revenue and statecraft:

[T]he revenue, which is the spring of all power, becomes in its administration the sphere of every active virtue. Public virtue, being of a nature magnificent and splendid, instituted for great things, and conversant about great concerns, requires abundant scope and room, and cannot spread and grow under confinement, and in circumstances straitened,

[190] Langford, *Writings and Speeches*, VIII, 215.
[191] Langford, *Writings and Speeches*, VIII, 216.
[192] Langford, *Writings and Speeches*, VIII, 281.
[193] Langford, *Writings and Speeches*, VIII, 273.

narrow, and sordid. Through the revenue alone the body politic can act in its true genius and character, and therefore it will display just as much of its collective virtue, and as much of that virtue which may characterize those who move it, and are, as it were, its life and guiding principle, as it is possessed of a just revenue. For from hence, not only magnanimity, and liberality, and beneficence, and fortitude, and providence, and the tutelary protection of all good arts, derive their food, and the growth of their organs, but continence, and self-denial, and labour, and vigilance, and frugality, and whatever else there is in which the mind shews itself above the appetite, are no where more in their proper element than in the provision and distribution of public wealth.[194]

Revenue is the source of public virtue, and the investment of money in particular enterprises reflects moral choices. Hence public virtue cannot be exercised by the state if revenue is exhausted. What is public virtue in theory? As Burke mentions, it is liberality and magnanimity, fortitude and benevolence. How do these virtues translate to concrete policy? He does not offer specifics, but we can surmise some likely possibilities with regard to his commentary on the political economy of England: investment in the arts[195] (which Burke does suggest in the quotation) and grand public buildings; support for the corn bounty; the perpetuation of a (reformed) pension system; the payment of salaries to judges and magistrates; and national defense.

The investment of government expenditure did not mean, however, that the state should act with unbounded extravagance and exploded license. "Self-denial" and "labour" and "frugality" were all central virtues in the supply and dissemination of public money. The imperatives of sound public administration called for conscientious selection and discrimination in deciding which government ventures were worthy of investment. One can immediately detect a convergence between these comments and Burke's commentary in *Speech on Economical Reform*: states should use public revenue – but they should do so wisely and on behalf of the public. Even more, the distribution of public wealth should advance the priorities of the state, such as, in the case of Burke's program on economical reform, the continuation of the pension system, which rewarded government servants for true public service.

Because national revenue was intimately connected with public virtue, the study of public finance, Burke admits, was a relatively noble endeavor. "It is therefore not without reason that the science of speculative and practical finance, which must take to its aid so many auxiliary branches of knowledge, stands high in the estimation not only of the ordinary sort, but of the wisest and best men," he writes.[196] Burke here praises speculative finance for its crucial role in the collection and distribution of public wealth – yet he lambastes the

---

[194] Langford, *Writings and Speeches*, VIII, 274.
[195] Note that "art" in the eighteenth-century English lexicon included trades.
[196] Langford, *Writings and Speeches*, VIII, 274.

monied interest throughout the *Reflections*. How does one square the seeming discrepancy between these two stances?

For Burke, the monied interest of the French Revolution militated against the ethical and practical duties of a responsible finance minister, properly construed:

The objects of a financier are, then, to secure an ample revenue; to impose it with judgment and equality; to employ it oeconomically; and when necessity obliges him to make use of credit, to secure its foundations in that instance, and for ever, by the clearness and candour of his proceedings, the exactness of his calculations, and the solidity of his funds.[197]

Once again, Burke's description of these responsibilities bears a telling resemblance to his own endeavors in support of economical reform in the early 1780s. Both were guided by a chief maxim of statesmanship: a secure revenue stream is established by the steadiness of government, not by the capricious schemes of public officials.[198] In other words, state receipts tend to rise when the whims of rulers are constrained, and when the taxation of private wealth is orderly, predictable, and narrow in scope. Regularity of collection and the limitation of arbitrary force produce the conditions for thriving industry and abundant public coffers.

Burke underscores that the French revolutionary government flagrantly executed the opposite approach. If it had honored the traditions of France and remedied its worst deformities, he writes, "You would have had an unoppressive but a productive revenue. You would have had a flourishing commerce to feed it."[199] Instead the government's fiscal policy shredded the sources of industry and stymied the growth of revenue in the long run. The "whole indeed of [revolutionaries'] scheme of revenue is to make, by any artifice, an appearance of a full reservoir for the hour, whilst at the same time they cut off the springs and living fountains of perennial supply."[200] Accordingly, Burke observes, "Far from any encrease of revenue in their hands," the national revenue of France, according to a report from a reputable authority on finance[201] in the National Assembly, "diminished by the sum of two hundred millions, or *eight millions sterling* of the annual income, considerably more than one-third of the whole."[202]

In the *Reflections*, Burke describes a number of French policies he thought epitomized the careless and reckless character of the French Revolution's fiscal reforms. After swiftly abolishing the *gabelle*, the burdensome tax on salt, on the grounds that it violated the rights of men, deputies did not have in place an alternative plan to make up for the lost revenue generated by the tax. Such lack

---

[197] Langford, *Writings and Speeches*, VIII, 275.
[198] Of course, revolutionaries believed the ancien régime's revenue system was anything but steady.
[199] Langford, *Writings and Speeches*, VIII, 87.
[200] Langford, *Writings and Speeches*, VIII, 278.   [201] Théodor Vernier.
[202] Langford, *Writings and Speeches*, VIII, 275.

of foresight granted an air of license to districts, including the salt provinces, to determine which taxes they would pay according to their particular preferences, thereby placing revenue streams on an even more arbitrary and unsteady basis than the fiscal policy of the ancien régime. Moreover, the French government's plan to receive "patriotic contributions" from citizens in exchange for *assignats*, all in the name of "voluntary benevolence," failed to meet the citizens' needs, in no small part because the "load [was] thrown upon productive capital."[203] As Burke notes, these voluntary contributions ended up being extracted from citizens by force. Additional "patriotic donations" led to the further seizure of property and the ruin of trades.[204]

Such rash policies flouted the principles of wise public administration. For judicious administration, in Burke's judgment, occasioned a greater revenue stream – and a greater revenue stream was a mark of shining public opulence:

[T]he prosperity and improvement of nations has generally encreased with the encrease of their revenues; and they will both continue to grow and flourish, as long as the balance between what is left to strengthen the efforts of individuals, and what is collected for the common efforts of the state, bear to each other a due reciprocal proportion, and are kept in a close correspondence and communication.[205]

The ascent of national wealth and the flow of public revenue formed a natural symbiosis. The enlightened administrator helped establish the conditions for such prosperity by carefully determining how much wealth should remain in private hands and how much should be collected on behalf of the state.

This imperative penetrated the essence of responsible statesmanship. "To keep a balance between the power of acquisition on the part of the subject, and the demands he is to answer on the part of the state, is a fundamental part of the skill of a true politician," Burke pronounces in the *Reflections*.[206] And recall his insight in *Speech on Army Estimates* (1778): "Prudence, and a calm review of the financial powers of a country, were the first objects of a Statesman."[207] These two comments embody the heart of Burke's conception of statesmanship regarding public finance. A good statesman does not relieve the miseries of a people by pulling down the vigorous springs of industry that generate revenue for the state. Instead, he preserves their constitutional liberties while also conveying that consistent and predictable contribution to public expense will confer advantages on the whole. "Whether it be more advantageous to the people to pay considerably, and to gain proportion; or to gain little or nothing, and to be disburthened of all contribution," Burke was in favor of

---

[203] Langford, *Writings and Speeches*, VIII, 276–277. See Doyle, *Oxford History of the French Revolution*, 133–134.

[204] Langford, *Writings and Speeches*, VIII, 276–277.

[205] Langford, *Writings and Speeches*, VIII, 274.

[206] Langford, *Writings and Speeches*, VIII, 290.   [207] Langford, *Writings and Speeches*, III, 396.

the former proposition.[208] Although he supported government restraint in the internal grain trade, his comments on national revenue here communicate Burke's attitude that the state needed *some* stream of wealth in order to sustain the proper functions of public administration and assist in the promotion of public prosperity.

Yet the blind faith of "philosophic financiers" in the *assignats* and church plunder corrupted this notion of financial statesmanship. In comparing this faith to the mysterious substance desired by alchemists that could transform ordinary metals into gold or silver, Burke writes in the *Reflections* that the "dream of the philosopher's stone induces dupes … to neglect all rational means of improving their fortunes." The reckless usurpation of private property and the unhinged flow of paper money were detrimental to building sustainable wealth rooted in sound market principles. Additionally, Burke writes, "Even those, whose natural good sense and knowledge of commerce, not obliterated by philosophy, offer decisive arguments against this delusion [of *assignats*]," still proposed the further issuance of the currency.[209] Even men who possessed economic wisdom about the dangers of paper-money despotism – those with "natural good sense" and "knowledge of commerce" – still retained the stubborn view that paper money should be issued. In employing the phrases "rational means" and "natural good sense," Burke is also associating the opposition of paper-money despotism with reason and nature, summoning tinctures of Enlightenment vocabulary to strengthen his argument in favor of commercial prosperity.

Burke thus understood his indictment of French revolutionary economic policy to be harmonious with his own beliefs about the virtues of market-based economies and sound public finance. In the *Reflections*, he notes that the Constituent Assembly's attempt to expropriate ecclesiastical land and sell it off exhibited a "defiance of oeconomical principles."[210] In *Second Letter on a Regicide Peace*, published in 1796, he writes, in referring to France, "In that country entirely to cut off a branch of commerce, to extinguish a manufacture, to destroy the circulation of money, to violate credit, to suspend the course of agriculture, even to burn a city, or to lay waste a province of their own, does not cost them a moment's anxiety."[211]

It is no coincidence that Burke draws attention in this sentence to the economic ramifications of the French Revolution; radical stratagems to control the nation's economy, as Burke observes, spearheaded the destruction of its commerce, manufacturing, money, credit, and agriculture. In addition, he writes, revolutionaries "seize upon the fruit of the labour; they seize upon the

---

[208] Langford, *Writings and Speeches*, VIII, 289.
[209] Langford, *Writings and Speeches*, VIII, 280.
[210] Langford, *Writings and Speeches*, VIII, 281.
[211] Langford, *Writings and Speeches*, IX, 288.

labourer himself."[212] The impulse to usurp property and direct the flow of economic resources crushed the individual and the farm. Consequently, the Revolution triggered a revolution not just in social institutions but also in the nature of *wealth*, previously commanded by the propertied classes but now possessed by the monied interest and government. This shift led to a revolution in authority, as hereditary family and privilege were thrust aside by the rebellious energies of speculating experimenters.

Burke, then, did not separate monetary policy from its political consequences, for the reestablishment of civil stability required the defeat of paper-money despotism. "The utter destruction of Assignats and the restoration of order in Europe are one and the same thing," he asserted in 1793.[213] Stable currency was the parent of a stable economy, which was a pillar of social and political order.

One must cast a critical eye at Burke's portrayal of the two classes in the *Reflections*, however, as its ad hominem panache struggles to paint a more nuanced picture of the historical relations between the landed nobility and new monied class. On the eve of the Revolution, it was not uncommon for nobles to engage in business and financial activities, nor was it unusual for merchants to be considered nobles.[214] Eighty-seven percent of deputies in the Third Estate of the Estates General represented wealth gained from traditional sources of property, or what George V. Taylor called the "proprietary"[215] economy – stable investments in land, venal office, annuities, and urban property. Only 13 percent were bankers, merchants, and manufacturers, and over half of this group lived in rural or underdeveloped areas.[216]

It was not unusual, moreover, for members of the first and second estates of the Estates General to act on their acquisitive impulses. "[T]here were nobles who were capitalists. There were merchants who were nobles," Taylor writes.[217] Burke never expressly creates a strict, impenetrable division between the two groups in the *Reflections*. Nevertheless, the fury he levels at French revolutionaries in the writing can lead readers to believe that his purpose was to roundly denounce the new bourgeoisie and recover the sole primacy of the ancient aristocratic nobility.

In the end, however, Burke's sharp insights into the frailty of the *assignats* continue to be vastly underappreciated. "[T]he assignats have repeatedly been treated as a barely coded message for future lawmakers: a warning to keep expenses low and stay away from the printing press," Rebecca L. Spang writes, referencing Andrew Dickson White's commentary on the gold standard in

---

[212] Langford, *Writings and Speeches*, IX, 288–289.

[213] Burke to Florimond-Claude, Comte de Mercy-Argenteau, [*circa* 6 August 1793], in *Correspondence of Edmund Burke*, vol. VII, 389.

[214] George V. Taylor, "Noncapitalist Wealth and the Origins of the French Revolution," *The American Historical Review* 72 (1967): 469–496.

[215] Taylor, "Noncapitalist Wealth," 471.   [216] Taylor, "Noncapitalist Wealth," 489n78.

[217] Taylor, "Noncapitalist Wealth," 489.

America in the 1870s and Marcel Marion's discussion of the connection between the French Revolution and the hyperinflation of Germany and Austria in the 1920s. "Such accounts bear an unacknowledged debt to Edmund Burke's famous *Reflections on the Revolution in France.*"[218] White declared in *Fiat Money Inflation in France* that the monetary policy of the Revolution "brought ... commerce and manufactures, the mercantile interest, the agricultural interest, to ruin."[219]

Such was the core of Burke's critique of the political economy of the Revolution. There remains much debate about whether the *Reflections* should be considered the founding text of "conservatism," but the letter was, at the very least, a profound statement on the general principles necessary for sound public finance. We should recognize the writing as such.

11.6 THE RELATION BETWEEN THE MONIED INTEREST AND THE LANDED INTEREST

Burke's criticism of the *assignats* was part of his broader vision of the proper relation between the monied and commercial interests and the landed interest in civil society. Unlike modern understandings of eighteenth-century political economy, which tend to separate commercial and financial activities and landed property into isolated concepts, Burke and many of his English contemporaries imagined them as an integrated whole. We can begin to understand his perspective on this matter by first recalling the connection he intimates in the *Reflections* between metallic money and the virtue of stability: the former established the condition of constancy that modulated the turbulence of paper currency.

This analogy can be stretched further to elaborate on Burke's distinction between the qualities spread by the combination of the monied interest and the literary cabal, on the one hand, and the landed interest, on the other. The *Account* offered early traces in Burke's intellectual life of his awareness of such differences. In their discussion of Britain's West Indian settlements, the Burkes write:

The disposition to industry has a variety of characters, and is by no means constantly of the same colour. Some acquiesce in a moderate labour through the whole of their lives, attended with no risk either to their persons or their gains; such sort of people, who form the best citizens in general, are fit to stay at home. Others full as remote from an indolent disposition, are of quite a different character. These are fiery, restless tempers, willing to undertake the severest labour, provided it promises but a short continuance, who love risk and hazard, whose schemes are always vast, and who put no medium between great

---

[218] Spang, *Stuff and Money*, 9.
[219] White, *Fiat Money Inflation in France*, 66. See also Gary North, "Edmund Burke on Inflation and Despotism," Foundation for Economic Education, February 1, 1973, http://fee.org/free-man/edmund-burke-on-inflation-and-despotism/.

and being undone. Characters of this sort, especially when they happen in low and middling life, are often dangerous members in a regular and settled community.[220]

Enterprising men of an ambitious disposition frequently constitute a hazard to social order, while men of "moderate labour" pose little, if any threat, to the community.

Burke summons this key distinction in the *Reflections* to distinguish the monied interest and literary cabal from the landed interest. The first two groups evinced the faculties of "ability," "innovation," "energy," and "enthusiasm." These terms carried insidious undertones in the *Reflections*, symbolizing the radical efforts of monied men and public intellectuals to deploy their talents in the service of philosophical and financial speculation – all in order to accelerate their fanatical pursuit of influence and power.[221] "[A]bility is a vigorous and active principle, and as property is sluggish, inert, and timid, it never can be safe from the invasions of ability, unless it be, out of all proportion, predominant in the representation," Burke writes.[222] The passions of men with ability – financial investors and speculative philosophers – threaten the secure status of the landed nobility unless the nobility are overrepresented in the legislature.

Remember that, for Burke, members of the landed interest were not innovators but men of hereditary distinction and status – including members of the Church – faithful to advancing the common good. The House of Peers, Burke writes in the *Reflections*, was "formed upon" the "principle" that the hereditary aristocracy perpetuated not only property but "society itself."[223] In addition, "Nothing can secure a steady and moderate conduct in such assemblies, but that the body of them should be respectably composed, in point of condition in life, or permanent property, of education, and of such habits as enlarge and liberalize the understanding."[224] The political threat represented by men of assertive ability and zealous enthusiasm, however, was the substitution of the landed interest in the national legislature with themselves. This threat was magnified when the monied interest formed alliances with similar men of innovation in and outside government.

Burke's subtle use of metaphor in his discussion in the *Reflections* of John Law's role in fostering the reckless Mississippi Bubble illustrates this point. The popular leaders of the National Assembly could not "bear to hear the sands of his Mississippi compared with the rock of the church, on which they build their

---

[220] *Account of the European Settlements*, vol. II, 106.
[221] For other discussions of this issue, see Pocock, *Virtue, Commerce, and History*, 193–212; and Tom Furniss, "Burke, Paine, and the Language of Assignats," *The Yearbook of English Studies* 19 (1989): 54–70.
[222] Langford, *Writings and Speeches*, VIII, 102.
[223] Langford, *Writings and Speeches*, VIII, 102.
[224] Langford, *Writings and Speeches*, VIII, 92.

system."[225] Burke is calling attention to the delicious irony of the revolutionary politicians unwittingly using the "rock" of the church, a fortress of stability, to inspire their speculative designs, while denying any similarity to the volatile financial fluxes perpetrated by Law's scheme – even though, like his plan, they were engaging in the feverish dissemination of paper money. In fact, the *assignats* were worse than Law's policy; unlike his program for trade, which, according to Burke, at least "aimed at an increase of the commerce of France" touching the East Indies and Africa, as well as French farms, the revolutionary diffusion of paper money simply promoted fraud through coercion.[226] Burke insists that French lawmakers should restrain their passions for innovation until they demonstrate "what piece of solid ground there is for their assignats."[227] He hints that *assignats* did not stand on any solid ground at all – unlike, literally and figuratively, landed property.

Even given his celebration of the landed interest, Burke, it is worth reiterating, accommodated the role of ability in a polity. He remarks in the *Reflections* that a state should represent "ability"[228] as well as property, just not in the same proportion as the latter. Of course, Burke considered himself to be a man of diligence and ambition. In 1770, according to Will Burke, Edmund declared in Parliament that he was a new man – "*novus homo*," evoking Cicero – while affirming that he used his "Industry" to study "the Commerce, the finances, and constitution of his country."[229] Six years after the *Reflections*, in *Letter to a Noble Lord*, Burke reprimanded the Duke of Bedford for being a lazy hereditary aristocrat while arguing that he, Burke, employed his natural talents and hard work on behalf of the nation. "My merits, whatever they are, are original and personal; his are derivative," he asserted.[230] We have also learned that Burke was a champion of the right of middlemen to trade freely in accord with their enterprising spirit. In general, the nourishment of initiative was of great benefit to the state: as Will Burke wrote, Edmund observed in 1770 that "[a]ll wise governments have encouraged rising merit, as useful and necessary."[231]

One flaw of the revolutionary temper of the monied interest, however, was that it fueled an intemperate dependence on literal and dispositional speculation – incoherent and unfounded guesses, gambles, presumptions, and theories – to stimulate the dispersion of paper money. This temper was further moved by the unbounded confidence that clever monetary policy would

[225] Langford, *Writings and Speeches*, VIII, 287.
[226] Langford, *Writings and Speeches*, VIII, 287.
[227] Langford, *Writings and Speeches*, VIII, 287.
[228] Langford, *Writings and Speeches*, VIII, 102.
[229] William Burke to William Dennis, [3, 6] April [1770], in *Correspondence of Edmund Burke*, vol. II, 128.
[230] Langford, *Writings and Speeches*, IX, 165.
[231] William Burke to William Dennis, [3, 6] April [1770], in *Correspondence of Edmund Burke*, vol. II, 128–129.

strengthen the French economy. Yet the odious effect of speculation was the conversion of settled social and political attachments of civil society into relations based on slippery risk:

> Your legislators, in every thing new, are the very first who have founded a commonwealth upon gaming, and infused this spirit into it as its vital breath. The great object in these politics is to metamorphose France, from a great kingdom into one great play-table; to turn its inhabitants into a nation of gamesters; to make speculation as extensive as life; to mix it with all its concerns; and to divert the whole of the hopes and fears of the people from their usual channels, into the impulses, passions, and super-stitions of those who live on chances.[232]

Speculation transforms a stable political community into a dangerous game of chance. Tradition holds no sway; prescription is overturned. Custom and habit are replaced by ad hoc policies and devious subterfuge, fed by a malign combination of conjecture and treachery and underwritten by no stabilizing principle.

In consequence, the economy experiences a rupture. As Burke emphasizes, paper-money despotism infused a destructive spirit of fraught uncertainty in the market economy. "With you a man can neither earn nor buy his dinner, without a speculation," he states. "What he receives in the morning will not have the same value at night."[233] Wealth based on speculation triggers fluctuations and instabilities that give no incentive for producers and consumers to work and save: "Industry must wither away. Oeconomy must be driven from your country. Who will labour without knowing the amount of his pay? Who will accumulate, when he does not know the value of what he saves?"[234] Paper-money despotism sentences market participants to commercial ruin.

The additional, and perhaps even more important, toxic defect of the monied interest was its role in detaching man from the roots of local community. While family and friends with landed property were bound together by timeless social associations, financiers thirsted for a quick profit, and could move their capital beyond the edges of the commonwealth. "The new dealers being all habitually adventurers, and without any fixed habits or local predilections, will purchase to job out again, as the market of paper, or of money, or of land shall present an advantage," Burke writes in the *Reflections*.[235] The monied interest thus was less concerned about protecting their wealth with propriety and responsibility. "Do we not see how lightly people treat their fortunes when under the influence of the passion of gaming?" he asks in *Appeal from the New to the Old Whigs*.[236] Paper-money despots sought refuge in speculation and risk, while

---

[232] Langford, *Writings and Speeches*, VIII, 240.
[233] Langford, *Writings and Speeches*, VIII, 241.
[234] Langford, *Writings and Speeches*, VIII, 241.
[235] Langford, *Writings and Speeches*, VIII, 239.   [236] Langford, *Writings and Speeches*, IV, 468.

man's little platoons received comfort from the local prejudices of affection and faith.

Land as a Foundation for Commerce

Accordingly, Burke's larger point in the *Reflections*, and throughout the entirety of his reflections on political economy, is that land should be the foundation of enterprise and revenue, not the other way around:

Too many of the financiers by profession are apt to see nothing in revenue, but banks, and circulations, and annuities on lives, and tontines, and perpetual rents, and all the small wares of the shop. In a settled order of the state, these things are not to be slighted, nor is the skill in them to be held of trivial estimation. They are good, but then only good when they assume the effects of that settled order, and are built upon it. But when men think that these beggarly contrivances may supply a resource for the evils which results from breaking up the foundations of public order, and from causing or suffering the principles of property to be subverted, they will, in the ruin of their country, leave a melancholy and lasting monument of the effect of preposterous politics, and presumptuous, short-sighted, narrow-minded wisdom.[237]

These comments mark the crux of Burke's understanding of the relation between mobile and immobile property: while both were essential for the flourishing of a commonwealth, the gifts of commerce and finance would not endure without the chastening effect of land. Merchants and speculators were held captive to short-term thinking and narrow views when corrupted by radical political movements, as exhibited by the revolutionary French government's frenzied issuance of *assignats*. In contrast, landed aristocrats presided over propertied estates that were long-lasting institutions, which served as the necessary and eternal supports of a commonwealth.

Burke captured this belief more than fifteen years prior to the outbreak of the French Revolution. In a 1772 letter he wrote to the Duke of Richmond, a fellow Rockinghamite who at times needed to be coaxed into political activity, Burke observed that while men of drive such as himself were characterized by the "Rapidity of our growth" and the "fruit we bear," the hereditary aristocracy held a higher function in civil society.[238] "You if you are what you ought to be are the great Oaks that shade a Country and perpetuate your benefits from Generation to Generation," he counseled, which was why "Persons in your Station of Life ought [to] have long Views."[239] These comments are often connected to Burke's political and social thought, but they hold an important implication for his political economy as well: hereditary families of great wealth

---

[237] Langford, *Writings and Speeches*, VIII, 290.
[238] Burke to the Duke of Richmond, [*post* 15 November 1772], in *Correspondence of Edmund Burke*, vol. II, 377.
[239] Burke to the Duke of Richmond, [*post* 15 November 1772], in *Correspondence of Edmund Burke*, vol. II, 377.

were stable vessels in a free nation that steadied the restless activities of ambitious men, whether the latter included engaged lawmakers or enterprising merchants.

This is why Burke, in the *Reflections*, avows that some property should be able to be retained through means beyond "the previous acquisition of money,"[240] such as inheritance laws. He further writes in *Appeal from the New to the Old Whigs* that the House of Lords was "the chief virtual representative of our aristocracy" and "the great ground and pillar of security to the landed interest."[241] Even more, England's "law of primogeniture," was, "with few and inconsiderable exceptions," the "standing law of all our landed inheritance, and which without question has a tendency, and I think a most happy tendency, to preserve a character of consequence, weight, and prevalent influence over others in the whole body of the landed interest," a tradition radicals aimed to destroy.[242] The preservation of private property sustained an element of permanence in a polity, thereby protecting men from the utopian projects of revolutionaries and calming the effusions of speculators.

Burke frames this position by contrasting France with England. What enabled England, unlike France, to flourish commercially without surrendering to an indomitable monied interest was the close integration of its landed interest with its commercial and financial interests. Recall Burke's point in *Third Letter on a Regicide Peace*: England's landed classes did not form a "separate body, as in other countries," but instead had been in "close connexion and union" with the other economic interests in the nation.[243] Hence it had been "spontaneously allowed to lead and direct, and moderate all the rest."[244] Landed property was the foundation of commercial and financial prosperity, not the other way around.

Burke had delivered a similar point years before the outbreak of the French Revolution. In 1765, in *Tracts relating to Popery Laws*, he observed, "[H]ow miserable must that nation be whose frame of polity has disjoined the landing and the trading interests."[245] During a parliamentary debate in 1770 on whether to allow the exportation of malt, wheat flour, and barley, a measure Burke supported, he insisted, "There is no such thing as the landed interest separate from the trading interest. What God has joined together, let no man separate."[246] In a speech in February 1787 assailing the Anglo-French Commercial Treaty of 1786, Burke, according to the *Morning Chronicle*, posited that in Britain, "the Landed Interest, the Monied Interest, and the

---

[240] Langford, *Writings and Speeches*, VIII, 212.   [241] Langford, *Writings and Speeches*, IV, 433.
[242] Langford, *Writings and Speeches*, IV, 433.   [243] Langford, *Writings and Speeches*, IX, 374.
[244] Langford, *Writings and Speeches*, IX, 374–375.
[245] Langford, *Writings and Speeches*, IX, 478.
[246] Wright, *Sir Henry Cavendish's Debates of the House of Commons*, vol. I, 476.

Commercial Interest formed one great partnership, making up through the medium of discount and interest one great national capital."[247]

The moderating character of the landed interest thus prevented England's commercial spirit from succumbing to the designs of unchecked ambition. "Thanks to our sullen resistance to innovation, thanks to the cold sluggishness of our national character, we still bear the stamp of our forefathers," Burke observes in the *Reflections*.[248] In his view, the monied interest joined together to contrive financial schemes at the expense of the people. By contrast, "The very nature of a country life, the very nature of landed property, in all the occupations, and all the pleasures they afford, render combination and arrangement (the sole way of procuring and exerting influence) in a manner impossible amongst country-people," Burke avers. "Combine them by all the art you can, and all the industry, they are always dissolving into individuality."[249] Because England's landed interest tamed the financial appetites of the monied interest, the nation was able to pursue commercial advantage at the same time that it retained its constitutional traditions and moral customs, forging a careful balance between the vigor of enterprise and the fixed composure of landed property.

In the case of the French Revolution, however, the radical victory of the monied interest over the landed interest marked the unhinging of commercial and financial activities from the bolts of land. This triumph was the culmination of a longer process that had developed from the stiffness of French settlement law and the lethargy of the nation's vast landed possessions:

By the ancient usages which prevailed in [France], the general circulation of property, and in particular the mutual convertibility of land into money, and of money into land, had always been a matter of difficulty. Family settlements, rather more general and more strict than they are in England, the *jus retractus*, the great mass of landed property held by the crown, and by a maxim of French law held unalienably, the vast estates of the ecclesiastic corporations, – all these had kept the landed and monied interests more separated in France, less miscible, and the owners of the two distinct species of property not so well disposed to each other as they are in this country [of England].[250]

This is one of the most important arguments of Burke's analysis of the political economy of the French Revolution: one fundamental deformity of the ancien régime was not that it permitted the commercialization of land, but that the traditional inflexibility of French law, and the extravagant possessions of royal and religious institutions, discouraged the landed interest from intermingling with the monied interest. The divisions between these two interests during the French Revolution derived from their growing estrangement in the eighteenth century, leading to the segregation of social orders.

---

[247] Langford, *Writings and Speeches*, IV, 237n2.
[248] Langford, *Writings and Speeches*, VIII, 137.
[249] Langford, *Writings and Speeches*, VIII, 242.
[250] Langford, *Writings and Speeches*, VIII, 158–159.

Burke's argument in the *Reflections* then takes an even more intriguing turn: the landed interest in France, as well as the French people, grew to begrudge the monied interest, and thus was partially responsible for the progressive alienation of that interest under the ancien régime. "The monied property was long looked after on with rather an evil eye by the people. They saw it connected with their distresses, and aggravating them," Burke writes. "It was no less envied by the old landed interests, partly for the same reasons that rendered it obnoxious to the people, but much more so as it eclipsed, by the splendour of an ostentatious luxury, the unendowed pedigrees and naked titles of several among the nobility."[251] The landed interest grew to resent the *nouveaux riches*, jealous of their pretentious lucre and suspicious of their enterprising ambitions.

Burke's following remarks in this passage are even more noticeable because they defend, in a sense, the monied interest against criticisms from the nobility. When the propertied nobility married into the family of the monied interest, even if the wealth of the monied interest had "saved the family from ruin," the landed interest would still vilify it, Burke notes, communicating that the monied interest at times helped preserve the strength of established families in France.[252] Yet the "enmities and heart-burnings" between the two parties gained intensity, even though the mixture of the landed and monied interests was the typical means by which "discord is made to cease, and quarrels are turned into friendship,"[253] a comment hinting at Burke's belief in the possibility of reconciliation between the landed and monied interests.

As a result of the landed interest's suppression of the monied interest, the latter group itself grew indignant. "They felt with resentment an inferiority, the grounds of which they did not acknowledge," Burke explains.[254] Therefore, the monied interest acquired a raw urge to take vengeance upon the landed interest: "There was no measure to which they were not willing to lend themselves, in order to be revenged of the outrages of this rival pride, and to exalt their wealth to what they considered as its natural rank and estimation."[255] The monied interest was poised to strike at the nobility.

Such comments hint at the merging of Burke's interpretation of the political economy of the French Revolution with his psychological analysis of the diffuse impact of wealth in civil society. He is laying blame on the shoulders of the French landed interest for creating such an acute stigma toward the monied interest that the nobility aroused the latter from its slumber, leading it to initiate a radical assault on the landed possessions of the ancien régime and ecclesiastical authorities. Such is one of the most misunderstood aspects of Burke's interpretation of the French Revolution: his censure of the French

[251] Langford, *Writings and Speeches*, VIII, 159.
[252] Langford, *Writings and Speeches*, VIII, 159.
[253] Langford, *Writings and Speeches*, VIII, 159.
[254] Langford, *Writings and Speeches*, VIII, 159.
[255] Langford, *Writings and Speeches*, VIII, 159.

revolutionaries, in the context of his political economy, was not a reflection of his inherent antipathy toward commercial and financial interests; it was, rather, an indication of Burke's belief that France's historical failure to fuse the monied interest with the landed interest aided in stimulating the despotic rise of the former.

Of course, for Burke, the French economy prior to the French Revolution was still far preferable to the revolutionary economy, even if it did discourage miscible relations between the monied and landed interest. Consequently, the National Constituent Assembly's confiscation of church land and selling of *assignats* delivered a blow to the steady edifice of landed property that had provided stability to France's (albeit sluggish) economy under the ancien régime. Not unlike the interests of the British landed aristocracy, the French nobility's struggle to protect their privileges "operates as an instinct to secure property, and to preserve communities in a settled state."[256]

During the Revolution, therefore, the issue for Burke was not that commerce and finance in themselves necessarily corroded the foundations of traditional morality, but that the corrupt integration of commerce and finance with political power – liberated from the soothing forces of land – subverted the political imperatives of moderation and contravened the rights to property. "[B]anks, and circulations, and annuities on lives, and toutines, and perpetual rents, and all the small wares of the shop" were "not to be slighted" in "a settled order of the state."[257] Yet they "are good, but then only good, when they assume the effects of that settled order, and are built upon it."[258] The landed interest furnished this settled order.

The French Nobility under the Ancien Régime

Burke's rendering in the *Reflections* of the weak connection between the landed interest and the monied interest in France discloses another key insight into his interpretation of the French Revolution: even if the former did alienate the latter in the kingdom in the eighteenth century, the propertied aristocracy in general was not in opposition to political and social reform in the late 1700s. "Read their instructions to their representatives," Burke writes, referring to the French nobility. "They breathe the spirit of liberty as warmly, and they recommend reformation as strongly, as any other order. Their privileges relative to contribution were voluntarily surrendered."[259] Indeed, the Vicomte de Noailles and the Duc d'Aiguillon had led efforts to abolish feudalism on

[256] Langford, *Writings and Speeches*, VIII, 187.
[257] Langford, *Writings and Speeches*, VIII, 290.
[258] Langford, *Writings and Speeches*, VIII, 290.
[259] Langford, *Writings and Speeches*, VIII, 184.

August 4, 1789. And Burke noted earlier in the *Reflections* that the ancien régime was open to reform.[260]

Burke's view on the liberal inclinations of the French nobility has been echoed by contemporary scholarship. "The nobility was a reformist elite, if not indeed a revolutionary one," writes Guy Chaussinand-Nogaret, capturing the revisionist turn away from the Marxist interpretation of the French Revolution in the twentieth century, "and in the second half of the eighteenth century it was preparing to press for changes that would break open the constricting straitjacket in which it accused the monarchy of trying to keep the system forever locked."[261] The nobility in many ways demonstrated a greater attraction to economic improvement and technological ingenuity than the lower classes, even if the scope of their projects did not match the scale of the productive activities of the emerging bourgeoisie.[262]

Burke's comments on the seeming disharmony between the landed interest and the monied interest in France warrant further explanation: how could the two groups be as segregated as Burke suggests in the *Reflections* if the former was dedicated to meaningful reform, including technological and industrial advance? Would this fact not indicate that they were closer than he lets on? Yet for Burke, the monied interest was not equivalent to the emerging bourgeoisie, although the two overlapped. The latter, like the French nobility, was open to modernization and improvement. What distinguished the monied interest from other associations was its conscious manipulation of public credit to provoke the bureaucratic enlargement of the French state. In addition, Burke's argument about the separation between the landed interest and the monied interest was a relative one: his point was that their detachment was greater in France than in England, not that they never overlapped under the ancien régime.

The difference between the landed interest and the monied interest, then, was not that one held a greater affinity for reform, but that the first order provided the anchor of stability that allowed commercial and financial activities to blossom with a steady, but not volatile, pace. As Burke observes in the *Reflections*, changing the entire nature and character of a country through total destruction, as French revolutionaries desired to do, is one thing. But, he goes on to say,

At once to preserve and to reform is quite another thing. When the useful parts of an old establishment are kept, and what is superadded is to be fitted to what is retained,

---

[260] "So far from refusing itself to reformation, that government was open, with a censurable degree of facility, to all sorts of projects and projectors on the subject" (Langford, *Writings and Speeches*, VIII, 180).

[261] Guy Chaussinand-Nogaret, *The French Nobility in the Eighteenth Century: From Feudalism to Enlightenment*, trans. William Doyle (Cambridge: Cambridge University Press, 1985), 85. Consult Bossenga, "Divided Nobility," 43–75.

[262] Chaussinand-Nogaret, *French Nobility in the Eighteenth Century*, 84–116.

a vigorous mind, steady, persevering attention, various powers of comparison and combination, and the resources of an understanding fruitful in expedients are to be exercised; they are to be exercised in a continued conflict with the combined force of opposite vices, with the obstinacy that rejects all improvement and the levity that is fatigued and disgusted with everything of which it is in possession.[263]

Preservation and reform require "old establishments" to moderate the excesses of those who seek immediate transformation. Balance and wisdom can counteract the passionate impulses of restless reformers. Just as individuals exercise "circumspection and caution"[264] when changing inanimate matter, Burke continues, they must do so especially when the object of change is a flesh-and-blood human being.

Therefore, the stubborn stability of the landed nobility actually aided ambitious reformers in the pursuit of new projects. "I have never yet seen any plan which has not been mended by the observations of those who were much inferior in understanding to the person who took the lead in the business,"[265] Burke writes in discussing the relationship between the landed aristocrat – who, in his view in this context, was ignorant of the particular undertaking but replete with wisdom, and the innovator, who was knowledgeable about his industry but lacked the virtue of moderation. "By a slow but well-sustained progress, the effect of each step is watched."[266] For the "good or ill success of the first, gives light to us in the second, and so, from light to light, we are conducted through the whole series."[267] Moderate resistance to innovative schemes provides a necessary check to reformers to ensure their enterprising energies do not threaten social order.

In the *Reflections*, Burke argues that the convergence between the landed aristocracy and innovative reformers formed the substructure for real progress that could endure over time. There was no inherent tension between the two interests: "We see, that the parts of the system do not clash," he states. "The evils latent in the most promising contrivances are provided for as they arise"[268]; and as we – Burke is speaking of Englishmen – confront the utility and the disadvantage of the system, "We compensate, we reconcile, we balance. We are enabled to unite into a consistent whole the various anomalies and contending principles that are found in the minds and affairs of men."[269] The interactions between the landed interest and the commercial interest produce a careful harmony, balancing and correcting one another when one interest tipped too far on the side of either undisciplined

---

[263] Langford, *Writings and Speeches*, VIII, 216.
[264] Langford, *Writings and Speeches*, VIII, 217.
[265] Langford, *Writings and Speeches*, VIII, 217.
[266] Langford, *Writings and Speeches*, VIII, 217.
[267] Langford, *Writings and Speeches*, VIII, 217.
[268] Langford, *Writings and Speeches*, VIII, 217.
[269] Langford, *Writings and Speeches*, VIII, 217.

reform or slothful inertia. Progress can be achieved and sustained when the two interests maintain this equipoise.

Burke's reflections on this relationship illustrate the application of his broader philosophy of gradual reform to his specific conception of political economy in the *Reflections*. For Burke, the growth of civilization requires a healthy degree of reverence for the achievements of the past: "People will not look forward to posterity, who never look backward to their ancestors."[270] But ancient customs and habits leave room for steady amelioration. "[T]he idea of inheritance furnishes a sure principle of conservation, and a sure principle of transmission; without at all excluding a principle improvement," he continues. "It leaves acquisition free; but it secures what it acquires."[271] Meaningful reform of political economy does not call for the destruction of property; instead, it summons the progressive expansion of opportunity to own property and pursue commercial undertakings. Speculative enterprise should not be denied, yet it should be disciplined by the softening presence of the landed aristocracy. Incremental change should guide not just the preservation of political institutions or constitutions but also activities relating to land, commerce, and finance.

Burke does not blindly endorse every aspect of the landed nobility's predominance of political authority. He even admits near the end of the *Reflections* that some "usages have been abolished on just grounds"[272] by the French Revolution. But he qualifies this statement by remarking that "[t]hey who destroy every thing certainly will remove some grievance,"[273] and by claiming that the perpetuation of such usages would not have harmed the "happiness and prosperity"[274] of the state. Burke's discussion of these abuses in the *Reflections* is lacking, however.

Overall, the delicate concrescence of the landed interest and commercial interest preserved the constitutional liberties of the people. "To form a *free government*; that is, to temper together these opposite elements of liberty and restraint in one consistent work, requires much thought, deep reflection, and a sagacious, powerful, and combining mind," he writes.[275] Free government was the distilled outcome of freedom *and* restraint: the freedom to "let go the rein" and permit people to act without guidance; and restraint in the form of government, which should simply "[s]ettle the seat of power" and "teach obedience."[276]

Therefore, the landed interest remained the guardian of liberty as well as the purveyor of stability. Recall one of the initial quotations in this book's

---

[270] Langford, *Writings and Speeches*, VIII, 83.
[271] Langford, *Writings and Speeches*, VIII, 83–84.
[272] Langford, *Writings and Speeches*, VIII, 292.
[273] Langford, *Writings and Speeches*, VIII, 292.
[274] Langford, *Writings and Speeches*, VIII, 292.
[275] Langford, *Writings and Speeches*, VIII, 291.
[276] Langford, *Writings and Speeches*, VIII, 291.

Introduction, as expressed by Burke in the *Reflections*: "We have an inheritable crown; an inheritable peerage; and an house of commons and a people inheriting privileges, franchises, and liberties, from a long line of ancestors."[277] Burke's point is not to defend the elite interests of the few at the expense of the many, but rather to stress that the preservation of liberty for all social ranks demanded the retention and modification of inherited traditions. In his view, this social order could not prevail unless the element of restraint inherent in the landed aristocracy was able to cool the passions of unbridled freedom.

This verdict clinches one of Burke's most important insights into the general compatibility between liberty and restraint: he does not locate the two imperatives into self-regulating spheres throughout the *Reflections*, as the conservation of one depended on the aid of the other. The reconciliation between the landed interest and the monied interest was the shining achievement of the British constitution. In addition, their self-perpetuating unity thus occasioned a far more constructive environment for liberty than the unshackled license of the French Revolution. The Revolution, Burke states, augured a "despotic democracy" whose leaders triumphed over "the principles of a British constitution."[278] Under the British constitution, Burke writes near the end of the *Reflections*, "Our people will find employment enough for a truly patriotic, free, and independent spirit, in guarding what they possess from violation."[279] He insists that this constitution stood on something that France's revolutionary schemes did not: "firm ground."[280]

---

[277] Langford, *Writings and Speeches*, VIII, 83.
[278] Langford, *Writings and Speeches*, VIII, 184.
[279] Langford, *Writings and Speeches*, VIII, 292.
[280] Langford, *Writings and Speeches*, VIII, 293.

12

The Real Rights of Men, Manners, and the Limits of Transactional Exchange

> [T]he state ought not to be considered as nothing better than a partnership agreement in a trade of pepper and coffee, callico or tobacco, or some other such low concern, to be taken up for a little temporary interest, and to be dissolved by the fancy of the parties.[1]
>
> Edmund Burke, *Reflections on the Revolution in France*, 1790

12.1 THE REAL RIGHTS OF MEN AND THE MENACE OF FRENCH REVOLUTIONARY EQUALITY

Burke does not simply issue a defense of the right to own landed property in the *Reflections*. He also makes a determined effort in the writing to contend that men possessed the right to reap the benefits of their labor. After berating French revolutionaries for justifying their abstract rights claims on the basis of spurious metaphysics, Burke puts forth a different conception of freedom, or what he called the "*real* rights of men"[2]:

In denying their false claims of right, I do not mean to injure those which are real, and are such as their pretended rights would totally destroy. If civil society be made for the advantage of man, all the advantages for which it is made become his right. It is an institution of beneficence; and law itself is only beneficence acting by a rule. Men have a right to live by that rule; they have a right to justice, as between their fellows, whether their fellows are in public function or in ordinary occupation. They have a right to the fruits of their industry and to the means of making their industry fruitful. They have a right to the acquisitions of their parents, to the nourishment and improvement of their offspring, to instruction in life, and to consolation in death.[3]

---

[1] Langford, *Writings and Speeches*, VIII, 147.   [2] Langford, *Writings and Speeches*, VIII, 109.
[3] Langford, *Writings and Speeches*, VIII, 109–110.

Among other rights, men hold the right to use what they produce and purchase; the right to engage in industry according to their desires, and against encroachment by others; and the right to inherit the property of their parents. Burke is declaring his firm belief in the right to economic freedom, including the right to build and acquire wealth. In painting a contrast with the French Revolution's "false claims" of right, he suggests further that these rights were not speculative propositions but tangible expressions of concrete liberties that emerged throughout the ages.

Burke conveys his approval of the right to produce and keep one's fruits elsewhere in the *Reflections*: "Whatever each man can separately do, without trespassing upon others, he has a right to do for himself."[4] As long as man does not usurp the rights of others, he preserves the right to produce freely. This invocation of commercial liberty veers toward a Lockean conception of a liberal polity – an ironic convergence, considering that Burke, in the *Reflections*, scolds Richard Price for adopting the Lockean reasoning that the Glorious Revolution was based on the abstract right of the people to rebel against unjust governments. Additionally, the writing in general is a broadside against Lockean contractarian thinking.

We may, then, propose a distinction: Burke was hostile to Price's and Locke's historiography of the Glorious Revolution (and abstract conceptions of politics and man overall), but his statements on the right to produce in the *Reflections* do overlap with Locke's defense of liberty in *Two Treatises*. This is not to equate Locke with Burke, but to claim that the notion of a right to industry is adopted by both Locke and Burke as a bedrock of their respective economic thought. For both thinkers maintained that the divine gift of nature was granted to man to exploit for material advantage.[5]

Burke's list of rights transcended claims over the private right to labor and accumulate, however. He also indicates that members of civil society possess the right to the "nourishment and improvement of their offspring"; to "instruction in life"; and to "consolation in death."[6] Such rights illustrated Burke's belief that human beings did not exist as solitary individuals but comprised part of a wider social community, one that held its own attendant rights and responsibilities to its members. Burke is ambiguous whether this community or the parents themselves within it carried the right to nourish and improve their offspring.

But the final two rights – instruction in life and consolation in death – suggest salient roles for members in the community, including parents, to educate children and to honor the deceased. The real rights of mankind, then, were not simply negative rights that prevented others from obstructing man's

---

[4] Langford, *Writings and Speeches*, VIII, 110.
[5] Burke and Locke invoked the same popular Bible verse, Psalms 115:16, to justify man's industrious exploitation of the earth. For Burke, see Langford, *Writings and Speeches*, IX, 515. For Locke, see Locke, *Two Treatises*, 286.
[6] Langford, *Writings and Speeches*, VIII, 110.

individual liberty to produce, but also included the affirmative rights to receive proper religious instruction and education and to be treated with dignity. These rights could only be realized through social associations.

Revolutionary Equality

Burke, in the *Reflections*, passes to a discussion on how French revolutionaries' vision of equality threatened economic liberty. Man "has a right to a fair portion of all which society, with all its combinations of skill and force, can do in his favour."[7] To the modern ear, his use of "fair" immediately evokes notions of government-mandated wealth redistribution programs seeking to establish a more equal society. Yet Burke follows this comment by arguing something different. In a statement that strikes the essence of his economic thought and political theory, he states, "In this partnership all men have equal rights; but not to equal things."[8]

Burke here is blasting one of the foremost tenets of French ideology, which was fueled by the principle of equality embedded in the *Declaration of the Rights of Man*: the abstract right to equality demanded that the government confiscate and reapportion property in order to reduce material disparities and create an egalitarian society. This ideal was motivated by the French Revolution's conception of an abstract state of nature, an environment of perfect equality stripped bare of distinctions and differences among men. For revolutionaries, the ancien régime's arbitrary system of revenue collection – and its struggle to facilitate the economic conditions under which the French people could produce and consume sufficient provisions – offended this vision by aggravating socioeconomic inequalities, thereby corrupting the intrinsic constitution of man. Therefore, the expropriation and redistribution of wealth was justified to fulfill a theoretical social contract between the revolutionary government and the French people that aimed to recover man's natural condition of equality.

Burke was not convinced by this rationale for state coercion. In his judgment, the right to produce did not translate into a right to equality based on wealth, or into a right to seize private wealth. He writes:

He that has but five shillings in the partnership has as good a right to it as he that has five hundred pounds has to his larger proportion. But he has not a right to an equal dividend in the product of the joint stock; and as to the share of power, authority, and direction which each individual ought to have in the management of the state, that I must deny to be amongst the direct original rights of man in civil society; for I have in my contemplation the civil social man, and no other. It is a thing to be settled by convention.[9]

---

[7] Langford, *Writings and Speeches*, VIII, 110.   [8] Langford, *Writings and Speeches*, VIII, 110.
[9] Langford, *Writings and Speeches*, VIII, 110.

The basis of true economic equality is process, not outcome. Liberty is a right that should be equally protected for all members in a commonwealth. While men have the equal right to use what they produce, however, they do not have the right to possess the same amount of wealth as one's neighbor.[10] (Nor do they have an equal right to rule, Burke suggests.)

In addition to equality of process, this principle reflected the conception of proportional equality: a man who holds five shillings has the right to use those five shillings – but not the shillings of others. A man who holds five hundred pounds has a right to use those five hundred pounds – but not the pounds of others. In both cases, the individual's right to own and use his private property is locked and secured – as is the right of other members of civil society to dispense their own wealth as they see fit.

Five years after the *Reflections*, Burke remarked that the broad diffusion of wealth in Europe prior to the French Revolution stimulated the anxieties and jealousies of ambitious men, who were disturbed that the spread of general opulence did not satisfy their visions of equality. "Men of talent began to compare, in the partition of the common stock of public prosperity, the proportions of the dividends, with the merits of the claimants," he wrote in a letter to his friend William Elliott. "As usual, they found their portion not equal to their estimate (or perhaps to the public estimate) of their own worth."[11] For Burke, the appalling manifestation of this covetous and resentful attitude was the campaign to impose equality in theory – but tyranny in fact – on the French people during the Revolution.

We must remind ourselves, however, that a corresponding moral duty accompanied Burke's notion of the individual right to use one's riches. His summoning of the "Gentleman of Fortune" in the *Reformer*, and his belief that the prosperity of the affluent derived from the toil of common laborers, denoted a conception of paternalism that called for voluntary charity in times of want. Men of indigence did not hold the right to seize the fortunes of others; yet men of means did bear the ethical obligation to provide support for the poor. Portraying Burke's economic thought as a defense of individual liberty is incomplete, then, without taking note of his heavy stress on the broader social responsibilities of those in possession of wealth.

Burke's economic analysis of the French Revolution did not rest simply on his advocacy of individual property rights. His belief in the right to property applied to corporate bodies as well as to individuals, as outlined by his previous remarks asserting the prescriptive property rights of the Gallican Church. Burke remarks critically in the *Reflections* that French confiscators allege that "ecclesiastics are fictitious persons, creatures of the state; whom at pleasure they may destroy, and of course limit and modify in every particular;

---

[10] This quotation also reiterates Burke's opposition to the idea of political equality in the national legislature.

[11] Burke to William Elliott, 26 May 1795, in Langford, *Writings and Speeches*, IX, 39.

that the goods they possess are not properly theirs, but belong to the state which created the fiction."[12] By invoking "fiction," Burke signals his acute disapproval of the idea that corporate bodies were fabricated entities whose property was unworthy of state protection. "Corporate bodies are immortal for the good of the members" he states, referring to nations as well as to churches and families.[13] And corporate institutions such as the Church, like landed men of wealth, held the moral duty to care for the impoverished.

In addition, Burke asserts in his *Remarks on the Policy of the Allies* (1793) that "no one can be so very blind" to believe the French monarchy could be supported "upon any other basis than that of its property, *corporate and individual*."[14] He then links the stability of these forms of property with the perpetuation of social union in France. The monarchy could not "enjoy a moment's permanence or security upon any scheme of things, which sets aside all the antient corporate capacities and distinctions of the kingdom, and subverts the whole fabrick of its antient laws and usages"[15] in order to form a polity based on the "supposed *Rights of Man, and the absolute equality of the human race*."[16]

For Burke, then, one abhorrent consequence of the revolutionary attempt to thrust the idea of abstract equality upon French civil society was the endangerment of mobile and immobile property rights. In a parliamentary speech in December 1792, at a time when the British government was debating how to respond to French territorial ambitions, Burke said he could not hear "without emotions of horror, the application made of [the rights] to property in frequent discussions on the French revolution."[17] He continued: "It was this kind of application which caused most of the horrors of the French revolution."[18]

The naked urge to equalize society by redistributing wealth targeted ecclesiastical and aristocratic property in particular. "When once the commonwealth has established the estates of the church as property, it can, consistently, hear nothing of the more or the less," Burke explains. "Too much and too little are treason against property."[19] Yet the revolutionary belief that one body held an excessive amount of property, and that other bodies did not possess a sufficient amount, was grounds to confiscate the estates of one to give to the other. In *Speech on the Army Estimates*, Burke asks MPs in the House of Commons to consider whether they "would like to have their mansions pulled down and pillaged, their persons abused, insulted, and destroyed; their title deeds brought out and burned before their faces" simply because they were "born gentlemen, and men of property."[20] Radical movements, in general, were

---

[12] Langford, *Writings and Speeches*, VIII, 156.   [13] Langford, *Writings and Speeches*, VIII, 189.
[14] Langford, *Writings and Speeches*, VIII, 459.   [15] Langford, *Writings and Speeches*, VIII, 459.
[16] Langford, *Writings and Speeches*, VIII, 459.   [17] Langford, *Writings and Speeches*, IV, 519.
[18] Langford, *Writings and Speeches*, IV, 519.   [19] Langford, *Writings and Speeches*, VIII, 153.
[20] Langford, *Writings and Speeches*, IV, 290.

especially hazardous to property: "Revolutions are favorable to confiscation; and it is impossible to know under what obnoxious names the next confiscations will be authorized," he writes in the *Reflections*.[21]

Burke's position – the belief that "too much" and "too little" are "treason against property" – illustrates a core premise of his philosophy of political economy: the drive for perfect equality through schemes of wealth redistribution compromises the very social order that allows civil society to endure and flourish in the first place. In the case of the French Revolution, it cracked the institutions of, or provided support for, the French monarchy, church, nobility, law, revenue, army, navy, commerce, arts, and manufactures.[22] And radical egalitarianism empowered the government to extinguish the right to property in French society. It "level[ed] all ranks, orders, and distinctions in the state; and utterly to destroy property, not more by their acts than in their principles," Burke writes in *Appeal from the New to the Old Whigs*.[23] It sunk that anchor of constitutional government, landed property, which offered stability to political communities and checked the tyrannical ambitions of the monarchy. The lust to equalize, therefore, carried consequences far beyond economic considerations: it put in jeopardy the essential political foundations of a community.

Still, these economic consequences were ruinous in themselves. As Burke observes in the *Reflections*, the French campaign to equalize society corroded the principles of market activity as well as prescriptive property rights. It led to "industry without vigour," "commerce expiring," and "the revenue unpaid," among a host of vicious effects.[24] This social and economic disorder created "a people impoverished," not to mention a "church pillaged."[25] Recall also Burke's statement that he would support the changing circumstances in France as long as he could be certain that the French citizen would be spared the "free use of his industry and his faculties."[26] Burke's belief that the French Revolution threatened the country's commercial growth conveys that the *Reflections* was not a mere defense of a sluggish hereditary aristocracy, but also a strong, if oblique, statement in favor of market activity.

Such a view is at fundamental odds with the Marxian view that the French Revolution was a bourgeois uprising against the established feudal order. Karl Marx wrote in *The Eighteenth Brumaire of Louis Bonaparte* (1852) that the "heroes as well as the factions and the general mass of the old French revolution, accomplished, in Roman dress and with Roman phrases, the taste of their time, the release and establishment of modern *bourgeois* society."[27] This view dominated the interpretation of the French Revolution for the first half of the

---

[21] Langford, *Writings and Speeches*, VIII, 204. [22] Langford, *Writings and Speeches*, IV, 285.
[23] Langford, *Writings and Speeches*, IV, 399. [24] Langford, *Writings and Speeches*, VIII, 89.
[25] Langford, *Writings and Speeches*, VIII, 89.
[26] Burke to Mons. Dupont, October 1789, in William and Bourke, *Works and Correspondence of the Right Honourable Edmund Burke*, vol. I, 559.
[27] Kamenka, *Portable Karl Marx*, 288.

twentieth century.[28] Similarly, conventional accounts of the *Reflections*, which have their roots in anti-Burke pamphlets of the 1790s, impose a division between his seemingly reactionary defense of tradition and hierarchy and the progressive and reformist inclinations of the bourgeoisie and the poor.[29]

This assumption demands fundamental rethinking. Burke's praise of "tradition," to the extent that it can be called that, included a *conscious affirmation of market economies*, tempered by the moderating forces of landed property, as a mark of social order and commercial vigor. This point cannot be emphasized enough. As his previously-mentioned comments demonstrate, Burke believed that the French Revolution brought about economic ruin beyond the violation of landed property rights: the upsetting of supply and demand laws, the discouragement of industry, the obstruction of trade, the debasing of the currency, and ultimately the impoverishment of a people, or what he called "an oppressive degrading servitude."[30] In *First Letter on a Regicide Peace*, Burke describes revolutionary France as a nation "with an annihilated revenue, with defaced manufactures, with a ruined commerce, with an uncultivated and half depopulated country, with a discontented, distressed, enslaved, and famished people."[31] Rather than being a reactionary eulogy of feudal traditions, then, the *Reflections* in many ways was a defense of the possibilities for commercial and civil progress – if the landed interest and the monied interest were carefully integrated in a manner that permitted the growth of commerce resistant to revolutionary destruction.

Burke's approval of market economies in the *Reflections* calls into question Emma Rothschild's argument that a noticeable discrepancy separates his positive conception of the state in the writing from his negative view of government in *Thoughts and Details*. This division reflected "Burke's changing economical views," according to Rothschild: Burke's "view of government was more positive [in the *Reflections*] than [Adam] Smith's; with respect, for example, to the good commercial consequences of national expenditure on bridges, religion, and public reverence."[32] Yet "[b]y 1795,"

---

[28] See Gary Kates ed., *The French Revolution: Recent Debates & New Controversies* (London and New York: Routledge, 1998), 1–20.

[29] Langford, *Writings and Speeches*, VIII, 15–36. See, most recently, Robin, *Reactionary Mind*. See also Steven Blakemore's account of the critical reactions to the *Reflections* in *Intertextual War: Edmund Burke and the French Revolution in the Writings of Mary Wollstonecraft, Thomas Paine, and James Mackintosh* (Madison and Teaneck, NJ: Fairleigh Dickinson University Press, 1997). Consult O'Brien, *Great Melody*, 605–615 for Conor Cruise O'Brien's exchange with Isaiah Berlin over whether Burke was a reactionary. Berlin conceded O'Brien's position that Burke should not be characterized as such. In popular journalism, see Christopher Hitchens, "Reactionary Prophet," *The Atlantic*, April 2004, www.theatlantic.com/magazine/archive/2004/04/reactionary-prophet/302914/. For a concise bibliography of writings on this matter, see Bourke, *Empire & Revolution*, 745n22.

[30] Langford, *Writings and Speeches*, VIII, 290.   [31] Langford, *Writings and Speeches*, IX, 191.

[32] Rothschild, "Adam Smith and Conservative Economics," 86.

she continues, "Burke had become doubtful about what he now called government 'interference,'" as exemplified by *Thoughts and Details*.[33]

Such remarks do not accurately capture the relation between the *Reflections* and *Thoughts and Details*. Burke did not swing from an advocate of heavy government involvement in the economy in the former to an eighteenth-century avatar of proto-libertarianism in the latter. The doubt he conveyed in *Thoughts and Details* was on the idea that government should meddle in the internal provisions trade and dictate the terms of agricultural employment contracts. Burke maintained this attitude throughout his entire public life (the corn bounty excepted) and throughout the pages of the *Reflections*, as displayed by his attack on the French Revolution for destroying the commerce and revenue of France and by his defense of the private right to industry. Burke's commentary on the political economy of the Revolution was thus harmonious with his opposition to state intervention in the grain trade; in both instances, the appearance of abstract reason in practical market life threatened the operation of supply and demand principles.[34] We must also remember that Burke, in *Thoughts and Details*, did carve out an important role for the government in supporting religion, the magistracy, and the military; generating revenue; and granting corporations legal recognition.[35] The memorial thereby represents firm continuities with his prior support for market liberty in the *Reflections* and elsewhere, and also contains similar exceptions to this belief in such writings.

Population Growth and National Wealth

Burke proffers two straightforward measures in the *Reflections* to strengthen his conclusion that the French Revolution thwarted progress. First, in using both Necker's calculations and Richard Price's extrapolations of Necker's data, Burke submits that the population of France had increased under the ancien régime,[36] an assertion that has proven to be true.[37] Burke did acknowledge the "faults and defects" of the old government,[38] imperfections that he had outlined more than twenty years prior in the *Observations*, as examined in Chapter 7. Yet even if the ancien régime's policies were not seamlessly conducive to the exercise of free industry, the growth in population must have indicated some state accommodation for commercial opportunity. "[T]hat decried government," Burke writes, "could not have obstructed, most probably it

---

[33] Rothschild, "Adam Smith and Conservative Economics," 86.
[34] As Rothschild does note, Burke in both writings maintained an allegiance to the role of selective state involvement in English society, including the establishment of religion. Of course, Smith also supported public investment in infrastructure. See Smith, *Wealth of Nations*, vol. II, 723–731.
[35] Langford, *Writings and Speeches*, IX, 143.   [36] Langford, *Writings and Speeches*, VIII, 177.
[37] Riley, *Seven Years War and the Old Regime in France*, 5–6.
[38] Langford, *Writings and Speeches*, VIII, 175.

favoured, the operation of those causes (whatever they were) whether of nature in the soil, or in habits of industry among the people, which has produced so large a number of the species throughout that whole kingdom, and exhibited in some particular places such prodigies of population."[39] This is a subtle but important theme in Burke's political economy: much as he associated population growth with productive industry in his speech on the Poor Removals Bill in 1774,[40] Burke in the *Reflections* is linking the expansion of the French population with economic development – and, as he notes soon after in the writing, the decline in population with commercial ruin.[41]

The second sign of progress Burke cites in the *Reflections* was the growth of national wealth. Burke, again invoking Necker's data, remarks that France had accumulated an increasing amount of specie throughout the century.[42] In his judgment, however, the possession of gold and silver was not the only measure of public wealth, a conclusion that carries intriguing resonance with his criticism of the Spanish Empire's acquisition of gold in the *Account*, and with his disapproval of balance of trade theory in the *Observations*. Instead the deeper sources of specie could be located in the springs of collective industry, which could not blossom under a government intent on strangling the people's liberties. "Causes thus powerful to acquire and to retain, cannot be found in discouraged industry, insecure property, and a positively destructive government," Burke states.[43] The ancien régime was not such a "destructive government," akin to Turkish despotism: for Burke, the state could not have inhibited the French economy *too much* because it, at the very least, furnished an environment that witnessed the rise in commercial activities necessary to purchase gold and silver for the Royal Treasury.

Six years later, Burke insisted that the fall of the French monarchy "was far from being preceded by any exterior symptoms of decline." And he dismissed the argument that financial instabilities were the source of revolutionary zeal. "The financial difficulties were only pretexts and instruments of those who accomplished the ruin of that Monarchy," Burke writes in *First Letter on a Regicide Peace*. "They were not the causes of it."[44] Contrary to the theatrical utterances of French demagogues, the ancien régime was neither a tyranny nor an unprosperous nation.

Burke infuses his survey of French national progress in the *Reflections* with his imaginative rhetoric, reminiscent of his greatest speeches on India. The French kingdom was characterized, among various traits, by "the multitude and opulence of her cities; the useful magnificence of her spacious high roads

---

[39] Langford, *Writings and Speeches*, VIII, 178.
[40] "Wealth Redistribution and Equality in *Thoughts and Details*," Chapter 3.
[41] Langford, *Writings and Speeches*, VIII, 182. "Already the population of Paris has so declined . . . It is said . . . that an hundred thousand people are out of employment in that city."
[42] Langford, *Writings and Speeches*, VIII, 179.   [43] Langford, *Writings and Speeches*, VIII, 179.
[44] Langford, *Writings and Speeches*, IX, 190.

and bridges; ... the excellence of her manufactures and fabrics ... ; the grand foundations of charity, public and private."[45] Let us concede that Burke's larger point holds true: relative to other nations, including European nations, France was a wealthy kingdom at the time.

Nevertheless, Burke's description of the social and economic conditions of France in these passages suffers from a lack of nuance. Areas with access to navigable waterways and foreign trading networks certainly witnessed commercial improvement in the eighteenth century, but the domestic condition of France remained visibly worse. "[M]ost of Louis XVI's subjects lived in the interior," William Doyle writes, "where communications were poor, economic life sluggish, and such improvements as good harvests had brought in mid-century were being eroded by climatic deterioration and an inexorably rising population."[46] Poverty in the countryside was a glaring blemish of the ancien régime. Even though Burke acknowledged the government's abuses, his portrayal of France's national opulence failed to sufficiently take note of the bitter reality of French indigence in many local communities. To the extent that such conditions account for the vehemence of the rhetoric of the revolution, and of the violence of some of its episodes, it is a cause to which Burke's *Reflections* struggles to do justice.

Disparities in Wealth

Still, by spreading the belief that the only legitimate political economy of the country was one based on equality of wealth, French revolutionaries, according to Burke, shook the foundations of acquisition that enabled men to pursue economic opportunity in France, even if they could not attain the riches of the hereditary aristocracy:

The means of acquisition are prior in time and in arrangement. Good order is the foundation of all good things. To be enabled to acquire, the people, without being servile, must be tractable and obedient. The magistrate must have his reverence, the laws their authority. The body of the people must not find the principles of natural subordination by art rooted out of their minds. They must respect that property of which they cannot partake. They must labour to obtain what by labour can be obtained; and when they find, as they commonly do, the success disproportioned to the endeavour, they must be taught their consolation in the final proportions of eternal justice. Of this consolation, whoever deprives them, deadens their industry, and strikes at the root of all acquisition as of all conservation. He that does this is the cruel oppressor, the merciless enemy of the poor and wretched; at the same time that by his wicked speculations he exposes the fruits of successful industry, and the accumulations of fortune, to the plunder of the negligent, the disappointed, and the unprosperous.[47]

---

[45] Langford, *Writings and Speeches*, VIII, 179–180.
[46] Doyle, *Oxford History of the French Revolution*, 13–14.
[47] Langford, *Writings and Speeches*, VIII, 290.

The people must accept that disparities in wealth will persist in civil society, and that all men have the right to private property. But these realities do not wholly suppress the opportunities of the middle class and lower social orders to obtain the means for economic advance. Quite the opposite: only when revolutionaries indoctrinate men into thinking that all inequalities are unjust do they "deade[n]" the "industry" of men, and "strik[e]" at the "root of all acquisition." An acknowledgment of the mixed varieties of civil society preserves the conditions for production and trade, because it draws a thick line around each person's personal possessions and acquisitions of wealth. Burke's comments, we should note, also volunteer to the poor the comfort of the thought of an afterlife, disclosing a quietist tinge reflective of eighteenth-century attitudes toward consolation. In the context of his economic thought, Burke's lesson, reduced to its essence, is that men should not lament inequalities as long as liberty is preserved, for some men will always possess more than others. "The characteristic essence of property, formed out of the combined principles of its acquisition and conservation," he writes in the *Reflections*, "is to be *unequal*."[48]

Let us be clear: Burke is defending the interests of the poor, as well as the rich, in these comments. In his view, the French crusade for absolutely equality, kindled in part by its speculative adventures in *assignats*, offended the principles of property rights, both mobile and immobile, that secured the means of gain for different social classes. The scheme to usurp and redistribute wealth, Burke remarks, sacrificed "successful industry" and the "accumulations of fortune" to the arbitrary powers of men. As he says in his *Speech on the Army Estimates*, the revolutionaries, by subsuming the clergy and aristocracy into the National Assembly, "laid the axe to the root of all property,"[49] a consequence further fueled by the radical egalitarian energies of commoners in the Third Estate. The fruits of those who were diligent and prosperous were seized by many who were unindustrious and covetous. For Burke, markets could not function when the imposition of absolute equality on a people disrupted the principles of production and consumption. Yet the French Revolution militated against this idea; it placed in danger the property rights of all – not just those of the nobility and clergy.

The Perils of Perfection in an Imperfect World

Accordingly, the pursuit of equality did not actually result in equality. This insight is essential to understanding Burke's conception of the relationship between politics and economics. From his perspective, the goal of establishing social and economic equality was a futile quest to create a perfect society in an imperfect world. As Burke insists in the *Reflections*, "those who attempt to

---

[48] Langford, *Writings and Speeches*, VIII, 102.   [49] Langford, *Writings and Speeches*, IV, 289.

level, never equalize."[50] The state's effort to level social orders will fail to achieve its aim of eliminating distinctions in civil society.

Why is this the case? We can begin to grasp Burke's frame of mind on the matter by referring back to *A Vindication of Natural Society*, in which Burke mocked Lord Bolingbroke's argument that a return to natural religion would serve as a corrective to the supposed corruptions of "Artificial Society," composed of political and religious institutions. Written from the perspective of a "Noble Writer" attracted to Bolingbroke's brand of deistic rationalism, the *Vindication* suggests that the variety of human differences in civil society reflected natural disparities among man, which a revival of natural society could not remove. This principle applied to politics: "[T]his artificial Division of Mankind, into separate Societies, is a perpetual Source in itself of Hatred and Dissention among them."[51] Burke is deriding Bolingbroke's belief that political factions were the cause of human misery.

But Burke also summons such reasoning in the case of inequalities in wealth. "The most obvious Division of Society is into Rich and Poor," the Noble Writer declares.[52] "The whole Business of the Poor is to administer to the Idleness, Folly, and Luxury of the Rich; and that of the Rich, in return, is to find the best Methods of confirming the Slavery and increasing the Burthens of the Poor."[53] The apparent evils of civil society sentenced the many to harsh labor:

I suppose that there are in *Great-Britain* upwards of an hundred thousand People employed in Lead, Tin, Iron, Copper, and Coal Mines; these unhappy Wretches scarce ever see the Light of the Sun; they are buried in the Bowels of the Earth . . . they have their Health miserably impaired, and their Lives cut short, by being perpetually confined in the close Vapour of these malignant Minerals.[54]

Even more were "tortured without Remission by the suffocating Smoak, intense Fires, and constant Drudgery necessary in refining and managing the Products of those Mines."[55]

The interpretive challenge of the *Vindication* stems from the book's tendency to blend Burke's ridicule of Bolinstems from the book'sgbroke's thought with plausible arguments in themselves highlighting the imperfections of civil society, making it difficult to separate Burke's derision of Bolingbroke from the Noble Writer's own beliefs. The comments quoted here are an apt example. Carefully read, they are not an attack on the industrializing character of Britain's economy, but on the pretense that a recovery of natural society would relieve men of the many burdens of civil society, such as human toil.

For Burke, however, toil was a reflection of man's needs for food and shelter. Consequently, divisions of labor and social function developed naturally in civil society, exhibited by the incongruities between diligent laborers and the

---

[50] Langford, *Writings and Speeches*, VIII, 100.   [51] Langford, *Writings and Speeches*, I, 153.
[52] Langford, *Writings and Speeches*, I, 177.   [53] Langford, *Writings and Speeches*, I, 177.
[54] Langford, *Writings and Speeches*, I, 177.   [55] Langford, *Writings and Speeches*, I, 178.

ostentatious rich. Burke exaggerates these disparities to further scorn the presumption that political society was the sole source of human pain: "The lower Part broken and ground down by the most cruel Oppression; and the Rich by their artificial Method of Life bringing worse Evils on themselves, than their Tyranny could possibly inflict on those below them."[56]

Yet, according to the Noble Writer, human sufferings and distresses of civil society could be remedied by a return to nature:

Very different is the Prospect of the Natural State. Here there are no Wants which Nature gives, and in this State Men can be sensible of no other Wants, which are not to be supplied by a very moderate Degree of Labour; therefore there is no Slavery. Neither is there any Luxury, because no single Man can supply the Materials of it, Life is simple, and therefore it is happy.[57]

Burke is ridiculing the idea that man's natural state was a condition free from want, or at least a condition in which man's wants could not be met by modest effort. Earlier in the *Vindication*, the Noble Writer admitted that the state of nature was not stripped of inconveniences.[58] But the logical conclusion of Bolingbroke's call to revive natural religion, Burke insinuates in these comments, was the formation of a community liberated from human misery, and from riches. According to Bolingbroke's vision of natural society, the simplicities of life would make man happy.

Burke's derision of Bolingbroke's philosophy holds at least two important implications for his attack in the *Reflections* on the idea of abstract equality. First, for Burke, the French mission to perfect the human condition neglected to confront the inherent constraints and limits of man's real nature. Want and vice could not be removed from man's constitution because man was a flawed creature who required food and shelter to survive. Second, man's natural state was in many ways a state in which the divisions and disparities of civil society slowly emerged from great variances in human desires, faculties, and preferences.

Therefore, all human associations naturally encompassed individuals of different backgrounds and abilities. Some may achieve distinction or eminence, and others may not. "In all societies, consisting of various descriptions of citizens, some description must be uppermost," Burke states in the *Reflections*.[59] An aristocracy naturally pulls away from the commoners by setting moral standards and pursuing the common good in the legislature.

---

[56] Langford, *Writings and Speeches*, I, 180.   [57] Langford, *Writings and Speeches*, I, 180–181.

[58] Langford, *Writings and Speeches*, I, 138. "In the State of Nature, without question, Mankind was subjected to many and great Inconveniences."

[59] Langford, *Writings and Speeches*, VIII, 100. Burke also noted in the *Reflections* that creating jurisdictions through geometric calculation offended the realities of human diversity. "It was evident, that the goodness of the soil, the number of the people, their wealth, and the largeness of their contribution, made such infinite variations between square and square as to render mensuration a ridiculous standard of power in the commonwealth, and equality in geometry

Through education and reflection, they acquire virtue and wisdom, capable of recognizing and reconciling the vast complexities of civil relations. "To stand upon such elevated ground as to be enabled to take a large view of the widespread and infinitely diversified combinations of men and affairs in a large society," Burke writes in *Appeal from the New to the Old Whigs*, was one essential mark of a natural aristocracy.[60] This natural aristocracy, in his judgment, also accommodated merchants, who distinguished themselves from the masses by exercising their ingenious capacities and commercial virtues in the pursuit of wealth.[61]

The ideological push for equality, however, was a gross affront to the idea that natural distinctions emerged among men and women in civil society. Hence the French revolutionaries rejected nature: "The levellers therefore only change and pervert the natural order of things."[62] In Burke's view, the naturally forming hierarchy of man exposed the French Revolution's idea of equality to be a naked and shallow concept, divorced from a historical reality that illuminated the infinite varieties of human beings. An attempt to eliminate distinctions among men would be an attempt to eliminate man.

Furthermore, it would eliminate civil society. French notions of equality that aspired to remove human wants and vices symbolized the radical culmination of the rationalistic excesses of Bolingbroke's political thought that Burke mocked in the *Vindication*. Why should we worship political society, the Noble Writer asks, if it has "made the Many the Property of the Few; if it has introduced Labours unnecessary, Vices and Diseases unknown, and Pleasures incompatible with Nature; if in all Countries it abridges the Lives of Millions, and renders those of Millions more utterly abject and miserable . . . ?"[63] Yet if the necessities of civil society are "rather imaginary than real," the writer concludes in the *Vindication*, "[W]e should renounce [the Theology of the Vulgar's] Dreams of Society, together with their Visions of Religion, and vindicate ourselves into perfect Liberty."[64] In the *Reflections*, Burke exposes the sheer delusion in the belief that man could create a natural state of perfect equality and liberty emancipated from human needs and inequalities. Eradicate want and division, and you eradicate civilization.

Burke's conclusion that revolutionaries were antagonists of the prescriptive rights of the French nobility was accurate, and his detection of a levelling tendency in their ideology was shrewd. We should recognize, however, that Burke may have exaggerated the prospect that this trend would introduce a French state of radical egalitarianism. The most thoroughgoing attempt to establish complete equality during the French Revolution – the Conspiracy of

---

the most unequal of all measures in the distribution of men" (Langford, *Writings and Speeches*, VIII, 222).

[60] Langford, *Writings and Speeches*, IV, 448. [61] Langford, *Writings and Speeches*, IV, 449.
[62] Langford, *Writings and Speeches*, VIII, 100. [63] Langford, *Writings and Speeches*, I, 181.
[64] Langford, *Writings and Speeches*, I, 183.

Equals, in which Babeuf, a militant egalitarian fond of extreme Enlightenment thought, aimed to overthrow the French Directory in May 1796 and create a French state inspired by socialist conceptions of wealth redistribution – was an utter failure. Babeuf was guillotined.[65]

We should also be aware that French revolutionary politics at the time Burke published the *Reflections*, in late 1790, did not carry a uniform voice in favor of radical equality. As Jonathan Israel observes, three general political factions comprised the National Assembly and exemplified the broader attitudes of the Revolution: democratic republicanism; centrist monarchical liberalism; and the most conservative of the three, a form of constitutional monarchism.[66] The first written constitution of the Revolution, adopted in 1791, merged the radical strands of the *Declaration of the Rights of Man* with republican forms of government but also retained the monarchy. As Israel writes, "For the first time in Europe's history, a constitutional monarchy emerged that blended a minimum of royal authority with a powerful republican tendency and equality on the basis of the Rights of Man."[67] Of course, the infusion of a democratic-republican spirit into a monarchy rested on a possible contradiction. Yet it bears remembering when reading Burke's writings on the Revolution that some of its leaders' political persuasions did not reflect the extreme levelling tendencies he attacked throughout the 1790s.

Ultimately, for Burke, the engine behind the confiscation and redistribution of landed and commercial property for the seeming aim of establishing equality was the desire for unbounded power. "The Revolution was made, not to make France free, but to make her formidable," Burke observes in *Second Letter on a Regicide Peace*.[68] Power, he writes early in the *Reflections*, is the product of men exercising their liberties in bodies. Thus, "Considerate people, before they declare themselves, will observe the use which is made of *power*."[69] In the case of the Revolution, power was first brandished by the Constituent Assembly when it usurped Church lands for the ostensible purpose of shoring up France's national debt, thereby promoting its "national faith" – the "most astonishing of all pretexts," Burke states.[70]

This benevolent intention transformed into tyranny: "Who but a tyrant ... could think of seizing on the property of men, unaccused, unheard, untried, by

[65] For historical background on the Conspiracy of Equals, see Jonathan Israel, *Revolutionary Ideas: An Intellectual History of the French Revolution from* The Rights of Man *to* Robespierre (Oxford and Princeton: Princeton University Press, 2014), 670–673; and Leo A. Loubère, "The Intellectual Origins of French Jacobin Socialism," *International Review of Social History* 4 (1959): 415–431. Doyle called the conspiracy "the most radical and imaginative attempt to achieve equality yet seen in history" (Doyle, *Oxford History of the French Revolution*, 421).

[66] Israel, *Revolutionary Ideas*, 110–111.   [67] Israel, *Revolutionary Ideas*, 104.

[68] Langford, *Writings and Speeches*, IX, 278.   [69] Langford, *Writings and Speeches*, VIII, 59.

[70] Langford, *Writings and Speeches*, VIII, 156.

whole descriptions, by hundreds and thousands together?" Burke asks hypothetically in the *Reflections*.[71] France "has sanctified the dark suspicious maxims of tyrannous distrust."[72] Burke cleverly equates the apparent tyranny of kings, most notably King Louis XVI, with, in his judgment, the real tyranny of the French democratic mob – the people ostensibly committed to overthrowing autocratic institutions:

The sophistic tyrants of Paris are loud in their declamations against the departed regal tyrants, who in former ages have vexed the world. They are thus bold, because they are safe from the dungeons and iron cages of their old masters. Shall we be more tender of the tyrants of our own time, when we see them acting worse tragedies under our eyes? Shall we not use the same liberty that they do, when we can use it with the same safety – when to speak honest truth only requires a contempt of the opinions of those whose actions we abhor?[73]

The government's claim to property over the church was an ominous prelude to the unmitigated excesses of popular democracy and of the state supervision of economic resources.[74] In abandoning all pretenses of repairing French national credit, revolutionaries' seizure of private property – justified to fulfill their monstrous vision of egalitarianism – degenerated into an impulse to usurp. Their government, Burke wrote in *Fourth Letter on a Regicide Peace*, was "force; and nothing but force."[75] The revolutionary gospel of equality masked the face of despotism.

Elements of Market Liberty in the French Revolution

Nevertheless, Burke's attack on revolutionary conceptions of equality does not fully resolve the puzzle posed at the outset of this book: how could the Burke who condemned the French Revolution also profess an allegiance to principles of political economy that intersected with French revolutionaries? Even though Burke admits, near the end of the *Reflections*, that he does "not deny that among an infinite number of acts of violence and folly, some good may have been done,"[76] he does not specify such instances in which the French Revolution advanced market freedom in particular instances.[77]

---

[71] Langford, *Writings and Speeches*, VIII, 155.   [72] Langford, *Writings and Speeches*, VIII, 89.
[73] Langford, *Writings and Speeches*, VIII, 156.   [74] See the conclusion to this chapter.
[75] Langford, *Writings and Speeches*, IX, 90.   [76] Langford, *Writings and Speeches*, VIII, 292.
[77] One must also keep in mind that the *Reflections* was not an objective history of the Revolution, nor did it intend to be. For example, Burke's interpretation of its rash anticlericalism conflicts with Schama's account that Talleyrand was "not in fact an anticlerical bishop" but one of "pragmatic and utilitarian" inclinations (Schama, *Citizens*, 483). Note also that the French Revolution did not actually overthrow all of French society. "[O]ne of the most striking features of post-revolutionary France was the survival of ideas, prejudices, and social relationships characteristic of the *ancien régime*," R. B. McDowell (Langford, *Writings and Speeches*, IX, 17).

For example, the Constituent Assembly abolished the guild system, and later the right of all corporate bodies to assemble, in 1791.[78] Proponents of guilds argued that the organizations set professional standards for their craft and closely supervised workers. But critics found fault with them for exploiting their privileged status to: raise the price of goods; exclude outsider artisans from practicing their craft; stifle innovation; reduce the wages of workers; and obstruct the efficient production of goods.[79] Although the associations served a seemingly useful purpose in promoting common ties and mutual aid among different craftsmen in a given industry, they were perceived by revolutionaries as an ugly remnant of France's medieval past. Under the premise that guilds did, in fact, harm commercial vitality by narrowing competition and regulating the production and selling of goods, the French Revolution's abolition of the system signified movement toward greater economic freedom.

In many ways, the question of guilds discloses a seeming tension in Burke's broader political philosophy. The corporate ethos of the guild would appear to capture his preference for social groups over atomistic individualism, while the dismantling of guilds would appear to lend harmony to his support for market liberty, as outlined most forcefully in *Thoughts and Details*. While Burke issues a powerful defense of corporate bodies in the *Reflections*, he does not appear to make explicit mention of guilds in his survey of France's political economy.

There was at least one instance in Burke's career, however, when he did act on behalf of a group of artisans that aimed to build guild-like barriers to entry in their trade. In March 1787, he introduced a petition from Scottish weavers in the House of Commons that would have lengthened the years for apprentices to receive instruction in the weaver trade. "[I]t is only the Hand of the skilful Artist who gives that decided Superiority to Goods of the same Quality, which is the surest Pledge for future Demands, as well as the better to enable us to cope with our rival Neighbours" the petition claims.[80] By emphasizing the indispensability of experienced craftsmen, the petition clearly intended to protect the interests of existing weavers and inhibit market opportunities for young apprentices.

Whether Burke really believed in the merits of raising barriers to entry was another matter. He provided lukewarm support for the initiative.[81] Years before, he condemned the penal laws for, among various reasons, imposing

---

[78] For an overview of the French Revolution's abolition of the guilds, see Doyle, *Oxford History of the French Revolution*, 149; Schama, *Citizens*, 519–520; Liana Vardi, "The Abolition of the Guilds during the French Revolution," *French Historical Studies* 15 (1988): 704–717; and William H. Sewell, Jr., *Work & Revolution in France: The Language of Labor from the Old Regime to 1848* (Cambridge: Cambridge University Press, 1997), 1–2.

[79] See Vardi, "Abolition of the Guilds during the French Revolution."

[80] *Journals of the House of Commons*, vol. 42 (London: H.M. Stationery Office, 1803), 433.

[81] See Lock, *Edmund Burke*, vol. II, 53n12. A couple years earlier, when Burke was in Scotland, William Windham noted that the Committee of Operative Weavers organized a meeting "in honour of Lord Maitland and Burke." See William Windham, *The Diary of the Right Hon.*

arbitrary regulations and fees that limited employment opportunities for Irish Catholics. Years later, in his critique of the East India Company, Burke lambasted the corporation for using increased production costs to strangle competition from Indian cultivators and traders.

Perhaps we can offer a distinction: Burke was a robust advocate of the corporate spirit of religious institutions, like the Church of England and the Gallican Church, and chartered firms that traded in foreign lands, like the East India Company, when it affected genuine national interests, such as the promotion of religion or foreign commerce. But he did not champion the corporate spirit when it had a negative impact on domestic market activity (the petition from Scottish weavers notwithstanding). In the end, however, Burke's thought and actions struggle to overcome the friction between his sympathies for market competition and his vigorous support for corporate religious and commercial bodies.

The French Revolution was responsible for promoting market freedom in other ways. On August 4, 1789, on the same day it abolished other feudal privileges,[82] the Constituent Assembly eliminated the *corvée*, France's system of coerced, unpaid labor.[83] It was replaced by a property tax. The same day the Assembly also voted to abolish the traditional tithe system.[84] On October 31, 1790, the body ended domestic customs trade barriers for goods dealt among French provinces – one day prior to the publication of the *Reflections*. The elimination of additional taxes on trade and consumption continued on through 1791. The direct taxes of *vingtièmes*, capitation, and *taille* were removed, as were special exemptions and privileges. The French government established three direct taxes (the property tax, a tax on commercial profit, and a tax on movables[85]) in place of the old byzantine system – the same system that Burke condemned in the *Observations* more than twenty years earlier, as exemplified in the speech by his description of the *taille* as "that grievous and destructive imposition."[86]

Such efforts at fiscal reform suffered from defects of their own. The implementation of new direct taxes was more difficult to enforce than indirect taxes. The expropriation of church land violated private property rights. (As Paul Lucas notes, however, French revolutionaries enacted a measure not unlike the *Nullum Tempus* bill Burke supported, which limited royal claims to private property.[87]) Later, of course, the French government issued a series of price and wage controls, confiscated additional private property, and intruded into the

---

William Windham, 1784–1810, ed. Mrs. Henry Baring (London: Longmans, Green, and Co., 1866), 61.

[82] These changes were formally codified on August 11.   [83] Schama, *Citizens*, 85.

[84] The inclusion of eliminating tithes in this paragraph assumes, of course, that doing so advanced the cause of economic freedom.

[85] Doyle, *Oxford History of the French Revolution*, 131.

[86] Langford, *Writings and Speeches*, II, 151.

[87] Lucas, "On Edmund Burke's Doctrine of Prescription," 55.

private lives of French citizens.[88] Admittedly, Burke's initial publication of the *Reflections* came after many of these economic regulations were implemented, and after the abolition of guilds, while the elimination of internal customs occurred the day before the writing was published. The purpose of the aforementioned analysis, however, is to highlight possible tensions between Burke's attack on the French Revolution and some of the Revolution's policies that overlapped with strands of Burke's science of political economy.

Yet perhaps such tensions sharpen the distinctions between his political philosophy and French revolutionary ideology. Because Burke desired steady and principled reform over sudden and radical change, his thought quite plausibly could have accommodated incremental alterations to France's decrepit tax system. As mentioned, Burke himself recognized the oppressive nature of the system more than two decades before the Revolution, and conceded at the end of the *Reflections* that the event might have brought about some good.[89] But, in his judgment, the radical character of French political leadership destroyed the possibility that steady reform could take place in such a tempestuous revolutionary environment. Any prospect for gradual revisions of France's economy was sacrificed at the altar of zealous utopianism.

12.2   THE IMPACT OF ABSTRACT THEORY ON POLITICAL ECONOMY AND THE GENERAL BANK AND CAPITAL OF NATIONS

The gap between the benevolent intentions of the French Revolution to promote human equality and the violent horrors that attended the course of the event reminds us of the most famous insight Burke summons repeatedly in his commentary on the Revolution: abstract theorizing is a perilous endeavor because it fails to take into account the primacy of human circumstance. Circumstances, Burke writes in the *Reflections*, "give in reality to every political principle its distinguishing colour, and discriminating effect. The circumstances are what render every civil and political scheme beneficial or noxious to mankind."[90] The test of principle was its application in context. Burke's observations on this matter are typically connected to his defense of Britain's inherited political, social, and legal traditions, but they also hold an eminent relevance to his conception of political economy.

---

[88] For recent libertarian assessments of the economic policies of the French Revolution, see Richard M. Ebeling, "Inflation, Price Controls, and Collectivism During the French Revolution," *Foundation for Economic Education*, November 9, 2016, accessed January 2, 2017, https://fee.org /articles/inflation-price-controls-and-collectivism-during-the-french-revolution/; and H. A. Scott Trask, "Inflation and the French Revolution: The Story of a Monetary Catastrophe," *Mises Institute*, April 28, 2004, accessed January 2, 2017, https://mises.org/library/inflation-and-french-revolution-story-monetary-catastrophe.

[89] Langford, *Writings and Speeches*, VIII, 292.   [90] Langford, *Writings and Speeches*, VIII, 59.

Burke's contempt for political abstractions made an early appearance in *Thoughts on the Present Discontents*, in which he famously defended the idea of party government. It is not "impossible," he insisted, for a prince to establish a government that

will give a great degree of content to his people; without any curious and anxious research for that abstract, universal, perfect harmony, which while he is seeking, he abandons those means of ordinary tranquillity which are in his power without any research at all.[91]

A campaign to establish perfection in government, and political society in general, will neglect to secure the solid grounds of peace and contentment that remain, in themselves, lofty objects of judicious statesmanship.

This line of reasoning guided Burke's political thought throughout his life. More than twenty years later, in *Appeal from the New to the Old Whigs*, he declares:

Nothing universal can be rationally affirmed on any moral, or any political subject. Pure metaphysical abstraction does not belong to these matters. The lines of morality are not like the ideal lines of mathematics. They are broad and deep as well as long. They admit of exceptions; they demand modifications. These exceptions and modifications are not made by the process of logic, but by the rules of prudence. Prudence is not only the first in rank of the virtues political and moral, but she is the director, the regulator, the standard of them all. Metaphysics cannot live without definition; but prudence is cautious how she defines.[92]

In Burke's understanding, the French Revolution's metaphysical abstractions hardened general rules into ironclad laws to be applied universally at all times and at all places. These laws did not accommodate the power of intuitive human experience drawn from habits, customs, and social relations – such as the experience of producers and consumers in exchange economies.

The spirit of this belief suffuses the pages of the *Reflections*. One of Burke's most steadfast beliefs about the relation between abstract theory and circumstance in the writing is that the former did little to encourage the flow of provisions in market economies. He writes:

What is the use of discussing a man's abstract right to food or medicine? The question is upon the method of procuring and administering them. In that deliberation I shall always advise to call in the aid of the farmer and the physician rather than the professor of metaphysics.[93]

---

[91] Langford, *Writings and Speeches*, II, 282. See also "Rationalism in *Thoughts and Details*," Chapter 4.

[92] Langford, *Writings and Speeches*, IV, 383.

[93] Langford, *Writings and Speeches*, VIII, 111. It must be stressed that Burke's pejorative reference to the "professor of metaphysics" is a specific rebuke to French and English thinkers who defended the notion of an abstract state of nature, not to classical and scholastic thinkers.

While the metaphysician in his study may lecture on the theoretical necessity of distributing food and medicine to the people in the name of universal equality, the person who actually *acts* in markets – toiling the fields, manufacturing and trading goods (and, in the case of physicians, serving patients) – is the one who fulfills this philosophical speculation in reality. Burke's argument complements his position on the qualifications to govern in the *Reflections*: while some men of moderate professions might not possess the wisdom necessary to govern, they did serve a vital role in steering the allocation of resources throughout civil society.

Burke does not elaborate specifically on his claim that the farmer and physician were more helpful than professors of metaphysics at procuring necessities, but it firmly aligns with his observations in *Thoughts and Details*. In the latter tract, Burke identifies the practical activities of farmers and laborers in cultivating farmland, including his own personal experiences in farming and trading crops. Recall Burke's description in *Thoughts and Details* of his dealing in the market following the poor winter harvest of 1794–1795: "My best ears and grains were not fine; never had I grain of so low a quality – yet I sold one load for 21l. At the same time I bought my seed wheat (it was excellent) at 23l."[94] The trial-and-error activities of crop production and bartering were responsible for the smooth circulation of provisions, not theoretical speculators professing on the perceived merits of abstract equality.

This insight illustrates the meaning behind Burke's statement in *Thoughts and Details* that state regulations require the "exactest detail of circumstances" in order to form "firm and luminous general principles"[95] to effectively regulate market activity. In his view, the French – and particularly the Jacobins in the early to mid-1790s – were quite adept at furnishing firm and luminous principles such as "equality"; what they lacked, however, was a sense of modesty that would have otherwise cautioned them from meddling in the private economic affairs of the people. (Remember that the flurry of Jacobin price controls was a key consideration that motivated Burke to write *Thoughts and Details*.) If revolutionary leaders had been more sensitive to the mystifying complexities of market activities, Burke suggests in the *Reflections* and *Thoughts and Details*, perhaps they might have tempered their faith throughout the 1790s in the power of abstract theory and government regulation to perfect the human condition.

Burke's related point is that the farmer and physician are physically closer to other participants in exchange relations than abstract speculators and thus are more familiar with their particular desires and wishes. As he writes in an important passage in *Thoughts and Details*:

Market is the meeting and conference of the *consumer* and *producer*, when they mutually discover each other's wants. Nobody, I believe, has observed with any

---

[94] Langford, *Writings and Speeches*, IX, 138. [95] Langford, *Writings and Speeches*, IX, 124.

reflection what market is, without being astonished at the truth, the correctness, the celerity, the general equity, with which the balance of wants is settled.[96]

The abstract theorist does not interact with flesh-and-blood human beings in the mart when philosophizing on the virtues of equality and liberty. But the producer, middleman, and consumer, by the very nature of their practical roles in market economies, experience the immediate presence of others. They become aware of individuals' market preferences and seek to satisfy them in order to receive advantages themselves, an observation that anticipates Hegel's notion of a "system of needs" as a market environment of reciprocal fulfillment.[97] In essence, proximity is a parent of knowledge, while market exchange is a process of mutual discovery and an arena of social codependence. For Burke, free enterprise demanded a level of intuitive human cooperation that soaring revolutionary rhetoric could not articulate using the empty vocabulary of the rights of man.

This temptation to regulate the economy reflected a deeper political division between the British constitution and the French revolutionary stratagems. Much as Britain's economy permitted liberty of trade by recognizing the diversity of preference in markets, its constitution accommodated a variety of principles that balanced each other out in an institutional structure. "The whole scheme of our mixed constitution is to prevent any one of its principles from being carried as far, as taken by itself, and theoretically, it would go," Burke explains in *Appeal from the New to the Old Whigs*.[98] Such discouragement of extremes allowed for practical agreements and settlements over political disputes: "[I]n the British constitution, there is a perpetual treaty and compromise going on."[99] This lesson strongly parallels Burke's argument in *Thoughts and Details* that market contracts allowed for barter and conciliation between two parties without needing to rely on a rigid rule to govern their private negotiations.

Revolutionary politicians' democratic scheme of "abstract and unlimited perfection of power in the popular part" allowed for no such balance.[100] "With them there is no compromise," Burke writes in *Appeal from the New to the Old Whigs*, for their "principles always go to the extreme."[101] Extremes militated against compromise and negotiation, happy mediums and necessary trade-offs. A mixed constitution secured liberty for the people to settle controversies without unsettling social order; the French Revolution did precisely the opposite, because its leaders aimed to impose uniformity on the complex.

---

[96] Langford, *Writings and Speeches*, IX, 133.
[97] Hegel, *Philosophy of Right*, 129. "When men are thus dependent on one another and reciprocally related to one another in their work and the satisfaction of their needs, subjective self-seeking turns into a contribution to the satisfaction of the needs of everyone else."
[98] Langford, *Writings and Speeches*, IV, 470.   [99] Langford, *Writings and Speeches*, IV, 471.
[100] Langford, *Writings and Speeches*, IV, 471.   [101] Langford, *Writings and Speeches*, IV, 470.

This violent enterprise cut to the very core of the contrast between Britain and France. According to Burke, the growth of British order from time immemorial was the diffused product of accumulated customs and habits, not the sole intellect:

We are afraid to put men to live and trade each on his own private stock of reason; because we suspect that this stock in each man is small, and that the individuals would do better to avail themselves of the general bank and capital of nations, and of ages.[102]

Britain's legal traditions communicated a similar lesson: "[T]he science of jurisprudence, the pride of the human intellect, which, with all its defects, redundancies, and errors, is the collected reason of ages, combining the principles of original justice with the infinite variety of human concerns."[103]

Man's capacity to reshape society was bound by the inherent constraints of the mind, for the individual could only comprehend a finite amount of knowledge. Yet the slowly accreted social, legal, and constitutional insights and practices generated by the many over time – the "general bank and capital of nations, and of ages" – reflected a reservoir of wisdom that had occasioned prosperity for Britain for generations.

These comments are typically linked to Burke's political defense of history and tradition, but one could easily apply their principles to his economic thought, as he himself did in *Thoughts and Details*. Commercial societies embody streams of specific contractual arrangements, fluid price fluctuations, and disparate market desires that are incapable of being penetrated by the individual mind. It would thus be impossible for men in power – such as French revolutionaries – to possess the amount of knowledge necessary to maintain the efficient functioning of supply and demand laws while also ensuring that producers, consumers, and middlemen were fairly rewarded for their investments and purchases. Even if rulers were capable of doing so for a single moment, it would be folly to think that rotating collections of public officials serving in government in different generations would be able to sustain such market order *over time*. Abstract theory was no match for the gradual expansion of economic wisdom throughout the ages.

Social Engineering

Therefore, Burke thought that granting authority to French revolutionaries to implement their abstract theory in practice set in motion a process of *social engineering* on the part of the state. In one of the most stirring metaphors ever conveyed on the matter, he asserts in *Letter to a Noble Lord* that speculative philosophers in France "consider men in their experiments, no more than they

---

[102] Langford, *Writings and Speeches*, VIII, 138.
[103] Langford, *Writings and Speeches*, VIII, 145.

do mice in an air pump, or in a recipient of mephitick gas,"[104] possibly summoning the image of Joseph Wright of Derby's celebrated painting, "An Experiment on a Bird in the Air Pump." As David Bromwich explains, "An air-pump sucked oxygen out of a glass container, often for the sake of observing the effects on an animal. It was therefore a convenient symbol of an experimental scientific attitude of heartless detachment."[105] Similarly, French revolutionaries, according to Burke, conceived men and women as laboratory animals to be used for grand political and social experimentation.

The pretense of radical experimentation was the belief that man could fully comprehend the deep mysteries of society and control them to produce prosperity for all. Burke writes in *Appeal from the New to the Old Whigs*:

An ignorant man, who is not fool enough to meddle with his clock, is however suffi-ciently confident to think he can safely take to pieces, and put together at his pleasure, a moral machine of another guise importance and complexity, composed of far other wheels, and springs, and balances, and counteracting and co-operating powers. Men little think how immorally they act in rashly meddling with what they do not understand. Their delusive good intention is no sort of excuse for their presumption.[106]

French leaders presume they know more than they actually do about the complicated anatomy of political and social order. One revolutionary might pause before tinkering with his personal contraptions, but he did not hesitate to attempt to alter society based on his shallow understanding of the complexities of civil society – complexities that could not be measured with exact precision. "They think there is nothing worth pursuit, but that which they can handle; which they can measure with a two-foot rule; which they can tell upon ten fingers," Burke writes in *Second Letter on a Regicide Peace*.[107] Even benevolent aims for political transformation did not excuse such gross ignorance of the limits of the human mind.

The revolutionary process of experimentation thus demanded the wholesale reconstruction of the French nation, overturning its settled traditions and controlling the wealth of corporate bodies and farmers in the name of advancing the common good. For Burke, the social engineer's impulse to seize private property crippled progress. "Never did a state, in any case, enrich itself by the confiscations of the citizens," he insists.[108] This was why "injustice is not always good policy, nor rapine the high road to riches."[109] Taking from one and giving to another cut the roots of public prosperity. The social engineer's radical desire to enlarge public credit further excited militaristic impulses, as shown by the French Revolutionary Wars.

---

[104] Langford, *Writings and Speeches*, IX, 177.
[105] David Bromwich, ed., *Romantic Critical Essays* (Cambridge: Cambridge University Press, 1987), 252n6. I am grateful to Professor Bromwich for alerting me to this connection.
[106] Langford, *Writings and Speeches*, IV, 472. [107] Langford, *Writings and Speeches*, IX, 267.
[108] Langford, *Writings and Speeches*, VIII, 284.
[109] Langford, *Writings and Speeches*, VIII, 284.

Burke's salvo against French abstractionism can be applied to his notion of political economy in the *Reflections* and in *Thoughts and Details*. In both writings, he admonishes the experiment of wealth redistribution. In the former, Burke assails French revolutionaries for transferring wealth from the church to the monied interest. In the latter, Burke condemns, among various ideas, the proposal for government to increase wage rates of agricultural laborers and regulate the grain supply. The *Reflections* placed a greater focus on landed property, and *Thoughts and Details* on the market of provisions. But Burke detected the same menacing tendency underlying both Jacobinism and British support for government regulation: the thirst to level social and economic classes for the supposed purpose of promoting egalitarianism. Both movements aimed to engineer civil society through the imperious designs of the state.

Yet, in Burke's view, no state official should hold the power to decide whether some have too much wealth and others too little. "[W]ho are to judge what that profit and advantage [of the farmer] ought to be? Certainly no authority on earth," he concludes in *Thoughts and Details*.[110] This comment echoed Burke's aforementioned remark that "[t]oo much and too little are treason against property"[111] in the *Reflections*. Similarly, in a letter he wrote to Captain Thomas Mercer on February 26, 1790, soon after he issued his first public statement condemning the French Revolution in *Speech on the Army Estimates*, Burke stated, "I do not find myself at liberty, either as a man, or as a trustee for men, to take a *vested* property from one man, and to give it to another, because *I* think that the portion of one is too great, and that of another too small."[112] Why should an individual, much less the state, retain the authority to determine the amount of land each citizen should possess?

In his categorical objection to wealth redistribution, however, is Burke not surrendering to the abstract impulses of the French Revolution that he attacked? This interpretation is certainly fed by Burke's vociferous denunciations of French radicals, but it rests on a misunderstanding of his criticism of abstract theory for at least two reasons. First, that Burke condemned such theory did not mean he rejected the truth of certain propositions, such as: religion was a force for good; a moral law reflected the common humanity of men and women; and, in relation to his political economy, private property should be protected. Second, as discussed in the conclusion to Chapter 4, Burke's defense of market exchange was predicated largely on his awareness of the compound intricacies of social life.

Burke's firm opposition to wealth redistribution, not to mention to the regulation of wages and prices in the internal grain trade, presents continuities

---

[110] Langford, *Writings and Speeches*, IX, 125–126.
[111] Langford, *Writings and Speeches*, VIII, 153.
[112] Burke to Captain Thomas Mercer, 26 February 1790, in *Correspondence of Edmund Burke*, vol. VI, 93–94.

with this way of thinking. Seizing the wealth from some – whether in the form of mobile or immobile property – signaled an air of exploded arrogance on the part of rulers in presuming they possessed sufficient knowledge and wisdom to reorganize the complexities of society into a perfect social arrangement, cleansed of inequalities. "They have no respect for the wisdom of others; but they pay it off by a very full measure of confidence in their own," he declares in the *Reflections*, referring to the fusion of the literary cabal and revolutionary politicians.[113] The reapportionment of wealth justified by seemingly pragmatic adjustments to economic circumstance, rather than by abstract theory, still appeared to Burke to display the tendencies of social engineering of Jacobinism.

In addition, we should take note of Burke's view that the indiscriminate spreading of *assignats* was also drawn from the same abstract theory of the French Revolution which motivated its schemes for social engineering. While Burke, in the *Reflections*, lambastes the paper money for triggering inflation and turning ecclesiastical property into cudgels for material gain, his deeper point was that the flood of *assignats* marked a philosophical disposition consumed by abstract faith. "With these philosophic financiers, this universal medicine made of church mummy is to cure all the evils of the state," Burke writes in the *Reflections*.[114] He continues: "These gentlemen perhaps do not believe a great deal in the miracles of piety, but it cannot be questioned that they have an undoubting faith in the prodigies of sacrilege."[115] In Burke's judgment, the dash to distribute *assignats* illuminated the blind theoretical and speculative impulse of revolutionary politicians to advance the welfare of the state through the plunder of private property. The *assignat* was the financial avatar of the Revolution's metaphysics.

Burke's observation connecting *assignats* to abstract theory captured actual revolutionary sentiments. When arguing in support of issuing the paper money, Pierre Hubert Anson, a French statesman and financier, had proclaimed, "Everything suggests that the circulation of *assignats* is the best of all operations; indeed, it is the freest, because it is founded upon the general will."[116] Anson's invocation of "general will" is reminiscent of Rousseau's abstract concept of the General Will, the idea that different members of a political community should transcend their selfish interests to join together to advance the common good.[117] For Burke, the flood of depreciating *assignats*

---

[113] Langford, *Writings and Speeches*, VIII, 138.
[114] Langford, *Writings and Speeches*, VIII, 280.
[115] Langford, *Writings and Speeches*, VIII, 280.
[116] Aftalion, *Economic Interpretation*, 74. See also Spang, *Stuff and Money*, 76–77.
[117] It must be said, however, that Burke thought Rousseau's baleful influence on the Revolution came in the form of a revolution in taste and morals rather than in political theory. See Burke's comments on Rousseau and the Revolution in *Letter to a Member of the National Assembly* in Langford, *Writings and Speeches*, VIII, 312–319. Burke admitted that even Rousseau, who had passed away in 1778, would have been astonished at the radical innovations of his revolutionary followers: "I believe, that were Rousseau alive, and in one of his lucid intervals, he

exemplified the venomous economic effect of thrusting the General Will upon a people: it threatened the smooth operation of market order – not to mention political order – by elevating the spirit of abstract philosophy in the form of paper currency over the concrete concerns of the people and the financial needs of the state.

The French Revolution's abstract conceptions of egalitarianism, in addition to abstract political theory, also permeated debate in the Constituent Assembly over *assignats*. Tapping into the egalitarian attitudes of the Assembly's leftist members, Mirabeau contended in an important speech that in order for the church land to be sold efficiently, it had to be accessible to the "less well-to-do"[118] French. His speech garnered "loud applause" and "continued to have an effect upon the Assembly throughout the very lively debate," according to Florin Aftalion.[119] Bergasse-Laziroule, a deputy from the Third Estate, recognized the arresting potency of high-sounding prose: "[A]bstract truths not being within the scope of all men, orators can easily gain a hold upon them, corrupt or mystify them as they will."[120] This remark captured one of Burke's greatest anxieties in regard to the Revolution: abstract philosophy could be employed to justify the aggrandizement of state power, which, in this case, signified issuing an avalanche of *assignats* in the name of repairing public credit and restoring national honor. For Burke, such a policy would establish the conditions for commercial decay, and political tyranny.

Interestingly enough, while Burke is known for defending the ancien régime in the *Reflections*, he actually criticizes it in *Thoughts and Details* for being too heavily involved in regulating France's economy before the Revolution. In the economic tract, Burke approvingly conveys the opinion of his "dear departed friend" – ostensibly his son Richard, who had passed away the year before – that "the leading vice of the French monarchy ... was in good intention ill-directed, and a restless desire of governing too much."[121] Thus the "hand of authority was seen in every thing, and in every place,"[122] reflecting the policy of *dirigisme*.

Burke goes further in suggesting, ever so slightly, that the ancien régime's heavy regulatory burden created the conditions for revolution. "[T]hough it's enemies were not enemies to it's faults, it's fault furnished them with means for it's destruction," he claims.[123] Even more, "All, therefore, that happened amiss in the course even of domestic affairs, was attributed to the Government; and, as it always happens in this kind of officious universal interference, what began in odious power, ended always, I may say without an exception, in contemptible imbecillity."[124] Burke acknowledges that the constitution of the French

---

would be shocked at the practical phrenzy of his scholars, who in their paradoxes are servile imitators; and even in their incredulity discover an implicit faith" (Langford, *Writings and Speeches*, VIII, 219).

[118] Aftalion, *Economic Interpretation*, 78.   [119] Aftalion, *Economic Interpretation*, 78.
[120] Aftalion, *Economic Interpretation*, 77.   [121] Langford, *Writings and Speeches*, IX, 144.
[122] Langford, *Writings and Speeches*, IX, 144.   [123] Langford, *Writings and Speeches*, IX, 144.
[124] Langford, *Writings and Speeches*, IX, 144.

monarchy had "much good."[125] But the crux of his insight is that the ancien régime's failure to relax its regulatory grip on France's economy laid the seeds for public discontent. These comments are reminiscent of Burke's admonition of the excesses of French taxes on commerce and land in the *Observations*.[126]

For Burke, the deeper philosophical consequences of imposing abstract equality on political economy penetrated the souls of men. The replacement of the farmer and physician – not to mention the landed aristocrat and the clergyman – with speculative politicians and philosophers as the engineers of civilization spelled a dark descent toward the dehumanization of men and women. Because French revolutionaries denied the sacred integrity of ancient social associations, including those between the landlord and tenant and producer and consumer, they acted on the hardened impulse to transform human beings into disembodied chess pieces, arranging and rearranging their property in order to satisfy the revolutionaries' own vision of equality, liberty, and fraternity. Radical ideologues perceived man as an instrumental abstract entity to exploit for the present, rather than as a flesh-and-blood human being to cherish for the ages.

12.3 MANNERS AND ETHICS AS A PRECONDITION FOR COMMERCE AND THE SCOTTISH ENLIGHTENMENT

Burke's protest against revolutionaries' social and economic schemes was part of his wider philosophical argument in the *Reflections* relating to political economy: the expansion of European commerce and the ascent of public riches grew out of particular ethical preconditions, a belief harmonious with Burke's contention that the landed aristocracy served as the necessary anchor for commercial and financial activities. Public opulence derived not simply from the wheel of exchange but from a code of manners. This argument is *the* moral core of Burke's theory of political economy.

Burke hinted at this insight decades before the French Revolution, when he praised the Gentleman of Fortune in 1748, in *Reformer No. 7*, for the humane behavior he demonstrated toward his tenants, as discussed in Chapter 3. There remains another noteworthy instance of Burke's attraction to the relation between ethics and commerce before he entered Parliament. In the *Annual Register* for 1764, the journal published a favorable review of Adam Anderson's book *An Historical and Chronological Deduction of the Origin of Commerce*.[127] After providing general comments on the need for a comprehensive history of commerce, the review states, "Trade is so much influenced by the manners of mankind, as well as so intimately connected with

---

[125] Langford, *Writings and Speeches*, IX, 144.
[126] Consult Langford, *Writings and Speeches*, II, 152–153.
[127] "An Account of Books published in 1764," *The Annual Register, For the Year 1764* (London: J. Dodsley, 1765), 250–256.

their policy and government, that it cannot fail of furnishing no less valuable lights for the history of the human mind in different ages and countries, than for advancing the riches and prosperity of nations."[128] This remark illustrates Burke's understanding that trading activity was intricately woven into the habits of culture. The serious study of commerce illuminated deeper truths about the character of a people and the constitution of human nature.

Burke integrates this moral dimension of economics into his meditations on the political economy of the French Revolution in the *Reflections* in a number of ways. One such instance was his attempt to dispute Talleyrand's argument that the transformation of church lands into instruments of monied exchange would give rise to agricultural improvements. Burke seeks to combat this view by recounting his experience with a monk of the Carthusians, a Catholic monastic order, whom he most likely met during his visit to France, in 1773.[129] "I have got more information, upon a curious and interesting branch of husbandry, in one short conversation with a Carthusian monk," Burke claims, "than I have derived from all the Bank directors that I have ever conversed with."[130]

Accordingly, Burke repudiates the pretense that the secular tendencies of revolutionaries and the monied interest aided in the amelioration of agricultural property. "I cannot conceive how a man's not believing in God can teach him to cultivate the earth with the least of any additional skill or encouragement," he writes.[131] This is why "usury is not a tutor of agriculture."[132] On the contrary, man's instinct to tinker and improve was enhanced by the power of faith. Burke paraphrases Cicero in *De Senectute*, who remarked that the farmer sows "for the immortal gods, who willed it that I should not only receive these things from my forebears but should also produce for posterity."[133] An abiding trust in God spurs agricultural improvement from which future generations would benefit. Fidelity to a transcendent power, rather than financial wizardry, provides inspiration to the steward in the cultivation of his land.

Burke's argument is far more significant than it first appears, for it delivers an implicit challenge to one of the most common assertions articulated by both proponents and critics of liberal market economies in modernity: the advent of

---

[128] *Annual Register, For the Year 1764*, 250. The review published two long excerpts from the book. One review noted that, after London, Bristol, the city Burke would represent from 1774 to 1780, "made the greatest figure of any in England in commerce and shipping in all this century" (252). Note that Samuel Johnson's *Dictionary of the English Language* defined "manners," in the plural, as: "General way of life; morals; habits"; and "Ceremonious behaviour; studied civility." See Johnson, *A Dictionary of the English Language*, 3rd ed. (Dublin: W. G. Jones, 1768), 132.

[129] Burke also visited France around 1757 (Langford, *Writings and Speeches*, VIII, 1).

[130] Langford, *Writings and Speeches*, VIII, 239.

[131] Langford, *Writings and Speeches*, VIII, 239.

[132] Langford, *Writings and Speeches*, VIII, 239.

[133] Langford, *Writings and Speeches*, VIII, 239n3.

classical liberalism and the Enlightenment set the conditions for the burst of commercial dynamism. Modernity's ennobling of individual freedom, private economic rights, and profit reflected a changing Western attitude increasingly tolerant of business and financial activities. The departure from religious dogma and the subsequent embrace of market liberty forged the path for economic prosperity. Most important for our purposes, this perspective contends that the rise in trade produced civilizing effects on mankind. Two parties with a mutual material interest will be more likely to satisfy their desires through transactional exchange than through war, thereby leading to greater prospects for international peace. In short, commerce gave rise to a new form of ethical behavior that served as the enlightened foundation for virtue and morality in modern Western civilization.[134]

As J. G. A. Pocock keenly observed in his seminal essay, "The Political Economy of Burke's Analysis of the French Revolution," Burke dared to reverse this causal historiography in the *Reflections*, which was increasingly endorsed by proponents of market liberty and contractarianism in the seventeenth and eighteenth centuries.[135] Burke's insights into this matter occur in one of his most famous, and lampooned, passages, in the *Reflections*, when he painted a romantic portrait of Marie Antoinette, the queen of France, in light of his broader discussion of the destruction of chivalry triggered by the French Revolution.[136] His commentary on the relationship between ethics and economics in this section relates to our present inquiry, however, and continues to suffer from scholarly neglect.

Burke begins his argument by presenting his principal assertion about chivalry: it was the moral basis for the growth of European civilization, one that protected honor, rank, and status and spawned fealty, order, and stability. The code of chivalric manners cemented the communal bonds of man, preventing civilized social relations from dissolving into savagery. The arts and letters supported it. And the clergy and the landed aristocracy were the leading members of civil society who carried out this code and set the moral tone for the rest of society. "Nothing is more certain," Burke writes, "than that our manners, our civilization, and all the good things which are connected with manners, and civilization," have depended on "the spirit of a gentleman, and

---

[134] Variations of this argument are found most recently in, among many, Steven Pinker, *Enlightenment Now*; Pinker, *The Better Angels of Our Nature: Why Violence Has Declined* (New York: Penguin Books, 2011); Mokyr, *Enlightened Economy*; and Deirdre Nansen McCloskey, *Bourgeois Equality: How Ideas, Not Capital or Institutions, Enriched the World* (Chicago and London: The University of Chicago Press, 2016).

[135] See J. G. A. Pocock, "The Political Economy of Burke's Analysis of the French Revolution," originally published in 1982 in *The Historical Journal* (*The Historical Journal* 25 (1982): 331–349). It was later republished in Pocock, *Virtue, Commerce, and History*. See pages 193–212.

[136] Langford, *Writings and Speeches*, VIII, 126–127.

the spirit of religion."[137] The nobility and religious institutions fostered the practice of manners and ethics, which built up social order throughout the ages.[138]

One unsettling effect of the French Revolution, Burke believed, was the corruption of this ethic of chivalry and its replacement with the speculative theories of radical monied men and *philosophes*, unmoored from the foundations of religious and aristocratic morality. "[T]he age of chivalry is gone. – That of sophisters, oeconomists, and calculators, has succeeded; and the glory of Europe is extinguished for ever," Burke famously writes.[139] He then blends this insight with his beliefs about the sources of commercial progress:

If, as I suspect, modern letters owe more than they are always willing to own to antient manners, so do other interests which we value full as much as they are worth. Even commerce, and trade, and manufacture, the gods of our oeconomical politicians, are themselves perhaps but creatures; are themselves but effects which, as first causes, we choose to worship. They certainly grew under the same shade in which learning flourished. They too may decay with their natural protecting principles. With you, for the present at least, they all threaten to disappear together. Where trade and manufactures are wanting to a people, and the spirit of nobility and religion remains, sentiment supplies, and not always ill supplies, their place; but if commerce and the arts should be lost in an experiment to try how well a state may stand without these old fundamental principles, what sort of a thing must be a nation of gross, stupid, ferocious, and at the same time, poor and sordid barbarians, destitute of religion, honour, or manly pride, possessing nothing at present, and hoping for nothing hereafter?[140]

These are the most significant comments from Burke that reveal his philosophical and historical understanding of the relationship between virtue and economics. Just as the flourishing of modern letters owed its origins to ancient manners, so did commercial prosperity. The development of trade and manufacturing was the product of a wider moral and cultural environment in which the softening influence of such manners provided the ethical substructure for the emergence of mass commerce.

The shade of manners furnished by religious authorities and the landed nobility, then, did not simply produce political and social order; manners also created economic order by setting the necessary preconditions for exchange economies to progress steadily within the broader growth of civilization. Commercial dynamism was threaded carefully into existing moral, cultural, and religious institutions that had governed Europe throughout the centuries. The civilizing constraints of family, church, and class prevented the healthy

---

[137] Langford, *Writings and Speeches*, VIII, 130.
[138] Michael Novak put forth a similar argument about the relation between ethics and markets. See Novak, "How Christianity Created Capitalism," *Wall Street Journal*, December 23, 1999, www.wsj.com/articles/SB945912385717198338. See also Randall Collins, *Weberian Sociological Theory* (Cambridge: Cambridge University Press, 1990), 53–55.
[139] Langford, *Writings and Speeches*, VIII, 127.
[140] Langford, *Writings and Speeches*, VIII, 130–131.

pursuit of profit from mutating into an uninhibited avarice, one that otherwise would have transformed all sacred social relationships into perilous mediums of instrumental exchange. The "naturally protecting principles" of ethics, as Burke conveys, retained the code of honor throughout the process of modern economic expansion. "This mixed system of opinion and sentiment had its origin in the antient chivalry," Burke writes.[141] Men relied on pre-commercial social attachments – not transactional dealing – as the cardinal means to strengthen their collective human ties. Love, trust, and ethical obligation built the moral foundation for widespread material gain.

Burke widens this argument in *Appeal from the New to the Old Whigs* in 1791:

We have obligations to mankind at large, which are not in consequence of any special voluntary pact. They arise from the relation of man to man, and the relations of man to God, which relations are not matter of choice. On the contrary, the force of all the pacts which we enter into with any particular person or number of persons amongst mankind, depends upon those prior obligations. In some cases the subordinate relations are voluntary, in others they are necessary – but the duties are all compulsive.[142]

For Burke, the most dangerous way the French Revolution exhibited this transactional understanding of a "voluntary pact" was conceiving the relationship between the ruler and the ruled as an ad hoc arrangement based merely on contractarian notions of mutual consent, as defined by the ideas of popular sovereignty and the General Will, and not grounded in any deeper foundation of moral commitment.

But these comments are also eminently applicable to his observations about the spirit of nobility and religion. Trade and barter are voluntary pacts; one party freely chooses to enter into contracts with another party to satisfy their individual preferences. In this scenario, one's duty emerges from the conditions of the agreement. But the perpetuation of commercial activity – and civil society, and empire, and civilization – required the fulfillment of moral commitments that preceded the formation of temporary contracts. "The most essential human obligations and relations – especially those involving the family but also many of those involving community, the nation, and one's religious faith – are not chosen and could never really be chosen," writes Yuval Levin, describing Burke's position, "and political and social life begins from these, not from acts of will."[143] Unlike economic exchange in a free society, such obligations were not voluntary but mandatory.

Burke believed that the code of manners that established this moral foundation was more powerful than the dictates of written law. As he declares in *First Letter on a Regicide Peace*,

---

[141] Langford, *Writings and Speeches*, VIII, 127.   [142] Langford, *Writings and Speeches*, IV, 442.
[143] Levin, *Great Debate*, 101.

Manners are of more importance than laws ... Manners are what vex or sooth, corrupt or purify, exalt or debase, barbarize or refine us, by a constant, steady, uniform, insensible operation, like that of the air we breathe in. They give their whole form and colour to our lives. According to their quality, they aid morals, they supply them, or they totally destroy them.[144]

Notice Burke does not argue that commercial exchange civilizes man. Manners – those that developed prior to widespread market activity – do.

In Burke's judgment, the French Revolution corrupted the integrity of this belief by consecrating transactional and speculative inclinations, instead of moral obligations and affections, as the genesis of social relationships. Rather than seeing commerce and trade as the material gifts of European civilization to be handled with care, thinkers captive to this mindset conceived them as deities in themselves – "the gods of our oeconomical politicians" – that should command relations among human beings and between the government and the people. The Gallican Church and the French nobility thus came under attack. Ethics and manners surrendered to the muscle of speculation. Morality was monetized.

One must not confuse Burke's point in this context with his other reflections on the merits of free enterprise. As we have learned, he was a vocal proponent of market liberty and a recognized authority on commercial questions throughout his parliamentary service. Why, then, did he lambaste "oeconomical politicians" for exalting commercial activity when he himself stated less than six years later, in *Letter to a Noble Lord*, that being an "oeconomist" – "well understood" – was a "good deal"?[145] Why did he condemn "sophisters, oeconomists, and calculators" in the *Reflections*? Why did he write in a private letter in 1791, "It were better to forget once for all, the *Encylcopedie* and the whole body of Economists and to revert to those old rules and principles which have hitherto made princes great and nations happy"?[146] Was not Burke a self-professed student of political economy?

Burke's "well understood" qualification, when combined with his commentary on the ethical preconditions of commerce, can help us answer this question. Based on Burke's own activities in Parliament, political economy in his view was a worthy object of study for the apprehension of foreign and domestic commercial relations; the implications of trade on foreign policy and the national interest; and the impact of government regulations on the flow of provisions, among various economic matters he confronted in his public career. The sober application of mind to political economy was the best means to master the complexities of supply and demand laws, and to understand the connection between the law of scarcity and the competitive price system. In order to grasp how man satisfied his needs for food and

---

[144] Langford, *Writings and Speeches*, IX, 242.   [145] Langford, *Writings and Speeches*, IX, 159.
[146] Burke to Claude-François de Rivarol, 1 June 1791, in *Correspondence of Edmund Burke*, vol. VI, 267. De Rivarol was a royalist sympathizer who had left France in 1790.

shelter, a thoughtful investigation into the science of political economy offered the most appropriate avenue for intellectual and empirical reflection.

Yet Burke conceived man as something more than an animal impelled to realize his basic biological necessities. As this book has emphasized, his conception of political economy cannot be fully comprehended if we confine our inquiry to his examination of commercial gain. Burke did not isolate his meditations on commerce from the wider ethical, cultural, and political implications of trade on civil society – the foremost being that man was defined by qualities beyond those of transactional exchange. For one guiding theme in the *Reflections* is that human beings should not be wholly subject to the perishable nature of voluntary agreements, as exemplified by market contracts.

The premise of this theme is that man is not a mere brutish creature, enslaved to the low pursuit of material self-preservation. Man distinguishes himself from other animals by his exercise of chivalry and morality, religion and ethics, which was not dependent on the satisfaction of sensual or material desire, and that outlasted the fleeting sparks of conditional commercial agreement. Human beings were not "poor and sordid barbarians" but men and women of honor crafted in the divine image of God and endowed by Him with the faculty of reason.

This is where Burke detaches himself from the thought of John Locke and other contractarian thinkers in the early modern period on the subject of political economy. Burke acknowledged the importance of property and commerce in civil society, but he believed that the essence of man transcended the demands of biological self-fulfillment, the calculus of pleasure and pain, and the fulfillment of transitory contracts. We must not paint a distorted caricature of Locke: he was not a blind individualist elevating the pursuit of profit above all other human endeavors, and he provided a credible defense of Christianity, if liberal for its time. But his thought tended to reduce social relations to the kind of interim contractual arrangements seeking self-preservation that Burke blasts with bitter force in the *Reflections*.

Therefore, Burke's reprimand of "oeconomists" and "oeconomical politicians" (along with sophisters and calculators) in the *Reflections* attempted to expose an historical and intellectual strand of Enlightenment political thought he believed spelled doom for Europe. Historically speaking, the "oeconomists" to which Burke refers most likely included the Physiocrats and their ally Turgot, both of whom advocated a free grain trade in prerevolutionary France and espoused liberal principles of political economy similar to those supported by Burke. Yet, in his view, they also were guilty of spreading abstract, doctrinaire notions of civil society untethered from France's ancestral connections that laid the intellectual seeds for radical political movements such as the French Revolution.

An additional "oeconomist," as well as sophister and calculator, was most likely Richard Price, the English natural rights theorist whose impassioned sermon in support of the French Revolution provoked Burke into writing the *Reflections*, and who was an authority on public finance and compound interest.[147] Furthermore, one "oeconomical politicia[n]" Burke had in mind, J. G. A. Pocock posits, may have been Josiah Tucker, a contemporary economist and Burke antagonist.[148]

More important, on an intellectual level, Burke's attack on "oeconomists," "oeconomical politicians," sophisters, and calculators drew attention to a particular attitude about human nature embraced not only by French revolutionary politicians, *philosophes*, and the monied interest, but also by radical strands of English and Scottish thought eager to sanctify the new creeds of transactional exchange and contractarianism. This attitude, from Burke's perspective, can be explained by a number of precepts: society should be conceived through notions of abstract reason; human relationships should be animated purely by the principles of voluntary association, contingent social arrangements, and temporary quid pro quo agreements; and transactional and speculative activity should precede chivalric virtue as the heartbeat of social relations. According to this line of thinking, as Burke saw it, human beings held no deeper goal than to optimize the value of conditional exchange, whether in politics or economics. Authority rested simply in the province of consensual agreement rather than in the ancient roots of time-honored morality and religion. Human relations were established by mere consent, and carried no elevated meaning beyond the gratification of the self. Man was bound to man by the chains of cold logic rather than by natural sentiment.

---

[147] See Jerry Z. Muller, ed., *Conservatism: An Anthology of Social and Political Thought from David Hume to the Present* (Princeton: Princeton University Press, 1997), 103n53.

[148] Pocock, *Virtue, Commerce, and History*, 199n17. (For Tucker's criticism of Burke's views in *Speech on Conciliation with America*, see W. G. Shelton, "Dean Tucker's A Letter to Edmund Burke," *Studies in Burke and His Time* 34 (1968–69): 1155–1161.) This interpretation is further fueled by William Warburton's remark that Tucker made "trade his religion" (Rev. John Selby Watson, *The Life of William Warburton, Lord Bishop of Gloucester from 1760 to 1779: With Remarks on His Works* (London: Longman, etc., 1863), 496). Dugald Stewart captured such suspicion about the abstract notions of commercial liberty when he observed that "it was not unusual" in the 1790s "to confound, studiously, the speculative doctrines of Political Economy, with those discussions concerning the first principles of Government which happened unfortunately at that time to agitate the public mind" (Hamilton, *Collected Works of Dugald Stewart*, vol. X, 87). See also "Introduction," Chapter 6. Consult Salim Rashid, "Economists and the Age of Chivalry: Notes on a Passage in Burke's *Reflections*," *Eighteenth-Century Studies* 20 (1986): 56–61. Rashid contends that the contemporary spelling of "oeconomist" referred to Quesnay and the Physiocrats, suggesting that Burke was channeling his ire toward them in the *Reflections*. This was most likely the case, although it should be noted that Burke was called an "oeconomist," and his proposals for economical reform were characterized as plans of "oeconomy," in specific regard to Burke's program in the early 1780s to tame the extravagance and promote frugality in the British government, which had nothing to do with the economic thought of the Physiocrats. See Robinson, *Life in Caricature*, 50–52. See also 68, 72–75.

Although the phrase arrived after him, Burke suggests that this group viewed human beings as *homo economicus*, economic man. For Burke, misguided economists, like other ill-informed observers of the human disposition, understood men as moved by economic considerations alone, their worth determined by the temptations of transactional barter. They saw men not as part of a broader cultural and ethical order but as dispersed atoms of rationalist and utilitarian calculation, perpetually conditioned to measuring the merit of human action based on perceived immediate advantage, not on unqualified love and pre-commercial ethical commitments. Under this reasoning, men held no responsibilities beyond their generation. The delight in conditional pleasures confined their minds and lowered their hearts to the present moment, exhibiting no reverence for their past or willingness to sacrifice any immediate enjoyments for the sake of posterity.

In Burke's judgment, however, man was best understood not as a rationalist utilitarian calculator but as a species whose instinctual affections and immemorial customs channeled liberty toward duty, duty toward reverence, and reverence toward awe. English society represented such communal attachments: "[W]e still feel within us, and we cherish and cultivate, those inbred sentiments which are the faithful guardians, the active monitors of our duty, the true supporters of all liberal and manly morals."[149]

Similarly, man was not an individual emerging out of an abstract state of nature merely seeking to preserve his pre-civil right to self-preservation, but rather a *social* being who held moral obligations to the society at large. "Men are never in a state of *total* independence of each other," he writes in *First Letter on a Regicide Peace*, objecting to the French revolutionary pretense, as he understood it, that men were free to act without being bound by any prior ethical duties to their community. "It is not the condition of our nature; nor is it conceivable how any man can pursue a considerable course of action without it's having some effect upon others; or, of course, without producing some degree of responsibility for his conduct."[150]

Burke's front against such insidious conceptions of man spread by economists, sophisters, and calculators exposed the dangerous union between abstractionism and utilitarianism, the former draining man of dignity, and the latter then exploiting him for grand social experimentation. This idea in Burke's writings on the French Revolution was part of his wider attack in the *Reflections* on the belief that human reality could be controlled by men in power and reduced to hardened precepts of speculative logic. The conceit that politicians and bureaucrats, revolutionaries and *philosophes*, could, and should, measure and compute and tinker with man's sentiments and customs for supposedly benevolent purposes reflected an impoverished understanding of the

---

[149] Langford, *Writings and Speeches*, VIII, 137.
[150] Langford, *Writings and Speeches*, IX, 249.

complexities of society and the depth of the soul. Men were not mice in an air pump.

The implications of Burke's argument about the ethical preconditions of commercial activity were not simply theoretical in nature. If the morality that preceded transactional exchange was destroyed, and if the essence of man was a rationalist calculator, then human relationships would melt into a swamp of political instrumentality. The practical effect would be the fracturing of the religious and aristocratic foundations that allowed commerce and economic activity to prosper in the first place. Men and women would associate merely for instant self-satisfaction, not out of friendship and affection. Families and communities would be tied together – if they were tied together at all – by heartless utility and speculation rather than warm sympathy and compassion. The value of man would be measured ultimately by those with raw power.

In his letter to William Elliott in 1795, Burke recognized that the prosperity of Europe prior to the French Revolution was partially responsible for the dissolution of the moral and religious basis of commercial affluence. "[T]his prosperity contained in itself the seeds of its own danger," he wrote. "In one part of the society it caused laxity and debility. In the other it produced bold spirits and dark designs." The growth of riches produced human complacency and apathy, for there became no higher object to strive for in society than earthly satisfaction, Burke implies. "General wealth loosened morals, relaxed vigilance, and increased presumption." Enterprising men harbored progressively stronger ambitions for the acquisition of more and more lucre, creating a struggle between "establishment and rapacity." The consequence of these trends was the disintegration of faith: "Religion, that held the materials of the fabrick together, was first systematically loosened." Because property was "left undefended by principles," it came under attack as well.[151] The subversion of the underlying ethical and religious structure of European prosperity invited the destruction of property rights – and civil order.

Burke's dread about the revolutionaries' consecration of transactional exchange explains his famous observation that the French Revolution brought about the radical transformation of moral affection, as well as political and commercial society. The events of October 5 and 6, 1789 – when a French mob laid siege to the Palace of Versailles and forced the royal family back to Paris[152] – occasioned "the most important of all revolutions," meaning "a revolution in sentiments, manners, and moral opinions."[153] The French Revolution was "an attempt to destroy within us every principle of respect."[154] This vanishing sense of respect laid the roots for the coercion of the French people.

---

[151] Burke to William Elliott, 26 May 1795, in Langford, *Writings and Speeches*, IX, 39.
[152] The mob was sparked on October 5 by Frenchwomen who began to riot over the scarcity of bread and cost of provisions. It besieged the National Assembly in addition to the royal family.
[153] Langford, *Writings and Speeches*, VIII, 131.
[154] Langford, *Writings and Speeches*, VIII, 131.

Hence the foundations of peace and liberty were not established by radical ideology, but by the power of faith, and the institution of marriage. "The Christian Religion, by confining it to the pairs, and by rendering that relation indissoluble, has, by these two things, done more towards the peace, happiness, settlement, and civilization of the world, than by any other part in this whole scheme of Divine Wisdom," Burke writes in *First Letter on a Regicide Peace*.[155] The Legislative Assembly's transformation of marriage into a transactional contract that could be dissolved by divorce and mutual consent exemplified the Revolution's demotion of unconditional social associations to mere acts of pleasure and convenience. The new French institutions "strike at the root of our social nature," Burke insists when describing their role in shredding the bonds of love and duty that had sustained human relationships throughout the centuries.[156] For religion, not markets, was the anchor of civilization: "[R]eligion is the basis of civil society, and the source of all good and of all comfort."[157]

As Burke observes, civilization might continue to persist even without optimizing a people's capacity to trade – as long as "nobility and religion"[158] remain. In this case, "sentiment," furnished by the aristocracy and clergy, "supplies" the place of commerce.[159] But if the "old fundamental principles" of religion and nobility perish, then civilization would collapse into a horde of barbarous and disconnected individuals, unrefined in taste and manners and devoid of pride and honor. Men would become "ferocious" and "gross" – not to mention "poor."[160] There would remain no civilizing constraints to guide individuals to interact with each other based on a sense of mutual respect and admiration. The defeat of ethics and virtue would liberate man to pursue individual self-gratification, inevitably leading to socially fragmented communities and psychologically tormented individuals.

The most diabolical consequence of this process was existential in nature. Stripped of the protecting presences of virtue and honor, men would exist not for any deeper moral purpose but merely to serve the radical aims of another man's ends. Encroachment on the inviolable dignity of man, then, could be justified by rulers as a necessary means for progress and prosperity, as conceived by such rulers. Burke's argument, distilled to its essence, is that the substitution of temporary contracts in place of pre-commercial ethics as the primary driver of social relations provokes the uninhibited expansion of the state and the rise of engineers of the soul.

---

[155] Langford, *Writings and Speeches*, IX, 243.   [156] Langford, *Writings and Speeches*, IX, 243.
[157] Langford, *Writings and Speeches*, IX, 141.
[158] Langford, *Writings and Speeches*, VIII, 130.
[159] Langford, *Writings and Speeches*, VIII, 130.
[160] Langford, *Writings and Speeches*, VIII, 131.

The Scottish Enlightenment

As J. G. A. Pocock has noticed, Burke's belief in the *Reflections* of the ethical preconditions of markets challenged the historiography of commerce put forth by Scottish Enlightenment thinkers, including Adam Smith, David Hume, William Robertson, and John Millar, all of whom, according to Pocock, were more likely to connect the genesis of commercial activity with a refinement in human behavior.[161] "Burke is asserting that commerce is dependent upon manners, and not the other way round; a civilized society is the prerequisite of exchange relations, and the latter alone cannot create the former," he writes.[162] Yet these Scottish thinkers "had all isolated the growth of exchange, production and diversified labour as the motor force which created the growth of manners, culture, and enlightenment."[163] Hence they had adopted the Enlightenment perspective of political economy that attributed the growth of civil order to the advent of market liberty.

Let us, then, briefly draw out the similarities and differences between Burke and the Scottish thinkers on the compatibility between commerce and ethics.[164] Like Burke, the Scots recognized the harmonious coexistence between exchange economies and traditional marks of high culture. In his essay, "Of Refinement in the Arts," David Hume observed, "The same age, which produces great philosophers and politicians, renowned generals and poets, usually abounds with skilful weavers, and ship-carpenters." Even more, "We cannot reasonably expect, that a piece of woollen cloth will be wrought to perfection in a nation, which is ignorant of astronomy, or where ethics are neglected."[165] Adam Smith himself was the living embodiment of the alliance between markets and morals: he served as a professor of moral philosophy, and wrote an influential book on moral and social philosophy, *The Theory of Moral Sentiments*, before crafting his celebrated defense of liberal commercial activity, *The Wealth of Nations*.

In addition, Burke, like the Scots, pierced the romantic aura of feudal institutions, as we recall from his critical remarks on the royal household in *Speech on Economical Reform*.[166] Spanning back to the late 1750s, Burke, in *Essay towards an Abridgment of the English History*, called a "feudal

---

[161] See, however, Edmund Burke, *Revolutionary Writings:* Reflections on the Revolution in France *and the First* Letter on a Regicide Peace, ed. Iain Hampsher-Monk (Cambridge: Cambridge University Press, 2014), 78n158.

[162] Pocock, *Virtue, Commerce, and History*, 199.

[163] Pocock, *Virtue, Commerce, and History*, 199.

[164] Of course, a "school" of thought, like the Scottish Enlightenment, includes a variety of intellectual permutations. The following analysis will attempt to draw out general patterns of thought in the Scottish school.

[165] Hume, *Essays*, 270–271.

[166] Consult Chapter 5. For the Scottish thinkers' critical views on how feudalism obstructed commercial prosperity, see Neil Davidson, *How Revolutionary Were the Bourgeois Revolutions?* (Chicago: Haymarket Books, 2012), 45–54.

aristocracy" the "worst imaginable government."[167] Therefore, while Burke did grant a measure of legitimacy to primogeniture entail that Smith did not,[168] it is also true that Burke and the Scottish thinkers issued sharp reprimands of feudal structures throughout their lives.

The seeming gulf between Burke and the Scottish school narrows further if we take into account Burke's other writings and speeches that illustrate the connection between commercial transactions and ethical behavior. In brief, the general Scottish view on this matter emphasized that the diffusion of market exchange promoted the rise in commercial virtues such as industry and diligence. "Whenever commerce is introduced into any country, probity and punctuality always accompany it," Adam Smith stated in his *Lectures on Jurisprudence*. "These virtues in a rude and barbarous country are almost unknown."[169] David Hume wrote in his essay, "Of Refinement in the Arts": "In times when industry and the arts flourish, men are kept in perpetual occupation ... The mind acquires new vigour ... and by an assiduity in honest industry, both satisfies its natural appetites, and prevents the growth of unnatural ones, which commonly spring up, when nourished by ease and idleness."[170] Commerce was the germ for a new conception of virtue in modernity characterized by productive energy, not contemplation.[171]

Consider *Thoughts and Details* in this context. Burke's message in the tract is not simply that the domestic grain trade should be lightly regulated, but that voluntary exchange encourages farmers and laborers to treat each other well. The incentive of self-interest compels the farmer to provide good working conditions for his laborer. The laborer is motivated to help the farmer produce a profit in order to maintain his employment and earn a wage. The voluntary contract prompts both parties to act in an ethical fashion, which produces a level of social concord not possible under an arbitrary government. In essence, commerce was a precondition of manners in *Thoughts and Details* – not the other way around.

Furthermore, as discussed in Chapter 8, Scottish Enlightenment thinkers held that robust commercial intercourse led to greater prospects for political tranquility.[172] Because trading countries received mutual advantages from the diffusion of foreign goods, commerce was a medium that defused the possibility of military conflict as a source of national gain. Trade occasioned peace.

---

[167] Langford, *Writings and Speeches*, I, 547.
[168] Burke provided a qualified defense of primogeniture. See Langford, *Writings and Speeches*, IV, 433–434; IX, 436–437; and VIII, 83, 102, 212. Smith criticized the practice because it impeded industry. See *Lectures on Jurisprudence*, 466.
[169] Smith, *Lectures on Jurisprudence*, 538.   [170] Hume, *Essays*, 270.
[171] Note, however, that Adam Ferguson was more critical of the corrupting effects of commerce. See Gary L. McDowell, "Commerce, Virtue, and Politics: Adam Ferguson's Constitutionalism," *The Review of Politics* 45 (1983): 536–552.
[172] Consult also Berry, *Idea of Commercial Society in the Scottish Enlightenment*.

Burke's statements on behalf of the Irish trade bills were stirred by a similar conviction. "[Y]ou trade very largely where you are met by the goods of all nations," we recall him writing in *Two Letters*.[173] And Burke's efforts endorsing the Free Port Act of 1766 were animated by the attempt to unite the trading interests of North American merchants and West Indian traders. Burke wrote that the "Passions and Animosities of the Colonies" were "allayed and composed, and the Foundation laid for a lasting Agreement amongst them."[174] Taking such examples into account, Burke, similar to the Scots, held that commerce could serve as an antidote to parochialism and anti-market prejudice. For Burke, economic reform – not chivalry – encouraged concord among the British colonies.

Of course, one could use Burke's argument in the *Reflections* about the primacy of manners and apply it to the aforementioned examples. A farmer and laborer could not enter into a mutual contract in the first place without recognizing the other party as an individual who merits respect. One nation could not enact free trade agreements with another without both powers arriving at a mutual understanding of the conditions of the commercial regulations, thereby achieving some measure of friendly unity prior to the act of exchange. Yet Burke does not make these points explicitly in many of his writings and speeches on political economy outside the *Reflections*, and instead stresses the harmonizing effects that resulted from commercial freedom and market competition.

Beyond his legislative activities in pursuit of commercial liberty, Burke's view of the historical trajectory of England reflected similarities with the Scottish Enlightenment's stadial historiography of the general progression of mankind.[175] This perspective is evident in Burke's *Essay towards an Abridgment of the English History*. Written in the late 1750s, the dissertation traces the development of Britain from its pre-Roman days to the rise and fall of Roman Britain, then to the growth of Christianity, and finally ending at Magna Carta. When outlining this history, Burke, in line with the Scottish philosophers, frequently uses language that suggests an advance from barbarity to civilized behavior. In the early days of ancient Britain, "the whole face of nature was extremely rude and uncultivated; when the links of commerce, even in the countries first settled, were few and weak," he writes.[176] Observe that Burke, like the Scots, is bracketing rudeness with commercial underdevelopment. He remarks of the Anglo-Saxons:

---

[173] Langford, *Writings and Speeches*, IX, 511.

[174] Langford, *Writings and Speeches*, II, 55–56.

[175] For an investigation into Burke as an historian, see Sora Sato, *Edmund Burke as Historian: War, Order and Civilisation* (London: Palgrave Macmillan, 2017). For a discussion of the Scots' approach to the study of history, see Ronald L. Meek, *Social Science & the Ignoble Savage* (Cambridge: Cambridge University Press, 1976).

[176] Langford, *Writings and Speeches*, I, 345.

Thus ignorant in sciences, and arts, and unpractised in trade or manufacture, military exercises, war and the preparation for war was their employment, hunting their pleasure. They dwelt in cottages of wicker work, plastered with clay, and thatched with rushes, where they sat with their families, their officers and domesticks, round a fire made in the middle of the house. In this manner their greatest princes lived amidst the ruins of Roman magnificence.[177]

Rather than demonstrating a facility for art and commerce, the Anglo-Saxons were intent on enhancing the prowess of their military. And their living standards were decrepit and underdeveloped. Neglect of commerce corresponded with the absence of civility.[178]

In the *Reflections*, Burke also associates commercial backwardness with barbarism in non-Western cultures. Under the "ferocious sword" of Nadir Shah in Persia, and the "barbarous anarchic despotism" of Turkey, these were countries where "arts are unknown, where manufactures languish, where science is extinguished, where agriculture decays, where the human race itself melts away and perishes under the eye of the observer."[179] Like the Scottish thinkers, Burke believed that civilized temper of man tended to align with the affluence of industry as collective indicators of societal growth, mirroring the general Whig vision of progress in the eighteenth century.

Based on this evidence, how can we best understand the relationship between Burke and the Scots on the historiography of commerce and ethics? First let us offer a clarifying note: Burke maintained that market activity stimulated the exercise not of ancient virtue but *commercial virtue*, such as diligence and industry, and assisted in the reduction of social tensions between parties. This is not to say that Scottish thinkers exerted a direct influence on his economic thought, but it is to say that Burke, beyond the pages of the *Reflections*, at times adopted reasoning similar to that of Scottish thinkers about the civilizing effects of free commerce. Of course, Burke's self-understanding of his intellectual convergence with the school is also evident in the anecdote conveyed in Robert Bisset's biography of Burke, in which Bisset reported that Smith, in Burke's telling, said he thought "exactly"[180] the same way as Smith did on economic matters.

But even if Burke's thoughts beyond the *Reflections* narrow the divide between his beliefs and Scottish historiography, they still do not close it. Though Burke believed that markets could bring about commercial virtue, he did indeed place a sharper accent than the Scots on the idea that religion and chivalry were necessary preconditions for the emergence of commercial activity in the first place, which, following the pattern of his logic, enabled commercial virtue to flourish. Before proceeding on this matter, we must acknowledge that

[177] Langford, *Writings and Speeches*, I, 393.

[178] Burke goes on to write that the introduction of Christianity "soon made a sensible change in these rude and fierce manners" (Langford, *Writings and Speeches*, I, 393).

[179] Langford, *Writings and Speeches*, VIII, 176.   [180] Bisset, *Life of Edmund Burke*, 429.

Scottish thinkers recognized that chivalry had *some* effect on the improvement of manners. "Valour, humanity, courtesy, justice, honour, were the characteristic qualities of chivalry" in the Middle Ages, wrote William Robertson in *A View of the Progress of Society in Europe*.[181] John Millar remarked that "the manners introduced by chivalry ... may still be observed to have a good deal of influence upon the taste and sentiments even of the present age."[182]

In regard to his own argument, Burke does admit in the *Reflections* that it was difficult to determine the degree to which ancient chivalry was responsible for public affluence: "How much of that prosperous state was owing to the spirit of our old manners and opinions is not easy to say; but as such causes cannot be indifferent in their operation, we must presume, that, on the whole, their operation was beneficial."[183] Yet the lasting distinction is that prominent Scottish thinkers did not appear to endorse the particular argument posed by Burke that the advent of mass markets could be traced back specifically to pre-commercial foundations of medieval Europe. For many Scots, as well as French and English thinkers keen on commerce, chivalric morality may have flourished in the Middle Ages, but this ethical code was not a necessary precursor to the modern ascent of trade. In Burke's judgment, it was.

The distinctions between Burke and Scottish Enlightenment thinkers return us to the intellectual relationship between him and F. A. Hayek. We learned in Chapter 4 that Burke and Hayek shared a disdain for the intrusion of abstract rationality into complex market activities. Yet their conceptions of political economy were not synonymous. Although Hayek invoked common morality as a basis for liberty[184] and believed that tradition and freedom were compatible,[185] he, like prominent Scottish thinkers, did not go as far as Burke in attributing commercial prosperity to ancient manners and religion.

Furthermore, Hayek thought that the values of society should derive from the influence of market desires. As he writes in *Constitution of Liberty*:

Though there is a presumption that any established social standard contributes in some manner to the preservation of civilization, our only way of confirming this is to ascertain whether it continues to prove itself in competition with other standards observed by other individuals or groups.

The competition on which the process of selection rests must be understood in the widest sense. It involves competition between organized and unorganized groups no less than competition between individuals.[186]

---

[181] Robertson, *Works of Wm. Robertson*, 63. See also Ryu Susato, "The Idea of Chivalry in the Scottish Enlightenment: The Case of David Hume," *Hume Studies* 33 (2007): 155–178.

[182] John Millar, *The Origin of the Distinction of Ranks*, ed. Aaron Garrett (Indianapolis: Liberty Fund, 2006), 141. See also Adam Ferguson, *An Essay on the History of Civil Society* (Philadelphia: A. Finley, 1819), 359–365.

[183] Langford, *Writings and Speeches*, VIII, 129.   [184] Hayek, *Constitution of Liberty*, 123.

[185] Hayek, *Constitution of Liberty*, 122.   [186] Hayek, *Constitution of Liberty*, 88.

Gradual experimentation in an environment of competition was the ultimate driver of civilization.

In the *Reflections*, however, Burke places far greater stress on the idea that the preservation of civil order relied on sources beyond the evolutionary capacities of transactional exchange.[187] Society was more than a drawn-out process of market competition among groups and individuals. Burke retained a stronger sense that some knowledge, and some virtue, and some religion, should remain beyond the grasp of exchange economies. From his perspective, the foundations of civil order and civil progress were animated by powers that transcended the laws of supply and demand. There was life beyond spontaneous order.

In the end, Burke's argument about manners and markets not only offered a compelling case that they were harmonizing chords in the growth of European civilization, but it also rested on a unique principle of cause and effect distinct from the political thought of other proponents of commercial liberty in the Enlightenment period: the steady hands of chivalry and the nobility and religion spawned the preconditions for economic vitality. Ancient virtue furnished the civil environment necessary for commercial virtue to blossom.

12.4 THE LIMITS OF VOLUNTARY CONTRACTS AND TRANSACTIONAL EXCHANGE

Burke's sharp emphasis on the moral roots of commerce illuminates the most important philosophical lesson in the *Reflections* that relates to his conception of political economy: civilizations cannot sustain themselves on the principles of transactional exchange and voluntary contracts alone. The origins of this idea in Burke's thought can be extracted from a seemingly unlikely source, the *Philosophical Enquiry*. Even though the book addresses aesthetics, not politics, it offers comments on the subjects of curiosity and novelty that anticipate Burke's attack on temporary political gratification in the *Reflections*. "The first and simplest emotion which we discover in the human mind, is Curiosity," he writes in the *Philosophical Enquiry*. "By curiosity, I mean whatever desire we have for, or whatever pleasure we take in novelty."[188] The shifting curiosities of children exemplify this notion, Burke explains.

Yet unbounded curiosity posed a hazard to social order. It

---

[187] Hayek did argue that there was an important role in civil society for the truly wealthy – those who did not need to rely on employment to sustain their livelihood – to promote the arts and culture (*Constitution of Liberty*, 184–196). We should also note that Hayek's faith in markets to drive civilization conveyed his unease toward established religion. He demonstrated deep respect toward faith but remained uncomfortable with Christian orthodoxy and the idea of a revelatory God. He remained an agnostic throughout his life. See Elzinga and Givens, "Christianity and Hayek," 53–68.

[188] Langford, *Writings and Speeches*, I, 210.

is the most superficial of all the affections; it changes its object perpetually; it has an appetite which is very sharp, but very easily satisfied; and it has always an appearance of giddiness, restlessness and anxiety. Curiosity from its nature is a very active principle; it quickly runs over the greatest part of its objects, and soon exhausts the variety which is commonly to be met with in nature; the same things make frequent returns, and they return with less and less of any agreeable affect.[189]

Formulated differently, the occurrences of life, by the time we come to know it a little, would be incapable of affecting the mind with any other sensations than those of loathing and weariness, if many things were not adapted to affect the mind by means of other powers besides novelty in them, and of other passions besides curiosity in ourselves.[190]

Curiosity and desire do not direct man's energies toward a constant object. They introduce and spark – curiosity is an "active principle," as Burke says, evoking the quality of the enthusiastic innovator he assails in the *Reflections* – but they do not settle and maintain. Novelty provides temporary satisfaction for human passions, but the recurring gratification of desire furnishes no enduring principle for mental repose and social stability. Curiosity and novelty should not be struck from civil society, but man should be aware of their limits, Burke suggests in the *Philosophical Enquiry*.

This insight into human emotion builds the psychological frame for his political argument in the *Reflections* that transactional exchange cannot preserve civil order by itself. For Burke, social relations should not be reduced to matters of voluntary barter, speculative adventure, or ad hoc contracts. Market exchange fulfilled the curiosities and ingenuities of man; it encouraged novelties, met human desire, and promoted activity and energy. But men and women were more than creatures of curiosity. The aims of civil society surpassed the enlivening of sensation or the enjoyment of pleasure.

In other words, states flourished and civilizations endured not simply because of exchange economies and the drive for self-preservation and the accumulation of riches. In his speech opposing the Anglo-French Commercial Treaty of 1786, Burke anticipated this perspective in the *Reflections* by remarking that if a nation lost its honor, it does did not matter if it remained materially prosperous because of "fine cambrics, of rich scarlet or good black cloth, of silks or sattins."[191] He thus asked, "When a man has once sacrificed his honor, in what respect is he better than a beast? What is he good for, but to fatten?"[192] Nations should not sacrifice integrity to the temptations of excess affluence.

Burke broadens this theme in the *Reflections* by redefining contractarian views of society that were popular in elite French and English circles in the eighteenth century:

---

[189] Langford, *Writings and Speeches*, I, 210.   [190] Langford, *Writings and Speeches*, I, 210.
[191] Langford, *Writings and Speeches*, IV, 240.   [192] Langford, *Writings and Speeches*, IV, 240.

Society is indeed a contract. Subordinate contracts for objects of mere occasional interest may be dissolved at pleasure – but the state ought not to be considered as nothing better than a partnership agreement in a trade of pepper and coffee, callico or tobacco, or some other such low concern, to be taken up for a little temporary interest, and to be dissolved by the fancy of the parties ... it is not a partnership in things subservient only to the gross animal existence of a temporary and perishable nature.[193]

The character of society transcends the collection of voluntary agreements made by autonomous individuals over goods or politics. There is more to life than the acquisition of fleeting riches.

Man could choose to enter into or leave ad hoc contracts, then, but he did not have the right to escape his ethical duties in civil society. "Now though civil society might be at first a voluntary act (which in many cases it undoubtedly was) its continuance is under a permanent standing covenant, coexisting with the society; and it attaches upon every individual of that society, without any formal act of his own," Burke writes in *Appeal from the New to the Old Whigs*.[194] For duties "are not voluntary."[195] Virtue, unlike commercial exchange, was not a matter of choice.

The existential danger of the French Revolution, and of the new Whigs' attraction to the Revolution, derived from France's attempt to apply the principles of temporary contracts to society at large, such as the transformation of marriage from a religious covenant to a civil contract.[196] As Burke writes, revolutionaries perceived society as a "partnership agreement"; men chose to enter into society and form government for the fulfillment of individual wants. (The revolutionaries themselves, of course, believed they were advancing the principles of liberty, equality, and fraternity.) Similarly, the new Whigs held that a sovereign people "may set up any new fashion of government for themselves, or continue without any government at their pleasure."[197]

Furthermore, if institutions did not satisfy these desires, men had a right to overthrow them and establish new modes and practices. "Are we to deny to a *majority* of the people the right of altering even the whole frame of their society, if such should be their pleasure?" Burke asks, condemning the revolutionaries' claim that their schemes were backed by "the *people*."[198] Such sweeping alterations limited contracts to one generation: "[I]f a contract *de facto* is made with [magistrates] in one age, allowing that it binds at all, it

---

[193] Langford, *Writings and Speeches*, VIII, 146–147. As Sunil M. Agnani notes, Burke's references to such commodities call attention to the global and historical influence of the British Empire, spanning from the empire's East Indian interests in the Old World (calico and pepper) to its North American colonies in the New World (tobacco). See Agnani, *Hating Empire Properly*, 72.

[194] Langford, *Writings and Speeches*, IV, 442. [195] Langford, *Writings and Speeches*, IV, 442.

[196] Consult Suzanne Desan, "The French Revolution and the Family," in Peter McPhee, ed., *A Companion to the French Revolution* (Chichester, UK: Wiley-Blackwell), 473.

[197] Langford, *Writings and Speeches*, IV, 410. [198] Langford, *Writings and Speeches*, IV, 440.

only binds those who were immediately concerned in it, but does not pass to posterity."[199] Apply this principle to exchange economies: market contracts, like revolutionary contracts, secure commitments from people for only a limited span of time.

Accordingly, because ad hoc contractual relations are deprived of the essential element of permanence necessary for an enduring political order, societies based on subordinate contracts of pleasure lead to radical swings in political institutions. Burke writes, "They may change it, say they, from a monarchy to a republic to-day, and to-morrow back again from a republic to a monarchy; and so backward and forward as often as they like."[200] The political community thus trembles at the mercy of rulers: "They are masters of the commonwealth; because in substance they are themselves the commonwealth."[201] Violent political transformation in the name of the people, then, not only subverts "all government" and "all stable securities to rational freedom," but also "all the rules and principles of morality itself."[202]

As Burke emphasizes, men in power do *not* have the right to dissolve existing political, social, and religious institutions based on mere indulgence when they deem them to be inconvenient – unlike traders, who could voluntarily join or withdraw from market contracts according to their subjective preferences (consistent with the terms of the agreement). "Neither the few nor the many have a right to act merely by their will, in any matter connected with duty, trust, engagement, or obligation," Burke states.[203] He continues: "The constitution of a country being once settled upon some compact, tacit or expressed, there is no power existing of force to alter it, without the breach of the covenant, or the consent of all the parties. Such is the nature of a contract."[204] An enduring contract in civil society is really a pledge of trust among men, rather than a temporary instrument for private advantage. And to the extent that such pledges are based on consent, as Burke intimates, this consent must be achieved through duty and engagement – such as the duty to seek the counsel of the people to gauge whether they would like to uproot existing institutions. French leaders in power did not execute this prior ethical obligation, in Burke's judgment.

Therefore, while Burke praised enlightened avarice for spreading commercial affluence, he denounced the commodification of that which, in his view, eclipsed considerations of trade and utility, convenience and pleasure. What were these considerations? Upon examining Burke's philosophy of political economy in this book, we are now able to arrive at an answer: religious establishments (such as the Church of England and the Gallican Church); families; marriages; moderate amounts of landed property; select public monuments and other structures of national significance; trading

---

[199] Langford, *Writings and Speeches*, IV, 411.   [200] Langford, *Writings and Speeches*, IV, 440.
[201] Langford, *Writings and Speeches*, IV, 440.   [202] Langford, *Writings and Speeches*, IV, 411.
[203] Langford, *Writings and Speeches*, IV, 440.   [204] Langford, *Writings and Speeches*, IV, 440.

companies (such as Britain's East India Company); foreign policy and the national interest (see following discussion); public service to the state; the code of ethics that governed social relations in civil society; and, ultimately, the lasting chords of friendship that warmed the heart and enriched the soul. As Burke famously writes in the *Reflections*, there was an "unbought grace of life,"[205] symbolized in particular by these last two imperatives, that commodification could not purchase.

Commerce and Diplomacy

Consistent with this manner of thinking, Burke further signaled in his commentary on the French Revolution that market exchange should not dictate diplomatic relations. This is one of the most overlooked dimensions of Burke's economic thought, and of his political theory in general, but it remains fundamental to his understanding of the delicate relation among political economy, statesmanship, and morals.

Burke conveyed his thoughts on this matter in a relatively obscure speech, *Speech on Traitorous Correspondence Bill*, which he gave on April 9, 1793, five or so months prior to the start of the Reign of Terror. The speech addressed a bill that would have discouraged British subjects from engaging in economic transactions with the French, such as exchanging commodities and purchasing land and securities in France. Violators could face charges of treason. Critics attacked the bill for its potentially injurious impact on commercial activity, as well as for eroding British civil liberties.

Burke, however, threw his firm support behind the bill. He first argued that it was grounded in precedent, while also admitting that war demanded the expansion of royal prerogative. His next argument confronted the issue of trade. In his speech, Burke contended that even if the bill discouraged intercourse with France, the imperatives of national honor and security warranted priority over the maximization of commerce:

England was a Commercial Nation – so was every other, as far as it could. But if, by Commercial Nation, it was implied that Commerce was her ultimate, her only end, he would deny it, her Commerce was a subservient instrument to her greater Interests, her Security, her Honour, and her Religion. If the Commercial spirit tended to break those, he insisted it should be lowered.[206]

These remarks are some of the most telling of Burke's economic thought, distilling to its core his notion of the connection between commerce and statecraft. We have already learned Burke was a stout advocate of foreign trade, as embodied by the Free Port Act and Irish trade bills. But we have also observed he harbored exceeding reservations toward promoting commercial

---

[205] Langford, *Writings and Speeches*, VIII, 127.   [206] Langford, *Writings and Speeches*, IV, 582.

ties with hostile enemies, such as France, as demonstrated by his opposition to the Anglo-French Commercial Treaty of 1786.

Burke's comments in *Speech on Traitorous Correspondence Bill* illustrate continuities with this latter approach. He thought that the elevation of trade above considerations of security and honor in the 1790s undermined Britain's national interests, particularly when trade connections would be forged with a seemingly implacable foe such as revolutionary France. "Nothing can contribute more to the destruction of that Idea of Local Patriotism – than the excessive predominance of *commercial principles*, money and traffick and getting them wholly to supersede the local Interest of the State," Burke wrote in draft notes for his speech.[207]

In light of his fervent support for market liberty throughout his life, Burke's sharp criticism of "commercial principles" here is striking, suggesting a possible contradiction in his economic thought. Burke's point, however, is not that trade should not be considered in the formation of foreign policy, but that it should remain subordinate to the wider national aims during times of military conflict, such as the French Revolutionary Wars.

The contrasting belief that commerce could soften relations between Britain and France was grounded in a dangerous premise, in Burke's judgment. The mood of the times called for a "more *enlarged* Benevolence; to throw down *the Barriers* which seperate communities; totally to destroy in the minds of men that moral relation called *our Country*; and to substitute in its place the Ideal of *Fraternity*."[208] Commerce between neighbors with preexisting mutual interests, such as England and Ireland, could in fact promote concord between the two nations. But the notion that commerce could generate benevolence between two enemies was a perilous assumption, particularly if one party – France – showed no intention of moderating its revolutionary ambitions. Burke was acutely aware that the fashionable presumption that commerce leads to peace – ever-present in his age and today – carried profound limitations, and rested on many preconditions.

Burke reinforced this message in *Fourth Letter on a Regicide Peace*, when he criticized the idea of a commercial treaty between European nations, including Britain, and revolutionary France. Burke wrote in the letter, "I have no objections to Treaties of Commerce, upon principles of commerce. – Traffick for traffick; – all is fair. But commerce, in exchange for empire, for safety, for glory! We set out in our dealing with a miserable cheat upon ourselves."[209] Reducing commercial restrictions between England and Ireland was a worthy aim, but using trade gestures to curry favor with a despotic government was capitulation. Much like social relations between men should be governed by principles beyond transactional barter, political relations between nations should be influenced by considerations that surpassed commercial activity.

---

[207] Langford, *Writings and Speeches*, IV, 585.   [208] Langford, *Writings and Speeches*, IV, 584.
[209] Langford, *Writings and Speeches*, IX, 94.

For Burke, national honor, much like individual honor, should not be up for the market.

The Great Primeval Contract

According to Burke, then, flourishing enterprise was an adornment of prosperous communities. But civil order, and growth, demanded something deeper: a humble commitment to honoring – and, when necessary, reforming – the traditions of the past, social bonds of affection, an ethical foundation, cultural renewal, religious piety, and a sense of honor. As he writes in the *Reflections*, society is "a partnership in all science; a partnership in all art; a partnership in every virtue, and in all perfection."[210] This social contract does not perish after each generation. "Each contract of each particular state is but a clause in the great primaeval contract of eternal society," Burke states.[211] Civilization endures even when transactional exchange is fleeting – if citizens fulfill their moral obligations to their fellow man that exist prior to the arrangement of voluntary contracts, and that remain even after such contracts dissolve.

While modern appraisals of free enterprise offer insights into political economy that Burke did not, the depth of his economic thought is illustrated by its greater awareness of the harmonious cooperation between change and stability; the limits of transient contracts; and the necessary roles of religion and virtue in preserving the integrity of man. If societies permit the principles of market exchange to dictate all social relations, Burke warns, the human essence will be crushed by the soft tyranny of temporary and convenient social partnerships.

12.5 THIRD LETTER ON A REGICIDE PEACE AND THE POLITICAL ECONOMY OF ENGLAND

Burke's insights into political economy during the age of the French Revolution were not confined to the pages of the *Reflections* and *Thoughts and Details*. As indicated throughout this chapter, he also provided compelling remarks on matters of property, commerce, and revenue in his various *Letters on a Regicide Peace*. Allow us to conclude our discussion of Burke's political economy of the Revolution, then, by probing his additional remarks on the subject in *Third Letter on a Regicide Peace*, which offers clarity to many of the themes on economics examined in this book. The thrust of *Third Letter* is Burke's resolute belief that the British government should not negotiate terms of peace with France. Rather than compromise with the revolutionaries, he maintains, Britain should continue to wage war against the nation in order to

---

[210] Langford, *Writings and Speeches*, VIII, 147.
[211] Langford, *Writings and Speeches*, VIII, 147.

check its militaristic and expansionist behavior that threatened to overwhelm Europe.

Perhaps the most significant insight Burke provides in *Third Letter on a Regicide Peace* in relation to his economic thought is the idea that individual interest is the impetus for broad opulence in a commonwealth. He writes:

> There must be some impulse besides public spirit, to put private interest into motion along with it. Monied men ought to be allowed to set a value on their money; if they did not, there could be no monied men. This desire of accumulation, is a principle without which the means of their service to the State could not exist. The love of lucre, though sometimes carried to a ridiculous, sometimes to a vicious excess, is the grand cause of prosperity to all States. In this natural, this reasonable, this powerful, this prolifick principle, it is for the satyrist to expose the ridiculous; it is for the moralist to censure the vicious; it is for the sympathetick heart to reprobate the hard and cruel; it is for the Judge to animadvert on the fraud, the extortion, and the oppression: but it is for the Statesman to employ it as he finds it, with all it's concomitant excellencies, with all it's imperfections on it's head.[212]

At face value, we can clearly detect a correspondence between these comments and Adam Smith's Invisible Hand: the pursuit of private interest generates advantages to the common good and is the germ of public prosperity.

We must also be aware, however, that these remarks in *Third Letter on a Regicide Peace* were addressing a specific historical episode: William Pitt's "loyalty" loan of £18,000,000, subscribed in December 1796 to help fund Britain's ongoing war against France at the time. What Burke is really conveying in this section is that financial investment should operate according to market principles – and one market principle was that private interest breeds public reward, which could then be used by the wise statesman in the service of the national welfare. Burke is applying his notion of the "benign and wise disposer" to the administration of public finance.

In this context, Burke supported Pitt's loan as part of the British government's broader campaign to continue to wage war against revolutionary France. "I liked the loan, not from the influence which it might have on the enemy, but on account of the temper which it indicated in our own people," he contends in the letter.[213] Burke proceeds to deliver three "capital points" in defense of the loan: it illustrated Britain's competence in rallying around a common cause that would serve the interests of Christian Europe, as well as Britain itself; it affirmed the courage and conviction of the English spirit, and this spirit's readiness to assume the burden of weighty responsibilities in times of strife; and it demonstrated the public's confidence in the British government. In essence, such a loan could unite and inspire a people to meet their

[212] Langford, *Writings and Speeches*, IX, 347.   [213] Langford, *Writings and Speeches*, IX, 345.

nation's moral obligations during war, which was waged "in defence of that very property which they expend for it's support."[214]

The terms of Pitt's loan were seen as an excessive bargain to subscribers. Burke suggests that the loan was indeed a "bargain," but proposes that radical economy was even more dangerous: "[T]here is a short sighted parsimony still more fatal than an unforeseeing expence."[215] Burke goes on to defend the liberty of investors to reap a profit and the justness in enabling money markets to operate according to the forces of supply and demand.[216]

The perceived generosity of the bargain was negated by a proposal, supported by Pitt, that would have compelled men of means to lend a percentage of their income to the government, in exchange for debentures issued by the Exchequer, in order to help pay for the interest of the loyalty loan.[217] Burke denounces this measure in *Third Letter on a Regicide Peace* for dissolving the integrity of financial investment. "The moment that shame, or fear, or force, are directly or indirectly applied to a loan, credit perishes," he writes.[218] Besides, it was wrongheaded to presume that the interests of government borrowers and those of private lenders were not aligned. "Constituted as our system of finance and taxation is, the interests of the contracting parties cannot well be separated, whatever they may reciprocally intend," Burke claims. "He who is the hard lender of to-day, to-morrow is the generous contributor to his own payment."[219]

The beneficial flow of man's expenditures confirmed this potent financial synergy between government and the people. Arguing against the claim that interest on the debt paid to private financiers diverted money from circulating throughout the British economy, Burke insists that interest payments placed more financial resources into the hands of "the capitalist" – monied men – for additional investments and expenditures, not to mention for the payment of their taxes, all of which contributed to the public stock. Hence "it is a fallacious estimate of the affairs of a nation to consider" public debt "as a mere burthen."[220] Burke's larger point is that the distribution of money reaches all sectors of society, indicating his firm belief in the power of financial investment to grant advantage to both public and private interests.

The graver danger of compelled contributions was the encouragement of a disposition fond of wealth redistribution, leaving "the comparatively indigent, to judge of the wealth, and to prescribe to the opulent, or those whom they conceive to be such, the use they are to make of their fortunes." Burke continues: "From thence it is but one step to the subversion of all property."[221] Beware of public officials who seek to coerce private men into

---

[214] Langford, *Writings and Speeches*, IX, 346. [215] Langford, *Writings and Speeches*, IX, 346.
[216] See "The Monied Interest and the *Assignats*," Chapter 11.
[217] See Langford, *Writings and Speeches*, IX, 349 and 349n2.
[218] Langford, *Writings and Speeches*, IX, 347. [219] Langford, *Writings and Speeches*, IX, 348.
[220] Langford, *Writings and Speeches*, IX, 348. [221] Langford, *Writings and Speeches*, IX, 350.

relinquishing their capital, as the best of government intentions can occasion the worst of results. "[T]he measure itself will lead them beyond their intention, and what is begun with the best designs, bad men will perversely improve to the worst of their purposes," he writes.[222] Burke summons the example of the "patriotick gifts" of revolutionary France as a prime instance in which a seemingly innocuous call for private contributions to the public stock led to the state's encroachment on property rights.[223]

Burke provides general comments on the British system of taxation and the roots of economic prowess that complement his defense of capitalists. First, England's taxes did not encumber the less fortunate: "Our taxes, for the far greater portion, fly over the heads of the lowest classes."[224] Commercial virtues, the springs of opulence, were common throughout the nation. "With us, labour and frugality, the parents of riches, are spread, and wisely too," Burke observes.[225] Yet he adds a twist to his reasoning: when the private capital of men fails to contribute to the common welfare, this money should be used for the public. "The moment men cease to augment the common stock, the moment they no longer enrich it by their industry or their self-denial," he declares, "their luxury and even their ease are obliged to pay contribution to the publick; not because they are vicious principles, but because they are unproductive."[226] Burke does not go so far as to argue that capitalists should be forced to contribute their money to government – if so, how would this be different from the French expropriation of private property? But it is compelling he suggests that idle capital should be transformed into a public utility.

Let us not overlook the broader significance of Burke's discussion: he is delivering a strong defense of the monied interest. "It is a good thing for a monied man to pledge his property on the welfare of the country; he shews that he places his treasure where his heart is," he states.[227] The preferences of speculators can align with the good of the nation, even during war. This belief contradicted the common suspicion (articulated by Burke in the *Reflections*, no less) that private financiers benefited from the ruins of military conflict.[228] How could Burke reconcile this apologia of the monied interest with his merciless reproach of financiers in France?

We can only offer possible explanations. For Burke, the monied interest performed a critical role in advancing the common welfare if it provided funds to the state for the prosecution of a *justifiable* war, such as, in his assessment, Britain's engagement with France. In his description of the monied interest in Britain, Burke affirms an elemental reality of war: private

[222] Langford, *Writings and Speeches*, IX, 350–351.
[223] See Langford, *Writings and Speeches*, IX, 351 and 351n1.
[224] Langford, *Writings and Speeches*, IX, 348.
[225] Langford, *Writings and Speeches*, IX, 348–349.
[226] Langford, *Writings and Speeches*, IX, 349.   [227] Langford, *Writings and Speeches*, IX, 349.
[228] See Brewer, *Sinews of Power*, 206–210.

financiers possessed an essential resource – capital – needed by the government to meet its military obligations.

We can further surmise that Burke did not harbor the same degree of apprehension toward the monied interest in Britain as he did toward the group in France. As we have learned in this chapter, he believed that the preservation of England's landed interest helped moderate the excesses of financial speculation – unlike the French landed interest, which, in Burke's telling, was not as closely tied to the monied interest in France throughout the eighteenth century and which came under attack during the Revolution. Perhaps he also thought that a defense of England's monied interest would strengthen his argument in favor of Pitt's loyalty loan, as part of his wider effort to support the continuation of Britain's war against revolutionary France.

Nevertheless, such explanations are not fully satisfying. Did Burke condemn the monied interest as such? Or did he condemn it for supporting causes, such as revolutions, that militated against property, and thus the public welfare? Why did Burke assume that the interests of British capitalists aligned smoothly with the common good, but those of French speculators did not? Even more, was there an inherent quality in speculation that undermined the general good, or was there a particular disposition of French financiers that inevitably fueled an attraction to zealous military aggrandizement and political influence? Burke does not offer adequate answers to these questions.

Burke's Assessment of the Condition of Britain's Economy

The section following Burke's appraisal of Britain's monied interest offers an intriguing portrait of the state of Britain's economy during its war with France. A prevailing opinion in England in the 1790s was that the nation's industry and commerce had suffered tremendous hardship during the war. Burke attacks this argument by calling attention to key principles of his economic thought.

Burke first contends that the common people had continued to profit from Britain's economic vitality, if one took into account "constant employment; proportioned pay according to the produce of the soil, and where the soil fails, according to the operation of the general capital; plentiful nourishment to vigorous labour; comfortable provision to decrepid age, to orphan infancy, and to accidental malady."[229] He goes on to note that population growth, improved agriculture, the construction of public works such as canals, the expansion of capital, the increase in manufactures, and climbing wages (including those for soldiers) were all signs of public prosperity, particularly for the laborer.

Burke had expounded some of the same matters – standards of living, wage rates, and agriculture – in *Thoughts and Details*. In *Third Letter*, then, Burke fortifies his argument in *Thoughts and Details* that the temporary high price of

[229] Langford, *Writings and Speeches*, IX, 352.

provisions could be traced back to the vagaries of nature: "An untimely shower, or an unseasonable drought; a frost too long continued, or too suddenly broken up, with rain and tempest; the blight of the spring, or the smut of the harvest; will do more to cause the distress of the belly, than all the contrivances of all Statesmen can do to relieve it."[230]

He then reiterates his view, as outlined in *Thoughts and Details*, that government interference in exchange economies should be narrowly confined:

Let Government protect and encourage industry, secure property, repress violence, and discountenance fraud, it is all that they have to do. In other respects, the less they meddle in these affairs the better; the rest is in the hands of our Master and theirs.[231]

Burke may have had in mind the corn bounty in his reference to the role of government in encouraging industry. The other responsibilities of the state – to secure property, repress violence, and discountenance fraud – all contained a clear public function. Otherwise, Burke conveys, legislators should check their desire to regulate private market activity. Up until his final years, he was advocating for state forbearance in internal economic affairs.

After denouncing the phrase "labouring poor" for conflating able-bodied workers with the infirm,[232] Burke in *Third Letter* underscores a brute fact of man's fallen state: he must labor to eat. He writes:

It is the common doom of man that he must eat his bread by the sweat of his brow, that is, by the sweat of his body, or the sweat of his mind. If this toil was inflicted as a curse, it is as might be expected from the curses of the Father of all Blessings – it is tempered with many alleviations, many comforts. Every attempt to fly from it, and to refuse the very terms of our existence, becomes much more truly a curse, and heavier pains and penalties fall upon those who would elude the tasks which are put upon them by the great Master Workman of the World, who in his dealings with his creatures sympathizes with their weakness, and speaking of a creation wrought by mere will out of nothing, speaks of six days of *labour* and one day of *rest*.[233]

Toil is necessary for the production and consumption of provisions. Nature and God made it so. To deny this reality would signal a gross ignorance of man's inherent constraints and imperfections – "the very terms of our existence" – and occasion far greater consequences than the burden of laboring to eat. In other words, Burke is implicitly attacking the pretensions of English and French ideologues who held that man's natural state of poverty could be remedied by the government control of economic resources. For Burke, the attempt to create a state of perfection in an imperfect world would grant a dark license to social

[230] Langford, *Writings and Speeches*, IX, 354–355.
[231] Langford, *Writings and Speeches*, IX, 355. This is the section in *Third Letter* where Burke noted that he had "lately written something" on the subject of government involvement in the agricultural economy, most likely referring to *Thoughts and Details*.
[232] See "Labor, the Laboring Poor, and the Rich as Trustees," Chapter 3.
[233] Langford, *Writings and Speeches*, IX, 355.

engineering. An acknowledgment of man's limits, however, could help set the conditions for prosperity by affirming that hard work and diligence, not the state, were the energizing sources of industry.

Burke proceeds to demonstrate that wartime taxes and duties did not discourage consumption and production, and thus did not hurt the British economy to the extent that critics had insisted. He consulted a wide variety of information to brace this argument with empirical support, much of which was included in the publication of *Third Letter* by Burke's executors.[234] The letter includes official statistical data on land taxes, bricks and tiles, plate, glass plates, groceries, teas, coffee and cocoa nuts, sugar and beer, wine, sweets, muslins and calicoes, printed goods, silk, and furs. Such data was introduced to show that revenue from duties on these items did not plummet during war. Eating, drinking, clothing, and entertainment industries remained strong. Bills relating to enclosure,[235] navigation, and canals increased. Revenue of the Post Office grew. The public income from the licenses of retail traders rose steadily, while internal and external trade flowed with sufficient vigor.[236]

Of course, statistics could not fully capture the health of an economy. "There is much gaiety, and dissipation, and profusion, which must escape and disappoint all the arithmetick of political oeconomy," Burke writes.[237] Yet empirical data, combined with general observation, conveyed *some* indication of Britain's relatively prosperous state. "When such is the vigour of our traffick in it's minutest ramifications, we may be persuaded that the root and the trunk are found," he states. "When we see the life blood of the State circulate so freely through the capillary vessels of the system, we scarcely need enquire, if the heart performs its functions aright."[238] Burke's analysis of the British economy in *Third Letter* casts light on his attraction to statistical information as a tool for persuasive argument, reflecting his lasting appreciation for the power of experience in testing the truth of human reasoning.

Burke's discussion on British commerce in particular includes remarks on the balance of trade that contain echoes of his sharp distrust of balance of trade theory he expressed more than twenty years earlier in the *Observations*. Critics had argued that the rate of British imports had not matched that of British exports, giving voice to the theory that a positive trade balance conferred net benefits to the importing nation. Burke breezily dismisses the argument in *Third Letter*. He references an "early tract" of his, ostensibly the *Observations*, which issued "many observations on the usual method of computing that balance," as well as objections to the entry-keeping of the Custom House. Yet misguided thinking on balance of trade theory persisted into the 1790s: "I am not surprised that the same trite objection is perpetually renewed by the detractors of our

[234] Lock, *Edmund Burke*, vol. II, 562.   [235] See "Enclosure," Chapter 3.
[236] See Langford, *Writings and Speeches*, IX, 362–384 for Burke's portrayal of the healthy state of the British economy, including his use of statistical tables.
[237] Langford, *Writings and Speeches*, IX, 369.   [238] Langford, *Writings and Speeches*, IX, 380.

national affluence," Burke writes.[239] He was "gratified," however, that the balance of trade was "now computed in a manner much clearer, than it used to be."[240] Britain's colonies near and far, its people's commerce and navigation, and its industry and skill had generated bountiful capital to the seat of empire that helped lighten the encumbrances of its national debt.[241] Such comments confirm Burke's keen examination of the merits and demerits of trade balances spanning his political life, revealing a depth of insight on political economy unusual for his time period.

Much like his reasoning in the *Observations*, Burke's economic argument in *Third Letter on a Regicide Peace* was not that war was the most effectual means for public opulence. "I am not considering whether, if the common enemy of the quiet of Europe had not forced us to take up arms in our own defence, the spring-tide of our prosperity might not have flowed higher than the mark, at which it now stands," he insists.[242] Considerations over commercial prosperity collided with "the question of the justice and the necessity of the war."[243] Based on such comments, and on the general spirit of *Third Letter*, we can reasonably surmise that Burke's motivation in the letter was to counteract the British temptation to negotiate with France based on the unfounded presumption that war had exacted grave harm on the English people. In his view, war had not seriously depressed the British economy. In any event, Burke suggests, were there not some things worth fighting for beyond the sparkle of commerce?

Third Letter on a Regicide Peace was not the most important writing of Burke that addressed matters relating to political economy. But it supplies a strong supplement to *Thoughts and Details* by broadening his reflections on the complicated anatomy of England's agricultural economy and commercial vitality (not to mention the salutary role of the monied interest in Britain). Most important, it cements Burke's argument in the *Reflections* that societies should be conceived as something more than a collection of perishable agreements between transacting parties. A defense of Christian Europe required the courage to confront revolutionary ideology – without conditions.

12.6 CONCLUSION

A full appreciation for Burke's critique of the French Revolution requires not simply recognition of his searing attack on abstract reason and the destruction of French tradition. It calls for acute attention to his economic argument. And because Burke did not perceive land and commerce to stand in irreconcilable tension, we must grasp that his economic critique was not just an economic critique; it was inextricably linked with larger questions of politics, morality, and history. Burke's thoughts on political economy, then, constructed a fertile

---

[239] Langford, *Writings and Speeches*, IX, 383.   [240] Langford, *Writings and Speeches*, IX, 383.
[241] Langford, *Writings and Speeches*, IX, 384.   [242] Langford, *Writings and Speeches*, IX, 361.
[243] Langford, *Writings and Speeches*, IX, 361.

intellectual path for his wider comprehension of the factors that drove civil growth and decay. The *Reflections* lies at the glowing intersection of Burke's economic thought and political philosophy.

The *Reflections* was not an objective history of the French Revolution, nor did it purport to be, even though the evidence and facts it furnished rested on solid grounds.[244] Reputable scholarship has both displayed sympathy for and conveyed strong opposition to the view Burke propounds in the writing.[245] And we must remind ourselves that the perspective of moderate revolutionaries, if we may permit the phrase, was not without merit; the French state was plagued by fundamental defects and contradictions in its political institutions and system of revenue collection. Although the French economy witnessed a slow expansion in the eighteenth century, the fluctuations in bread prices and the capricious appearances of scarcity certainly compels us to sympathize with the plight of the lower orders. Burke argued that he lamented the downfall of Louis XVI and the spread of revolutionary sentiments espoused by Richard Price because "it is natural"[246]; was it not also natural for a commoner to seethe at the ostentatious luxury of the French monarchy?

Burke's prognosis of the French Revolution proved to be eerily prescient, however. In the *Reflections*, Burke famously predicted the rise of a military dictator, a prophecy that Napoleon Bonaparte fulfilled in November 1799 as a result of the Coup of 18 Brumaire, when he became first consul of the new French government. Less famously, but with no less prescience, Burke in the letter anticipated the disastrous effects of France's revolutionary economy. He accurately forecast that the mix of the monied interest, the flood of *assignats*, and the augmentation of the French state would fuel rampant speculation and aggravate food prices; that the burst of *assignats* would induce further depreciation and hyperinflation[247]; and that the government's economic schemes would largely disturb – not facilitate – the flow and pace of industrious activity and commercial transactions.

Indeed, the Revolution would occasion the swift enlargement of the state bureaucracy and the centralization of the economy,[248] including the government control of wages and trade. Violent rioters attacked the businesses of shopkeepers and grocers who were not Jacobin supporters.[249]

---

[244] Consult Lock, *Edmund Burke*, vol. II, 288–292.

[245] For a survey of recent literature on the French Revolution, see Kates, *Recent Debates & New Controversies*, 1–20.

[246] Langford, *Writings and Speeches*, VIII, 131.

[247] At the time Burke wrote the *Reflections*, the *assignats* had depreciated – but not nearly as much as after its publication, particularly between August 1794 and December 1795. See Harris, *Assignats*, 186–205. Note that Brezis and Crouzet argue that up until 1792, *assignats* did not cause inflation. They contend that starting in 1792, there was a direct correlation between the two. See Brezis and Crouzet, "Role of Assignats," 26–27.

[248] See Aftalion, *Economic Interpretation*, 138–162.

[249] Israel, *Revolutionary Ideas*, 310–311.

Such revolutionary upheaval also crippled French foreign trade and enhanced protectionist trade measures, which, Florin Aftalion writes, came to generate "incalculably destructive consequences" in France.[250]

More important, Burke divined that the breakdown of the French revolutionary economy would lead to violence. Consider his keen insight that foresaw the French farmer's struggle to make a profit when dealing crops in towns:

The truly melancholy part of the policy of systematically making a nation of gamesters is this, that though all are forced to play, few can understand the game; and fewer still are in a condition to avail themselves of the knowledge. The many must be the dupes of the few who conduct the machine of these speculations. What effect it must have on the country people is visible. The townsman can calculate from day to day, not so the inhabitant of the country. When the peasant first brings his corn to market, the magistrate in the towns obliges him to take the assignat at par; when he goes to the shop with his money, he finds it seven per cent the worse for crossing the way. This market he will not readily resort to again. The townspeople will be inflamed; they will force the country people to bring their corn. Resistance will begin, and the murders of Paris and St. Denis may be renewed through all France.[251]

The farmer would be compelled to accept the *assignat* at the government-mandated price. Because of the depreciating value of the *assignats*, however, he would realize he could not receive strong market value for his crops in towns, and would stop trading in those towns.[252] But then the townspeople would force farmers to trade their corn in markets. Resistance and violence would ensue.

Burke's apprehensions over the direction of the French economy bore out in reality. Under the Reign of Terror, France fortified its control over "goods of the first necessity"[253] for the purposes of alleviating food shortages and punishing farmers who allegedly hoarded their crops, coercing them into selling their goods in marts. This intervention demanded an "unprecedented intrusion into the rural economy by the bureaucratic state," Simon Schama writes. "[V]ery often it degenerated into the sans-culotte *armées révolutionnaires*, sent to enforce the economic Terror, ransacking villages for concealed sacks of wheat or guarding fields, lest the peasants cut the crop while it was still green rather than surrender it at dictated prices."[254]

In a larger sense, Burke recognized that the *assignats* epitomized the broader ideological temptation to grasp for power at the expense of the corporate body

[250] Aftalion, *Economic Interpretation*, 193. See also Alfred Cobban, *The Social Interpretation of the French Revolution* (Cambridge: Cambridge University Press, 1999). Cobban writes, "It has hardly been claimed by any historian that the revolution was other than a disaster for France's colonial and foreign trade" (74).

[251] Langford, *Writings and Speeches*, VIII, 241.

[252] See also Henry E. Bourne, "Maximum Prices in France in 1793 and 1794," *The American Historical Review* 23 (1917): 110.

[253] Schama, *Citizens*, 757.   [254] Schama, *Citizens*, 757.

and the individual, which sowed broader political and social consequences beyond the disruption of supply and demand laws. He predicted correctly that the seizure of church lands threatened the property rights of all French citizens. The control of the economy would lead to unbridled coercion and force. Bonds of trust between politicians and its people, and among market actors within France, would dissolve. Confidence in government would be shattered.

Hence the wider the French state expanded for its revolutionary politicians, the smaller the zone of autonomy shrunk for the ordinary Frenchman. This illuminated a paradox of power Burke shrewdly discerned in his commentary on the French Revolution: the more individual rights the French government asserted, the more individual liberties it suppressed. "Individuality is left out of their scheme of Government," Burke states in *Second Letter on a Regicide Peace*. "The state is all in all."[255]

For Burke, however, the malign consequences of the Revolution's scheme of property confiscation and the selling of *assignats* transcended the confines of fiscal or commercial questions. The event itself represented a fundamentally new *form* and *spirit* of political economy, one that invited the state to launch a complete transformation of social and economic relations among members in French society. Burdensome taxation was one thing; the shameless usurpation of private property, the destruction of prescription, the fueling of paper-money despotism, the discouragement of industry, and the relentless train of price controls were quite another. By overturning settled principles of market liberty and public finance that permitted steady, if moderate, commercial improvement, the Revolution in Burke's judgment acquired a terrible new face of economic despotism previously unseen in Europe.

One detects a strong correspondence between Burke's observations on the political economy of the French Revolution and his critique of the East India Company's rule in British India. In both instances, a monied interest endeavored to influence government policy through patronage and pecuniary ambitions. The encroachment on property rights by despotic forces – the French state and the Company – led to the monetization of land, damaging not only the landed interest but the commercial interest as well. These institutions disturbed the flow of economic activity and uprooted the traditions of communities. And their arbitrary rule impelled the transfer of power from localities to centralized institutions, for both French revolutionaries and the corporation eliminated the thick layers of social authority that shaded the common people from the might of the state. In doing so, they made the people servile to the rulers, and the former's commerce dependent upon the latter's arbitrary indulgences. This abuse of power frayed the implicit trust between rulers and the ruled in France and India – trust that was essential, in Burke's judgment, to sustaining a strong and free political community.

---

[255] Langford, *Writings and Speeches*, IX, 288.

In a letter to Lord Loughborough in 1796, Burke observed this frightening convergence between French revolutionaries and Britain's corruption of Indian culture. He wrote that "[o]ur government and our Laws are beset by two different Enemies, which are sapping its foundations, Indianism, and Jacobinism."[256] According to Burke, the former was "the worst by far" for it "furnishe[d] Jacobinism with its strongest arms against all *formal* Government."[257] In both France and in India, rulers shocked existing market structures and landed estates with sparks of unbounded tyranny.

Burke's Political Economy and the French Revolution

Yet the striking implication of Burke's broader theory of political economy – including but not limited to the *Reflections* – is that it might penetrate the boundaries of French revolutionary economic thought, even though his attack on the radical movement glides over any plausible intellectual harmonies. For example, some French leaders arrived at similar conclusions about the importance of protecting private property. Remember the statement of Abbé Sieyès, who had been even more critical of ecclesiastical authority than Talleyrand: "I don't see how a simple declaration can change the nature of rights," he said in opposition to Mirabeau's resolution calling for expropriation.[258] The confiscation of church property breached the inviolable right to property enshrined in the *Declaration of the Rights of Man*. In addition, the new revolutionary government initially attempted to establish a free internal grain trade, and then tried to do so again in the mid-1790s following the failed policies of *dirigisme*.

Consider for a last time, the French Revolution, seen now in this light. It was inspired in part by the idea that natural economic activity was hindered by the abuse of government regulations and the granting of special privileges. The draft of the *Declaration of the Rights of Man* stated that each citizen had the right to "acquire, possess, manufacture and sell, and use his abilities and skills ... as he pleases."[259] Besides the phrase "as he pleases," which suggests an air of license, Burke's economic thought certainly embodied the principle that the individual held a right to acquire, possess, manufacture, and sell market goods, as he states explicitly in the *Reflections*, when he insisted that man had a "right to the fruits of their industry and to the means of making their industry fruitful."[260]

Even more, the final document of the *Declaration of the Rights of Man* avowed that property is an "inviolable and sacred right," in Article XVII, and

[256] Burke to Lord Loughborough, [*circa* 17 March 1796], in *Correspondence of Edmund Burke*, vol. VIII, 432.
[257] Burke to Lord Loughborough, [*circa* 17 March 1796], in *Correspondence of Edmund Burke*, vol. VIII, 432.
[258] Schama, *Citizens*, 485.   [259] Vardi, "Abolition of the Guilds," 712.
[260] Langford, *Writings and Speeches*, VIII, 110.

that the "natural and imprescriptible rights of man" include "liberty" and "property."²⁶¹ As shown in this book, Burke believed that private property was imbued with a sacred quality that warranted protection from the designs of the state. And the French Revolution's multiple efforts to establish a free internal grain trade is certainly consistent with *Thoughts and Details*.

Such common areas suggest there may be more overlap between Burke's economic ideas and French strands of thought than he lets on in the *Reflections* – and between his ideas and the economic thought of moderate and radical classical liberals such as John Locke, Richard Price, Thomas Paine, and Joseph Priestley. Recall the intellectual puzzle outlined at the start of this book: Burke's conception of political economy blended significantly with Adam Smith's economic theory. Yet Smith was seen as an intellectual inspiration behind the French Revolution; Pierre Samuel Dupont de Nemours, who served as president of the Constituent Assembly, told Smith, "You have done much to speed this useful Revolution, the French *Économistes* will not have harmed it."²⁶² The Smith-Burke problem and Das Edmund Burke Problem hence arises in its fullest light: how was Burke able to defend a conception of tradition and custom in the *Reflections* while also praising a relatively novel phenomenon – market liberty – in *Thoughts and Details* and in his other writings and speeches, including the *Reflections* itself? Was Burke a secular classical liberal in disguise?

We can offer an answer by taking note of several historical details. First, Smith was employed by French revolutionaries to justify a range of positions, which included, but was by no means limited to, support for free markets.²⁶³ "[A]ll sides of patriotic opposition to the ministries and the crown claimed Smith as one of their own," Richard Whatmore writes.²⁶⁴ Linking Smith to the French Revolution at its face discloses little about the possible tensions in Burke's own thought.

Second, it is true that Burke endorsed economic principles that were embraced by classical liberals such as Locke and Price. The question, however, is whether Burke championed market principles on the same

---

²⁶¹ "Declaration of the Rights of Man – 1789," *Avalon Project*, Yale Law School, accessed January 2, 2017, http://avalon.law.yale.edu/18th_century/rightsof.asp.

²⁶² See Whatmore, "Adam Smith's Role in the French Revolution," 74n31. In addition, Condorcet oversaw the publication of extracts from a French translation of the *Wealth of Nations* in 1790, as part of his larger project to promote the importance of virtue in inculcating a strong sense of French citizenship (74, 83–84). The translation was reprinted often in the 1790s. Abbé Sieyès utilized Smith's argument about the necessity in cleansing the public sphere of ravenous mercantile competitors and arbitrary rulers to inform his applied theory of national sovereignty (77). Sieyès did not identify himself as a doctrinaire Smith disciple, however, because he believed Smith's thought led to a defense of the landed aristocracy (78).

²⁶³ See Whatmore, "Adam Smith's Role in the French Revolution."

²⁶⁴ Whatmore, "Adam Smith's Role in the French Revolution," 82.

grounds as classical liberals, such as the sanctity of individual freedom, the merit of acquisitive self-preservation, or the virtues of voluntary contracts.

Burke indeed flirts with these ideas, as illustrated by his defense of "laudable avarice" and his unwavering support for a free internal trade and the steady relaxation of commercial entanglements. Yet Burke's economic thought suggests that a defense of the pursuit of profit, the right to industry, and the virtues of market competition need not be associated simply with "classical liberalism." His exertions on behalf of voluntary exchange demonstrated a steadfast fidelity to free enterprise – but he did not sanctify the philosophical principles of a Lockean state of nature that conventional classical liberals endorsed in the seventeenth and eighteenth centuries.

This was because support for market liberty in the eighteenth century could rest on different suppositions about human nature and human association. French Physiocrats and (some) revolutionaries championed a free grain trade like Burke, but they tended to submit to abstract conceptions of society, prone to the rigidness of ironclad logic and mathematical proofs, distinct from Burke's political thought. Burke's life, however, displayed a greater effort to defend the imperatives of commercial liberty in a traditional, historically informed Anglo-American framework, not in conformity to the speculative theories of the Physiocrats or to the contractarian notions of civil society championed by English radicals.[265]

If we locate Burke's economic thought in a broader intellectual context, moreover, we find that his belief in exchange economies was not driven by the premise that individuals emerged out of an abstract state of nature and assented to a voluntary contract to secure their pre-civil right to private liberty, a core premise of classical liberalism and libertarianism. Rather, it was moved by the idea that the markets reflected the steady interactions and arrangements among men and women already living within a communal setting seeking to meet their practical needs for food and shelter. Markets were provinces of social interaction and part of a wider ethical and religious order; they were not mere mediums for the maximization of personal autonomy and material wealth.

Burke's defense of market liberty, then, fits neatly into his conception of prejudice in the *Reflections* as the distilled wisdom of many generations. The historical development of Britain was the product not only of slowly accumulated political traditions and social customs, but also of the gathered insights and adaptations of market activities stemming from the shifting preferences of consumers and producers. If markets were tempered by land and virtue, they could be reconciled with existing institutions to promote prosperity without poisoning the character of civil society.

---

[265] Scottish Enlightenment liberal thinkers, we should add, also did not embrace Lockean conceptions of an abstract state of nature. They instead favored a historical approach not unlike Burke, although their causal historiography of commercial activity differed from his notion of the relation between markets and morals, as discussed.

We must emphasize that this conception of market prejudice accommodated reform in order to alter existing conditions of commercial policy, as epitomized by Burke's economic statesmanship. Yet his reform efforts – such as the Free Port Act, the Irish trade bills, and the repeal of bans on middlemen trading practices – were all carried out in a preexisting political and social framework, pursued in a forum of stable and deliberative institutions and protected by the secure foundations of Britain's ancestral constitutional heritage. While Burke, in *Thoughts and Details*, professed a confidence in the natural laws of commerce to channel the flow of internal provisions in an efficient manner, he understood that such conceptions of nature, ever popular in eighteenth-century Europe, operated in wider social, ethical, and religious contexts. He thus never called for the expropriation of church lands or the property of the landed nobility, or for the radical democratization of English political institutions, or for the large expansion of British administrative bureaucracy, or for stern obedience to enlightened legislators aspiring to remake states in the name of rights and benevolence.

Thus, unlike French revolutionaries and strands of Physiocratic thinking, Burke did not promote the spirit of market liberty by aiming to swiftly conform the complex dimensions of society to unbendable notions of nature. For such rapid change based on speculative logic would unsettle civil stability and uproot prevailing institutions that had a calming influence on social and economic fluxes, thereby subverting the foundations of progress and injecting new vices into a commonwealth. "[A]ny thing which unnecessarily tore to pieces the contexture of the state, not only prevented all real reformation, but introduced evils which would call, but, perhaps, call in vain, for new reformation," Burke stated in *Speech on the Army Estimates*.[266] Real reform was lasting change that did not self-implode: "A spirit of reformation is never more consistent with itself," he wrote in *Appeal from the New to the Old Whigs*, "than when it refuses to be rendered the means of destruction."[267]

An underlying implication of Burke's argument can be felt in the force of these comments, and in the *Reflections*: French revolutionaries, rather than Burke, exhibited reactionary sentiments by revolting against the steady forces that had propelled the growth of European civilization up to 1789. The blossoming of modern commercial society was the effect of a firm moral code. The sublimation of man's baser passions created a climate of civility in which trade could flourish. Liberty governed by order induced disciplined affluence.

French political innovators and *philosophes* reacted reflexively against this foundation, however, by undermining the very principles that sustained such civil improvement. The "mixed system of opinion and sentiment" that originated in "the antient chivalry," Burke writes in the *Reflections*, had "given its character to modern Europe."[268] But the moment when "antient

---

[266] Langford, *Writings and Speeches*, IV, 288.   [267] Langford, *Writings and Speeches*, IV, 404.
[268] Langford, *Writings and Speeches*, VIII, 127.

opinions and rules of life are taken away" is when "we have no compass to govern us; nor can we know distinctly to what port to steer."[269] Revolution shattered this compass for progress, since social upheaval discouraged the growth of commerce to the detriment of posterity. The *Reflections* was not simply a defense of the past but a defense of the future.

What difference does it make if Burke's defense of market liberty should be located in the ancestral and conservative traditions of Anglo-American thought rather than in strands of doctrinaire classical liberalism (both of which, admittedly, overlap to a certain extent)? The crux is that Burke offers an imperfect yet instructive way to support market competition that is more resistant than strands of Enlightenment philosophy to the debilitating effects of commercial and speculative excess on social relations. Burke's economic thought protected commercial freedom from disintegrating into disorder and atomism, because he placed a sharper accent than other market enthusiasts did on the importance of a strong religious ethos, time-honored institutions, and moral virtue as sturdy checks against the human impulse to continuously enter into voluntary contracts for immediate gain, in both economic and political realms. As he wrote in *Thoughts on French Affairs*:

It is the natural operation of things where there exists a Crown, a Court, splendid Orders of Knighthood, and an Hereditary Nobility; – where there exists a fixed, permanent, landed Gentry, continued in greatness and opulence by the law of primogeniture, and by a protection given to family settlements; – where there exists a standing Army and Navy; – where there exists a Church Establishment, which bestows on learning and parts an interest combined with that of Religion and the State; – in a country where such things exist, wealth, new in it's acquisition, and precarious in its duration, can never rank first, or even near the first; though wealth has it's natural weight, further, than as it is balanced and even preponderated amongst us as amongst other nations, by artificial institutions and opinions growing out of them.[270]

In a nation with a monarchy, established church, and hereditary nobility, new wealth will not be able to shake the foundations of civil society, since it will be embedded in wider and more stable institutional frameworks and tempered by sober minds.

Accordingly, Burke's understanding of the ethical preconditions of commercial exchange helped build a conception of individual liberty that was able to coexist with and complement social order. In *Speech at Arrival at Bristol*, Burke said:

The distinguishing part of our constitution is its liberty. To preserve that liberty inviolate, seems the particular duty and proper trust of a member of the House of Commons. But the liberty, the only liberty I mean, is a liberty connected with order; that not only

---

[269] Langford, *Writings and Speeches*, VIII, 129.
[270] Langford, *Writings and Speeches*, VIII, 347.

exists along with order and virtue, but which cannot exist at all without them. It inheres in good and steady government, as in its substance and vital principle.[271]

He repeated the same remarks in *Appeal from the New to the Old Whigs*.[272] Ordered liberty – not just liberty – embraced the possibilities of commercial enrichment while preventing ad hoc social relations from collapsing into driftlessness, moral turpitude, or anarchy. "Men are qualified for civil liberty, in exact proportion to their disposition to put moral chains upon their own appetites," Burke writes in *Letter to a Member of the National Assembly*, in 1791.[273] Self-rule demands virtue. "[W]e cannot be too cautious in our communication with those, who seek their happiness by other roads than those of humanity, morals, and religion," he states in *Fourth Letter on a Regicide Peace*, "and whose liberty consists, and consists alone, in being free from those restraints, which are imposed by the virtues upon the passions."[274] Burke's economic thought defended a notion of liberty whose enduring moral basis could withstand the vicissitudes and temptations of human weakness.

Soon before the *Reflections* was published, Burke remarked in a private letter that his primary concern was Britain: "In reality, my Object was not France, in the first instance, but this Country."[275] He was not doing his work justice. The *Reflections* was indeed a warning to Burke's fellow Englishmen about the menacing contagion of French political radicalism, but it also conveys a grander lesson about civil society: one must be aware of both the potentialities and the limits of transactional exchange in steering the growth of social and political order. Sociability and religion, virtue and chivalry, define man. Temporary contracts do not.

---

[271] Langford, *Writings and Speeches*, III, 59. Burke does go on to note that England at the time was still not immune from the destabilizing effects of new monied men.
[272] Langford, *Writings and Speeches*, IV, 394.   [273] Langford, *Writings and Speeches*, VIII, 332.
[274] Langford, *Writings and Speeches*, IX, 110.
[275] Burke to Charles-Alexandre de Calonne, 25 October 1790, in *Correspondence of Edmund Burke*, vol. VI, 141. Burke even admitted that the French Revolution did not produce the Jacobinism embraced by English radicals but "only discovered it, increased it, and gave fresh vigour to its operations" (Langford, *Writings and Speeches*, IX, 83).

Conclusion

Burke was one of the most prominent and influential advocates of commercial liberty in eighteenth-century British politics. He played a central role in shaping public policy on foreign and domestic trade from the 1760s to the 1790s, displaying an acuity on matters pertaining to commerce, revenue, and finance unusual for the era while deftly utilizing empirical information to strengthen his mode of reasoning. We should not think of him simply as a wise political theorist or shrewd statesman, then, but also as a profound thinker on the science of political economy.

This conclusion suggests we should modify the conventional interpretation of Burke as an inflexible defender of the ancient aristocratic order against the restless rising classes of enterprising men. Burke was in close contact with merchants throughout much of his political life, and consistently sought to advance their interests by promoting the cause of economic freedom in Parliament. At times he followed their advice, such as in the case of the Free Port Act, and at other times he rejected it, such as in the case of the Irish trade bills; but his legislative activities were always informed by a warm sympathy toward liberal commerce. In short, Burke was a steadfast champion of both hereditary aristocrats of great pedigree and entrepreneurial dealers from more modest backgrounds.

Burke's impact on economic debates and controversies has eclipsed his time period, however. One of the most telling facts about his intellectual and political life is that Burke introduced or clarified arguments regarding the political economy of the internal grain trade, French Revolution, paper money, British India, Anglo-Irish trade relations, and Anglo-American colonial relations that have remained influential and clear-eyed interpretations of the subjects to this day. Additionally, his work on economical reform had a lasting effect in reconstituting the administrative and financial architecture of the British government. Burke's economic thought was, and is, of much consequence. We should recognize it as such.

The guiding principles of Burke's approach to political economy, however, escape the paradigms of contemporary economic theory. Modern labels used to describe economic doctrines – free-market capitalism, classical liberalism, libertarianism, individualism, progressivism, socialism, Communism – emerged after Burke's death in 1797. That Burke was a practicing statesman as well as a philosophical thinker makes it even more difficult to fit his thought neatly within tidy analytic frameworks of political economy. Burke encountered a wide range of commercial and financial matters in his parliamentary career that were specific to a particular time and place, provoking a body of statements from him that might not lend itself, at first glance, to congruity of theoretical form. Even though this book has frequently described Burke's statements on political economy as a "philosophy" or "theory," how could a legislator even possess a "philosophy" of political economy, or of any other subject, if his views were determined by the fluidities of contingent circumstance?[1] Accordingly, some commentaries on Burke hesitate to ascribe firm principles to his intellectual thought.

This book is not one of them. Burke's remarks on political economy illustrate an underlying coherence that incorporated, but transcended, elements of prudence, utility, and tradition. Burke arrived at these principles much as he approached questions relating to other political affairs as a philosopher-statesman: he concentrated his mind on the particular circumstances and details at hand, and then broadened his gaze to acquire an understanding of their implications for Britain, its empire, the foreign arena, and civilization as a whole. "There are but very few, who are capable of comparing and digesting what passes before their eyes at different times and occasions, so as to form the whole into a distinct system," he wrote in *Thoughts on the Present Discontents*.[2] Burke was one of the few such men in his time. This faculty of mind allowed him to offer one of the most comprehensive visions of political economy in the eighteenth century that aimed to sustain the virtues of market liberty while protecting against its debasing tendencies.

Burke's economic thought can be captured in a number of general principles. In domestic industries, government should not disturb the private diffusion of goods and services; supply and demand laws help circulate goods throughout civil society, including to needy areas; the competitive price system is a more effectual instrument than the magistracy in regulating wages and contracts; commerce thrives best when freed from the burden of arbitrary regulations; trade restrictions heighten the cost of goods and labor; middlemen increase the

---

[1] Of course, the belief that human affairs cannot be categorized neatly according to rationalist principles is itself a tenable philosophy.
[2] Langford, *Writings and Speeches*, II, 256.

efficiency of the flow of provisions; and currency should not be devalued by the excesses of paper money.

In addition, a providential force – Burke's "benign and wise disposer of all things"[3] – transforms individual self-interest into collective advantage; laudable avarice in an environment of market competition is a stimulus for public opulence; market competition lowers the cost and enhances the quality of goods; voluntary exchange advantages members from different social orders, including the poor; market liberty promotes commercial virtues such as industry and diligence; and the security of private property is necessary for a flourishing trade.

On the matter of foreign commerce, Burke's tenets of political economy include: government should pursue the relaxation of foreign trade barriers, as long as this mission does not subvert the imperatives of national security and national honor; the wealth of nations derives from international trade, not simply from bullion; balance of trade theory is premised on the misguided assumption that a surplus of imports over exports impairs the nation's economy; commercial intercourse can ease social tensions and strengthen relations between different nations, particularly between those that have a joint interest in forging such relations; and market liberty, in general, elevates the fortunes of the many.

Furthermore, we must not forget the pillars of Burke's conception of public finance: a government that enacts low and moderate taxes occasions a far healthier revenue stream for posterity than an arbitrary system of high taxation; the employment of revenue to stimulate trade diminishes government receipts in the long run and discourages the growth of public riches; a powerful and effectual state is a trim and selective one; government should not be run by a large administrative bureaucracy; government should establish and carry out definable tasks in accord with its responsibilities and capabilities; and public accounting practices should be implemented with consistency and transparency.

Our survey of Burke's economic thought would be incomplete without summoning his reflections on the primacy of landed property: landed property is the counterpoise to the political ambitions of the Crown; landed property is the ballast of constitutional government and constitutional liberty; estates are fertile provinces of agricultural and technological innovation; inherited land furnishes the stability that allows for the gradual expansion of commerce from generation to generation; and the right to private property is derived from the law of nature and acquires authority through prescription. Most important, the seizure of private property is tyranny.

As this book has contended, however, the precepts of Burke's political economy cannot be sufficiently understood without stressing his insights into the limits of commerce: commercial culture cannot sustain itself without prior

[3] Langford, *Writings and Speeches*, IX, 125.

ethical commitments; religion and time-honored virtue are more important for the growth of civil order than material affluence; commerce was not fully responsible for the creation of modern civilization; Europe's code of manners established the ethical preconditions necessary for the rise of commercial economies; man has a moral duty to provide charity to the poor when supply and demand laws are inadequate to meet their needs; avarice unhinged from the disciplining effect of markets and manners breeds persecution and corruption; the slave trade violates the moral law and should be gradually abolished; and liberty requires virtue.

In taking into account all of these principles, the broader aim of this book has been to illuminate the significance of Burke's philosophy of political economy as a statement that surpassed considerations of Whiggism, free market doctrine, or public finance. Burke's study of commerce included the examination of supply and demand laws, but it also outlined a larger argument about civilization: societies decay when the imperatives of market competition dispense with the pre-commercial ties of love and sentiment. Unconditional ethical obligations precede the fulfillment of voluntary contracts. A political community includes markets, but its soul transcends them: "[C]ommonwealths are not physical but moral essences," Burke wrote in *First Letter on a Regicide Peace*.[4] *Thoughts and Details*, Burke's chief economic tract, and the *Reflections*, his most famous writing, were both written near the end of his life, but they represent that harmonizing bookends of his conception of political economy: social order is enhanced by the power of commerce – but only when transactional exchange is governed by a sense of its limits.

THE RELATIONSHIP BETWEEN BURKE'S ECONOMIC THOUGHT
AND POLITICAL THEORY AND THE QUESTION OF BURKE'S
CONSERVATISM

Drawing from these central principles of Burke's economic thought, we can discern lines of consistency between his philosophy of political economy and his political theory. The most fundamental similarity is a judgment on individual reason. Burke's aversion to the swift intrusion of abstract rationality into markets is similar to his condemnation of French ideology in the *Reflections*: in both instances, a corrupted form of theoretical reason scorned the infinite complexities of human activities. The perimeters of the human intellect – man's "private stock of reason" – constrained man from comprehending the limitless bits of knowledge necessary to ensure the smooth functioning of market economies. Therefore, the imposition of abstract reason on civil society unsettled the stable foundations for commercial enterprise and social union.

---

[4] Langford, *Writings and Speeches*, IX, 188.

Burke's distaste for abstract reason exposed his bitter antipathy toward the concentration of economic and political power in few hands. Much like his legislative activities were defined by efforts to prevent the Crown from becoming the gravitational center of British politics, Burke endeavored to prevent public officials from controlling the distribution of provisions and the regulation of contracts in the internal grain trade. In his view, however, one crucial role of the state was to establish legal protections for the individual to enjoy a monopoly on his own capital, which would safeguard his property from the grasping hands of government and other market actors. On questions of foreign commerce, Burke's diligent resistance to the establishment of excessive duties and prohibitions illustrated his opposition to combining power between the state and powerful mercantile constituencies for the aim of thwarting competition.

When Burke did defend a monopoly in foreign commerce, he did so by highlighting the precarious nature of trading in distant lands, as exemplified most famously by his defense of the East India Company. Even on this matter, Burke conveyed stern opposition to the control of internal trade. While the Company warranted commercial privileges in the East Indies, its mixing of economic power with political monopoly fueled an upsurge in the firm's despotic behavior toward Indian natives. For Burke, the convergence of these forces brought about the suppression of supply and demand laws, the usurpation of profit and property, the dictation of terms of contract, and the encouragement of bribery and corruption – not to mention the oppression of Indians.

Burke's defense of the landed aristocracy complemented his hostility to the unchecked fusion of economic and political power. The propertied classes in Parliament stood as the moderating influences between the king and the people, thereby securing constitutional liberty and social protection for the people. Further, landed aristocracies performed a crucial role in market economics by being incubators of agricultural ingenuity and technological advancement. Burke himself represented this blend: he was a member of the landed gentry but also a farmer known for his progressive cultivation techniques and knack for reducing costs while maximizing returns.[5] Landed property, in essence, provided for the diffusion of political and economic decision-making in private hands, not the state, and served as the steady support for the growth of the arts and manufactures.

A third prominent similarity between Burke's economic thought and political philosophy is that his respect for local custom was moved by a humane spirit. The gift of liberty was not confined to Englishmen: Burke advocated for the rights of the Americans, Indians, Irish, and Africans to possess property and trade freely at the same time that he defended their distinctive cultural heritages.

---

[5] See Cone, "Edmund Burke, the Farmer," 65–69. See also "The Roots of Burke's Interest in the Science of Political Economy," Chapter 1.

Commercial liberty could furnish reciprocal benefits to traders regardless of blood, family, or social order.

Fourth, Burke's economic thought and political philosophy were woven together by the idea of progress. Burke is famous for promoting the notion that a society can change by renewing and modifying the accumulated traditions of the past in order to meet the needs of contemporary circumstances. Secondary accounts typically stress how this conception of progress encompassed a belief in the reform of political and social institutions. But, as this book has emphasized, it also included a healthy confidence in the possibilities for *commercial* improvement, orchestrated by the symbiotic power of market competition and landed property rights, that spread prosperity to the many over time.

Inspired by such considerations of his political economy, Burke in many ways aimed to drain politics from the commercial arena. He regularly argued for the liberation of economic activity from the intrusive supervision of politicians and state administrators (the corn bounty being one important exception). His efforts to repeal the statutes against middlemen trading practices; his support for the relaxation of trade restrictions between England and Ireland; his opposition to the government regulation of wages and contracts; his attempt to free Indians from the internal monopoly of the East India Company; and his defense of salutary neglect in the context of Anglo-American economic relations all testified to Burke's stance that political meddling frequently discouraged the expansion of commerce.

Nevertheless, one glaring difference between Burke's economic thought and political thought was that the former was ultimately subordinate to his broader defense of the British Empire. Although the enlargement of trade was a chief object of Burke's legislative activity, he believed that commerce should not dictate the foreign policy of Britain. If existing trade laws such as the Navigation Acts were responsible, at least in part, for the growth of Anglo-American opulence and stability, and if the Acts were not the cause of colonial tumults in North America, Burke did not see why they should be hastily abolished. In addition, if nations hostile to Britain, such as France, aspired to use trade to gain imperial and military advantages over Britain, Burke was keen on sacrificing a measure of commercial prosperity for the sake of preserving the integrity and security of the British Empire. The wealth of nations was a worthy aspiration, but the honor of nations was an even nobler aim.

Burke and American Political Traditions

Mindful of these beliefs of Burke's political economy, how can we better understand his place in conservative and liberal political traditions in Anglo-American history? While Burke is known as the father of modern conservatism, it is important to remember that at the time he lived, he championed economic policies that aligned with what today we would consider to be the liberal persuasions of his time period – the relaxation of trade obstacles between nations, the release of commerce from the grip of the state, the endorsement of property rights for oppressed groups, and the defense of the competitive price system. Burke's philosophy of political economy embodied his liberal instinct for change.

This consideration cannot be stressed enough. Alfred Cobban, communicating a widely-held perspective of Burke, maintained that he represented a "revolt" against the eighteenth century by swearing an allegiance to tradition as a check against the liberal passions of the 1700s.[6] Most recently, Steven Pinker has written that Burke "suggested that humans were too flawed to think up schemes for improving their condition and were better off sticking with traditions and institutions that kept them from the abyss."[7] Such comments typify a slanted interpretation of his thought. As this book has sought to demonstrate, Burke's commitment to "tradition" included a commitment to preserving the underlying ethical sources for civil progress, including economic progress, since the destruction of these sources by way of radical ideology would destroy the roots of social order and occasion commercial decay.

Burke's economic thought, then, suggests that we adjust our understanding of Anglo-American conservatism, a creed whose emphasis on tradition, aesthetics, and culture is often contrasted with classical liberalism's and libertarianism's (and neoconservatism's) attraction to free-market economics and business and finance. As we have learned, Burke's political and philosophic life illustrated a firm commitment to the principles of economic liberty and prolonged engagement with concrete matters of commercial policy and public finance. If, indeed, Burke is the godfather of conservatism, his recurrent support for market enterprise suggests harmonious cooperation between this intellectual and political heritage and commercial freedom.[8]

The distinctive aspect of Burke's economic thought, however, was its attempt to blend liberal commercial principles with the distilled wisdom of Europe's

---

[6] Cobban, *Edmund Burke and the Revolt against the Eighteenth Century*.

[7] Pinker, *Enlightenment Now*, 363.

[8] For scholars who have attempted to identify distinctions between the characteristics of tradition-alist conservatism and those of neoconservatism, classical liberalism, and libertarianism, see Kirk, *Conservative Mind*; Peter Viereck, *Conservatism Revisited: The Revolt against Ideology* (New Brunswick, NJ: Transaction Publishers, 2005), including Claes G. Ryn's introduction; Stephen J. Tonsor, "Why I Am Not a Neoconservative," in *Conservatism in America since 1930*, ed. Gregory L. Schneider (New York and London: New York University Press, 2003), 373–378; Samuel Francis, "Beautiful Losers: Why Conservatism Failed," in *Conservatism in America since 1930*, 414–423; and Deneen, *Why Liberalism Failed*. For a helpful overview, see Dan Himmelfarb, "Conservative Splits," in *Conservatism in America since 1930*, 383–393. See also Hayek's essay "Why I Am Not a Conservative," in *Constitution of Liberty*, 519–533; and Meyer, *What Is Conservatism?*; and, most recently, Yoram Hazony, "Is 'Classical Liberalism' Conservative?" *Wall Street Journal*, October 13, 2017, www.wsj.com/articles/is-classical-liberalism-conservative-1507931462.

past prior to the advent of mass markets. In this sense, there is no "Burke-Smith Problem" or "Das Edmund Burke Problem": Burke did not apprehend tensions between traditional virtue and modern economies that could not be integrated and reconciled, for a properly balanced state mixed market vibrancy with the pre-commercial pillars of religious instruction, social affection, and aristocratic moderation. As Burke argued throughout his political life, no inherent conflict persisted between ancestral institutions such as the church and the landed nobility, on the one hand, and exchange economies, on the other. In fact, clerical authorities and landed aristocrats were the guardians of vigorous commercial activity by building and retaining the stable conditions under which trade could thrive.

Accordingly, because Burke was a man of letters before he was a political economist, he held that a society's cultural heritage was more important to sustaining civil order than mere compliance with supply and demand laws or the formation of commercial policy in Parliament. Culture indeed included economics; but it also expressed a carefully refined wisdom drawn from the insights of philosophers, theologians, legal thinkers, artists, and writers that predated the blossoming of widespread trade. For Burke, if a commonwealth could not shield this culture from the baser aspects of transactional exchange, it would struggle to preserve its political and social institutions – and potential for commercial enrichment.

APPLICATIONS FOR TODAY

What wisdom does Burke's economic thought supply for contemporary debate over capitalism and its limits? We can start by highlighting its shortcomings. It is difficult to declare whether Burke would have supported particular tax rates, trade regulations, or government welfare programs, given the many historical differences between the agriculturally-based economy of eighteenth-century England and the industrial and post-industrial economies of twenty-first-century America and Europe. Even the simple question of whether Burke would have championed specific policy prescriptions – an inquiry in any event that lies outside the scope of this book – is premised on the idea that policy reform was the chief object of his economic reflections, when in reality it represented the surface level of his deeper meditations on political economy.

The import of Burke's commentary, moreover, is weakened by his insufficient discussion on key questions relating to the relationship between politics and economics. Was there really no tension between the stability of landed property and the dynamism of commercial activity that could not be reconciled? What were the conditions under which it would be appropriate for government to intervene in domestic industries? Burke mentions fraud and abuse in passing, but he never offers a satisfying answer to this question.

Additionally, even if liberal commercial intercourse spreads opulence to many nations, does government not hold the moral responsibility to assist traders or farmers who lose business to foreign competition? If trade restrictions should be retained to promote a country's national interest, such as the Navigation Acts, how does one define national interest? Is private charity alone an adequate tool for the alleviation of poverty? Most important, did Burke underestimate, or not even anticipate, the extent of the socially unsettling effects of widespread market industrialization on local communities?

The horizon of Burke's intellectual attention to these matters derives from a number of considerations noted in this book: he was not an economist removed from the demands of government activity but a practicing statesman; he wrote tracts that addressed ad hoc contingencies rather than sweeping treatises (although his tracts did consistently weave theoretical commentary into them); and his exertions were consumed by a slew of intellectual and political pursuits, of which economics played an important but by no means overwhelming role.

Given such limitations, however, Burke's reflections do supply timely insights into contemporary economic debates and controversies. *Thoughts and Details*, for instance, highlighted the difficulties in imposing uniform rationality through legislation on a mixed mass of social and economic arrangements. The unending stream of transactions and contracts in market economies should give lawmakers pause before they enact a hardened rule that ignores the complicated nature of private market activity. In Burke's view, voluntary exchange between two parties was often more effectual than third parties in arriving at mutually beneficial agreements. This does not mean that regulations should or should not be implemented, but that a sensitive awareness of the complexities of civil society is a precondition for informed judgment on economic affairs.

Burke's thoughts on political economy also offer a cautionary message for reflexive proponents of market-based solutions for social ailments in civil society. While Burke praised the spirit of commercial enterprise, he believed that there was more to life than transactional exchange, and that a fully formed person was alert to the deeper religious and moral traditions that sustained civilization. This lesson applies in particular to philosophers and historiographers of the political economy of the Enlightenment, who perceive the dawn of modernity to have ushered in an enlightened epoch of economic freedom unburdened by the dead weight of Europe's medieval past.[9]

Burke's economic thought is uncommon in this respect. As this book has documented at length, he avidly supported the flowering of commercial liberty, but, unlike many champions of liberal commerce in the contemporary West and in eighteenth-century Europe, he maintained that the flourishing of markets was the product of the West's ancestral heritage, not a departure from it. What is his lesson for modernity? Market liberty is integral for material affluence and commercial virtue, but religion and morality are even more indispensable for

[9] See, most recently, Pinker, *Enlightenment Now*.

civil order and social progress. "Better this Island should be sunk to the bottom of the sea," Burke writes in *Fourth Letter on a Regicide Peace*, "than that (so far as human infirmity admits) it should not be a country of Religion and Morals."[10]

In this sense, although Burke is often located in the conservative intellectual tradition, his political economy even accommodates strands of progressive thought by highlighting the limits of commercial opulence and voluntary contracts. Conservatives, classical liberals, and libertarians are fond of extolling the benefits of commodification and competitive capitalism,[11] yet Burke's thought discloses an awareness that life is not simply about entering into temporary socioeconomic arrangements, maximizing one's investment, and satisfying one's material desires. It is admittedly difficult to reconcile Burke's antipathy to wealth redistribution with the desire of progressives for an expansive welfare state, but his emphasis on the bonds of community overlap with particular conceptions of modern liberalism (and of traditionalist conservatism) anxious about social atomism – and, increasingly, with conservative trepidations over unfettered globalization.[12]

On this last note, Burke's economic statesmanship may offer an instructive path forward for debates over globalization between free trade enthusiasts and advocates of protectionism. Burke was a supporter of free trade on principle, but he strove to ensure that legislation promoting commercial intercourse would not create lasting social and economic disorder. He was further aware that a nation should act with caution before exposing its commerce and manufactures to hostile enemies (such as, in Burke's time, France), which he thought might use such economic opportunities to their military and imperial advantage. A commercial policy that promotes steady intercourse with friendly nations, and that displays greater prudence in enhancing trade relations with global adversaries, might thus reflect a Burkean approach to foreign trade, thereby combining libertarian and conservative approaches to the art of economic statecraft.

Finally, Burke's attention to the limits of transactional exchange and temporary contracts illuminates the most important lesson his political economy offers for conservatives, classical liberals, libertarians, and progressives. Burke lends a strong degree of dignity to the market activity of the farmer, middleman, laborer, but, in his commentary on the French Revolution, he cautions that the radical commodification of *all* social relationships would presage the descent of human beings into an unpitied abyss. Burke's economic thought delivers a stark warning to modernity about

---

[10] Langford, *Writings and Speeches*, IX, 115.

[11] A recent book that captures this attitude is Jason Brennan and Peter M. Jaworski, *Markets Without Limits: Moral Virtues and Commercial Interests* (New York: Routledge, 2016).

[12] See, among many, Deneen, *Why Liberalism Failed*; and Yoram Hazony, *The Virtue of Nationalism* (New York: Basic Books, 2018).

the menace of social engineering, endeavoring to turn men into mice and crush the human soul.

Therefore, man should control wealth, not the other way around. As Burke writes in *First Letter on a Regicide Peace*:

If wealth is the obedient and laborious slave of virtue and of public honour, then wealth is in it's place, and has it's use: But if this order is changed, and honor is to be sacrificed to the conservation of riches, riches which have neither eyes nor hands, nor any thing truly vital in them, cannot long survive the being of their vivifying powers, their legitimate masters, and their potent protectors. If we command our wealth, we shall be rich and free: If our wealth commands us, we are poor indeed.[13]

In the age of the French Revolution, Burke was imploring his fellow countrymen to protect and treasure England's national honor, which included but was not defined by its commercial affluence. His message penetrates the minds of modern men and women: political communities built on the foundation of ordered liberty are worth defending because of their moral essences, not simply because of their earthly riches.

In the end, Burke's conception of political economy, seen in its fullest philosophical dimensions, teaches us to be on watchful guard against the seduction of perishable agreements, and to strive to maintain objects of permanence in our lives that can withstand the vagaries of markets and the transient nature of voluntary contracts. We should make sure that the temptation for gain in the commercial economy does not overwhelm our deeper social obligations to our fellow neighbor. We should recognize both the possibilities and limits of trade in order to prevent a healthy appreciation for market liberty from transforming into the crass monetization of all social relations. We should be aware that our deepest friendships are those of an unconditional nature. Burke himself attempted to heed these lessons. For at the same time he was passionately defending the laws of supply and demand in *Thoughts and Details*, Burke knowingly violated them by offering high-quality bread to the poor in his neighborhood below the going rate,[14] thereby making markets obedient to charity, and calculation to grace.

---

[13] Langford, *Writings and Speeches*, IX, 194.
[14] See Prior, *Life of Edmund Burke*, 422–423. One year later, Burke further violated supply and demand laws by offering to house a French émigré family in a cottage under his name free of charge. See Lock, *Edmund Burke*, vol. II, 553–554.

Bibliography

EDMUND BURKE, PRIMARY WRITINGS

Note: Burke's edited journal, The Annual Register, *will be included in the Secondary Sources section. Burke most likely relinquished his editorial duties on the periodical after 1765. Burke's joint work with William Burke,* An Account of the European Settlements in America, *will also be included in the Secondary Sources section.*

The Correspondence of Edmund Burke. Edited by Thomas Copeland et al. 10 vols. Cambridge: Cambridge University Press, 1958–1978.

Revolutionary Writings: Reflections on the Revolution in France *and the First* Letter on a Regicide Peace. Edited by Iain Hampsher-Monk. Cambridge: Cambridge University Press, 2014.

Thoughts and Details on Scarcity, Originally Presented to the Right Hon. William Pitt, in the Month of November 1795. London: F. and C. Rivington, 1800.

The Writings and Speeches of Edmund Burke. Edited by Paul Langford et al. 9 vols. to date. Oxford: Clarendon Press, 1970–.

Samuels, Arthur P. I., ed. *The Early Life Correspondence and Writings of The Rt. Hon. Edmund Burke.* Cambridge: Cambridge University Press, 1923.

William, Charles, Earl Fitzwilliam, and Sir Richard Bourke, eds. *Correspondence of the Right Honourable Edmund Burke: Between the Year 1744, and the Period of His Decease, in 1797.* Vols. I–IV. London: Francis & John Rivington, 1844.

The Works and Correspondence of the Right Honourable Edmund Burke. Vol. I. London: Francis & John Rivington, 1852.

MANUSCRIPTS AND NEWSPAPERS

17th and 18th Century Burney Collection Newspapers, British Library.
British Museum.
Centre for Research Collections, Edinburgh University Library.
Division of Work and Industry, National Museum of American History, Smithsonian Institution.
Egerton, British Library.
Osborn Files, Beinecke Library, Yale University.

Wentworth Woodhouse Muniments, Sheffield City Archives.
The Wentworth Woodhouse Papers have been accepted in lieu of Inheritance.
Tax by HM Government and allocated to Sheffield City Council.

SECONDARY SOURCES

Aftalion, Florin. *The French Revolution: An Economic Interpretation.* Translated by Martin Thom. Cambridge: Cambridge University Press, 1990.

Agnani, Sunil M. *Hating Empire Properly: The Two Indies and the Limits of European Anticolonialism.* New York: Fordham University Press, 2013.

Anderson, Adam. *An Historical and Chronological Deduction of the Origins of Commerce.* London: A. Millar et al., 1764.

Anderson, Gary M. and Robert D. Tollison. "Sir James Steuart as the Apotheosis of Mercantilism and His Relation to Adam Smith." *Southern Economic Journal* 51 (1984): 456–468.

The Annual Register, of the Year 1759. London: R. and J. Dodsley, 1762.

The Annual Register, of the Year 1762. London: R. and J. Dodsley, 1763.

The Annual Register, For the Year 1764. London: J. Dodsley, 1765.

The Annual Register, For the Year 1767. London: J. Dodsley, 1768.

The Annual Register, For the Year 1776. London: J. Dodsley, 1788.

The Annual Register, For the Year 1778. London: J. Dodsley, 1779.

The Annual Register, For the Year 1798. London: T. Burton, 1800.

Anson, Sir William R., ed. *Autobiography and Political Correspondence of Augustus Henry Third Duke of Grafton.* London: John Murray, 1898.

Aquinas, Thomas. *Summa Theologica.* Vol. III. Translated by Fathers of the English Dominican Province. Allen, TX: Christian Classics, 1981.

Arendt, Hannah. *The Human Condition.* Chicago: The University of Chicago Press, 1998.

Aristotle. *The Politics.* Translated by T. A. Sinclair. London: Penguin Books, 1981.

Armytage, Frances. *The Free Port System in the British West Indies: A Study in Commercial Policy, 1766–1822.* London: Longmans, Green and Co., 1953.

Aston, Nigel. *Religion and Revolution in France, 1780–1804.* Washington, DC: The Catholic University of America Press, 2000.

Bargar, B. D. "Matthew Boulton and the Birmingham Petition of 1775." *The William and Mary Quarterly* 13 (1956): 26–39.

Barnes, Donald Grove. *A History of English Corn Laws: From 1660–1846.* London and New York: Routledge, 2014.

Barrington, Donal. "Edmund Burke as an Economist." *Economica* 21 (1954): 252–258.

Barrow, Thomas C. "Background to the Grenville Program, 1757–1763." *The William and Mary Quarterly* 22 (1965): 93–104.

Barry, James. *The Works of James Barry, Esq. Historical Painter.* Vol. I. London: T. Cadell and W. Davies, 1809.

Basye, Arthur Herbert. "The Secretary of State for the Colonies, 1768–1782." *The American Historical Review* 28 (1922): 13–23.

Bayly, C. A. *The New Cambridge History of India.* Vol. II, *Indian Society and the Making of the British Empire.* Cambridge: Cambridge University Press, 2002.

Beales, Derek. "Edmund Burke and the Monasteries of France." *The Historical Journal* 48 (2005): 415–436.

Berry, Christopher J. *The Idea of Commercial Society in the Scottish Enlightenment.* Edinburgh: Edinburgh University Press, 2015.

Bisset, Robert. *The Life of Edmund Burke.* London: George Cawthorn, British Library, 1798.

The Life of Edmund Burke. Vol. II. London: George Cawthorn, British Library, 1800.

Blackstone, William. *Commentaries on the Laws of England.* Vol. II. Edited by Thomas M. Cooley. Chicago: Callaghan and Company, 1876.

Blakemore, Steven. *Intertextual War: Edmund Burke and the French Revolution in the Writings of Mary Wollstonecraft, Thomas Paine, and James Mackintosh.* Madison and Teaneck, NJ: Fairleigh Dickinson University Press, 1997.

Blakemore, Steven, ed. *Burke and the French Revolution: Bicentennial Essays.* Athens and London: The University of Georgia Press, 1992.

Blane, Sir Gilbert. *Inquiry into the Causes and Remedies of the Late and Present Scarcity and High Price of Provisions.* London, 1817.

Bohstedt, John. *The Politics of Provisions: Food Riots, Moral Economy, and Market Transition in England, c. 1550–1850.* Farnham, England: Ashgate, 2010.

Bond, Jr., Beverley W. "The Quit-Rent System in the American Colonies." *The American Historical Review* 17 (1912): 496–516.

Bossenga, Gail. "A Divided Nobility: Status, Markets, and the Patrimonial State in the Old Regime." In *The French Nobility in the Eighteenth Century: Reassessments and New Approaches.* Edited by Jay M. Smith. University Park: The Pennsylvania State University Press, 2006, 43–75.

Boswell, James. *The Life of Samuel Johnson, LL.D.* Vol. II. London: Henry Baldwin, 1791.

Bourke, Richard. *Empire & Revolution: The Political Life of Edmund Burke.* Princeton: Princeton University Press, 2015.

Bourne, Henry E. "Maximum Prices in France in 1793 and 1794." *The American Historical Review* 23 (1917): 107–113.

Bowen, Huw V. "The 'Little Parliament': The General Court of the East India Company, 1750–1784." *The Historical Journal* 34 (1991): 857–872.

Bowen, H. V. *The Business of Empire: The East India Company and Imperial Britain, 1756–1833.* Cambridge: Cambridge University Press, 2006.

Bowen, H. V., Margarette Lincoln, and Nigel Rigby, eds. *The Worlds of the East India Company.* Suffolk, UK: The Boydell Press, 2006.

Boyd, Richard. "'The Unsteady and Precarious Contribution of Individuals': Edmund Burke's Defense of Civil Society." *Review of Politics* 61 (1999): 465–491.

Brands, H. W. *Reagan: The Life.* New York: Anchor Books, 2016.

Braudel, Fernand. *The Wheels of Commerce.* Vol. II, *Civilization & Capitalism, 15th–18th Century.* Translated by Siân Reynolds. New York: Harper & Row, 1982.

Brennan, Jason and Peter M. Jaworski. *Markets Without Limits: Moral Virtues and Commercial Interests.* New York: Routledge, 2016.

Brewer, John. *The Sinews of Power: War, Money and the English State, 1688–1783.* Cambridge, MA: Harvard University Press, 1990.

Brezis, Elise S. and François H. Crouzet. "The Role of Assignats during the French Revolution: An Evil or a Rescuer?" *Journal of European Economic History* (1995): 7–40.

Britnell, R. H. "Forstall, *Forestalling and the Statute of Forestallers.*" *The English Historical Review* 102 (1987): 89–102.

Bromwich, David. *The Intellectual Life of Edmund Burke: From the Sublime and Beautiful to American Independence.* Cambridge, MA: The Belknap Press, 2014.

Bromwich, David, ed. *Romantic Critical Essays.* Cambridge: Cambridge University Press, 1987.

Brown, Christopher L. "Empire without Slaves: British Concepts of Emancipation in the Age of the American Revolution." *The William and Mary Quarterly* 56 (1999): 273–306.

Moral Capital: Foundations of British Abolitionism. Chapel Hill: The University of North Carolina Press, 2006.

Brownson, O. A. *The American Republic: Its Constitution, Tendencies, and Destiny.* New York: P. O'Shea, 1866.

Bryant, Gerald. "Officers of the East India Company's Army in the Days of Clive and Hastings." *The Journal of Imperial and Commonwealth History* 6 (1978): 203–227.

Buckle, Henry Thomas. *History of Civilization in England.* Vol I. London: Longman, etc., 1864.

Burke, Edmund. *Reflections on the Revolution in France.* Edited by J. G. A. Pocock. Indianapolis/Cambridge: Hackett Publishing Company, 1987.

Burke, Peter. *The Public and Domestic Life of the Right Hon. Edmund Burke.* London: Nathaniel Cooke, 1854.

Burke, William and Edmund Burke. *An Account of the European Settlements in America.* 2 vols. London: R. and J. Dodsley, 1760.

Burns, Richard Dean, Joseph M. Siracusa, and Jason C. Flanagan. *American Foreign Relations since Independence.* Santa Barbara, CA: ABC-CLIO, 2013.

Campbell, Bruce M. S. et al. *A Medieval Capital and Its Grain Supply: Agrarian Production and Distribution in the London Region c. 1300.* Belfast: The Queen's University of Belfast and the Centre for Metropolitan History, Institute of Historical Research, University of London, 1993.

Canavan, Francis. "Burke on Prescription of Government." *The Review of Politics* 35 (1973): 454–474.

The Political Economy of Edmund Burke: The Role of Property in His Thought. New York: Fordham University Press, 1995.

Catalogue of the Library of the Late Right Hon. Edmund Burke, 1833.

Chanel, Gerri. "Taxation as a Cause of the French Revolution: Setting the Record Straight." *Studia Historica Gedanensia* TOM 6 (2015): 65–81.

Chapman, Richard A. *The Higher Civil Service in Britain.* London: Constable, 1970.

Chaussinand-Nogaret, Guy. *The French Nobility in the Eighteenth Century: From Feudalism to Enlightenment.* Translated by William Doyle. Cambridge: Cambridge University Press, 1985.

Christelow, Allan. "Contraband Trade between Jamaica and the Spanish Main, and the Free Port Act of 1766." *The Hispanic American Historical Review* 22 (1942): 309–343.

Christie, Ian R. "Economical Reform and 'The Influence of the Crown', 1780." *The Cambridge Historical Journal* 12 (1956): 144–154.

Myth and Reality in Late-Eighteenth-Century British Politics and Other Papers. Berkeley and Los Angeles: University of California Press, 1970.

"Sir George Savile, Edmund Burke, and the Yorkshire Reform Programme, February, 1780." *Yorkshire Archaeological Journal* 40 (1962): 205–208.

Wilkes, Wyvill and Reform: The Parliamentary Reform Movement in British Politics 1760–1785. London: Macmillan, 1962.

"The Yorkshire Association, 1780–4: A Study in Political Organization." *The Historical Journal* 3 (1960): 144–161.

Christie, I. R. "Henry Cruger and the End of Edmund Burke's Connection with Bristol." *Transactions of the Bristol and Gloucestershire Archaeological Society* 74 (1955): 153–170.

Claridge, Jordan and John Langdon. "Storage in Medieval England: The Evidence from Purveyance Accounts, 1259–1349." *The Economic History Review* 64 (2011): 1242–1265.

Clark, Henry C. *Commerce, Culture, & Liberty: Readings on Capitalism before Adam Smith.* Indianapolis: Liberty Fund, 2003.

Compass of Society: Commerce and Absolutism in Old-Regime France. Lanham, MD: Lexington Books, 2007.

Clarke, John J. *Social Administration Including the Poor Laws.* London: Sir Isaac Pitman & Sons, 1922.

Clarkson, Thomas. *The History of the Rise, Progress, and Accomplishment of the Abolition of the African Slave-Trade by the British Parliament.* Vol. I. London: Longman, etc., 1808.

Coats, A. W. "Changing Attitudes to Labour in the Mid-Eighteenth Century." *The Economic History Review* 11 (1958): 35–51.

Cobban, Alfred. *Edmund Burke and the Revolt against the Eighteenth Century: A Study of the Political and Social Thinking of Burke, Wordsworth, Coleridge and Southey.* London: George Allen & Unwin, 1962.

The Social Interpretation of the French Revolution. Cambridge: Cambridge University Press, 1999.

Cobbett's Parliamentary History of England. Vol. XVII, *1771–1774.* London: T. C. Hansard, 1813.

Cobbett's Parliamentary History of England. Vol. XVIII, *1774–1777.* London: T. C. Hansard, 1813.

Cobbett's Parliamentary History of England. Vol. XX, *Comprising the Period from the Seventh of December 1778, to the Tenth of February 1780.* London: T. C. Hansard, 1814.

Cobbett's Parliamentary History of England. Vol. XXI, *Comprising the Period from the Eleventh of February 1780, to the Twenty-Fifth of March 1781.* London: T. C. Hansard, 1814.

Cobbett's Parliamentary History of England. Vol. XXVI, *Comprising the Period from the Fifteenth of May 1786, to the Eighth of February 1788.* London: T. C. Hansard, 1816.

Cobbett's Parliamentary History of England. Vol. XXIX, *Comprising the Period from the Twenty-Second of March 1791, to the Thirteenth of December 1792.* London: T. C. Hansard, 1817.

Cobbett's Parliamentary History of England. Vol. XXXII, *Comprising the Period from the Twenty-Seventh Day of May 1795, to the Second Day of March 1797.* London: T. C. Hansard, 1818.

Collins, Gregory M. "Edmund Burke on the Question of Commercial Intercourse in the Eighteenth Century." *Review of Politics* 79 (2017): 565–595.

"Edmund Burke on Slavery and the Slave Trade." *Slavery & Abolition* 40 (2019): 494–521.

"Edmund Burke, Strauss, and the Straussians." *Perspectives on Political Science* 48 (2019): 192–209.

"The Limits of Mercantile Administration: Adam Smith and Edmund Burke on Britain's East India Company." *Journal of the History of Economic Thought* 41 (2019): 369–392.

Collins, Randall. *Weberian Sociological Theory*. Cambridge: Cambridge University Press, 1990.

"Committee on the Reports of the Secret Committee for East-India Affairs." *The Gazetteer*. 16 April 1782.

Cone, Carl B. *Burke and the Nature of Politics: The Age of the American Revolution*. Lexington: University of Kentucky Press, 1957.

Burke and the Nature of Politics: The Age of the French Revolution. Lexington: University of Kentucky Press, 1964.

"Edmund Burke, the Farmer." *Agricultural History* 19 (1945): 65–69.

Conniff, James. "Burke on Political Economy: The Nature and Extent of State Authority." *The Review of Politics* 49 (1987): 490–514.

The Useful Cobbler: Edmund Burke and the Politics of Progress. Albany: State University of New York Press, 1994.

Correspondence of William Pitt, Earl of Chatham. Vol. I. London: John Murray, 1838.

Correspondence of William Pitt, Earl of Chatham. Vol. III. Edited by William Stanhope Taylor and John Henry Pringle. London: John Murray, 1839.

Courtney, C. P. *Montesquieu and Burke*. Oxford: Basil Blackwell, 1963.

Cowen, Tyler. "Why I Don't Believe in God." *Marginal Revolution*, May 25, 2017. Accessed September 12, 2017. http://marginalrevolution.com/marginalrevolution/2017/05/dont-believe-god.html.

Cowherd, Raymond G. "The Humanitarian Reform of the English Poor Laws from 1782 to 1815." *Proceedings of the American Philosophical Society* 104 (1960): 328–342.

Crowley, John E. "Neo-Mercantilism and *The Wealth of Nations*: British Commercial Policy after the American Revolution." *The Historical Journal* 33 (1990): 339–360.

Cullen, L. M. *Anglo-Irish Trade 1660–1800*. Manchester: Manchester University Press, 1968.

Customs Tariffs of the United Kingdom, from 1800 to 1897. With Some Notes Upon the History of the More Important Branches of Receipt from the Year 1600 (London: Her Majesty's Stationery Office, 1897).

Davidson, Neil. *How Revolutionary Were the Bourgeois Revolutions?* Chicago: Haymarket Books, 2012.

Davis, Ralph. "The Rise of Protection in England, 1689–1786." *The Economic History Review* 19 (1966): 306–317.

Deane, Phyllis and W. A. Cole. *British Economic Growth 1688–1959: Trends and Structure*. Cambridge: Cambridge University Press, 1967.

"Declaration of the Rights of Man – 1789." *Avalon Project*, Yale Law School. Accessed January 2, 2017. http://avalon.law.yale.edu/18th_century/rightsof.asp.

Deneen, Patrick J. *Why Liberalism Failed*. New Haven: Yale University Press, 2018.

Desan, Suzanne. "The French Revolution and the Family." In *A Companion to the French Revolution*. Edited by Peter McPhee. Chichester, UK: Wiley-Blackwell, 470–485.

Dickerson, Oliver M. *The Navigation Acts and the American Revolution*. New York: A. S. Barnes & Company, 1963.

Dickerson, Oliver Morton. *American Colonial Government 1696–1765: A Study of the British Board of Trade in Its Relation to the American Colonies, Political, Industrial, Administrative*. Cleveland, OH: The Arthur H. Clark Company, 1912.

Dickson, P. G. M. *The Financial Revolution in England: A Study in the Development of Public Credit, 1688–1756*. London: Macmillan, 1967.

Doyle, William. *The Oxford History of the French Revolution*. Oxford: Oxford University Press, 2002.

Duckham, Baron F. "Selby and the Aire & Calder Navigation 1774–1826." *The Journal of Transport History* 7 (1965): 87–95.

Dunn, William Clyde. "Adam Smith and Edmund Burke: Complementary Contemporaries." *Southern Economic Journal* 7 (1941): 330–346.

Dutt, Romesh Chunder. *The Economic History of India Under Early British Rule: From the Rise of the British Power in 1757 to the Accession of Queen Victoria in 1837*. London: Kegan Paul, Trench, Trübner & Co., 1906.

Earle, Edward Mead. "Adam Smith, Alexander Hamilton, Friedrich List: The Economic Foundations of Military Power." In *Makers of Modern Strategy from Machiavelli to the Nuclear Age*. Edited by Peter Parent. Princeton: Princeton University Press, 1986, 217–261.

Ebeling, Richard M. "Inflation, Price Controls, and Collectivism During the French Revolution." *Foundation for Economic Education*, November 9, 2016. Accessed January 2, 2017. https://fee.org/articles/inflation-price-controls-and-collectivism-during-the-french-revolution/.

Ebenstein, Alan. *Friedrich Hayek: A Biography*. New York: Palgrave, 2001.

Edie, Carolyn A. "The Irish Cattle Bills: A Study in Restoration Politics." *Translations of the American Philosophical Society* 60 (1970): 1–66.

Elofson W. M. *The Rockingham Connection and the Second Founding of the Whig Party, 1768–1773*. Montreal & Kingston: McGill-Queen's University Press, 1996.

Elzinga, Kenneth G. and Matthew R. Givens. "Christianity and Hayek." *Faith & Economics* 53 (2009): 53–68.

Epstein, Richard A. *The Classical Liberal Constitution: The Uncertain Quest for Limited Government*. Cambridge, MA and London: Harvard University Press, 2014.

"The Libertarian: Discrimination, Religious Liberty and How We Undervalue Free Association." *The Federalist*, April 2, 2015. Accessed September 12, 2017. http://thefederalist.com/2015/04/02/the-libertarian-discrimination-religious-liberty-and-how-we-undervalue-free-association/.

Erikson, Emily. *Between Monopoly and Free Trade: The English East India Company, 1600–1757*. Princeton and Oxford: Princeton University Press, 2014.

Evans, Eric J. *William Pitt the Younger*. London and New York: Routledge, 1999.

Faccarello, Gilbert. "'Nil Repente!': Galiani and Necker on Economic Reforms." *The European Journal of the History of Economic Thought* 1 (1994): 519–550.

Fasel, George. "'The Soul That Animated': The Role of Property in Burke's Thought." *Studies in Burke and His Time* 17 (1976): 27–41.

Fay, C. R. *Burke and Adam Smith: Being a Lecture Delivered at The Queen's University of Belfast, April 27, 1956*. Belfast: Queen's University of Belfast, 1956.

The Corn Laws and Social England. Cambridge: Cambridge University Press, 1932.

Ferguson, Adam. *An Essay on the History of Civil Society*. Philadelphia: A. Finley, 1819.

Fetter, Frank Whitson, ed. *The Economic Writings of Francis Horner in the Edinburgh Review 1802–6*. London: The London School of Economics and Political Science, 1957.

Flinn, M. W. "Trends in Real Wages, 1750–1850." *The Economic History Review* 27 (1974): 395–413.

Ford, Worthington C., ed. *Journals of the Continental Congress 1774–1789*. Vol. I. Washington, DC: Government Printing Office, 1904–1937.

Foster, Ralph T. *Fiat Paper Money: The History and Evolution of Our Currency*. Edited by Paul J. Myslin. Berkeley, CA: Ralph T. Foster, 2010.

Frazer, Michael L. "Seduced by System: Edmund Burke's Aesthetic Embrace of Adam Smith's Philosophy." *Intellectual History Review* 25 (2015): 357–372.

Friedman, Milton. *Capitalism and Freedom*. Chicago and London: The University of Chicago Press, 2002.

  Money Mischief: Episodes in Monetary History. New York: Harcourt Brace Jovanovich, 1992.

Furniss, Tom. "Burke, Paine, and the Language of Assignats." *The Yearbook of English Studies* 19 (1989): 54–70.

Garber, Peter M. *Famous First Bubbles: The Fundamentals of Early Manias*. Cambridge, MA and London: The MIT Press, 2001.

General Advertiser. 14 May 1778.

"Genesis: Chapter 3." *King James Bible*. Accessed August 31, 2016. www.kingjamesbibleonline.org/Genesis-Chapter–3/.

The Gentleman's Magazine. Vol. 70. London: Nichols and Son, 1800.

Goodman, Rob. "*Doux Commerce*, Jew Commerce: Intolerance and Tolerance in Voltaire and Montesquieu." *History of Political Thought* 37 (2016): 530–555.

Gray, W. Forbes. "Alexander Donaldson and His Fight For Cheap Books." *Juridical Review* 38 (1926): 180–202.

Gregg, Samuel. "Trade, Nations, and War in an Enlightened Age." *Law & Liberty*, November 15, 2018. www.lawliberty.org/2018/11/15/trade-nations-and-war-in-an-enlightened-age/.

Grossman, Jennifer Anju. "Can You Love God and Ayn Rand?" *Wall Street Journal*, November 10, 2016. Accessed September 13, 2017. www.wsj.com/articles/can-you-love-god-and-ayn-rand–1478823015.

Hadfield, Charles. *The Canals of Yorkshire and North East England*. Vol. I. Newton Abbot: David & Charles, 1972.

Halévy, Elie. *The Growth of Philosophic Radicalism*. Translated by Mary Morris. New York: The Macmillan Company, 1928.

Hamilton, Sir William, ed. *The Collected Works of Dugald Stewart*. Vol. X. Edinburgh: Thomas Constable and Co., 1858.

"Hamilton, William Gerard." In *The History of Parliament: The House of Commons 1754–1790*. Vol. II, *Members A-J*. Edited by Sir Lewis Namier and John Brooke. London: Her Majesty's Stationery Office, 1964, 572–574.

Haque, Akhlaque. "Edmund Burke: Limits of Reason in Public Administration Theory." PhD thesis, Cleveland State University, 1994.

Harris, Robert D. "Necker's *Compte Rendu* of 1781: A Reconsideration." *The Journal of Modern History* 42 (1970): 161–183.

  Necker: Reform Statesman of the Ancien Régime. Berkeley: University of California Press, 1979.

Harris, Ron. *Industrializing English Law: Entrepreneurship and Business Organization, 1720–1844.* Cambridge: Cambridge University Press, 2000.

Harris, S. E. *The Assignats.* Cambridge, MA: Harvard University Press, 1930.

Harte, N. B. "The British Linen Trade with the United States in the Eighteenth and Nineteenth Centuries." *Textile Society of America Symposium Proceedings* (1990): 15–23.

"The Rise of Protection and the English Linen Trade, 1690–1790." In *Textile History and Economic History: Essays in Honour of Miss Julia de Lacy Mann.* Edited by N. B. Harte and K. G. Ponting. Manchester: Manchester University Press, 1973, 74–112.

Hayek, F. A. *The Constitution of Liberty.* Edited by Ronald Hamowy. Chicago: The University of Chicago Press, 2011.

The Fatal Conceit: The Errors of Socialism. Edited by W. W. Bartley III. Chicago and London: The University of Chicago Press, 1991.

Law, Legislation, and Liberty. Vol. II, The Mirage of Social Justice. Chicago: The University of Chicago Press, 1976.

The Road to Serfdom. Edited by Bruce Caldwell. Chicago: The University of Chicago Press, 2007.

"The Use of Knowledge in Society." *The American Economic Review* 35 (1945): 519–530.

Hazony, Yoram. "Is 'Classical Liberalism' Conservative?" *Wall Street Journal*, October 13, 2017. www.wsj.com/articles/is-classical-liberalism-conservative-1507931462.

The Virtue of Nationalism. New York: Basic Books, 2018.

Heckscher, Eli F. *Mercantilism.* Vol II. Translated by Mendel Shapiro. Edited by E. F. Söderlund. London: George Allen & Unwin Ltd., 1962.

Hegel, Georg. *Philosophy of Right.* Translated by T. M. Knox. Oxford: Clarendon Press, 1958.

Henderson, W. O. "The Anglo-French Commercial Treaty of 1786." *The Economic History Review* 10 (1957): 104–112.

Herbruck, Wendell. "Forestalling, Regrating and Engrossing." *Michigan Law Review* 27 (1929): 365–388.

Himmelfarb, Gertrude. *The Idea of Poverty: England in the Early Industrial Age.* New York: Vintage Books, 1985.

The Roads to Modernity: The British, French, and American Enlightenments. New York: Alfred A. Knopf, 2005.

Hirschman, Albert O. *The Passions and the Interests: Political Arguments for Capitalism before Its Triumph.* Princeton and Oxford: Princeton University Press, 2013.

Hitchens, Christopher. "Reactionary Prophet." *The Atlantic.* April 2004. www.theatlantic.com/magazine/archive/2004/04/reactionary-prophet/302914/.

Hodge, Helen Henry. "The Repeal of the Stamp Act." *Political Science Quarterly* 19 (1904): 252–276.

Hoffman, Ross J. S. *Edmund Burke, New York Agent with His Letters to the New York Assembly and Intimate Correspondence with Charles O'Hara 1761–1776.* Philadelphia: The American Philosophical Society, 1956.

Hont, Istvan and Michael Ignatieff. *Wealth & Virtue: The Shaping of Political Economy in the Scottish Enlightenment.* Cambridge: Cambridge University Press, 1985.

Hoselitz, Bert F. "The Early History of Entrepreneurial Theory." *Explorations in Entrepreneurial History* 3 (1951): 193–220.

Hume, David. *Essays: Moral, Political, and Literary*. Edited by Eugene F. Miller. Indianapolis: Liberty Fund, 1994.

Hunt, E. K. and Mark Lautzenheiser. *History of Economic Thought: A Critical Perspective*. 3rd ed. Armonk, NY and London: M. E. Sharpe, 2011.

Inca, Onur Ulas. *Colonial Capitalism and the Dilemmas of Liberalism*. New York: Oxford University Press, 2018.

Irwin, Douglas A. *Against the Tide: An Intellectual History of Free Trade*. Princeton: Princeton University Press, 1996.

Israel, Jonathan I. *Conflicts of Empires: Spain, the Low Countries and the Struggle for World Supremacy 1585–1713*. London and Rio Grande, OH: The Hambledon Press, 1997.

Revolutionary Ideas: An Intellectual History of the French Revolution from The Rights of Man *to Robespierre*. Oxford and Princeton: Princeton University Press, 2014.

Janzen, Olaf U. *War and Trade in Eighteenth-Century Newfoundland*. Liverpool: Liverpool University Press, 2013.

Jebb, John. *The Works Theological, Medical, Political, and Miscellaneous, of John Jebb, M.D. F.R.S. with Memoirs of the Life of the Author*. Edited by John Disney. Vol. III. London: T. Cadell et al., 1787.

Johnson, Phillip. "The Myth of Mr Burke and Mr Watt: For Want of a Champion!" *Queen Mary Journal of Intellectual Property* 6 (2016): 370–379.

Johnson, Samuel. *A Dictionary of the English Language*, 3rd ed. Dublin: W. G. Jones, 1768.

Jones, P. M. *Reform and Revolution in France: The Politics of Transition, 1774–1791*. Cambridge: Cambridge University Press, 1995.

Journals of the House of Commons. Vol. 30. London: H.M. Stationery Office, 1803.

Journals of the House of Commons. Vol. 31. London: H.M. Stationery Office, 1803.

Journals of the House of Commons. Vol. 33. London: H.M. Stationery Office, 1804.

Journals of the House of Commons. Vol. 38. London: H.M. Stationery Office, 1803.

Journals of the House of Commons. Vol. 42. London: H.M. Stationery Office, 1803.

Journals of the House of Commons. Vol. 51. London: H.M. Stationery Office, 1803.

Journals of the House of Commons. Vol. 52. London: H.M. Stationery Office, 1803.

Kamenka, Eugene, ed. *The Portable Karl Marx*. New York: Penguin Books, 1983.

Kates, Gary, ed. *The French Revolution: Recent Debates & New Controversies*. London and New York: Routledge, 1998.

Kearney, H. F. "The Political Background to English Mercantilism, 1695–1700." *The Economic History Review* 11 (1959): 484–496.

Kimball, Roger, ed. *The New Leviathan: The State versus the Individual in the 21st Century*. New York and London: Encounter Books, 2012.

King, Steven. *Poverty and Welfare in England 1700–1850: A Regional Perspective*. Manchester: Manchester University Press, 2000.

Kirk, Russell. *The Conservative Mind: From Burke to Eliot*. Washington, DC: Regnery Publishing, 2001.

Klinge, Dennis Stephen. "Edmund Burke, Economical Reform, and the Board of Trade, 1777–1780." *The Journal of Modern History* 51 (1979): 1185–1200.

Knox, William. *An Appendix to* The Present State of the Nation. *Containing a Reply to the Observations on that Pamphlet*. London: J. Almon, 1769.

The Present State of the Nation: Particularly with Respect to Its Trade, Finances, &c. &c. London: J. Almon, 1768.

The Present State of the Nation: Particularly with Respect to Its Trade, Finances, &c. &c. 4th ed. London: J. Almon, 1769.

Koehn, Nancy F. *The Power of Commerce: Economy and Governance in the First British Empire*. Ithaca and London: Cornell University Press, 1994.

Kramnick, Isaac. *The Rage of Edmund Burke: Portrait of An Ambivalent Conservative*. New York: Basic Books, 1977.

Kristol, Irving. *The Neoconservatism Persuasion: Selected Essays, 1942–2009*. Edited by Gertrude Himmelfarb. New York: Basic Books, 2011.

LaHaye, Laura. "Mercantilism." In *The Concise Encyclopedia of Economics*. Edited by David R. Henderson. Indianapolis: Liberty Fund, 2008, 340–343.

Lambert, Elizabeth R. *Edmund Burke of Beaconsfield*. Newark: University of Delaware Press, 2003.

Langford, Paul. *The First Rockingham Administration 1765–1766*. London: Oxford University Press, 1973.

Langworthy, Edward, ed. *Memoirs of the Life of the Late Charles Lee, Esq*. London: J. S. Jordan, 1792.

Latimer, John. *The Annals of Bristol in the Eighteenth Century*. Bristol: Butler & Tanner, 1893.

Lawson, Philip. *The East India Company: A History*. London and New York: Longman, 1993.

Lawson, Philip and Jim Phillips. "'Our Execrable Banditti': Perceptions of Nabobs in Mid-Eighteenth Century Britain." *Albion* 16 (1984): 225–241.

Leadbeater, Mary. *Poems by Mary Leadbeater*. Dublin: Martin Keene, 1808.

The Leadbeater Papers: A Selection from the MSS. and Correspondence of Mary Leadbeater. Vol. II, *Unpublished Letters of Edmund Burke: and the Correspondence of Mrs. Richard Trench and Rev. George Crabbe*. London: Bell and Daldy, 1862.

Letwin, William L. "The English Common Law Concerning Monopolies." *The University of Chicago Law Review* 21 (1954): 355–385.

Levasseur, E. "The Assignats: A Study in the Finances of the French Revolution." *The Journal of Political Economy* 2 (1894): 179–202.

Levin, Yuval. *The Great Debate: Edmund Burke, Thomas Paine, and the Birth of Right and Left*. New York: Basic Books, 2014.

Levis, R. B. "Sir James Lowther and the Political Tactics of the Cumberland Election of 1768." *Northern History* 19 (1983): 108–127.

Lipscomb, George. *The History and Antiquities of the County of Buckingham*. Vol. III. London: J. & W. Robins, 1847.

Lock, F. P. *Edmund Burke*. Vol. I, *1730–1784*. Oxford: Clarendon Press, 2012.

Edmund Burke. Vol. II, *1784–1797*. Oxford: Clarendon Press, 2009.

Locke, John. *Two Treatises of Government*. Edited by Peter Laslett. Cambridge: Cambridge University Press, 1993.

The London Magazine, For the Year 1776. Vol. 45. London: R. Baldwin, 1776.

Loubère, Leo A. "The Intellectual Origins of French Jacobin Socialism." *International Review of Social History* 4 (1959): 415–431.

Love, Walter D. "Edmund Burke's Idea of the Body Corporate: A Study in Imagery." *Review of Politics* 27 (1965): 184–197.

Lucas, Paul. "On Edmund Burke's Doctrine of Prescription; Or, an Appeal from the New to the Old Lawyers." *The Historical Journal* 11 (1968): 35–63.

MacIntyre, Alasdair. *After Virtue: A Study in Moral Theory.* Notre Dame: University of Notre Dame Press, 1984.

Macpherson, C. B. *Burke.* Oxford and New York: Oxford University Press, 1990.

Mahoney, Thomas H. D. *Edmund Burke and Ireland.* Cambridge, MA: Harvard University Press, 1960.

Malthus, Thomas. *An Essay on the Principle of Population.* Edited by Geoffrey Gilbert. Oxford: Oxford University Press, 1993.

Mandeville, Bernard. *The Fable of the Bees.* London: J. Tonson, 1724.

Mansfield, Harvey C. *Statesmanship and Party Government: A Study of Burke and Bolingbroke.* Chicago and London: The University of Chicago Press, 2013.

Marczewski, Jan. "Some Aspects of the Economic Growth of France, 1660–1958." *Economic Development and Cultural Change* 9 (1961): 369–386.

Marshall, Alfred. *Principles of Economics.* Vol. I. London: Macmillan and Co., 1895.

Marshall, P. J. *East Indian Fortunes: The British in Bengal in the Eighteenth Century.* Oxford: Clarendon Press, 1976.

Edmund Burke & the British Empire in the West Indies: Wealth, Power, & Slavery. Oxford: Oxford University Press, 2019.

"A Free though Conquering People": Eighteenth-Century Britain and Its Empire. Burlington, VT: Ashgate, 2003.

Marzagalli, Silvia. "Commerce." In *The Oxford Handbook of the Ancien Régime.* Edited by William Doyle. Oxford: Oxford University Press, 2012, 252–266.

Mathias, Peter. "Agriculture and the Brewing and Distilling Industries in the Eighteenth Century." *The Economic History Review* 5 (1952): 249–257.

McCloskey, Deirdre Nansen. *Bourgeois Equality: How Ideas, Not Capital or Institutions, Enriched the World.* Chicago and London: The University of Chicago Press, 2016.

McConnell, Michael W. "Establishment and Toleration in Edmund Burke's 'Constitution of Freedom.'" *The Supreme Court Review* 1995 (1995): 393–462.

McDowell, Gary L. "Commerce, Virtue, and Politics: Adam Ferguson's Constitutionalism." *The Review of Politics* 45 (1983): 536–552.

McGee, Robert W. "The 'Austrian Economics' of the Early Italian Economists." *Austrian Economics Newsletter* 6 (Spring 1987): 9–10.

McLain James J. *The Economic Writings of Du Pont de Nemours.* Newark: University of Delaware Press. London: Associated University Presses, 1977.

McLoughlin, T. O. *Edmund Burke and the First Ten Years of the "Annual Register," 1758–1767.* Salisbury: University of Rhodesia, 1975.

Meek, Ronald L. *Social Science & the Ignoble Savage.* Cambridge: Cambridge University Press, 1976.

Mencher, Samuel. *Poor Law to Poverty Program: Economic Security Policy in Britain and the United States.* Pittsburgh: University of Pittsburgh Press, 1967.

Meyer, Frank S., ed. *What Is Conservatism?* Wilmington, DE: ISI Books, 2015.

Millar, John. *The Origin of the Distinction of Ranks.* Edited by Aaron Garrett. Indianapolis: Liberty Fund, 2006.

Minchinton, W. E., ed. *Politics and the Port of Bristol in the Eighteenth Century: The Petitions of the Society of Merchant Venturers 1698–1803.* Vol. 23. Bristol: Bristol Record Society, 1963.

Minchinton, W. E., ed. *The Trade of Bristol in the Eighteenth Century*. Vol. 20. Bristol: Bristol Record Society, 1966.

Mitchell, B. R. *British Historical Statistics*. Cambridge: Cambridge University Press, 1988.

Mitchell, L. G. *Charles James Fox*. Oxford: Oxford University Press, 1992.

Mokyr, Joel. *The Enlightened Economy: An Economic History of Britain 1700–1850*. New Haven and London: Yale University Press, 2009.

Montesquieu. *The Spirit of the Laws*. Translated and edited by Anne M. Cohler, Basia Carolyn Miller, and Harold Samuel Stone. Cambridge: Cambridge University Press, 1994.

The Monthly Review. Vol. XIX. London: R. Griffiths, 1796.

Morgan, Edmund S., ed. *Prologue to Revolution: Sources and Documents on the Stamp Act Crisis, 1764–1766*. Chapel Hill: The University of North Carolina Press, 1959.

Morgan, Gwenda and Peter Rushton. "The Magistrate, the Community and the Maintenance of an Orderly Society in Eighteenth-Century England." *Historical Research* 76 (2003): 54–77.

Morgan, Kenneth. *Bristol and the Atlantic Trade in the Eighteenth Century*. Cambridge: Cambridge University Press, 1993.

Mori, Jennifer. "The Political Theory of William Pitt the Younger." *History* 83 (1998): 234–248.

Morley, John. *Burke*. London: Macmillan and Co., 1879.

Morning Post. Issue 7399. 26 October 1795.

Mossner, Ernest Campbell and Ian Simpson Ross, eds. *The Correspondence of Adam Smith*. Indianapolis: Liberty Fund, 1987.

Muller, Jerry Z. *The Mind and the Market: Capitalism in Western Thought*. New York: Anchor Books, 2003.

Muller, Jerry Z., ed. *Conservatism: An Anthology of Social and Political Thought from David Hume to the Present*. Princeton: Princeton University Press, 1997.

Murphy, Antoin E. *John Law: Economic Theorist and Policy-Maker*. Oxford: Clarendon Press, 1997.

Murray, Robert H. *Edmund Burke: A Biography*. Oxford: Oxford University, Press, 1931.

Muthu, Sankar. *Enlightenment against Empire*. Princeton and Oxford: Princeton University Press, 2003.

Nakazawa, Nobuhiko. "The Political Economy of Edmund Burke: A New Perspective." *Modern Age* 52 (Fall 2010): 285–292.

Namier, Lewis. "The Character of Burke." *Spectator*, 19 December 1958, 895–896.

England in the Age of the American Revolution. London: Macmillan, 1963.

The Structure of Politics at the Accession of George III. London: Macmillan, 1982.

Necker, Jacques. *De l'Administration des Finances de la France*. Lausanne: J.-P. Heubach, 1784.

A Treatise on the Administration of the Finances of France. Vol. III. London: J. Walter, 1785.

Neill, Thomas P. "The Physiocrats' Concept of Economics." *The Quarterly Journal of Economics* 63 (1949): 532–553.

Nisbet, Robert. *Conservatism: Dream and Reality*. New Brunswick, NJ and London: Transaction Publishers, 2008.

The Quest for Community: A Study in the Ethics of Order and Freedom. Wilmington, DE: ISI Books, 2010.

Nock, Albert Jay. *Our Enemy, The State.* Caldwell, ID: The Caxton Printers, 1950.

Norman, Jesse. *Edmund Burke: The First Conservative.* New York: Basic Books, 2013.

North, Gary. "Edmund Burke on Inflation and Despotism." Foundation for Economic Education. February 1, 1973. http://fee.org/freeman/edmund-burke-on-inflation-and-despotism/.

Novak, Michael. "How Christianity Created Capitalism." *Wall Street Journal,* December 23, 1999. www.wsj.com/articles/SB945912385717198338.

   The Spirit of Democratic Capitalism. New York: Touchstone, 1983.

Nozick, Robert. *Anarchy, State, and Utopia.* New York: Basic Books, 1974.

O'Brien, Conor Cruise. *The Great Melody: A Thematic Biography and Commented Anthology of Edmund Burke.* Chicago: The University of Chicago Press, 1993.

O'Gorman, Frank. *Edmund Burke: His Political Philosophy.* Bloomington: Indiana University Press, 1973.

O'Hearn, Denis. *The Atlantic Economy: Britain, the US and Ireland.* Manchester, UK: Manchester University Press, 2001.

Olson, James S., ed. *Historical Dictionary of European Imperialism.* New York: Greenwood Press, 1991.

O'Neill, Daniel I. *Edmund Burke and the Conservative Logic of Empire.* Oakland: University of California Press, 2016.

The Oracle, Public Advertiser. 17 December 1795, British Library.

Owen, Hugh. *Two Centuries of Ceramic Art in Bristol: Being a History of the Manufacture of "The True Porcelain" by Richard Champion.* London: Bell and Daldy, 1873.

Paganelli, Maria Pia and Reinhard Schumacher. "Do Not Take Peace for Granted: Adam Smith's Warning on the Relation between Commerce and War." *Cambridge Journal of Economics* 43 (2019): 785–797.

Paine, Thomas. *Rights of Man: Being an Answer to Mr. Burke's Attack on the French Revolution.* London: J. S. Jordan, 1791.

Parker, David. *Class and State in* Ancien Régime *France: The Road to Modernity?* London and New York: Routledge, 1996.

Peterfreund, Stuart. "Burke and Hemans: Colonialism and the Claims of Family." In *Global Romanticism: Origins, Orientations, and Engagements, 1760–1820.* Edited by Evan Gottlieb. Lewisburg, PA: Bucknell University Press, 2015, 19–36.

Petrella, Jr., Frank. "Edmund Burke and Classical Economics." PhD thesis, Notre Dame, 1961.

   "Edmund Burke: A Liberal Practitioner of Political Economy." *Modern Age* 8 (Winter 1963–64): 52–60.

Pike, E. Royston, ed. *Human Documents of Adam Smith's Time.* Vol. 5. London and New York: Routledge, 2010.

Piketty, Thomas. *Capital in the Twenty-First Century.* Translated by Arthur Goldhammer. Cambridge, MA and London: The Belknap Press, 2014.

Pinker, Steven. *The Better Angels of Our Nature: Why Violence Has Declined.* New York: Penguin Books, 2011.

   Enlightenment Now: The Case for Reason, Science, Humanism, and Progress. New York: Penguin Books, 2019.

"Pitt, Hon. William." In *The History of Parliament: The House of Commons 1754–1790.* Vol. III, *Members K-Y.* Edited by Sir Lewis Namier and John Brooke. London: Her Majesty's Stationery Office, 1964, 299–301.

Pitts, Jennifer. *A Turn to Empire: The Rise of Imperial Liberalism in Britain and France.* Princeton and Oxford: Princeton University Press, 2006.

Plucknett, Theodore F. T. *A Concise History of the Common Law.* Indianapolis: Liberty Fund, 2010.

Pocock, J. G. A. *The Ancient Constitution and the Feudal Law: A Study of English Historical Thought in the Seventeenth Century.* Cambridge: Cambridge University Press, 1987.

"Burke and the Ancient Constitution: A Problem in the History of Ideas." *The Historical Journal* 3 (1960): 125–143.

"The Political Economy of Burke's Analysis of the French Revolution." *The Historical Journal* 25 (1982): 331–349.

Virtue, Commerce, and History: Essays on Political Thought and History, Chiefly in the Eighteenth Century. Cambridge: Cambridge University Press, 1985.

"The Policy of a Repeal of the Corn Laws." *The British and Foreign Review; or, European Quarterly Journal.* Vol. 12 London: Richard and John Edward Taylor, 1841, 462–515.

Pownall, Thomas. *Considerations on the Scarcity and High Prices of Bread-Corn and Bread at the Market; Suggesting the Remedies in a Series of Letters.* Cambridge: Francis Hodson, 1795.

Preece, Rod. "The Political Economy of Edmund Burke." *Modern Age* 24 (Summer 1980): 266–273.

Prendergast, Renee. "The Political Economy of Edmund Burke." In *Contributions to the History of Economic Thought: Essays in Honour of R. D. C. Black.* Edited by Antoin E. Murphy and Renee Prendergast. London and New York: Routledge, 2000, 251–271.

Priestley, Joseph. *Historical Account of the Navigable Rivers, Canals, and Railways, Throughout Great Britain.* London: Longman, Rees, Orme, Brown and Green, 1831.

Prior, James. *Life of the Right Honourable Edmund Burke.* London: George Bell & Sons, 1878.

"Psalms: Chapter 115." *King James Bible.* Accessed August 31, 2016. www .kingjamesbibleonline.org/Psalms-Chapter-115/.

Putnam, Robert D. *Bowling Alone: The Collapse and Revival of American Community.* New York: Simon & Schuster, 2000.

Rae, John. *Life of Adam Smith.* New York: Augustus M. Kelley, 1965.

Raeder, Linda C. "The Liberalism/Conservatism of Edmund Burke and F. A. Hayek: A Critical Comparison." *Humanitas* 10 (1997): 70–88.

Rashid, Salim. "Economists and the Age of Chivalry: Notes on a Passage in Burke's *Reflections.*" *Eighteenth-Century Studies* 20 (1986): 56–61.

Reid, John Phillip. *Constitutional History of the American Revolution: The Authority to Legislate. Vol. II, The Authority to Tax.* Madison: The University of Wisconsin Press, 1987.

Reitan, E. A. "The Civil List in Eighteenth-Century British Politics: Parliamentary Supremacy versus the Independence of the Crown." *The Historical Journal* 9 (1966): 318–337.

Reitan, Earl A. *Politics, Finance, and the People: Economical Reform in England in the Age of the American Revolution, 1770–92.* Basingstoke, UK: Palgrave Macmillan, 2007.

Reports from Committees of the House of Commons. Vol. IX, Provisions; Poor: 1774 to 1802. House of Commons, 1803.

Robertson, William. *The Works of Wm. Robertson, D.D.* Vol. III. London: W. Pickering, 1825.

Robin, Corey. *The Reactionary Mind: Conservatism from Edmund Burke to Donald Trump.* Oxford: Oxford University Press, 2018.

Robinson, Eric. "Matthew Boulton and the Art of Parliamentary Lobbying." *The Historical Journal* 7 (1964): 209–229.

Robinson, Nicholas K. *Edmund Burke: A Life in Caricature.* New Haven and London: Yale University Press, 1996.

Rodd, Thomas, ed. *Original Letters, Principally from Lord Charlemont, the Right Honorable Edmund Burke, William Pitt, Earl of Chatham, and Many Other Distinguished Noblemen and Gentlemen, to the Right Hon. Henry Flood.* London: J. Compton, 1820.

Rodgers, Nina. "Edmund Burke and the Abolition of the Slave Trade." In *Politics and Political Culture in Britain and Ireland 1750–1850: Essays in Tribute to Peter Jupp.* Edited by Allan Blackstock and Eoin Magennis. Belfast: Ulster Historical Foundation, 2007, 91–106.

De Roover, Raymond. "Scholastic Economics: Survival and Lasting Influence from the Sixteenth Century to Adam Smith." The Quarterly Journal of Economics 69 (1955): 161–190.

Rose, J. Holland. "The Franco-British Commercial Treaty of 1786." *The English Historical Review* 23 (1908): 709–724.

Rothbard, Murray N. "Free Market." In *The Concise Encyclopedia of Economics.* Edited by David R. Henderson. Indianapolis: Liberty Fund, 2008, 200–202.

Rothschild, Emma. "Adam Smith and Conservative Economics." *The Economic History Review* 45 (1992): 74–96.

Roy, Rama Dev. "Some Aspects of the Economic Drain from India during the British Rule." *Social Scientist* 15 (1987): 39–47.

Sabine, George H. and Thomas Landon Thorson. *A History of Political Theory.* 4th ed. Fort Worth, TX: The Dryden Press, 1978.

Sandel, Michael. *What Money Can't Buy: The Moral Limits of Markets.* New York: Farrar, Straus and Giroux, 2012.

Sarason, Bertram D. "Edmund Burke and the Two *Annual Registers.*" *PMLA* 68 (1953): 496–508.

Sato, Sora. *Edmund Burke as Historian: War, Order and Civilisation.* London: Palgrave Macmillan, 2017.

Le Saux, Jean-Yves Michel. "Commerce and Consent: Edmund Burke and the Imperial Problem during the American Revolution, 1757–1775." PhD thesis, Princeton University, 1992.

Schama, Simon. *Citizens: A Chronicle of the French Revolution.* New York: Alfred A. Knopf, 1989.

Schindler, D. C. *Freedom from Reality: The Diabolical Character of Modern Liberty.* Notre Dame: University of Notre Dame Press, 2017.

Schneider, Gregory L., ed. *Conservatism in America since 1930.* New York and London: New York University Press, 2003.

The Scots Magazine. Vol. 42. Edinburgh: A. Murray and J. Cochran, 1780.

Scott, William Robert. *The Constitution and Finance of English, Scottish and Irish Joint-Stock Companies to 1720.* Vol. I, *The General Development of the Joint-Stock System to 1720.* Cambridge: The University Press, 1912.

Seccombe, Wally. *A Millennium of Family Change: Feudalism to Capitalism in Northwestern Europe.* London and New York: Verso, 1995.

Semmel, Bernard. *The Rise of Free Trade Imperialism: Classical Political Economy the Empire of Free Trade and Imperialism 1750–1850.* Cambridge: Cambridge University Press, 1970.

Seth, Vijay K. *The Story of Indian Manufacturing: Encounters with the Mughal and British Empires (1498–1947).* London: Palgrave Macmillan, 2018.

Sewell, Jr., William H. *Work & Revolution in France: The Language of Labor from the Old Regime to 1848.* Cambridge: Cambridge University Press, 1997.

Shain, Barry Alan, ed. *The Declaration of Independence in Historical Context: American State Papers, Petitions, Proclamations & Letters of the Delegates to the First National Congresses.* New Haven and London: Yale University Press, 2014.

Sheldon, Richard. "Practical Economics in Eighteenth-Century England: Charles Smith on the Grain Trade and the Corn Laws, 1756–72." *Historical Research* 81 (2008): 636–662.

Shelton, George. *Dean Tucker and Eighteenth-Century Economic and Political Thought.* London and Basingstoke: The Macmillan Press, 1981.

Shelton, W. G. "Dean Tucker's A Letter to Edmund Burke." *Studies in Burke and His Time* 34 (1968–69): 1155–1161.

Sheridan, Richard B. *Sugar and Slavery: An Economic History of the British West Indies, 1623–1775.* Kingston, Jamaica: Canoe Press, 2007.

Shklar, Judith N. *After Utopia: The Decline of Political Faith.* Princeton: Princeton University Press, 1969.

Smith, Adam. *An Inquiry into the Nature and Causes of the Wealth of Nations.* Vol. I. Edited by R. H. Campbell and A. S. Skinner. Indianapolis: Liberty Fund, 1981.

An Inquiry into the Nature and Causes of the Wealth of Nations. Vol. II. Edited by R. H. Campbell and A. S. Skinner. Indianapolis: Liberty Fund, 1981.

Lectures on Jurisprudence. Edited by R. L. Meek, D. D. Raphael, and P. G. Stein. Indianapolis: Liberty Fund, 1982.

The Theory of Moral Sentiments. Edited by D. D. Raphael and A. L. Macfie. Indianapolis: Liberty Fund, 1984.

Smith, Charles. *Three Tracts on the Corn-Trade and Corn-Laws.* London: J. Brotherton, 1766.

Smith, Robert W. "Edmund Burke's Negro Code." *History Today* 26 (1976): 715–723.

Smith, Steven B. *Modernity and Its Discontents: Making and Unmaking the Bourgeois from Machiavelli to Bellow.* New Haven and London: Yale University Press, 2016.

Somerset House. "History." Accessed March 12, 2017. www.somersethouse.org.uk /history.

Somerset, H. V. F. "Some Papers of Edmund Burke on His Pension." *The English Historical Review* 45 (1930): 110–114.

Sowell, Thomas. *Basic Economics: A Citizen's Guide to the Economy.* New York: Basic Books, 2004.

"Are Jews Generic?" In Thomas Sowell, *Black Rednecks and White Liberals.* San Francisco: Encounter Books, 2005, 65–110.

On Classical Economics. New Haven: Yale University Press, 2006.

Spang, Rebecca L. *Stuff and Money in the Time of the French Revolution.* Cambridge, MA: Harvard University Press, 2015.

St. James's Chronicle. Issue 2201. 23–25 March 1775.

St. James's Chronicle. Issue 5912. 12–14 November 1795.

Stanlis, Peter J. *Edmund Burke and the Natural Law*. Shreveport and Lafayette, LA: Huntington House, 1986.

Stephen, James Fitzjames. *A History of the Criminal Law of England*. Vol. I. London: Macmillan, 1883.

Stephen, Leslie. *History of English Thought in the Eighteenth Century*. Vol. II. Cambridge: Cambridge University Press, 2012.

Stern, Philip J. "The English East India Company and the Modern Corporation: Legacies, Lessons, and Limitations." *Seattle University Law Review* 39 (2016): 423–445.

Stern, Walter M. "The Bread Crisis in Britain, 1795–96." *Economica* 31 (1964): 168–187.

Stevens, David. "Adam Smith and the Colonial Disturbances." In *Essays on Adam Smith*. Edited by A. S. Skinner and Thomas Wilson. Oxford: Clarendon Press, 1975, 202–217.

Strauss, Leo. *Natural Right and History*. Chicago and London: The University of Chicago Press, 1965.

Susato, Ryu. "The Idea of Chivalry in the Scottish Enlightenment: The Case of David Hume." *Hume Studies* 33 (2007): 155–178.

Sutherland, Lucy S. *The East India Company in Eighteenth-Century Politics*. Oxford: Clarendon Press, 1952.

Sutherland, Lucy S. and J. Binney. "Henry Fox as Paymaster General of the Forces." *English Historical Review* 70 (1955): 229–257.

Sutherland, L. Stuart. "Edmund Burke and the First Rockingham Ministry." *The English Historical Review* 47 (1932): 46–72.

Tawney, R. H. "The Assessment of Wages in England by the Justices of the Peace." *Vierteljahrschrift für Sozial- und Wirtschaftsgeschichte* 11 (1913): 307–337.

Religion and the Rise of Capitalism: A Historical Study. London and New York: Verso, 2015.

Taylor, George V. "Noncapitalist Wealth and the Origins of the French Revolution." *The American Historical Review* 72 (1967): 469–496.

Thomas, R. P. and Donald McCloskey. "Overseas Trade and Empire 1700–1860." In *The Economic History of Britain since 1700*. Vol. I, *1700–1860*. Edited by Roderick Floud and Donald McCloskey. Cambridge: Cambridge University Press, 1981, 87–102.

Thompson, E. P. *The Making of the English Working Class*. New York: Vintage Books, 1966.

Timbs, John. *Anecdote Lives of William Pitt, Earl of Chatham, and Edmund Burke*. London: Richard Bentley & Son, 1880.

The Times. 28 December 1795. British Library.

Tocqueville, Alexis de. *Democracy in America*. Translated and edited by Harvey C. Mansfield and Delba Winthrop. Chicago and London: The University of Chicago Press, 2000.

Trask, H. A. Scott. "Inflation and the French Revolution: The Story of a Monetary Catastrophe." *Mises Institute*, April 28, 2004. Accessed January 2, 2017. https://mises.org/library/inflation-and-french-revolution-story-monetary-catastrophe.

Tribe, Keith. "'Das Adam Smith Problem' and the Origins of Modern Smith Scholarship." *History of European Ideas* 34 (2008): 514–525.

Tucker, Josiah. *Four Tracts on Political and Commercial Subjects*. Glocester: R. Raikes, 1774. http://oll.libertyfund.org/titles/tucker-four-tracts-on-political-and-commercial-subjects.

Turner, M. E., J. V. Beckett, and B. Afton. *Agricultural Rent in England, 1690–1914*. Cambridge: Cambridge University Press, 2002.

Underdown, P. T. "Edmund Burke, the Commissary of His Bristol Constituents, 1774–1780." *The English Historical Review* 73 (1958): 252–269.

Vardi, Liana. "The Abolition of the Guilds during the French Revolution." *French Historical Studies* 15 (1988): 704–717.

Velde, François R. "John Law's System." *American Economic Review* 97 (2007): 276–279.

Viereck, Peter. *Conservatism Revisited: The Revolt against Ideology*. New Brunswick, NJ: Transaction Publishers, 2005.

A View of the Grievances of Ireland by a True Patriot. Dublin: George Faulkner, 1745.

Viner, Jacob. "Early Attitudes toward Trade and the Merchant." In Jacob Viner, *Essays on the Intellectual History of Economics*. Edited by Douglas A. Irwin. Princeton: Princeton University Press, 1991, 39–44.

Voegelin, Eric. *The New Science of Politics: An Introduction*. Chicago and London: The University of Chicago Press, 1987.

Wagner, Kevin M. "Understanding the Divisions within Conservative Thought: Edmund Burke vs. Adam Smith." *Florida Political Chronicle* 21 (2012): 11–24.

Wall, Maureen. "The Rise of a Catholic Middle Class in Eighteenth-Century Ireland." *Irish Historical Studies* 11 (1958): 91–115.

Walpole, Horace. *Memoirs of the Reign of King George the Third*. Vol. II. Edited by Denis Le Marchant. Philadelphia: Lea & Blanchard, 1845.

Walsh, David. *The Growth of the Liberal Soul*. Columbia and London: University of Missouri Press, 1997.

Watson, Rev. John Selby. *The Life of William Warburton, Lord Bishop of Gloucester from 1760 to 1779: With Remarks on His Works*. London: Longman, etc., 1863.

Weare, George Edward. *Edmund Burke's Connection with Bristol, from 1774 till 1780; with a Prefatory Memoir of Burke*. Bristol: William Bennett, 1894.

Wecter, Dixon. "Burke's Theory concerning Words, Images, and Emotion." *PMLA* 55 (1940): 167–181.

"Edmund Burke and His Kinsmen: A Study of the Statesman's Financial Integrity and Private Relationships." In *The University of Colorado Studies*, vol. I, Series B, Studies in the Humanities. Edited by Francis Ramaley, Irene P. McKeehan, and Hugo G. Rodeck. Boulder: University of Colorado, 1939, 1–113.

Wells, Roger. *Wretched Faces: Famine in Wartime England, 1793–1801*. New York: St. Martin's Press, 1988.

Westerfield, Ray B. *Middlemen in English Business: Particularly between 1660 and 1760*. New Haven: Yale University Press, 1915.

Wharton, Mary. "Sir Gilbert Blane Bt (1749–1834)." *Annals of the Royal College of Surgeons of England* 66 (1984): 375–376.

Whately, Thomas. *Considerations on the Trade and Finances of This Kingdom*. London: J. Wilkie, 1766.

Whatmore, Richard. "Adam Smith's Role in the French Revolution." *Past & Present* 175 (2002): 65–89.

Whelan, Frederick G. *Edmund Burke and India: Political Morality and Empire.* Pittsburgh: University of Pittsburgh Press, 1996.

"The Place of Contract in Burke's Political Theory." In Frederick G. Whelan, *The Political Thought of Hume and His Contemporaries: Enlightenment Projects Volume I.* New York and London: Routledge, 2015, 87–115.

White, Andrew Dickson. *Fiat Money Inflation in France: How It Came, What It Brought, and How It Ended.* New York and London: D. Appleton-Century Company, 1933.

Whitworth, Sir Charles. *State of the Trade of Great Britain in Its Imports and Exports, Progressively from the Year 1697: Also of the Trade to Each Particular Country, during the above Period, Distinguishing Each Year.* London: G. Robinson et al., 1776.

Wiles, Richard C. "The Theory of Wages in Later English Mercantilism." *The Economic History Review* 21 (1968): 113–126.

Willis, Kirk. "The Role in Parliament of the Economic Ideas of Adam Smith, 1776–1800." *History of Political Economy* 11 (1979): 505–544.

Winch, Donald. "The Burke-Smith Problem and Late Eighteenth-Century Political and Economic Thought." *The Historical Journal* 28 (1985): 231–247.

Riches and Poverty: An Intellectual History of Political Economy in Great Britain, 1750–1834. Cambridge: Cambridge University Press, 1996.

Windham, William. *The Diary of the Right Hon. William Windham, 1784–1810.* Edited by Mrs. Henry Baring. London: Longmans, Green, and Co., 1866.

Woehl, Arthur Lensen. "Burke's Reading." PhD thesis, Cornell University, 1928.

Woodfall, William, ed. *An Impartial Report of the Debates That Occur in the Two Houses of Parliament.* Vol. I. London: T. Chapman, 1795.

Woods, Michael E. *Emotional and Sectional Conflict in the Antebellum United States.* Cambridge: Cambridge University Press, 2014.

Woodward, Donald. "The Background to the Statute of Artificers: The Genesis of Labour Policy, 1558–63." *The Economic History Review* 33 (1980): 32–44.

Wright, J., ed. *Sir Henry Cavendish's Debates of the House of Commons. Vol. I. May 10, 1768–May 3, 1770.* London: Longman et al., 1841.

Wright, J., ed. *Sir Henry Cavendish's Debates of the House of Commons. Vol. II.* London: Longman et al., 1841.

Wu, Chi-Yuen. "Mercantilism vs. Free Trade: The Early Years." *Mises Institute*, September 14, 2013. Accessed January 31, 2018. https://mises.org/library/mercantilism-vs-free-trade-early-years.

Wyatt-Walter, Andrew. "Adam Smith and the Liberal Tradition in International Relations." *Review of International Studies* 22 (1996): 5–28.

Young, Arthur. *The Autobiography of Arthur Young.* Edited by M. Betham-Edwards. London: Smith, Elder, & Co., 1898.

The Farmer's Tour Through the East of England. Vol. IV. London: W. Strahan, 1771.

Young, Arthur, ed. *Annals of Agriculture and Other Useful Arts.* Vol. VII. Bury St. Edmund's: J. Rackham, 1786.

"'Your World' Interview with Economist Milton Friedman." *Fox News*, November 16, 2006. Accessed September 12, 2017. www.foxnews.com/story/2006/11/16/your-world-interview-with-economist-milton-friedman.

Index

Account of the European Settlements in America
  exclusive trading companies, 225–226, *See also* East India Company, Britain's
  Georgia, 220–222, *See also Speech on Economical Reform*
  metals, 219, 226–227, *See also* mercantilism
  paper money, 229–230, 432–433, *See also* assignats
  quitrents, 221
  slavery. *See* slavery
  Spanish Empire, 218–219
Acts, Navigation, 219
Aiguillon, Duc d'. *See* Plessis-Richelieu, Armand-Désiré
Aire & Calder Navigation, 356
Alam II, Shah, 387
al-Daula, Shujah, 387
Allen, Benjamin, 307, 308
Anderson, Adam, *An Historical and Chronological Deduction of the Origin of Commerce*, 27, 303, 487
Anglo-French Commercial Treaty of 1786, 337–338, 452
Annual Register, 22
  letter to editor on free trade, 303
  on EB as farmer, 25
  on EB's hospitality, 26
  on English and French public finance, 259
  on forestalling, regrating, and engrossing, 75
  review of Adam Anderson's *History of Commerce*, 487–488
  review of *Wealth of Nations*, 141
Anson, Pierre Hubert, 485
Aquinas, Thomas, 126

Aristotle, 69, 70, 112, 223, 295, 417
Armytage, Frances, 258
assignats, 433–434
  EB on, 436–441
  economic consequences of, 435–436, 517–519, *See also* French Revolution
  issuance of during French Revolution, 434–435
avarice, 116, 174, 320, 393–395

Babeuf, François Noël, 474
Bacon, Francis, 22
balance of trade
  in *Observations*, 253–257
  in *Third Letter*, 515–516
Barnes, Donald Grove, 82, 86
Barwell, Richard, 365
Beauchamp, Francis Seymour Conway, styled Viscount, 106, 107
Bedford, Francis Russell, 5th Duke of, 449
  on EB's pension, 27
Belloni, Girolamo, 302
Benfield, Paul, 429
Bergasse-Laziroule, 486
Bible
  Genesis, 324
  Psalms, 324
Blackstone, William, 58, 125, 126, 289
Board of Trade, 28, 164–169, 190, 198, 199, 200, 206, 261, 262, 388
Bohstedt, John, 39, 41, 122
Boisgelin, Jean Raymond de Cucé de, Archbishop of Aix, 439
Bolingbroke, Henry St. John, 1st Viscount, 22, 132, 395, 471, 472, 473

Bonaparte, Napoleon, 465, 517
Booksellers Bill. *See* monopoly, EB on
Boswell, James, 30
Bourke, Richard, 239, 302, 413
British Museum, 186
Bromwich, David, 483
Burgh, Thomas, 315, 317, 329, 330, 334
Burke, Edmund, background interest in and
    knowledge of political economy, 240
  as farmer, 23–25
  contemporary testimonials, 29–31
  Debating club, 20
  EB library with works discussing
    commerce, 27
  in *Letter to a Noble Lord*, 27–29
  Reformer. See Reformer, The
  regarding economical reform, 155–156
Burke, Edmund, on
  Butcher's Meat Bill, 138
  corn bounty. *See* Pownall's Act of 1773
  Corn Laws, 80–82
  Insolvent Debtors Bill, 106–107
  Linen Bill, 85
  Navigation Acts, 241, 249, 266, 267,
    276–281, 282, 292–294, 297–298, 340,
    341, 531
  Poor Removals Bill, 102–105, 468
  Pownall's Act of 1773, 82–84, 87–88
  Scottish weavers petition, 476
  Shipwreck Bill, 326–327
Burke, Jane Nugent, 22
Burke, Richard Jr. (son), 22, 31, 96
Burke, William, 217, 272, 349, 355, 361, 449
Burke-Smith Problem, 5, 533

Cabot, Sebastian, 223
Campbell, John, 217
Canavan, Francis, 9, 12, 211
capitation tax, 477
Carthusians, 488
Cazalès, Jacques Antoine Marie de, 439
Champion, Richard, 356
Chapman, Richard A., 348
charity, 108–109
  EB's care for poor, 25–26
  EB's school for French émigrés, 101–102
  in *Speech on Poor Removals Bill*, 105
Charles II, 166, 300, 392
Civil Establishment bills, EB's, 155, 168, 190
  Establishment Act, 190
Clarkson, Thomas, 224
Clive, Robert, 351, 352

Cobban, Alfred, 8, 9, 127, 211, 319, 532
Columbus, Christopher, 217
Condorcet, Marquis de, 2, 439, 521
Cone, Carl B., 23, 24, 25, 75, 211
Conniff, James, 9, 10, 211
Conspiracy of Equals. *See* Babeuf, François
    Noël
Corn Laws
  EB on. *See* Burke, Edmund, on
  history of, 79–80
corvée, 408, 477
Cowen, Tyler, 7
Cromwell, Oliver, 214

Das Edmund Burke Problem, 5, 521, 533
Depont, Charles-Jean-François, 411
diwani, 351, 359, 360, 383
Domat, Jean, 422, 423
Dow, Alexander, 398
Dowdeswell, William, 32, 155, 239, 241,
    252, 262
Dundas, Henry, 38, 43, 56, 94, 316, 354
Dunn, William Clyde, 319
Dupont de Nemours. Pierre Samuel, 2, 521
Dutch Republic, 214

East India Company, Britain's. *See also Ninth
    Report of Select Committee* and *Speech
    on Fox's India Bill*
  Bengal Judicature Bill of 1781, 354
  dastak, 381
  EB against parliamentary intrusion into its
    affairs, 353
  EB and free trade, 384
  EB offered to serve on commission
    regarding, 352
  EB on institutional credibility of, 384
  EB on monopoly of, 357–358, *See also*
    monopoly, EB on
  EB on Regulating Bill of 1773, 353–354
  EB's financial interests in, 355–356
  Eleventh Report of Select Committee, 372
  First Report Select Committee
    "Observations," 399
  Fox's India Bill, 372
  history of, 348–349, 350–352
  poligars, 385
  Regulating Act of 1773, 354, 371
  Select Committee (both iterations), 354
  Speech on Nabob of Arcot's Debts, 393
économistes. *See* Physiocrats
Eden, William, 168, 335

Egerton, Sir Thomas, 331, *See also* Irish trade
Eleventh Report of Select Committee. See East
India Company, Britain's
Elliott, William, 463, 496
enclosure, EB on, 88–92, 515
EB chart, "English Enclosure Bills,
1789–1796," in *Third Letter*, 91
Epstein, Richard A., 7

First Letter on a Regicide Peace
public credit, 428
First Rohilla War, 387
forestalling, regrating, and engrossing, 75–76
EB's opposition to attempts to revive statutes
banning (1787). *See Speech on Motion
for a Bill against Forestalling*
EB's role in repeal of statutes banning (1772),
70–72
Fox, Charles James, 42, 47, 54, 61, 191, 335
Fox-North coalition, 26, 335, 355, 371, 397
Francis, Philip, 32, 367, 368, 369, 397,
398
Free Port Act of 1766, 237–247, 267, 299, 339,
340, 500
as an expression of party, 246, 247
EB on organizing meetings with merchants
regarding, 271, *See also* Stamp Act
EB on protectionists' resistance to, 244
EB's role in crafting, 237, 239, 246
history of, 237–239
Observations on a Late State of the Nation
on, 270–275
Short Account of a Late Short Administration
on, 241
free trade, 244–245
and Britain's East India Company, 384
EB on Irish trade in *Two Letters of the Trade
of Ireland* et al., 307–318
EB on limits of, 337–338, 507–509, *See also*
Anglo-French Commercial Treaty of
1786 and *Speech on Traitorous
Correspondence Bill*
in *Account of the European Settlements*,
230–232
in *Speech on St Eustatius*, 309–310
French Empire
in *Account of the European Settlements*,
228–229
French Revolution
EB on ethics as precondition of commerce,
487–492
EB on general critique of, 405–406

EB on impact of abstract theory on political
economy, 479–482
EB on limits of transactional exchange,
503–509
EB on revolutionary notions of equality,
462–465, 472–473
EB on social engineering, 482–487
EB on wealth redistribution. *See* wealth
redistribution
historical context, 407–410
Remarks on the Policy of the Allies, 464
revolutionary notions of equality, 473–474
Friedman, Milton, 7, 434

gabelle, 407, 443
Gallican Church, 420, 421, 430, 438,
506
Gascoyne, Bamber, 331, 332
General Will, 485–486, 491
George I, 361
George III, 74, 153, 154, 184, 429
Georgia. *See Account of the European
Settlements in America*
Gibbon, Edward, 139, 168
Goldsmith, Oliver, 139
Gordon, Lord George, 200
Grenville, George, 105, 116, 237, 246, 249,
251, 252, 253, 267, 270, 274, 275, 276,
279, 281, 299, 339
Guadaloupe (Guadeloupe), 254
guilds, 476
Gulliver's Travels, 388

Halévy, Elie, 319
Hamilton, William Gerard, 21, 22, 173,
261, 262
Harford, Cowles & Co., 308
Hastings, Warren, 109, 347, 354, 367, 371,
372, 381, 382, 387, 389, 390, 392, 393,
394, 395, 396, 397, 399, 401
Hayek, F. A., 7, 15, 63, 139
EB and, 53–54, 136–137, 312, 502–503
Hegel, Georg, 481
Henderson, Archibald, 240
Himmelfarb, Gertrude, 40, 127, 146, 319
Hoheb, Samuel. *See Speech on St Eustatius*
Horner, Francis, 142
Howard, John, 108
Hudson's Bay, 225–226
Hudson's Bay Company, 225
Hume, David, 7, 27, 139, 320, 321, 342,
498, 499

India. *See* East India Company, Britain's, *Ninth Report of Select Committee,* and *Speech on Fox's India Bill*
India Act of 1784, 397
Insolvent Debtors Bill. *See* Burke, Edmund, on intellectual property rights. *See* monopoly
Intolerable Acts, 250, 294
    Boston Port Bill, 294
    Massachusetts Government Act, 295
Invisible Hand, 61, 97, 320, 510
Irish trade. *See also Two Letters on the Trade of Ireland*
    Committee on Irish Trade, 307, 314, 316
    EB on Bamber Gascoyne's amendment, 331
    EB on bills limiting Irish trade ports, 303–304
    EB on importation of Irish potatoes and pulses, 327
    EB on Irish soap bill, 305
    EB on Pitt's commercial propositions, 334–337
    EB on sailcloth and iron industry, 314–315
    EB on Thomas Egerton's amendment, 331–333
    EB's letter to Thomas Burgh on, 315–316, 329, 330–331, 334
    EB's parliamentary activity in support of, 307–308
    history of, 300–302
    Irish trade bills in the 1770s, historical context of, 306–307

Jackson, Richard, 30
Jamaica
    and the Free Port Act, 238
    in *Account of the European Settlements,* 222, 235–237
    in *Observations,* 257–258
Johnson, Samuel, 30, 139, 238, 352, 488
    A Dictionary of the English Language, 488
Jolliffe, William, 200

Khan, Faizullah, 387
Khan, Mir Kasim Ali, 359
Kirk, Russell, 196
Knox, William, 251, 252, 253, 257, 258, 259, 260, 261, 262, 263, 264, 266, 267, 268
Kramnick, Isaac, 9, 97, 108, 197, 198

labouring poor, 94
    abstract words, in *Philosophical Enquiry,* 96
    in *Third Letter,* 95
    in *Thoughts and Details on Scarcity,* 95

Lambert, Elizabeth R., 22
Law, John, 230, 408, 409, 433, 448
León, Juan Ponce de, 229
Letter to a Noble Lord, 176, 239, 244, 321, 449, 482, 492
Levin, Yuval, 491
Lipscomb, George, 23
Linen Bill, 84, 85
Lock, F. P., 24, 25, 211, 231, 336
Locke, John, 7, 10, 22, 113, 423, 461, 493, 521
Louis XVI, 3, 187, 408, 410, 469, 475, 517
Lowther, James, 178, 412

Macpherson, C.B., 9, 127, 145, 146, 211
Malthus, Thomas, *An Essay on the Principle of Population,* 38
Mandeville, Bernard, 320
Mansfield, Harvey C., 413
Marshall, P.J., 352, 355, 397, 398
Martinique, 253, 254, 257, 262
Marx, Karl, 55, 465
    EB and, 54–55
mercantilism, 239
    EB and, 339–342
middlemen, 57–59, *See also Ninth Report of Select Committee* and *Thoughts and Details on Scarcity*
Mill, John Stuart, 7
Millar, John, 498, 502
Mirabeau, Honoré-Gabriel-Victor, comte de, 2, 421, 486, 520
Mississippi Bubble. *See* Law, John
monopoly, EB on. *See also Ninth Report of Select Committee*
    Booksellers Bill, 356
    general principles of, 356–358
    of authority, 64–65
    of capital, 64
    Richard Champion's china clay patent renewal, 356
    Selby-Leeds Canal, 356
Morley, John, 335
Mughal Empire, 387

natural law, 396–397, 422–423, *See also Two Letters on the Trade of Ireland*
natural rights, 295, 323–325, 328, 356, 376–380, 400
Navigation Acts, 129, 241, 245, 249, 266, 267, 276, 277, 278, 279, 280, 281, 282, 285, 286, 292, 293, 297, 313, 340, 341, 531
    history of, 214–215

Necker, Jacques, 86, 187, 188, 189, 201,
    407, 408, 409, 410, 430, 439, 467,
    468
New York agent, EB as, 164–165
Newfoundland, 255, 256
Newhaven, William Mayne, Lord, 333
Ninth Report of Select Committee
    dalals (Indian middlemen), 365, *See also*
        Thoughts and Details on Scarcity
    monopoly of Indian markets (opium,
        saltpeter, salt), 366–369, *See also*
        monopoly, EB on
    profit-and-loss, 362
    raw silk market, 363–365
    revenue-for-investment scheme, 360–361, 390
Nisbet, Robert, 202
Noailles, Louise-Marie, Vicomte de
    Noailles, 455
North Carolina, 222
North, Frederick, Lord North, 153, 183, 189,
    190, 292, 353, 371
Novak, Michael, 7
Nugent, Robert, 1st Viscount Clare and 1st Earl
    Nugent, 307
Nullum Tempus affair. *See* property, EB on

O'Hara, Charles, 31, 237, 240, 242, 243,
    304, 305
Observations on a Late State of the Nation
    balance of trade, 253–257
    cost of living, 265
    EB's use of empirical data in, 253–254,
        257–259, 260–263
    France, 259–260, 265
    Free Port Act. *See* Free Port Act
    historical context, 251–253
    land tax, 268
    Navigation Acts, 267, *See also* Navigation Acts
    public economy, 267
    revenue, 268
    supply and demand, 265–266
    taxes, 263
    variety of imperial circumstance, 264, 269

Paine, Thomas, 108, 521
Pery, Edmund Sexton, 330
Petrella, Jr., Frank, 9, 319
Physiocrats, 2, 10, 319, 493, 494, 522
Pitt, William (the Elder), 1st Earl of Chatham, 243
Pitt, William (the Younger), 38, 42, 43, 94, 318,
    334, 335, 337, 380, 397, 510, 511,
    See also Irish trade

commercial propositions. *See* Irish trade
Plassey, Battle of, 351, 360, 366
Plessis-Richelieu, Armand-Désiré Vignoret du,
    Duc d'Aiguillon, 455
Pocock, J. G. A., 9, 145, 489, 498
Poor Laws, 103, 115
Postlethwayt, Malachy, 27
Pownall, Thomas, 59, 82, 83, 84, 86, 87,
    119, 141
Pownall's Act of 1773, 82–84, 87–88
Preece, Rod, 9, 198
prescription. *See* property
Price, Richard, 7, 461, 467, 493, 517, 521
Priestley, Joseph, 7, 521
profit, EB on, 64, 127, 175
property, EB on, 411–414, 420
    as a foundation for industry, 414–416
    during French Revolution. *See* French
        Revolution
    Nullum Tempus affair, 411–414, 422
Protestant Ascendancy, 96, 337

Rand, Ayn, 7
Rawlinson, Abraham, 240
Reflections on the Revolution in France
    assignats. *See* assignats
    confiscation of church property, 420–422,
        425–426
    ethics as precondition of commerce. *See*
        French Revolution
    impact of abstract theory on political
        economy. *See* French Revolution
    land as foundation for commerce,
        451–453
    landed property, 417–419, 422–423, *See also*
        property
    limits of transactional exchange. *See* French
        Revolution
    monastic orders, 424–425
    monied interest, 428–429, 431–432
    real rights of men, 460–462
    relation between monied and landed
        interests, 456–459
    revenue, 441–445
    revolutionary notions of equality, EB on.
        See French Revolution
    social engineering. *See* French Revolution
    sophisters, oeconomists, calculators, and
        oeconomical politicians, 493–496
    wealth disparities, 469–470
    wealth redistribution, 464–465, 484–485,
        See also wealth redistribution

Reformer, The, 21, 463
  "Gentleman of Fortune,", 98–99
  desire of lucre, 59
  on Irish poverty and property, 99–100
Regulating Act of 1773. *See* East India
  Company, Britain's
Regulating Bill of 1773. *See* East India
  Company, Britain's
Rex v. Rusby, 76, *See also* forestalling,
  regrating, and engrossing
Reynolds, Joshua, 139
Ricardo, David, 239
Richmond, Charles Lennox, 3rd Duke of, 451
Robertson, William, 342, 498, 502
Rockingham Whigs, 154, 155, 191, 250,
  275, 412
Rockingham, Charles Watson-Wentworth,
  Marquess of, 22, 262
Rothschild, Emma, 466
Rousseau, Jean-Jacques, 485
Royal Mint. *See Speech on Economical Reform*

Savile, Sir George, 171, 200
Scottish Enlightenment, 50, 312, 342
  EB and, 498–502
Second Letter on a Regicide Peace,
  430–431
Selby-Leeds Canal. *See* monopoly, EB on
Semmel, Bernard, 211
Sheffield, John Lord, *Observations on the
  Manufactures, Trade, and Present State
  of Ireland*, 301
Sheridan, Richard B., 224, 244
Shipwreck Bill. *See* Burke, Edmund, on
Shklar, Judith N., 8, 127, 143
Sieyès, Abbé Emmanuel-Joseph, 2, 270,
  520, 521
slavery, 55–57
  in *Account of the European Settlements in
    America*, 224–225
  in *Speech on Conciliation*, 289–290
  Sketch of a Negro Code, 56–57, 129, 224
Smith, Adam, 2, 5, 7, 10, 13, 15, 27, 29, 50, 68,
  71, 85, 86, 94, 211, 215, 231, 239, 244,
  247, 272, 301, 335, 341, 342,
  343, 348, 374, 498, 499, 501,
  510, 521
  EB's intellectual relationship with, 139–143,
    318–322
  Invisible Hand. *See* Invisible Hand
  Lectures on Jurisprudence, 142, 320, 499
  on Navigation Acts, 341

Theory of Moral Sentiments, 5, 141, 142,
  320, 498
Wealth of Nations, 27, 50, 68, 85, 86, 94,
  139–141, 142, 215, 272, 318–322
Smith, Charles, 79
Society of Merchant Adventurers of Bristol, 308
Somerset House, 185, 186, 201
  Speech on Somerset House, 185–186
South Carolina, 222
Sowell, Thomas, 52
Span, Samuel, 308, 309, 313, 323, 325,
  330
Spanish Empire, 214, *See also Account of the
  European Settlements in America*
Speech on American Taxation
  historical context, 276
  Navigation Acts, 276–280, 281, *See also*
    Navigation Acts
Speech on Butcher's Meat Bill, 138
Speech on Conciliation with America
  American fishery, 285–286
  authority to tax, 287–288
  EB's use of trade data, 283–284
  English roots of American liberty, 287
  historical context, 282
  link between liberty and religion, 288–289
  Navigation Acts, 292–294
  plan of imperial reform, 294–295
  revenue, 296–297
  slavery. *See* slavery
  study of law, 289
Speech on Economical Reform
  Abolition of royal offices, 178, 182, 183
  American Secretary, 164, 190
  Civil List, 184–185
  Costly subordinate jurisdictions, 176–178
  EB's plan summarized, 181
  Georgia, 166, *See also Account of the
    European Settlements in America*
  government contracts, 161–163
  Pension reform and patent places, 171–176
  Royal Mint, 163
  selling off royal land, 159–161
Speech on Fox's India Bill
  corrupt bargains and sales, 386–387
  Indian middlemen, 389–390, *See also Ninth
    Report of Select Committee*
  mercantile administration, 374–375
  natural rights and chartered rights,
    376–380
  six mercantile principles, 373–374
  zamindars, 387, 389

Speech on Motion for a Bill against Forestalling,
 72–74
 on free market, 73
 on price fluctuations, 73
Speech on Nabob of Arcot's Debts. See East
 India Company, Britain's
Speech on St Eustatius
 free trade in Dominica, 241
 Hoheb, Samuel, 62–63
 St. Eustatius as global market, 309–310
 the Jewish people as merchants, 62–63
Speech on the Army Estimates, 406
Speech on Traitorous Correspondence Bill,
 507–508
Stamp Act, 27, 237, 238, 249, 250, 252, 274,
 275, 276, 283, 339
 EB receiving petitions and consulting
 merchants on, 241
Statute of Artificers of 1563, 41, 118
Stevens, David, 211
Stewart, Dugald, 140, 210, 494
Strauss, Leo, 196, 329
Sutherland, Lucy S., 246
Swift, Jonathan, *Gulliver's Travels,* 388

taille, 260, 407, 477
 EB on, 260
Talleyrand-Périgord, Charles Maurice de, 421,
 475, 488, 520
Third Letter on a Regicide Peace
 balance of trade, 515–516
 landed property, 416–417, 420
 love of lucre, 510, *See also* Invisible Hand
 monied interest, 512–513
 Pitt's loyalty loan, 510–511
 war and taxes, 515, 516
Thompson, E.P., 40, 122
Thoughts and Details on Scarcity
 abstract reason, 133–136
 commercial virtues, 123–125
 complexities of labor, 92–94, 111–112
 equality, 113–114
 government restraint, 114–115
 historical context, 38–43, 118–119
 implied contract, 120, 123, 125–126
 laissez-faire, 127–130
 middlemen, 59–70
 minimum wage, 41, 42, 45, 46, 94, 118
 monopoly of capital. *See* monopoly
 nature, 49–52
 poverty, 112–113
 price theory, 52–55

rich as trustees of the poor and charity,
 97–98, *See also Reformer, The,*
 "Gentleman of Fortune"
 supply and demand, 44–49
 wealth redistribution. *See* wealth
 redistribution
Townshend Acts, 249, 250, 276
 EB on, 249
Townshend, Charles, 239, 279, 303, 304
Townshend, Thomas, 81
Treaty of Alliance, 313
Treaty of Amity and Commerce, 313
Trustee theory of representation, EB's, 105,
 191–192
 in *Speech on Economical Reform,* 192–193.
 See also Speech on Economical Reform
 in *Thoughts and Details,* 106
 regarding Insolvent Debtors Bill, 106–107
 regarding Irish trade, 328–330, *See also* Irish
 trade
Tucker, Josiah, 32, 293, 494
Turgot, Anne-Robert-Jacques, 3, 187, 408,
 410, 493
Two Letters on the Trade of Ireland
 historical context, 308
 mutual advantages of trade, 308–309
 nature and trade, 322–325
 political and social benefits of trade, 310–313

Utrecht, Treaty of, 255, 337

Verney, Ralph, 2nd Earl, 355, 361
Vindication of Natural Society, A, 131–132,
 395, 471–472
vingtièmes, 477
Voltaire, François-Marie-Arouet-de, 7

Walpole, Horace, 253
Walpole, Robert, 215
Wealth of Nations. See also Smith, Adam
 Annual Register review of, 141
 EB on, 139–140
 EB's influence on, 141–142
wealth redistribution. *See also Reflections on
 the Revolution in France*
 in *Observations on a Late State of the
 Nation,* 264
 in *Third Letter on a Regicide Peace,* 511–512
 in *Thoughts and Details,* 109–112
 regarding French Revolution, 464–465,
 484–485
Whatmore, Richard, 521

Whelan, Frederick G., 126, 351
Whitbread, Samuel, 41, 42, 45, 46, 94, 118
White, Andrew Dickson, 434, 446
Whiteboys, 21, 92
William III, 164, 213, 215, 300, 361
Wright of Derby, Joseph, "An Experiment on a Bird in the Air Pump," 483
Wyvill, Christopher, 153, 154, 200

Yorkshire Association, 153
Young, Arthur, 24, 31, 42, 43, 70, 71, 86, 115

zero-sum economic reasoning, EB on, 70, 104, 231, 247, 256, 284–285, 291–292, 297, 309–310, 311, 337, 398–399, 400